HISTORY
OF
WILLIAMSBURG

Something About the People of Williamsburg County, South Carolina, from the First Settlement by Europeans About 1705 until 1923.

BY

WILLIAM WILLIS BODDIE

Southern Historical Press, Inc.
Greenville, South Carolina

Copyright 1923
By: William Willis Boddie

Copyright Renewed 1950
By: Helen Scott Boddie

All rights reserved. No part of this publication may be reproduced, stored in a retrieval system, transmitted in any form, posted on to the web in any form or by any means without the prior written permission of the publisher.

Please direct all correspondence and orders to:

www.southernhistoricalpress.com
or
**SOUTHERN HISTORICAL PRESS, Inc.
PO BOX 1267
Greenville, SC   29601**
southernhistoricalpress@gmail.com

ISBN #0-89308-754-8

Printed in the United States of America

INTRODUCTION

Preparing what I have called the History of Williamsburg has given me great pleasure. It was designed to give statements of fact to one who cares simply for such, as well as to lure the student who wants to learn something of Williamsburg's place in the world. Practically everything herein contained is based on ancient documents or official records.

I am very grateful to Mr. A. S. Salley, Jr., Secretary of the Historical Commission of South Carolina, for his sympathetic patience with me while gathering material from his office and for much aid given me; and, likewise, to the authorities in the office of the Secretary of State and the Charleston Library. Miss Mabel L. Webber, Secretary of the South Carolina Historical Society, gave me many helpful suggestions. Judge of Probate W. E. Snowden and Clerk of the Court John D. Britton, of Williamsburg, Judge of Probate Frank M. Bryan, of Charleston, and Judge of Probate Thomas E. Richardson, of Sumter, were always very kind and helpful when I worked in their offices.

Mr. B. E. Clarkson allowed me the use of the Confederate War Diary of his late father, William J. Clarkson; Mr. E. C. Epps furnished me a copy of the Retaliation War Prison Diary of his father, the venerable William Epps; and Mrs. J. B. Morrison, Jr., permitted me to gather much material from "Ervins and Their Kin" manuscript of her late father, Reverend E. E. Ervin. Nothing helped me with the early history of this County more than Colonel J. G. Wardlaw's "Genealogy of the Witherspoon Family." Mr. Louis W. Gilland allowed me to make a copy of the old Session Record Book of Williamsburg Presbyterian Church, and Mr. D. E. McCutchen one of the Indiantown Presbyterian Church. I have used freely "The Register Book for the Parish Prince Frederick Winyaw," edited by the late Mrs. Elizabeth W. A. Pringle. I have drawn at will from all the published histories of South Carolina, the biographies of men of Williamsburg, and the newspaper files in the Charleston Library.

Mrs. D. C. Scott, during many years, collected historical material in connection with her work in the patriotic societies of Williamsburg and the Pee Dee Historical Society. I became heir to all this. It was she who first told me the story of the people of Williamsburg and influenced me to undertake this delightful labor. Dr. D. C. Scott, out of his more than seventy years of comprehensive understanding of Williamsburg, and Mrs. Boddie, from her naturally beautiful enthusiasm for my work, have both been continuously helpful. They have been most generous in avoiding even an attempt to color my scheme and I desire that no questionable opinion herein be charged to them.

Mr. Samuel R. Mouzon, Mr. Harvey J. Brown, Mr. William M. McKnight, and Mr. Alonzo W. Flagler, all Confederate Veterans of more than four score years of age, whose minds are clear and whose memories are vivid, gave me invaluable information. Mr. J. J. B. Montgomery told me a thousand good stories that he would not allow me to publish and helped me to understand many things. Peter G. Gourdin, C. E., contributed for use in this volume his excellent map of Williamsburg, 1923. Mrs. John A. Scott allowed me to copy the Robert Frierson map of Williamsburg (Kingstree) 1801, which greatly adds to the value of this History.

Miss Ann Fulton (now Mrs. Glenn E. Scott, Sarasota, Florida,) used her good judgment, both in including and excluding material, in copying for me thousands of pages from old manuscripts. Miss Adeline Shuler prepared from dictation the manuscript for this book. Out of her keenly intelligent interest, she made many helpful suggestions, both as to form and content, that have been incorporated in the work.

WILLIAM WILLIS BODDIE.

Kingstree, South Carolina,
June 22, 1923.

TABLE OF CONTENTS

CHAPTER		PAGE
I.	Before Williamsburg Had a Name	1-7
II.	The King's Tree and Williamsburg Township	8-20
III.	Original Settlers	21-26
IV.	The People Who Settled Williamsburg	27-37
V.	Economic Conditions	38-43
VI.	Churches and Churchmen	44-58
VII.	Growing Pains and Petitions	59-72
VIII.	Colonial Wills	73-86
IX.	Political and Social Matters	87-93
X.	The War of the Revolution	94-113
XI.	Williamsburg Soldiers in the Revolution	114-130
XII.	Government by the People	131-136
XIII.	The Town of Williamsburg, 1788	137-153
XIV.	Williamsburg Census, 1790	154-170
XV.	Presbyterianism Regnant	171-198
XVI.	Williamsburg Taxpayers, 1811	199-206
XVII.	Roads and Ferries from 1788 to 1830	207-212
XVIII.	Government and Officials, 1783-1830	213-219
XIX.	Old Wills and Notes on Them	220-246
XX.	Economic and Social Life, 1783-1830	247-257
XXI.	Indiantown Church, 1819-1830	258-265
XXII.	The Nullification Movement, 1832	266-270
XXIII.	Puritanism, Calvinism, and Arminianism	271-303
XXIV.	Things, Political and Social, 1830-1860	304-322
XXV.	Transportation, 1830 to 1860	323-328
XXVI.	Slavery and Secession	329-342
XXVII.	Williamsburg, C. S. A., 1861	343-378
XXVIII.	Williamsburg, C. S. A., 1862	379-396
XXIX.	Williamsburg, C. S. A., 1863	397-402
XXX.	Williamsburg, C. S. A., 1864	403-412

TABLE OF CONTENTS

CHAPTER		PAGE
XXXI.	WILLIAMSBURG, C. S. A., 1865	413-432
XXXII.	WILLIAMSBURG, U. S. A., 1865	433-439
XXXIII.	RECONSTRUCTION	440-457
XXXIV.	ANOTHER WILLIAMSBURG	458-466
XXXV.	PUBLIC EDUCATION SINCE 1880	467-479
XXXVI.	RELIGIOUS DENOMINATIONS, 1865-1923	480-495
XXXVII.	BANKING IN WILLIAMSBURG	496-502
XXXVIII.	THROBBING WAR DRUMS CALL	503-516
XXXIX.	MANY THINGS	517-532
XL.	GENERAL PROGRESS	533-548

ILLUSTRATIONS

Lieutenant Joseph Scott	123
Lieutenant Colonel John G. Pressley	343
Colonel James F. Pressley	349
Major C. S. Land	359
Colonel James McCutchen	379
Lieutenant Junius E. Scott	400
Lieutenant William Epps	418
Lieutenant David Ervin Gordon	419
Lieutenant Colonel Edward C. Register	505
Sergeant Leroy W. Smith	511
Honorable R. C. Logan	521

LIST OF MAPS.

Proposed Town of Williamsburg, 1737—Williams	8
Williamsburg Township. Mouzon's Map, 1775	87
Town of Williamsburg, 1788—Old Map	137
Williamsburg, 1801—Frierson	257
Williamsburg District, 1825—Mills	257
Williamsburg County, 1923—Gourdin	533

ERRATA

There are certain errors in the *History of Williamsburg* which this is written to correct.

The third sentence, first paragraph, page one, should read: "This territory, however, had been designated Carolana by Charles I when he made in 1629 a grant of land to Sir Robert Heath."

The record in the Will Book in the office of Judge of Probate, Williamsburg, is responsible for the statement on page 242 that James McConnell refers in one part of his will to his wife "Mary" and in another to his wife "Sarah." I allowed that to pass without having read over the original will, which does not allow the statement. The punctuation in the record book warrants the observation which my secretary made.

About the middle of page 305, there is a reference to the "University of South Carolina" when the name for that institution was "South Carolina College" until 1866. There are two or three of the same errors on other pages.

On page 429 and others, I am unfair to the memory of General Potter, although many of the most intelligent men of these parts who were living at that time and when my book was written gave me the ideas incorporated. General Potter led his army across the Santee near Georgetown and raided only on the south side of Santee River. Robber bands, masquerading as Potter's forces, were responsible for the outrages committed south of Black River in Williamsburg. The quotation beginning "The old Mokish law," etc., on the bottom of page 365, explains much of what has passed as facts about "Potter's Raiders" in Williamsburg.

Wm. W. Boddie

Kingstree, South Carolina,
December fourth, nineteen twenty eight.

CHAPTER I.

BEFORE WILLIAMSBURG HAD A NAME.

The territory in Southern North America claimed by the British at the beginning of the seventeenth century was called Virginia. In 1663, that portion South of the parallel of latitude 36° 33' was separated from Virginia and named Carolina in honor of Charles II, King of England. This territory, however, had been designated Carolina by Charles I when he made in 1629 a grant of land to Sir Robert Keith.

Charles II granted Carolina in 1663 to eight noblemen, known as Lords Proprietors. At that time, there were a few scattered settlements along the Roanoke and Chowan Rivers, in what is now North Carolina, but none other in all the vast territory denominated Carolina. These Lords Proprietors believed that they could establish almost at once in this naked country a feudalistic civilization more complex than had grown up in many centuries in their mother country. They secured John Locke, a celebrated English philosopher, then under the patronage of Ashley, one of the Lords Proprietors, to write a Constitution for Carolina.

While Locke was one of the most influential thinkers of modern times and wrote a Constitution for Carolina from which Jefferson, Hamilton, and Marshall, a century later, drew many valuable suggestions, he had never visited Carolina and had only his vast store house of learning and his imagination to aid him in creating his remarkable scheme for the government of the widely scattered settlements in these wilds. His Fundamental Constitution for Carolina was accepted by the Lords Proprietors and made the law of the land. It was a beautiful theory which Locke had created and he and the Lords

Proprietors had many hopeful dreams that their plans would materialize.

The Lords Proprietors did all they could to consummate the ideal empire that had its origin in the brain of Locke. They made large grants of land in Carolina to seemingly eager English noblemen, expecting these pampered products of wealth and ease to migrate with their retainers to this wilderness and soon establish an aristocratic Carolina.

These English lords did not come to Carolina to live on their estates. They attempted to send hirelings to overcome the pioneer matters and create a condition their masters could endure. But hirelings never make a wilderness a garden unless severely superintended.

The English government gave the Lords Proprietors a free hand for more than a half century while Carolina was a Proprietary Province, but the plans of Locke would not work. Finally, seven of the Lords Proprietors ceded back to the King their claims to Carolina, and in 1719 it became a Royal Province. In 1729, Carolina was divided into the provinces of North Carolina and of South Caroling along the lines now obtaining.

In 1729, there were only two small settlements in South Carolina. These were Charleston and Beaufort, both along the coast. These two settlements had no back country to support them and nothing for maintaining their existence except the nominal trade with the Indians. Charleston and Beaufort then produced practically nothing. Besides, they were dangerously near the Spanish territory of Florida, and the Spaniards were forever foraying on them. The Indians from the West were likewise frequently disturbing them and constantly threatening their existence.

King George knew that up to 1730 but little of practical value had been done towards the creation of a successful colony in South Carolina. He realized that the colonies at Charleston and Beaufort were not self sustaining and could not be made so without the development of the back country; and, furthermore, that the Spaniards and the Indians might at any time unite and exterminate these two towns on the coast. In 1730, he gave the following instructions to Governor Robert Johnson of South Carolina:

"Whereas, it has been found by long experience in our province of New Hampshire and Massachusetts Bay, that the settling of such persons as were disposed to become planters there hath redounded very much to their advantage, not only with respect to the assistance they have been able to afford each other in their civil concerns, but, likewise, with regard to the security they have thereby acquired against the insults and incursions of the neighboring Indians:

"We have thought it for our service, and you are hereby required to mark out and set apart eleven townships in our said province, on the banks of rivers, at sixty miles distance from Charleston; that is to say, two townships on the Altamaha, two on the Savannah River, one on Ponpon River, two on Santee River, one on Wateree River, one on Black River, and one on Waccamaw River. Each of these townships must consist of twenty thousand acres of land, to be laid out in square plots,—one side thereof to front the respective rivers on which they shall be settled.

"In each of these townships, you shall mark out proper place for the situation of a town, contiguous to the river, where the township lies, to consist of so many lots, and each lot of such quantity of land as you shall judge convenient, and to each inhabitant, at their first settling there, besides their respective town lots, you shall grant fifty acres, part of the above mentioned twenty thousand, for every man, woman, or child, of which the grantee's family shall consist, which grants shall be augmented from time to time as the abilities of the respective inhabitants shall render them capable of cultivating more lands, always taking care to proportion profitable and unprofitable land in each grant and to mark the same out in such manner that every grantee, by the situation of his land, may reap equal advantage of access to the river to which the township shall be contiguous, and to the intent that land near the said township may not be wanting for the convenience of the inhabitants, as their substance shall increase.

"No person, except the inhabitants, shall be allowed to take up land within six miles of the said townships, respectively, to which the said township shall be contiguous.

"Each of these townships, together with all the lands on the same side of the river, lying within six miles of the said townships, respectively, be erected into a distinct parish, and that when any of the said intended parishes shall have one hundred householders, it shall be entitled to send two members to our Assembly and to enjoy all such other privileges as of right and common usage belong to other parishes in our said province.

"As other encouragement to such persons as shall be disposed to settle in these townships, we are graciously pleased to allow the inhabitants there the right of common and herbage in and through all such lands contained within the extent of the said townships as shall not be taken up by grants made to the said inhabitants; and that a quantity of land not exceeding three hundred acres contiguous to the said town shall be set apart for a common in perpetuity to each of the said towns free from quitrent; and it is our pleasure that no person claiming right to take up land in South Carolina by former grant from the Lords Proprietors be allowed to take up lands within six miles of these townships by virtue of such grant.

"We have been informed that the number of white men in our said province bears a small proportion to that of the blacks, which is not only a hindrance to the peopling and settling of the same but may be also of dangerous consequence from the attempts of an enemy and from an insurrection of the negroes. It is our will and pleasure that you recommend in the strongest terms to the Assembly that it pass an Act giving suitable encouragement to all who shall import servants into the province, either men or women; and, as an encouragement for white servants to come, we are gracious to allow you to grant fifty acres of land, free of quitrent, to all white servants, men or women, who shall have served their masters the whole term of their agreement, and shall be allowed afterwards to become planters or settlers in the said province.

"You will not make any grants of land to any person whatsoever under a less quitrent than four shillings, proclamation money, for over one hundred acres, except for the first ten years to white servants as mentioned in the foregoing article and for those who shall undertake to settle the eleven aforementioned townships, or any of them.

"And to the end, the Ecclesiastical Jurisdiction of the Lord Bishop of London may obtain in that, our province, so far as conveniently may be, we do think fit that you do give all countenance and encouragement to the exercise of the same.

"No school master shall be allowed to teach school in the province without the license of the Lord Bishop of London.

"A table of marriages established by the Canons of the Church of England must be hung up in every orthodox church and duly observed, and you must get a law passed in the Assembly of that province, if not already done, for the strict observance of said table.

"We have granted unto Edmund, Lord Bishop of London, the Right Reverend Father in God, and under our great seal of Great Britain, whereby he is empowered to exercise ecclesiastical jurisdiction by himself, or by such commissaries as he shall appoint in our several plantations in America. And you must give all commissaries due encouragement to the said Lord Bishop of London, in the legal exercise of such jurisdiction.

"You must cause all laws already made against blasphemy, profaneness, adultery, fornication, polygamy, incest, profanation of the Lord's Day, swearing, and drunkenness to be vigorously executed. You are so to punish the above named vices that, by such example, infidels may be invited and persuaded to embrace the Christian religion.

"You must recommend the Assembly to enter upon proper methods for erecting and maintaining schools in order to be training up youths to read and to the necessary knowledge of the principles of religion; and you are also, with the assistance of the Council and Assembly, to find out the best means to facilitate and encourage the conversion of Negroes and Indians to the Christian religion.

"You are particularly enjoined to use all possible ways and means for regaining the affections of the Indians and to preserve a good correspondence with such of them as remain faithful to our interest, but especially to the Cherokees. You are hereby directed to recommend in strongest terms to Indian traders to be just and reasonable in their dealings with the native Indians, and to recommend to the Assembly the passing of such laws as may be necessary for the encouragement and protection of such Indians as shall adhere to our interest.

"You shall take care that all planters and inhabitants and Christian servants be fitly provided with arms, and that they be listed under good officers, mustered, and trained, to be in readiness for the defense of the province, and especially in those parts bordering upon the Indians.

"Give due encouragement and invitation to merchants and others who shall bring trade to the province, particularly to the Royal African Company, and others, to the end that the province may have a constant and sufficient supply of merchantable negroes at moderate rates." (B. P. R. O., copy in archives Historical Commission of South Carolina, Columbia.)

In compliance with these orders of the King in 1730, nine townships in South Carolina in the interior on the banks of rivers were laid out. In establishing and settling these townships, the English government laid the foundation for the prosperous colony of South Carolina, which later became the State. Until these townships were settled, the colony of South Carolina at any time might have failed.

CHAPTER II.

THE KING'S TREE AND WILLIAMSBURG TOWNSHIP.

Some explorer, whose name has been lost, long before 1730, laboriously rowed his pettiagua from Winyaw Bay up the sinuous channel of Black River to a large white pine tree on the north bank, which he marked and called the "King's Tree." This explorer went no further westward up the river but returned to Charleston and reported to the Colonial Governor that he had worked his way up the Wee Nee River for more than a hundred miles to a place where he found a white pine tree, one like those growing on the New England hills, and that he had chopped into the sap of this "King's Tree" a broad arrow just as the King's trees in New England had been marked. This explorer told wonderful tales about the King's Tree section, and the "King's Tree" became a basal point in the "back country".

White pine trees grow normally only on highlands in Northern latitudes. It was purely by chance that this white pine tree, christened by that nameless explorer the "King's Tree", grew in Williamsburg. Only to the poet's mind can its history be known. Possibly some Indian brave, coming southward from the Great Lakes, camped on this bluff on the Wee Nee River and unwittingly dropped the seed that grew into the King's Tree. Or did some bald old eagle, bloody from his battle in the mountains, rest a while on this spot, and in a cooling shower, have washed from his matted feathers the little bit of life that grew into the King's Tree?

This white pine tree on the Wee Nee River possibly caused King George to reserve in every grant of land in these parts all white pine trees forever as the sole property of the King. In those days of sailing ships, white pine made the best masts available and the King kept them

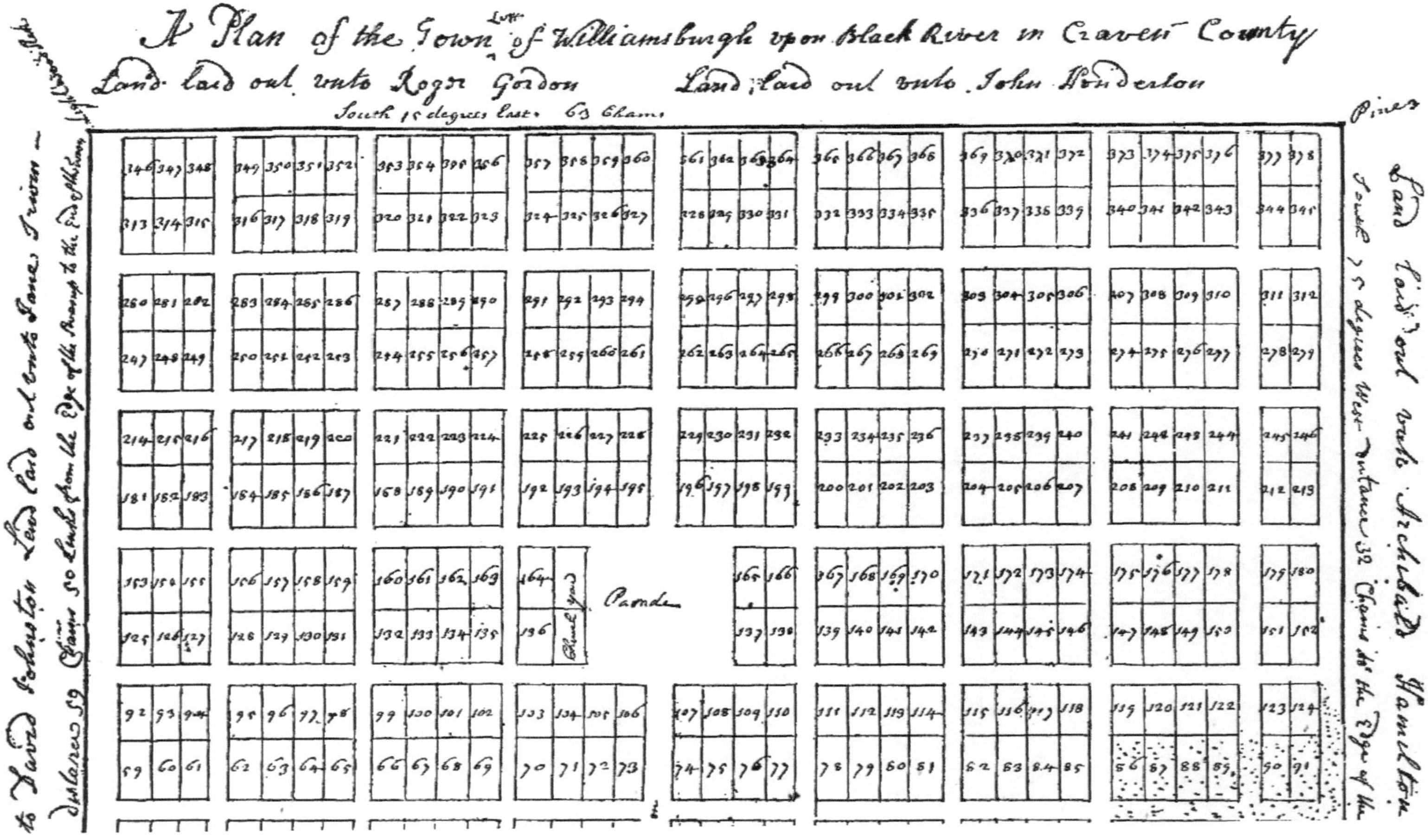
A Plan of the Town of Williamsburgh upon Black River in Craven County
Land laid out unto Roger Gordon
Land laid out unto John Henderson
South 15 degrees East 63 Chains
Pines
Land laid out unto Archibald Hamilton
South 75 degrees West distance 32 Chains to the Edge of the
to David Johnston Land laid out unto Same Town
distance 59 Chains 50 Links from the Edge of the Swamp to the End of the Town
Parade
Canal

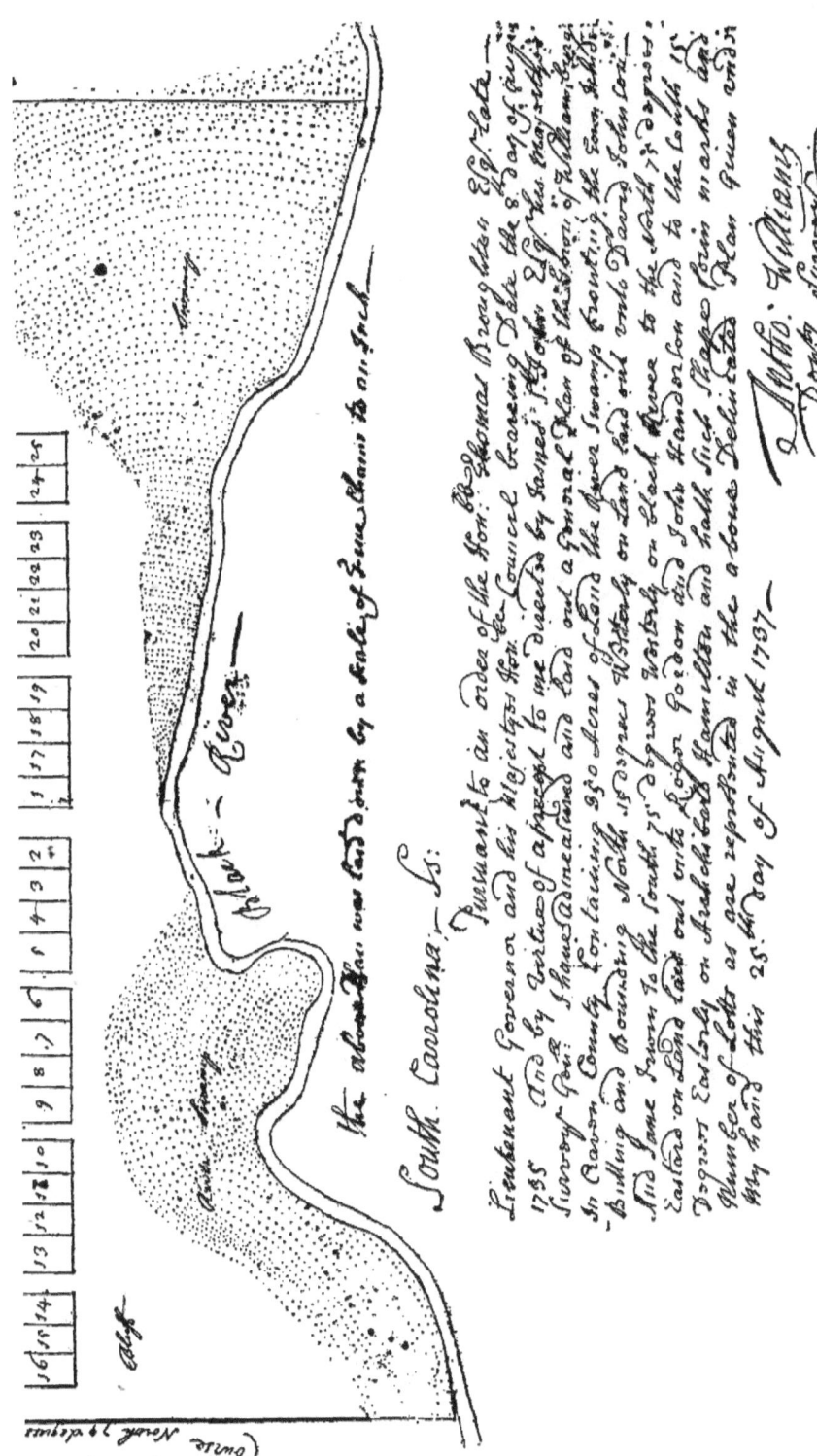

PLAN OF THE TOWN OF WILLIAMSBURG, 1737.

THE KING'S TREE AND TOWNSHIP 9

for his own. Few of these white pine trees had ever grown in Williamsburg and none of them ever went into a ship flying a Royal Banner.

Although even the English Government at this time had begun practical schemes for the development of South Carolina, it had not entirely lost hope that it would find a land of gold. When these eleven townships were decreed established in 1730, in every grant of land in them, there was reserved to the King one-tenth of all the gold and silver mined.

The Township on Black River had the King's Tree as its basal point and its establishment conformed to the order of the King made in 1730. The Township, as surveyed with the reserved lands surrounding, consisted of one hundred ninety-eight thousand and twenty-three and seven tenths English acres. It was admeasured and laid out by Anthony Williams, Deputy Surveyor, on the 18th day of March, 1736. On August 28, 1737, the Town of Williamsburg was laid out by the same surveyor. The King's Tree was located on town lot No. 1 of the plat then made. In 1923, the colored Methodist Episcopal parsonage on Main Street was situate on this spot of ground.

Williamsburg Township was a part of Craven County, one of the four original political divisions of South Carolina. In 1734, Craven County was divided into parishes, and the territory later becoming Williamsburg was a part of Prince Frederick's Parish. Prince Frederick's Parish was named in honor of one of the many imbecile sons of King George II, who never ascended the throne. It was due, probably, to the influence of William James, who settled on Black River in 1732, that the township was named Williamsburg, in honor of William of Orange. Captain John James, father of William, served under the Prince of Orange before he came to the British throne, and had great admiration for that excellent Protestant.

The wonderful tales that had been told about Charleston of the King's Tree country, and from thence had been retold in England, Scotland, and Ireland, made many poor Protestants in those countries look longingly across the Sea. Finally, they began coming. When they reached the King's Tree and saw endless pine barrens enmeshed in impenetrable swamps, from whence came strange shrill screams of unknown birds, rasping cries of savage beasts and war whoops of still more savage men, and when they realized that they must begin against primeval conditions, under unknown skies, and by black waters, they needed all the firmness of mind and body they had accumulated through a hundred generations of struggle against severity.

In 1732, a colony of forty Scotch-Irish under the leadership of Roger Gordon settled about the King's Tree on Black River on lands now within the immediate vicinity of Kingstree. Making up this colony of forty, were the families of the following men: Roger Gordon, Edward Plowden, Robert Ervin, James Armstrong, David Johnson, Adam McDonald, William James, Archibald Hamilton, David Wilson, and John Scott. This colony came up Black River and, disembarking from their vessel at Brown's Ferry, blazed their way through the forests along what is now the Kingstree-Georgetown road to the King's Tree. These were the first settlers in Williamsburg Township.

In 1734, John Witherspoon and his seven children, six of whom were married and brought children of their own, came up Black River as far as Potato Ferry; and, from this point, settled in various parts of the Township. Robert Witherspoon, grandson of John, in 1780, wrote the following account of the Witherspoon Colony, the original manuscript, of which this is a true copy, is in the possession of the descendants of the late Dr. J. R. Witherspoon, of Alabama.

"John Witherspoon and Janet Witherspoon were born in Scotland about the year 1670. They lived in their younger years near Glasgow, at a place called Begardie, and were married in 1693. In 1695, they left Scotland and settled at Knockbracken, in the Parish of Drumbo, County of Down, Ireland, where they lived in comfortable circumstances and good credit until the year 1734. He then removed with his family to South Carolina.

"We went on board the ship called 'The Good Intent' on the 14th of September, and were detained by headwinds fourteen days in the Lough at Belfast. On the second day after we set sail, my grandmother, Janet, died and was interred in the boisterous ocean, which was an affecting sight to her offspring.

"We were sorely tossed at sea with storms, which caused our ship to spring a leak; our pumps were kept incessantly at work day and night for many days together and our mariners seemed many times at their wits' end. But it pleased God to bring us all safe to land, except my grandmother, about the first of December.

"But to return,—my grandfather and grandmother had seven children. Their names were as follows, viz.: Janet (or Jennet), David, James, Elizabeth, Robert, Mary, and Gavin. Their daughter Janet was born in Scotland and was married to John Fleming in Ireland. They had a large family of children born in Ireland and brought seven of them to this place, Williamsburg, viz.: Isabella, John, Elizabeth, James, Janet, Penelope, and William. My uncle, John Fleming, died in 1750, in a good old age; my aunt Janet died in 1761 in the sixty-sixth year of her age. My uncle David was born in 1697, married to Ann Pressley and brought with him to this place two children, viz.: Sarah and Janet. He died in the year 1772 in the sixty-seventh year of his age.

"My aunt Elizabeth was married to William James and they brought with them to this place four children, viz.: Mary, Janet, John, and William. They both died in the year 1750, he forty-nine and she forty-seven years of age.

"My uncle Robert was married to Mary Stuart and by her had two children, Mary and John; his first wife, Mary, died in Ireland. He married his second wife, Hester Jane Scott, a short time before he left Ireland and brought his two children with him to this place. His wife, Hester Jane, died in 1756, aged forty years; he died in 1758, aged fifty-three years.

"My aunt Mary was married to David Wilson in Ireland, and brought to this place two children, William and John. My uncle David died in 1750, aged fifty years, and she died in 1765, in the fifty-eighth year of her age.

"My uncle Gavin, the youngest son of my grandparents, was born in 1712, and was unmarried when he left Ireland.

"It is to be remembered that we did not all come over in one ship, nor in the same year, for my uncles, William James and David Wilson, and their families, with uncle Gavin, left Belfast in 1732, and uncle Robert followed in 1736. As I said, we landed in Charleston three weeks before Christmas in 1734. We found the inhabitants very kind. We remained in that place until after Christmas and were put on board an open boat, with tools, one year's provisions, and one steel mill for each family. Our provisions consisted of Indian corn, rice, wheat flour, beef, pork, some rum, and salt; and, for each hand over sixteen years of age, one axe, one broad and one narrow hoe.

"We were much distressed in our passage, as it was in the depth of winter and we were exposed to the inclemency of the weather by day and by night; and that which added to the grief of all persons on board were the profane and blasphemous oaths and expressions of the patroon and his boatmen. They brought us up as far as Potato Ferry on Black River, about twenty miles from Georgetown, where they put us on shore.

"We lay for some time in Samuel Commander's barn, while the boat made her way up to the King's Tree, with the goods and provisions on board, and was probably the first boat that had ever ascended the River to that place. While the women were left at Commander's the men went up to build dirt houses, or rather potato houses, to take their families to. They also brought up a few horses and what help they could get from the few inhabitants, in order to carry their families, children, and other necessary articles up; as the woods were full of water, and the weather very cold, it made it go very hard with the women and children.

"We set out in the morning the last of January, a part reached Mr. McDonald's, others as far as Mr. Plowden's, and Mr. James Armstrong's, and a part to my uncle, William James'. Their little cabins were as full that night as they could hold and the next day every one made the best he could to his own place. This was on the first of February, 1735, when we came to the place called the Bluff, three miles below the King's Tree. My mother and we children were still in expectations of coming to an agreeable place, but when we arrived and saw nothing but a wilderness, and instead of a comfortable house, no other than one of dirt, our spirits sank; and what added to our trouble was that the pilot who came with us from uncle William James' left us as soon as he came in sight of the place. My father gave us all the comfort he could by telling us that we would soon get all the trees cut down and in a short time there would be plenty of inhabitants and that we would be able to see from house to house.

"While we were here, the fire went out that we brought from Boggy Swamp. My father had heard that up the river swamp was the King's Tree. Although there was no path nor did he know the distance, he followed up the meanderings of the swamp until he came to the branch and by that means he found Roger Gordon's place. We watched him as far as the trees would let us see and returned to our dolorous hut, expecting never to see him or any human being more. But after some time, he returned with fire and we were somewhat comforted, but evening coming on the wolves began to howl on all sides. We then feared being devoured by wild beasts, as we had neither gun nor dog, nor even a door to our house, howbeit we set to and gathered fuel and made a good fire and so we passed the first night.

"The next morning being clear and moderate, we began to stir about, and about midday there arose a cloud at Southwest, attended with high wind, lightning, and thunder. The rain quickly penetrated through the poles of the hut and brought down the sand with which it was covered and which seemed for a while to cover us alive. The lightening and claps were very awful and lasted for a good space of time. I do not remember to have seen a much severer gust than that was. I believe we all sincerely wished to be again at Belfast. But the fright was soon over and the evening cleared up comfortable and warm.

"The boat that brought up the goods arrived safe at King's Tree. People were much oppressed in bringing away the articles, for as there were no houses near, they were obliged to toil hard and carry them on their backs, consisting of clothing, beds, chests, provisions, tools, pots, bowls; and, as at that time there were but few roads or paths, every family had to travel the best way it could, which was near double distance to some, for they had to follow swamps and branches as their guides at first and after some time, some men got such a knowledge of the woods as to be able to blaze paths, so that the people soon found out to follow blazes from place to place.

"As the winter season was far advanced, the time to prepare land for planting was very short, yet the people were generally healthy and strong. All that could do anything wrought diligently and continued clearing and planting as long as the season would admit. So they made provisions for that year. As they had but few beasts to feed, a little served them; and as the range was good, there was no need of feeding creatures for several years.

"I remember that the first thing my father brought from the boat was his gun, which was one of Queen Anne's muskets. He had her loaded with swan shot, and one morning while we were at breakfast there was a travelling 'possum passing by the door, my mother screamed out, "There is a great bear!" Mother and we children hid ourselves behind some barrels and a chest at the far end of the hut, while father got his gun and steadied her past the fork that held up the other end of our house and shot him about the hinder parts, which caused him to grin in a frightful manner. Father was in haste to give him another bout, but the shot, being mislaid in the hurry, could not be found, and we were penned up for some time. Father at last ventured out and killed him with a pole. Another circumstance which gave us much alarm was the Indians when they came to hunt in the Spring. They came in great numbers like the Egyptian locusts, but were not hurtful.

"We had a great deal of trouble and hardships in our first settling, but the few inhabitants were favored with health and strength. We were also much oppressed with fear on divers other accounts, especially of being massacred by the Indians, or bit by snakes, or torn by wild beasts, or of being lost and perishing in the woods, of whom there were three persons who were never found.

"My uncle Robert, with his second wife and two children, Mary and John, arrived here near the last of August, 1736. He came on the fine ship called the 'New-built', which was a ship of great burthen and brought a great many passengers, who chiefly came and settled here and had to travel by land from Georgetown, and instead of being furnished with provisions, etc., as we were, they had money given them by the public. When they arrived, our second crop had been planted and was coming forward, but the season being warm and they much fatigued, many were taken sick with ague and fever, some died and some became dropsical and also died.

"About this time, August or September, 1736, the people began to form into a religious society, built a church and sent to Ireland for a minister. One came whose name was Robert Herron, who staid only three years and returned to Ireland. The first call was made out for Reverend John Willison of Scotland, author of the 'Mother's Catechism', 'A Practical Treatise on the Lord's Supper', and of the 'Discourses on the Atonement'.

"The following anecdote is handed down by tradition of Mr. Gavin Witherspoon; meeting a neighbor one day, this conversation is reported to have taken place. Witherspoon—'Wull, we must have a minister.' 'Wull, Mister Witherspoon, wha wull ye git to be your minister?' 'Wull, wha but Mister Willison o' Dundee?' 'But the minister must have a muckle sight o' money for his living,' 'And that we must gie him,' says Mr. Witherspoon. 'An' how much, Mr. Witherspoon, wull ye gie?' 'Ten pounds', was the ready reply. 'But, Mr. Witherspoon, whar'll ye git the ten pounds?' 'Why if wus comes to wus, I ien can sell my cow,' says he. Mr. Willison, of Dundee, was accordingly sent for to preach the Gospel in the wilds of America.

"In the fall of the year 1737, my grandfather, John Witherspoon, took a disease called Rose-in-the-leg, which occasioned a fever from which he died. He was the first person buried at the Williamsburg Meeting House, which he had assisted to erect. About the same time, 1737, my father had a daughter, Elizabeth, that died, aged three years, born at the place called the Bluff, where we lived.

"My grandfather was a man of middling or common stature, of a fine, healthy constitution, of fair complexion, and somewhat bow-legged. He was well acquainted with the Scriptures, had volubility in prayer, and was a zealous adherent to the principles of what was called in his day the Reformed Protestant Church of Scotland. He had also a great aversion to Episcopacy, and whoever will impartially read the history of the times of his younger years in Scotland will see that his prejudices were not without cause. It was his lot to live in a time of great distress to the persecuted Church, during the reign of James the Seventh of Scotland and Second of England. Being one who followed field-meetings, he and some others of his kindred were much harassed by the Papists. Yet, notwithstanding, if his younger years were attended with some trouble, he still enjoyed great peace and tranquility in his after life and had the comfort and happiness of living to see his seven children all creditably married and settled for themselves; and, except the death of my grandmother, his beloved wife, he never knew what it was to part by death with one of his own immediate family, a blessing which few persons have granted to them, especially at his advanced age.

"My father's name was James, the third child and second son of my grandparents. He was born at the beginning of the present century, lived with his parents at Drumbo, County of Down, until he was twenty-five years old, when he married my mother, whose name was Elizabeth McQuoid, in the twentieth year of her age.

"My grandfather, Robert McQuoid, married Sarah Campbell. They both died in Ireland, he in 1728, aged eighty-six, and she was aged about eighty. My father and mother settled in the Parish of Graba, near the Canningburn Mills, where they lived about nine years and sold their possessions to embark for America. My father brought the family to my grandparents at Knockbracken about the 1st of May, 1734, and left us there until the 1st of September. In the meantime, he wrought at the reed-making business. He brought four children on board of the ship, viz.: David, Robert, John, and Sarah. Sarah died in Charleston shortly after their arrival, and was the first person buried in the Scotch Meeting House Yard.

"In May, 1743, the Reverend Mr. John Ray arrived here from Scotland. He came upon a call which his congregation had sometime before sent to the Reverend Mr. John Willison, of Dundee. Mr. Ray continued a faithful, zealous, and laborious worker in the congregation until 1761. He being abroad on a visit up Black River was taken sick with the pleurisy and died. The remains of this eminently pious man were brought down from Salem, where he died, and buried at the church where he had for eighteen years successfully labored, being about forty-six years of age. 'Blessed are the dead that die in the Lord from henceforth: Yea, saith the spirit, that they may rest from their labors, and their works do follow them.'

"I was born in Ireland on the 20th day of August, 1728, was my father's second son; in my youth he taught me to weave, as he also taught my elder brother, David, to make reeds. The family lived together at the Bluff until March, 1749. My father then moved to Thorntree, a place situated between the Lower Bridge on Black River and Murray's Ferry on the Santee. I there went out and wrought at the weaving business with my uncle, Gavin Witherspoon, who lived at a place called Megart's (McGirts) Swamp, until the September following. I went next to overseeing for a Mr. Fleming, near Black River Church, twenty-five miles below King's Tree, where I remained until January, 1752, and then returned to my father's.

"The reason of my return was that it had pleased God—in the last awful epidemic that prevailed in Williamsburg in the year 1749 and 1750, usually called the 'Great Mortality', and which had carried off near eighty persons, many of them the principal people or heads of families—to remove by death my elder brother, David, and my sister, Jane, both in the year 1750. My father being then in a very feeble and infirm state of health and unable to attend to his own business, I left my own to take care of his. I remained with my parents until 1758, when, on the 2nd of March, I married Elizabeth Heathly, a young lady then in the eighteenth year of her age, and settled for myself four miles below King's Tree and near the River.

"I afterwards removed and settled one mile higher up the River nearer King's Tree, in 1761, and immediately on the public road leading from that place to the Lower Bridge on Black River. Here I had a more comfortable and healthy residence, and here also, I expect to spend the remainder of my days.

"Our first son, James, was born on the 20th of March, 1759; our second son, Thomas, was born on the 22nd of March, 1761, and died on the 8th of September, 1765, aged four years and six months; our first daughter, Ann, was born January 4, 1763; our third son, John, was born January 20, 1765, and died on the 24th of July, 1767, aged two years and six months; our fourth son, Robert, was born January 29, 1767; our second daughter, Mary, was born March 20, 1769; our third daughter, Elizabeth, was born July 25, 1771; our fifth son, John, was born March 17, 1774; our sixth son, Thomas, was born July 23, 1776.

"My honored mother departed this life on the 22nd day of January, 1777, in the seventy-second year of her age, and was the last surviving branch of the old stock of our family. As I have had an intimate personal knowledge of their lives and deaths, I bear them testimony that they were servers of God, were well acquainted with the Scriptures, were much engaged in prayer, were strict observers of the Sabbath, in a word, they were a stock of people that studied outward piety as well as inward purity of life.

"Indeed God blessed this settlement at first with a number of eminently pious and devoted men, out of whom I chose to set down some of their names, viz.: William Wilson, David Allen, William Hamilton, John Porter, William

James, David Wilson, John James, James McCleland, Robert Wilson, Robert Paisley, James Bradley, John Turner, William Frierson, to whom I add my own father and my three uncles, David, Robert, and Gavin. These were men of great piety in their day, indeed they were men of renown. May the glorious King and Head of the Church for His own glory still maintain and keep up men of piety and holiness as a blessing to this place and congregation to the latest posterity is the heart request of the unworthy scribe."

CHAPTER III.

ORIGINAL SETTLERS.

From 1735 to 1737, a great many settlers came to the new township on Black River and practically every acre of land had been taken up by these settlers within a year after the township had been surveyed. Every man settling here was granted a half acre town lot and fifty acres of land in the township for himself, his wife, and each one of his children.

These are the names of the heads of families who had settled in Williamsburg Township up to 1737: Robert Allison, John Anderson, James Armstrong, David Arnett, James Adams, John Athol, John Ballentine, John Barnes, George Barr, Joseph Barry, John Basnett, Benjamin Bates, Matthew Bernard, Joseph Bignion, James Blakely, John Blakely, John Bliss, John Borland, Jonathan Bostwick, James Bradley, Thomas Brown, George Burrows, William Camp, William Campbell, William Cochran, John Connor, William Copeland, William Cooper, James Crawford, Thomas Dale, John Dick, Nathaniel Drew, Thomas Dial, Robert Ervin, Francis Finley, Robert Finley, James Fisher, John Fleming, John Frierson, William Frierson, Aaron Frierson, David Fulton, James Gamble, Roger Gibson, Gabriel Girrand, John Gotea, Roger Gordon, Francis Goddard, Hugh Graham, Hugh Green, George Green, Richard Hall, Thomas Hall, Archibald Hamilton, William Hamilton, Christopher Harvey, William Harvey, John Herron, George Hunter, Peter Hume, John James, William James, John Jamison, William Johnson, Joseph Johnson, David Johnson, Abraham Jordan, Samuel Kennedy, John Knox, Crafton Kerwin, Richard Lake, John Lane, James Law, Patrick Lindsay, William Lowry, Richard Malone, John Matthews, Samuel Montgomery, Daniel Mooney, John Moore, William Morgan, Joseph

Moody, John McCullough, Nathaniel McCullough, Daniel Murray, David McCants, John McCants, James McCauley, James McCutchen, James McClelland, Alexander McClinchy, William McCormick, William McKnight, John McElveen, Thomas McCrea, Alexander McCrea, William McDole, Hugh McGill, David McEwen, James McEwen, Andrew McClelland, James McGee, Edward McMahan, Matthew Nelson, John Nicholson, William Orr, James Pollard, John Porter, John Pressley, William Pressley, Edward Plowden, John Robinson, Joseph Rhodus, Andrew Rutledge, John Scott, James Scott, William Scott, James Smith, Charles Starne, James Stuart, John Stubbs, John Sykes, William Syms, James Taylor, William Turbeville, William Troublefield, Matthew Vannalle, John Whitfield, William Williamson, Henry Williams, Anthony Williams, David Wilson, John Wilson, William Wilson, David Witherspoon, Gavin Witherspoon, James Witherspoon, John Witherspoon, Robert Witherspoon, Robert Wilson, and Robert Young.

These original settlers in Williamsburg Township came from England, Ireland, Scotland, Germany, Holland, and from the New England States, Pennsylvania and Virginia. They were all about the same class of men. They were people who had been non-conformists as to State-Church religion, and nearly all of their families had lost their property in the religious conflicts of the seventeenth century. The greater number of them had lived in Ireland for many years before coming to America. They had migrated from England and from Scotland to Ireland on account of fair promises on the part of the English King. These failing them, they sought refuge in America.

The Blakelys, Bradleys, Browns, Finleys, Gambles, Halls, Humes, Johnsons, Matthews, Murrays, Nelsons, Plowdens, Rutledges, Taylors, and Wilsons were of English blood. The Barrs, Dials, and others were of German descent. The Bignions, Janneretts, Vanalles, and Orrs were of Swiss origin. The Barrys, Kennedys, Lindsays, Lowrys, Malones, and Morgans were Irish. The Arnetts, Campbells, Crawfords, Ervins, Friersons, Fultons, Flemings, Grahams, Hamiltons, Montgomerys, McColloughs, McCreas, McGills, Pressleys, Scotts, and Witherspoons were Scotch-Irish. The Williams and the James families were Welsh.

Within the territory limits of what is now Williamsburg County, but outside of Williamsburg Township as surveyed in 1736, and whose names have not heretofore been mentioned, had settled the following: William and Hesther Brown; John and Sarah Lane; Daniel and Sarah Shaw; Caleb and Mary Avant; Samuel and Mary Miller; John and Hannah Avant; John and Martha Thompson; Anthony and Mary Atkinson; Anthony and Mary White; John and Elizabeth Green; John and Anne Brunson; John and Mary McIntosh; John and Elizabeth Cribb; Thomas and Elizabeth Cribb; John and Margaret Henlin; Thomas and Mary Harrington; William and Mary Barton; John and Rebecca Evans; William and Mary Heathly; William and Lydia Green; William and Margaret Turbeville; Joseph and Ann Rhodus; James and Priscilla McGirt; Joseph and Mary Cantey; Samuel and Anne Cantey; William and Mary Snow; Robert and Mary Oliver; Abraham and Lydia Michaux; Michael and Mary Murphy; James and Elizabeth McPherson; John and Lucretia McDowell; William and Elizabeth Chicken; William and Elizabeth McGee; John and Sarah Frierson; Henry and Rebecca Bennett; Paul and Margaret Jaudon; William Cooper, Francis Cordes, Peter Guerry, William Saunders; John and Ann Leger; Daniel and Mary McDaniel; Jonathan and Hesther Christmas; John and Ann Conyers; Bryan and Mary Kennedy; James and Frances Jenner; John and Isabella Jamison; James and Cassiah Crawford; Hardy and Elizabeth Futhy; Thomas and Mary McCormick; Anthony and Ann Phillips; Alexander and

Priscilla Campbell; John and Elizabeth Kelly; John and Elizabeth McDonald; Thomas and Dorothy Jenkins; Richard and Elizabeth Jones; John and Philadelphia Turbeville; John and Margaret Lee; Stephen and Elizabeth DuBose; John and Rebecca Hodges; John and Mary Singleton; William and Sarah Purvis; John and Arabella Scott; Lodowick and Anne Hudson; Daniel and Susannah McGinney; William and Jane Green; John and Elizabeth Dozier; John and Hannah Davis; James and Mehitabel Boyd; John and Mary Britton Sinkler; William and Sarah Tompkins Dinkins; Moses and Hester Jolly Britton; Alexander and Elizabeth Ball Davidson; Charles and Susannah Sanders Turbeville; Moses Britton; Daniel and Elizabeth Hyrney Britton; George and Hannah Saunders; and Peter and Isabel Tamplet.

These people settled along Black River from the point where it turns abruptly Northward, just after entering Georgetown County from Williamsburg County, and along the present Williamsburg-Georgetown County line to the Pee Dee River. This settlement was called Winyaw, and this was the first part of the present County of Williamsburg that was inhabited by white people. Some of these people lived there in 1710. They organized Prince Frederick's Church in 1713.

Reverend William Screven and his Congregation of Dissenters from the Church of England were the first permanent settlers in the Winyaw section. They were granted a large part of the territory on both sides of that section of Black River flowing through ancient Winyaw. While Mr. Screven was a militant Antipaedo-Baptist, many of the Dissenters who came with him were of the Presbyterian faith.

The names of some of these Baptist and Presbyterian Dissenters who settled in Winyaw along Black River and Black Mingo from 1700 to 1736 were: Reverend William Screven, and his sons, Elisha, Robert and William; John

Peter Somerhoeff, Dugal MacKeithan, John Nesmith, William Brockinton, John Godfrey, Jonah Collins, Sabrine Burnett, Alexander McGuinness, David Fulton, Dr. Thomas Potts, William Shepard, Dr. James King, John Hendlin, Samuel Commander, Joseph Commander, John Commander, Joshua Green, Samuel Vareen, Thomas Wood, Jeremiah Vareen, Jonathan Westberry, Nathaniel Pygott, John McNally, Joseph Chandler, James Armstrong, Isaac Brunson, Thomas Boone, James Hoole, Joshua Jolly, John Wallace, Thomas North, Dr. John A. Fincke, William Davis, Sr., Francis Futhy, William McFarland, Ebenezer Jones, James Cunningham, Samuel Jenkins, Charles Baxter, William Fraser, George Powell, Dr. John Cantzor, David McIver, Abraham Giles, Daniel Myers, and William Daniel.

From the South from 1720 to 1737, there crossed over the Santee River at Lenud's Ferry into Williamsburg many French Huguenots, who had fled in 1685 from their native land after the Revocation of the Edict of Nantes to Charleston and had gradually gone Northward. Among these were John Leger, Peter Lequex, John Perret, Noah Sere, Henry Bedon, James Sinclair, Abraham Perdreau, Henry Mouzon, Francis Lesesne, Abraham Michau, Paul Jaudon, Peter Gourdin, Theodore Gourdin, James Ferdon, Daniel Bluset, Abraham Lenud, Paul Bonneau, and Rene Richbourgh.

There were a large number of settlers who came to Williamsburg during the period from 1737 to 1775. Among them were John Gregg, John Boone, John Burgess, William Burgess, William Byrd, John Cameron, James Kennedy, Charles Cantley, Benjamin Capell, George Chandler, William Cockfield, Arthur Cunningham, Daniel Epps, James Ferguson, Henry O'Neal, Ebenezer Bagnal, James Conyers, Charles F. Gordon, William Gordon, David Gordon, Dr. John Graham, John Grant, James Harper, Drury Harrington, Daniel Holliday, William Holliday, Samuel

Haselden, George McCutchen, Andrew Patterson, William Reagin, William McDonald, Jeremiah Rowell, Peter Salters, Richard Singletary, Matthew Singleton, William Douglas, John and Mary Dickey, James Dickey, Charles McCallister. These were nearly all Scotch-Irish, coming here, in most cases, from the Scotch-Irish settlement in Pennsylvania. Some of them, however, came directly from Ireland.

While there were among these original settlers in Williamsburg men and women of English, Scotch, French, Irish, Welsh, German, and Danish descent, most of them came to this district from Ireland. The Scotch-Irish element, largely influenced by the French Huguenot, soon gained the ascendency, and has remained the dominant element in the life of Williamsburg.

CHAPTER IV.

THE PEOPLE WHO SETTLED WILLIAMSBURG.

The history of the Scotch-Irish for more than two thousand years is one continuous story of hardihood made splendid by heroism. Some students think they were descendants of the Gog of Magog, of whom Ezekiel writes, and connected with the Scythians whom Alexander fought and failed to conquer. Others believe they were the backbone of the warlike tribe of Sahi that so disturbed the Assyrian King Asurbanipal (668-626 B. C.)

It is generally accepted that these Scotch-Irish were the same nomad tribes that worked their way eastward along the shores of the Black Sea, by the Danube through Switzerland and France and Spain, from whence they went into Ireland before the days of Saint Patrick. After spending six centuries in Ireland, some of them crossed over the Irish Sea into North Britain. Here they fought the Picts continuously for hundreds of years. After remaining in Scotland for almost a thousand years, during which time they gave this land a name and made it a "thing of the soul," in the seventeenth century, they turned again home into Ireland, and settled in Counties Down and Antrim, along the northern shores.

In his wars on the Roman Catholics in Ireland, James I destroyed almost all of the people who lived in the northern portion of Ireland, Counties Donegal, Londonderry, Tyrone, Armagh, Antrim, and Down. This part of Ireland was left a wilderness after his forces had completed their conquest.

There were, in Scotland, at this time, a great many men of influence and power who were Roman Catholics, and who continuously made the lives of these Presbyterians burdensome and their condition intolerable. After this northern part of Ireland had been cleared of Roman Catholics and their property confiscated, the English Government induced a great many of these Scotch Congregationalists, living in Argyll, Sterling, Renfrew, Glasgow, Lanark, Ayr, and Bute, to cross the North Channel into Counties Antrim and Down, Ireland, and there repopulate the country. These Scotch were made fair promises, both as to the ownership of the land and as to permission to enjoy their own religion. They came in great numbers. When William of Orange ascended the throne of England, it seemed that these Congregationalists, or Presbyterians, in Scotland, and especially in Ireland, would enjoy the right to work out their own spiritual salvation according to their own notions. It was at this time that most of the Scotch, who later came to Williamsburg, migrated into the Counties Down and Antrim, Ireland.

For about thirty years, the Scotch, who had gone into the north of Ireland, thought that they had found the promised land. They understood they had received absolute titles to the lands on which they lived and went to work immediately to develop them. They were industrious and frugal by nature. Later, after they had transformed a wilderness into a pleasing place for human habitation, they realized that they had been tricked when they were forced to submit to the imposition of enormous rents imposed by absentee landlords.

Many of these Scotch-Irish, as they then had begun to be called, chose to leave the foundations which they had laid in Ireland, and migrate to America. Many of them about 1720 came to the New England States, Pennsylvania and South Carolina, but most of the original settlers in Williamsburg elected to remain in Ireland until about 1735, when they came direct to Williamsburg Township. A few of them had come to this section between 1725 and 1732 and had settled on Black River.

Many of these original Scotch-Irish settlers can trace their lineage until pleasing records run into beautiful tradition. The following are taken as types:

John Nesmith settled North of Black Mingo in Williamsburg in 1725. He was the progenitor of all the Nesmiths of this section. He was born on the shores of the River Bann in the North of Ireland in 1670 and died in Williamsburg in 1750.

The Nesmiths have owned land on the Tweed since the thirteenth century. Twelve miles from Glasgow are two ancient homes of the family, one at Hamilton and another at Auchingraymont. The name is said to have originated in this way: Between September 8, 1249, when Alexander III, of Scotland, was crowned King, and March 16, 1286, when he died, the story goes, an aide-de-camp of the King on the eve of a battle was required by him to mend his armor. Though a man of powerful physique and a brave warrior, he was unsuccessful as a mechanic. For his prowess, great daring, and achievements in the battle, he was knighted by the King, with this laconic saying, "Although he is nae smith, he is a brave gentleman." The armorial bearings of the family refer to this remark: A drawn sword between two war "martels" broken, with the motto in old Scotch dialect, "Not by knavery, but by bravery."

John Scott settled at the King's Tree on Black River November 1, 1732. From that day until this, March 7, 1923, there has lived a John Scott at the King's Tree in Williamsburg. The original settler was born in Galloway, Scotland, in 1665, migrated to County Down, Ireland, in 1690, and died in Williamsburg in 1749.

Legend says two brothers of Galloway, banished for participation in a rebellion, retired to Rankelburn in Ettrick Forest, where the keeper received them gladly on account of their skill in the chase. Soon afterwards, Kenneth MacAlpin, King of Scotland, came to hunt in this royal forest and pursued a buck from Ettrick to the glen now called Buccleuch. Here the stag stood at bay on the top of a steep hill, and the King and his attendants were thrown when attempting to reach the object of that chase. John, one of the brothers from Galloway, had followed the hunting party on foot; and, coming in, ran up the hill, seized the buck by the horns, threw him across his shoulders and ran about a mile to Cracracross, where Kenneth had halted, and laid his prey at his sovereign's feet. Kenneth then said:

> "And for the buck thou stoutly brought
> To us up that steep heuch,
> Thy designation ever shall
> Be John Scott in Bucksleuch."

This line of Scotts is one of the most illustrious and ancient in Scottish history. As well at Flodden as on other famous fields, the banner of the Scotts has ever shone in the far flung battle line. The coat of arms is thus described in Burke: Gold on a bend a mullet of six points two crescents gold; Crest, a stag proper horned and hoofed gold.

John Witherspoon settled on Boggy Swamp in Williamsburg in 1734, and died in 1737. He was the first person buried at the Williamsburg Meeting House. He was born near Glasgow in 1670, moved to County Down, Ireland, in 1695, from whence he came to this country.

He was the great grandson of John Knox and his second wife, Margaret Stuart. From his Stuart great grandmother, he drew some of the blood of Robert Bruce as well as that of other Scotsmen of great strength and power —even from the Laird who became Shakespere's Banquo's Ghost.

Witherspoon is an old Scottish name and is frequently mentioned in accounts of ancient battles. A description of the coat of arms may be found in Burke's Armory. The cross and crescents thereon indicate crusader ancestry and the engrailed cross denotes possession of landed estates.

Dr. John Witherspoon, President of Princeton, member of the Continental Congress, and signer of the Declaration of Independence, was a nephew of the John Witherspoon, original settler in Williamsburg.

John Gregg settled on Cedar Swamp in Williamsburg in 1752. He was a son of Captain David MacGregor of the army of William of Orange. After the war, Captain MacGregor settled in Londonderry, Ireland, where later he was massacred by Irish Roman Catholics. John Gregg's mother migrated with him and his three brothers to Boston in 1717. As an old man, he finally came to this township.

The Gregg family is one of the most ancient and most honorable of the Irish-Scots. A Celtic proverb says, "The mountains, the MacGregors and the Devil are coeval." Another Highland saying runs, "Where MacGregor sits, that is the head of the table." Gregg, or Gregory the Great, as he is known in history, was the fourth King of the Alpin line and reigned from 876 to 893. He was of mixed Scottish and Pictish descent. The next Gregg King of Scotland was ninth in line after Gregory the Great. His grand daughter, Lady Gruoch, was the Lady MacBeth of history and of Shakesperian drama. A description of the Gregg crest and coat of arms may be found in Burke's Peerage. The ancient motto of the family was "S'rioghail Mo Dreahm," (My race is royal.)

Much romantic interest attaches to the Gregg clan. It lived under act of attainder for about three centuries, during which time it was unlawful to name a child Gregg or MacGregor. They called themselves outwardly Drummond or Murray, but every Gregg knew his name. Notwithstanding this terrible ordeal of attainder for such a long time inflicted by their government, and even though they could not call themselves by their own name, when Charles

II sought to regain the throne of England from the younger Cromwell, every member of the clan, by whatsoever name known, promptly enlisted under the banner of the man who had the royal blood. The Greggs remembered that they had occupied the throne, and it was then the Stuart's turn. For this supreme evidence of loyalty, Charles II, immediately after the Restoration, removed the attainder from them and they used their rightful name.

Probably one half of the white people of present day Williamsburg have in their veins some of the blood of one of these four original settlers, John Nesmith, John Scott, John Witherspoon, and John Gregg. All of their descendants seem to have believed in marrying early and as often as the law allowed. Their tribes have increased.

It is an old Scotch custom which seals the lips of elders everywhere but around their own firesides. No Nesmith, nor Scott, nor Witherspoon, nor Gregg, of the "straitest sect," would tell the foregoing tales of royal lines and loyal service, save to his own sons, when a look would seal the story within the family circle. Centuries of severe struggles as non-comformists have taught these Scotch-Irish or Irish-Scots many things, not the least of which is the value of keeping within yourself what little concerns only yourself.

This habit of concealing within the family as much as possible of its history has made tradition in Williamsburg exceedingly rich. Further, the effect of these tales told by fathers in sacred secrecy to sons has made a wonderful morale among these Scotch-Irish. Follow down the years the several Scotch-Irish names on the roll of original settlers in Williamsburg and some uncanny force will be felt calling all generations to answer the first roll call to war and to respond effectively in every emergency.

The French Huguenots who came to Williamsburg were strikingly like the Scotch-Irish in fundamental racial traits and instinct. It is believed that the Huguenots were derived from the same nomads that passed through France on their way to Scotland, some of these having elected to remain along the Rhone. The easy union of the sons of Francis Lesesne, Theodore Gourdin, and Henry Mouzon, who dwelt along the North bank of the Santee, with the sons of Samuel Montgomery, John McCullough, and Hugh McGill, who lived at the King's Tree, in all essential pioneer matters, notwithstanding the fact they spoke different languages, shows much to the student.

History tells no more pathetic tale than the story of these French Huguenots,—how persecution, in the name of the merciful Fisherman, drove them from the citron groves and sunny vineyards of France into the wilderness of America. A traveler in this Santee country in 1721 wrote most vividly of what he saw among these people and of how bravely and uncomplainingly they were struggling with famine and fever in this strange land. They won. Sacred fire, older than the Caesars, still burns in their bosoms.

Another distinctive race out of which Williamsburg has come was the English that settled along Black Mingo and Black River. Among these, when they came, there were two distinct and well defined factions, to wit: Those who were communicants of the Church of England and those who were Dissenters. Each of these two classes showed factional differences. The stricter sectarians of the Church of England along Black River, of whom Anthony White and Meredith Hughes are selected as typical, struggled along for years with the ever increasing Dissenter forces and finally abandoned Prince Frederick's Church and the community. The other element of these adherents of Prince Frederick's Church, of whom Edward Plowden, James Gamble, and Thomas McCrea are representative, finally joined the Dissenters becoming members of the Presbyterian Congregations of Black Mingo and of Indiantown. This element has remained in Williamsburg to this day.

The two elements among the original Dissenters of the Winyaw country were the Presbyterian and the Antipaedo Baptists. Typical of the Presbyterians were Alexander McKnight and David McIver. Their descendants supported the ancient Black Mingo Church until it failed and then united with other Presbyterian Congregations. This class were Scotsmen of the ancient faith and traditions. The Antipaedo Baptist Dissenting element was dominated by Elisha Screven and his brothers. This element was composed almost entirely of the Screven family and the descendants of the retainers that the Reverend William Screven had brought with him into Carolina.

The Reverend William Screven was the Father of the Baptist denomination in South Carolina and his influence on the religious history of the South has not been less than that of Roger Williams in the North. In his youth, he was educated for priesthood in the Church of England. Later, he was overcome by the idea that immersion was the only authorized form of baptism and dissented from the Church of England. He married Bridget Cutt, daughter of the Governor of Jamaica, whose mother married a Champernown the second time, and hence became connected with some of the oldest and most distinguished families of England. On account of his faith in immersion and of the feeling of his wife's Church of England relatives against him for preaching to dissenting congregations, he migrated to Kittery, Maine, where he had expected to preach the Gospel according to his own notion, and without let or hindrance. But, even in this wild, unsettled Colony of Maine, the Church of England still persecuted him; and, for some of his preaching, the Ecclesiastical Courts had him arrested and placed under bond not to preach the Antipaedo Baptist doctrine in Maine.

In 1696, be brought with him from Kittery, Maine, his congregation to Charleston, South Carolina, obtained a grant of land in what is now Berkeley County, and settled there on his plantation, "Somerton". A few years later, Mr. Screven abandoned his Somerton plantation and moved to Charleston, where he organized the first Baptist Church in that city. Afterwards, about 1705, he secured land on Black River and there located as the first English settler in the Black Mingo country. He saw the future for a seaport, about twenty miles down the River from his Winyaw plantation, and there planned to lay out Georgetown. He died, however, in 1713, before that work had been done.

Mr. Screven was a strong man. It seems that one drop of his blood will make a deep water Baptist, even two centuries after his death. An excellent illustration of this is found in the McCullough family of Williamsburg. John McCullough, original settler in 1736, was a Presbyterian of the severest type. He married a daughter of William James, herself a Presbyterian of the same kind. All of the McCulloughs were Presbyterians until one of them married a woman of Screven blood. All generations of the McCulloughs descended from this woman have been Baptists. One of them now living in Williamsburg, John Graham McCullough, is a leader of his denomination in this section.

The Reverend Elisha Screven was a director of both temporal and spiritual affairs in Winyaw. In 1734, he made a deed of trust to two hundred seventy acres of land for the city of Georgetown, granting plots for the necessary public buildings and for the churches of all religious denominations then represented in the Colony of South Carolina.

The people of Williamsburg were strikingly alike, although born of many nations. Probably no part of the American continent began its existence with a more homogenous colony. They were known as "poor Protestants," those who had been reduced to poverty on account of the politico-religious wars of the seventeenth century.

During the seventeenth century, there were three great Church factions in Great Britian continuously warring for supremacy. These schemes were called by Green Popery, Prelacy, and Presbyterianism. While each one claimed that it, only, knew and offered the way, the truth and the life from this world to a better one, students of history know full well that the leaders of each one of these three great Church systems were seeking more for temporal power and dominion than for spiritual grace and salvation. The fact is, in the seventeenth century, Popery and Prelacy and Presbyterianism were simply three great relentless political parties that worked for success and counted not the cost of human suffering and human woe.

It may be said, however, that the party denominated Prelacy did not use such fearful means for promoting its ends as did Popery or Presbyterianism. By Prelacy is meant the scheme of the Church of England. The Presbyterian idea and the Papal idea had been, up to this time, the two great warring Church factions. The Church of England grew out of an attempted compromise between the other two uncompromising schemes. It essayed to appropriate the body of Roman Catholicism and to breathe into it the breath of Presbyterianism.

The severities practiced by the Roman Catholic Church and by the Presbyterians in the name of the merciful Nazarene were limited only by the mental abilities of their leaders. Both Papacy and Presbyterianism used the gibbet, the rack, the torch, the screw, and the cross, in England and in Scotland and in Ireland, whenever they had opportunity, up to the time of Oliver Cromwell. Oliver Cromwell and his Ironsides made the English speaking world realize the inhumanity and the absurdity of both Roman Catholicism and of Presbyterianism at that time.

Oliver Cromwell was the first man who applied the rule of reason to the Christian religion in England.

It is true that much of the absurdity in Puritanism grew out of his labors; but when he made the average man in England realize that neither the Roman Catholic Church nor the Presbyterian Congregations controlled the keys to the Kingdom of Heaven, he made a great contribution to the world. He hated alike Roman Catholicism and Presbyterianism, and cared but little for the compromise, the Church of England. John Milton, his Latin Secretary, recorded that he said, "Presbyter is but priest writ large." Cromwell punished alike the criminal priests and the presbuteros, who were violating the principles of humanity in the names of their political religions.

It was out of these fierce religious wars that the settlers of Williamsburg came. Many of them had lost their fathers in Scotland and Ireland, when, incited by their religious leaders, their own tribes had undertaken to exterminate a settlement of Roman Catholics or a force of Roman Catholics had attacked them.

The deepest desire of every one of the original settlers, who came to Williamsburg, was to be let alone by everybody and by everything, from his nearest neighbor to the King of England; and every settler in Williamsburg Township realized that every other settler was dominated by the same desire. Each man built his pioneer hut as far away from the blazed trails, called roads, as was possible, and where it was most inaccessible from these beaten ways. They found abiding peace in these wilds of Williamsburg.

CHAPTER V.

ECONOMIC CONDITIONS.

Priests and kings could not make these Scotch-Irish conform to a religion which was not of their very own, but these same priests and kings could withhold lands from them and could confiscate what little worldly goods the Scotch-Irish accumulated from time to time.

The original settlers of Williamsburg came to this wilderness for economic reasons—to secure titles to land and to make it bring forth what was necessary for their sustenance and comfort. They were called "Poor-Protestants" when they came and were so described in official records of South Carolina until the War of the Revolution. Their struggles against the fearful power of the mediaeval political state church gods had made them poor, and had bereft them of all save their strong bodies and their unconquerable spirits.

These Scotch-Irish paid their passage to this province, but accepted aid from the King in the way of provisions and agricultural implements for the first few years. It takes a strong imagination to conceive the conditions the first forty found when they arrived at the King's Tree on Black River in 1732. Immediately surrounding the King's Tree were swamp lands within which sandy pine barrens were scattered. These swamps were thickly covered with cyprus trees bearded with long gray moss. Underneath these cyprus trees were massed and matted luxuriant undergrowth tangled with muscadines, Cherokee roses, and jessamine. Over the tree tops, strange birds screamed. From the dark recesses about their roots, wolves and panthers howled; venomous snakes crawled here and there; and swarms of death-dealing insects shaded the sunny skies. But in the midst of all this rampant nature, the mocking bird sang and the wild dove called, and the Scotch-Irish knew that a benevolent God reigned and rewarded righteousness. They found dry places in the pinelands and there they erected rude huts as they had known in Ireland.

Clearing this thickly wooded land was a labor of Hercules, but these Scotch-Irish toiled until they had prepared and planted grain in a soil of which they knew but little. The soil here was not like that in Northern Ireland, and their first harvest brought but little reward for their labor.

In 1734, Samuel Eveleigh, a merchant in Charleston, wrote to George Morley, Provost Marshal of the Colony of South Carolina, who was then in London, a letter from which the following is an extract: "Last November was twelve months came over a party of Irish Protestants from the North of Ireland, which the Governor got settled at a Township called Williamsburg at Winyaw on Black River, where the land is good. They immediately made up some huts to cover them from the weather and then went to clearing the land, which they planted and made very good crops so that they had grain enough for themselves and five hundred bushels to spare. There are several families since arrived and gone there to settle and I believe in the usual time, it will be a considerable settlement. I can not tell you the particular allowance they have out of the public exactly, but I think it is a cow and a calf and a sow to two families, one hundred weight of beef, half a hundred of pork, one hundred weight of rice and five bushels of corn to each person, besides tools. This is and will be a considerable charge to the Province." This letter refers to the Colony under Roger Gordon, which first settled about the King's Tree.

In 1734, among the estimates made by the several colonial officials is found the following: "To allowance for one year to Mr. Roger Gordon and forty Highlanders in one of the Northern Townships (Williamsburg) and to Mr. William York with sundry Palatines from Philadelphia and also to several from England, £5,000." The allowance made that year was to each adult eight bushels of corn or peas, two hundred pounds of rice, four hundred pounds of beef or three hundred pounds of beef and fifty of pork; to each child under twelve years of age, half these amounts.

From the beginning, the men produced an abundance of corn. They did not succeed in wheat cultivation. The rivers and swamps swarmed with enormous quantities of excellent edible fish and the forests were full of herds of deer. Wild turkeys were abundant. Fifty years later Cornwallis said "Williamsburg is worth capturing for the fish in Black River;" and a hundred years afterwards, John Ervin Scott, who lived in the Cedar Swamp section, said that he never went early in the morning to his hog pens, about a mile from his home, without seeing three or four deer.

Every two families among the original settlers were given a cow and a calf. These found abundant grazing lands all over the District and soon there were large herds of half wild cattle roaming the country. Cattle have been, from the first days of Williamsburg until the present time, the thing which has given hope to the people of this section, when everything else seemed wanting. They flourish in these meadows without any food except what they find themselves. From cow hides these pioneers made not only their harness for horses, but leather breeches for men, aprons for women, coverings for their chairs, and used them in the place of modern springs on their high posted beds.

Sheep and hogs were also brought to Williamsburg and they have proved continuous assets to the section. Both of these useful animals live well in the wildwood and multiply rapidly. Much of the clothing of ancient Williamsburg was made on the plantations from wool produced at home. The first articles exported from the township were deerskins, pork, and lard. There were many horses in the colony. The original settlers brought some with them and they, too, multiplied rapidly in the swamps. Whenever a man needed another horse, he called together his friends, and they drove these half wild horses into a specially made pen from which the party selected such as it needed.

The settlers, who came to Williamsburg, had learned the cultivation of flax in Ireland and many of them were expert weavers. In 1742, William Lowry, of Williamsburg, exhibited before the Governor and his Council in Charleston a sample of Holland's cloth, which he had made on his own plantation by his own hands, from the flax seed to the finished product. He was granted the sum of twenty pounds as an encouragement. There were many plantations in the District at that time making linen and some of it then made is yet held as heirlooms in the old families of Williamsburg. Some cotton was produced for plantation purposes. The seed were laboriously separated by hand from the lint on long winter nights and the lint spun and woven into cloth.

For many years, these people fought the forests and the swamps, enduring and overcoming handicaps inconceivable. Slowly they prospered. Within a few years, they began to sell their surplus products in Charleston. In 1749, they had a crop failure; it did not rain that year. In August, they gathered together in the Williamsburg Meeting House to offer prayers for rain. The rains did not come in time to fill the ears of the withered corn. They bought corn from North Carolina, but that winter nearly one-fourth of the people of the colony died. Some strange sickness, probably influenza, overtook them, and caused eighty newly made graves in the Williamsburg Churchyard.

About that time, the planting of indigo was begun. Some few negro slaves had already been brought in the

Township, and used in the cultivation of this indigo. Within five years after its first introduction, prosperity came to this people and riches were not far away. They bought more negro slaves and blooded horses from Charleston. It is said that indigo sold for such enormous prices that at this time a planter could fill his wallet with this product, ride horseback to Charleston and exchange it for a slave.

Indigo covered the country and every plantation had its indigo vats. These vats were holes in the ground about thirty feet square at the top, shaping downward to resemble half of a broken inverted pyramid. These holes were lined with a composition of sand and pitch which was waterproof. In these vats they poured water, into which they packed and crushed the plant. The water absorbed the dye from the bruised plant after a certain period of time. Another deeper pit was dug by this vat and from the bottom of this vat, a line of wooden pipe permitted the drainage of the water filled indigo to pass into casks in the pit below. This indigo filled water had to be drained from the vat at the proper time or the whole product would spoil.

Now these Scotch-Irish were the most God-fearing people in the world. On Saturday evenings they made their small sons go out into the fields and shut down their bird traps and their rabbit gums. They took their pocket knives from these youngsters at the same time. Promptly on Monday morning these boys were given back their knives and allowed to place their traps in proper condition to receive unwary game.

But these Scotch-Irish brethren simply had to devise some scheme to start their indigo tanks draining when their product would be damaged by waiting until the following morning. One beautiful Sunday afternoon, when an Elder was strolling out with his family on its solemn service, he passed one of his indigo vats that was rich and ripe for draining. Monday morning his indigo would be ruined. This good Elder's foot accidently struck the peg that held the rich, ripe indigo fluid in leash, the peg fell out and the casks below began receiving the bluish drippings. They had the future Revolutionary hero up in the Church for his accident, but the good Session of Elders finally decided that accidents would happen and that men could not be held too strictly accountable for them. Similar accidents often happened after that time, and much indigo was saved thereby for the commerce of the world.

CHAPTER VI.

CHURCHES AND CHURCHMEN.

While the original settlers of Williamsburg came to the township on Black River primarily for economic reasons, yet the congregational religious principle, which had grown in the majority of them for centuries and which was largely responsible for their temporary impoverished condition, was, in fact, the cause of their migration into this wild country.

Until the adoption of the United States Constitution in 1789, the Church of England determined the ecclesiastical polity of South Carolina. The colonists were forced by law to support the Church of England and this was the only church recognized as such by law. No man could hold office under the government unless he were a communicant of the Church of England and would take an oath that for one year prior to his accession to office he had not received the sacrament of communion except from the hands of a priest of the established religion, and, when a man took the oath of office, he was required, then and there, to receive the Holy Sacrament administered according to the ritual of the Church of England. Furthermore, no man was allowed to teach school in the colony unless a communicant of the Church of England and duly licensed for such purpose by the Lord Bishop of London.

When Williamsburg Township was surveyed and laid out on August 28, 1736, the most desirable acre of ground in the town of Williamsburg was reserved for the Church of England, and an adjoining acre was granted for the Churchyard. These two acres of land were those making up the northwestern half of the block in Kingstree whereon the Bank of Kingstree now stands. At the same time, one hundred acres of glebe land on the northern boundary of the town of Williamsburg, adjoining the lands of John

Henderson, were surveyed and granted to the use of the minister of the town of Williamsburg.

But the Church of England and its "Society for the Propagation of the Gospel in Foreign Parts" were never too seriously concerned about the religious condition of the "Poor Protestants" of Williamsburg. A few times between 1735 and 1750, the Rev. John Fordyce, minister of Prince Frederick's Church of Winyaw, and the Rev. Joseph Bugnion, minister of Orangeburg, visited the town of Williamsburg on Easter, Whitsuntide, and Christmas, and conducted services, baptized a few children, and received nominal contributions from these poor Protestants in Williamsburg, but no Church of England was erected or even undertaken in this township on Black River.

Practically all of the original settlers in Williamsburg Township were of the Congregational or Presbyterian faith and their exceeding enthusiasm was shown in the promotion of Presbyterian principles. Although many of them inclined to the Church of Scotland as "reformed" by John Calvin and John Knox, yet in heart they were adherents of the untouched ancient doctrines.

On July 2, 1736, the following "indwellers in Williamsburg" met and formed the Williamsburg Presbyterian Congregation, which congregation has maintained its organization continuously until the present day: John Witherspoon, John Fleming, William James, David Wilson, James Bradley, Robert Wilson, John Porter, David Pressley, Robert Ervin, William Pressley, John Henderson, William Frierson, Thomas Frierson, William Syms, David Allen, John James, James McClelland, and David Witherspoon.

This congregation petitioned for a grant of land for erecting thereon their Meeting House, but the Colonial Governor did not act promptly on their petition. Two years later, in 1738, they secured from Captain Roger Gordon two acres of land on the eastern boundary of the platted "Town of Williamsburgh", and there built the Williamsburg Meeting House. On this spot, the congregation worshipped continuously until 1890, when the church was moved to Academy Street in the town of Kingstree. The lot was then devoted exclusively to the use of the white people of the vicinity as a burying ground.

The title to this property was made to the following as trustees of the Congregation: James Bradley, William Syms, David Allen, William James, John James, John Porter, James McClelland, and David Witherspoon. This Congregation chose as its first elders, John Witherspoon, John Fleming, James McClelland, James Bradley, William James, and David Witherspoon. This Session of Elders and its successors have played a remarkable part in the administration of the law of Williamsburg, civil and religious, until this day.

The first Williamsburg Meeting House was built of logs and was used until 1746, when the log structure was replaced by an excellent house of worship. William Swinton, a prominent member of Prince George's Church, left a legacy of one hundred pounds in his will for aiding the erection of this second Meeting House.

This was the largest building in the township until the War of the Revolution. It faced the East and was located in the Western part of the present Williamsburg cemetery. As one entered he came first to the Deacons' seats, elevated about six inches above the floor of the aisle. Back of the Deacons' seats, and elevated twelve inches higher, was the pew for the Ruling Elders, larger than that of the Deacons', and about square. Back of the Elders' pew and three feet higher and up against the wall was the pulpit. The pews were all high-backed. The head of each family owned a pew and the Church and the Minister were supported by a tax on these pews. Some of the pew owners were not members of the Church, yet each pew owner had an equal voice and vote in the congregational meetings. This rule resulted in serious conditions in later years.

In 1770, on account of the rapid growth of the colony, both by birth and by new immigrants from Ireland, this house of worship was doubled in size, which was done by extending the side opposite the pulpit.

It was customary among the Presbyterians of ancient Williamsburg to leave something, if not more than one hundred pounds or fifty acres of land, in their wills to their church. Among the first bequests to the Congregation were those of James McClelland, John Blakeley, James Blakeley, John Watson, John Scott, and Nathaniel Drew. Frequently, outsiders remembered this Congregation at the King's Tree and made bequests. Henry Sheriff, of James Island, and William Swinton, of Georgetown, were among this class of non-residents. When one now looks over the list of valuable bequests to this congregation during the first century of its existence, he wonders why the present Williamsburg Presbyterian Church corporation is not as wealthy as some other ancient church organizations in America.

The first minister of the Williamsburg Presbyterian Congregation was the Reverend Robert Heron, of Ireland, who served three years, returning to his native land in 1740. The next minister was the Reverend John Rae, installed in 1743. He was a "high church" Presbyterian and saw that everything done in this pioneer settlement congregation was according to the ritual of the most elect and select Church of Scotland. He required his congregation to fast and pray on Saturday, listen to his four hour sermon on Sunday, and spend Monday in thanksgiving that they had heard such a wonderful discourse.

Mr. Rae was not much of a Puritan, since he did not preach about drinking whiskey, horse racing, and permitting slaves to work for themselves on Sunday, but he was a great Presbyterian advocate. His sermons were remarkable displays of theological learning. He hated the Roman Catholic Church a great deal more than he did the Devil, and feared God to the limit of his capacity.

May 19, 1752, the following officers of the Williamsburg Congregation signed the Confession of Faith: John Rae, minister; John James, James McClelland, James Witherspoon, John Leviston, Robert Witherspoon, Samuel Fulton, Robert Wilson, Robert Paisley, Gavin Witherspoon, William Dobein, Elders.

Mr. Rae served the congregation eighteen years and died in 1761 at Salem. He was buried in the Williamsburg churchyard, although the exact location of his grave is unknown. He was a man of strong personality and was very influential in his congregation. Dr. J. R. Witherspoon says he went about "with unwearied diligence and fidelity reproving the negligent, encouraging the doubtful and desponding, visiting the sick, comforting mourners, and relieving the distressed."

This Williamsburg Presbyterian Congregation was the only religious organization maintained in Williamsburg Township until 1786. Out of the township, prior to the Revolution, there went several colonies who formed Presbyterian Congregations in other sections, and the Williamsburg Church may rightfully regard them as offspring. Among these may be mentioned: Salem Black River, Aimwell on the Pee Dee, and Indiantown.

The first House of Worship or Church built on the territory now known as Williamsburg County was the Black Mingo Meeting House located on Church Creek in the corner where the Williamsburg-Georgetown County line road leads to the South from the Georgetown-Kingstree highway. This was an excellent brick structure, forty by sixty feet, and was erected in 1726 for use by the religious Dissenters in that Black Mingo community. The Reverend Elisha Screven, an Antipaedo Baptist Minister, was the moving spirit in the building of this Church, contributed the greater part of its cost and preached the first sermon from its pulpit.

Although it was largely through Screven influence, money, and energy that the Black Mingo Church was built, since there were few of the Baptist faith in the community, this ancient Church was soon dominated by the Presbyterian element in the Congregation; and, after the death of the Reverend Elisha Screven, it became known as the Black Mingo Presbyterian Meeting House. It was used, from its beginning, by dissenting congregations, first come, first served. The Reverend John Baxter was the first Presbyterian Minister who preached there. In 1729, he baptized John Nelson, son of George and Helen Nelson, the first baptism among the Calvanists in Williamsburg. This Church was the first structure erected by a dissenting congregation between the Santee and the Cape Fear Rivers.

The records of this old Church have all been lost. Here and there one finds reference to it and its congregations in old diaries written in that period. The last reference to it is found in the Indiantown Session Records of June 20, 1824, and reads as follows: "Mrs. Margaret McConnell was received into this Church on reputable testimony of her having been an acceptable member of the Black Mingo Church, this Church being now extinct."

The walls of this old Church stood until about 1890, when the bricks were hauled away and used for plantation purposes. The church site is yet plainly discernible, and about four acres of ancient graves, with a few old tombstones, still tell simple tales of the men and women who there more than a century ago lived and labored.

Indiantown Presbyterian Congregation consisted of John James, Robert Wilson, David Wilson, William Cooper, Sr., William Cooper, Jr., Robert McCottry, George McCutchen, George Barr, Thomas McCrea, Robert Witherspoon, James McCutchen, and about fifteen other heads of families when it was organized in 1757. The first Indiantown Church was built that year on the four acre lot of ground left in the will of William Thompson for that purpose. Mr. Thompson also bequeathed one hundred pounds sterling towards the building. John James, Robert Wilson, and David Wilson were its first elders and the Reverend John Knox its first minister.

There were many causes contributing to the founding of Indiantown Church. Williamsburg Township had overflown into this district, as had the Black Mingo section, and those who had settled in the Indiantown community had prospered. The founders of the Indiantown congregation were, for the most part, the sons of settlers in Williamsburg Township.

At that time, there were two flourishing Presbyterian Churches in Williamsburg, the Williamsburg and the Black Mingo Churches. The founders of these two churches had come from Europe and were belligerent dissenters. Many of them had actually witnessed, and some of them felt, the fires of religious persecution administered by the political state church. These Presbyterians represented one of the extreme factions in the religious life of the English speaking peoples for many generations. While the Roman Catholic Church had been the organization of the other faction, and while the Church that was created with the view of reconciling these two extreme factions had succeeded in becoming the Church of England, neither the extremists of the Presbyterian faction nor those of the Roman Catholic faction accepted the Church of England as constituted, but both factions hated it to the limit of their ability.

These Scotch-Irish Presbyterians, who came to Williamsburg, were, for the most part, uncompromising in their religious conceptions. The ancient Presbyterian doctrine was very largely monotheistic, strikingly similar to that of Judaeism. The Roman Catholic Church made

Jesus Christ outstanding in the Holy Trinity. The Church of England adopted very largely the Roman Catholic idea of Jesus Christ. Scotch-Irish Presbyterians hated anything that had in it a suggestion of the Roman Catholic Church, and so the Presbyterian Churches at Black Mingo and at Williamsburg, following the doctrines of the Church of Scotland, were practically Unitarian. Their ministers were called to preach by virtue of their being entitled to certain hereditary rights under the British Government, the right of presentation to a benefice inherent in certain families, were educated in Scotland and Ireland, and preached in this country the doctrines of the Church of Scotland.

There are now, in old diaries, minute books, and other ancient documents, references to more than one hundred sermons preached by these ministers in these two old Williamsburg Churches and not one of these sermons was based on a text taken from the New Testament. The Church of Scotland ministers of that day seemed to overlook the New Testament. One finds among the original Presbyterians who came to Williamsburg Abraham, Isaac, and Jacob, Moses and Aaron, Nathan and David and other Old Testament names, but he looks in vain to find a man called Matthew, Mark, Luke, Paul, Silas, or Cornelius.

In all the wills of the pre-revolutionary period, the first paragraph dedicates the soul of the testator to God. There are shown in them two ideas of Christ—the Presbyterian, which does not call His Name; and that of the Episcopalians and the Baptists, which does. A typical Church of Scotland Presbyterian was James McCown, who says, "Principally and first of all, I give and recommend my soul into the hands of God that gave it, and my body I recommend to the earth to be buried in decent Christian burial, nothing doubtful but at the general resurrection, I shall receive the same again by the mighty power of God."

Contra, the first clause in the will of Nathaniel Snow, Church of England: "First and principally recommending my immortal soul into the hand of Almighty God, my Heavenly Father, trusting in the merits of my Blessed Saviour for pardon and remission of all my sins and an happy admission into the regions of Bliss and Immortality." Also, the will of Isaac Chandler, Baptist: "Principally, I commend my soul into the hands of Almighty God and my body to the earth to be decently buried in the hopes of a joyful resurrection at the last day unto Life Eternal by the Mighty Power and through the merit of Jesus Christ, our Mighty God and Saviour."

The original Presbyterians who came to Williamsburg scorned the celebration of Easter or Christmas, declaring that they were of heathen origin and unworthy of the Church. Until this day, some men and women in Williamsburg seriously object to special Easter and Christmas decorations and music, even in other churches than their own.

While the Church of England exercised over lordship of the colony of South Carolina until the War of the Revolution, and built its churches and supported its ministers out of public funds, it allowed a large measure of freedom to dissenting congregations. The young men who grew up in Williamsburg gradually assimilated the American Presbyterian idea and accepted Jesus Christ and the Holy Trinity. The Black Mingo Church from 1726, when it was founded, until 1811, when it became extinct, was, for all practical purposes, a Unitarian Church. The Williamsburg Presbyterian Church did not worship Jesus Christ nor say much of His Divinity until its union with the Bethel congregation in 1828, ninety-two years after it was organized. The Indiantown Church was dedicated to the Holy Trinity at its foundation and many of these younger Presbyterians from Black Mingo and Williamsburg united with the Indiantown Church for the reason

CHURCHES AND CHURCHMEN   53

that it was Trinitarian in conception and American in its organization.

An act of the Colonial Assembly of 1706, generally known as the Church Act, divided South Carolina into ten parishes. Craven County was one of these Parishes. In 1721, the Parish of Prince George Winyaw was established —bounded on the Southwest by the Santee River, on the northeast by the Cape Fear River, on the east by the ocean, and on the west by the Indian country.

In 1734, Prince Frederick's Parish was divided from that of Prince George Winyaw. In 1713, on a beautiful bluff on Black River, probably the most striking river scene in South Carolina, Prince Frederick's Church was built. When Prince Frederick's Parish was separated from Prince George's Parish, it was intended that this Prince Frederick's Church should be included in Prince Frederick's Parish; however, the eastern line of Prince Frederick's Parish as established by law was afterwards found to be west of the church. This church remained, however, for nearly half a century the place of worship for the few adherents of the Church of England in Prince Frederick's Parish, which later became Williamsburg.

The pew holders in Prince Frederick's Church in 1734 were as follows: John Brown, John Lane, Reverend Thomas Morritt, John Thompson, Daniel Shaw, Francis Avant, John Wallace, Esq., Captain Anthony White, Anthony Atkinson, John White, Paul Laroche, William Swinton, John Borrell, Josias Dupre, and Caleb Avant. All of these men lived along Black River, some of them as far westward into the present Williamsburg County as Indiantown and Cedar Swamp. This Prince Frederick's Church was wealthy. The Reverend Mr. Morritt, who conducted services one Sunday in each month of 1735 in Georgetown and three Sundays at Prince Frederick's, admitted that his income was more than $7,500.00 a year.

In 1736, the Reverend John Fordyce became the minister of Prince Frederick's Parish "in the room of" Reverend Mr. Morritt. Mr. Fordyce resigned in 1741. In 1743, Reverend Mr. Fordyce held communion services at the King's Tree on April 3rd and July 1st. His collection taken on these two occasions amounted to about $55.00.

Prince Frederick's Church had an eventful history. Its records were kept and throw much light on the beginnings of Williamsburg. In 1756, the Church wardens and vestrymen wrote a letter to the Lord Bishop of London complaining of spiritual conditions in Prince Frederick's Parish. The letter was signed by John White, George Atkinson, William Green, Anthony White, James McPherson, William Walker, James Crockett, and Charles Woodmason, and begged for a Minister to succeed the Reverend Michael Smith, who, they said, had done more injury to the cause of virtue, religion, and the Church in three years time than "his successors could repair in many." They wrote that this Parish was the largest and most populous in the province, yet, "though numerous in inhabitants, the members of the Church are widely scattered and but few in number."

They state that the people of this section were for the most part of the communion of the Church of Scotland, being settlers from Scotland from the North of Ireland. The Church of Scotland then had two Meeting Houses in the Parish, one at Black Mingo and one at Williamsburg and large congregations at each of these places. They say that "Our back country", meaning Williamsburg, "is filled with numbers who never saw a minister of the Church of England."

The letter also states that the Reverend Mr. Smith did make "a Tour into these remote Parts of the Parish, But He had better stay'd at home, for the Consequence has been, that thro' his indiscreet Carriage, (We shd rather say immoral Conduct), among them, instead of bringing them over, and joining them to the Communion of our Church, he has unhappily driven them to send for Anabaptist Teachers from Philadelphia, who dip many, and form them into Congregations; so that the regaining of them, and making them Members of the Established Chh will (we judge) be attended with great Pains, if not an impossibility."

In the following year, Charles Woodmason, Register of Prince Frederick's Parish, wrote the Lord Bishop of London the following: "Our Parish Church, Parsonage & Glebe is daily falling to Ruin by being unoccupied. That there are now 4 Meeting Houses in this Parish, and two more talked of being built, (wch Increase would not have been except thro' Weakness, Supineness, & Immorality of our Incumbents) Whereas, had we Godly Ministers, Chapels of Ease would probably be raised in their places, and less Room for the Sectaries to spread themselves. That the People of the Lower Part of our Parish, are a sober, sensible & literate People, those of the upper part, far otherwise; whose Numbers daily increase by Refugees from ye other Provinces. That if a Minister be not settled here soon, the defection from the Church will be so great, as hardly to leave enough Church Members to form a Congregation.

"That Itinerant Teachers from the Noard, are Yearly making of Converts that illiterate Persons set up for Pastors; That the Presbyterian Missionaries from the Northern Colleges, use unwearied pains & Diligence to extend their Influence & Interest, to the hazard of this whole Parish being soon entirely in their Hands; That this Prospect grieves every true Son & Well-wisher to the Church of England, while our Establish'd Clergy calmly look on, But that our Assembly, Alarm'd at our Situation, has lately divided into this extensive Parish, taking a New one out of it, to be called by the Name of St. Mark alloting also 100 L stg. pr. ann. for an Itinerant Minister to officiate the Waterees, & ye Catawba Settlemt So that we want 3 Ministers Sir at present, in this one Parish only."

On August 10, 1756, thirty-two Acadians were sent to Prince Frederick's Church and distributed among the good people of that Parish for sustenance and support. Among these Acadians were Joseph Durong (Durant) and his wife, Ann Lambert; and their children, Mary, Josette, Ann, Margaret, Mary Ann, and Rosalie; John Daigle and his wife, Rosalie Richard, and their child, John Baptist; Peter Lambert and his sons, Peter and John; Francois LaBlanc and his wife, Magdalene Comie, and their children, Josetta, Ozick, Magdalene, Tesslie, and Margaret; Paul Oliver and his wife, Magdalene Bourk; Margaret Daigle Forrait and her three children, Paul, Larion, and John Baptist; John Baptist Porrier; Michell Porrier, Peirre Caisee; Michell Lapierre; and Renaie Drowhanny.

On the 3rd of November, 1770, Mary Bonnell died under suspicious circumstances. The matter of her sudden passing created great interest in all this community. After she had been buried thirty-six days, her body was raised from its grave and examined by Samuel Nesmith, Esq., Coroner, "For our said Lord the King," and his Coroner's jury composed of James Lane, Foreman, Bartley Clark, Elias McPherson, Richard Green, Francis Green, William Green, William Green, Sr., Francis Futhy, John Glenn, Sr., Daniel Williams, James McPherson, and John McCrea. The first sessions of this Jury were held in the Prince Frederick's Church but later meetings were had at Black Mingo.

The last record in "the Register Book" of this old Prince Frederick's Church on Black River is a petition to the Church wardens for the assistance of an old woman who had been of good behavior and of good reputation in Williamsburg for more than thirty years. It was dated the 21st day of January, 1778, and signed by the following: James McCollough, Andrew Patterson, John Jones, William Scott, William Cooper, James Daniel, George McCutchen, John Scott, Thomas McConnell, Alex. H. Crasener, William Miller, William Dobien, William Hamilton. This petition was filed, but never was heard, for the last meeting of the officers of this old Church had been held and its doors had been closed forever, but for nearly a hundred years thereafter people of the community used this old Churchyard as a burying ground. It is situated on a high bluff on the convex side of the river where its deep dark waters form a crescent, the horns of which seem to pass into infinite distance, fading away in fringes of live oak and cypress.

Prior to this time, many, even of its officers, had withdrawn from the Church and united with the Black Mingo and the Indiantown Presbyterian Churches. Among these may be mentioned William Wilson, Thomas G. Scott, John Ervin, Thomas Goddard, Francis Britton, Jr., Daniel McGinney, John McDowell, Moses Britton, John James, Hugh Ervin, James Lane, William McCottry, Adam McDonald, James McPherson, George Burrows, Edward Plowden, William Gamble, William McGee, Moses Brown, John Futhy, Alexander McCrea, Benjamin Duke, Thomas Potts, William Hamilton, and Thomas McCrea. The communicants of this Church who retained their connection with the Church of England transferred their membership to the Church at Georgetown.

The Santee French Huguenots built a Chapel of Ease a few miles North of Lenud's Ferry on the Britton's Ferry road about 1730, and another Chapel of Ease on Murray's old field near Murray's Ferry, where they worshipped in their native tongue but according to the ritual of the Church of England. The use of the French language in these Chapels of Ease along the Santee for more than half a century had a great influence in determining the language used in Williamsburg. Until the present day, one finds many French idioms in the speech of the Williamsburg people and their pronunciation shows a strong Romance language influence.

At the beginning of the War of the Revolution, there were large congregations supporting the Williamsburg Church at Kingstree, and the Black Mingo Church on the Kingstree-Georgetown road, which two churches were connected with the Presbytery of Scotland; about one hundred families supporting the Indiantown Presbyterian Church, which belonged to the Presbytery of Orange, an American organization; a few members of the Church of England living along what is now the Williamsburg-Georgetown County line, some of whom worshipped in Georgetown and others at the Chapel of Ease near Lenud's Ferry; and a few other communicants of the Church of England, who worshipped at the Chapel of Ease at Murray's old field near Murray's Ferry. There were probably a dozen Baptists in the Black Mingo community and nearly every one of these was a lineal descendant of the Reverend William Screven. At the outbreak of the Revolution, at least ninety-five per centum of the people of Williamsburg were Presbyterians.

CHAPTER VII.

GROWING PAINS AND PETITIONS.

Ancient inland communities all grew up on the banks of rivers. With few exceptions, the world depended upon water transportation until recent modern times. King George decreed that Williamsburg Township should be laid out on the banks of Black River, and that every grantee of land in the Township should have free access to the River. He also decreed that no grant of land should border the River for a distance more than one-fourth the distance it extended backward into the forest. This rule was established to give as many settlers as possible actual as well as constructive access to the river. The river was planned as a highway over which transportation to and from this back country was to be effected.

In 1730, for a great part of the year, Black River seemed almost a large inland sea as far westward as the King's Tree. Generally it was then very deep and the King's mariners reported that it would be navigable as far westward as the King's Tree for all the King's vessels. But, during the long summer seasons, Black River sometimes decreased until it became at the King's Tree a very small stream. The River from Georgetown westward to Kingstree is one continuous series of elbows, and, at some points, frequently shows dangerous sandy shallows. The very large trees that grow along its banks have frequently fallen into the current and have always been serious menaces to the navigation of the river.

On Friday, December 10, 1736, Robert Finley, Crafton Kerwin, and Richard Middleton, residents of Williamsburg, petitioned the Colonial Council to clear Black River and make it navigable. This petition brought the first act of the Colonial Government applying specially to Williamsburg Township, which was passed in 1738, "An act for clearing, cleaning and making navigable Black River from the 'Narrows' to the western boundary of Williamsburg Township, inclusive." This act created a district for taxation for raising necessary funds to clear the river. This district was all North of a line half way between Santee River and Black River and all South of the line half way between Black River and Pee Dee River, from ten miles above Phineas Spry's plantation to the "Narrows" on Black River. Every man under sixty years old, white and black, free or slave, should be a unit for taxation, and every two hundred and fifty acres of land should be counted as a man for taxation. The commissioners appointed were so to clear Black River that it would be navigable for "boats, barges, pettiaguas, lighters, and other vessels."

In 1732, the Roger Gordon colony came up Black River, disembarked at Brown's Ferry and blazed its way through the country to the King's Tree. This blazed trail, which is now a part of the Kingstree-Georgetown highway, was the first trail the white men made to the King's Tree. It has been continuously used as a road since 1732.

In 1734, John Witherspoon came from Belfast, Ireland, by way of Charleston, Georgetown, and thence up Black River to Potato Ferry, where he and his people disembarked and blazed a trail westward to the King's Tree. This blazed trail became the Kingstree-Potato Ferry road and has been open to wayfarers since 1734. Many years before this time, a trail had been made from the Black Mingo community southward to Lenud's Ferry on the Santee. The Williamsburg-Georgetown County line road follows this ancient trail. The Wee Tee Indians had a trail from Lenud's Ferry westward along the north bank of the Santee River to where the abandoned Lower Saint Mark's Church now stands, and to the West. This Indian trail grew into the Santee River road.

GROWING PAINS AND PETITIONS 61

The first public road established by law in Williamsburg was that from Murray's Ferry to the King's Tree. This road was laid out by Act of the Colonial Council on the 8th day of March, 1741. All of the inhabitants and owners of slaves on the North side of the Santee River, within so many miles of Murray's Ferry as the commissioners of the public roads judged proper, were obliged, made liable, and directed to make and keep in repair the Murray's Ferry road to the King's Tree in the same manner as was described by the Highway Act of the General Assembly of the province.

By the same Act, Murray's Ferry over the Santee River, connecting this road with the road to Charleston, was vested in Joseph Murray. By the terms of this Act, Joseph Murray, his executors, administrators, or assigns, were required to provide and keep at the said ferry for a term of seven years "one good and sufficient boat with at least two able men (one of which shall be a white man) fit for transporting passengers, horses, and cattle." He was allowed to charge ferriage for each passenger on foot two shillings and sixpence; for each horse, three shillings and nine pence; for a man and a horse, five shillings; for neat cattle, per head, ferried or swam, one shilling; for calves, sheep, or hogs, per head, six pence. "When the 'freshes' are so high that they are obliged to go from highland to highland, then all persons passing the ferry shall be obliged to pay double the rates above mentioned." This ferry was to be free at all times to all persons sent on His Majesty's service.

About 1750, somebody blazed a trail from Kingstree to Camden over Broad, Clapp's and Pudding Swamps, and about the same time, a trail from Kingstree northward by Effingham toward Cheraw. The Witherspoons made a trail from Kingstree over Black River at what is now known as the Lower Bridge about 1740.

On the 25th day of May, 1745, Thomas McKeithen, John McIver, David Allen, Nathaniel Drew, and John McCants were appointed commissioners for cutting and clearing the lakes and water courses in the swamp at the head of Black Mingo Creek from the plantation of Colonel Anthony White to the mouth of Heathley's run and to make the stream navigable for flats and canoes. These persons were allowed to charge toll rates on everything passing through the canal and required to render an account yearly of the money collected by them.

The highway commissioners for the township of Williamsburg, or said part of Prince Frederick's Parish as lies on Black River, in 1747, were as follows: Robert Gibson, William Young, William Frierson, Isaac Brunson, John Leviston, Roger Gordon, Robert Wilson, John Jones, and John Allen. This board of commissioners was ordered to meet on Easter Monday and on the first Monday of August of every year. They were authorized to exercise general supervision over the roads and ferries in the district.

In 1748, the following commissioners were instructed to build a bridge over Black River at the King's Tree: Nathaniel Drew, John Allen, William Young, John Leviston, William Frierson, William Nelson, and William James. In 1756, the inhabitants of Williamsburg Township petitioned the Council that "a ferry be established from the plantation of Theodore Gaillard on the South side of Santee River to Murray's Landing on the North side of the River; and have a more convenient passing when the freshes are up; that the Creek called Ferry Creek on the South side of the River and the Creek leading to the North side of the river to Murray's house be cleared and cleansed." This ferry was vested in Theodore Gaillard. The Council ordered that the Creek on the North side of Santee River leading from Murray's house to the River be cleared and thereafter kept clean and clear so that there might be free passage for the ferry boat or boats in the said Creek when the river was high, by the male inhabitants from sixteen to sixty years of age living and residing in the township of Williamsburg, or within five miles of Murray's Ferry. John Leviston, William Young, and William Nelson were appointed commissioners for clearing this Creek.

The Williamsburg section was thought to offer great opportunities and all of the land in the Township was taken up by grants within a very short time after the lines of the township had been established. In 1737, John Hamilton petitioned the King for a grant of two hundred thousand acres of land as near as possible to Williamsburg Township. In his petition, he stated that he could bring over immediately about one hundred forty Protestant families, skilled in the production of wine, currants, raisins, oil, coffee, cocoa, hemp, flax, wax, honey, saffron, and all kinds of grain and cattle, and that this section was well adapted to the production of all of these things.

John Hamilton's grandfather, John, and Robert Montgomery, were the two leading spirits in the migration of the Scotch into Northern Ireland during the seventeenth century, and the John Hamilton of 1737 hoped to found a colony in this section. His petition, however, for the grant of two hundred thousand acres of land for his colony was not given action by the King, and John Hamilton became an ordinary citizen of Williamsburg.

Another petition of interest, dated 1742, and signed by Thomas McCrea, Alexander McCrea, Crafton Kerwin, and William McNeedy, represents to the Colonial Council that these four petitioners had been granted lands in the Northeastern corner of the Township as originally surveyed; that they had settled thereon and had gone through much labor and expense in making their plantations suitable for habitation and for the production of salable articles; that some time later the Colonial Council had sent a man purporting to be a surveyor to this section and that this man had gone to the hospitable home of John Peter Somerhoeff, about fifteen miles from any point of Williamsburg Township, and, without approaching any nearer the Township than Mr. Somerhoeff's piazza, had made another plat of the township which so changed the lines that the grants of these petitioners therefore made in good faith, accepted, and acted upon, had been left outside of the Township and had thereafter been included in grants to other persons. These four petitioners further said that they had been caused great annoyance and expense in defending their claims to original grants and submitted bills for the damages they had sustained. This matter was finally adjusted to the satisfaction of these petitioners.

Many grants of land were made in Williamsburg Township in violation of the order of the King establishing the Township. By decree, land in Williamsburg Township should have been granted only to bona fide settlers, but there were a great many influential people in Charleston, suspecting the value the lands in Williamsburg would probably have, secured grants within the territory without having any intention of actually settling thereon. These grants greatly damaged the Township and were a source of much ill feeling among the bona fide settlers. The two petitions following represent something of public opinion in Williamsburg in 1742 in regard to these illegal grants.

"Representation of the inhabitants of Williamsburg, complaining to His Majesty's Forty-third instruction being broke thro' by the Governor and Council.

"To Henry McCulloh, Esq., the Humble Representation of the inhabitants of the town of Williamsburg showeth that, being informed, His Majesty has been graciously pleased to constitute and appoint you as His Commissary with full power to inquire into the abuses with respect to the grants of land and the quitrent payable thereupon and towards preventing and determining all matters in relation to the premises:

"We beg leave to represent that by His Majesty's Forty-third instruction to his Governor of this province, there were eleven townships set apart for the reception of such Protestants as might come and settle in this province; that in consideration of the encouragement given us by the Government and Council and from the certainty we apprehended with it, under His Majesty's Royal Instructions to His Governor, had secured our properties and the remainder of the township lands would remain only for the uses, direct by his Majesty's instructions, which would have enabled us to have brought over our friends and relatives to settle in our neighborhood. We, under these encouragements, transported ourselves and families to this province and settled in Williamsburg Township.

"But to our great concern, we have found the land in this township a common unrestrained range to all persons, and the best land therein taken up by persons, who have not at this time settled the same nor, in all probability, will at any time reside thereon. Some of us have been sued for trespass on land pointed out to us by the Deputy Surveyor and have been caused considerable damage and others have become tenants rather than remove their families. Some time past, we presented our humble petition to the Governor's Council setting forth our said grievances and praying, but we could obtain no answer. We, therefore, take leave to trouble you with a copy of the same, wherein the hardships we have labored under here are, which we humbly submit to your consideration.

"The river, by which we can have any convenience of our goods to a market, is rendered difficult in the navigation, by reason of great trees, which fall therein and which the General Assembly should pass a law for clearing same. Now the whole burden of that work falls on us, the residenters, while those who are possessed of large tracts of the most valuable lands contribute nothing to it.

"We have letters from our friends in Ireland, acquainting us of their desire to come here, if we could in any shape encourage them, which we have to decline because of the lands being run and possessed by others. We take leave, Sir, to assure you that every tract alleged in our said petition and in this, our humble representation, shall be effectually proved, with the addition of many more particulars, when you will please to require it.

"We pray, therefore, you will take the premises into consideration and that you will relieve us of the many oppressions and hardships we labor under, in relation to our possessions in the said Township of Williamsburgh. And we shall ever pray.

"Williamsburg Township, the 19th day of January, 1742. (Signed) James Bradley, Thomas McCrea, Alexander Scott, John Fleming, James Scott, John Bradley, William Bradley, Thomas Bradley, Samuel Bradley, William Dick, Thomas Scott, Patrick Lindsay, William McCormick, Joseph Anderson, James Armstrong, John Moore, Henry Montgomery, William Pressley, John James, John Fleming, John Hamilton, Robert Witherspoon, John Dick, Robert Wilson, Roger Gibson, George Burrows, Adam Strain, John Watson, Avagbel Campbell, David Witherspoon, John McCullough, James Gamble, George Montgomery, John McKnight, William James, Alexander McCrea, Robert Wilson, John Pressley, Hugh McGill, John Matthews, John Anderson, James Dick, John Lemon, Robert McCottry, John McFadden, John Anderson, Jr., James McClelland, John Blakeley, James Law, Roger Gordon, William McKnight, David Wilson, Thomas McCrea, John Scott, John Leviston, John Porter, Gavin Witherspoon, John Ervin."

The following is a copy of first petition in the same matters.

"To the Honorable William Bull, Esq., Lieutenant Governor, and Commander-in-chief in and over His Majesty's Honorable Council.

"The humble petition of several subscribing persons, inhabitants of Williamsburg Township, showing that your petitioners and the rest of the inhabitants of the said Township are chiefly Irish Protestants, who came over from their native country to this province at their own expense, to settle in the said Township, encouraged by an account they received that the lands in the said township were for the most part good and fertile, and the same wholly reserved for such distant Protestants as should come here from Europe to settle same and particularly for Irish Protestants.

"That your petitioners were informed and apprehended a scheme of settling as well the said Township as other townships; were strictly enjoined by His Majesty's Royal Instructions to His Late Excellency, Governor Johnson, with the view of encouraging back inhabitants who would make no great use of slaves in these parts but from their own labor that they might have a competent maintenance and, upon any occasion, be the more ready to unite for the public safety, for the said instructions, as your petitioners are informed, have been not altered from their first frame in that particular, since the demise of the said Government, but continues still in force as His Majesty's stated plan for the settling of the said Township; that several of the said inhabitants, who first arrived in the said Township, were obliged by the Deputy Surveyor to settle on contiguous tracts of land laid out for them in square forms beginning at a certain place there called the King's Tree, which your petitioners thought a great hardship, to be debarred from making any choice, for rather the said lands were for the most part infertile, pine bearing lands, and not likely to afford any produce or profit to compensate the trouble of cultivating same, but as they were given to understand that the said Deputy Surveyor was instructed by the Government to settle them in such a manner, that a square of land six miles round the township line was reserved for the further accommodating of the said Township inhabitants, the said inhabitants proceeded to improve and settle the said squares in tracts to the best of their power in hopes of being afterwards better provided for out of the said reserved lands.

"That the second set of people who arrived in the second ship to settle the said township were subject to the same strictness and hardships, but were nevertheless encouraged with the same hopes of having better lands in the parish line, as well for themselves as for their relatives and countrymen who they expected would follow them.

"But, your petitioners cannot but represent to your Honor how greatly disappointed in finding the lands of the said Township afterwards become a common unrestrained range for other people. All of the good lands of both are taken up by gentlemen residing in other parts of the province who were better able to pay surveyors, and were residing at Charleston, to get their grants passed for them so that only these first families who came over last to settle with their countrymen in the said Township were greatly disappointed.

"Many of them have been obliged to become tenants in the said Township to gentlemen who had lands there granted them in great tracts, who were directed by the Township Surveyor to settle with their families in particular places, and had the misfortune to find their possessions granted others and so became subject to actions at law attended with great expenses, and others obliged to struggle into other parts of the province.

"Your petitioners cannot but further represent your Honor that, notwithstanding the many discouragements they have labored under, yet they have adhered to each other and the said Township still consists of about one hundred and fifty able male persons willing and ready to furnish their assistance in defense of the province against any of His Majesty's enemies, but must at the same time, humbly desire that the scheme for settling them directed by His Majesty be fulfilled to have that said Township lands rendered wholly for the Township inhabitants and that the township be made a parish with the privileges of sending representatives to the Assembly as His Majesty has most graciously directed; otherwise, most of your petitioners must think it prudent to remove to some other of His Majesty's provinces where they may hope to meet with less danger and more encouragement.

"Your petitioners take leave to set forth the names of several persons who have had lands granted to them in the said township, but who reside in other parts of the province, viz.: George Hunter, John Ballentine, Captain John Cleland, the Reverend John Baxter, Charles Starnes, Andrew Rutledge, Esq., Thomas Monk, Bridget Hughes, Samuel Pontovine, Captain James Fisher, John Scott (of Charleston), Elisha Screven, Captain John Whitfield, Sarah Blakeway, Jane Eldridge, John Wilson, Lieutenant Thomas Farrington, and Captain James Atkins, and many others, upon the view of which list your petitioners have reason to hope your Honor will take the premises into consideration and grant such relief as your Honor in your great wisdom, shall think most meet. And your petitioners will ever pray."

In 1742, when a number of citizens of Williamsburg petitioned the King for the redress of certain grievances, among other things, they stated that they stood ready at all times to serve His Majesty and to fight his battles. Not many years after this time France and England began the final war which determined that England should control this continent. The French enlisted the services of the Indians in this war and the Cherokee tribe threatened South Carolina. It is very interesting to note that in

1759, when the King called for volunteers to serve in this French and Indian War, two companies from Williamsburg immediately responded. The first company: Captain William Scott; Sergeant Alexander Scott; privates, George Davis, Thomas Davis, Matt Young, John Anderson, John Garrison, James Barr, George Whitby, Robert Wilson, George Crawford, John McNally, Samuel Ervin, Hugh Ervin, Samuel Ford. The second company: Captain David Anderson; Ensign Robert Lewis; Sergeant Thomas Hume; privates, Peter Mellett, William Grimes, Thomas Dial, Joseph Chandler, Roger McGill, Charles McCoy, Thomas Player, Thomas Newman, John Rowell, John Kennedy, James Ferdon, John McIntosh, John DuBose, John Lloyd, Thomas Commander, Daniel Butler, John Bradley, Aaron Frierson, James Armstrong, William Westberry, Sylvester Dunn, Nathaniel Pygott, Stephen Motte, James Berwick, James Gordon, Henry Price, Daniel Bluset, Alexander Chosewood, John Dubush.

Since one of the reasons expressed by the King for the creation of Williamsburg Township was the protection of Charleston and Beaufort from the incursions of the Indians from the West, it was natural that those colonists, who first came to the Township, feared the Red Men. The first colony elected Roger Gordon as Captain of the Militia Company at the King's Tree and all able bodied men in the township immediately enlisted. They built a stockade fort on Roger Gordon's land near where the Williamsburg cemetery stands at present. It was planned that all the colonists in this vicinity should take refuge within this stockade whenever an Indian attack was impending, but the Indians never disturbed the Williamsburg colony.

As the territory of Craven County was settled from time to time, other communities organized militia companies and these were mustered into the regiment. Roger Gordon became the first colonel of this Regiment, which played a distinguished part in the history of South Carolina so long as the territory belonged to Great Britain.

The first regimental mustering ground in Craven County was on the spot where the Williamsburg Court House now stands. Later, the Regiment sometimes was mustered near Willtown on Black Mingo. Sometimes the various companies gathered at Murray's Ferry on the Santee. Among the colonels of this Craven County Regiment were Roger Gordon, George Pawley, John White, Anthony White, and Richard Richardson; Captains, Abram Michaux, John Waites, William Scott, John McDonald, David Anderson, William Nelson, John McDaniel, Isaac Brunson, John Jannerett, John James, Daniel Horry, Henry O'Neal, James McGirt, and James Crockett; and the lieutenants, William Frierson, Peter Robertson, John Leviston, Daniel McDaniel, Samuel Cantey, Abraham Lenud, Paul Bonneau, Edward German, Charles Woodmason and Robert Lewis.

Long before the Scotch-Irish came to Williamsburg, the Indians had abandoned the section as a place for permanent residence. Sometimes, however, they came to fish and hunt in the swamps of Black River and the Santee. They did not like these parts during mosquito season.

Tradition says that there were three small tribes of Indians that had their headquarters within the territory now known as Williamsburg County, and there is yet some evidence visible to sustain it. It is said that the Mingoes had their camp ground in the fork made by the junction of Indiantown Swamp and Black Mingo Creek. Their burying ground on the bluff at this point has yielded many relics of the time of their occupation. The word "Mingo", in one Indian language, means black; in another, a kind of officer. Possibly, the Mingoes were Indian chiefs who spent their vacations in the Indiantown-Black Mingo country and hoped to find there after death the "happy hunting ground." The Americans who dwell in this section now will tell you that it is the favored spot on earth and give reasons from the past and present to prove their statement.

The Wee Nee Indian camp was located in the forks of Black River near the present Williamsburg-Clarendon line. Many war clubs, arrow heads, and other Indian implements of battle may be found in this community. Marion's Men fought many skirmishes in this section during the War of the Revolution. Perhaps this might be called the "dark and bloody" ground of Williamsburg. Wee Nee is a favorite name for associations in Williamsburg, all the way from sewing societies to banking corporations.

The Wee Tee Indians lived once in the vicinity of Lenud's Ferry and several miles westward along the Santee. They built mounds all over this section. Excavations in these mounds have brought to light many things that Indians loved and treasured. B. E. Clarkson says when he was a boy, about 1875, he dug into one of those mounds. Among the interesting things he found was a baby skeleton enmeshed in beads. This was contained within two pieces of pottery attached.

It is said that these three bands of Indians, the Wee Nees, the Wee Tees, and the Mingoes, belonged to the five great nations that had their headquarters along the Great Lakes. It is believed, however, that these Indian camping grounds in Williamsburg were not places of permanent residence, but that they were occupied from time to time by hunting and fishing parties from the North and the West.

CHAPTER VIII.

COLONIAL WILLS.

The wills of the people of Williamsburg who died during the Colonial period are recorded in the office of the Judge of Probate, Charleston. To those who can see, these wills contain a vast amount of historical material. One reads in them that the average man of Williamsburg who came about 1735, without a material possession, amassed a considerable estate within a score of years. When he died, his will and inventory of his goods show that he owned many broad acres of land, a number of valuable slaves, droves of horses, and herds of cattle. It shows, too, that sometimes he wore silver shoe buckles and a "Wigg," and was ready to furnish a "pair of pistols" whenever the code duello demanded. The rapid recuperation of these Scotch-Irish of Williamsburg under these pioneer conditions proves what manner of men they were. Their sustained strength under further development is simply additional evidence.

In these old wills, the women, wives and daughters and sisters, are called by name. And well may they be remembered, for women have borne the burdens of the day since the curse was pronounced in Eden. When one looks into the first life of these "Poor Protestants" in Williamsburg and regards the women, he draws on all his virtuous manhood to salute them. These ancient women of Williamsburg were the real "Colonial Dames of America." Whether or not their fathers had been commissioned by the King for service in the colonies, their sons were called by God Almighty for the accomplishment of American freedom and for the establishment of the American Commonwealth. And right worthily did these sons fulfill their high calling!

Here follow some statements taken from these ancient wills, and a few comments. All are described as planters unless otherwise specified.

William Anderson married Ann Baxter, a widow. He left a son, Alexander Anderson, and a daughter, Ann Anderson. Charles Baxter was his stepson. William Anderson died in 1746.

John Avant died in 1750 leaving two sons, Francis and John; and three daughters, Lydia, Hannah, and Rebecca. One of his daughters married a Green, for he left two grandsons, William and Francis Green.

James Bradley died in 1775. He left an annuity of one hundred pounds to be paid to his mother, Jane, who, when a widow, married William Burrows. His sister, Mary, married Robert McConnell. He had three half-brothers, George, Samuel, and Joseph Burrows; and one half-sister, Jane Burrows. He had a cousin named James Bradley, who was the son of his uncle, Samuel Bradley.

Moses Britton died in 1773. His will shows that he left a widow named Ann; two sons, Daniel Lane and Benjamin; and a daughter, Rebecca. He had three brothers, Philip, Henry, and Francis.

Joseph Britton died in 1773. His wife was named Ann. He left eight children, Elizabeth, Philip, Thomas, Martha, Mary, Moses, Joseph, and John.

William Barr died in 1764. His wife was named Esther. His children were James, Margaret, Isaac, Nathaniel, Rachael, Caleb, Jacob, Silas, Esther, John, and William. He instructed his executors to have each one of his children taught a trade.

William Brockinton died in 1741. He and his wife, Sarah, lived on the South side of Black Mingo Creek. His sons were William, John, and Richard; his daughters, Elizabeth, afterwards wife of James Hepburn; Mary, married Joshua Jolly; Hannah, married James Hoole; and Sarah Jane. Sarah, wife of William, died in 1759, leaving a will in which she made her son Richard executor. William and Sarah Brockinton were ancestors of all the South Carolina Brockintons.

William Brockinton, Jr., married Rachel Commander in 1742 and died in 1743. He left all of his property to his wife, providing for an unborn child. This "unborn child" became, in all probability, the Joseph Brockinton of whom Bishop Gregg writes in his "History of the Old Cheraws."

William Borland died in 1741. His wife was named Mary. He left two sons, William and Archibald; and three daughters, Mary, Jean, and Elizabeth.

Timothy Britton died in 1749. He divided his property between his wife, Mary, and his child, who was not named. His executors were his wife, Mary, his brother, Joseph, and his brother-in-law, Francis Goddard.

Philip Britton died in 1749. He left a wife named Jane, but no child. He bequeathed property to his brothers, Joseph, Moses, Francis, and Timothy Britton; his nephew, John Rae; his nieces, Ann and Rachel; and, also, gives some property to Walter Martin's two children and to William and Francis Goddard.

Daniel Britton died in 1748. He left property to his wife, Elizabeth, and to his unborn child.

John Blakeley died in 1747. He left a wife, who was born Elizabeth Fleming, and four children who were not named in his will. He designated James Armstrong, William Pressley, and James McClelland, and his brother James, executors, and ordered that if his wife, Elizabeth, remarried, his brother James was to have control of his children and of his estate. He left fifty acres of land to the Williamsburg Presbyterian Congregation.

Elizabeth Clapp died in 1751. She was the daughter of Gibson Clapp, for whom Clapp Swamp was named. In her will, she mentions her grandfather, Colonel Thomas Lynch; her uncle, the Honorable Joseph Blake; her beloved sister, Mary Clapp; her mother, Sarah Hopton, wife of William Hopton; her aunt, Sarah Blake, half-sister to her father; and her aunt, Mary Acheson, daughter of her grandfather, Thomas Lynch.

Isaac Chandler died in 1748. He left a widow named Elizabeth; two sons, Samuel and Isaac; and a daughter, Ann. He was an Antipaedo Baptist minister and was trained under the Reverend William Screven, the elder. Mr. Chandler was a member of the Baptist colony which came with Reverend William Screven from Kittery, Maine, and settled at Somerton. He was at his death a man of considerable wealth, much learning, and liberal culture. His will indicates that he owned one of the largest private libraries of his day, and many heirlooms of silver and gold.

John Dick died in 1749. His will names his wife, Jane; his sons, Robert, John, and William; his daughter, Jannet, who married Packer; his daughter, Elizabeth, who married John Leviston; his daughter, Margaret, who married John Scott; his daughter, Mary, who married Runnels; and his daughter, Susannah, who married Wirter. He names two of his grandchildren, John and Samuel Leviston.

Nathaniel Drew died in 1750. His wife was born Margaret Barr. He mentions in his will his son, Samuel Drew; his brother, David Drew; and his sister, Mary Drew, who married Thomas Ervin, of Fog's Manor, Pa.; and his son-in-law, John Barr. He left some money for the education of his two grandsons, John and Samuel Nesmith, sons of John Nesmith, deceased. After specific bequests, he instructed his executors to sell the remainder of his estate and place one-third thereof in the hands of Reverend John Baxter, Thomas Carne, and Alexander McCants, trustees, for the use and benefit of the Presbyterian Congregation at Black Mingo Creek. The remaining two-thirds he gives to James McClelland and John Leviston, trustees, for the benefit of the Presbyterian Congregation at Williamsburg. He provides that these trustees shall give security for this money and that none of it shall be paid to any minister but one who preached and taught the doctrines and submitted to the rules and discipline of the Church of Scotland and who was of moral conduct.

Margaret Drew died in 1762. She was the widow and relict of Nathaniel Drew. She mentions her son, Samuel Drew, and makes her trusty and well beloved sons-in-law, John Brockinton and Samuel Nesmith, her executors.

John Frierson died in 1760. He left four sons, Aaron, Moses, John, James, and a daughter, Mary.

John Fleming died in 1750. He left three sons, John, James, and William; and three daughters, Elizabeth, who married Blakeley; and Jannet, who married James; and Isabella, who married John Pressley.

David Fulton died in 1745. In his will, he mentions his wife, Rebecca, and his son, Samuel. After making specific bequests to them, he leaves the remainder of his property to his son, Samuel Fulton, subject to the payment of one hundred pounds to Jean Fulton, only daughter of his son, Paul Fulton, deceased, when she attains the age of fifteen years.

Paul Fulton died in 1742. He mentions his wife, Mary; his daughter, Jean; his nephew, David Fulton; and his brother, Samuel Fulton.

Roger Gordon died in 1750. His wife was named Mary. He had three sons, James, John, and Moses; and four daughters, Sarah, who married Hugh McGill; Margaret, who married Robert Wilson; Elizabeth and Mary. He mentions his granddaughter, Mary, and his grandsons, Roger Wilson and Roger McGill.

Peter Gourdin died in 1774. He gives his son, Peter Gourdin, all of his property when he shall arrive at the age of nineteen years. He instructed that his son should have as good an education as could be had in the province of South Carolina. He directed that his negro man,

Billy, should not be put to any field work but to be kept jobbing on the plantation and, in proper seasons, to tend the indigo works about the vats, and further that Billy should not be under the power or authority of any overseer which should be put on his plantation after his decease. His first wife was named Esther Sullivan. He wills, if his son, Peter, die before he arrives at the age of nineteen years, that the property coming to him from his wife, Esther, shall return to his brother-in-law, John Sullivan, and to his sister-in-law, Margaret Richbourgh. If his son, Peter, die before reaching the age of nineteen, the property which came to him from his late wife, who was Ann Lester, should return to his brother-in-law, John Lester, and to his sister-in-law, Martha Lester. He mentions his niece, Mary Ann Finley; his nephews, Theodore and Samuel Gourdin; and his brother, Isaac Gourdin.

Elizabeth Jaudon died in 1743. She left three young children, Paul, David, and Elisha. Paul was the oldest and yet a minor. She waived his age and made him her sole executor.

John Hamilton died in 1744. His wife was Christian McClelland. They left no children. He bequeathed three hundred acres of land in Williamsburg Township for the support of the Williamsburg Presbyterian Church, then under the management of Reverend John Rae.

William James died in 1750. His widow was named Elizabeth. He had four sons, John, William, Robert, and Samuel; and four daughters, Jannet, Elizabeth, Esther, and Sarah. He mentions his sons-in-law, David Wilson, Gavin Witherspoon, James McCullough, and Nathaniel McCullough.

William Heathly died in 1742. He mentions his wife, Mary; his son, William; and his daughter, Elizabeth.

William Jamison died in 1756. He left a large estate which he gave to his sister, Agnes Still, widow of James Still, who lived in Ireland. Agnes Still came to Williamsburg with James McDowell, who was married to her granddaughter, Agnes Davidson. Agnes Still died soon afterwards and left her property to James McDowell. When James McDowell died, his widow, Agnes, was made attorney for them by the following heirs, who then lived in Ireland; Archibald Drew, Margaret Drew, Adam Wilson, William McCormick, James McCormick, George Maxwell, Dorothy Maxwell, Robert Adams, and Sarah Adams.

Crafton Kerwin died in 1747, leaving a widow, Mary; and a son Thomas. His widow afterwards married the Reverend John Fordyce, minister of Prince Frederick's Church.

Sarah Mongtomery died in 1770. She mentions her two sons, William and Henry; and her two daughters, Janet, who married Dunn; and Mary, who married Armstrong; and her niece and her nephew, Margaret and John Barr.

William McCalla died in 1750. He mentions his daughter, Jannet; his daughter, Margaret, wife of Alexander McCrea; his daughter, Sarah; and his daughter, Jean, wife of John James.

John McCormick died in 1752. He mentions his sister, Isabella McCormick; and his three other sisters, Mary Averton, Agnes Carson, and Jean Dick.

William McCormick died in 1750. He mentions his son, John McCormick; his daughter, Mary, who married John Dick; and his daughter, Isabelle.

James McCown died in 1750. He left all of his property in the hands of William Young, Samuel Montgomery, and Gavin Witherspoon, to apply so much of same as was necessary for the "Christian education" of his children, and the remainder to be paid to his sons, David, Thomas, and James.

John McCrea died in 1765. He mentions his wife, Martha; his sons, Thomas, William, John, and Joseph; and his daughter, Sarah.

Joseph McCrea died in 1762. His wife was named Mary. He left two daughters, Mary, and Ann, who married John Matthews.

James McClelland died in 1761. His wife was named Mary. He had six children, James, John, Leonard, Bryce, Samuel, and Grizelle.

Abraham Michaux died in 1767. His wife was named Lydia. He had four sons, Peter, Daniel, Paul, and William. Of his daughters, Lydia married Clegg; Julia married Perry; and Hester married Cromwell.

Samuel Montgomery died in 1751. He left his wife, Jeleba, his plantation and all his slaves so long as she remained his widow. He mentions his sons, Nathaniel and William.

Jonathan Murrill died in 1743. He left legacies to his children, Anthony, William, Elizabeth, Susannah, Sarah, Mary, and Martha.

John Matthews died in 1750. His wife was Ann McCrea. He left four sons, William, John, Isaac and Abraham; and four daughters, Mary, Sarah, Elizabeth, and Jean.

Matthew Nelson died in 1742. He mentions his eldest son, George; his daughter, Mary, and his daughter, Elizabeth; and his four grandsons, Matthew, son of the oldest son, George; Samuel, son of his son, John; William, son of his son, William; and William, son of his son, Samuel.

George Nelson died in 1742. His wife was named Eleanor. He had two sons, Matthew and Jared; and three daughters, Mary, Jane, and Isabelle.

John Porter died in 1750. He had a son named James and a daughter named Mary and a brother-in-law named Joseph Bradley.

Dr. Thomas Potts died in 1760. His wife was named Sarah. He had a son named Thomas, and four daughters, Mary, Ann, Elizabeth, who married Swinton, and Margaret, who married Potts. He had a grandson named Thomas Johnson.

Robert Paisley died in 1761. His wife was named Mary. He had four sons, John, Robert, James, and William; and two daughters, Mary and Elizabeth.

John Rae died in 1760. He was the first Minister of the Williamsburg Presbyterian Church. His wife was named Rachel. They left no children.

Samuel Scott died in 1774. He married Margaret Gregg. They had two daughters, Janet and Elizabeth. His widow married second William Gordon, third William Flagler. She was the Margaret Gregg Gordon of the Revolution.

Reverend Elisha Screven died in 1756. His wife was named Hannah. He had six sons, Joseph, Elisha, Joshua, Samuel, William, and Benjamin; and two daughters, Elizabeth, wife of James Fowler, and Hannah. This man was the founder of the city of Georgetown.

Nathaniel Snow died in 1760. He had three sons, George, James, and John; and two daughters, Mary and Ann.

James Scott died in 1750. He left all of his property to his two brothers, Alexander and John.

John Scott died in 1750. He left his property to his wife, and children, not named, and made his brother William Scott, Richard Richardson, and William Cantey, his executors.

Samuel Vareen gives all of his property to his granddaughters, Martha and Elizabeth Crousby and Elizabeth Harbin. He makes his son-in-law, Francis Harbin, and his daughter, Ann Harbin, executor and executrix.

John White died in 1750. His wife was named Mary Ferguson. They left one son, Blakely White.

John Watson died in 1760. He left two hundred pounds to the Williamsburg Presbyterian Church and the remainder of his estate to be equally divided among the duaghters of Thomas Scott, of Williamsburg, deceased.

James Witherspoon died in 1768. He married Elizabeth McQuoid. They had four sons, James, Gavin, Robert, and John; and one daughter, Ann, who married Archibald McKee. In his will, he mentions his granddaughter, Elizabeth McKee.

Elizabeth Mouzon died in 1748. She mentions her five sons, Louis, James, Peter, Samuel, and Henry; and two daughters, Elizabeth and Ann.

Henry Mouzon died in 1749. His wife was named Ann. He had seven children, Henry, Ann, Esther, Jane, Sarah, Susannah Elizabeth, and Mary Ann.

John Pressley died in 1750. His wife was named Margaret. He left legacies to his son, William; his daughter, Susannah, of tender age; his daughter, Sarah; his daughter, Jane McCullough; and his daughter Eleanor Thompson. In his will, he directs that if his house, which he leaves to his wife, should become unfit to live in, that his son, William, should build her a house twenty-eight feet in length, and eighteen feet in breadth and that he shall keep her comfortable.

Joshua Screven died in 1764 and is buried on the North side of Big Dam Swamp. The tombstone standing at the head of his grave is the oldest monument in Williamsburg County. He endows his wife, Hannah, and gives to his brother, Benjamin Screven, his plantations on the North side of the North bank of Black River. He gives his silver knee buckles to his brother, William Screven, and his watch to his brother, Benjamin Screven; and some negroes to his mother, Hannah Screven.

William Matthews died in 1760. He left legacies to his wife, Elizabeth, and to his son, William.

William Sabb died in 1765. His wife was named Deborah. He left two sons, Thomas Sabb and William Sabb; and four daughters, Deborah, Anna, Elizabeth, and Mary. In this will, he mentions his brother, Thomas Sabb.

John McBride died in 1766. He gives his wife, Elizabeth, a liberal share of his property and his family Bible.

He provides for his five children, John, James, William, Samuel, and Rebecca, and for an unborn child.

Esther Vanalle died in 1749 and gave all of her property to her husband, Matthew Vanalle.

John Scott died in 1788. He mentions his wife, Sarah; his mother-in-law, Mrs. Elizabeth Williams, and his sister-in-law, Mrs. Rebecca Screven.

Thomas Scott died in 1766. He provides for his wife, Jannet, and his seven daughters, Elizabeth, Jean, Mary, Jannet, Katherine, Margaret, and Sarah, and gives all of his real estate to his son, William. These seven daughters were given much property in the will of John Watson.

John Scott died in 1769. His wife was named Catherine. He left three sons, Samuel, Joseph, and Moses, and one daughter, Isabelle.

Thomas McCrea died in 1760 without leaving a will. His oldest son, William McCrea, did not come to this country with his father but remained in Belfast, County Antrim, Ireland. Thomas McCrea left some children living in Williamsburg. When he died, his brother, Robert McCrea, of Lisnabrin, County Down, Ireland, made affidavit to these facts, aiding William McCrea to appoint attorneys in South Carolina.

Jannet Scott of Williamsburg. She mentions her grandson, Thomas Scott; son, William Scott; seven daughters, Elizabeth, Jean, Mary, Jannet, Catherine, Margaret, and Sarah; and her son-in-law, John Burrows. This will was probated on the 29th day of March, 1772.

James Fowler, planter and merchant, died in 1772. He mentions his father, Richard Fowler; his mother, Sarah Fowler, and his sister, Joanna Fowler, all of whom then lived in England; his wife, Elizabeth Screven, and his only child, Martha Fowler. He provides that his daughter, Martha, should inherit when she reached the age of eighteen years, and appointed his friends, John Scott, William Scott, and his wife, Elizabeth Screven, his executors.

William Frierson died in 1773. In his will, he mentions his wife, Mary; his son, Robert, and his son, John James. William Brown, William Campbell, and Isaac Nelson were his executors.

Theodore Gourdin's will was probated January 8, 1774. He mentions his brothers, Isaac and Peter Gourdin; his sons, Theodore and Samuel; and his niece, Marian Boisseau. He left legacies to John Buddin, Esther McDonald, daughter of the late Captain John McDonald, and Edward Howard, son of George Howard. He wills that in the division of his negroes families should not be separated. His will was witnessed by James Lynch, William Buford, and Daniel Rhodus.

Francis Britton's will was proven before Samuel Nesmith, Esq., March 24, 1768. He mentions his sons, Moses, Francis, and Henry, and his daughter, Mary; his grandson, Daniel Lane Britton, son of Moses; Martha Britton; and Philip Britton, son of Joseph, his brother.

Isaac Brunson's will was proved September 7, 1770. He mentions his wife, Mary; his son, Daniel; and his other children—his sons, David, Isaac, Josiah, Matthew, Moses, and Joshua; and his daughters, Mary Mellett and Susannah.

John Fleming's will was proved before James McCants, Esq., May 11, 1768. He mentions his wife, Elizabeth; his brother's daughter, Elizabeth; his cousin, Samuel Shannon; his sister, Agnes Cooper alias Fleming, and her two sons, James and Thomas Cooper; his sister's son, George, and daughter, Elizabeth Cooper; his wife's daughter, Jannet, and her daughter, Elizabeth Blakeley; his brother, James Fleming and his son, Peter Blakeley Fleming.

Henry Montgomery's will was proved January 26, 1769. He mentions his wife, Sarah; his sons, William and Henry; his daughters, Sarah Jannett Dunn and Mary Armstrong and his nephew, Hugh Montgomery. This will was witnessed by Alexander McCrea, John McElveen, and William McCullough.

Jeremiah Vareen's will was proved July 5, 1767. He mentions his wife, Mary Vareen; his sons, William, Jeremiah, and Ebenezer; his son-in-law, James Sullivan; his daughters, Sarah Lewis, Ann Jenkins, Rebecca, Hannah, Rachel, Jane, and Martha.

Thomas Frierson's will was proved December 27, 1770, before James McCants, Esq. He mentions his wife, Mary Frierson; his daughter, Mary Wilson, and his daughter, Sarah Scott; and his grandson, Thomas Wilson. He makes his two sons-in-law, Roger Wilson and John Scott his sole executors.

Mary Gordon's will was proved the 23rd day of May, 1766. She mentions her six children, Moses, Elizabeth, Sarah, Margaret, Jean, and Mary. She left a legacy to Mary Wilson and also one to John Gordon, if he come to this province. She makes her son, Moses, Samuel Bradley, and William Frierson, Jr., her executors. This will was witnessed by James Dickey and Robert Wilson.

Royal Spry's will was proved December 27, 1770. He mentions his wife, Rebecca; his four children, Jean, John, Elizabeth, and Rebecca. He wills that his old slave Phyllis should have her freedom immediately after his death and be maintained and clothed out of his estate.

Thomas McKnight's will was proved November 29, 1772. He mentions his sons, Robert, James, and William; and his daughter, Mary; and his brother, Robert. His will was witnessed by William Law, George Dickey, and Richard Tyser.

John McFadden's will was proved July 19, 1773. He mentions his five children, John, James, Robert, Thomas, and Mary. His executors were Robert Wilson, Sr., and his son, John McFadden, at the age of twenty years, William Orr, and Robert Paisley, and Joseph McKee.

John Gregg's will was proved October 3, 1775. He mentions his wife, Eleanor; his sons, James, John, Robert, and William; and his daughters, Margaret, Mary, and Janet. "It is my desire that my sons, Robert and William, and my daughter, Jannet, be learned to Read, and Right, and Cypher through the common rules of Arithmetick."

Archibald McKee's will was proved October 3, 1776. He mentions his wife, Elizabeth; his five children, Adam and Joseph McKee, Martha Cooper, Jane Miller, and Archibald Knox, and his two sons-in-law, William Miller and Samuel Knox.

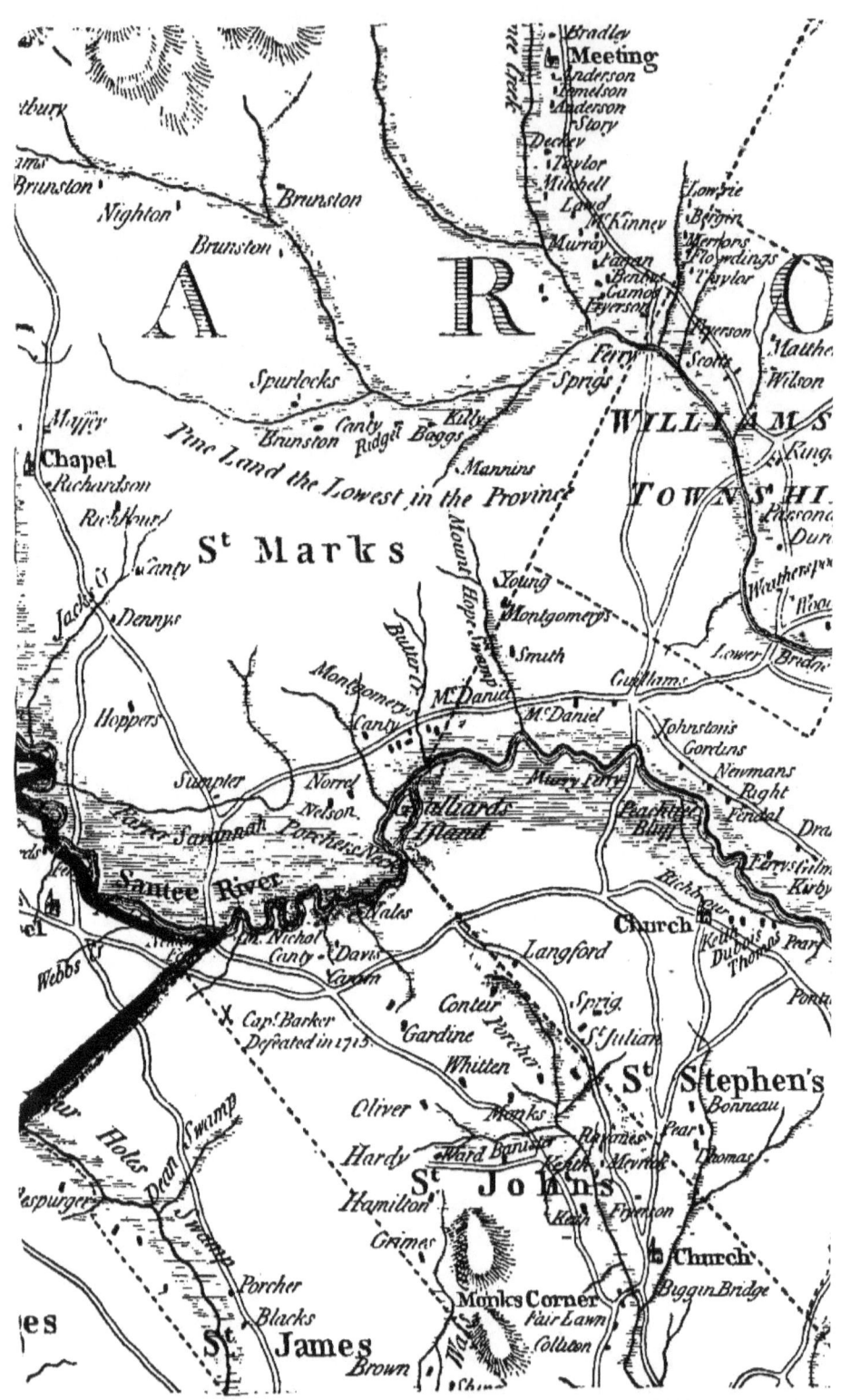

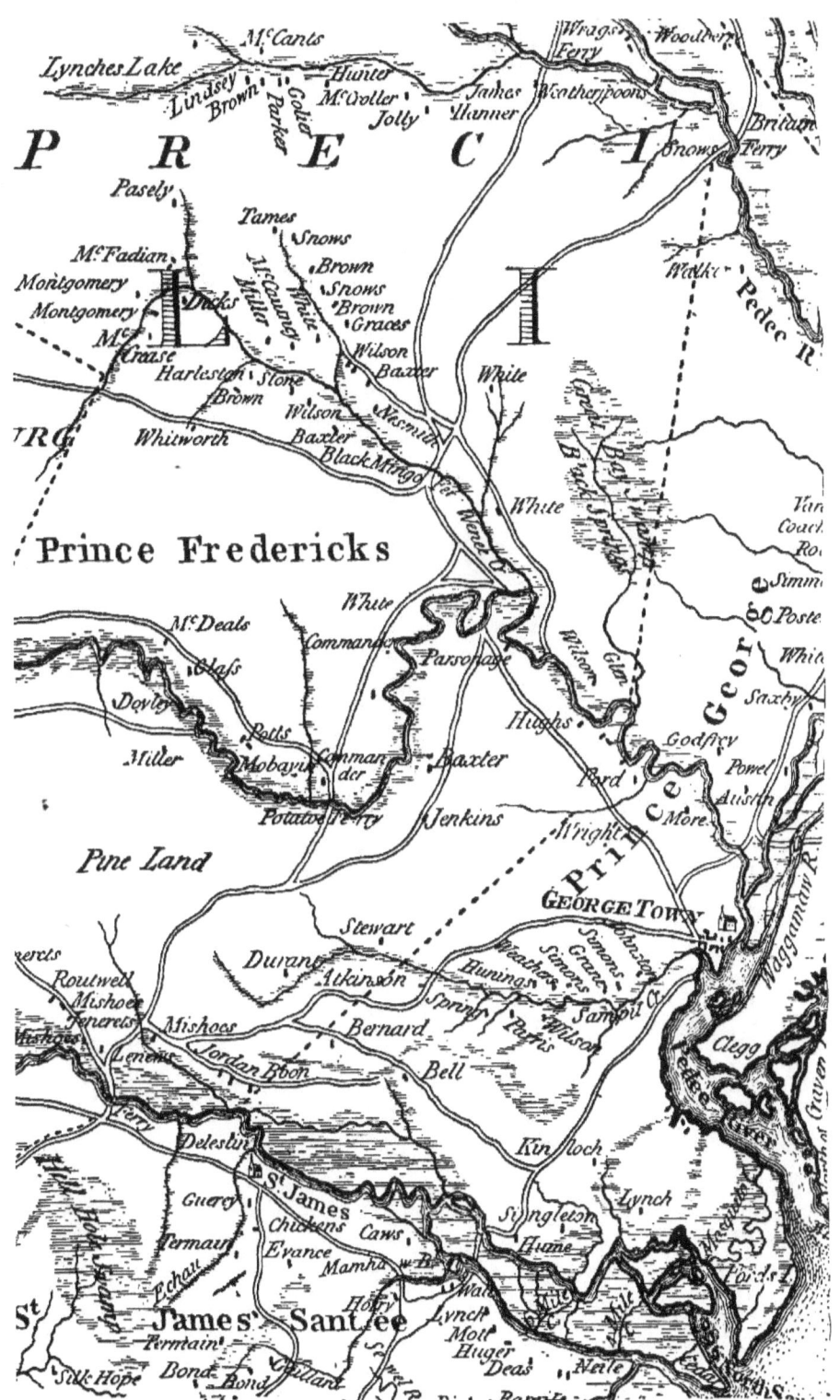

FROM MOUZON'S MAP, 1775.

CHAPTER IX.

POLITICAL AND SOCIAL MATTERS.

It is probable that Williamsburg lived from 1735 to 1745 as nearly within itself as any part of the civilized world. Its citizens had been made sick of other peoples, and their means of transportation during this period were nominal. These pioneers cleared enough land to produce the required amount of corn and vegetables, flax, and cotton for their own use. Their horses, cattle, hogs, and sheep grew unattended in the swamps.

When anything was needed from outside markets, these pioneers drove a herd of cattle to Charleston, or sent a consignment of deer skins, and from the proceeds secured the required supplies. Rounding up cattle and horses in cowpens and horsepens taught these people how to ride and control horses. Further, it made them love horses and obtain good ones. Hunting deer was a productive occupation. Venison is excellent food and deerskins sold at high prices.

Herdsmen and hunters did not need many slaves. No slaves were brought in 1732 when the first settlers came, and but few had been imported up to 1745. Indeed, the average citizen of this time owned not more than five. John Matthews had six; Samuel Montgomery, two; William James, nine; Joseph Burgess, four; Roger Gordon, five; Richard Middleton, eleven; Robert McCottry, five; William Pressley, one; John Scott, nine.

The Williamsburg woman of this pioneer period existed solely for the use of her husband. Even on the Church books her name was not recorded, and she had no interests outside of her home. Her husband held her at home and she conformed completely to his habits and his will. Sometimes he took her to church, and once or twice each year he carried her to her mother's home for a few hours visit. She never left home unless under his cautious care. The jealous zeal with which the original settler in Williamsburg guarded his wife and the complete dominion which he exercised over her may be better imagined when it is known how the exceptionally conservative man of the old stock now in the County regards his wife and how fully he believes his life should completely circumscribe her very own.

The man made the corn and hauled it to his barn; the woman shucked and shelled it, ground it into meal and baked it into bread. The man killed and dressed a steer at the slaughter pen; the woman cured and cooked the meat, and made the hide into breeches for her husband, moccasins for her children, and aprons for herself. The man sheared the sheep; the woman picked the burrs from the wool, carded, spun, and wove in into cloth from which she made the family clothing.

The average woman of this time married about fifteen years old, bore her husband about ten children, at least half of whom did not survive infancy, and she died about thirty years of age. About one year after her death, her husband married another fifteen year old girl. Her life was similar to that of the first wife. The man probably married a third time. The average man of Williamsburg of seventy-five years of age had probably been married three times and had fifteen living children and an equal number who had died in infancy. The average colonial Williamsburg man married young and kept married all his life.

Sometimes, however, a woman survived the strenuous life of the day and showed wonderful virility. Mary Frierson was born in Ireland in 1701, came to Williamsburg in 1735, and died in 1791. She married Thomas Frierson when she was very young. Her youngest child, Mary Frierson, afterwards wife of John Scott, was born when her mother was more than fifty years old.

Mary Heathly married first William Brady and bore seven children to him. He died and she married Thomas Witherspoon, to whom she bore seven children. Afterwards, she married Thomas McCrea and bore three children to him. She survived her husband, Thomas McCrea, but did not marry again.

James Witherspoon was married five times. He seems to hold the record in old Williamsburg, although there were many of his friends who were married four times, according to the records; but possibly some of these old fellows omitted recording one or two of their marriages.

The thing a fifteen year old boy of 1750 most wanted was the finest rifle to be bought in the world. He desired one that would bring a squirrel from the highest cypress on the Santee and fell a deer at three hundred yards. His father wanted the finest looking and fastest running horse in the colony. Soon after the cultivation of indigo was begun, this father and son became more concerned as to where their hearts' desire might be obtained than about the price they would have to pay. Planters on the lower Wee Nee and the Santee allowed their rice paddies to fail while digging and cementing indigo vats. All the Williamsburg country cultivated indigo and it brought forth an hundred fold.

These old indigo holes may yet be seen in all parts of the present County. There is one within a hundred yards of Sutton's Methodist Church and is plainly visible from the Santee road. A series of them may be found in George's field on Cedar Swamp, and some on the Flagler plantation on Finley Bay. These indigo vats were made by digging out a cavity in the earth and plastering this cavity with a waterproof composition of pitch and sand. The story goes that the secret of this composition for lining indigo pits came with African slaves, and that they so jealously guarded it that their masters never discovered it. But few slaves had the secret and could successfully line indigo vats. They were invaluable to their masters. When an indigo planter discovered that he had a slave possessing this valuable secret, he immediately made that slave the prime minister of the plantation, clothed him in purple and fine linen, and caused him to fare sumptuously every day.

Cattle made Williamsburg substantial; indigo made it rich.

By 1765, Williamsburg citizens were far removed from want. Nearly all of them had a considerable surplus and their estates grew until the Revolution. Wealth brought no specially noticeable change in their manner of living. Cultivating indigo and herding cattle did not require much labor, so a very few slaves were all that a planter could use. Consequently, nobody in the District ran riot accumulating negro slaves. Nobody in this section built a colonial mansion, as did most of the wealthy men in many other parts of the country. Nobody in Williamsburg ever has until this good day erected such an "old Southern home" as Henry W. Grady remembered and described in his Boston banquet speech. The people of this community have elected to live in modest comfortable homes, although many of them might have erected splendid mansions. Is it that the cryptomnesic content of forty generations of nomad life on the continent and a thousand years of warring and wandering in Ireland and Scotland deter them? Is there an unconscious yet determining instinct in them that "something might happen to move me and I could not carry a mansion?"

Yet no people on earth ever had a deeper land love than did the Colonial Scotch-Irish masters of plantations. Every one ruled his little realm as absolutely as any ancient monarch attempted in his sphere, and every one knew his rights, required them, and respected those of his neighbors. This same idea still obtains in Williamsburg. "Woe to trespassers—all others welcome" might well be graven over all its gates.

Prior to the War of the Revolution, no person could teach school in the colony unless he were a communicant of the Church of England and duly licensed by the Lord Bishop of London. These Presbyterians in Williamsburg at that time had much rather have employed the Devil to teach their children than a member of the Church of England. Consequently, Colonial Williamsburg children were taught in their own homes. Remarkable it may be, but the truth is the average man and woman of Williamsburg in 1776, although born and reared under severe pioneer conditions, were more familiar with letters that at any period since that time. Not more than one man out of the first one hundred wills and transfers of property made and recorded between 1765 and 1775 had to make his mark, nor did a greater per centum of women releasing rights fail to write legibly their names. Out of more than three hundred of Marion's Men from Williamsburg who filed their statements for pay, only six made their marks where they should have signed their names. Almost every one of these men was born in Williamsburg later than 1740. The old manuscripts of the Colonial period, though written with goose quill pens and red oak ball ink, are beautiful in general appearance and the chirography is almost perfect.

All office holders in the colonial period were required to take communion according to the ritual of the Church of England and from the hands of a priest of the Established Church. This eliminated nearly all of the indwellers in Williamsburg from official duties, for no Presbyterian of that day would have touched the elements after blessed by a priest of the Established Church sooner than he would have torn out his tongue. Besides, the Scotch-Irish in Williamsburg desired only to be let alone and they had too much caution to enter where they would be disturbed. Williamsburg Township was entitled to two representatives in the Colonial Assembly from the day it was surveyed in 1736, since then it had more than one hundred heads of families, yet it did not choose to exercise this right until the war drums sounded.

Prince Frederick's Parish, or Williamsburg, elected these men to the Provincial Congress of August, 1775: Thomas Gilliard, Jr., Thomas Port, Anthony White, Benjamin Screven, Archibald McDonald, John James. This Provincial Congress, on March 26, 1776, resolved itself into the first General Assembly of the State of South Carolina. This general assembly appointed the following as Justices of the Quorum for this Parish: Anthony Bonneau, John Brockinton, Sr., Francis Britton, Benjamin Gause, Peter Simons, William Wilson, John James, Thomas Lynch, James McDonald, William Snow, Anthony White, Gavin Witherspoon, William Michau, Samuel Nesmith, John Plowden, Benjamin Screven, and John Witherspoon.

The legal holidays in South Carolina for many years prior to the Revolution were as follows: All Sundays; Circumcision Day, January 1, Martyrdom of Charles I, January 30; Good Friday; Monday in Easter Week; Tuesday in Easter Week; King George's birthday, June 4; Monday in Whitsuntide; Tuesday in Whitsuntide; Nativity of Our Lord, or Christmas, December 25; St. Stephen's Day, December 26; St. John Evangelist's Day, December 27. These were all fast or feast days of the Established Church and the Scotch-Irish Presbyterians of Williamsburg scorned to recognize them or even to know their names.

It must not be understood, however, that Williamsburg observed no holidays. The fact is the making of a living was then, is now, and ever will be an easy matter in Williamsburg, and its people were then inclined to holidays. Once every two months, the militia companies mustered. Twice a year, the militia battalions were assembled. Once a year, the Craven County Regiment of Militia was called together. All of these days were holidays in ascending degree of intensity. Every man essayed his utmost to make a "perfect day" on the regimental muster ground.

Besides these muster occasion holidays, there were the midsummer and midwinter racing seasons. Sometimes, these lasted for many days before all were satisfied. At that time a horse provided the most rapid means of transit available. No colony knew more the value of good horses than did Williamsburg, nor anywhere was the racing spirit more rampant. These old pioneers introduced the best breed of horses they could find and developed some fast racers. All the section gathered to witness these biennial races, and no winners ever more appreciated a victory. Owners trained and rode their own horses and the keenest possible rivalry existed.

These races were not Sunday School picnics, nor were they religious communion occasions. The distillers of North Carolina knew well the dates of these races and always kept the gentlemen of Williamsburg well supplied with old, ropy corn whiskey, and rich, ripe apple brandy.

Sometimes a Puritan minister would preach about these ungodly races and say all manner of evil things about them. Who can say that such a one was declaring the way of God to man? Grant it that John James always participated in these races, sometimes swore a combination of Scotch and Welsh oaths, and occasionally drank himself into dreamland before the night came—was it not he who rode from Georgetown to the King's Tree on "Thunder" and called all Williamsburg to "Liberty or Death?" And could Mouzon and Macaulay and McCottry and McDonald and Witherspoon and Scott and their Selim and Saladdin and Mecca and Medina and Bucephalus and Buddha have come out of other times and things than these?

CHAPTER X.

THE WAR OF THE REVOLUTION.

> I hear the drums of War's alarum beat,
> I see them seize their arms, rise to their feet,
> Their enemies—and Liberty's—to meet!
> Roselle Mercier Montgomery.

Williamsburg was peaceful and happy in 1775. Its doors were never locked and its windows were never barred. Its cornfields produced abundantly and its meadows were overflowing with cattle. Indigo ran riot so that cleared acres could not contain it. Tobacco and flax flourished wherever their seeds were sown. Roses bloomed and geraniums grew about the doorways. Morning suns came fresh out of the sea and evening showers brought peace to the troubled sands.

Williamsburg had not been disturbed by outsiders for half a century. It had been left alone to work out its own political and social and religious salvation. And it had accomplished that for which it had come. It had builded its foundation on the Rock of Ages and its dreams were continuously coming true.

The "Mother Country" had been good to Williamsburg. It required in theory that this Township comform to the Established Church, but in fact it permitted Presbyterianism to rule this little realm. No meddling colonial officers came this way and the Stamp Act was but a name. Williamsburg produced its own tea and a surplus. It had no use for commercial papers that were taxed. The only people who came not to stay were traders from North Carolina and from Georgetown and Charleston. These traders bought Williamsburg cattle and indigo and sold tape and buttons. Williamsburg fixed the prices. Traders are the practical diplomats of the ages—the promoters of good feeling—the unifiers of peoples.

The people of Williamsburg heard about the Edenton Tea Party, where fifty-two colonial dames had gathered in the home of Mrs. Thomas Barker and signed a solomn agreement to use no more tea so long as it was taxed by London authority. They knew something of the Boston Tea Party where a number of men, disguised as Indians, boarded a ship in the harbor and threw all of its cargo of stamped tea into the depths of the sea. Charleston and Georgetown business men had told these planters how burdensome the stamp taxes were and how the Tory party in England had the ascendency and was trying to force upon the American colonies such a policy as Spain had practiced. Williamsburg knew that Lord North and others had swung the pendulum as far as possible from William Pitt.

These things made Williamsburg think seriously. It was happy. Reason revolted from breaking the longest and most beautiful peace that these Scotch-Irish had known. One summer day in 1776, young Thomas Lynch came from Philadelphia to his plantation home on Lynch's River, and told Williamsburg that he had, with some other South Carolinians, signed the Declaration of Independence on July Fourth, and that the thirteen colonies were at war with Great Britain.

A youth in whose veins there runs the blood of a hundred generations of men of war and into whose ears a thousand times have been poured tales of the valor and the heroism of his fathers does not hesitate when he hears the war drums. No wonder the Montgomerys and Nesmiths, Gordons and Gambles, McDonalds and McCottrys, Scotts and James, the Witherspoons and Wilsons sniffed the noise of battle from afar and volunteered for service in the first South Carolina troops. From these young men, Williamsburg sent as many in the beginning as the colony desired from the district. These men showed the fighting force of their fathers. Captain John James was cited for valor and conspicuous ability in the skirmish of Tulifinny Bridge.

After Charleston had fallen on May 12, 1780, the citizens of Williamsburg, many of whose sons had served in the seige of that city, decided that "something must be done." That was the darkest day of the Revolution in South Carolina. One who knows and understands the Williamsburg people of 1780 can see these Scotch-Irish discussing the situation. There were no mass meetings held at the King's Tree, no brass bands playing martial music, no eloquent orators sounding striking climaxes, no raising of liberty poles, and nothing of the spectacular. No fiery cross summoned the clans to council, but somehow every Scotchman determined on "liberty or death."

John James just before that time had been sent from Charleston to Williamsburg to organize the district into a fighting force. He knew the people of Williamsburg and the people of Williamsburg knew him. Quietly and without the waving of banners, he went to the several clan leaders in Williamsburg and told them in low tones that "something must be done," and every clan leader repeated the statement John James had made to every member of his clan personally and individually, and every member of every clan repeated the statement, "something must be done." For some time, men and women of Williamsburg looked seriously into each others' faces and said but little. They decided to send Captain John James to interview the British commander at Georgetown, and to ascertain just what would be expected of the people of Williamsburg. Their sons had been paroled after the fall of Charleston and their status was not clearly understood.

When Captain James referred to the people "whom I represent," the British Commander shouted, "I shall require unqualified submission from them; and, as for you, I shall have you hanged." The Britisher drew his sword, which Captain James parried with a chair. In a moment,

Captain James had escaped and mounted "Thunder," and that celebrated war horse was moving towards Williamsburg. Here is where the historian calls the poet. But even the historian must see that coal black charger, outside the house of that interview, unhitched, the reins falling separate to the ground, there standing alert and understanding his master; the strained nervousness and assembling strength of that thoroughbred as he saw his master hurriedly approaching; the furious power he felt with his master's mounting; and his haughty scorn of distance. Here were a man and a horse that Williamsburg had produced. They were both necessary.

Captain John James reached the King's Tree that night. He told his story to John and Joseph Scott and William Frierson and David Witherspoon. John Scott saddled his horse and went to Pudding Swamp and told the story to Henry Mouzon; Joseph Scott, to Cedar Swamp and advised Robert McCottry; William Frierson, to Thorntree Swamp and informed John Macauley; and David Witherspoon to Lynch's Lake and notified John James, Jr. Captain John James remained at the King's Tree and rested the following day.

The third day the Ervins, Scotts, Burgess', Dickeys, Friersons, Nelsons, McClarys, Montgomerys, and Campbells came with Henry Mouzon and elected him Captain of the King's Tree Company; from South of Black River, the Gambles, McGills, Friersons, Watsons, Boyds, Gordons, and Witherspoons chose John Macauley Captain; from Lynch's Lake, the James', McBrides, McCallisters, Matthews', Haseldons, McFaddens, and Rodgers called John James, Jr., to command them; and from Cedar Swamp and Black Mingo, the McCants', McConnells, McCulloughs, McKnights, McCreas, McCutchens, and Nesmiths, made Robert McCottry Captain. These four companies assembled at the King's Tree, formed a battalion, and elected

John James Major. This battalion became the nucleus of Marion's Brigade.

Williamsburg began again the War of the Revolution when it organized James' battalion. This district dedicated all its strength to the cause of Liberty. There were only three hundred men in James' battalion. There were a thousand between the ages of sixteen and and sixty who were alert and strong and who begged for service. And there were a thousand women in Williamsburg who had the capacity and the will to sustain these thousand men in the field. Everybody saw the possibility for the future Brigade. There were hundreds outside of Williamsburg who would join the Brigade. The leader was the thing for which they looked.

Major James and Captain Mouzon knew Lieutenant Colonel Francis Marion. They had been close to him under fire. Many others of James' battalion knew him. He did not talk very much. He did things. Williamsburg called Francis Marion to command and he came. He was a French Huguenot by descent. So was Captain Mouzon.

Scotch clan leaders have an uncanny control over their clansmen. A McDonald will follow a McDonald to the ends of the earth; a Campbell will help a Campbell swim a lake of fire. But, place the McDonalds and the Campbells under either a Campbell or a McDonald, and soon they forget the common enemy and fight each other. Nobody knew this better than Major James. His knowledge of Scotch character made him suggest Francis Marion to Williamsburg. No man ever commanded several Scotch companies with greater success than did this "silent man."

General Marion took command of this Williamsburg Battalion on Lynch's Creek. There was nothing of the spectacular in his assuming command. When it is realized that he was of Latin blood and was a trained soldier accustomed to command, it may seem strange that no formalities were observed,—no roll of drums, no presenting of arms. These four companies were resting under some oaks on the side of a swamp close by the river when he came.

William James, then fifteen years old and a soldier, who afterwards became Judge James, the Historian, was an eyewitness. He says, "The officers and men flocked about General Marion to obtain a sight of their future commander, who was rather of bold and middle stature, lean and swarthy. His body was well set, but his knees and ankles were badly formed, and he still limped upon one leg. He had a countenance remarkably steady; his nose was aquiline, his chin projecting; his forehead, large and high; he was then forty-eight years old, with a frame capable of enduring fatigue and every privation. He was dressed in a close round-bodied crimson jacket of a coarse texture and wore a leather cap, part of the uniform of the Second Regiment, with a silver crescent in front inscribed with the words, 'Liberty or Death'." General Marion knew the minds of the men before him, was in perfect harmony with their purposes, took the position which they had assigned to him; and, from that moment until the end in view had been accomplished, commanded their highest respect, enjoyed their supreme confidence, and directed them to utmost endeavor.

Weems says that when Marion took command he formed the men into a circle and swore them upon their swords never to yield until the liberty of their country had been accomplished, but neither James nor Horry describes the event in such a manner, nor would Marion have instigated such a spectacle in the presence of those Scotch-Irish whom he knew. Marion secured and held the faith of his command by simple, prudent, and severe action and conduct. While he was exceedingly daring in the exercise of many of his activities, the security of his forces seemed always his first consideration. His ability to strike the enemy a hard blow with the minimum loss to himself soon gave his command a wondrous faith in him.

Marion had from the beginning a remarkable faculty for securing information. Probably his spy system has never been improved. The women of the district were his dependable aids in all things but especially in furnishing him information. Many of the women of the district at this time could ride horses as well as their brothers. They looked to Marion for protection and they gave him all they could. General Marion made his headquarters on Snow's Island. From that point, he conducted his campaigns throughout eastern Carolina. It has been said of him that he was never beaten, never surprised, and it does not appear that he ever made a serious military mistake.

After Charleston had fallen into the hands of the British, Lord Cornwallis marched with about twenty-five hundred men and five pieces of artillery from Charleston by way of Lenud's Ferry to Camden. At Lenud's Ferry, his army was met by the American troops under Colonels White, Washington, and Jamison, and engaged in a severe battle. The Americans lost five officers and thirty-six men, killed; and seven officers and sixty men, all the horses, arms, and accoutrements, captured. The three American colonels escaped by swimming. The British lost two dragoons and twenty-four horses. This was a complete victory for the British.

Cornwallis led his army westward along the Santee River road by Murray's Ferry and St. Mark's Church toward Camden. Tarleton separated from the main army at Lenud's Ferry and went to Georgetown, taking with him the Legion and a detachment of the Seventeenth Dragoons, "to take prisoners of all violent enemies of the British Government and to receive the allegiance of others." Cornwallis encountered no resistance on this journey along the Santee.

Tarleton remained in Georgetown about six weeks, during which time he suffered a severe attack of fever. On August 1, he led a cavalry command from Georgetown to Lenud's Ferry and thence to Black River where he crossed at the Lower Bridge. His command reached the King's Tree on August 6, and pitched camp on the parade ground where the County Court House now stands. Major James, who was then at Witherspoon's Ferry on Lynch's Creek with his command, learned of Tarleton's progress in the district and advanced to meet him. That afternoon Tarleton learned that Major James' Battalion, with McCottry's riflemen as advance guard, was approaching the King's Tree, whereupon Tarleton immediately decamped and proceeded toward Camden. McCottry's men arrived a few hours later.

Tarleton took with him on that evening as prisoners of was several men from the King's Tree, among whom was Samuel McGill. That night he burned the mansion house and fourteen buildings of the messuage of Captain Henry Mouzon, about eight miles from the King's Tree. This was the first dwelling house burned by the British in Williamsburg. When Tarleton reached Salem, he disguised himself as an American officer and went to the home of James Bradley, a former citizen of Williamsburg, and passed himself off as Colonel Washington. Mr. Bradley was expecting Colonel Washington and was deceived by Tarleton. Tarleton persuaded him to lead him across the swamps of Black River, when he threw off his disguise and made his aged guide a prisoner.

Colonel Tarleton was sent on this campaign through Williamsburg, as he admits, "to punish the inhabitants in that quarter for their late breaches of parole and perfidious revolt." The breaches of parole to which he refers came about in this way. There were some of the soldiers of Williamsburg taken by the British at the fall of Charleston. Among them were John James, Jr., John Watson, and Isaac Matthews. These Williamsburg soldiers taken at Charleston were paroled on condition that they would no longer carry arms against the British Government. Afterwards, all Williamsburg was ordered by the British to enlist in the British army for the suppression of the American cause. This order, emanating from British authorities to the men of Williamsburg, who had been paroled, they rightly regarded as relieving them from their parole; and, after Major James' interview with Captain Ardesoif at Georgetown, practically all of Williamsburg enlisted in the American cause. The names of only three Tories of Williamsburg are now known. They were Captain John Brockinton, Major John Hamilton, and Major William Sabb, all three of them merchants.

Colonel Tarleton was a typical English Cavalier of his time. He was a game fighter, chivalrous in his treatment of women, and apologetic in the severities which orders required him to practice upon the people of this section. The fact is the only house which he burned in Williamsburg County was that of Captain Henry Mouzon. Tarleton knew Captain Mouzon was one of the leading spirits and the ablest exponents of the American idea in Williamsburg and was, at that very time, engaged in severe warfare against the British. Furthermore, Colonel Tarleton had an abiding hatred for France, growing out of the series of wars between England and France that had recently ended and from the French aid then being given the American colonies by Lafayette and others. Colonel Tarleton knew Captain Mouzon was of French descent, spoke the French language, and hated the English as earnestly as he himself hated the French.

Colonel Tarleton took Samuel McGill as a prisoner of war from Kingstree to Camden, and held him there in irons for some time. It is possible that the only way that Tarleton could have held Samuel McGill was to have put him in irons. For, Samuel McGill was about forty years

THE WAR OF THE REVOLUTION 103

old at that time and was a real man. He had in him all the daring of his wild Welsh, the craftiness of his Scotch, the magnetism of the Irish, and the perseverance of his English ancestors.

While Colonel Tarleton was encamped on the Witherspoon plantation below the King's Tree, there were a number of the Williamsburg young women within his lines. Record and tradition indicate that Tarleton and his officers accepted with becoming grace the frequent sallies of sharpness coming from the tongues of their fair, spirited captives, and were as gracious to them as conditions permitted.

The war path of the British from Camden to Charleston at that time was by way of Nelson's Ferry on the Santee River. Unconquered Williamsburg lay dangerously near to this warpath, less than ten miles in many places, and it was very important from a military standpoint to the British that they should crush this Williamsburg spirit. The British first sent Tarleton through Williamsburg, but Tarleton was too chivalrous a foe to do the destructive work the British authorities deemed necessary, so, a few days later, Lord Cornwallis sent Major Wemyss through Williamsburg to do the work that Tarleton had left undone.

Major Wemyss crossed Black River on the west side at Benbow's Ferry on the western boundary of Williamsburg August 20, 1780, and destroyed all the dwelling houses, cattle, and sheep in that community. He burned the homes of John Gamble, Major James Conyers, James Davis, Captain John Nelson, Robert Frierson, John Frierson, Robert Gamble, and others. The Reverend James A. Wallace says that, "Wemyss laid waste a tract of country between Black River and the Pee Dee, seventy miles in length and in some places fifteen miles wide."

Major Wemyss proceeded without hindrance on his way of destruction from Benbow's Ferry to the King's Tree. Just about the time he arrived at the King's Tree on

August 27, 1780, Major James met him and killed fifteen of his men and took a number of prisoners. Major James lost thirty men in this action. It was a sharp, severe conflict for a few minutes, after which Wemyss withdrew and hurried on the Indiantown road to Georgetown. Major James' forces were constantly attacking him from the rear. It was on this campaign through Williamsburg that Wemyss burned the Indiantown Church and the home of Major James.

In August, 1780, Marion's Brigade was the only body of American troops in South Carolina. The Continental forces had all been dispersed or captured; the Virginia and North Carolina Militia in this State had been scattered and disorganized, and Sumter's Legion had been destroyed by Tarleton. The British had a strong garrison at Georgetown and one at Camden. Williamsburg and Francis Marion alone and unconquered stood in the way of complete domination in South Carolina. The Georgetown and Camden road by way of Black Mingo to Kingstree ran through the heart of Williamsburg. The British planned to establish a chain of strongholds along this way from Georgetown to Camden, to fortify these points, and to keep them strongly garrisoned with men and full of supplies and munitions of war.

The first one of these strongholds along this road, which the British strategists had planned, was about twenty miles on the way from Georgetown to Kingstree on Black Mingo Creek. The British under Colonel Elias Ball proceeded up Black River and a short distance up the Black Mingo to Patrick Dollard's Inn, known as the Red House, just South of Shepherd's Ferry. The British made this Red House headquarters, and from this point they dug communicating trenches to the Black Mingo, along the banks of which they entrenched for about a mile so as to command this navigable stream for such distance. From the point at the Red House, the two trenches communicating with the stream formed an angle of about sixty degrees. These trenches are yet discernible along the banks of the River and were visible to the point where they converged at the Red House until about thirty years ago, when they were filled for the purpose of making the land available for corn fields. The British expected to complete this chain of fortifications through Williamsburg. They did considerable work on this stronghold at Black Mingo and placed a large body of troops there.

Marion knew all about this British plan and this fort on Black Mingo. He was then at his headquarters on Snow's Island. On the 14th of September, 1780, he collected his troops and proceeded in the night southwestward from Snow's Island to Willtown, the only place he could cross Black Mingo in that vicinity, except at Shepherd's Ferry, too near the British stronghold. Marion crossed the bridge over Black Mingo at Willtown in the night, and the noise his cavalry made in crossing warned the British at the Red House and they came out to meet him. A sharp engagement ensued in which seventy-one patriots under Marion were killed and seventy-four of the British, including Colonel Ball, the commander of the garrison. Half of the soldiers under Marion and half of the British were probably wounded within a few hours. At daybreak, the British retreated into their stronghold and there remained. General Marion held his ground and kept up almost a continuous firing on the entrenched British for two days, when they embarked in their boats and proceeded to Georgetown, taking away their wounded but leaving their dead.

General Marion buried his seventy-one dead in the field on the left hand side of the road about five hundred yards going South from Shepherd's Ferry. He interred the British dead at the Red House about one mile further South on the same side of the same road. This battle of Black Mingo resulted in the abandonment of the British plans for building a chain of forts through Williamsburg and was a turning point of the Revolutionary War in the South.

Captain Mouzon's and Captain James' companies from Williamsburg suffered most severely in this battle. Captain Mouzon's company was almost wiped out. Captain Mouzon and Lieutenant Joseph Scott were both so severely wounded that they were rendered useless for further military service in the War and made cripples for life.

It is strange that there is no monument on this Black Mingo battlefield. It is stranger still that years ago somebody was permitted to move away for building chimneys to cabins the brick which had walled in the spot where the seventy-one of Marion's valiant dead were buried.

The Historian Simms thinks that Marion was in error in permitting his troopers to make so much noise in passing over the Black Mingo Bridge that the British at the Red House knew of his coming. Simms says Marion learned a lesson from this and henceforth whenever he crossed a bridge with cavalry his troopers covered the bridge with their saddle blankets so that the horses might pass over without making noise.

With due deference to Simms, it would seem that the noise which Marion's horses made in crossing the bridge was just exactly what the "Swamp Fox" desired. General Marion knew that the number of the British under Colonel Ball at the Red House equalled his own of Americans, and certainly Marion preferred attacking these British in the open and about the swamps to besieging them in a stronghold. Marion's force of cavalry and riflemen would have stood little show against these British in their trenches with their excellent artillery. Colonel Ball would not have led his forces out in the open if he had known the strength of Marion's command. Colonel Ball attempted by scattering his forces to surround Marion and capture him, since the capture of General Marion was the one thing the British forces desired. This fighting of small detachments of troops in the swamps was Marion's strongest point. For, like Brer Rabbit, who was "born and bred in the briar patch," so Marion's men were born and bred in the swamps.

Late in September, 1780, Marion left Snow's Island and proceeded up Lynch's Creek for the purpose of driving out the British and the Tories under Colonel Harrison, who were threatening Williamsburg. While on his way, General Marion learned that Colonel Tyrnes was at Tarcote, in the forks of Black River, where he had collected large supplies of provisions and war material. Marion's forces were sorely in need of rifles, powder, and balls, and clothing, and Tyrnes was stirring up much trouble in the Black River vicinity. General Marion camped near where the town of Cades now stands while he was on his way to Tarcote. His camping there gave the name "Camp Branch" to that vicinity for a hundred years. From that point, General Marion proceeded on his way to Tarcote, crossing the lower ford on the North branch of Black River at Nelson's plantation, and came upon the camp of Tyrnes at midnight. Tyrnes and his Tories were enjoying themselves. Some of them were sleeping, others were eating and drinking, and others were playing cards, but none of them were looking for the "Swamp Fox." Marion fell upon them immediately, killing twenty-six, capturing Tyrnes and two of his officers, and many of his men, without resistance on their part. Most of the Tories escaped in the swamp and never reassembled. General Marion secured many valuable supplies and was enabled from them to outfit his entire brigade.

A little later than this, Tarleton, with a very superior force, attempted to capture Marion, while on the South branch of Black River. The story goes that Tarleton followed up Marion for many miles until the Britisher reached Ox Swamp. Looking over the way that Marion had gone, this miry waste, he exclamed to his Legion. "Come, my Boys! Let us go back. We will soon find the Game Cock, (meaning Sumter) but as for this 'Swamp Fox', the Devil himself could not catch him." It was from this expression that General Marion became known as the "Swamp Fox."

Another invasion of Williamsburg was attempted in 1781 when Lord Rawdon undertook to crush Marion in his rendezvous on Snow's Island. It was planned that Colonel Watson with a British Regiment and a large body of Loyalists should proceed from Fort Watson down the Santee and thence through Williamsburg, reach Snow's Island about the time that another British Regiment and a band of Tories under Colonel Doyle, which was directed to proceed by way of McCallum's Ferry and down Jeffry's Creek to the Pee Dee, where these forces under Colonel Watson and Colonel Doyle were to form a junction and take Snow's Island. Marion was advised by his scouts of these approaching British armies almost as soon as they had left Fort Watson. He hurried forward and met Colonel Watson at Wiboo Swamp about half way between Nelson's and Murray's Ferries.

The first point of contact between these forces at Wiboo was that of the Tory Cavalry under Colonel Richbourgh and Marion's Cavalry under Colonel Peter Horry. These advance guards fell back on their main bodies. Finally, a troop of Tory Cavalry under Harrison attempted to pass over the narrow causeway toward Marion's army. It was here that Gavin James, a private soldier, mounted on a strong gray horse and armed with a musket and bayonet, advanced in front of his comrades directly in the path of the enemy. He fired his rifle and felled the leader and drew a volley from the platoon approaching, not a shot of which took effect. A dragoon rushed upon James but was stricken down by the bayonet, another rushed forward to the assistance of his comrade and shared the same

THE WAR OF THE REVOLUTION 109

fate, but, in falling, laid hold of the muzzle of James' musket and was dragged in the retreat about fifteen yards.

Captains Macauley's and Conyers' troops of cavalry resisted the oncoming Tories and Captain Conyers here killed Harrison, the Tory leader. Marion's force was not sufficiently strong to resist Watson, so he withdrew, marching down the river. Marion contested Watson's advance again at Mount Hope in Williamsburg. He burned the bridges that crossed Mount Hope Swamp; and, while Watson's engineers were rebuilding them, his sharpshooters killed and wounded many. Watson had several pieces of artillery and finally succeeded by shelling the swamps in driving out Marion's men.

Watson led his command towards the Lower Bridge. General Marion sent Major James, commanding a detachment of fast moving cavalry, thirty of whom were McCottry's expert riflemen, by a nearer way to the Lower Bridge. He crossed toward the King's Tree, destroyed the bridge and placed his riflemen on the North side of the River before Watson's command arrived. Later, General Marion, having come by way of the King's Tree, reinforced Major James at the bridge. Marion arrived before Watson.

The river at this point at the bridge is about fifty yards wide. Some distance below, it was fordable. On the southwest, the bank of the river is a high bluff; on the northeast, the land is low and swampy. Watson approached the river from the southwest and opened up his field pieces upon the ford. Watson's artillery could not fire effectively upon the ford without placing their guns in a position exposed to the deadly fire of McCottry's riflemen. Every attempt made to bring the field pieces to bear upon the low ground occupied by Marion's men resulted fatally for the artillerists. Watson attempted to rush the ford. The officer leading this forlorn hope fell from Captain McCottry's rifle. Captain McCottry's first shot was a signal for his riflemen along the banks to fire; and, as fast as the British approached, they fell before the unerring aim of McCottry's men. Watson was terrified at the fierce resistance that he had received. He said that he had never before seen such shooting in all of his life. At night the firing ceased and Colonel Watson retired and took up his quarters at the house of John Witherspoon. The losses to the British in this battle have never been known to the Americans. They buried their dead in the river.

This defeat of Watson at the Lower Bridge possibly saved Marion's Brigade from destruction. Watson remained on the Witherspoon plantation a few days, where he was constantly harassed by Marion's forces. It was here that Sergeant McDonald climbed a tree on the Witherspoon Avenue and shot the British Lieutenant Toriano at a distance of three hundred yards, a marvelous feat of marksmanship with a rifle at that time. Realizing that Marion was collecting sufficient forces to cross the river and attack, Watson proceeded by forced marches toward Georgetown. He was constantly annoyed on his way by troops of Marion's Brigade; and as he crossed the Sampit Bridge, was given a parting volley by McCottry's riflemen.

In the meantime, Colonel Doyle had reached Snow's Island unresisted. When General Marion set out from Snow's Island to meet Colonel Watson, he left Colonel Hugh Ervin in command. Colonel Ervin realized that he had too small a force to resist Colonel Doyle's command, so he threw all of his stores and ammunition into Lynch's Creek and retreated. By that time, Marion was hurrying toward Snow's Island, having driven Watson out of Williamsburg. He arrived too late to meet Doyle; however, his brigade fired on Doyle's forces as they were crossing Witherspoon's Ferry on their way back to Camden. Soon after this time, Lee's Legion joined General Marion and the American cause found brighter hopes out of frequent victories.

Marion's Brigade brought light out of Williamsburg in the darkest hours of the Revolution. When Williamsburg invited General Marion to marshal its forces in the cause of Liberty, hope for independence in South Carolina had fled from all but the Scotch-Irish of Williamsburg. Out of action, which seemed suicidal, there came independence. Some time the American people will realize that Marion's campaigns in Williamsburg kept the fires of liberty burning when its flames were flickering low and then lovers of patriotism will visit these unmarked shrines in Williamsburg and will then do honor by placing marble and bronze on so many places where valiant dust reposes. One might place immortelles on almost any spot in Williamsburg and the muse of history would commend.

Half a century of pioneer conditions in which Williamsburg lived, almost shut off from communication with the other parts of the world and rejoicing in the fact, had made them self-reliant, self-supporting and strong. Hunting and stalking wary game had taught them the secrets of field, forest, and stream. Rounding up horses and cattle had made them fearless riders. Marion's horsemen and their horses knew the topography of all this country and how to overcome the difficult natural conditions. Shooting squirrels, on the Santee, made many of Marion's riflemen for the Revolution.

When Williamsburg formed James' battalion, the nucleus of Marion's Brigade, it was equipped entirely in the district. It had the finest rifles and the best horses and the strongest men in America; and Marion's troops, from that time until the war had been practically won, were supplied largely from the resources of Williamsburg and from the material obtained by capture from the enemy.

It is true that Marion's men were sometimes poorly supplied with clothing and with provisions and that often they dressed in the skins of animals they had slain and lived on sweet potatoes and fish, and fought with swords their women had filed out of handsaws and shot the bullets these same women had moulded from their pewter spoons. Cornwallis said after the War, on being taunted on account of his inability to destroy Marion in Williamsburg, "I could not capture web-footed men who could subsist on roots and berries." He was thinking of the ability of Marion's Men to cross the swamps in Williamsburg and of their potato diet.

All of the men of Williamsburg from fifteen to sixty fought under General Marion for more than two years. The women of the district showed remarkable adaptability in doing their men's work about the home and on the plantation. These Williamsburg Revolutionary women deserve much notice from history. Tales of their labors, their hardships, and their triumphs have never been told. Knowing how the average man of that time in Williamsburg dominated completely and how little exercise of discretion and authority he allowed his wife and the women of his family, it is remarkable, to say the least, how these Williamsburg women apparently all at once emerged out of their restricted spheres and managed plantations and controlled slaves with such excellent judgment. They kept the home fires burning, the cornfields growing, and the cattle breeding.

On of the best known heroines of Revolutionary Williamsburg was Margaret Gregg, wife of Captain William Gordon. For her and her soldier husband, the Margaret Gregg Gordon Chapter, Daughters of the American Revolution, is named. Two stories of her are told in Wallace's History of the Williamsburg Church as follows:

"Pending the predatory warfare of Hamilton, in Williamsburg, a party of marauding Tories went to the house of Captain William Gordon, and commenced plundering the house. But conscience makes men cowards. The alarm was given, whether false or not does not appear, that the Whigs were coming, when the whole party fled. One of them becoming fastened in some way on the fence, was unable to get over. Mrs. Gordon ran and caught the fellow, and pulling him down on her own side of the fence, detained him until help came, and he was secured.

"At another time, the free-booters came and carried off all Mr. Gordon's horses, while he was absent fighting the battles of his country. Mrs. Gordon, unable to prevent the robbery, followed the party at a distance, and observed where the horses were enclosed. That night she went alone, caught the best horse in the lot—a better than any one of her own, and mounting him rode away in safety with her reprisal."

CHAPTER XI.

WILLIAMSBURG SOLDIERS IN THE REVOLUTION.

So far as is known, all records of Marion's Brigade have been lost; indeed, it is not certain that General Marion kept any rolls of his soldiers. Tradition is full of tales of these men of valor, but it is difficult to obtain authentic information of many who must have been among them. Some years after the War, those soldiers who submitted accounts for services and supplies were paid. There are a great many of these "Pay Indents" in the office of the Historical Commission of South Carolina and from these records it has been established that nearly all of the following served under General Marion. There are a few names on the list that have other incontestable evidence to warrant their worthiness among these mighty men.

Colonels: John Baxter, Hugh Ervin, John Ervin, Archibald McDonald.

Majors: John James, William Buford, James Conyers, Morgan Sabb, James Postell.

Captains: John Armstrong, Philip Frierson, William Frierson, John Graham, James Green, William Gordon, John James, Hugh Knox, Andrew Lester, John Macauley, Robert McCottry, John McKenzie, John Mills, Henry Mouzon, Robert Paisley, William Spivey, John Nelson, Samuel Taylor, James Wilson, James Witherspoon, John Witherspoon, David Witherspoon, Gavin Witherspoon, Daniel Conyers, Andrew DuBose, Mark Huggins.

Lieutenants: James H. Allison, Daniel Britton, Daniel Cottingham, John Frierson, William Gamble, James Gordon, Roger Gordon, James Hamilton, John Hinds, Alexander James, Thomas Kerwin, Andrew Lester, James McDowell, Hugh Postell, John Reed, Joseph Scott, John McKenzie, James McDowell, John Wilson, William Wilson, James Davis, William Huggins.

SOLDIERS IN THE REVOLUTION 115

Sergeants: George Frierson, Gavin James, Thomas McGee, David Simms, William Nelson.

Soldiers: Alexander Adair, Benjamin Adair, James Adair, John Adair, James Allison, James Armstrong, John Armstrong, William Armstrong, John Arnett, Francis Austin, John Austin, Thomas Austin, John Anderson.

Israel Baxter, Samuel Bennett, John Blakeley, James Bradley, John Borland, John Boyd, John Bradford, Joshua Braveboy, John Brockinton, James Brown, John Brown, James Brunson, William Brunson, Joseph Burgess, William Burgess, John Burns, William Burrows.

David Campbell, Duncan Campbell, George Campbell, James Campbell, Thomas Campbell, William Campbell, John China, George Chandler, Isaac Chandler, Jesse Chandler, Jacob Coleman, Benjamin Coker, Nathan Coker, West Cook, William Cook, Samuel Cordes, Dill Cottingham, John Cunningham Thomas Clark, John Cantey, Charles Cantley, Thomas Coker, John Cousar.

John Daniel, John Davis, James Davis, Robert Davis, John Dial, John Dickey, Peter Dubose, Ben Duke, William Duke, John Dye, Isaiah Dennis.

Daniel Eaddy, Henry Eaddy, James Ervin.

Hugh Ferguson, John Ferguson, Thomas Ferguson, James Fleming, John Fleming, William Fleming, Absalom Frierson, George Frierson, Joshua Frierson, Robert Frierson, William Frierson, William Frierson, Jr., John Ford, William Fullwood, Moses Ferguson, James Frierson, James Fleming, Jr., Robert Fraser, William Fraser.

Hugh Gamble, James Gamble, John Gamble, Robert Gamble, Samuel Gamble, Stephen Gamble, Samuel Garner, Jesse George, Richard George, William George, James Gordon, James Gibson, Robert Gibson, Roger Gibson, William Godwin, Moses Gordon, John Gordon, James Green, James Graham, William Graham, Samuel Garner, Benjamin Green, William Green, Andrew Gillespie.

James Hamilton, John Hamilton, William Hamilton, Richard Hanna, Sr., Robert Hanna, Jr., William Haselden, Richard Haselden, Robert Heathley, John Huggins, James Hodge, Benjamin Hodge, William Hodge, Benjamin Howard, Edward Howard, John Hutson, William Hutson, John Howard.

Gavin James, William D. James, Robert Jamison, Nathaniel James, David James, James James, Robert James.

Abraham Keels, Isaac Keels, John Keels, James Kelly, John Kelly, Samuel Kelly, Alexander Kennedy, James Kennedy, Joseph Kennedy, Stephen Kennedy, Thomas Kennedy, Robert Knox, Archibald Knox.

Andrew Lee, John Lee, Henry Lenud, Peter Lequex, Samuel Lequex, Daniel Lesesne, Francis Lesesne, John Lesesne, James Lester, Robert Lowry, William Lowry.

David Matthews, John Marshall, Isaac Matthews, Joseph Matthews, Samuel Matthews, William Matthews, Samuel Mayes, David McCants, John McCants, Thomas McCants, William McCants, John McCown, Samuel McCown, Moses McCown, John McCreary, James McCreight, Alexander McCown, John McConnell, James McConnell, Hugh McConnell, Thomas McConnell, Robert McCormick, Hugh McBride, James McBride, Barkley McClary, John McClary, Matthew McClary, Jr., Thomas McClary, Samuel McClary, William Michau, James Macauley, James McCutchen, James McCullough, John McCullough, Hugh McCullough, Nathaniel McCullough, William McCullough, Francis McDonald, James McDonald, John McDonald, William McDowell, James McDowell, William McElveen, Edward McFaddin, John McFaddin, Thomas McFaddin, William McFaddin, Adam McKee, Robert McKee, Thomas McKee, John McKnight, Moses McKnight, Robert McKnight, James McGee, Thomas McGee, William McGee, John McGill, Samuel McGill, Thomas McGinness, Charles McGinney, John McCrea, Thomas McCrea, Thomas McCrea, Jr., James McCutchen, William McPherson, Andrew

Miller, Jesse Mills, Thomas Mills, Thomas Mitchum, William Moffat, Hugh Montgomery, James Montgomery, Robert Montgomery, Samuel Montgomery, Norman Montgomery, Benjamin Morris, Thomas Morris, William Morris, Edward Murphy, John Murphy, James Murphy, William Murrell, John Mills, John Morris, George Morris, Andrew McMuldrow, John McMuldrow, James McMuldrow, William McMuldrow, Hugh McMuldrow, David McMuldrow.

Isaac Nelson, Samuel Nelson, Thomas Nelson, William Nelson, John Nesmith, Lemuel Nesmith, Robert Nesmith, Samuel Nesmith, Thomas Nesmith, Joseph Nettles, Robert Nettles.

William Oliver, William Orr.

John Perdreau, John Paisley, James Parnell, James Parsons, John Postell, Joshua Patrick, James Patrick, Patrick Pendergrass.

James Richbourg, John Robinson, William Robinson, Andrew Rodgers, John Rodgers, Jr., Nathanial Rodgers, William T. Rodgers, Benjamin Reeves.

Morgan Sabb, Peter Salters, Alexander Scott, James Scott, John Scott, Samuel Scott, Thomas Scott, William Scott, Daniel Shaw, William Sellers, David Simms, Thomas Simms, Richard Singleton, Peter Sinkler, Samuel Smiley, William Smiley, James Smith, John Smith, William Smith, James Snow, William Snow, John Staggers, Alexander Stewart, Hugh Stewart, James Steele, William Steele, Robert Strong, Hugh Sutton, Robert Swan, William Swinton, Shadrack Simons, Edward Sexton, James Steele, William Shaw, Jacob Sutton.

Edward Thomas, William Thompson, Archibald Thomson, James Thomson, John Tomlinson, James Thomas, Nathaniel Tomlinson, William Thomas.

Michael Wallace, James Wallace, John Wallace, William Wallace, John Watson, James Watson, Robert Watson, John Wheeler, John White, Jesse Williamson,

Sterling Williamson, William Williamson, Hugh Wilson, James Wilson, Edward Wingate, Gavin Witherspoon, John Witherspoon, John Workman, Robert Workman, John Wilson, John Woodberry, David Watson.

Among those who furnished supplies for Marion's brigade were the following: John Armstrong, John Burns, David Campbell, John Cantey, Charles Cantey, Thomas Ferguson, Moses Gordon, Thomas Kerwin, James Lester, James Macauley, John Macauley, Robert McKnight, James McCullough, Samuel Montgomery, Nathaniel Montgomery, Mrs. Susannah Parsons, William Thompson, Michael Wallace, John Watson, Mrs. Catherine Watson, John Wilson, Mrs. Mary Wilson, Captain Hugh Knox, Robert McKee, John Mills, John Mills, Jr., William McFaddin, William Nelson, Alexander Kennedy, Robert Gibson, James Gibson, John White, Benjamin Screven, Benjamin Singleton, John Woodberry, Daniel Lesesne, Edward Thomas, William James, Mrs. Sarah James, Thomas Kennedy, Thomas Simms, John Lee, Archibald McDonald, Mrs. Rachel McDonald, Daniel Kelly, Abraham Keels, John Kennedy, Charles McGinney, John Gordon, John Arnett, Daniel Eaddy, William Graham, Robert Lowry, Peter Lequeux, William Michau, Isaac Nelson, James Richbourg, Peter Sinkler, Samuel Cordes, James Brunson, Henry Lenud, John Staggers, Joseph McKee, John McGill, Thomas McCants, William Burgess, John Perdreau, James Armstrong, John Adair, William Burrows, John Dye, Samuel Bennett, Nathaniel McCullough, James McCullough, John Scott, William Scott, Mrs. Jane Arnett, Mrs. Martha Boyd, John Boyd, Absalom Frierson, Hugh Gamble, Theodore and Peter Gourdin Estates, Mrs. Mary Lesesne, Thomas McFaddin, Mrs. Mary Salters, Morgan Sabb, Ben Duke, Mrs. Elizabeth Dobbin, Henry Lenud, Hugh McCullough, James Belin, John Dickey, Mrs. Elizabeth Bradley, George Chandler, James McCullough for estate of Paul Fulton,

William Snow, John Gamble, Allard Belin, James Belin, Mrs. Margaret Gordon.

Colonel John Baxter was a son of the Reverend John Baxter, minister of the Black Mingo Presbyterian Church in 1733. Colonel Baxter was born and reared in Williamsburg, where his father was a successful planter as well as a vigorous preacher. Colonel Baxter was severely wounded at Quinday, from which wound he never fully recovered.

Colonel John Ervin commanded the Britton's Neck Regiment and served in Marion's Brigade. He was born March 25, 1754, and died June 10, 1820, the son of John and Elizabeth Ervin. He married Jane Witherspoon, daughter of Gavin and Jane James Witherspoon, January 10, 1775. Their children reaching maturity were Samuel, who moved to Georgia and married Harriette Keith; Elizabeth, who married Mr. Ford of Mississippi; and James Robert, who married Elizabeth Powe. Jane, wife of John Ervin, died September 20, 1790, and he, on October 6, 1799, married his cousin, Margaret Ervin. Two of their children reached maturity, Hugh and John. Colonel Ervin was born in the Cedar Swamp section of Williamsburg County but moved just before the War of the Revolution to the Aimwell community of the great Pee Dee River. He was one of the founders of the Aimwell Presbyterian Church and one of its first Session of Elders. It is probable that he was the youngest man who attained to the rank of colonel during the War of the Revolution.

Colonel Hugh Ervin was second in command of Marion's Brigade. He was as a general rule left in command at Marion's headquarters when the general was in the field. He was a son of Hugh Ervin, Sr., and was born in the Cedar Swamp community of Williamsburg. He moved to the Aimwell community on Pee Dee just before the War of the Revolution and was one of the founders and first Elders of the Aimwell Presbyterian Church.

Colonel Archibald McDonald was born in Orangeburg and later moved to Williamsburg and served in the Revolution from this district.

Major William Buford lived on the Santee River and was a valuable officer in Marion's Brigade.

Major James Conyers was one of the most dashing officers South Carolina furnished in the Revolution. He was born on his father's plantation in the Brewington community where a lake is still known as Conyers' Lake. He first enlisted in Captain Fullwood's company in 1775 along with his younger brother, Daniel. James Conyers was a major in Wade Hampton's Regiment of State Cavalry in 1782 and served under General Sumter in the northwestern section of South Carolina, and under General Green in his campaigns in northern South Carolina. Major Conyers was the officer chosen by General Green to bear his confidential communications to General Marion, evidencing unmistakably the high esteem in which he was held by the Commander-in-chief of the Revolutionary Armies of South Carolina.

Judge James, in his Life of Marion, relates how Major Conyers, when attacked by cavalry force of the British by night, rather than fall back on the main body in camp where he knew it must be asleep and liable to disastrous surprise, took the dangerous risk of leading the enemy off on another road, continuing a running fight, and by so doing, saved the camp. Major Conyers was killed after the British in South Carolina had been driven into the City of Charleston and the War of the Revolution had been practically won. One day late in the year 1782 his body servant came home leading his master's horse and telling that Major Conyers had been killed by a foraging party of the British at the Round O near Charleston.

Captain John Nelson was born September 17, 1753, and died December 27, 1803. In the War of the Revolution, he first enlisted as a private in Fullwood's Company, September 30, 1775, and afterwards became a captain in Marion's Brigade. He married a Miss Kingswood who was born 1768 and died 1864. Captain Nelson lived on his plantation in the Brewington community. Close by was the ford across Black River Swamp frequently used by General Francis Marion in his military forays. A few miles from this Nelson plantation Marion fell on the Tories at Tarcote and scattered them with great loss. Captain John Nelson's house was burned by Wemyss, the British Commander, but rebuilt on the same spot.

Captain Nelson was an interesting character and his home was the center of the social life of the Brewington community. As long as he lived, Captain Nelson kept at his home a cannon that had been used in the War of the Revolution; and, whenever he desired that his friends and Revolutionary comrades gather at his home for a few hours of feasting and fellowship, he would fire this old cannon and everybody in the community would hasten to his home. They knew very well that Captain Nelson had already roasted many pigs, and a barrel of good old brandy had been skidded out in the grove and made ready for tapping. His bread was baked in a large brick Dutch oven built out under the oaks. Sometimes a hill of luscious sweet potatoes was baked all at once in this oven. The corn meal used on his plantation was all ground in a hand mill and his slaves knew how to bake corn bread in a manner not known in the present day. The fact is the baking of corn bread is as much a lost art in Williamsburg as the tempering of Damascus' swords is in the world at large.

Captain Nelson loved his friends and hated his enemies. The story is told that after the War a man who had been a troublesome Tory during the conflict and who afterwards wanted the Captain's friendship and to "neighbor" with him rode up the long avenue one day and, prudently remaining on his horse outside the gate, hailed. When Captain Nelson appeared on the porch, the former Tory began to announce his errand, which was never finished, for the old Captain stepped back within the door where his loaded rifle always hung and the kind hearted housewife or somebody who understood, cried out, "Ride, Tory, ride," and when Captain Nelson with his rifle appeared on the porch, the only thing visible in the land was a cloud of dust.

Captain William Gordon was a native of Pennsylvania. He settled in the Cedar Swamp section in 1770. Some time later, he married Margaret, widow of Samuel Scott, and daughter of John Gregg. In 1774, William Gordon moved into the Aimwell community. He died in 1783, before any claims for the services of Marion's men were paid. When his widow submitted her claim for his services, the separate items amounted to a considerable sum. Endorsed on this claim for payment and signed by Robert Baxter, Justice of the Quorum, is the following: "Captain Gordon is dead; there is therefore no person to prove his account; however, I can assure the Auditor that Mr. Gordon was as constantly and as regularly in the service of his country as any Militia officer in the Pee Dee Regiment; and, from the character of the officers who have given his service, I really think his account must be just." The claim was paid in full. Captain Gordon was elected a member of the General Assembly of South Carolina for the district "East of the Waterees" in 1782.

Captains John McKenzie, William McKenzie, and John Mills were from the northwestern section of Williamsburg and served under General Sumter. Captain Samuel Taylor lived in the Pudding Swamp community and was an aide-de-camp to General Sumter and one of his most dashing officers.

Lieutenant Roger Gordon was a grandson of Colonel Roger Gordon, an original settler in Williamsburg in 1732. In 1781, General Marion sent him out to patrol on Lynch's Creek. He and his company were surrounded by a much

LIEUT. JOSEPH SCOTT, MARION'S BRIGADE

larger body of Tories; and, after having capitulated, he and all his men were murdered. Lieutenant Gordon left a widow and one son, who was an infant. They lived afterwards in Sumter District.

Lieutenant Joseph Scott was born August 18, 1747, son of John Scott, an original settler in Williamsburg. He married Jannet McCrea, born August 5, 1747, daughter of Alexander McCrea, original settler in Williamsburg. They had four daughters, Margaret, Jannet, Elizabeth, and Mary, and one son, John. Lieutenant Joseph Scott was one of the most daring officers in Marion's Brigade. He served under Marion but a short time, from the formation of the Brigade in June until wounded by a rifle ball which shattered his thigh in the Battle of Black Mingo, which prevented him from further active duty with troops. His record was such that he has always been a favorite Revolutionary hero in Williamsburg, and fiction writers have frequently found material in his exploits. The bullet which shattered his thigh still remains in the possession of one of his descendants in Kingstree.

Major John James was born in Ireland, April 12, 1732, son of Elizabeth Witherspoon and William James, who brought him to Williamsburg when he was less than a year old. Major James' grandfather was John James, Captain of Dragoons, under William of Orange against James II. Major James was a powerful man from every point of view, broadshouldered, clearminded, and commanding in appearance and character. He was captain of militia under George III in 1775 and immediately resigned when the Revolutionary War began and served with distinction during that seven year conflict. He gained special distinction in commanding a company at the battle of Tulifinny's Bridge before the fall of Charleston.

Major James, before the fall of Charleston, was sent by Governor Rutledge to Williamsburg to organize the district into a fighting force for service in the Revolution.

While doing this work, Charleston was taken by the British and thus Major James escaped capture. A number of the men of Williamsburg were soldiers in the American forces at the fall of Charleston, May 12, 1780. These soldiers were paroled and allowed to come home on condition that they would refrain from further active participation in the war against the King's forces. Major James had already begun his work organizing and training soldiers in Williamsburg for service in the Revolution when these paroled soldiers reached home. Their coming on parole gave an element of uncertainty in the district. The men who Major James had already incited to action and enlisted in the service of the colonies did not know just what to do. Major James was sent to Georgetown to interview Captain Ardesoif, British Commander at that time. The military record of Major James is shown along with the story of the participation of Marion's Brigade in many battles of the Revolution. History is full of records of his daring deeds. Frequent references to him are found in Weems' Life of Marion, Simms' Life of Marion, McCrady's History of South Carolina, and Ramsay's Revolution.

Major James was Ruling Elder in the Indiantown Church, represented his people in the Provincial Assembly, and was a member of the Legislature after the formation of the State. His statesmanship is well shown in his services in the State Legislature during the trying time when the colony was being transformed into the State. January 18, 1753, Major James married Jean, daughter of William Dobein, of Indiantown, and to them were born four children; John, who was a Captain in the Revolution; William Dobein, a seventeen year old soldier in the Revolution, later a Chancellor in Equity and the author of the Life of Marion; and two daughters, Elizabeth and Jannet.

Captain John Witherspoon, the son of Gavin and his cousin, Jane James, was born in Williamsburg in 1742 and died in 1802. He married Mary Conn. He was an Elder in the Hopewell Church and lived in the Pee Dee section. He was a captain in the Revolutionary War. Simms in his life of Marion says of him, "Like his brother, Gavin, he is distinguished for great coolness, strength, and courage, and delighted in rash adventure, the rashness giving a sort of relish to the danger."

Gavin Witherspoon, son of Gavin, was born in Williamsburg in 1748 and died in 1834. Marion called him an extraordinary soldier. He was a great athlete all of his life. He died at eighty-five years old; and, on the day of his death, he rode thirty miles on horseback and died in his chair. The children of Gavin Witherspoon all gave distinguished service in the Revolutionary War: John and Gavin as captains, and Robert and William as private soldiers, while two of his daughters married the Colonels Ervin, who ranked next to Marion in his Brigade.

Captain James Witherspoon, son of Robert and Elizabeth Heathly, was born March 20, 1759, and died September 9, 1791. On July 15, 1781, he was commissioned first Lieutenant of Captain John McBride's company, Colonel Archibald McDonald's Regiment. On April 16, 1782, he was promoted to be Captain of the Kingstree Company. In transmitting his commission, as Captain, General Marion in a letter thus referred to him, "A man whose conduct and spirit I have been an eye-witness of, whom I have always had the highest opinion and the highest regard for." Captain Witherspoon was one of the most popular officers in Williamsburg. He was engaged in most of the battles of the Revolution fought in South Carolina. He is buried in the old Indiantown Churchyard. No stone marks the spot. He married Miss Nancy White January 8, 1782, and to them were born four children, Robert Lynn, James Harvey, George White, and Martha Ann.

John Witherspoon, son of John and his first cousin, Mary Witherspoon, was born in 1755 and died in 1827. He was an active soldier in Colonel Taylor's Regimnet during the Revolution. He married Rebecca Ervin, widow, whose maiden name was McBride. He lived near Midway Church and served for a time as Judge of Probate in Williamsburg District.

Captain David Witherspoon lived near Salem Church. He was an active officer under Marion. He married twice: first, Elizabeth Bradley; and second, Mary Story.

Gavin Witherspoon was a Corporal in Captain Daniel Conyers' company of Marion's Brigade.

Captain Daniel Conyers was a daring officer under Marion. Many tales of his exploits are told. One story in which the young woman who afterwards became his wife figures. The British were encamped on the Witherspoon plantation about seven miles South of the King's Tree. They held possession of the place for several days. It seems that the British protected the Witherspoon women and showed them commendable courtesies. Mary Witherspoon, daughter of the house, was affianced to Captain Conyers. He was then serving under Marion and Marion's forces were preparing to drive the British from the Witherspoon plantation. Before Marion had made his final successful attack on the British at the Witherspoon house, Captain Conyers had ridden up the Witherspoon Avenue and challenged any British officer to mortal combat. On the afternoon of the day on which Captain Conyers had issued this challenge, a British officer was taunting Miss Mary with the hopelessness of the American cause and telling her how soon Captain Conyers would be his prisoner. Miss Mary pulled off her slipper, struck the British officer in the face, saying at the same time,

"He is ready to meet you; go out and fight him, you coward."

From these old pay vouchers on file in the office of the South Carolina Historical Commission, Columbia, S. C., the following statements are taken: "Thomas Ferguson furnished Marion with seventy-five thousand feet of lumber which Marion used in the Brewington vicinity; Samuel Montgomery made boots and shoes for Marion's men; Alexander Kennedy, a saddler; James Hamilton, a paymaster; William Murrell, commissary; Richard George frequently ferried Marion's men across the Pee Dee; Daniel Eaddy was a bootmaker; John Perdreau was Marion's ferryman at Lenud's; Ben Duke was saddler for Colonel Peter Horry; John Dickey was one of Marion's purchasing commissaries; James Armstrong was a wagon master; Governor Rutledge in 1781 impressed five hundred thirty-four pounds of indigo from Allard Belin; John Hamilton was one of the keenest observers in Marion's remarkable secret service."

The four Nesmith brothers, John, Robert, Samuel, and Lemuel, were General Marion's bodyguard. These Nesmiths were herdsmen in their boyhood days and knew the country from following the cattle. They were exceptional physical men, each one of them more than six feet, straight, active, and alert as Indians, and every one an expert rifleman. They all loved their leader with surpassing loyalty and devotion. Tradition says that General Marion and a Continental officer, who had a message from General Green to General Marion, were discussing one day at Tarcote conditions then existing when a body of Tories under Major Gillis appeared in the distance. General Marion and the Continental officer stood their ground but the four Nesmith brothers disappeared immediately behind a little milk house. Marion understood, but the Continental officer doubted. The Tories came on. When their leader had arrived at a point about three hundred yards from General Marion, four rifles from behind the milk house shot as one and the Tory leader fell. His followers fled. General Marion and the Continental officer walked up to the body of the dead Tory. General Marion placed his hand over the heart of the dead man and asked the Continental officer to locate the wound. The four Nesmith brothers had each placed a bullet in the space covered by Marion's hand. The Continental officer then told General Marion that he would go back to General Green and tell him that the swamps of South Carolina were safe for liberty.

The four captains, Henry Mouzon, Robert McCottry, John Macauley and John James, Jr., who organized the companies forming the Williamsburg battalion about which Marion's Brigade grew, are outstanding officers in the War of the Revolution.

Captain Mouzon was of French Huguenot descent, had been schooled in France, and spoke French as fluently as English. He was one of the peculiarly active influences in the amalgamation of the Huguenot and the Scotch-Irish elements in Williamsburg. It was largely due to him that these two peoples lived so harmoniously in the first days of contact and finally united in the Americans of the present time. He was a civil engineer of the first rank. He made the first map of North and South Carolina drawn anything like to scale, which map became the basis of all maps of these States made since 1775. It was in that year that his map was first published in London and afterwards in Paris. He made the first survey for the Santee Canal. Within a month after Marion's Brigade began its work, Captain Mouzon was so severely wounded in the battle of Black Mingo that he could not further participate on the field. He was buried in the Mouzon graveyard near where he lived on Pudding Swamp.

Captain Robert McCottry developed, in all probability, the most effective fighting unit of his age. Tales of

McCottry's riflemen told by Tarleton and Wemyss and Ardesoif in London caused all the world to wonder; and it may be that the marksmanship displayed in battle by these men of Cedar Swamp and Black Mingo has had much to do with the careful training of modern riflemen. Captain McCottry was the leading man of his organization, from every point of view. When he fired, a victim fell. Many stories are told of his unerring aim. One tale of him goes: He saw across Black River a Tory leader, raised his rifle, drew a bead on the Tory, and the men looked to see the Tory fall. But Captain McCottry lowered his rifle without firing. The unconscious Tory did not know. Three times Captain McCottry raised his rifle, and every time he refused to fire. His men wondered. "That Tory is one of my neighbors, Captain John Brockinton," he explained, "and I cannot kill him." Captain McCottry is buried in George's Field and no stone marks his grave. McCottry's Lake, a favorite pleasure ground of Williamsburg, is named for him.

Captain John Macauley was the conservative force in the Williamsburg battalion. He was of the scholar type. It must not be understood from this statement that he was wanting in daring, dash, and executive ability, for no man could have commanded his company a single day unless he had these qualities. But, rather, that his understanding was a positive factor. When Captain Macauley expressed an opinion, his soldiers ceased to think and translated it into action. Captain Macauley was elected to the General Assembly for many years after the Revolution, and was of great usefulness and strength in that body while it was building the State on the broken

---

*Captain McCottry was called "Robert" by his family and his namesakes for generations have been Roberts. Family records refer to him as Robert. He is known, however, as "William" in the South Carolina General Assembly Journal, and so denominated by some historians who have referred to Williamsburg in the Revolution. His name was probably William Robert McCottry.

colonial foundation. He was for some time Major of the upper Williamsburg battalion of Militia. He was buried with his fathers in the Frierson graveyard. No stone shows the spot.

Captain John James, son of Major John James, was born in 1754. Although young and somewhat overshadowed by his illustrious father, Captain James was worthy of his place in the "Big Four" captains of Revolutionary Williamsburg. He was the chief actor in many thrilling exploits during the War wherein he added reputation for valor to his name and to the lines of his blood. He was a soldier in the War before the fall of Charleston. After he had joined Marion's Brigade, he was, therefore, outlawed by the British. Once they captured him and he escaped the halter merely because the British soldiers who could identify him would not testify against him. He was long a useful, substantial citizen and a ruling elder in the Indiantown Church. He was buried in his churchyard, and his family placed a tombstone to mark his grave.

Nearly every man in the foregoing lists of officers and men of Marion's Brigade now has descendants living in Williamsburg County. Careful study indicates that less than one per centum of the people now living in Williamsburg have none of the blood of these heroes of the American Revolution in the veins.

CHAPTER XII.

GOVERNMENT BY THE PEOPLE.

During the Revolution, the State of South Carolina considered few matters than those directly related to prosecuting the War to its successful conclusion. The General Assembly did, however, virtually abolish the overlordship of the Church of England. It enabled men who were not communicants of this Church for the first time to hold official positions. This permitted the Scotch-Irish to enter politics.

In 1782, Williamsburg, or Prince Frederick's Parish, sent to the House of Representatives the following: Colonel John Baxter, Major John James, Major John Macauley, Captain Robert McCottry, and Dr. Thomas Potts. All of these men were serving as officers in the Revolutionary War at that time. Dr. Potts was a surgeon in Marion's Brigade. James Postell was the sixth member chosen from Williamsburg, but he was elected at the same time from St. Philip's and St. Michael's Parishes in Charleston and represented these parishes.

The General Assembly of 1783 began real constructive work for the permanent welfare of the State of South Carolina. Williamsburg was fortunate in having in this Legislature such an able delegation. This General Assembly found the State in a most precarious condition. The people of the state had determined to form a republic and had little precedent for guiding them along the way they had chosen.

The Whig or Patriot element in the state, while victorious and dominating, had the defeated Tory faction always present and portending evil to the new state. This Tory element included most of the men who had theretofore governed the colony and were therefore conversant with conditions and experienced in controlling. A majority of the men who lived in Beaufort, Charleston, and Georgetown had opposed the Revolution and had remained loyal to the Mother Country during that great struggle. The "back country" in South Carolina, of which Williamsburg formed a part, was composed almost entirely of men who had favored the Revolution and fought the war for independence to its successful conclusion. Beaufort, Charleston, and Georgetown, before the Revolution, had paid but little attention to this "back country" and this "back country" had no special bond of union with these places. When a certain element of these three cities elected to remain loyal to England and the men of the "back country" determined to struggle for independence, this breach was widened.

The Tories in South Carolina, while in the minority and defeated in war in 1783, for the most part were even then unwilling to accept the result of the War and to enter enthusiastically into the formation of the independent State of South Carolina. This Legislature of 1783 had this Tory opposition to face. The Patriots were in the majority in the Legislature, however, and passed laws confiscating the property and banishing many of the leading Tories from South Carolina. Of the three Tories of Williamsburg, Major Sabb died during the War; Major Hamilton left the colony when the British finally evacuated Charleston and did not return; and Captain John Brockinton remained on his plantation on Black Mingo. This Legislature ordered that his property be confiscated and that he be banished. Immediately in 1783 upon the passage of this act naming him for banishment, he petitioned the General Assembly to waive the penalties provided in the act so far as he was concerned and his petition was referred to the delegates from this parish and from Saint David's. Every member of this committee knew Captain Brockinton personally before the War of the Revolution and liked him.

This committee, although composed entirely of men who had served under Marion, among whom were Major John James and James Bradley, took a large view of the whole situation, and their decision to remove the disabilities imposed upon Captain Brockinton had much weight in determining the future liberal policy of the State of South Carolina toward the Tories. Perhaps that one act dissipated more of the hatred then existing between the Whigs and Tories in South Carolina than any other, and opened the way for all men to unite for the upbuilding of the commonwealth. A few of the Tories were banished and the estates of some of them were confiscated; however, the State very soon began to welcome these men, once so hated, as valuable citizens of the new nation, which they so soon proved themselves.

While a majority of the people realized that the Whigs and Tories were simply, in the beginning, two great political parties in England and America, and that a colonial citizen, in all good conscience, might have espoused the cause of the "Mother Country," some regarded the Tory taint as ineradicable. In 1787, when a bill to restore the civil rights of a certain Tory was before the General Assembly, the Williamsburg delegation voted as follows: Aye, Robert Paisley, John Dickey, and Benjamin Porter; Nay, John Thompson Green.

From the close of the Revolution in 1783 until South Carolina became a member of the Federal Union in 1788, Williamsburg was concerned primarily in working out its own economic salvation. No other section in South Carolina suffered so severely during the Revolution as did Williamsburg. When the War began, Williamsburg had grown rich producing indigo and tobacco and raising cattle and sheep. This indigo that Williamsburg produced was exported to England; and, when the War of the Revolution began in South Carolina, the sale of indigo ceased. The one thing upon which Williamsburg had for so long depended for its economic prosperity failed all at once. Its immense stock of indigo on hand rotted. Its indigo tanks decayed and its indigo fields grew into wild wood. During the Revolution, the large herds of cattle that fed and flourished along the swamps and creeks and rivers emptying into Black River had either been exhausted in supplying Marion's men with beef or wantonly destroyed during the several British campaigns in this district.

After the Revolution, Williamsburg had to come again almost from pioneer conditions. Of course, pessimists preached that the end had come, but this district then evidenced its most striking recuperative powers, which have been evident ever since in the many calamitous conditions that have befallen the section. For several years, the men of Williamsburg paid especial attention to cattle raising, and, within a few seasons, many were abundantly rewarded. It is said that Captain John Nelson, whose home was burned, whose plantation was destroyed, and whose cattle were all lost in the Wemyss destruction of 1780, by 1790 was marking more than a thousand calves every season, while in other sections of the district, Major John James, Major John Nesmith, William Wilson, Benjamin Screven, Alexander McCrea, and John Snow owned herds as large as Captain Nelson. Ready markets for these cattle were found in Charleston and Georgetown. They were driven by cow boys across Murray's Ferry to Charleston and Brown's Ferry to Georgetown.

Much tobacco was grown in Williamsburg immediately after the War and was a source of great revenue. Some cotton for market was grown on the Santee. Rice for plantation use was grown all over the section, but only along Big Dam Swamp was it produced in marketable quantities.

The State Convention for the purpose of considering and ratifying or rejecting the Constitution framed for the United States by a Convention of Delegates assembled in Philadelphia in May, 1787, met in Charleston on May 12, 1788. One hundred delegates from the various districts in South Carolina were present. The members of this Convention from Williamsburg, or Prince Frederick's Parish, as it was then called, were William Wilson, Patrick Dollard, Alexander Tweed, William Frierson, William Reed, James Pettigrew, and John Burgess, Jr. A temporary organization was effected and the Convention adjourned until the following day. When it reassembled, there were two hundred twenty-four delegates present. General Thomas Sumter moved the postponement of further consideration of the proposed Constitution, which motion was lost. Ayes, 89, and nays, 135. The delegates from Prince Frederick's Parish voted as follows: Patrick Dollard, William Reed, James Pettigrew, and John Burgess, Jr., aye; William Wilson, Alexander Tweed and William Frierson, nay.

This Convention considered in detail every article of the proposed Constitution. William Wilson of Williamsburg was appointed a member of the committee of seven from this South Carolina Convention to suggest to Congress amendments to this Constitution. One of the points most feared was its failure to limit the eligibility of the President of the United States to re-election after the expiration of one term of four years. This section was hotly contested. It was urged that the failure to limit the President to one term of four years was dangerous to the liberties of the people and calculated to perpetuate in one person during life the high authority and influence that inheres in the chief magistracy; and that in a short time unlimited terms of office for the President would terminate in a hereditary monarchy. The Convention voted on a resolution to limit the tenure of the President to one term of four years. The final vote stood: ayes, 68, and nays, 139. The delegates from Prince Frederick's Parish voted as follows: William Wilson, William Frierson, and

James Pettigrew, nay; Patrick Dollard, William Reed, and John Burgess, Jr., aye. The following resolution was passed: "This Convention doth declare that no section or paragraph of the said Constitution warrants a construction that the states do not retain all powers not expressly relinquished by them and vested in the General Government of the Union."

South Carolina ratified the proposed United States Constitution on May 23, 1788, the vote of the Convention being ayes, 149, and nays, 73. The delegates from Williamsburg voted as follows: For ratification, William Wilson, Alexander Tweed, William Frierson, James Pettigrew; against ratification, Patrick Dollard, William Reed, John Burgess, Jr. Thus it will be seen that four of the seven delegates from Williamsburg in the South Carolina Constitutional Convention of 1788 voted for the ratification of the United States Constitution as adopted by the Thirteen States and three voted against it. The four delegates who voted for ratification were sons of original settlers who came from Ireland to Williamsburg in 1736 and were Scotch-Irish; the three delegates who voted against ratification had themselves come directly from Ireland to Williamsburg about 1770 and were of Irish ancestry. William Wilson was one of the leaders of the Convention for ratification; while Patrick Dollard was especially earnest and eloquent in opposing South Carolina's entering the Union.

In 1788, South Carolina had been a free and independent republic for twelve years. A very substantial minority of its people most vigorously opposed the surrender of one jot or tittle of its sovereignty.

This tract is said to have been granted to Jane

Lines Shaded Blue
This tract was granted to David Johnston in 1736 but was resurveyed and returned in Feby 1734

Lines Shaded Red
This tract was surveyed for the town of Williamsburgh Returned in August 1737

Black River

This part of the town is claimed by Robert Grierson Aiken

Lines Shaded green
tract was Surveyed for Wm James
& returned in Feby 1734

Lines Shaded dark green
this tract was granted to Jas Witherspoon
in 1786.

CHAPTER XIII.

THE TOWN OF WILLIAMSBURG, 1788.

In 1730, when King George contemplated the establishment of a township on Black River, which afterwards was named Williamsburg, and the others in the colony, he had in mind the townships that he had formed in New England and their development. He believed that he could establish these townships on the rivers in South Carolina and that they would work out their own salvation in the same manner and after the same plan as those in New England. The settlers in New England built their pioneer homes close together in little towns. Each householder held a half-acre lot in the town on which he lived and a tract of land in the vicinity of the town whereon he raised his crops. The waste land in these New England communities formed a commons on which everybody grazed cattle and from which everyone secured the fire wood and lumber required for general purposes.

So, when Williamsburg township on the bank of Black River in South Carolina was laid out and established, the King decreed that each settler should have a one-half acre lot in the proposed town and a grant of land within the township, believing that the settlers who came would dwell in the town and would go out every morning to their plantations in the township. But those settlers who came to Williamsburg between 1730 and 1745 built their homes on their respective plantations in the township and paid practically no attention to their half-acre lots granted them within the town. The fact is that until 1788, within the township of Williamsburg as surveyed, there was practically nothing except a cleared space whereon the Court House now stands, which was used as a parade and muster ground for the Colonial Militia, and a race track in the northeast portion of the town whereon horses and men frequently were tried in athletic games for the amusement and entertainment of the people of the township. The plot of land in the town granted to the Church of England had been cleared of pine trees.

There were in the town in 1788 five small buildings, not one of them more than 20 x 20 feet. Two of them were located about where the Wee Nee Bank now stands. In one of these, William Bracey lived; in the other he kept a mercantile establishment. His stock of merchandise usually consisted of one barrel of whiskey, one bag of buckshot, one bag of squirrel shot, one bag of turkey shot, one keg of powder, a few tallow candles, and a few sealing wax wafers. Occasionally, when an especially prosperous season indicated a good trade, he would add five pounds of linen writing paper to his stock of goods. Powder and shot and whiskey were the only salable articles all the year round. On the other side of Broad Street were three little houses. Patrick Cormick lived in one of these. It was located about where the Hammett residence now stands. He had a little store near his home, which store was similar to that of William Bracey across the street. John Brady lived in a little house about where the Court House now is. There were some remains of old indigo vats to the rear of the Court House lot, about where the office of Kelley and Hinds now stands. At that time, the Branch ran through the town a few feet west of where is now located the Atlantic Coast Line station.

Outside of the town as surveyed and on the road to Black Mingo about half way between the King's Tree and the Presbyterian Meeting Houses was the James Davidson settlement, where the Harper home now is. This was one of the most pretentious mansion houses in the district. Further east along the Black Mingo road and where it was crossed by the Cheraw-Santee road was located the Williamsburg Presbyterian churchyard. There

THE TOWN OF WILLIAMSBURG, 1788

were two Presbyterian Churches on this lot at this time. The road from Darlington to Santee did not then curve eastward as now when it reached the churchyard, but went straight through the lot, passing directly east of the front door of the original Williamsburg Church. On the East side of this road and about fifty yards directly east of the original Williamsburg Church was the other Presbyterian Congregation's house of worship. It will be remembered that the original Williamsburg Presbyterian Congregation had divided in 1786 and these two churches were the meeting houses of the respective factions.

From the foregoing, it will be seen that more than fifty years had not made a town at the King's Tree, as seemed so desirable and necessary. This King's Tree was the central point in Williamsburg. It was on Black River, which was still regarded as a natural outlet to the sea, and all roads in Williamsburg led to the King's Tree. The King's Tree was therefore the logical point in the district for establishing the seat of government.

On March 12, 1785, the General Assembly created "one other county beginning at Lenud's Ferry on Santee River, thence along said river to the parish line, thence along said line to Lynch's Creek, thence along said creek to Great Pee Dee River, thence along said river to Britton's Ferry, thence along the boundary of Winyaw County to the beginning, and shall be known by the name of Williamsburg County."

In 1788, the General Assembly of South Carolina passed an ordinance authorizing and appointing commissioners to resurvey and lay out the town of Williamsburg in the District of Georgetown. "Be it ordained, by the Honorable, the Senate and House of Representatives, in General Assembly met, and by authority of the same, that the persons herein named, to wit: John Macauley, John Burgess, Sr., James Witherspoon, Jr., William Frierson,

John Scott, Robert McConnell, Thomas McConnell, James Fleming, Sr., and Robert Frierson, shall be commissioners, and have authority to cause to be resurveyed and laid out in half-acre lots all that parcel of land allotted by law for the town of Williamsburgh, in Georgetown District, and bounding as follows, viz.: on the southwest, by Black River; on the northwest, by land of John Scott; on the northeast, by lands of James Witherspoon, Jr., and Moses Gordon; and on the southeast by the lands of Thomas Lansdale.

"And as sundry grants of land had passed between the year one thousand seven hundred and thirty, and the year one thousand seven hundred and forty-five, under the name of bounty lands, the proprietors whereof were entitled to lots in the said town, many of which lots were not laid out or ascertained to the proprietors; be it ordained by the authority aforesaid that all proprietors of lands under the said description and having a right to a lot or lots in the said town, shall within six months after the passing of the Ordinance, make known to the said commissioners their claims by producing their titles to enable their commissioners to assign each claimant the quantity he is entitled to; and thereupon the commissioners shall locate and lay out the same in such manner as shall be reasonable. The said commissioners shall reserve such lots as they shall deem necessary for two churches, for a public school, market house, and other public purposes, and shall sell or dispose of the residue by public auction or otherwise as they shall deem most advantageous. And the moneys arising therefrom, after paying the surveyor and other necessary charges, shall be appropriated for establishing a public school for the education of youth in the said town, under the direction of the said commissioners.

"And be it further ordained by the authority aforesaid that any five of the said commissioners shall have au-

THE TOWN OF WILLIAMSBURG, 1788

thority to act under this Ordinance, and to fill any vacancies which may happen by the death, refusal, or removal of any of the other commissioners.

"And be it further ordained by the authority aforesaid that if any person shall be sued for anything done by virtue of this Ordinance, he may plead the general issue and give this Ordinance and the special matter in evidence." (In the Senate House, the twenty-seventh day of February, 1788. John Lloyd, President of the Senate. John J. Pringle, Speaker of the House of Representatives.)

This board of commissioners met at the King's Tree on Monday, December 8, 1788. There were present John Burgess, Sr., James Fleming, John Macauley, Robert McConnell, James Witherspoon, Jr., William Frierson, Sr., Thomas McConnell. The first act of the board was to elect John Dickey a commissioner "in the room of John Scott," who had died between the time of his appointment by the General Assembly and the first meeting of the board. The board employed John Burgess, Jr., and Robert Witherspoon, surveyors, to resurvey and lay out the town of Williamsburg according to the plat made by Anthony Williams in 1737, which plat was delivered to them. The board then adjourned to meet at the King's Tree on March 25, 1789, for the purpose of assigning to rightful claimants lots within the town of Williamsburg granted between the years 1730 and 1745, and on the day following to sell all lots not claimed. The commissioners advertised their action and invited the original grantees of these half-acre lots in the town of Williamsburg to come forward and establish their claims, warning them that all lots not claimed would be sold at public vendue.

Until this time, practically no attention had been paid to these half-acre lots by their owners, but this advertisement of the commissioners stirred all Williamsburg from center to circumference. Every original settler in the district immediately searched his home for his grant of land in the township and his half-acre town lot. Most of these old papers had been lost or destroyed, so many men in Williamsburg went to Charleston to see if they could secure a copy of the grants made to them entitling them to these half-acre lots.

When the commissioners met on March 25, 1789, all Williamsburg was there to present claims for these lots. Here follows a list of claims allowed:

Granted in	Persons granted to	Present Proprietors	Lot No.
1735	James Gamble	Heirs Will Gamble	147
1734	James Bradley	James Bradley	228
1733	Robert Ervin	Robert Ervin	235
1735	Richard Middleton	Ebenezer Gibson	99
1735	Robert Young	Samuel Wilson	320
1735	James Law	Isaac Barrineau	272
1742	John Borland	Heirs Will McConnell	205
1736	Crafton Kerwin	James Blakely, Jr.	353
1736	William Troublefield	Thomas McCants	42
1734	John Moore	Sarah Witherspoon	392
1735	Hugh Graham	} John McClary {	276
1736	Edward Plowden		234
1736	William Chambey		70
1735	John Boling	Heirs David Witherspoon	140
1735	Jane McClelland	Heirs David Witherspoon	288
1736	David Johnston	Heirs John Scott	292
1736	John Anderson	Heirs John Scott	253
1736	Nathaniel Drew	Matthew Camlin	139
1734	David Wilson	William Wilson	154
1736	Daniel Mooney	} Gavin Witherspoon {	289
1736	Mary McElroy		294
1738	John Anderson		391
1735	Richard Hall	William Heathley	237
1735	William Hamilton	Samuel Adair	390
1735	John Whitfield	Robert McConnell	249
1738	William James	James Witherspoon	341
1745	John McBride	John Macauley	280
1739	Francis Goddard	John Burgess	257
1737	John McElveen	Hugh McCullough	373
1734	William Wilson	John Wilson	214
1736	John Porter	John Wilson	260
1734	David Witherspoon	William Bracey	236

THE TOWN OF WILLIAMSBURG, 1788

Granted in	Persons granted to	Presents Proprietors	Lot No.
1736	Roger Gordon	⎫	255
1739	John Baxter	⎬ Heirs,	243
1736	John Jamison	⎭	369
1736	Gavin Witherspoon	⎫	281
1736	John Witherspoon	⎬ Robert Witherspoon	382
1736	James McClelland	⎭	48
1736	Margaret Barr	Joseph Scott	232
1735	Thomas Farrington	John McBride	233
1739	Francis Goddard	James Fleming, Sr.	307
1736	William James	James Fleming, Sr.	293
1735	William James	James Fleming, Sr.	208
1735	John Fleming	James Fleming, Sr.	247
1741	Archibald Hamilton	Cong. Williamsburgh	41
1736	James Armstrong	Heirs Thomas Lansdale	245
1734	James Witherspoon	John M. Kinder	204
1740	Archibald McKee	John Boyd	225
1735	Crafton Kerwin	William Frierson, Sr.	215
1735	John Baxter	Ruffin Taylor	203
1735	James Fisher	Thomas McConnell	309
1736	Roger Gibson	James Witherspoon, Jr.	362
1737	John Pressley	William Frierson, Jr.	259

It was decided to allow until April 16, 1789, to others to present their claims to titles to town lots and on that day to sell those not claimed. Seven lots were claimed under original grants on April 16, 1789, as follows:

Date	Granted to	Present Proprietors	Lot No.
1735	William Cochran	⎫	210
1734	Jane Ross	⎬ Samuel McClelland	302
1735	Theodore Monk	⎭	235
1735	Andrew Rutledge	Heirs, Thomas Frierson and Isaac McKnight	184
1735	James Scott	⎫	291
1736	John Blakely	⎬ Congregation Williamsburg	297
1736	James Blakely	⎭	318

John Dickey was selected vendue master and allowed five per centum commissions. The following lots were sold:

Persons Names	Lot No.	£.	S.	P.
Archibald Connor	7	2	10	6
Samuel Kennedy resold	8	2	5	6
Isaac Matthews	10	1	15	7
Robert Fullwood	11	1	5	..

Persons Names	Lot No.	£.	S.	P.
Irvin Dawson	12	1	11	..
James Heathley to James Gowdy	14	..	13	..
Adam Connor	15	1	3	..
Adam Connor	16	1	13	..
Adam Connor	27	1	1	9
Robert Fullwood	30	..	11	9
Robert Fullwood	31	1	2	9
James McCullough	32	2	..	6
Ebenezer Gibson	33	1	3	..
Samuel Kennedy	34	2	15	..
Archibald Connor	35	3	6	..
Hugh McCullough	36	3	10	..
Hugh McCullough	37	3	11	2
John Macauley	43	1	16	6
James McBride	44	2	3	6
John Humphreys	46	3	2	6
James Witherspoon	47	3	2	..
John Humphreys	49	1	1	2
Andrew Early	50	..	15	1
Andrew Early	51	..	15	2
James McConnell	20	3	..	2

After this sale, the clerk was ordered to advertise the sale of all vacant lots remaining unclaimed to be held at the King's Tree on Captain James Witherspoon's Muster Day on June 11, 1789. A number of lots were sold on this day as follows:

Persons Names	Lot No.	£.	S.	P.
Isaac Nelson	74	3	11	..
George McConnell	75	2	10	..
Samuel Maxwell	76	1	12	..
Samuel Maxwell	77	1	1	..
John McClary	79	3	..	6
John McClary	80	3	..	6
John McClary	81	2	2	6
Samuel Maxwell	82	..	16	..
Samuel Maxwell	83	..	13	..
Samuel Maxwell	84	..	11	6
Samuel Maxwell	110	..	10	6
James Bradley	115	..	14	..
James Witherspoon, Jr.	114	2	10	..
Thomas McConnell	105	3	7	..
John Wilson	112	2	4	..
James Witherspoon, Jr.	106	5	16	6

THE TOWN OF WILLIAMSBURG, 1788

Persons Names	Lot No.	£.	S.	P.
Samuel Maxwell	98	..	6	..
John Burgess, Jr.	97	..	10	..
John Burgess, Jr.	96	..	5	..
John Burgess, Jr.	95	..	6	..
John Burgess, Jr.	93	..	5	..
John Wilson	60	..	5	6
John Wilson	62	..	4	6
Samuel Maxwell	63	..	5	..
John Burgess, Jr.	64	..	4	..
Samuel Douglass	65	..	4	8
Samuel Douglass	66	..	5	..
John McClary	67	..	7	..
Samuel Maxwell	68	..	19	..
Samuel Maxwell	69	1	10	..
Thomas McConnell	70	3	..	..
Robert McConnell	71	3	18	6
Robert McConnell	72	4	2	..
James Burgess	73	5	17	..
Robert Gamble	137	4	18	..
Robert Gamble	138	..	8	5
Robert Gamble	141	2	10	..
James Burgess	142	3	2	6
William Law	143	1	1	6
Michael Harding	144	1	2	..

For some time the titles to the town lots that were being sold were questioned and the board adjourned until the advice of attorneys could be secured. In 1790, Major John Macauley, a commissioner, died, and on January 4, 1791, Lieutenant Joseph Scott was elected to succeed him. At the meeting of the commissioners held at the house of James Alexander on August 1, 1791, there were present John Burgess, James Fleming, James Witherspoon, William Frierson, Robert Frierson, Robert McConnell, Thomas McConnell, and Joseph Scott. At this meeting, Thomas Williams was elected a commissioner "in the room of" John Dickey. Robert Witherspoon was paid £12. 3s. and 6p. for surveying the town of Williamsburg; John Fleming was paid £1. 12s. and 8p. for chain carrying; William Douglass was paid £2. 2p. for chain carrying; William Bracey was paid £2. 5s. and 2p. for sundries (liquors);

Samuel Douglass was paid 9s. 4p. for serving liquor on two of the sales days. The commissioners voted at this meeting to fine any commissioner £1. sterling for being absent at any meeting of the commissioners.

At the meeting of the commissioners held on September 5, the following men were given titles to certain town lots: Samuel Maxwell, James Witherspoon, John McClary, John Wilson, James Bradley, Samuel Douglass, James Burgess, John Burgess, John McBride, William Bracey, George Gamble, James Gilbraith, Michael Hardy, Robert McConnell. Robert McConnell was paid £7. 18s. and 8p. for drawing up deeds to the lots sold to the above named men. William Bracey presented an account as follows: To 6 gals. rum at 7s.—£2. 2s. 0p.; 1 quire of paper, 2s. 0p.; 1 box wafers, 1s. 2p. This bill was paid. After the payment of this bill, Captain William Frierson resigned and "declined to act as commissioner any more." It is believed that Captain Frierson was a prohibitionist and that he did not approve of the use of liquors at the sale of the town lots nor at the meetings of the commissioners.

At the next meeting, Robert Frierson and Thomas Williams resigned, and James Witherspoon had died. James Burgess, John McClary, Captain John Fulton, and Robert Witherspoon were duly elected to fill the vacancies. Robert Witherspoon and John McClary were chosen to lay off and stake every lot in the town of Williamsburg, since the former stakes had fallen down. These men were required to lay off one-half acre lots in each corner of the Parade Ground. On the 24th of October, 1792, it being Captain Jones' Muster Day, the commissioners sold the following lots:

Persons Names	Lot No.	£.	S.	P.
John Humphrey	423	4	2	6
Robert Hanna	421	3	4	..
James Tisdale	422	5	..	..
Samuel Snowden	420	4	12	..

Persons Names	Lot No.	£.	S.	P.
Benjamin Durant	401	3	18	..
James Fleming, Sr.	402	3	14	..
James Fleming, Sr.	403	2	5	6
James Fleming, Sr.	404	2	11	..
James Fleming, Sr.	405	..	8	..

On April 10, 1793, John Burgess declined to act as commissioner of the town, and Robert Ervin was elected in his place. On January 2, 1796, George McConnell was elected commissioner in the place of Robert McConnell, deceased. An August 30, 1800, Captain John Fulton resigned as commissioner and Captain Samuel Malcolmson was appointed in his place. Robert Ervin and James Fleming had died prior to this meeting and William Flagler and Robert Hamilton were appointed to succeed them. On November 27, 1800, the Board met at Mr. Robert Hamilton's. There were present Captain William Flagler, Chairman, John McClary, Robert Hamilton, George McConnell, Thomas McConnell, James Burgess, and Joseph Scott. Captain Samuel Malcolmson was absent.

On February 25, 1801, lot No. 425 was set apart for a market house. At this time, Captain Samuel Malcolmson, George McConnell, Robert Hamilton, and John McClary were appointed a committee to have the town resurveyed entirely and it was resolved to advertise in the Georgetown Gazette that all persons claiming land in the town should come forward and present their claims and take possession of them on or before April 22, 1802.

On April 30, 1801, John McClary resigned as commissioner and Eliphalet H. Hewitt was appointed in his place. James Burgess resigned and Captain James Campbell succeeded him. At the meeting on August 22, 1801, it was resolved that no person should further trespass on the public lots in the town and that a man be appointed to keep the streets open. It was also resolved that any person who had planted any public lots in the town under fence should pay the sum of 2s. 4p. per year per lot. On January 1, 1802, the Reverend James Malcolmson offered the board $2.00 for each of the unclaimed sixty one-half acre lots on the south side of Broad Street (Main) on both sides of the Branch. The board accepted this offer and made quit claim deeds for each one of these sixty lots. On August 19, 1803, Arthur Cunningham was elected in the place of George McConnell and made clerk and treasurer of the board.

In 1801, Robert Frierson made a survey and drew a map of the "Town of Williamsburg" at the King's Tree. As originally platted, the two blocks in the centre of the proposed town had been reserved for the parade ground and the churchyard, and Broad Street had not been planned to divide this reservation. Frierson's map shows Broad (Main) Street passing through this reservation eastward, and that the parade ground had been limited to two lots—that land east of Main Street between Academy and Long Streets. The Williamsburg Court House now stands on this lot. The churchyard, as then reserved, was one hundred and five feet in breadth from Academy to Long Streets of present Kingstree. Heller's stables stand on a part of this land.

The market house lot was set apart at the corner of present Main and Long Streets where Miss Andy Lockamy's home stands. Lots 420, where the Post Office now stands; 421, Silverman's building, occupied by McIntosh Motor Company; 422, Long Street tenements; 423, Kellahan brick stores on Academy Street; and 424, Bank of Kingstree; all were taken from the parade ground and churchyard reservations and sold to individuals.

On this Map of 1801, the present Kingstree Main Street is known as Broad; Mill as Washington: Church as Adams; and Brooks as Jefferson. Beginning at the river, streets running North and South were numbered serially. Academy Street was then called Fourth Street. Later,

THE TOWN OF WILLIAMSBURG, 1788

it was named Bay Street. In 1805, the commissioners set apart a lot where the residence of W. I. Nexsen stands for a public school and a building was erected thereon. This academy finally gave the name to this handsome residence street in Kingstree.

On January 15, 1805, Joseph Scott was chairman of the board and Arthur Cunningham, secretary and treasurer. Arthur Cunningham was appointed agent to carry on a suit against T. T. Woods for conspiracy. The commission had on November 27, 1800, employed T. T. Woods as surveyor to lay out the parade ground on which it was found that John Brady had built his house. Woods had been employed also as clerk of the board. At this meeting of the board on January 15, 1805, it is recorded in the minutes that the board adjourned to meet on the first Monday in February after the meeting of the committee appointed to place a Court House in Williamsburg.

In 1805, Joseph Scott died and Thomas Rodgers was elected in his place. In 1806, after many surveys of the town had already been made, Theodore Gourdin and John Scott, of Kingstree, obtained a restraining order from the court in the matter of the boundary lines of the town. Captain Samuel Malcolmson, Major John Nesmith, and Samuel Fluitt were appointed a committee to have the boundaries of the town confirmed by the courts. Henry Mouzon and Isaac Singletary were appointed as surveyors to determine the boundaries of the town and to make a new plat. On October 10, 1806, the commissioners attended the first court held in the town of Williamsburg and there sought an order confirming the boundary line as made.

On February 22, 1808, James G. McGill and James B. McConnell were appointed commissioners to succeed Major John Nesmith and E. H. Hewitt. In 1809, the board of commissioners consisted of Thomas D. Beard, Samuel Malcolmson, Thomas Rodgers, James B. McConnell, Arthur Cunningham. At this meeting, Patrick Cormick was elected in the place of William Moore, and Robert Witherspoon vice Samuel Fluitt. Patrick Cormick did not accept, so John Broome was elected. The next year Dr. T. M. Brown filled the vacancy caused by the resignation of Thomas G. Beard.

On the 29th of January, 1810, Thomas Rodgers was ordered to pay $50.00 for the destruction of the old plat of the town of Williamsburg, otherwise to have a new plat made. Colonel Robert L. Witherspoon was given liberty to fence twelve feet of Broad Street (Main) and twelve feet of Church Street in order to plant out shade trees to form a pavement. At this meeting, it was decided to prosecute all men who trespassed on the streets. Dr. T. M. Brown introduced a resolution which was passed that the ground appropriated for Church and yard be kept sacred. At this meeting, the board entered suit against Theodore Gourdin for planting corn in one of the streets of the town. Thomas Rodgers was fined $10.00; Martin Staggers, $8.00; William Staggers, $8.00; Samuel Fluitt, $5.00; and Samuel Malcolmson, $2.00 for cultivating crops in the streets. A resolution was passed that Broad Street should be forever the center street in the town and on no account be thereafter changed. John Matthews and Patrick Cormick were elected members of the board to succeed John H. McConnell and James B. McConnell. At the meeting of the board of July 6, 1821, Patrick Cormick was sold that portion of a lot of land lying in front of his house extending to Broad Street, directly between the Court House and the Jail, at the rate of $1.03 per foot.

In 1800, the following men or their heirs owned lots as follows: 1, James Fisher; 2, Thomas Hall; 3, Richard Hall; 4, William Morgan; 5, John Basnet; 6, Robert Finley; 7, Archibald Connor; 8, Samuel Kennedy; 9, Francis Goddard; 10, Isaac Matthews; 11, Robert Fullwood; 12, John Dawson; 13, Thomas Lake, Esq.; 14,

THE TOWN OF WILLIAMSBURG, 1788   151

John Harshey to James Gowdy; 15, 16, Adam Connor; 20, John Hamilton; 21, John Sykes; 22, Robert Pringle; 23, Thomas Monk; 24, John McClary; 25, Henry Williams; 26, Thomas McCullough; 27, Adam Connor; 28, Samuel Kennedy; 29, John McClary; 30, 31, Robert Fullwood; 32, James McCullough; 33, Elisha Gibson; 34, Samuel Kennedy; 35, Archibald Connor; 36, 37, Hugh McCullough; 38, Margaret Morgan; 39, John Cleland; 40, William Morgan; 41, Congregation of Williamsburg; 42, Thomas McCants; 43, John Macauley; 44, James McBride; 45, Hugh Copeland; 46, John Humphreys; 47, James Witherspoon; 48, Heirs Robert Witherspoon; 49, John Humphreys; 50, 51, Andrew Early; 52, John Pennyfather; 53-58, John McClary; 59, John Knox; 60, John Wilson; 61, John Pressley; 62, John Wilson; 63, Samuel Maxwell; 64, John Burgess, Jr.; 65, 66, Samuel Douglass; 67, John McClary; 68, 69, Samuel Maxwell; 70, Thomas McConnell; 71, Robert McConnell; 73, 74, James Burgess; 75, George McConnell; 76, 77, Samuel Maxwell; 78-81, John McClary; 82-84, Samuel Maxwell; 85-92, John McClary; 93, John Burgess, Jr.; 94, James Smith; 95-97, John Burgess, Jr.; 98, Samuel Maxwell; 99, Ebenezer Gibson; 100, Charles Starnes; 101, David Arnett; 102, Jane Carge; 103, Matthew Vanalle; 104, John Scott; 105, Thomas McConnell; 106, James Witherspoon, Jr.; 107, James Moody; 108, Sarah Blakeway; 109, Samuel Malcolmson; 110, Michael Harding; 111, John Bliss; 112, John Wilson; 113, Samuel Malcolmson; 114, James Witherspoon, Jr.; 115, James Bradley; 116, Samuel Maxwell; 117, Thomas Forrest; 118, John Hewitt; 119, John Mooney; 120-134, John McClary; 135, John Holden; 136, John Dick; 137, 138, Robert Gamble; 139, Matthew Camlin; 140, John McClary; 141, Robert Gamble; 142, James Burgess; 143, William Law; 144, Michael Harding; 145, 146, John McClary; 147, Heirs of Will Gamble; 148, John McClary; 149, Heirs of David

Witherspoon; 150-153, John McClary; 154, William Wilson; 155-159, John McClary; 160, James Seawright; 161, Doctor Lining; 162-167, John McClary; 168-180, I. Fluitt; 181, 182, Samuel Snowden; 183, Heirs of Thomas Frierson and Isaac McKnight; 184, Robert Hamilton, Jr.; 185, Robert Dixon; 186, 187, Robert Hamilton, Jr.; 188, George Durant; 189-191, Samuel Malcolmson; 192-194, Joseph Scott; 195, James Galbraith; 196, William Bracey; 200, John Ballentine; 201, Benjamin Bates; 202, Margaret Bowlee; 203, Ruffin Taylor; 205, Richard Malone; 206, Richard Hughes; 207, John M. Kinder; 208, James Fleming, Sr.; 210, James McClelland; 214, John Wilson; 215, William Frierson, Sr.; 216, 217, Robert Hamilton, Jr.; 218, John Scott, Jr.; 219-221, Robert Hamilton; 222, 223, William Witherspoon; 224, Andrew Patterson, Sr.; 225, John Boyd; 226, Samuel Wilson; 227, Andrew Patterson; 228, James Bradley; 229, 230, William Hiddleston; 232, Joseph Scott and A. Cunningham; 233, John McBride; 234, John McClary; 235, Robert Ervin; 236, William Bracey; 237, William Bracey; 238, William Heathley; 243, Heirs Robert Witherspoon; 247, James Fleming, Sr.; 248, Heirs Thomas Landsdale; 249, Robert McConnell; 250, Ama Hardger; 251, James Scott, Sr.; 252, L. Snowden; 255, Heirs Robert Witherspoon; 256, William McCormick; 259, William Frierson, Jr.; 260, John Wilson; 262, Henry Montgomery; 263, Heirs John Scott; 265, Heirs William McConnell; 269, John Burgess; 272, Isaac Barrineau and I. Malcolmson; 276, John McClary; 279, Joseph Rhodes; 280, John Macauley; 281, Heirs Robert Witherspoon; 284, William Frierson; 286, Samuel McClelland; 288, Heirs David Witherspoon; 289, Gavin Witherspoon; 292, Heirs John Scott; 293, James Fleming, Sr.; 294, Gavin Witherspoon; 296, 297, Congregation of Williamsburg; 301, Reverend J. Bignion; 302, Samuel McClelland; 303, Samuel Malcolmson; 307, James Flem-

THE TOWN OF WILLIAMSBURG, 1788

ing, Sr.; 309, Thomas McConnell; 310, William Williamson; 313, Hugh McCollough; 314, Henry Postell; 315, Francis Finley; 317, Mary Gladden; 318, Congregation of Williamsburg; 319, William Hamilton; 327, John Lemon; 328, William Montgomery; 329, David McCants; 330, John Barns; 331, William Orr; 332, John Cornell; 333, George Burrows; 334, Robert Witherspoon; 335, Robert Allison; 336, Wllliam McKnight; 337, John Watson; 338, William Scott; 340, Patrick Lindsay; 341, James Witherspoon; 348, Robert Little; 349, David M. Owen; 350, John Danner and James G. McGill; 352, James McCrea; 353, James Blakeley, Jr.; 354, William Hamilton; 355, James Stewart; 356, John Watson; 357, 358, John and Nathaniel McCullough; 359, Matthew Barr and James Frierson; 360, James Dickson; 361, William Pressley; 362, James Witherspoon; 365, John Dick; 366, Robert Little; 367, David McCants, Sr.; 368, John Athol; 369, Heirs Robert Witherspoon; 370, William Young; 371, Christopher Harvey; 373, James Pettigrew; 374, William Campbell; 375, Abraham Gordon; 376, William Harvey; 377, John Matthews; 378, Hugh McGill; 380, Roger Gibson; 381, William McDonald; 382, Heirs Robert Witherspoon; 383, John Cleland; 387, William Hamilton; 390, Samuel Adair; 391, Gavin Witherspoon; 392, Sarah Witherspoon; 399, Richard Johnson; 400, Martin Staggers and G. Gamble; 402-405, James Fleming, Sr.; 406, Samuel Malcolmson; 407, 408, Martin Staggers; 409, 410, James Campbell; 420, Samuel Snowden; 421, Robert Hanna; 422, James Tisdale; 423, John Humphreys.

CHAPTER XIV.

WILLIAMSBURG CENSUS, 1790.

The census of 1790 shows the names of every householder in Williamsburg County, first column in the list following; the number of white males sixteen years of age, or upwards, of his household, second column; the number of white males under sixteen, third column; the number of white females, fourth column; and the number of negro slaves the head of the house owned, fifth column. This list is about as full of history as so much space can contain.

Heads of Families	Males over 16	Males under 16	Females	Slaves
Ard, Barbary,	2	1	1	..
Axson, Elijah	2	4	6	5
Avant, Francis	1	1	2	1
Avant, Francis, Jr.	1	4	3	10
Allison, Sarah	..	2	1	3
Altman, Jane	..	..	2	16
Armstrong, James	1	1	3	6
Arely, Andrew	1	..	..	..
Adair, Samuel	1	3	3	14
Adams, Margaret	1	..	2	2
Allen, John	1	..	1	..
Allen, Henry	2	1	4	..
Anderson, William	1	1	2	..
Adams, John	1	1	2	..
Anderson, James	2	..	..	57
Brown John	1	3	2	..
Biggen, James	3	2	4	..
Braveboy, Joshua	..	..	..	..
Baxter, John	1	1	1	83
Bartell, Jacob	1	3	2	..
Barefield, Charles	1	2	8	3
Brockinton, John, Jr.	1	..	2	..
Bates, Isaac	2	2	2	2
Brown, Jeremiah	2	3	2	..
Beard, Henry	1	..	1	..
Burbage, Jonathan	1	1	2	..
Butler, Sarah	1	1	3	9
Birch, Joseph	2	2	3	36

WILLIAMSBURG CENSUS, 1790

Heads of Families	Males over 16	Males under 16	Females	Slaves
Brown, Ann		1	5	..
Benton, Cress	1	1	4	..
Buxton, Nancy	1	2	3	..
Barefoot, John	1	2	4	..
Blunt, Jesse Gashum	1	..	2	..
Boyd, Evan	1	1	1	7
Blakely, James, Jr.	3	4	4	36
Bland, Thomas	2	3	6	5
Bostwick, Jonathan	1	3	2	8
Boyd, John	2	1	4	14
Brown, John	3	..	3	..
Barrineau, Isaac	2	2	3	1
Barrineau, Arthur	1	1	2	..
Berry, Lydford	1	1	1	..
Bradley, James, Jr.	1	3	3	17
Bracey, Wm. and John Graham	2	2	1	2
Burrows, John	2	3	2	22
Burrows, Joseph	1	..	..	4
Barr, James	3	2	3	3
Brown, James	2	4	2	10
Butler, Sarah	..	1	3	6
Barker, John	1	..	3	1
Blackborn, Gabriel	1	..	1	..
Bernard, Paul, Jr.	2	..	3	13
Barber, John	1	1	2	..
Boutwell, Joseph	1	..	1	3
Boone, John	2	..	..	21
Bernard, Paul	3	1	3	25
Boone, Thomas	2	3	..	42
Barns, John	1	..	..	5
Brockinton, John	1	1	4	20
Bineau, Michael	1	..	2	5
Bates, Isaac	1	..	..	..
Berry, James	1	..	1	..
Burrows, George	1	2	1	29
Booth, Robert	1	..	4	1
Bulloch, Ephrain	1	4	2	..
Boone, Mary	..	..	1	1
Berry, Thomas	3	2	3	..
Boone, Capers	1	..	1	6
Boone, Robert	2	1	3	20
Burrows, Samuel	2	1	2	..
Barren, John	1	1	4	..
Buford, William	1	3	5	9
Coupland, John	2	..	1	4

HISTORY OF WILLIAMSBURG

Heads of Families	Males over 16	Males under 16	Females	Slaves
Cooper, George	1	..	3	5
Callum, John	2	..	1	24
Commander, James, Jr.	1	1	1	4
Cooper, James	1	1	3	5
Comb, Ann	2	..	3	..
Cooper, John	1	1	..	17
Cooper, William James	1	..	1	26
Callebuff, Elizabeth	..	..	1	1
Cook, Joseph	1	2	4	..
Cook, Benjamin	1	1	1	..
Commander, James	2	4	2	35
Cheesborough, John	2	2	2	38
Camlin, William	1	2	1	..
Cunningham, James	2	3	2	..
Carlisle, Alexander	1	..	2	..
Carter, Zachary	1	1	3	4
Coleman, Robert	2	2	2	2
Cox, William	1	..	..	..
Carter, Josiah	1	..	3	..
Cummins, David	1	3	2	..
Crosby, Sarah	..	..	3	..
Calcot, Henry	1	1	3	..
Conner, Adam	1	1	1	19
Conner, Archibald	2	2	1	18
Cantley, John	1	..	3	..
Cannon, John	1	2	1	16
Calcot, James	1	..	3	..
Clark, James	1	..	1	..
Campbell, Mary	1	1	2	13
Coleman, Jacob	1	1	4	..
Cunningham, Mary	1	1	4	26
Cunningham, Alexander	1	..	1	·8
Clark, Henry	1	4	1	5
Camlin, Matthew	1	..	2	1
Cockfield, Josiah	1	3	5	10
Campbell, James, Jr.	1	..	1	...
Carter, William	1	4	2	2
Cribb, John	1	4	3	..
Craps, William	1	..	3	..
Chovin, Alexander and Collins, Alexander	2	1	4	49
Campbell, James	2	2	2	..
Campbell, Archibald	3	..	2	..
Dickson, John	1	1	1	..
Davis, Mary	1	1	2	9

WILLIAMSBURG CENSUS, 1790

Heads of Families	Males over 16	Males under 16	Females	Slaves
Day, John	2	..	2	8
Digman, Robert	1	2	2	..
Davis, Robert	1	1	2	1
Dickey, John	1	5	4	45
Durant, Benjamin, and Durant, Paul	2	..	..	4
Douglas, Sarah	1	..	2	..
Durant, George	1	2	1	6
Douglas, Samuel	1	1	2	5
Dawson, John, and Brady	2	..	1	6
Dick, Robert, and Jonas Win.	2	2	2	27
Davison, Mary, and William Menkelroy	1	1	1	13
Dollard, Patrick, and Jno. O'Bryan	2	..	1	27
Davidson, William	1	..	4	11
Daniel, James	1	2	5	2
Dupre, James	1	1	2	13
Dowen, James	1	3	2	..
Dobbin, William	1	2	1	..
Downing, Ranatus	2	3	2	..
Douglas, William	1	..	2	..
Dickey, George	1	3	4	..
Dickey, Stuart	1	2	5	..
Ervin, Hugh	1	1	2	19
Ervin, John	1	2	1	29
Edmonds, Lattemore	3	..	7	..
Evans, Barwell	1	..	..	..
Ervin, Elizabeth	...	..	3	11
Ervin, Robert	1	..	3	13
Eaddy, James, Jr.	1	4	3	7
Eaddy, James	1	..	..	..
Evans, Francis	2	4	3	10
Early, Andrew	1	3	2	..
Edwards, Simon	2	..	1	..
Freeman, James	1	4	3	..
Flagler, William	1	3	3	16
Finkly, John	1	1	3	2
Finkly, Thomas	1	..	4	10
Finkly, Charles	2	..	1	7
Falcon, Peter	1	2	2	..
Francis, Richard	1	3	3	..
Fryer, Joel	3	..	2	..
Fraser, William	1	..	..	4
Fryer, Drure	2	2	5	..

158 HISTORY OF WILLIAMSBURG

Heads of Families	Males over 16	Males under 16	Females	Slaves
Frierson, William, Jr.	1	..	1	8
Frierson, Samuel	1	..	1	10
Frierson, Robert, Sr.	2	2	6	29
Frierson, William	3	3	2	18
Frierson, Robert, Jr. and Mary Witherspoon	1	..	2	7
Frierson, John	3	1	3	15
Fulton, John	1	1	2	14
Fleming, Ann	2	..	5	1
Felps, Samuel	1	..	..	..
Futhy, John	1	1	2	18
Futhy, Henry	3	..	..	12
Foxworth, Thomas	1	..	2	..
Forrister, Anthony	1	3	2	..
Ford, Hephen	2	4	2	98
Fleming, John, Jr.	1	..	1	..
Fleming, John	1	3	4	..
Fleming, John	1	2	3	..
Fleming, John, Jr.	1	..	1	..
Gibson, John	1	6	2	..
Gordon, John	2	2	4	..
Gaskin, Sarah	..	1	3	1
Green, Samuel	1	..	2	8
Gamble, Robert	2	..	2	12
Gilley, John	1	1	1	..
Gregg, John	1	3	2	..
Gaskin, Ezekiel	1	5	2	6
Gardner, John	1	2	2	..
Gibson, Daniel	..	..	..	..
Gregg, Joseph	1	2	4	11
Gregg, John	1	6	4	19
Gregg, James	1	3	6	16
Gregg, Robert	1	1	1	2
Gourley, Joseph, and Thomas McKeney	2	3	4	8
Goodwin, Abel	2	2	4	9
Green, Richard	1	3	1	16
Goddard, William, and Francis Billum	2	..	..	70
Gorman, Catherine	..	1	2	..
Ginn, Shadrach	3	3	5	..
Going, Bathiah	..	..	2	..
Griffis, David	1	..	2	..
Gibson, Ebenezer	1	..	1	9
Gillespie, John	1	2	2	7

WILLIAMSBURG CENSUS, 1790 159

Heads of Families	Males over 16	Males under 16	Females	Slaves
Gibson, James	1	..	5	1
Graham, John, and Robert Moore, and Margaret Raffell	2	..	2	16
Gourdin, Theodore	1	1	3	150
For John James Estate	1	..	1	13
Gilbert, James, and John Roulet	2	..	..	..
Gotea, James	1	3	3	11
Gamble, John	1	3	1	3
Graham, Hugh	1	3	6	5
Gamble, William	1	..	..	..
Gibbons, Michael	3	..	6	..
Wilson, Godfrey (Est.)		..	1	6
Green, William	1	..	2	7
Graham, William	3	..	2	9
Gregg, Hugh, and Samuel Thomson	2	..	..	8
Green, John Thomson	1	..	3	18
Gamble, Robert	1	1	2	..
Grant, Hugh, and Richard Taylor	2	..	..	2
Green, Francis	1	2	4	33
Green, John	1	..	..	12
Green, James	1	2	2	18
Green, John (son of Richard)	1	..	2	46
Glass, Joseph Alexender	2	..	3	9
Gibson, John	1	5	2	8
Grier, John	1	..	1	..
Graham, Robert	1	..	..	..
Gaskin, Vincent	1	1	2	..
Gouge, John	1	..	..	..
Gordon, John	2	3	3	18
Gaskin, James	2	3	3	9
Gibson, Ebenezer	1	..	2	..
Gasque, Aaron	1	..	..	..
Gadsden, Christopher (negroes)		..	..	90
Guerry, Benjamin	1	1	3	..
Gibson, Thomas	1	3	3	..
Goudge, John	1	2	1	..
Gibson, James	1	4	2	..
Gibson, Alexander	1	3	1	..
Gibson, Thomas	1	..	1	..
Gibson, George	1	1	1	..
Gilbraith, James	1	3	2	..
Holland, James	1	2	2	1
Horn, Richard	2	1	4	..
Hickman, Isaac, and Joshua Hickman	2	..	..	12

Heads of Families	Males over 16	Males under 16	Females	Slaves
Hudson, Hannah, Sr. 1		3	5	4
Hudson, Benjamin 1		1	4	..
Harrell, Lewis 1		3	3	14
Harmon, Thomas		..	..	..
Hudson, Joseph 1		..	3	..
Hutchenson, Aaron 1		..	2	..
Hutchenson, Arthur 1		..	2	..
Hagan, Zachariah 4		4	7	..
Harmon, William 1		1	3	..
Harmon, Shemeraft 1		..	..	..
Hartley, James 1		..	..	..
Hagan, Obediah 1		..	..	..
Hains, Samuel 2		2	5	..
Herren, Eleanor 1		1	4	1
Humfrey, John, and James Perry 1		..	1	..
Hill, Isaac 1		1	1	..
Hickson, John 1		3	3	..
Howard, John 1		2	2	10
Hope, Ralph 1		1	1	..
Hannah, William 3		2	5	3
Hannah, Hugh 1		..	1	4
Halcher, Isham 1		2	1	2
Howell, Joshua Joseph 2		..	2	7
Hambelton, Rebecca 1		2	1	2
Ham, William 1		..	1	7
Hart, Hyman, and Joseph McCrea 2		..	..	6
Hart, Simon 1		1	2	..
Hoddy, Elizabeth		1	3	..
Herren, William 1		2	5	..
Hannah, James 1		3	1	..
Hickson, Peter 1		1	1	..
Hughs, John 1		..	..	2
Harelson, William 2		2	5	9
Hart, Daniel 2		..	3	6
Harth, Simon 1		1	1	..
Howard, Martin 2		1	1	..
Hydecker, John Arthur 1		..	1	1
Heathly, William 1		1	2	24
Hughes, Sarah 1		2	2	..
Hix, William 1		3	2	..
Hepburn, James 1		1	1	11
Halcher, Moses 1		2	2	..
Holden, Shoemach 1		..	..	..

WILLIAMSBURG CENSUS, 1790

Heads of Families	Males over 16	Males under 16	Females	Slaves
Herren, Eleanor	1	1	4	1
Hendlen, John	1	3	2	..
Harrington, Thomas	1	2	1	..
Harden, Thomas	1	4	2	..
Harden, Michael	1	2	1	..
Houldon, Samuel	1	1	..	..
Hull, Joseph	1	..	1	..
Henlin, Benjamin	1	4	3	..
Howard, Rachael	..	..	4	..
Harvey, Judith	1	3	3	..
Howard, John	1	1	3	..
Hickson, John	1	..	4	..
Hiddleston, William	1	2	2	..
Johnson, William	1	2	2	..
Jolly, Joseph	1	..	8	12
James, William	1	..	..	1
James, Robert	1	..	..	..
Jones, Peter	1	3	1	..
Ivey, John	1	1	1	..
Ironmonger, Recten	2	3	3	..
Johnson, George	1	..	..	..
June, Stephen	1	..	..	7
Jones, William	1	1	1	20
Jones, Mary	1	..	1	2
Jenkins, Margaret, and James Jenkins	1	2	1	2
Jolly, Archibald	1	1	7	3
Irwin, James	2	1	3	6
Johnson, Thomson	1	5	3	..
Simon, Joseph	2	..	1	..
James, Jane	1	..	3	31
Jaudon, Martha, and Margaret Bowen	..	2	2	6
James, John	1	1	3	11
Johnson, Jacob	1	2	2	..
Jackson, William	1	..	4	..
Jackson, John	1	..	..	3
James, Samuel Winter	1	..	..	1
Johnston, James	1	1	2	..
Joseph, Lazarus	1	2	3	..
Jenkins, Samuel	1	1	2	..
Jones, Samuel	1	2	4	..
Jones, James	1	1	3	..
Knight, Catherine	1	..	2	..
Keith, Sarah Ann	2	1	2	11

Heads of Families	Males over 16	Males under 16	Females	Slaves
Keels, Isaac	1	1	3	7
Kelty, John	1	2	4	2
Knox, Archibald	1	2	4	10
Kinder, John Michael	1	1	3	3
Kennedy, Samuel	1	2	1	17
Knox, Mary	2	1	3	2
Knox, William	1	2	2	4
Kennedy, Mary	..	..	1	..
Keels, John	1	2	3	3
Keith, William	2	2	4	..
Knox, Samuel	1	..	2	..
Knox, John	1	3	1	..
Kirkpatrick, James	1	..	..	..
Lee, Needum	1	4	3	6
Lowry, John	1	..	2	1
Ligneager, Isaac	..	..	..	..
Lane, John	1	2	2	..
Lane, Hannah	..	2	2	..
Latham, Amos	1	..	3	..
Lee, Samuel	2	1	2	..
Lee, James	2	1	1	..
Levy, Aaron	1	..	4	..
Lacey, Sarah	..	..	3	..
Leger, John	1	..	2	6
Lifrage, William, and James Meek	2	2	3	2
Law, William	1	..	1	14
Lowry, Robert	1	..	1	..
Layman, David	1	1	1	3
Lane, Rebecca	..	2	1	..
Leger, William	1	2	1	1
Lamb, Javin	1	..	2	..
Leger, James	2	2	3	..
Leger, Daniel	1	..	4	1
Lequex, Sims	2	1	..	26
Lequex,	..	1	2	6
Luiser, Thomas	1	1	1	..
Lacey, James	3	2	1	..
Lester, William	1	..	2	25
Lamb, Levy	2	..	2	..
Leger, Daniel	1	2	3	8
Linson, Thomas	1	1	1	..
Lequex, John	1	1	1	21
Lawremore, William	1	1	2	..
Lamb, Joseph	1	1	1	..

WILLIAMSBURG CENSUS, 1790

Heads of Families	Males over 16	Males under 16	Females	Slaves
Lanels, Thomas	1	1	2	..
Lee, Fernay	3	..	1	..
March, Tarenah	1	1	1	2
McDowell, William	1	..	..	1
McKindru, John	1	1	2	..
McDonald, John	1	4	1	..
Malpess, Joel	1	1	3	4
Martin, Zachariah	1	1	3	4
McGinney, James	1	4	1	1
Mikell, Jane	..	1	2	..
McKee, John, and Thomas Seabrook	2	1	2	20
Murfee, Moses	2	3	2	..
McIntree, Thomas	1	..	..	..
March, John	1	1	5	..
Montgomery, Nathaniel	1	..	1	15
Montgomery, Samuel	1	1	2	1
McKnight, James	1	1	2	20
McDonald, Adam	2	..	3	17
McDonald, Sam	1	..	..	8
McDonald, Daniel	1	..	..	7
McDowell, Samuel	1	..	..	..
McDonald, Archibald	1	..	..	5
McKnight, Thomas	1	3	2	26
Marlow, James, and William Bailey	2	2	3	..
Marlow, Richard	1	..	1	..
McCracker, David	1	..	1	..
Macauley, Sarah	..	1	6	15
McMullen, Hugh	1	..	..	..
McCullough, James	1	2	1	2
McBride, James, and Samuel McBride	2	2	3	7
Mouzon, Henry	3	2	5	4
Manning, James	1	3	4	..
Montgomery, Hugh	2	2	3	52
McCullough, William	1	2	2	21
McCants, Thomas	2	4	4	17
Matthews, John	1	1	4	42
Marner, Charles	1	1	2	..
McConnell, Thomas	1	6	3	15
Murphy, Archibald	1	..	2	6
McKee, Joseph, and James Stephenson	2	..	2	14
Matthews, Isaac	1	2	6	35

HISTORY OF WILLIAMSBURG

Heads of Families	Males over 16	Males under 16	Females	Slaves
(For Abraham Matthews, Est.)...1	..	..	14	
Marsden, Elizabeth	..	1	13	
Maxwell, Samuel, and Margaret McCarty 1	5	3	3	
McClary, John 3	1	4	4	
McGill, Samuel 1	2	2	11	
McConnell, Robert 1	2	4	33	
McConnell, George 1	1	2	3	
McCrea, Susanna, and Samuel Panton 1	2	3	54	
McConnell, Mary 2	2	2	12	
McConnell, James 1	3	3	8	
McCants, Alexander 1	..	2	1	
McCutchen, George 1	4	2	11	
McKnight, Allen	1	5	58	
McKee, James 1	..	1	..	
McGill, Roger 2	2	3	24	
McCutchen, James 2	..	4	8	
McCrea, Thomas 1	..	3	26	
McCrea, James 1	..	1	..	
McElveen, William 3	2	4	12	
Mulhollen, Jeannet	..	3	..	
McAlister, John 1	4	3	..	
Marlowe, Charles 1	1	3	..	
McKnelly, James 1	..	5	4	
McElveen, William, Jr. 1	1	1	12	
McGee, William 2	1	2	1	
McDowell, John 1	..	..	7	
McDowell, William 1	8	1	..	
McKnight, John 1	3	3	17	
Miller, Moses, Jr. 1	3	3	14	
Marlow, William 4	1	4	..	
Moore, William 1	3	3	4	
McCullough, Elizabeth 1	..	3	..	
Messers, John 1	3	4	..	
McFadden, Robert 1	1	1	..	
Michau, Paul 1	..	8	21	
Perdreau, John (Est. of) Guerry, Lydia	1	3	5	
Michau, Manassel 2	3	5	25	
McCullough, John 1	..	..	..	
Murfee, Moses 1	3	2	87	
McBride, John 1	2	3	4	
McKissick, Archie 1	..	..	2	
Mason, John, and John Paisely...2	..	..	2	

WILLIAMSBURG CENSUS, 1790

Heads of Families	Males over 16	Males under 16	Females	Slaves
McCottry, Robert	2	..	6	30
Michau, Peter	2	..	..	31
McKee, John	2	1	2	20
McCrea, John	1	2	3	9
McElroy, William	1	2	3	1
Miller, Moses	2	..	2	45
Meerse, Daniel	2	1	2	11
McCullough, Hugh	1	4	1	12
McGinney, Samuel	1	..	1	12
Michau, Peter	3	..	..	32
May, Enoch	1	..	2	..
Morris, William	1	..	..	..
McAllister, Charles	2	1	3	9
McKnight, Robert	1	..	..	17
Moore, William	1	3	3	4
Marler, Richard	1	..	2	..
McKable, Alexander	1	..	..	..
McMelly, Mary	2	1	2	16
Murray, John	1	1	4	17
McCullough, John	2	..	2	8
March, John	1	1	5	..
Matthews, Jonas	1	..	..	..
Marlow, William	3	2	5	..
McClary, John	1	..	..	..
Morris, John	1	1	1	..
McCrea, Joseph	1	2	3	..
McCrea, Farquher	3	2	2	..
Mills, John	1	..	1	..
Miller, Stephen	2	1	1	..
McDowell, Forgas	1	1	1	..
McBane, Daniel	1	2	4	..
McDonald, Jane	1	2	2	10
Mammon, John	1	1	4	..
Night, Thomas	1	..	3	..
Nelson, Letitia	1	..	4	40
Nalton, Caleb	1	..	1	..
Nesmith, Samuel	5	..	1	9
Nesmith, Drew Nathaniel	1	1	3	1
Nesmith, Samuel	2	..	3	21
Nesmith, John	1	2	3	5
Nesmith, Samuel	1	..	..	..
Nesmith, Elizabeth	1	..	2	1
Nesmith, Robert	1	..	1	10
Nettles, Isham	1	2	2	..
Nesbit, James	1	..	1	..

HISTORY OF WILLIAMSBURG

Heads of Families	Males over 16	Males under 16	Females	Slaves
Orr, John	1	3	1	3
Orr, Mary	..	..	1	8
O'Neill, John, and Lachlen McIntosh	2	1	2	5
Owens, James	1	1	3	..
Orr, William, Sr.	3	1	2	4
Orr, William, Jr.	1	1	1	..
Owen, Lewis	1	1	1	5
Owen, James	4	..	6	4
Ogelby, Lewis	1	..	3	..
Owens, Zacheriah	1	..	1	..
O'Brian, John	1	1	2	..
Owens, Peter	1	..	3	7
Ogelby, Daniel	1	4	5	..
Pritchard, Simon	1	..	1	1
Porter, John	1	1	2	4
Perkins, Mary	..	..	3	11
Poston, James	1	..	3	..
Poston, John	1	3	3	..
Port, Francis	3	1	5	26
Perkins, Lewis	1	..	..	9
Pilkenton, DuRay	1	..	2	..
Pritchard, Stephen	1	3	2	..
Pilkenton, John	1	1	1	..
Perritt, James	1	1	3	5
Price, Henry	2	1	1	11
Patterson, Andrew	4	..	3	1
Paisley, Thomas	1	1	5	11
Paisley, William	1	..	1	8
Paisley, Robert	2	..	5	25
Pell, Gilbert	1	..	2	1
Perrit, Abraham	1	2	4	29
Potts, Thomas	1	3	5	28
Potts, William	1	1	1	17
Perkins, David	1	..	3	11
Perrit, Francis	1	3	1	15
Porter, William	1	..	4	9
Pettigrew, James	2	3	1	11
Port, Benjamin	1	..	2	9
Payne, John	1	2	3	..
Pigott, Nathaniel	2	1	2	3
Parsons, Amos	3	1	5	1
Patterson, Andrew	1	..	3	1
Parkerson, John	2	3	5	..
Paisley, Hugh	1	..	1	13

WILLIAMSBURG CENSUS, 1790

Heads of Families	Males over 16	Males under 16	Females	Slaves
Paisley, William, Jr.	1	..	..	3
Parsons, William	1	..	..	1
Porter, Benjamin	3	..	3	67
Porter, John	1	..	..	14
Plat, Elizabeth	..	2	1	..
Parker, John	2	3	4	..
Paidey, Peter	3	1	3	..
Poston, Joseph	1	..	1	..
Russell, Thomas	..	..	..	..
Rawls, Elisha	2	4	5	..
Rodgers, Isaac	1	1	3	..
Rodgers, Shadrach	1	2	3	..
Rhodes, John	1	5	3	..
Roberts, Peter	1	..	..	24
Rhodus, Solomon	1	..	1	5
Russell, Andrew	1	..	1	..
Reed, Hugh	1	..	2	7
Rodgers, Micajah	1	..	2	..
Rowlin, Margaret	..	..	2	..
Rigden, Ephraim	2	2	3	..
Roland, Elizabeth	..	1	5	18
Riche, Anthony	1	1	1	..
Rambart, Joachem	1	2	2	..
Roland, Abraham	1	..	2	..
Raney, Herbert	1	..	3	..
Riche, James	1	2	3	1
Reaves, Benjamin	1	2	4	..
Rasberry, Nathaniel	1	1	1	..
Reaves, James	1	2	1	..
Royals, James	2	1	3	..
Raphield, James	1	..	1	..
Reed, William	1	2	3	..
Richardson, David	1	4	2	..
Robinson, John	1	3	3	..
Roland, Benjamin	1	..	2	..
Stevens, Ruben	1	1	1	2
Spring, Ann	..	1	2	2
Stone, William	1	2	2	3
Scarf, Edward	2	..	6	..
Smith, John	1	..	1	..
Shackelford, Jean	..	3	5	..
Stapleton, Levi	1	..	..	..
Stapleton, Sarah	..	4	?	..
Swab, John George	1	1	1	..
Smith, James	1	..	1	..

Heads of Families	Males over 16	Males under 16	Females	Slaves
Staggers, Barbary	1	2	1	..
Smith, Adam	1	..	1	..
Scarf, William	1	..	1	..
Scott, James	3	5	4	20
Scott, Joseph, and William Reed	3	1	3	34
Scott, Joseph (for his father's estate)	2	2	2	26
Smith, Henry	1	3	4	..
Smith, Hugh	1	1	2	..
Scison, Ebenezer	1	4	3	..
Singletary, Ebenezer	1	4	4	12
Spring, Robert	1	..	1	..
Smith, James	1	..	2	..
Small, Christopher	1	3	5	1
Sessions, John	3	2	5	..
Sessions, Wm., and Francis Martin	3	1	6	..
Sullivan, Joseph	1	2	4	..
Smith, Thomas	1	..	3	..
Staggers, John	2	2	1	..
Savage, Nathan	3	2	3	22
Stone, Austin	2	4	5	..
Snow, James	1	1	..	..
Snow, William	4	2	7	43
Spears, William	1	..	..	9
Skrine, Thomas	1	2	..	7
Scott, Alexander	2	4	2	8
Smith, Abner	1	1	5	..
Scott, John	1	3	1	10
Sparkman, Richard	1	1	3	..
Smyth, Thomas	1	..	3	..
Sheed, John	1	2	1	..
Shealds, John	3	1	2	..
Swinton, Hugh	2	2	3	..
Smith, Benjamin	1	2	1	..
Simons, Due	1	3	1	..
Smith, William	1	..	3	..
Starnes, Charles	1	4	2	..
Smith, John	1	2	1	..
Tomson, James	1	3	3	1
Turner, John	1	1	1	..
Tomson, George	3	2	3	8
Tyler, Samuel	1	..	7	..
Thomas, David	1	..	4	..
Thomas, Jesse	1	1	1	..

WILLIAMSBURG CENSUS, 1790

Heads of Families	Males over 16	Males under 16	Females	Slaves
Timmons, John	3	3	4	6
Timmons, James	1	..	2	1
Timmons, Levi	1	..	3	..
Turner, Amos	1	2	5	..
Tucker, John	1	..	..	4
Tisdale, James	1	..	1	5
Thorp, Samuel	1	2	2	5
Thomson, Alexander	1	4	4	2
Tucker, John	1	..	1	..
Thomson, Ruben	1	..	2	..
Thomson, James	2	1	1	1
Tyler, Benjamin	1	1	2	5
Taylor, Ruffin	1	2	1	15
Thomas, Alexander	1	..	..	..
Thomson, John	1	2	1	4
Turner, Ruben	1	1	4	..
Turner, Benjamin	1	1	2	..
Watrous, Abner	1	..	..	..
Whitfield, William	1	2	1	11
Wickham, Thomas J.	1	..	1	13
Wilson, Robert	1	..	..	..
White, Daniel	2	3	2	..
Williams, Hannah	1	1	2	..
Wilson, Captain William	2	3	2	..
Wilson, William	1	..	3	..
Wilson, John	1	1	5	..
Ward, James	1	2	2	..
Watson, George	3	2	..	11
Witherspoon, John	1	..	..	3
Witherspoon, Sarah	1	..	1	14
Witherspoon, Gavin, and John Perry	2	2	3	27
Do. for James Witherspoon's est.	1	3	3	31
Do. for Hugh Macauley	1	..	1	..
Watson, Hugh	1	4	3	12
Wimper, John	1	..	..	..
Wilson, John	1	1	2	10
Do. for Grace Wilson's	1	1	1	15
Witherspoon, Elizabeth	1	1	3	38
Witherspoon, Elizabeth	....	..	2	5
Do. for James Witherspoon's est.	1	3	1	21
Do. for James Grier	1	..	1	..
Walters, Jacob	1	2	2	..
Wilson, Samuel	1	1	1	15
Williams, Thomas	1	3	2	26

Heads of Families	Males over 16	Males under 16	Females	Slaves
Wood, William	1	..	1	3
Winters, Robert, and John Patterson	3	2	2	40
Wilson, William	1	..	..	1
White, George	1	1	2	22
Windom, Jesse	1	2	2	..
Wilkes, Ester	1	3	2	7
Whitacre, Isaac	1	1	3	..
Williams, William	1	1	3	1
Walker, James, and Benjamin Kuel	2	1	4	18
Whitfield, Thomas	1	2	2	..
Witherspoon, William	1	..	1	..
Walter, Patrick	1	1	3	..
Weaver, William	1	..	2	..
Wilson, David	1	1	5	19
Weatherly, Isaac	1	2	2	5
Wilson, Robert	3	2	2	21
Walker, James	1	..	4	37
Witherspoon, John	1	1	1	40
Wilson, William	2	3	2	14
White, Anthony	3	6	8	73
Witherspoon, Gavin, Jr.	1	4	7	38
Williams, John George	1	3	5	9
Westberry, William	1	4	2	5
Williams, William	3	1	2	1
Wilson, Charles	3	..	..	2
Winter, Robert	2	2	2	47
Walters, Priscilla	1	..	1	..
Wilkes, Lemuel	1	2	2	10
Young, Elizabeth	3	2	4	..
Young, William	1	1	3	..
Zuill, James	2	..	3	4

CHAPTER XV.

PRESBYTERIANISM REGNANT.

Whoever would understand the history of Williamsburg and its present life must first know its religious history. The dominant element among the original settlers of Williamsburg comes from a peculiar people whose spirit has remained unchanged in fundamental principles for more than a thousand years. In the sixth century, a colony of Irish-Scots migrated to North Britain, settled in the County Argyle, subjugated the Pictish tribe, and established there their kingdom. Ancient Caledonia has been since that day Scotland. These ancient Caledonians held the Presbyterian belief more than a thousand years before Calvin and Knox were born. Later, these Scots fell under the influence of Rome but never have until this day surrendered to its authority. Talliessin, a Latin poet who lived about 620 A. D., thus expressed the feeling of these Presbyterians in those far off ancient days: (Translation English of about a thousand years later).

> "Wo be to that priest yborn,
> That will not cleanly weed his corn,
> And preach his charge among.
> Wo be to that shepherd, I say,
> That will not watch his fold alway,
> As to his office doth belong.
> Wo be to him that doth not keep
> From Romish wolves his erring sheepe,
> With staff and weapon strong."

Calvin and Knox were both born, trained, and educated under Roman Catholic influences and were mature men before they partially embraced Presbyterian principles. The second wife of Knox was Lady Margaret Stuart, a militant Romanist. Both of these men undertook to color

Presbyterianism with their own views. Neither one of them accepted the ancient Presbyterian faith as he found it. Both of them had a wonderful influence on Presbyterianism, although results did not reach great proportions until more than a century had passed. There are yet in Scotland and in Williamsburg County, South Carolina, two factions in the Presbyterian Church, one of which is distinctly the ancient Presbyterianism, and the other the Presbyterianism growing out of the influence of John Knox and of John Calvin.

After the War of the Revolution had closed, in 1783, there were three Presbyterian Congregations functioning in Williamsburg. In two of these, the Williamsburg Presbyterian Church and the Black Mingo Presbyterian Church, the majorities held to the ancient Presbyterian idea, while in the other, the Indiantown Presbyterian Congregation, the Calvin-Knox majority obtained. These three Presbyterian Churches were the only religious organizations existing in Williamsburg in 1783. There were a handful of Episcopalians and Baptists in the Black Mingo community and a few Episcopalians along the Santee River, but more than ninety-five per centum of the people in Williamsburg were Presbyterians.

After South Carolina had adopted the Constitution of the United States in 1788, the Presbyterian Church had in Williamsburg, for the first time in its history, an unhindered opportunity to work out its own salvation. It had here, in all probability, a fairer field than it had enjoyed theretofore at any time or place in the world.

In 1783, the Williamsburg Church had sent to it, out of the patronage scheme of the Church of Scotland, the Reverend Samuel Kennedy, a native of Ireland. He was employed for a term of three years. The faction in his Church that inclined to the ancient Presbyterian doctrine of Scotland enjoyed his ministry. The Calvin-Knox faction of the congregation declared that he preached Socinianism, that he denied the Divinity of Jesus Christ, and that his sermons were more blasphemous than the sayings of infidels. During his first three years ministry, these two factions became sharply defined and each of them was enthusiastic in promoting its own idea in the matter.

When the three years time for which Mr. Kennedy had been engaged expired in 1786, the issue was drawn as to whether or not Mr. Kennedy's services as minister to the congregation should be retained. The "auld lichts" were in the majority in the congregation and so Mr. Kennedy was re-elected to serve the Church for another term of years. The "new lichts," or the minority faction, immediately withdrew and declared that no longer would it listen to a man who profaned by atheistic preaching the sanctuary which its fathers had built. The minority element said that the majority element was composed largely of settlers who had but lately come into the community, and did not represent the faith of the original founders of the Church. Since the voting in the congregation at that time was done by pew holders and many of the pew holders were not members of the Church, the minority element also charged that it had been voted out of the Church, which its fathers had founded, by men who did not even profess the true faith. The minority element could not be reconciled nor would it participate in worship in the old church. The majority element attended services conducted by the Reverend Samuel Kennedy in the old church and, while it said nothing, evidently enjoyed the situation.

Among the "auld lichts" were the McCulloughs, Strongs, Nelsons, McClarys, Flaglers, Hamiltons, Maxwells, McCants, Macauleys, Porters, Pressleys, Burgess', McGills, McKnights, McIntoshs, McDonalds, Flemings, and McElveens. Among the "new lichts," or minority faction, were the Friersons, Bradleys, Grahams, Wilsons, Witherspoons, McCulloughs, Blakelys, McBrides, Dickeys,

Ervins, Scotts, Matthews, Hendleys, and McClellands. It is interesting to note that the Witherspoons, Wilsons, Fultons, Ervins, and Blakelys of this minority element were all lineal descendants of the Reverend John Knox.

The minority element, immediately after its withdrawal from the old congregation, erected another church on the same plot of ground about fifty yards east of the old church. For some months, these two congregations, that of the old Williamsburg Church and that of the new church, worshiped in their respective buildings. These two congregations held their services at the same hour every Sunday morning, and while no member of either congregation would defile his feet by touching a grain of sand on the ground by common consent controlled by the other, yet when the congregation in one of these churches began to pray, the congregation in the other would immediately begin to sing an old familiar hymn,—and those were days when hymns were sung. One old sinner, who lived more than a half mile from the church at this time, when reproached by his minister for not attending, replied, "I sit on my piazza every Sunday morning during the services and can hear distinctly every word preached, prayed or sung."

The feeling between these two congregations, within a very few months, grew so intense, that one night in August, 1786, the minority element took about one hundred slaves to the old church, tore it down, and removed even its foundations from the spot. They carried the pulpit of the old church three miles in the country and hid it in Samuel McClelland's hay loft. The minority element claimed that its fathers had built this old church and its act in tearing it down was an act of virtue, for that within its sacred walls the name of Christ was being notoriously profaned. Just exactly what the "auld lichts" said when early that morning they saw nothing where their church had stood is left to the imagination.

The Kennedy faction brought action in the Courts at Georgetown against the individuals composing this minority element that had destroyed its church. The Courts held that the title to the property of the church obtained in the Kennedy faction and the seceding faction that had destroyed the church was forced to pay in full for the damage it had done. The old Williamsburg Congregation then rebuilt its church on the same spot the original had stood.

From 1786 until 1789, the Reverend Samuel Kennedy was minister of the ancient Williamsburg Church, from which time until 1792 the congregation was unsupplied. In that year, the Reverend James Malcolmson of Belfast, Ireland, was called. He served the Williamsburg Church until 1804, when he went to Charleston. Dr. Malcolmson had received the title of Doctor of Medicine from the University at Edinburgh and was a licensed physician. He practiced medicine in his congregation. In addition to his pastoral charge and his practice of medicine, he taught a large grammar school at Kingstree and was the moving spirit in the establishment of the Academy in Kingstree. The Reverend James Malcolmson, Theodore Gourdin, Robert Witherspoon, James Davis, John Nesmith, and John Frierson were incorporated by the General Assembly of South Carolina, December 19, 1795, as trustees of the Williamsburg Academy and were empowered to raise by lotteries a sum not exceeding five thousand dollars to defray the necessary building expenses of the school. From this money raised by lotteries, this board of trustees erected an academy building at the head of Bay Street. Dr. Malcolmson possessed a pleasing personality and was probably one of the ablest men who ever preached in Williamsburg. He died of yellow fever in Charleston in 1804, in the thirty-sixth year of his age.

From 1804 until 1819, the Williamsburg Church remained without a minister, although the Reverend William Knox, of the Black Mingo Church, and other ministers of the Church of Scotland preached in the church and the Elders kept up the organization. In 1819, the Reverend John Covert, a native of New York and a graduate of Princeton Theological Seminary, who had been serving the Indiantown and the Bethel Congregations most acceptably for two years, withdrew from the Presbytery of South Carolina and resigned as minister of the Bethel and Indiantown Churches. He was then ordained by the Congregational Association of South Carolina "in the Independent Order" that he might be qualified to become the minister of the old Williamsburg Congregation.

This reordination of Mr. Covert "in the Independent Order" after he had been ordained by the American Presbyterian Church, that he might become minister of the old Williamsburg Presbyterian Church, is a most significant fact. It throws much light on the controversy existing between the two factions in the Williamsburg Congregation. Mr. Covert brought life and vigor into the old Williamsburg Congregation, although he died in 1822 after having served the congregation for but a short period. He was a young man of force and played well the difficult part he had. After the death of Mr. Covert, the old Williamsburg Church had no minister until 1828.

The minority faction that had seceded from the old Williamsburg Church in 1786, on account of the retention of the Reverend Samuel Kennedy as minister and which had built its church across the road about fifty yards from the original church, called its organization the Williamsburg Presbyterian Congregation until 1803. So, from 1786 until 1803, there were two Presbyterian churches at Kingstree, within fifty yards of each other, each one claiming the rights of the ancient Williamsburg Congregation and denominating itself by the original name.

The minority element, immediately after its secession in 1786, united with the Presbytery of South Carolina and petitioned that body for the services of a minister, and the Reverend Thomas Reece was secured for this Church one Sunday in each month. In 1788, Reverend James Edwards, Reverend Robert McCullough, and the Reverend Thomas Reece each preached one Sunday in a month at this church. In 1789, the Reverend Robert Finley preached one Sunday each month. In October, 1789, the Reverend James W. Stephenson became minister for this church at the King's Tree and the Indiantown Church. This faction in the Williamsburg Church and the Indiantown Church belonged to the Presbytery of South Carolina and were united in their efforts as well as their faith in the Trinity.

Dr. Stephenson served this part of the Williamsburg Congregation, known after 1803 as the Bethel Congregation, and the Indiantown Congregation, for nineteen years, and was possibly the most influential minister who ever lived in Williamsburg. He was born of Scotch-Irish stock in Augusta County, Virginia, in 1756. Soon after that time, his parents moved to the old Lancaster District, South Carolina, and settled near old Waxhaw Church. He was educated at Mount Zion College and taught school in the vicinity of old Waxhaw Church. President Andrew Jackson was one of his pupils. He was a valiant soldier under General Sumter in the Revolution and participated in the battles at Blackstock, Hanging Rock, and other engagements.

When Dr. Stephenson served the Bethel faction of the Williamsburg Congregation, he found a most difficult task. His congregation and another congregation of the same name had been at daggers' points for about four years. The individuals composing these two congregations lived in the same community, but a member of one would have no relations whatsoever with a member of the other. This condition continued all during Dr. Stephenson's ministry in

Williamsburg. He showed great tact and discretion in handling the complicated condition.

"In the reproval of vice, as well as its removal, Mr. Stephenson was not less successful than in the more welcome functions of his office. A number of pernicious practices were found prevalent in the congregations when he entered upon his duties in them, which he felt conscientiously bound to correct, trusting to God for the consequences. The principal of these were dancing, horse-racing, and treating at funerals. In the last century, the practice of drinking at the burial of the dead prevailed to a melancholy extent; and not a few instances are given of ministers being disciplined for indulging too freely on such occasions. And too frequently the living were not sufficiently sober to follow with becoming decorum their departed friends to the grave. The people, convinced by the warning voice of their pastor, put an end to the practice. Another monster evil which he was successful in opposing was horse racing, usually followed by music and dancing, and kindred amusements. Regarding these as wholly inconsistent with Christian character, he ceased not to denounce them as such until they were mostly discontinued. And it is but justice to state, that to Mr. Stephenson belongs the honor, so far as it is known, of commencing, in this part of the country, the benevolent work of evangelizing the negroes and preventing them from laboring on the Sabbath for themselves as they had to generally been permited to do." (Howe's History of the Presbyterian Church, page 586.)

Indiantown Presbyterian Church and the Bethel faction of the Williamsburg Presbyterian Congregation both promoted American Presbyterian principles and had the same minister from 1790, until 1828. These two churches were so closely related in faith and works for all this period that they may be considered together. It will be recalled that the Indiantown Church was destroyed by the Tories under the command of Major Wemyss in 1780. The congregation assembled for worship until 1783, the close of the War, under bush arbors where the original church had stood. One of the first cares of this congregation at the close of the War was the rebuilding of its church. The Reverend Thomas Hill supplied it in 1783 and 1784; the Reverend Thomas Reese in 1787; the Reverend Robert McCollough in 1788, and the Reverend Robert Finley in 1789, when Dr. Stephenson took charge of the congregation. Under the ministry of Dr. Stephenson, the Bethel Church and the Indiantown Church grew in numbers and influence. In 1802, the Bethel Church had one hundred and four communicants and the Indiantown Church had ninety-six.

In 1803, the Bethel faction secured three acres of land from the estate of James Witherspoon, Jr., on the north side of the road leading from Kingstree to Cedar Swamp, one mile east of the present Williamsburg Court House, whereon it built the Bethel Church. When this building had been completed, this faction abandoned the Church it had built in 1786 across the road from the old Williamsburg Church and worshipped thereafter in its new sanctuary. The heads of families of the Bethel Congregation in 1803 were as follows: Joseph McKee, Robert Frierson, Sr., James Bradley, John Graham, Samuel Wilson, John Wilson, John Frierson, Sr., Robert P. Witherspoon, Gavin Witherspoon, William Frierson, Sr., James McBride, Elias Frierson, Joseph Witherspoon, William McElroy, William McCullough, William Dobbin, James Blakely, James Witherspoon, John Blakely, Jennett Blakely, Margaret Frierson, Samuel Frierson, William Frierson, Mary Fleming, James Armstrong, Moses J. Frierson, Robert Frierson, Jr., John Arnett, John Frierson, Jr., William Frierson, Jr., David Frierson, John Dickey, Paul Fulton, Joshua Frierson, George Frierson, David McClary, Jane Ervin, John Scott, William Wilson,

Robert L. Witherspoon, Isaac Matthews, John Matthews, Jr., John Fulton, Robert Frierson, (son of Robert), Thomas Stephenson, Robert Witherspoon, Elizabeth Witherspoon, John Knox, Elizabeth Heathly, and Thomas Witherspoon.

This Bethel Congregation was composed of markedly pious people. While they were Puritanic in their conceptions of life, they were progressive in spirit. They organized and promoted the first Sunday School and the first Bible Society in Williamsburg and fostered many new ideas in religious worship which now prevail. Out of this congregation came many exceptionally religious men and women who helped in a large measure to direct the saner religious thought of that day.

The intensity of the unpleasant feeling existing between the Bethel and the Williamsburg Congregations was so repulsive to the Bethel Congregation that a large majority of it migrated from this section. From 1805 until 1815, a great many of them moved into Marion and Sumter Districts in South Carolina; some went to Georgia and others to Alabama.

On March 25, 1805, Moses B. Frierson and family, James Armstrong and family, James Blakely and family, Paul Fulton and family, members of the Bethel Congregation and part of the Reverend James Stephenson's charge, emigrated to Maury County, Tennessee, and there settled on lands purchased from the heirs of General Green. On March 6, 1806, the following families from the Bethel Congregation followed: John Dickey, Esq., and family; Mrs. Margaret Frierson and children; Mrs. Janette Blakely and children; Samuel Frierson and family; Thomas Stephenson and family; William Frierson and family; William J. Frierson and family; Samuel Witherspoon and family; Mrs. Mary Fleming and children; and John W. Stephenson and family. A little later, Robert Frierson, Joshua Frierson, and Samuel Mayes and their families left Williamsburg and settled with their friends in Tennessee. The Reverend James W. Stephenson, pastor of Bethel and Indiantown Churches, resigned his charges in Williamsburg and became the pastor of that part of his flock that had settled in Tennessee. These people and their descendants have since that time played a most substantial and a worthily conspicuous part in the development of Tennessee.

The Reverend Andrew Flynn succeeded Mr. Stephenson as pastor of Bethel and Indiantown Churches in 1808. Mr. Flynn was succeeded within less than a year by the Reverend Daniel Brown. At the same time Mr. Brown was pastor of the Indiantown Church. He served these two congregations for about ten years. He did signal service Christianizing negro slaves and bettering their conditions. He fell dead on his way between Indiantown and Bethel Churches. On his person was found $425.00 in currency, which was an enormous amount of money for any man to have in possession at that time.

In 1818, the Reverend Robert Wilson James, a graduate of South Carolina College and of Princeton and a grandson of Major John James, was chosen as pastor of the Bethel and Indiantown Churches. He was ordained in 1819.

The elders of the Bethel Church, prior to the ministry of Mr. James, were: Robert Frierson, Samuel Frierson, Dr. John Graham, Samuel Wilson, John Wilson, William Wilson, and Thomas Witherspoon. When Mr. James began his ministry, of these Samuel Wilson, William Wilson, Robert Frierson, and Thomas Witherspoon were still living and these were added by ordination to the Session: David McClary, Robert I. Wilson, Samuel E. Fulton, Robert S. Witherspoon, and I. B. Witherspoon. Bethel and Indiantown Churches were served by the Reverend Robert W. James until 1827, when he removed to Salem Black River Church, Sumter District.

From 1786 until 1828 the Williamsburg Congregation was divided. Great bitterness between the congregations of Williamsburg and Bethel made social relations so unpleasant that they were impossible. In 1802, fifteen years after the disunion, a great camp meeting was held by the Reverend James W. Stephenson and others at the Sandhills, about three miles west of Kingstree, yet the burning eloquence of these powerful preachers even at such a time was not able to sear deeper into the souls of these religious feudists than their old hate. It is said that members of both congregations attended this camp meeting, but, even in moments of supreme religious ecstasy, no member of the one would touch or speak to the other, nor would the slave of the one regard the slave of the other.

The faithful labors of the Reverend Mr. James and the Reverend William Wilson, both of the blood of both factions and men of power, had much to do with the failing of the hate between these two congregations. The venarable John McClary seemed to hold the confidence, respect, and veneration of both congregations, the Bethel and the Williamsburg. He alone was a member of each of the churches and a ruling elder in both of them. In 1828, after a separation of forty-two years, he secured the consent of both congregations to attend and hear a sermon in the old Williamsburg Church on Tuesday, June 15, 1828. Mr. McClary on the Sunday preceding had induced the Session of Elders of the Bethel Church to propose terms of union to the Williamsburg Church. The Williamsburg Church immediately thereafter invited the the Bethel Congregation to unite with them in hearing Mr. Ervin's sermon on Tuesday. After Mr. Ervin's sermon, Mr. McClary was called to the chair and a union of the two congregations was effected without a dissenting vote. The property rights of the Williamsburg Congregation were retained and the ecclesiastical connection of the Bethel Congregation with the Presbytery of South Carolina was accepted by the reunited congregation. The Williamsburg Congregation had theretofore held its connection directly with the Church of Scotland.

Here follows a copy of the minutes of the joint meeting of the Williamsburg and the Bethel Congregations, when union was effected:

"At a Meeting of the Members of the old Presbyterian Church and the Members of the Bethel Church held at the old church on Tuesday, the 17th June, 1828, there being a Majority of the Members of each congregation present, they proceeded to business. John McClary, Esq., was appointed chairman and R. G. Ferrell, secretary.

"1st Resolved that these two churches become United and that the two become one Congregation and that they Worship in the old or original Church.

"2nd Resolved that this Congregation Join with the Indiantown Congregation and employ a Minister, and the Minister so employed Preach one half of his time in this Church and the other half in the Indiantown Church.

"3rd Resolved that Mr. William Wilson, Colonel William Salters, Samuel E. Fulton, Isaac Nelson, Sr., Dr. James Bradley, and H. D. Shaw be a Committee to Inform the Reverend John McKee Ervin that we wish to give him a call as our Pastor for one half of his time.

"4th Resolved that the Members of this Congregation do meet at the Church on the last Saturday in this Month in order to regulate the business of the Church."

"At a Meeting of the Members of the Church on Saturday, the 28th June, 1828. The Committee appointed to say to the Reverend John M. Ervin that we intended giving him a call as our Pastor report that they have done so and that they think there is a prospect of our getting him.

"1st Resolved that H. D. Shaw, Dr. James Bradley, Samuel E. Fulton, Thomas Duke, and Robert G. Ferrell be appointed a Committee to meet the Indiantown Committee to give the Reverend John McKee Ervin a call as our Minister.

"2nd Resolved that Robert Strong, Daniel Frierson, and Isaac Nelson, Sr., be a Committee to regulate the Seats of the Church and to make what repairs to the Church they may find necessary.

"3rd Resolved that the Committee appointed to meet the Indiantown Committee be authorized to inform the Reverend John M. Ervin that this Congregation will give him three hundred and fifty dollars for the half of his time with the use of the Glebe Lands of this Church should he prefer living on them to living in Indiantown.

"4th Resolved that the salary of the Minister be raised by subscription.

"5th Resolved that the Committee appointed to regulate the Seats of the Church cause all the seats to be numbered and that the heads of families draw their numbers with this exception, that is, when families are small, the Committee shall have to themselves the power of putting two in one seat.

"6th Resolved that Colonel William Salters, Captain William S. Brockinton, Isaac Nelson, Jr., and D. H. McClary be trustees for the said congregation.

"7th Resolved that Captain Isaac Nelson be appointed treasurer.

"8th Resolved that the trustees be authorized to invite a minister to preach occasionally in our Church until the Reverend John M. Ervin take charge of the Congregation, should he accept our call, and that the ministers so invited by the trustees be paid by the congregation five dollars for each sermon preached by them.

"Adjourned—R. G. Ferrell, Secretary."

It is interesting to note that Captain William S. Brockinton was not a member of this or of any other church.

He was, however, a pew holder in the church, and by virtue of that fact was eligible for appointment as trustee.

There were several Presbyterian Churches in the territory surrounding Williamsburg that had considerable influence on this district during the period between 1780 and 1830. These congregations had been organized by people migrating from Williamsburg; and, notwithstanding the condition of what they called roads, kept up communication with their friends and relatives in this district. Of these churches, Salem Black River in the Sumter District and Hopewell and Aimwell on the Pee Dee had been founded between 1760 and 1770 and were large and aggressive churches. They were about forty miles from the King's Tree. This great distance meant much at that time, although the congregations of these churches usually came to Williamsburg to attend spring and fall communion services and camp meetings.

In September, 1801, John Witherspoon, John Witherspoon, Jr., Archibald Knox, William McIntosh, Thomas Rhodus, Daniel Epps, John McFadden, Thomas McFadden, and Samuel Fleming met at the home of Mrs. Mary Conyers, who lived about half way between the Williamsburg Church and the Salem Black River Church, and organized a Presbyterian Congregation for their community. John Witherspoon, John Witherspoon, Jr., and Archibald Knox were named as its first elders. On November 10, 1802, the building was completed and called Midway because it was half way between the two well known churches just named. The Reverend C. G. McWhorter gave one-fourth of his time to this new church.

In 1809, Midway had twelve members. That year the Reverend John Cousar preached two Sundays every month at Midway and the other two at the Brewington Church. Midway Church is located on the northeastern branch of Black River in what is now Clarendon County. In 1811, the Brewington Presbyterian Church, south of the southwestern branch of Black River, was built. The Nelson, Plowden, Pendergrass, and Montgomery families composed its membership. Midway and the Brewington churches grew rapidly in strength. In 1829, Midway had one hundred forty-one members and Brewington one hundred fourteen. These two communities were at that time enjoying much material prosperity. Probably half of the membership in these two churches lived in Williamsburg District.

Lower Saint Mark's Church (Protestant Episcopal) was built in 1809 on the south side of the Santee road where it was crossed by what is now the Clarendon-Williamsburg County line. In this section, there lived many descendants of French Huguenot families and many of English and Scotch descent who had always been conformists in religion and were communicants of the Church of England. The Friersons, Lesesnes, Keels, McDonalds, Connors, Olivers, Gourdins, Canteys, Cordes, and Doughtys built this Lower Saint Mark's Church. The land for the site was donated by Charles Frederick Lesesne. William Doughty, Major William McDonald, and Joseph Francis Cantey were the first lay readers in this church. Lower Saint Mark's had difficulty in all its history in securing ministers. However, it frequently had services conducted by visiting priests of the Church. In 1825, Bishop Bowen confirmed the following as communicants of this Church: Richard Keels, Archibald McDonald, William J. R. Cantey, Miss Susan McDonald (Mrs. John L. Felder), Miss Laura McDonald (Mrs. Henry B. Singleton), and Miss Mary M. Keels (Mrs. A. C. McKnight).

Frequently, Methodist ministers on the Santee Circuit held services in this church. In 1835, Charles Lesesne, a vestryman, invited the Reverend John R. Pucket, the junior Methodist preacher on the Santee Circuit, to preach regularly at Saint Mark's; and, from that time,

Saint Mark's became a part of the Santee Circuit, Methodist Episcopal Church, and nearly all of its communicants became members of the Methodist Episcopal Church. However, J. W. Keels, who died in 1865, retained his membership in Saint Mark's Episcopal Church until the time of his death. The silver christening basin used in Saint Mark's Church, while it belonged to the Protestant Episcopal Church, was left in the possession of Charles Lesesne, surviving vestryman, in 1835. On this basin was engraved, "Presented the 12th of January, 1820, to Lower Saint Mark's Church, Williamsburgh, by Mrs. Mary Grimke Ward." (These statements about Lower St. Mark's Church were taken from the History of St. Mark's Church, by Dr. James M. Burgess.)

On February 13, 1785, Bishop Francis Asbury, under the guidance of the Reverend Jesse Lee and the Reverend Henry Willis, entered South Carolina at Cheraw. The party spent some time in prayer in Saint David's Church and proceeded on its journey to Long Bluff Court House, thence to Mr. Kimbrough's, thence across Lynch's Creek, Black Mingo, and Black River, and by the usual road of travel to Georgetown, where they arrived on February 23. On March 13, the party travelled from Georgetown to the King's Tree and visited at Mr. Durant's. From the King's Tree, Bishop Asbury went to Wilmington, North Carolina. The next year, Bishop Asbury crossed over Lynch's Creek into Williamsburg and proceeded along the way he had made the year before to Georgetown. He writes, in his diary, "We crossed Lynch's Creek and wet my books coming to Black Mingo where we were lodged at a tavern and were well used, sleeping upstairs. I was afraid, if not the roof, the shingles would be taken away with the wind. On Saturday, January 7, I preached at Georgetown twice to about eighty people each time. Georgetown is a poor place for religion." From Georgetown, Bishop Asbury went to the vicinity of Lenud's Ferry where he was entertained at the home of Thomas Boone and also at Robert Sutton's. From that point, he preached along the Santee River road to Murray's Ferry, where he was entertained at the homes of Isaac Keels and of Darby Pendergrass. After remaining in the vicinity of Murray's Ferry for a few days, he proceeded on his way to Charleston.

Bishop Asbury made many visits to South Carolina during the next thirty years and usually followed this same route through Williamsburg. He preached a new doctrine and prepared the way for a new church. The part of Williamsburg that he usually visited along what is now the Georgetown-Williamsburg County line and the Santee River were the only portions at that time not completely within the control of the Presbyterian Church; and these outlying sections along which his journey lay were inhabited by people who had been communicants of the Church of England. Even these people did not look upon this great organizer with anything like favor. The reception which he received at the King's Tree on his only visit to this Presbyterian territory was very much like that accorded a Mormon missionary in Kingstree in the year 1923.

Even among the Episcopalians, Bishop Asbury was hardly welcome, and but few homes on his route would receive him. However, Samuel Haselden, who lived on Muddy Creek in the northeastern corner of Williamsburg, was always glad to entertain him and so were Robert Sutton, of Suttons, and Isaac Keels and Darby Pendergrass, of Murray's Ferry.

With the coming of Bishop Asbury into South Carolina, there came the Methodist Episcopal Church. When he came into Williamsburg, the Methodist denomination was practically unknown in these parts. He preached and prayed and labored for many years without realizing what results would come from his ministry. Wherever he went, he conducted services whenever permitted. He sent missionaries and circuit riders into this territory for nearly forty years before there was a Methodist Church within the limits of Williamsburg District.

On many of these missionary journeys of Bishop Asbury through Williamsburg, he records interesting experiences. In 1787, he writes of his attempting to cross at Murray's Ferry. "In one place," he says, "the planters had laid down about a hundred logs of wood, which they called puncheons, in order to mend the road. These, owing to the heavy rains, were loosened and floated on the water which covered the road. We were obliged to turn back into the dark, miserable road until we arrived at the house of a little planter who very kindly took us in and gave us a roasted turkey for our supper and the best beds in his house to lie on." "On March 30, 1804, we lodged at Henry Britton's, where we were most kindly entertained."

"Saturday, November 14, 1805, I committed the remains of Elijah Rembert to the dust. He was sixty-two years old and for the last sixteen years of his life had been a member of our society. There is a revival in the society here, so much for camp meetings. I am now in the fortieth year of my labor in the ministry, thirty-four years of my time having been spent in America."

"October 27, 1806, we made twenty-five miles to Murray's Ferry. We were five hours in the swamp. Heat, mosquitoes, and gallinippers—plenty. Monday, January 1, 1810, we crossed Potato Ferry. Missing our way, we dropped in upon Mr. John Graham. He was a Presbyterian, but showed us much kindness. December 16, 1810, I visited Thomas Boone. His father was the first to entertain me at lower Santee Ferry." Bishop Asbury often refers to Theodore Gourdin, "that excellent gentleman who owns all the ferries on Black River."

From 1785, when Bishop Asbury came into Williamsburg, until 1820, there was no Methodist Church in Williamsburg, but, during all that time, it was kept on Methodist circuits, and Methodist circuit riders preached and prayed and sang in private homes wherever they were received, in barns on plantations wherever they were permitted, in bush arbors erected for them and most frequently at cross roads gatherings. Up to 1820, there were very few men in this district who would admit without half apology that they belonged to a Methodist Society. It was not a popular doctrine that Bishop Asbury and his followers preached. It required that men and women walk in the straight and narrow way. It had no history.

In 1820, Ebenezer Methodist Church was built on Muddy Creek in Williamsburg on the land of Samuel Haselden. When Mr. Haselden died in 1822, he left in his will two acres of land on which this church was located to the Methodist Episcopal Church. This was the first parcel of land that the Methodist Church ever owned in Williamsburg District. Samuel Haselden was one of the men in Williamsburg who received Bishop Asbury kindly from his first visit. This old Ebenezer Church has maintained its organization until the present day and is now one of the churches of the Hemingway Circuit.

In 1825, Robert Sutton gave the following deed which is recorded in Book C at page 229, Williamsburg County Registry. "State of South Carolina. To all people to whom these presents shall come: Know ye, that I, Robert Sutton, of Williamsburg District in the State aforesaid, Planter, for and in consideration of the love, good will, and affection which I have and do bear towards the Methodists of this place, have given, granted and by these presents do freely give and grant for the use of the Methodists of this place, one hundred yards square, whereon the new Meeting House is now building, in Williamsburgh District, and State aforesaid, butting and bounding about Southeast on land belonging to the Estate of Duplessus Michau, about Southwest on the public road and on all other sides of lands of my own, now being my right and property in district aforesaid: I do hereby nominate and appoint my friends Samuel Perdreau, Dr. William J. Buford, John Perdreau, and Edward Peter Perret, trustees, to whom I leave the said one hundred yards square of land in trust for the use of the said Methodist Society of this place; and, in case of the death of one of the Trustees, the others are hereby authorized to appoint another in his room; and, in case the house wants repair, they may have timber off my adjoining land to repair said house as long as the property remains mine or the right of my heirs. July 5, 1825." Signed by Robert Sutton. Witnessed by Samuel Guild, Sarah Tamplet, and Mary C. Michau.

In 1800, the religious camp meeting fever began in Kentucky. It reached Kingstree in 1803, when one was held at the Sandhills about three miles west of Kingstree. Dr. Stephenson had been preaching to the Bethel Congregation in Kingstree for thirteen years and had great influence over its people. He was assisted by Dr. John Brown, of the Waxhaw Church, who had just finished a wonderful camp meeting at Waxhaw; Reverend Duncan Brown of Hopewell; and the Reverend C. G. McWhorter of Salem. Crowds flocked to this camp meeting. They came in wagons loaded with provisions and fitted up for temporary lodging. Dr. Stephenson opened the meeting with a sermon in explanation and defense of the revival. At these revivals, excitement became intense and was attended in many cases with remarkable bodily contortions as well as trance conditions. These pulpit orators preached the "Day of Wrath" with such fearful eloquence that frequently strong men and women lost control of themselves and did all manner of things under the hypnotic spell.

Dr. Malcolmson was then pastor of the old Williamsburg Church. It will be remembered that the Williamsburg Congregation and the Bethel Congregation, the two factions of the old Williamsburg Congregation, were at that time exceedingly hostile toward each other. Dr. Malcolmson disapproved these revivals and did not conceal his contempt for so much religious frenzy.

Dr. Stephenson's camp meeting was a great success from the attendance standpoint as well as for the intensity of emotion shown by the people attending. Similar camp meetings were held in many parts of South Carolina and by the Methodist denomination as well as the Presbyterian for many years. One of these camp meetings held in the summer of 1806 at Remberts was attended by William Capers, afterwards a Bishop in the Methodist Church. The following description which he gives applies to practically all of them held in this section at that time.

"The number of people occupying tents was much greater than it had been at the two previous meetings of the same kind in 1802 and 1803, in that neighborhood, both of which I had attended with my uncle's family, and at which wagons and awnings made of coverlets and blankets were mostly relied on in place of tents. The tents too (of this meeting in 1806), though much smaller and less commodious than in later years, were larger and better than at the former meetings. But, still, at the tents as well as at the wagons of the camp, there was very little cooking done, but every one fed on cold provisions, or at least cold meats. Compared to those first two camp meetings, this one differed also in the more important respects of management and the phases of the work of God. At the first one (1802), particularly (which was held on McGirt's Branch, below the point where the Statesburg and Darlington road crosses it), I recollected little that looked like management. There were two stands for preaching, at a distance of about two hundred yards apart; and sometimes there was preaching at one, sometimes at the other, and sometimes at both simultaneously. This was evidently a bad arrangement, for I remember seeing the people running hastily from one place to the other as some sudden gush of feeling vented itself aloud, and perhaps with strange bodily exercises, called their attention off. As to the times of preaching, I think there were not any stated hours, but it was left to circumstances; sometimes oftener, sometimes more seldom. The whole camp was called up by blowing a horn at the break of day; before sunrise it was blown again, and I doubt if after that there were any regular hours for the services of the meeting. But what was most remarkable both at this camp meeting and the following one, a year afterward (1803), as distinguishing them from the present meeting of 1806, and much more from later camp meetings, was the strange and unaccountable bodily exercises which prevailed there. In some instances, persons who were not before known to be at all religious, or under any particular concern about it, would suddenly fall to the ground and become strangely convulsed with what was called the jerks; the head and neck, and sometimes the body also, moving backward and forward with spasmodic violence, and so rapidly that the plaited hair of a woman's head might be heard to crack. This exercise was not peculiar to feeble persons, nor to either sex, but, on the contrary, was most frequent to the strong and athletic, whether men or women. I never knew it among children, nor very old persons. In other cases, persons falling down would appear senseless, and almost lifeless, for hours together; lying motionless at full length on the ground, and almost as pale as corpses. And then there was the jumping exercise, which sometimes approximated dancing, in which several persons might be standing perfectly erect, and spring upward without seeming to bend a joint of their bodies. Such exercises were scarcely, if at all, present among the same people at the camp meeting of 1806, and yet this camp meeting was not less remarkable than the former ones, and very much more so than any I have attended in later years, for the suddenness with which sinners of every description were awakened, and the overwhelming force of their convictions, bearing them instantly down to their knees, if not to the ground, crying for mercy. At this meeting I became clearly convinced that there was an actual, veritable power of God's grace in persons then before me, and who were known to me, by which they were brought to repentance and a new life; and that with respect to the latter (a state of regeneration and grace), the evidence of their possessing it was as full and satisfactory as it was that they had been brought to feel the guilt and condemnation of their sins. I did not fall at any time, as I saw others do, but with the conviction clear to my apprehension as to what was the true character of the work before me, that it was of God, while I feared greatly, I could not but desire that I might become a partaker of the benefit. Still I kept myself aloof, I knew not why."

About 1820, Isaac Carraway, wheelwright and carpenter, and a handful of Free Will Baptists, Noah Floyd, Jesse Floyd, Sam McKenzie, John James Matthews, Jesse Osborn, William Brown, Muldrow Kennedy, John Hutson, Joe Hutson, and Coker Flowers, built Pine Grove Church in the northwestern corner of Williamsburg and this congregation and their descendants have worshipped there until this day. The Reverend Sam McKenzie was its first regular minister. When this Pine Grove Church was erected, there were no sawmills in that section. In fact, most primitive conditions obtained. The church was built of pine logs drawn to the spot by means of ox-carts. The tires on these old ox-carts were made of white oak slats affixed to the rims with handmade blacksmith shop nails. The spirit which has kept alive the worship of this congregation for more than a century most forcefully appeals to one who knows it. The ministers who have preached in this church have received but little monetary reward, yet the sacred fires have been kept continuously burning.

There were a very few of the missionary Baptist faith in Williamsburg until 1770, and these were nearly all of the blood of William Screven and lived in the vicinity of Black Mingo. Until this time, they had no house of worship in the district. From the building of the Black Mingo Congregational Church in 1726, visiting ministers of that denomination had frequently preached in that church and some people in the section had always held to the belief that immersion was the only scriptural mode of baptism. Among the Baptist preachers from time to time holding services in that community up to 1830, were the Reverend Elisha Screven, Reverend Phillip James, Reverend John Brown, Reverend Joshua Edwards, Reverend Robert Williams, Reverend Nicholas Bedgegood, Reverend Elhannan Winchester, Reverend Joseph Reese, Reverend Oliver Hart, Reverend John Botsford, Reverend John Gano, Reverend Jeremiah Dargan, and the Reverend Richard Furman.

About 1810, there came to Black Mingo from Georgetown a boy, by name, Cleland Belin. His mother had died and his father had married again. Cleland did not consider his stepmother's treatment worthy to hold him at his father's house, so he ran away and lived thenceforth at Willtown in the home of his uncle, John Screven. Cleland Belin became a Baptist, and for more than fifty years, the Baptist denomination at Black Mingo centered in him. About 1820, the Baptists built a small meeting house near Willtown; and for many years the little congregation worshipped in this building and baptized their candidates for admission in Black Mingo.

About 1820, John R. Easterling came from Charleston to Williamsburg and purchased a mill site from R. G. Ferrell on Poplar Hill Swamp, where he established a grist and a saw mill. Mr. Easterling was a man of intelligence and piety and as soon as he had made his family comfortable, began a movement for the building of a church. Men of all denominations in that community, whether members of a church or not, assisted him. The building committee was composed of John R. Easterling, William Belin, and Reverend Jeremiah Russell. It was the plan of these people to erect a community church where all denominations might worship and that any denomination might use the building when not in service for another. The rule "first come, first served" was adopted and held for many years.

This building committee applied to Colonel David D. Wilson, who owned the land in that vicinity, and who presented them with the lot on which the Union Church was first built and gave them a liberal money subscription. Colonel Wilson was an elder in the Indiantown Church and a militant Presbyterian as well as a man of exceptional force and personality. Benjamin Britton subscribed liberally and aided in many ways. He was a Methodist, one of the first Methodists of wealth and influence in Williamsburg. Captain John Dozier gave of his means and assisted the building of the church in many ways.. He was an enthusiastic member of the Protestant Episcopal Church. Cleland Belin, the Arch-Baptist of his day, a man of remarkable natural ability and of much wealth, made contributions. Among the others assisting were Captain John Graham, Henry Smith, Matthew Bellune, Thomas McConnell, Richard Cribb, and the Coachmans, Russells, and Greenes.

Of the contributors to the building of this Union Church, the Episcopalians were the most numerous, but all four of the denominations were well represented on the subscription list. This Union Church was used in common by these four denominations for many years. Later it became a Methodist Church. All records and tradition concerning this period indicate that this church played a beautiful part in the community and that all denominations worked in it for the glory of God and the good of the people.

In 1830, there were, in Williamsburg District, the following living churches: The Williamsburg Presbyterian Church, the Indiantown Presbyterian Church, the Willtown Baptist Church, the Ebenezer Methodist Church on Mill Branch, Suttons Methodist Church, and the Pine Grove Free Will Baptist Church. The Williamsburg Presbyterian Congregation and the Indiantown Presbyterian Congregation included and controlled fully ninety-five per centum of the population of the district. The other four churches had very few members and but nominal influence. The Presbyterian Congregations outside of Williamsburg and within the surrounding country were composed largely of people who had been connected with the Williamsburg and the Indiantown Churches, were of like religious principles, and loyally supplemented these two Williamsburg Churches in all of their undertakings.

The Presbyterian denomination felt that this County was its very own and its communicants labored with a crusader's zeal to make its conquests complete and to control the territory forever. The Methodist Churches in the district were small. Very few people regarded the Methodists or the Baptists seriously, and still fewer admitted membership in their societies, as the churches were called.

In 1828, the Reverend John M. Ervin began his pastorate at the Williamsburg Church and the Indiantown Church. He divided his time between them. Mr. Ervin was born in Mecklenburg County, North Carolina, in 1769. His parents were Presbyterians of the "straitest sect." Indeed, it is traditional that the Ervin family has produced Presbyterian elders and ministers in every generation, since the memory of man runneth not to the contrary.

Mr. Ervin was a strong man. He believed that the one way to God was through the Presbyterian Church, and the errors which he made were due most largely to this delusion. He practiced and promoted the belief that the Presbyterian Church should determine the temporal as well as the spiritual affairs of the district. When he came to Williamsburg and Indiantown, he found these Presbyterian Churches conditioned for dominating. He surveyed the field and made well his plans. With such a preponderance of Presbyterians in the district, he thought it needless to use tact or discretion, but sought to make the session of elders in his two churches the supreme arbiters of their respective communities. Mr. Ervin had then a remarkable session of elders in each of his two churches. The elders of the Williamsburg Church were Daniel Frierson, Henry D. Shaw, Isaac Nelson, John McClary, and James E. Fulton. The elders of the Indiantown Church were George Barr, George McCutchen, David D. Wilson, and Samuel J. Wilson. It is believed that no two stronger committees of men in any capacity, religious or secular, ever labored in this district.

CHAPTER XVI.

WILLIAMSBURG TAXPAYERS, 1811.

There is copied on the fly leaves of Book B, Williamsburg District Registry, in the office of the Clerk of Court of Common Pleas, a list of the taxpayers in the district in 1811, with the amount levied on each individual. The taxes assessed at that time on the property in this district probably indicates more nearly the relative wealth of the men of the district than the tax list of 1923 would show the wealth of the several men of Williamsburg at such time.

Theodore Gourdin paid that year $158.10 in taxes; Francis Cordes, $56.89; James Burgess, $35.52; Stephen Miller, Jr., $27.22; Moses Glover, $24.99; William McDonald, $24.49. The man who paid next in amount was Isaac Matthews, $19.77. There were only fifty-three in the district then whose taxes were more than $10.00 a year. These fifty-three were wealthy. A man who paid $5.00 to support the government in 1811 had little trouble in keeping the wolf from the door.

Here follows a list of all the taxpayers and amounts levied in Williamsburg District in 1811: John Arnett, $2.94; Joseph Adams, $1.05; James Atkinson, $0.06; Stephen Atkinson, $0.24; Benjamin Ard, $0.03; James Ard, $0.03; Barnard Ard, $0.02; Thomas Ayers, $0.17; John Benton, $0.15½; Solomon Budden, $0.35; John Blakely, Jr., $3.60; Moses Benton, $0.60; William Benton, $0.09; John Brockinton, $2.95; John Boyd, (Estate) $0.49; Henry H. Bostwick, $2.60; John Barr, $5.03½; Daniel Brown, $2.10; Sarah Brown, $0.35; William Brown, $0.46; James Brown, $9.60; Robert Brown, $0.98; Maurice Braveboy, $2.93; James Bradley, $16.30; James Barr, $3.25; William Brockinton (minor), $1.55; John Brockinton (Estate), $0.45; Joseph Benton, $0.05; James

Bailey, $0.06; George Burrows, $11.70; John Burrows, $4.78; William Burrows, $4.69; Thomas Burrows, $5.51; Levi Barrineau, $0.19; Asa Bradshaw, $0.06¼; Manuel Barrineau, $0.35; Benjamin Britton, $11.00; Silas Bradshaw, $0.22; Samuel Bradshaw, $0.02; James Burgess, $35.52; Jonathan Bostwick, $4.64; Benjamin Bradham, $0.03; John Broome, $3.59; Robert Benton, $1.35; Risdon Barrineau, $0.35; Mary Bradshaw, $0.03; Margaret Barrineau, $0.07½; Abner Brown, $0.91; Benjamin Blanchard (Estate), $1.75; Thomas Browder, $0.03; Arthur Barrineau, $2.99; Hugh Boyd, $2.25; Isaac Barrineau, $4.61; John Blakely, $7.20; James Ballentine, $2.78; Jesse Blount, $0.09; Martha Brockinton, $3.85; Joshua Baxley, $0.12; Timothy Britton, $1.78; Francis Britton, $3.66½; Aaron Bradley, $1.35; John Barker, $0.06; Thomas Blackwell (Estate), $11.33; Michael Blackwell, $9.72; Thomas M. Brown, $2.35; John Cooper, $7.69; John Coward, $0.19; William Camlin, $0.56; James Campbell, $10.49; James Calhoun (Estate), $3.25; Washington Cockfield, $0.70; George Carter, $0.15; Sarah Clark, $0.35; George Chandler, $2.96; Mary Cunningham, $0.38; Bryant Cameron, $0.03; John Cetty, $2.90; Joseph Cockfield (minor), $1.14; John Connor (minor), $3.77; Ann Cockfield, $1.87; Margaret Cockfield, $0.78; Ann Cockfield, Jr., $0.76; William Cockfield, $1.14; Robert Cade, $3.74; Patrick Cormick, $3.25; William Cooper (Estate), $18.76; Samuel Coleman, $0.05; Jacob Coleman, $0.37; Thomas Connel, $3.31; John Collum, $0.20; William Carter, $0.02; George Cooper, $6.38; Rebecca Campbell, $4.20; Francis Cordes, $56.89; Joseph Clark, $0.09; Abram Connor, $0.08; James Cooper (Estate), $6.72; Arthur Cunningham, $9.67½; James Cunningham (Estate), $5.72; John Dick, $4.87; George Durant, $4.98; William Dick, $9.16; Thomas DuPre, $7.39; Margaret DuPre (Estate), $9.70; John Dickson, $0.83; William Daniel, $0.35; James

WILLIAMSBURG TAXPAYERS, 1811

Daniel, $0.25; Martha Daniel, $0.35; Benjamin Durant (Estate), $1.47; William Douglass, $3.14; Martha Downing, $0.02; Samuel Douglass, $2.04; Ben Duke, (Estate), $2.10; James Dickey (Estate), $2.21; Thomas Drake, $2.80; Samuel E. Dickey, $0.79; William Dobein, $18.51; John Dickey (Estate), $1.40; William Dollard, $8.05; James Eaddy, $0.85; Robert Ervin (Estate), $12.10; Daniel Epps, $7.69; Barbara Early, $2.19; James Eaddy, Jr., $0.20; Samuel Eaddy, Jr., $0.35; Jenny Eaddy, $0.70; James Fleming, $5.53; James Fleming (Estate), $6.21; John Fullwood (Estate), $0.81; William Flagler, $2.39; John Fleming, $5.53; James Fleming (Estate), $0.18; Robert Frierson, Jr., $10.46; Robert Frierson, $3.49; John Frierson, $5.60; William Frierson, $9.65; Joanna Jaudon, $3.65; William Felps, $0.03; John Fulton, $16.35½; Samuel E. Fulton, $4.30½; Mary Ferrel, $0.11½; Harmon Flower, $0.12½; John Fleming, $0.03; James Folly, $0.12; Mary Folly (Estate), $0.05; Samuel Fluitt, $7.84; Theodore Gourdin, $158.10; John Gotea, Jr., $2.15; Roger Gordon, $9.76; Elizabeth Gordon, $3.75; John Gordon, $0.58; Robert Greene, $1.26; John Goode, $0.30; James Gamble, $9.23; Gillespie Scott, $2.65; William Gamble, $5.04; Moses Glover, $24.99; James Gibson, $0.73; Ebenezer Gibson, $2.76; James Gowdy (Estate), $0.03; Daniel Gillespie, $0.09; William Graham, $0.33; Nelson Graham (Estate), $0.42; William Graham, Jr., $0.75; William Graham, $3.65; Ebenezer Gibson (Estate), $0.24; William Graham, $0.31; John Graham, $0.81; John Graham, $5.34½; John Gotea, Jr., $1.87; John Gibson (Estate), $6.72; John Gamble, $4.40; Lewis Glenn, $0.04; Dr. John Graham, $16.70; John Glenn, $0.05; George Gamble, $3.50; Samuel Gordon, $4.20; James Graham, $17.46; David Gordon (Estate), $11.43; John Hickson, $0.76; Hugh Hanna, $6.13; William Hanna, Jr., $0.24; James Hanna, $0.13; Samuel Hazeldon, $1.33; Thomas Hazeldon, $0.02; Samuel Hawthorn, $0.14; John Haseldon, $1.05; George Hawthorn, $1.51; John Hawkins, $0.11; John Howard, $1.84; Eliphalet H. Hewitt, $3.02; William R. Howard, $1.05; Margaret Hamilton, $5.06; John Hedelston, $0.51; William Hiddleston, Jr., $3.03; Gilles Hemmington, $0.18; Micajah Hicks, $0.03); Elisha Hicks, $0.03; Jesse Hicks, $0.36; John Hamilton, $0.79; James Hepburn (Estate), $3.36; Jonathan Helms, $0.03; John James, $10.92; Samuel W. James, $2.45; Mary J. Johnston (Estate), $5.39; William Johnston, $5.68; Mary Johnston, $0.09; Jacob Johnston, $0.10; Sarah Jordan, $0.03; Archibald Jolly (Estate), $1.66; William Johnston, Sr., $2.26; William James, $5.97; Gavin James, $2.75; Jane James (Estate), $3.20; James Johnston, $0.56; Samuel Jones, $0.36; William Jones (Estate), $14.50; John June, $4.20; Samuel Jenkins, $1.16; Edward D. Johnston, $0.36; Samuel James, $6.30; Samuel Knox, $1.19; Isaac Keels, $12.76; Samuel Keels, $4.76; John Keels, $7.42; John M. Kinder, $3.11; John Kelty, $0.06; Archibald Knox, $0.03; John Kennedy, $0.03; Timothy Lee, $0.05; Elijah Lee, $0.03; Needham Lee, $4.00; Sherrod Lee, $0.03; James Lever, $0.03; Levi Lamb, $0.14; John Lane, $3.50; William Lifrage, Jr., $0.02; William Levy, $0.11; William Lester, $16.60; Robert Lowry, $12.05; David McClary, $5.29; Samuel McClary (Estate), $1.40; William McGill (Estate), $1.75; Thomas Miles, $0.10; John McAlister, $0.09½; Moses Miller, $7.72; William McConnell, $1.45; Samuel Miller, $0.70; Stephen Miller, Jr., $27.22; William Manning, $0.04; James Menely, $0.22½; Robert Morris, $0.43; James McDonald, $1.17; Daniel McGee, $0.21; Alexander McCants (Estate), $3.25; Jeremiah Matthews, $0.06; William McFaddin, $7.00; Alexander McKnight, $11.68; Samuel McGill, $1.84; John McGill, $4.05; Thomas McCrea, Jr., $12.42; George McCutchen, $9.48; John Montgomery, $3.78; George McConnell, Sr., $3.75; John M. Matthews, $5.43; Mary McConnell, $4.26;

WILLIAMSBURG TAXPAYERS, 1811

Robert McConnell, $2.73; Isaac Montgomery, $2.26; John Matthews, Sr., $0.09; Henry Mouzon (Estate), $2.42; William H. Mouzon, $3.21; Elizabeth McGill, $2.19; Philip McRea, $1.30; James J. McCullough, $0.05; William McDonald, $24.49; John McLaughlin, $0.70; Thomas McCants, $2.56; Samuel Malcolmson, $0.25; John McClary, $9.58; James McGill, $8.86; James McCutchen, $4.07; Elam Mills, Jr., $3.28; Thomas McCrea, Sr., $13.87; Joseph McKee (Estate), $1.75; David McCave, $0.04; James McBride, Sr., $12.85; William McElroy (Estate), $1.79; Abraham Matthews (Estate), $9.72; John Matthews, Jr., $11.82; John Maxwell, Jr., $0.50; David Matthews, $0.04; Hugh McCutchen, $3.40; Thomas McCutchen, $0.35; Robert McCottry (Estate), $12.47; Mary McCottry, $0.07; David McCottry (Estate), $0.04; John McCullough, Jr., $0.49; William McCrea, $1.11; Thomas Miller, $0.05; Alexander Miller, $0.03; Solomon McClam, $0.96; William Matthews, $0.07; William McCutchen, $0.10; Richard Matthews, $0.12; Jemina Mon, $0.11; Jonah Matthews, $0.11; William Matthews, $0.06; Janet Montgomery, $14.13; Archibald Murphy, $5.03; Henry McNealey, $0.48; Bryant McClam, $0.25; Thomas McConnell, $0.75; William McCollough, $1.57; James McMurray, $0.05; Samuel R. Mouzon, $7.95; Alexander McCrea, $10.42; George McConnell, $1.30; James McConnell, Sr., $4.15; James McFaddin, $13.20; Elizabeth Matthews, $7.00; John McMurray, $0.82; Andrew McElroy, $0.03; William McCullough (Estate), $5.38; Nathaniel McCullough, $0.35; Peter Mouzon, $2.98; John McCullough, $3.90½; Alexander McCullough, $1.54; Elizabeth Morris, $0.12; John Morris, $0.03; Samuel McCants, $3.58; William Moore, $2.81; Paul Michau (Estate), $10.67; Duplessus Michau, $3.08; Alexander Michau, $1.40; James Marshall, $0.06; Joseph Marler, (Estate), $0.94; Isaac Matthews, $19.77½; Charles McCallister, $0.89½; William McElveen

(Estate), $1.96; James McElveen, $0.85; Jacob Norton, $0.49; Elizabeth Nesmith, $0.70; Robert Nesmith, $0.16 2/3; John Nesmith; $0.09; Samuel Nesmith, Sr., $2.86; William Nelson, $14.65; Isaac Nelson, $10.05; Lemuel Nesmith, $2.50; Robert Nesmith, Jr., $4.98; Samuel Odear (Estate), $3.65; Aaron Odom, $0.14; Zachariah Owen, $0.17; Samuel Perdreau, $5.79; John Perdreau, $2.55; John Penny, $1.05; Andrew Patterson, $7.94; Jannet Patterson, $1.88; Mary Parsons, $0.35; Sarah Parsons, $0.35; Elizabeth Parsons, $0.35; Solomon Parsons, $1.47; Robert Patterson (Estate), $0.70; Andrew L. Patterson, $1.14; Thomas Potts (Estate), $0.45; Rebecca Potts, $5.95; Thomas Potts, $1.70; Henry Price (Estate), $1.14; Hugh Paisley, $9.94; John Price, $0.45; Edward R. Plowden, $1.92; Isaac Pitman, $1.05; Francis Perrett, $3.36; Ann Perrett, $1.43; Peter E. Perrett, $4.35; John Pressley, $3.52; Hannah Paisley, $7.07; Nicholas Punch, $1.40; William Parsons (Estate), $1.64; Amos Parsons (Estate), $0.05; William Parker, $0.12; Ann Robinson (Estate), $1.74; William Rogers, $0.18; John Rodgers, Sr., $0.05; Thomas Rogers (Estate), $3.69; Rebecca Rowell, $1.40; James Riche, $3.21; Isaac Rogers, $0.09; Mary Reid (Estate), $0.04; Micajah Rogers, $0.09; John Rogers, Jr., $0.24; William Reid, $0.04; Noah Smith, $0.24; Robert Strong, $1.75; Philip Stone, $0.17; John Session, $0.05; Austin Stone, $0.21; Elizabeth Swinton, $12.60; Thomas Steel, $2.89; Alexander Scott, Jr., $9.43; Samuel Scott, $5.20; Jennet Scott, $2.45; John Scott, Jr., $11.21; Samuel Strong, $2.36; William Staggers, $4.40; Robert Sutton, $13.17; William Salters, $3.06; Thomas D. Singleton, $5.28; Mary Stretch, $7.19; John Stephenson, $0.64; Martin Staggers, $3.16; Agnes Singletary, $0.35; Ebenezer Singletary (Estate), $1.89; Samuel Singletary, $0.53; Richard Spring, $0.16; Abner Smith, $0.12; Robert Spring, $0.49; Ann Spring, $0.04; Samuel Snowden,

$2.21; Joseph Scott, $5.03; Alexander Scott, $5.98; Caleb Stephens, $0.09; John Scott, Sr., $10.41; John Staggers, $0.75; Henry Smith, $0.94; Dottson Stone, $0.14; Edward Sessions, $0.37; Richard Sessions, $1.47; John D. Singletary, $0.35; Ebenezer Singletary, $2.36; William Turner, $0.11; Benjamin Turner, $0.43; Hannah Thompson, $3.50; William Thompson (Estate), $0.11; William Thompson, $0.34; William and William A. Thompson (Estate), $0.30; James Tisdale, $15.35; Elizabeth Thomas, $0.03; Levi Timmons, $0.15; Alexander Thompson, $0.58; John Tharp, $1.14; John R. D. Witherspoon, $0.50; Thomas Williams, Sr., $5.67; Robert Wilson, Jr., $9.47; Robert Wilson, Sr., $7.12; Jane Wilson (Estate), $7.26; John Wilson (Estate), $10.19; David Wilson, Jr., $6.73; Samuel Wilson, Sr., $15.35; William Wilson, $7.71; Jane Wilson, $6.17; George Wisner (Estate), $0.04; James Witherspoon (Estate), $6.17; Robert Witherspoon, $16.07; Hugh Wilson, $12.81; James Witherspoon, $10.36; Gavin Witherspoon, $11.99; Thomas Witherspoon, $8.25; Elizabeth W. Witherspoon, $3.15; Robert B. Witherspoon, $1.50; Robert P. Witherspoon, $7.13; Samuel Witherspoon, $0.03; John Williams (Estate), $2.08; Willis Woods, $0.19; Sarah Watson, $4.55; Andrew Watson, $4.38; Joseph Witherspoon, $7.30; Robert L. Witherspoon, $9.49; John Wilson, Jr., $0.70; David Wilson, Sr., $9.88; James Ward, $1.51; Jacob Walters, $0.12; James Zuill (Estate), $7.68; Michael Blackwell, $0.28½; James Burgess, $0.17; William Cooper (Estate), $2.42; John Dozier, $1.43; John Dozier, $0.15; Samuel Douglass, $0.03; Leonard Dozier (Estate), $0.09; Samuel Fluitt, $1.50; William Flagler, $0.30; Ebenezer Gibson, $0.38; Moses Glover (Estates), $0.12; Moses Glover (Estates), $0.08; Hugh Giles (Estate), $7.26; William Hiddleston, Sr., $0.03; Thomas Lane, $0.22; John Mc-

Callister, $0.08; William Nelson, $0.11; Isaac Nelson, $0.18; William Reid (Estate), $0.38; John Steel, $0.03; Samuel Wilson, Sr., $4.83; Andrew Watson, $0.15.

CHAPTER XVII.

ROADS AND FERRIES FROM 1788 UNTIL 1830.

The road from the Lower Bridge on Black River to Lenud's Ferry on the Santee was made a public highway in 1788. Captain William Frierson, Gavin Witherspoon, Esq., Peter Lequeux, and Abraham Perret were appointed commissioners to lay out this highway.

Murray's Ferry over the Santee was held by Joseph Murray and his son, James Murray, until 1786, when it became vested in the heirs of Adam McDonald for a term of fourteen years. In 1789, Samuel Matthews, Needham Lee, Henry Mouzon, John Robinson, and Dr. John Graham were appointed to make and keep in repair the road from Lynch's Creek to Murray's Ferry already established. In 1792, a ferry was established on Black Mingo Creek at the plantation of James Baxter, and he was authorized to receive fees for ferriage for a term of fourteen years.

In 1795, the road from Effingham Saw Mills to the King's Tree Meeting House on Black River was made a public highway. Captain John Fulton, Hugh Reed, Needham Lee were appointed commissioners and empowered to call out all the male inhabitants who resided within six miles of the said road but for no longer term than twelve days in the year. In 1795, the road from Lenud's Ferry on the Santee River to Potato Ferry on Black River was established. Edward Thomas, Thomas Boone, and Theodore Gourdin were appointed commissioners and were empowered to keep the same road in good order and repair by the labor of all male inhabitants from the age of sixteen to fifty years, and with all the male slaves from the age of sixteen to fifty years residing within ten miles of the road.

In 1796, Murray's Ferry and Skrine's Ferry were vested in Theodore Gourdin, Esq., for a term of fourteen years. In 1798, Samuel Jenkins, Zachariah Owens, and Shadrack Simons were appointed commissioners for keeping in repair the road leading from Black Mingo to Britton's Ferry on the Pee Dee. In 1798, Peter Mouzon, Sr., James Burgess, Robert Frierson, and Henry Mouzon, Sr., were appointed commissioners on the north side of Black River, and James Campbell, William Buford, and Isaac Keels were appointed commissioners on the south side of Black River, to clean and keep in repair the present road leading down the south side of Lynch's Creek to Pudding Swamp on Black River, and to continue the same to Mouzon's landing on Black River, thence over Mouzon's Bridge, the most direct course toward Santee so as to fall into the road leading from Benbow's Ferry on Black River to Murray's Ferry on the Santee.

In 1799, James Blackmon, Josias Dupre, and John McClary were appointed commissioners to re-establish a road leading from Kingstree to Cooper's Ferry on the north side of Black River. In 1799, a public road was laid out from Brewington Lake on the south branch of Black River to Gamble's muster field on McGirt's Swamp and thence to Murray's Ferry on the Santee. William Taylor, John Conyers, James Campbell, William Nelson, Isaac Keels, and Theodore Gourdin were appointed commissioners for the said road. Allison's Ferry was vested in John Allison in 1798.

The commissioners then composing the several boards in the District of Williamsburg were convened at the house of Samuel Snowden on the first Monday in April, 1801, to proceed further with the discharge of their duties. Witherspoon's Ferry on Lynch's Creek was vested in John Witherspoon in 1801. A ferry on Black River at the landing, or the ferry commonly known by the name of North's Ferry, was established in 1803. That on the northeast side of the river was vested in Martha Brockinton and the southeast side of the river in James Cooper for a term of fourteen years. A toll bridge across Black River known as Mouzon's Bridge was vested in Henry Mouzon for a term of seven years from 1805. He was allowed to charge 50¢ for every man and horse; 6¼¢ for every horse and chair or cart and horse; 37½¢ for every hogshead of tobacco; 12½¢ for every head of cattle, sheep, goats, or hogs; and 2¢ for every led horse or foot passenger.

In 1806, the commissioners of the roads for Winyaw and Williamsburg were ordered to lay out and cause to be cleared a road from the road from the Williamsburg Court House to Potato Ferry across the parish line to William Rowell's plantation and from thence to Gapway road. That same way or ferry was established across Black River where the road crossed it and the ferry vested in William Rowell for a term of fourteen years. Samuel Commander and William Rowell were the commissioners for this road.

In 1803, Ezekial Pickens, Theodore Gourdin, and J. B. Richardson were appointed a committee to revise the general road laws in the State and to report at the next session what amendments in the road laws were necessary.

In 1809, Captain William Graham, Needham Lee, and Robert Cade, in the District of Williamsburg, were appointed commissioners to erect a bridge over Lynch's Creek at the place called Effingham Mills at the joint expense of the inhabitants of Darlington and Williamsburg Districts.

In 1811, the road leading from the causeway at and passing through Black Mingo or Willtown was discontinued as a public road and the road passing over Black Mingo Creek at the old ferry below Black Mingo or Willtown was re-established as a public road. The commissioners of the districts of Williamsburg and of Winyaw were authorized to build a good and sufficient bridge over Black Mingo Creek at the old Black Mingo ferry.

It was provided that said bridge be so constructed as to leave and afford a full and sufficient passage above and below said bridge to all rafts and unmasted boats, flats, or other craft. All male inhabitants from sixteen to fifty years residing not exceeding ten miles from Black Mingo and who made use of said creek to send produce to market and who were not liable or compelled by law to work on any other water course were liable to work on the same. John James, James McConnell, Loveless Gasque, John Dozier, Francis Greene, John Bossard, and Aaron Gasque were appointed commissioners to effect this ordinance.

In 1813, a new road was laid out five hundred eight yards from the junction formed by the Indiantown road and the post road from Witherspoon's Ferry on Lynch's Creek, the road leading by Loveless Gasque's plantation in the most direct way from the said State road to the Black Mingo bridge where the old ferry was established. This road was laid out at the expense of Thomas Williams, Sr., of Williamsburg. In 1813, James M. Grier, Nathan Gasque, Loveless Gasque, John Dozier, Benjamin Britton, and David Wilson, Jr., were appointed commissioners for the purpose of erecting and building a bridge over Black Mingo Creek.

In 1814, Potato Ferry over Black River was re-established and vested in Thomas Skrine for a term of seven years.

In 1815, Witherspoon's Ferry over Lynch's Creek was vested "in J. D. Witherspoon, executor of John Witherspoon, deceased, for a term of fourteen years in trust for and having the sole use and benefit of the incorporated Presbyterian Church at Aimwell on the Pee Dee River, in conformity to the last will and testament of the said John Witherspoon, deceased."

In 1818, Mouzon's bridge over Black River was established as a toll bridge and vested in Samuel R. Mouzon for a term of seven years, and he was allowed to demand and receive the same rates of toll as were allowed at Lowry's bridge on the same river. In 1818, the ferry at the Episcopal Church on Black River heretofore vested in William Avant was then vested in John Avant, the owner of the land on the south side of the river, and John J. Greene, the owner of the land on the north side.

In 1819, a dispute between Thomas McConnell and John Dozier respecting the old road leading across Black Mingo Creek at Willtown had arisen. The Legislature of that year appointed John Gotea, Jr., on the part of Thomas McConnell, and Hugh McCutchen, on the part of John Dozier, to make a survey of this road and a plat of the same which they should return to the board of commissioners of roads of Williamsburg District. This board was required to report to the next Legislature the propriety or impropriety of opening said road by the said Thomas McConnell's.

In 1820, Loveless Gasque, Matthew Allen, and William Small, on the part of Georgetown District, and John Gordon, Sr., John Dozier, and Benjamin Britton, on the part of Williamsburg District, were appointed commissioners to have repaired the bridge over Black Mingo Creek.

A public ferry was established on Black River Swamp at Kingstree in 1822. Such ferry was vested in the commissioners of roads for Williamsburg District for a term of ten years. The following rates were established: for every wagon or other fourwheeled carriage, 50¢; for every cart or chair, 25¢; for every man and horse, 2¢; for every head of hogs, sheep, goats, and turkeys, 1¢; for every head of black cattle, 4¢; for every head of horses, 2¢.

In 1822, William Frierson, Ebenezer Gibson, Robert Frierson, Sr., William Montgomery, John B. McClary, William Camlin, Jr., Henry Miller, John Hawkins, Robert Lester, and Isaac Nelson, Jr., were appointed a board of commissioners to open and improve the navigation of Black River from Benbow's Ferry to North's Ferry and all the male inhabitants between the ages of sixteen and fifty living within six miles of the said river were required to work on the same under the direction of these commissioners six days in the year and no more.

In 1828, the old road in Williamsburg District called the Samuel James' road, from an old field opposite to William Brown's to its intersection with the main road near William Cooper's plantation in Indiantown, was re-established as a public road and kept in repair.

CHAPTER XVIII.

GOVERNMENT AND OFFICIALS, 1783-1830.

Until the Revolution, elections in Prince Frederick's Parish were held at Prince Frederick's Church on Black River, which was located about three miles east of Prince Frederick's Parish line. In 1787, it was enacted that all elections in the future for Prince Frederick's Parish should be held at George White's at Indiantown. By Act of 1789, the elections for members of the Legislature for Prince Frederick's Parish were held on the same day at the King's Tree Bridge, at house of George White at Indiantown, the house of Captain John McCrea, and also at the Episcopal Church of the Parish. Two managers were appointed for the holding of these elections at each one of these places and on the day following the election, these managers were required to meet at the house of George White at Indiantown and then and there open the ballot boxes and declare the persons elected for the General Assembly.

The South Carolina Constitutions of 1776 and 1778 were adopted under the storm and stress of war, and the Supreme Court held they were merely legislative actions. The Constitution adopted in 1790 is a remarkable body of fundamental law. At that time, South Carolina had the experience it gathered from other state constitutions as well as far-sighted, clear-thinking, and vigorous-acting statesmen. This Constitution placed almost absolute control of everything in the hands of the wealthy slaveholding aristocracy.

There was a property qualification required for membership in the General Assembly. A representative must own in the district five hundred acres of land or real estate of one hundred fifty pounds sterling. He need not reside in the district, if he owned property of the value of five hundred pounds sterling. A senator must own real estate in the district to the value of three hundred pounds; or, if a non-resident, have one thousand pounds sterling. A man might vote in any district in which he owned fifty acres of land or a town lot; or in the district in which he lived, if he paid three shillings tax. The Legislature was given almost unlimited power. In addition to its law making functions, it elected governor, presidential electors, United States senators, and almost every other official down to county coroners.

In his Sectionalism in South Carolina, Dr. W. A. Schaper of the University of Minnesota says: "The slave holding planters—a mere handful of the white population—became the absolute masters of the situation and remained so to the end. They had almost unlimited power to oppress the up country people, and it must be recorded to their credit that they never used their power for that purpose, nor was a single charge of corruption brought against the government in the heated controversy which led to the reform in the representation in 1808. Their administration seems to have been singularly fair and it speaks well for the wisdom and manhood of the South Carolina planters."

The working of this Constitution of 1790 divided South Carolina into two factions which have existed until the present day. The "low country" consisted of the old judicial districts of Georgetown, Charleston and Beaufort. It was the strip of land about sixty miles in width from the seashore westward. Williamsburg was included in this "low country," and has proven loyal to its idealism in all periods of South Carolina history. The "low country" was settled many years before the "up country," and by people who emigrated directly from Europe; while the "up country" immigrants came largely from the states to the North, following southward the foothills of the Appalachian Mountains.

During colonial times, Charleston had been the seat of the Government. After the Revolution, the "up country," where probably four-fifths of the population of the State resided, succeeded by one vote in making Columbia the capital of the State. However, a sort of duplicate government was created and the predominancy of the low country in a great measure was preserved. The low country, with one-fifth of the white population, kept control of the Legislature. The Governor was required to reside in Columbia during the sittings of the General Assembly and was permitted to live elsewhere as in his judgment conditions required. That meant that he lived in Charleston at least four-fifths of his time. Nineteen out of the first twenty governors' terms in South Carolina were filled by citizens of Charleston and the twentieth by Governor Alston who was from Georgetown and held "low country" ideals.

This Constitution of 1790 also provided for two treasurers, one to hold office in Columbia and the other in Charleston. The offices of the Secretary of State and Surveyor General were to be kept open at both these places, the principals to reside in one and the deputies in the other. The Supreme Court sat at Charleston as well as at Columbia.

The story of the working of this dual government and the dominance for three-fourths of a century in South Carolina of the relatively small aristocracy in the "low country" over the ever increasing democracy of the "up country" is exceedingly interesting to students of sociology and of government. During this period, South Carolina more nearly approached the conditions obtaining in Greece in the age of Pericles than has any other people up to this time. Dr. David Duncan Wallace called South Carolina during this period "an aristocratic republic."

From 1730 until 1769, all official matters of the citizens of the District of Williamsburg received attention in the city of Charleston and all official records were kept there. From 1769 until 1806, Williamsburg, then known as Prince Frederick's Parish, was a part of Georgetown District, and its official matters received attention in that city. However, many of the wills and deeds from Williamsburg during that period were filed and recorded in Charleston.

In 1804, an Act was passed establishing Williamsburg District according to the boundaries of Williamsburg County named in the Act of 1785 into a Circuit Court District. By Act of 1805, court was required to be held at Williamsburg Court House at the King's Tree on the 21st days of March and of October of each year, and to sit for any time not exceeding five days. All suits and prosecutions then pending in the Court of Common Pleas and General Sessions at Georgetown wherein the defendants resided in the District of Williamsburg were transferred to the Courts of Williamsburg, there being finally determined.

Major James Campbell, Major John Nesmith, and Theodore Gourdin, Esq., were appointed commissioners for the purpose of taking bond and security from the Clerk and Sheriff appointed for Williamsburg, for securing a court house for the use of the people of the Williamsburg District, and for attending to such other business as should be required in the organization of the new district.

When Messrs. Campbell, Nesmith, and Gourdin undertook to secure a court house at the King's Tree for Williamsburg District, they found that the land set apart as a public parade ground in 1736, and which belonged to the district, was in the possession of William Brady, who had built a house on it and claimed the lot. This committee was unable to secure this lot until Mr. Brady died in 1820. In 1805, they leased a store house of Patrick Cormick's which was located near where Mr. Hammett's home now is at the cornor of Main and Long Streets, Kingstree, for use as a court house.

The sessions of the District Court about this time were seasons of great dignity and solemnity. The High Sheriff of the district always escorted with a drawn sword at carry the presiding judge from his hotel to his seat on the bench, and the assembled multitude in strict harmony with these formalities paid respectful homage. Court was opened with a sermon preached at length in the "holy tone" by some venerable minister. The Reverend William Knox, of the Black Mingo Church, was usually the "sermonizer." He was paid $12.85 for each of these sermons, $10.00 fee and $2.85 for mileage. After the sermon, the grand jury was drawn and the presiding judge delivered a formidable charge. Immediately after the charge, the session adjourned for the day and everybody hurried across the street to Bracy's bar and there refreshed themselves. The next morning everybody was ready to decree woe to the unfortunates coming on for a hearing.

The first trial in the court of Williamsburg District was entitled, "The State against Daniel S. Eaddy, Moses Brown, Samuel Eaddy, Jr., and James Eaddy—assault and battery." These gentlemen had held a good old Irish "discussion with sticks," plead guilty, paid their fines, and doubtless regarded their money well spent.

In 1820, the General Assembly of South Carolina appropriated $10,000.00 for the building of the Williamsburg District Court House. This money was made available at once and the front part of the present Court House was built from plans of Architect Robert Mills and occupied in 1823. This structure was erected with greatest care and for overcoming chance and time. Its walls are thirty inches of solid brick. These brick seem to resist decay. Tradition says that they were brought from Charleston.

Samuel R. Mouzon was the first sheriff of Williamsburg District; J. McMurray, the first clerk of the Court of Common Pleas; David McClary, the first ordinary: all chosen and qualified in 1806. For about twenty years, either Samuel R. Mouzon or Peter Mouzon was sheriff of the district. One seems to have been elected for one term and the other for the next. At that time, Williamsburg District and Winyaw formed one senatorial district. Major James Campbell, of Williamsburg, was its first senator. R. L. Witherspoon and John Dozier composed the first delegation from Williamsburg District in the House of Representatives. David McClary was ordinary for Williamsburg District for more than thirty years.

John Dozier was elected senator in 1815; and William Burrows and Thomas Brown, members of the House of Representatives. In 1819, T. P. Davis and Thomas Witherspoon were elected representatives; Moses Matthews, sheriff; Hugh McCutchen, commissioner of location of lands, and James McCutchen, coroner. In 1823, T. P. Davis was senator; William Salters and John Graham, representatives; T. D. Singleton, sheriff; J. Gotea, Clerk of the Court of Common Pleas; and W. Hiddleston, coroner.

In 1825, Peter Mouzon was sheriff; R. G. Ferrell, Clerk of the Court; John Graham, senator; James D. Singleton and David D. Wilson members of the House of Representatives. In 1830, William Cooper was elected a member of the House of Representatives and Samuel E. Graham became sheriff.

During this period, the militia was an important factor in the district. Once every two months all of the men of the district reported to their company headquarters for instruction in military matters and these gatherings were influential in politics and in society at large. Among the officers of the companies and battalions in the Williamsburg District from the War of the Revolution to 1830 may be named the following: Colonel Robert L. Witherspoon, Colonel William Cooper, Major John Macauley, Major John Nesmith, Major James Campbell, Captains William Flagler, John McCrea, John Fulton, William Graham, Samuel Malcolmson, Isaac Nelson, John Scott, R. L. Gourdin, William Frierson, John Graham, John Coachman, John Dozier, Leonard Dozier, William G. Flagler, and Abraham Michau. These militia organizations were punctilious in the matter of observing military forms and ceremonies. They always attended Fourth of July celebrations and other official occasions. When one of their officers died, a military funeral was held. In 1798, Lieutenant Alexander Cunningham died and was buried in the Williamsburg cemetery at Kingstree with military honors. It was a very imposing ceremony.

A great many of the younger men of the district volunteered and served in the War of 1812. There were three well known officers from Williamsburg in this War, Major James Campbell, Captain Isaac Nelson, and Captain R. L. Gourdin. Captain Gourdin was adjutant of the Forty-Third United States Infantry, stationed at Georgetown, and signed the discharges of many of the men of Williamsburg who served in that regiment.

CHAPTER XIX.

OLD WILLS AND NOTES ON THEM.

From 1805 until 1835, nearly all of the men of Williamsburg, who had served in the Revolutionary War under General Francis Marion, died. Almost every old man who died in Williamsburg during that period had been a soldier in the War of the Revolution. The only migrations to this district during that period were some officers and men of General Greene's army who liked this country when they saw it and settled here immediately after they were discharged from the service.

Here follow some notes gathered from the wills of these ancient warriors and from other dependable sources. From these notes on wills and from others on preceding pages, probably three-fourths of the present inhabitants of Williamsburg may trace their ancestry to original settlers of 1735.

The will of Edward Howard was the first one recorded in Williamsburg District. It was dated December 29, 1805, and proved before David McClary, ordinary, February 24, 1806. In this will, he mentions his brother, William Howard, and his nephew, John Howard. John Scott, of Kingstree, and John Scott, of Cedar Swamp, were appointed executors. Witnesses, John Burgess and William McCullough. Inventory of the estate was made by James McFadden, Thomas McCrea, Jr., and John McCullough.

The second will recorded in Williamsburg records was that of Susannah V. Mouzon, spinster, who died September 15, 1817. This was a holograph will. She left all of her property to her sister, Anne Mouzon. The ear witnesses to this will were Elizabeth Mouzon, Mary B. Mouzon, and James G. McGill.

The will of Isaac Barrineau, Sr., of Black River, is dated February 24, 1806. He mentions Ferreby, his wife; his daughters, Margaret Lifrage, Nancy Hinson, Levina Bradshaw, Sarah Barrineau, and Margaret Barrineau; and his sons, Jesse, Isaac, and Mandewell. He appointed William Lifrage and Arthur Barrineau his executors. Witnesses, William Flagler, Jesse Barrineau, and James Bradshaw. Appraisement made by James Campbell, Robert Frierson, Jr., and James G. McGill.

The will of Solomon Rhodus is dated September 18, 1804. He mentions his wife, Nancy Rhodus; his brother, William Rhodus; the heirs of his brothers, Nathaniel, David, and John; and the heirs of his sister, Mary, and of his sister, Patience Hill. He also mentions his sister, Anne Perrett. This will is witnessed by Jonathan Bostwick and Martha Fluitt. Appraisement made by William McCullough, John Hickson, and William McConnell.

George Burrows made his will July 5, 1797. He mentions his sons, William and George Washington. His executors were William Burrows, Charles Williams, George McCutchen, and James Campbell. Witnesses, George Dickey, Sarah Dickey, Sr., Sarah Dickey, Jr. Appraisement by John James, John Winter, and Hugh McCutchen.

John D. Burgess dated his will June 30, 1806. His beneficiaries were his brother-in-law, George Cooper; his mother, Margaret Burgess; his sisters, Jane M. Magdalene, Mary Ann Elizabeth, Louisa, Caroline Sophia, and Pomelia. His executors were Dr. William Dollard, Hugh McCutchen, and Thomas P. Davis. Witnesses, William Cooper, J. P. Montgomery, and Frank Walsh.

James Gowdy's will is dated December 15, 1806. He left his property to his children, Mary Frances, and James Malcolmson. In case of the death of these two children, his estate was to be divided between the children of his brother, Ebenezer Gibson, and the children of his sister, Frances McConnell. Executors, Gavin Witherspoon and James McBride. Witnesses, Jonathan Bostwick, William Frierson, and Peter Morland. Appraisement made by Robert P. Witherspoon, William Frierson, and James Witherspoon.

Ebenezer Gibson's will is dated August 1, 1806. He mentions his son, Ebenezer; his daughter, Frances; his grandchildren, James Malcolmson Gowdy and Mary Gowdy; his son-in-law, William McConnell; his daughter, Frances McConnell; and his grandsons, Ebenezer Franklin McConnell and William Gibson McConnell. His executors were John Watson, James Tisdale, and William McCullough. Witnesses, Robert Cantley, Mary Cantley, and Thomas Gibson. Appraisement made by Gavin Witherspoon, William McCullough, and James McBride.

William McElveen's will was not dated but was proven January 19, 1807. He mentions his wife, Margaret; his sons, William, James, Henry, and Thomas; his daughters, Mary Ann, Margaret, and Jane; and his daughter-in-law, Eleanor Matthews and her son, John. Executors, William and James McElveen, William James Cooper, and Robert Gregg. Appraisement made by John James, Samuel Scott, and Benjamin Britton.

John Gotea, Sr., dated his will March 24, 1818. The beneficiaries were his wife, Elizabeth; his son, George Cooper Gotea; and his daughter, Eleanor, who married Douglass. Executors, Hugh McCutchen, Alexander McKnight, and William Gibson, Jr. Witnesses, T. M. Brown, William Gibson, and John McKnight.

Anne Spring's will is dated February 10, 1807. The beneficiaries were her son, Cornelius; her daughter, Anne Byrd; granddaughter, Orpha Byrd. Witnesses, John McCallister, John Rodgers, and Margaret Rodgers. Proven before John Nesmith, J. Q. Appraisement made by Robert Cade, Robert McCallister, and John McCallister.

William McElroy's will is dated December 30, 1806. The beneficiaries were: sons, John, Andrew, and William; daughter, Elizabeth; his six younger children, Mary, Jane Tisdale, James, Margaret McConnell, Sarah Dobein, and Samuel Adair. His wife, Jane, and Robert L. Witherspoon were made his executors. Witnesses, Gavin Witherspoon, Joseph Witherspoon, and Ebenezer Gibson. Appraisement made by Gavin Witherspoon, John Watson, and Ebenezer Gibson.

John Gibson's will is dated November 21, 1807. The beneficiaries were his wife, Elander; sons, William, John, George, Thomas, James; and his stepchildren, John and Jane Gotea, children of John Gotea, deceased. Executors: his wife, Jane Gotea, William Gibson, and Alexander McKnight, and Hugh McCutchen. Witnesses, James McConnell, Mary McConnell, and William Hitch. Appraisement made by William Burrows, James McConnell, and Alexander Scott.

William J. Cooper's will is dated February 3, 1808. The beneficiaries are his wife, Jane; daughter, Mary; son, George; daughter, Nancy McCottry Cooper and one other child not named. He gave the Presbyterian Church at Indiantown $800.00 and the estate of Robert McCottry, one sulky. Executors, wife, Jane; brother, George Cooper; Hugh McCutchen and Joseph McCottry. Witnesses, David Gordon, John Winter, and Thomas McCutchen. Appraisement made by John James, George McCutchen, and Thomas McCrea, Sr.

John McCallister's will is dated June 28, 1806. The beneficiaries were his four oldest children, John, Charles, William, and Anne. He mentions his younger sons, Ezekial and Sampson; his younger daughters, Sarah and Mary; his son-in-law, David Lee; and his sister, Ann Spring; and his wife, Catherine. Executors, James Graham, William Graham, and William McCallister. Witnesses, John McBride, William McCutchen, and Elam

James Mills. Appraisement made by Robert Cade, William Dickey, and Eison Atkinson.

Stephen Owens' will is dated April 20, 1808. The beneficiaries were his brother, Peter Owens; sisters, Mary Hannah, Jane Price, Cemmy Johnson, Ann Haselden, and Elizabeth Haselden. The heirs of his deceased brother, Zacine Owens, and James Hanna, husband of his sister, Lucy, deceased, and Edward Johnson, husband of his sister, Ann. Executors, Peter Owens, Samuel and John Haselden, and John Price. Witnesses, James Dobbin, Henry Snow, and Thomas Jenkins. Appraisement made by William Johnson, Sr., William James, and William Johnson, Jr.

James G. Calhoun's will is dated August 6, 1808. The beneficiaries were his wife, not named; son, William Alexander McKnight Calhoun; children of his sister, Ruth Durant, except Jane C. Bellune who has already been provided for; and the children of his sisters, Ann Brown and Mary Rodgers. Executors, Alexander McKnight, Sr., William Burrows, and Nathaniel Snow. Witnesses, James McGinney, A. L. McGregor, and Samuel Grier. Appraisement made by Samuel Nesmith, John Graham, and George Cooper, Sr.

Eliphalet H. Burdick's will is dated September 2, 1820. The beneficiaries were his brother, Elam C. Burdick; Elizabeth M. Hewitt, Sarah Hewitt, John J. Hewitt, Francis Marion Hewitt, Thomas N. Hewitt, and Anna Hewitt, his aunt Mary's children. Executors, uncle William J. Burrows, and aunt Mary Hewitt. Witnesses, John Tharp, Robert Wisner, and James Gibson.

John Keels dated his will April 27, 1818. The beneficiaries were his wife, Mary Keels; sons, Peter R., James W., Richard T., and Robert F., daughter, Mary Maria. Witnesses, Benjamin Blanchard, William F. Blanchard, and William M. McDonald.

OLD WILLS AND NOTES ON THEM 225

Robert Gamble's will is dated December 5, 1809. His only son, James Gamble, is mentioned. Executors, his son, James Gamble, and his nephew, James Burgess. Witnesses, William H. Mouzon, Mary Mouzon, and James G. McGill.

Patrick Cormick, of the village of Williamsburg, dated his will June 11, 1820. He mentions his wife and three children, Ann, Jane, and Elizabeth, and one other child not named. Mrs. Cormick is made sole executrix, and Thomas P. Davis, Esq., is designated in the will as her legal adviser. Witnesses, James Bradley, T. D. Singleton, and Joseph Adams.

Hugh Graham's will is dated October 11, 1809. The beneficiaries were his wife, Sevil Graham; his sons, John Graham, William Graham, and James Graham and his daughters, Sarah Graham, Elizabeth McCallister, Sevil Hathhorn, Ann, Jean, Hester, and Mary. Executors, his wife, Sevil; his son, William Graham, and William Graham, Esq. Witnesses, James Myers, Philip McRae, and William Dick. Appraisers, Philip McRae, Solomon McClam, and William Duke.

Benjamin Durant's will is dated January 3, 1810. He mentions his wife, Mary; his son, John; and his daughters, Hannah Fleming and Martha Mary. Executors, his wife, Mary, and George Chandler. Witnesses, Robert Frierson, Jr., Margaret Hamilton, and David Benton. Appraisers, Robert Frierson, Jr., Martin Staggers, and William Douglass.

James Zuill of Willtown dated his will March 20, 1810. He mentions his wife, Margaret. He gives to his son, John Zuill, his real and personal estate in the parish of Belpon, in North Britain (Scotland.) He refers to John and Jane Pressley as "my two little children." His excutors were his wife, Margaret, and Thomas McConnell. Witnesses, William Hitch, David Martin, and

Cleland Belin. Appraisers, John Dozier, John Pressley, and John Graham.

Joseph McKee dated his will March 23, 1810. He mentions his wife; his daughter, Elizabeth; his grandson, John White; his granddaughter, Elizabeth McClary; his grandson, Samuel M. Knox; his grandchildren by his daughter, Elizabeth Fleming, wife of James Fleming. He mentions his father, Archibald McKee. Executors, his wife, his brother, John Shaw, and his nephews, Robert and Thomas Witherspoon. Witnesses, John R. McClary, Roger Wilson, and Roger G. Cantley. Appraisers, Gavin Witherspoon, John McClary, and Hugh Wilson.

Henry Price dated his will April 27, 1810. His wife, Margaret, and her sons, William and Hugh McFaddin, are mentioned. Witnesses, James McFaddin, John Montgomery, and William D. Scott.

Elizabeth McKee's will is dated July 2, 1810. The beneficiaries were Peter, David, and William Shaw, nephews; Elizabeth, Lillie, and Sarah, nieces. Witnesses, Jannet Austin and Samuel M. Knox.

William Buford's will is dated October 25, 1810. The beneficiaries were his son, William June; his daughters, Emma Corbett, wife of William Richardson, Esq.; Frances Fraser, wife of Reverened Hugh Fraser; and Elizabeth, wife of John S. Richardson, Esq. Executors, his son and three sons-in-law. Witnesses, T. D. Singleton, Daniel McDonald, and William Lesesne. In a codicil, he mentions Peter Fraser, his grandson. Appraisers, Daniel McDonald, John Blakely, and John Watson.

Thomas Rodgers dated his will April 12, 1811. The beneficiaries were Margaret Rodgers, his wife; daughter, Mary Ann Rodgers; and his sons, William and David Rodgers. Executors, Captain John Scott and John Matthews, Jr. Appraisers, William Wilson, George McConnell Fulton, and Samuel Fulton.

Jane James dated her will April 16, 1811. She mentions her sons, John, William, and Samuel; grandsons, Robert Sidney, James Edwards, and John Benoni, sons of Robert Witherspoon; granddaughter, Jane Wilson, wife of William Wilson; granddaughter, Sarah Jane James, daughter of son, William. Executors, John, William, and Samuel James. Witnesses, William Ervin, Colwell Crawford, and William Johnson, Jr.

Paul Michau's will is dated December 30, 1811. The beneficiaries were his daughters, Ann, Dorothy, and Charlotte; his son, Alexander Michau; his daughter, Lyda Singletary, and his grandson, Isaac Samuel Singletary. The executors were his nephews, Samuel Perdreau and John Perdreau, and his son, Alexander Michau. Witnesses, Hugh Fraser, Alexander Glass, and Frances Fraser. Appraisers, Henry H. Bostwick, Solomon Budden, and John Arnett.

Isaac Matthews dated his will 1811. His sons, John and Isaac; his daughter, Ann, wife of Captain John Screven; his daughter, Sarah, wife of William Lester, and his daughters, Jane and Mary; are mentioned. Executors, his two sons and his two sons-in-law. Witnesses, Thomas Scott, Moses Matthews, and Robert Lowry.

Dr. John Graham dated his will February 13, 1813. Dr. Graham was one of the wealthiest men in the county. He left no descendants. Just before the Revolutionary War, his mother, with her three small boys, migrated from Chester, Pa., to Fayetteville, North Carolina, where they lived a number of years. Dr. Graham studied medicine and settled on Black River near Kingstree. His two brothers remained in North Carolina and one of them later became a general in the War of the Revolution and the other, Secretary of the Navy. From these two men have descended many distinguished Grahams of the State of North Carolina. Dr. Graham was buried in the Williamsburg cemetery.

John McNicholl Connor dated his will April 10, 1813. The beneficiaries were his wife, Susannah; his daughters, Ann and Sarah, and an unborn child. Executors, Joseph Horton, John Keels, and his wife, Susannah. Witnesses, William Lesesne, Benjamin Blanchard, and David Brunson. Appraisers, Charles F. Lesesne, Francis Cordes, and John Keels.

John McMurray dated his will April 2, 1813. He requests that he be buried in James G. McGill's burying ground. In his will, he mentions his wife, Sarah Strong; his brother, James McMurray; and his daughter, Mary Ann. He refers to his mother but does not name her. Executors, William H. Bostwick, Elijah H. Bostwick, and Elizabeth McMurray. Appraisers, William Flagler, Martin Staggers, and Samuel Fluitt.

Captain Joseph Coachman's will is dated September 7, 1813. The beneficiaries were his wife, Margaret; his daughters, Mary Lynch Simons and Hannah Greene; and his sons, Benjamin and Isaac. Executors, his wife, Margaret, and his brother, John Coachman. Witnesses, T. M. Brown, Samuel Fluitt, and T. D. Singleton. Appraisers, T. D. Singleton, Gavin Witherspoon, and Robert Wilson.

Paul Jaudon's will is dated July 15, 1814. The beneficiaries were his wife, Elizabeth; his children, Paul, James, Samuel, Esther, and Sarah. Executors, Alexander Glass, Samuel Perdreau, and wife, Elizabeth. Witnesses, Caleb Charles Lenud, Joseph Logan, and Benjamin Guerry.

Jacob Coleman's will is not dated. He mentions his wife, Susannah; grandson, Jacob W. Williams; his daughters, Susannah Coleman, Elizabeth Murphy, Margaret Barrineau, and Hetty Williams. He mentions the heirs of his son, George, deceased, and his grandson, George, son of Samuel Coleman. Witnesses, John Staggers, Isaac Montgomery, and Christian Rae.

John Hickson's will is dated June 15, 1813. He mentions his son, Moses; his daughters, Ann Bostwick and Elizabeth Hawkins, and his three youngest children, James, Solomon Rhodus, and Richard Sessions. Witnesses, Nathaniel McCullough, Daniel J. Williams, and William Miller. Appraisers, Nathaniel McCullough, William Dobbin, and John Sessions.

James Barr's will is dated June 21, 1812. He mentions his son, John, and his heirs; daughter, Elizabeth, and her husband, Hugh Hanna; grandchildren, George Alexander Barr and Elizabeth Kirkpatrick Barr, children of son, Daniel, deceased; daughter, Jane, and her sons, George and James. Witnesses, Samuel McGill, Edward D. Johnson, and Roger Gordon.

Hannah Paisley's will is dated September 12, 1815. She mentions her daughter, Sarah, wife of William Gamble; daughter, Susannah, wife of John Matthews, Jr.; granddaughter, Sarah Hannah Adaline Matthews; grandson, Samuel McGill Gamble. Executors, Samuel R. Mouzon, John Matthews, Jr., and William Taylor, of Sumter District. Witnesses, William Wilson, Samuel E. Fulton, and Robert J. Wilson.

Janet Scott's will is dated December 2, 1815. She mentions her daughters, Janet Burgess and Elizabeth Scott; granddaughter, Janet Martha Lemira Burgess; son, John Scott, Jr. Witnesses, Thomas Burgess, Mary M. Patterson, and John McCottry. Appraisers, John Montgomery, John McLaurin, and William McCullough.

Eliphalet H. Hewitt's will is dated January 16, 1816. He mentions his wife, Mary Hewitt, daughter of John Burrows; daughter, Jane M. Hewitt; and other children are mentioned in the will but not named. Executors, Mary Hewitt, William J. Burrows, James McElveen, and Hugh McCutchen. Witnesses, Sarah Burdick, George McConnell, Sr., and Daniel H. Gillespie. Appraisers, James Gibson and Thomas Burrows.

James Bradley's will is dated January 1, 1816. He mentions his wife, Mary; son, Samuel, to whom he gives a tract of land granted to his father, Samuel Bradley; daughters, Mary Stewart, Sarah, Janet Martha; his sons, William Wilson, Robert, and James, to whom he gives a tract of land granted to his grandfather, James Bradley. Witnesses, Moses Matthews, Robert J. Wilson, and Mary S. Wilson. Appraisers, John Fulton, Moses Matthews, and George McConnell.

John Fleming's will is dated January 20, 1816. He mentions his wife, Anne Fleming; his youngest son, Pinckney, and refers to other sons without naming them. He refers to his daughters, Elizabeth Hamilton McCullough and Jane Bennet Snowden. Executors, his sons, William, Thomas, and John McCullough, and Alexander McCrea. Witnesses, James Fleming and James Daniel. Appraisers, John Scott, Jr., William McCullough, and Abner Brown.

James Burgess dated his will May 27, 1806. He mentions his wife, Margaret, and "his sons and daughters," not named. Executors, Margaret, "my wife and my son, John Burgess." Witnesses, Raphael Bell, William Dollard, and J. B. Cummings. Estate appraised by William Dollard, Daniel Epps, and Samuel R. Mouzon, in June, 1816.

James McConnell dated his will January 25, 1816. He mentions his wife, Mary; children, George, Thomas, Janet Dick, Mary McCottry, Elizabeth Gotea, and Sarah McConnell. He mentions also in his will John Gotea, Matthew Alling, Susan Gibson, James McConnell Dick, and Elender Gotea. Executors, George and Thomas McConnell, Robert McCottry, and John Gotea. Witnesses, William Hiddleston, Jr., John Lane, and Susannah Gibson. Appraisers, William Hiddleston, Jr., John Gamble, and John Pressley.

James McBride's will is dated February 10, 1816. He mentions his wife, Elizabeth; his son, John Dobbin McBride; his daughters, Rebecca Frances and Mary Ann. Executors, cousin William Wilson, Samuel McBride, Samuel M. Witherspoon, William Dobbin, and John M. Witherspoon. Witnesses, Ebenezer Gibson, James M. Gowdy, and Francis Gibson.

Thomas McCrea, Jr., dated his will February 25, 1816. He mentions his wife, Mary; his three children, Mary Ann, Susannah, and Thomas Armstrong. Executors, wife, Mary, Alexander McCrea, and James McFaddin. Witnesses, James McFaddin, Alexander McCrea, and John Scott, Jr. Appraisers, John Scott, Jr., James McElveen, and James Montgomery.

William Campbell's will is dated February 27, 1816. He mentions his wife, Mary; son, William McKnight Campbell. Executors, wife, Mary; brother, James, and William Salters. Witnesses, J. B. Cummings, Alexander McKnight, and James Graham. Appraisers, George McCutchen, Alexander McKnight, and Samuel Scott.

Moses Benton's will is dated October 15, 1816. He mentions his children, Mary, Simon, Ann, and Sarah. Executors, his friends and brothers-in-law, Simon and Isaac Timmons. Witnesses, James Myers, Moses Benton, Jr., and William Timmons. Appraisers, Benjamin Turner, William Turner, and John Coward.

Abner Smith's will is dated February 1, 1816. He mentions his sons, Abner, Simon, James, and Pat; daughters, Mollie, Mary Ann Elizabeth Garland, and Drusila Nancy Becky; and Mollie, his wife. Executors, John Steele, Abner Smith, Mollie Smith, and William Graham. Witnesses, William Graham, Mary Taylor Graham, and Aaron F. Graham. Appraisers, James Graham, Andrew Patterson, Robert Green, and Bryant Cambrahan.

George McConnell, Sr., dated his will August 6, 1816. He mentions his granddaughter, Jane M. Hewitt, (proviso—"that Jane M. Hewitt shall not marry either Elam Cheeseborough Burdick, Eliphalet Herbert Burdick, or Frederick Allen Burdick, in which case, my granddaughter shall not inherit anything); sister, Rachael McConnell; nephew, George McConnell, son of James McConnell; and nephews, James, Robert, and Thomas McConnell; niece, Eleanor Gotea. Executors, nephews, George McConnell and William Wilson and Rachael McConnell. Witnesses, Elam J. Mills, John Matthews, Sr., and John Lane. Appraisers, James Bradley, W. P. McConnell, and Thomas Burrows.

Alexander Glass dated his will April 15, 1816. He mentions his wife, Elizabeth; children, not named; the children of my sister, Avagale Wilson, deceased, wife of Robert Wilson, namely, Thomas, Avagale, and Margaret Wilson. Executors, Thomas Witherspoon, and Colonel William Salters. Witnesses, Robert Sutton, John Fort, and C. S. Osborne. Appraisers, Robert Sutton, Alexander Michau, and John Perdreau.

Mary Stretch's will is dated October 26, 1808. She mentions her grandson, William Newman Murrell; nieces, Elizabeth Todd, Agnes Brown, and Mary Campbell; and her nephew, William Campbell. Witnesses, T. D. Singleton, M. M. Singleton, and Isaac Nelson.

William Moore's will is dated February 16, 1810. He mentions his daughter, Sarah Lane, wife of Thomas Lane, Sr.; grandchildren, Elizabeth Lane, James Lane, and Sarah Ann Lane. Executors, Dr. John Graham, William Dobbin, Moses Miller, Jr., and Stephen Miller, Sr. Witnesses, Stephen Miller and Hannah Miller.

John Leger's will is dated March 2, 1808. He mentions his daughter, Dorothy Blakely, and children of Dorothy Blakely, and cousin William Leger's children. Executors, Archibald Campbell and Dorothy Blakely. Witnesses, Francis Leger, John David, and Jannet David.

Robert Benton's will is dated June 13, 1817. He mentions his wife, Susannah; sons, Elijah, Moses, and John; daughters, Sarah, Elizabeth, Rachael, Vila, and Martha. Executors, Elijah Benton and Samuel Timmons. Witnesses, Benjamin Turner and Hugh Turner.

Susannah Mouzon's will is dated March 19, 1817. She mentions her sons, Peter, William, and Samuel R.; daughters, Sarah Gamble, and Mary McGill; three single children, Ann Mouzon, Susannah V. Mouzon, and Henry Mouzon. Executors, Samuel R. Mouzon, and son-in-law, James McGill. Witnesses, Caroline M. Dollard, Louisa Scott, and Samuel P. Taylor. Appraisers, John D. Burgess, Daniel D. Epps, James Frierson, Samuel E. Dick, and Daniel Frierson.

Jacob Singletary's will is dated October 27, 1817. He mentions his wife, Elizabeth. He refers to his "bodily heirs." Executors, his wife, Elizabeth, and son, Joseph Sion Singletary. Witnesses, Philip Snow, Barnabas Ard, and William Ard.

Catherine Dickey's will is dated November, 1817. She mentions her daughter, Letitia S. Durant, wife of John H. Durant; Catherine C. Blanchard, Sarah McDonald Dickey, and Martha Elvira Dickey. Executors, brother-in-law, Samuel E. Dickey. Witnesses, Isaac Nelson, William M. Murrell, and William Nelson. Appraisers, James G. McGill, Robert Frierson, and John Staggers.

Samuel Wilson, Sr., dated his will April 10, 1816. He mentions his wife, Mary Stuart Wilson; sons, James Edmund, Samuel McClelland, John Witherspoon, William Calvin, and David Elisha, and daughter, Mary Grace. He mentions his mother-in-law, Elizabeth Witherspoon. Executors, James E. and Samuel M. Wilson, and wife's brothers, James Bradley and Robert Bradley, and

Thomas Witherspoon. Witnesses, Samuel E. Fulton, William Wilson, and Robert J. Wilson.

Gavin Witherspoon's will is dated January 10, 1816. He mentions the children of his daughter, Janet, and of his son, Robert Pinckney. His son, Samuel, Thomas Reece and John Miller; and his daughters, Elizabeth and Mary. Witnesses, William Frierson, Joseph Witherspoon, and James B. Witherspoon. Appraisers, Gavin Witherspoon, William Salters, and Robert Frierson, Jr.

Sarah Watson's will is dated October 19, 1817. She mentions her nephew, John Watson; niece, Sarah Ann Watson; brother, John Watson. Executors, John Watson, David P. Rodgers, William Salters, and James M. Gowdy.

Samuel Nesmith's will is dated September 16, 1816. He mentions his son, Samuel; daughters, Mary, Martha, and Sarah. The name of his wife is not given. Witnesses, L. Nesmith, Robert Nesmith, and James Baker. Appraisers, John Gamble, John Baker, and John Pressley. His daughter Sarah married John Brockinton and was consequently bequeathed but a peppercorn for her portion. The John Nesmith and the William Brockinton, who settled on Black Mingo in 1725, were very close business and personal associates. Their descendants have intermarried so many times since then that it is difficult to determine whether a present Nesmith is more of a Brockinton, or a Brockinton of a Nesmith. Too, these families have always been closely associated in business. Yet, every time a marriage has further related them, disinheritances have resulted. These Sabines have usually been able to reconcile husband and father in all things except statements in wills.

William McDonald's will is dated September 8, 1808. He mentions his sons, William Nelson, Thomas Edwin, and Archibald Couterier; his daughters, Martha Harriette Grenerager Davis, Mary Esther Charlotte McDonald,

Susannah Emily Ann McDonald, Catherine Laura Singleton McDonald, Eliza Maria Cantey McDonald, and Louisa Margaret Augusta McDonald. Executors, son, William Nelson McDonald; son-in-law, John G. Davis. Witnesses, Charles Lesesne, Thomas S. Cantey, and Margaret A. Lesesne. Appraisers, John Keels, Jane Cantey, and Charles F. Lesesne.

John Kelty's will is dated September 18, 1818. He mentions his wife, Jean; son, James; grandson, John, son of James; daughters, Susannah Michau; grandson, William Dickey. Executors, James Kelty, William Dobbin, and Alexander Michau. Witnesses, Jacob Norton, Allen Norton, and Miles Norton. Appraisers, Samuel Perdreau, William Dobbin, and John Perdreau.

Samuel Bradshaw's will is dated September 16, 1815. He mentions his wife, Amelia; and his sons, Asa, Moses, and Silas. Witnesses, Caleb Stephens and Abraham Davis. Appraisers, Abraham Martin, Levi Barrineau, Ebenezer Martin, and Abraham Connor.

James Eaddy's will is witnessed September 24, 1819. He mentions his wife, Mary; his sons, John, Edward D., and Henry; his daughters, Mary Stone and Sarah Prosser. Witnesses, Philip Stone, Isaac Carter, and William Tilton. Appraisers, George Carter, John D. Singleton, and Ebenezer Singletary.

Mary Bradley's will is dated July 14, 1817. She mentions her sons, William Wilson, James and Robert Bradley; daughters, Mary Stuart Wilson, Sarah, and Janet Martha Bradley; granddaughters, Elizabeth Westberry Bradley and Margaret Elvira Fulton.

Solomon McClam, Sr., dated his will July 2, 1819. He mentions his sons, Daniel, Solomon, and Bryant; and daughters, Ann Jane Smith, and Eliza Singletary. Witnesses, Philip McRae, James J. Douglass, and James Lacey. Appraisers, Robert Cade, Andrew Patterson, Sr., and Noah Smith.

Samuel Strong's will is dated December 24, 1819. He mentions his brother, Robert Strong, and sister, Eleanor Boyd. Executors, Robert Strong, Hugh Boyd, and John Scott, Jr. Witnesses, John J. McClary, A. Douglass, and Samuel D. McClary.

John Scott, Sr., dated his will April 29, 1820. He mentions his sons by his first wife, Joseph, John Thomas, William Robert, Albert Alexander McCrea, and Samuel James Washington; his wife, Rebecca Gordon, and his unborn child who became John Ervin Scott. Executors, Rebecca, his wife; Joseph Scott, his brother; and John Thomas, his son. Witnesses, James McFaddin, Mary M. Flagler, and Samuel Scott. Appraisers, James McFaddin, Samuel Scott, and John Montgomery.

Elizabeth Witherspoon's will is dated June 7, 1820. She mentions her sons, Robert, Thomas, John R. Witherspoon; grandsons, James H. Witherspoon, James E. Wilson, and Robert P. Frierson; granddaughters, Mary A. Witherspoon and Sarah A. Frierson; and grandsons, John R. and George Witherspoon; great grandchildren, James E. Wilson, Eliza A. Wilson, Thomas E. Wilson, and Robert M. Wilson, children of David Wilson; and great grandchildren, Esther D. Witherspoon and Langdon Witherspoon. She bequeathed $50.00 to the Bethel Congregation.

Samuel Snowden's will is dated August 25, 1819. He mentions his wife, Mary; sons, William, Samuel Mouzon, and Thomas James; daughters, Elizabeth Margaret, Sarah R. Gibson, Jane Burrows, and Mary Murphy. Witnesses, John Montgomery, James McFaddin, and Benjamin E. Gordon.

Benjamin Turner's will is dated January 3, 1821. He mentions his wife, Phœbe; sons, Reuben and Hugh and four others, not named. Witnesses, Solomon Coward; Moses Buddin, and William Turner. Appraisers, William McCallister, William Turner, and William Cockfield.

John Pressley dated his will May 14, 1821. He mentions his wife, Mary B.; sons, William J., John B., and James F.; daughters, Martha and Eliza. Witnesses, Thomas McConnell, William S. Brockinton, and Thomas Hiddleston. Appraisers, Thomas McConnell, William S. Brockinton, and John Gotea.

Jannet Patterson dated her will September 18, 1818. She mentions her daughters, Jean Murphy and Jannet Wizner; son-in-law, Robert Greene; grandsons, Robert P. Greene, Robert P. Wizner, and Robert James Patterson; and granddaughters, Margaret Patterson, Jane Hamilton Patterson, and Mary M. Flagler. Executors, Andrew Patterson and Samuel Gaskin.

Samuel Haselden's will is dated August 1, 1822. He mentions his wife, Ann; sons, James and Samuel Wyatt; daughter, Violetta L. Haselden. "Two acres of land I give for the use of the church, whereon the Methodist Church now stands." Witnesses, William W. Johnson, Samuel Marsh and Thomas Haselden. Appraisers, John Murphy, John Tharp, and Asa Brown.

David McClary dated his will October 5, 1827. He mentions his wife, Mary; sons, Samuel G. and William D.; daughters, Mary Elizabeth Hiddleston, Sarah F. Wilson, Margaret S. McGill, and Louisa J. Dollard. Witnesses, John B. McClary, Samuel Fluitt, and James B. McGill.

Archibald Murphy's will is dated September 18, 1827. He mentions his wife, Jane; son, John; daughter, Elizabeth, who married Fleming; daughter, Janet, who married Thorp; and Mary and Catherine.

Sarah Singleton dated her will April 17, 1829. She mentions her brother, William Purse, Sr.; son, Thomas D. Singleton; granddaughters, Esther Gibson Singleton,

Mary Magdalene Burgess Singleton. Witnesses, William J. Gamble, R. G. Ferrell, and William Purse.

James Ward dated his will March 10, 1829. He mentions his daughter, Eliza, wife of Thomas Hetchinhan. Witnesses, James S. Donnelly, Robert James, Sarah Kennedy, and Archibald Kennedy.

John Singletary dated his will January 16, 1826. He mentions his granddaughter, Sophronia Pervis Singletary; daughter, Martha Dickey; mother, Sarah Singletary; wife not named. Executors, son-in-law, James Dickey, and cousin, Elam T. Mills.

Thomas McCutchen's will is dated December 13, 1822. He mentions his wife, Nancy; sons, Robert George, Joseph White, and Thomas; daughter, Mary Julina. Executors, wife, Nancy, Hugh McCutchen, George McCutchen, Jr., Thomas Williams, Jr., and George W. Cooper. Witnesses, Alexander McKnight, William Cooper, and George Gotea Cooper.

Robert Frierson's will is dated July 31, 1827. He mentions his wife, Hesther; grandson, Samuel Flavale Wilson; nephew, Daniel Frierson; brothers, William and Samuel; sister, Jane Smith. He bequeaths to the Bethel Congregation $100.00.

Hugh Paisley dated his will August 5, 1827. He mentions his wife, Janet; son, William; daughters, Sarah G., Elizabeth, and Susannah.

Daniel Epps dated his will May 28, 1826. He mentions his wife, Martha; sons, Edward, Daniel, James, Peter, John, David, and Robert. He did not name his daughters, but made a bequest "to each of my daughters."

Nancy McCottry dated her will March 20, 1826. She mentions her daughter, Nancy McCutchen; son-in-law, George McCutchen; granddaughter, Elizabeth W. McCutchen; grandson, George W. Cooper. She gives the Indiantown Congregation $20.00. Witnesses, D. D. Wilson, William Cooper, and William E. James.

Elizabeth Graham dated her will October 18, 1826. She mentions her son, John; and daughter, Mary Ferrell. She named Mary Frierson's children, Mary S. Frierson, Robert G., Benjamin T., and William Ferrell; and Catherine L. Blakely.

Isaac Keels, Sr., dated his will July 2, 1821. He mentions his wife, Susannah; sons, Samuel John, Isaac, and George W.; daughter, Catherine Gamble; grandchildren, John Isaac James and Peter R. Keels. Executors, wife, Susannah; son, Samuel John; Morgan Sabb, and William Salters. Witnesses, Morgan Sabb, Joseph Holding, and P. M. Oliver.

John Montgomery dated his will October 9, 1824. He mentions his wife, Jane; his brothers, Isaac, William, James, Samuel S., and Henry; his sisters, Rachael Macauley, and her two daughters, Amarynthia Macauley and Mary Jane Plowden. Witnessed by Isaac Bagnall, John B. Bagnall, Henry James, and Samuel Montgomery.

Robert Cade dated his will March 2, 1823. He mentions his wife, Violet; sons, John, Charles, Andrew, Erasmus, and Felix Brown; daughters, Jane, Agnes, Elizabeth, and Adeline. Witnesses, James Fulmore, Violet Cade, and Jannet C. Cade.

Robert Lowry dated his will July 1, 1825. He mentions his nephew, Robert Lowry, in Statesville, N. C., and his brother, Joseph, in Ireland; John Lowry, studying medicine under Dr. Dollard; and Sarah Douglass, Elizabeth Douglass, and Isaac Matthew Douglass; children of his brother, David Lowry; and of his brother, William Lowry; and of his brother, Samuel, who lived in Sumter. He also mentions his sister, Elizabeth, wife of Joseph Caswell, and their two sons, John and Samuel Caswell, who lived in Ireland.

William McConnell dated his will January 23, 1829. He mentions his wife, Margaret; the following children by his first wife: sons, William Gibson and Robert

Franklin; daughters, Mary Bradley, Ann Elizabeth, and Frances Jane. Witnesses, Charles Barrineau, Francis Gowdy, and James Gowdy.

Thomas McCrea dated his will January 23, 1832. He mentions his wife, Esther; daughters, Sarah, Mary Cooper, Catherine DuBose McDowell, Esther L. Witherspoon, and Mary E. White. Witnesses, William S. Brockinton, William Burrows, and James Gamble. Appraisers, James McFaddin, George McCutchen, and Alexander Cunningham.

William Hiddleston dated his will March 7, 1834. He mentions his son, John Hiddleston, and his grandsons, John and William Hiddleston; his daughter, Margaret Nesmith, wife of Samuel, who first married Gibson.

James Folly dated his will June 12, 1835. He mentions his son James Lafayette Folly; and daughter, Margaret Ann Folly. Witnesses, William Turner, Robert Spring, and James Carraway.

John McClary dated his will January 12, 1831. He mentions his sons, John J. McClary, and his children, Mary, James, John Calvin, Alexander, David Manton, and George Frierson; and his daughter, Mary F. Duke, wife of Thomas; the children of said Mary, David McClary, Sarah Thermutas, and Mary Eleanor; his son, Samuel Blackwood, and the children of the said Samuel, Margaret H., John Milton, Hannah R., Sarah Blackwood McClary; and his son, David Sidney McClary. Witnesses, John J. Tisdale, Samuel Tisdale, and William Tisdale. Appraisers, H. D. Shaw, P. G. Gourdin, and Robert Strong.

Jane Wilson dated her will May 30, 1828. She mentions her son, David D. Wilson; her grandsons, Robert Harvey, David Edward, and John Calvin; her granddaughters, Jane Isabella, Sarah Elmira, and Mary Louisa; her stepdaughter, Mary Greene. Witnesses, John Gordon, William Hiddleston, and James H. McElveen.

Daniel McKenzie dated his will August 22, 1815. He mentions his sons, William, Samuel, Peter, and John; his daughters, Nancy and Mary. Executors, Thomas Rose and William Kennedy. Witnesses, Thomas Kennedy, Ann Kennedy, and David Muldrow.

William J. Pressley dated his will September 17, 1830. He mentions his wife, Elizabeth; daughter, Sarah, and one other child, not named. Executors, his uncle, William S. Brockinton, his brothers, John B. Pressley and James F. Pressley.

William Frierson, Jr., dated his will September 9, 1830. He mentions his grandson, William Frierson Rodgers; brother, Samuel Frierson, in Alabama; his nieces and nephews, Susannah Chandler, John H. Smith, Martha Kennedy, Rebecca McElveen, James Frierson, and Daniel Frierson; and his brothers, Joshua and George, in the State of Tennessee. Executors, Henry D. Shaw, William Lifrage, Jr., and Joseph Chandler. Witnesses, Henry J. Smith, Hampton Draughn, and W. C. Reardon.

Jane Murphy dated her will January 3, 1831. She mentions her son, John Murphy; daughters, Jannet, Mary, and Elizabeth. Her grandsons, Andrew James, John, James Calvin Murphy. Her granddaughters, Sarah Jane and Mary Catherine Murphy; and her grandchildren, Hesther Jane and Henry Singletary.

George McConnell dated his will April 13, 1832. He mentions his sons, William Scott, and Thomas James; his daughters, Catherine Ann, Mary Rachael, Sarah Elizabeth, and Margaret Eleanor.

Sarah Graham dated her will June 13, 1834. She mentions her husband, John Graham; son, John Graham; her nieces, Sarah McConnell, Mary McCutchen, Elizabeth Gotea, and Jannet P. Duke.

William S. Brockinton dated his will September 7, 1832. He mentions his wife, Louisa; his children, John Fowler, William Robinson, James Screven, Burrows

Pressley, Caroline Matilda, and Martha Ann; brother, John.

Thomas D. Singleton, Sr., dated his will May 11, 1826. He mentions his wife, Mary Magdalene; sons, Thomas Day and Henry B.; daughters, Esther, Mary, and Susannah Elizabeth Gourdin, wife of Peter G. Gourdin. He requested to be buried in the family burying ground on Santee, along side the remains of his father-in-law, Henry Blanchard.

John Watson dated his will June 10, 1821. He mentions his wife, Mary F.; son, John; and daughter, Sarah Ann.

John Belin's will is dated June 18, 1821. He mentions his brothers, James F. and Cleland Belin; his sister, Mary Gamble; his niece, Esther J. McDonald. Witnesses to this will, William S. Brockinton, Mary B. Pressley, and Martha Brockinton.

James McConnell dated his will January 25, 1816. In the beginning of this will, he speaks of his wife, Mary. Later in the will, it is written "my wife, Sarah." He mentions his sons, George and Thomas; and his daughters, Jannet Dick, Mary McCottry, and Elizabeth Gotea.

Robert Strong dated his will May 13, 1821. He mentions his wife (second) Sarah; his sons, Robert, William, and James; and his daughter, Amea Byrd, children by his second wife.

Martin Staggers dated his will October 10, 1822. He mentions his three brothers, William, John, and George. Witnesses, William Salters, Thomas D. Singleton, Jr., and William Dollard.

Martha Brockinton's will is dated April 3, 1822. She mentions her sons, John and William S.; daughter, Mary B. Pressley; grandson, William Burrows.

William Graham's will is dated June 14, 1821. He mentions his wife, Susannah; daughter, Mary Turner, wife of William Frierson; Jannet M., Susannah, and

Sarah; his sons, Aaron Frierson, Samuel E., William J., John F., Daniel B., Charles N., and Alexander J. W.

John Montgomery dated his will July 7, 1821. He does not name his wife nor his three daughters but his two sons, John Milton and William Rue.

James McDaniel dated his will September 19, 1810. He mentions his wife, Catherine; his daughters, Honour Bow, Catherine, Mary, Elizabeth, and Isabella, wife of Thomas B. Abrams; sons, James, Enos, Randol; son-in-law, Thomas B. Abrams; grandson, William James Cooper. Executors, wife, Catherine; and son, Enos. Witnesses, Hugh McCutchen, Samuel James, and Robert W. James.

Rachael McConnell dated her will April 1, 1824. She mentions her nieces, Eleanor Douglass, Sarah McConnell, Jane M. Miller, Catherine Gordon, Rachael Connor; and John H. McConnell, her nephew. Executors, nephews, George McConnell, son of James, and John Miller. Witnesses, Henry Miller and John G. Hewitt. Appraisers, Stephen Miller, William Morris, and Thomas Steele.

Elizabeth Wilson's will is dated January 19, 1822. She mentions her sons, John Wilson, David Wilson, Samuel J. Wilson, and Robert Wilson, in Louisiana; daughter, Elizabeth James, and her husband, John James; grandchildren, Elizabeth M. Wilson, Martha Wilson, Robert D. Wilson, children of John, by his former wife, Jane. Executors, David and Samuel J. Wilson. Witnesses, Samuel McGill and Samuel James.

John James dated his will June 16, 1824. He mentions his wife, Elizabeth, (books formerly of her father, Robert Wilson.); sons, William E., Robert W., John T.; daughters, Mary E., who married Greene; E. Lavinia, and Sarah Ann James; grandson, John L. Wilson, son of William; and granddaughter, Mary L. Wilson. He gives to his sister, among other things, a tract of nine hundred acres granted to Henry Perineau, dated April 28, 1732, at Indiantown. Executors, wife and three sons, Robert

W., John T., and William E. James, and brothers-in-law, David and S. J. Wilson. Witnesses, Samuel James, Mary Ann McGill, and Elizabeth A. McGill. Appraisers, Benjamin Britton, George Barr, Samuel McGill, Thomas McDaniel, and William Cooper.

Robert Sutton's will is dated October 6, 1824. He mentions his daughters, Elizabeth, Ann, Margaret, Dorothy, Magdalene; and son Robert Edward Glenn; his wife, Mary; and Sarah Tamplet. Executors, wife, Mary, and Dr. William J. Buford. Witnesses, John Perdreau, Peter Michau, Jr., and John Lequeux. Appraisers, Isaac Barrineau, Samuel Guilds, John Perdreau, and Francis W. Perrett.

James Gibson's will is dated June 16, 1825. He mentions his daughters, Jannet Greene, Margaret Cameron, Martha Gibson, and Mary Fluitt; sons-in-law, George Greene, Henry Cameron, and Samuel Fluitt; and grandson, Robert James Patterson. Executors, Samuel Fluitt and James Gamble. Witnesses, A. J. McGinnis, Benjamin Blanchard, and Charles Lesesne.

William Johnson's will is dated October 3, 1823. He mentions his wife, Celia; children and grandchildren, not named. Executor, Francis Johnson, son. Witnesses, Dotson Stone, John Frost, and David D. Dawsey. Appraisers, John Barr, Austin Stone, and Samuel W. Haselden.

Ann Perrett's will is not dated. She mentions her granddaughters, Ann Budden and Martha McColl; grandsons, John Lequeux, James Budden, and Solomon Budden. Executor, Peter E. Perrett, friend. Witnesses, Benjamin Whitfield, Elizabeth Frances and Sarah Barrineau. Appraisers, William Lifrage, Jr., Samuel Guild, and James Ward.

James Campbell's will is dated March 4, 1825. He mentions the following beneficiaries, Susannah Covert, Laura Covert, and Isaac Nelson; nephew, William Campbell; sister, Agnes Brown, Elizabeth Todd, and Mary Campbell. Executors, William Salters, Isaac Nelson, and S. Covert. Witnesses, T. D. Singleton, Morgan Sabb, and P. M. Oliver. Appraisers, Morgan Sabb, Robert Frierson, Sr., and James G. McGill.

Lemuel Nesmith dated his will August 29, 1820. He mentions his brother, Robert Nesmith, and his children. Executor, Robert Nesmith. Witnesses, John Baker, William North, and John Pressley.

George McCutchen, Sr., dated his will July 1, 1826. He mentions his sons, Hugh, George, and William; daughter, Jannet Barr; and grandchildren, Robert George, Joseph White, Mary Julina, and Thomas McCutchen. Executors, Hugh and George McCutchen and George Barr. Witnesses, John S. Dick, Jannet B. Dick, and Thomas S. Thomson. Appraisers, Alexander McCrea, James McFaddin, and Samuel Scott.

Elizabeth James dated her will July 10, 1820. She mentions her daughters, Sarah Ann James, Mary E. Greene, and Elizabeth L. James; sons, Robert W., William E., and John T. Executors, John T. and William E. James, and son-in-law, Samuel Greene. Witnesses, J. M. Witherspoon, W. Lifrage, Jr., and Samuel James.

Joanna Ferdon's will is dated February 14, 1820. She mentions her daughter, Mary Ann Blackwell; sons, Thomas B. Hamlin, John P. Ferdon, and William Ferdon; grandsons, John William Ferdon Gamble and John Ferdon Nesmith; and daughter, Maria A. Nesmith. Executors, Samuel Nesmith, John P. Ferdon, and William Ferdon. Witnesses, J. Dozier, R. R. Gamble, and Leonard Dozier.

Mary Parsons dated her will November 3, 1825. She mentions as her beneficiaries: nephew, David Parsons, Jr.; and Joseph Parsons, nephew; brothers, David Parsons, Sr., and Solomon Parsons; niece, Mary McDonald; children of her sister, Isabella McDonald, deceased, viz.:

James McDonald, Enos McDonald, Randal McDonald, Isabella Abrams, and Elizabeth Eaddy; children of brother, William Parsons, viz.: Elizabeth Powell, Josiah Parsons, and Ann Parsons. Executors, David Parsons, Sr., and Jr., and witnesses, John Gotea, George Gibson, and Thomas McCants.

James Blake dated his will October 11, 1826. He mentions his wife, Mary; and his daughters, Margaret Ann Norton, Sarah Bates, and Jane Blake; and his son, John Blake. Executors, Miles Norton and William N. Dickerson. Witnesses, Joseph Dickerson, Tobias Bates, and Margaret Norton. Appraisers, John Mims, William Craps, and Jobe Driggers.

Samuel Eaddy's will is dated January 28, 1827. He mentions his daughter, Jenny Eaddy; son, James A. Eaddy's children: Margaret D., Elizabeth M., Samuel J., and Frances Eaddy; son, James A. Eaddy. Executor, son, J. A. Eaddy. Witnesses, Philip Stone, James H. Stone, and Jacob Singletary.

Gavin James dated his will October 2, 1816. He mentions his nephew, William; nieces, Mary Wilson, Jannet Scott, and Mary Ann McGill, wife of Samuel; grandnieces and nephews, not named. Executors, John McGill and Alexander McCrea. Witnesses, Samuel Scott, D. D. Wilson, and William Cooper.

CHAPTER XX.

ECONOMIC AND SOCIAL LIFE, 1783-1830.

The original settlers of Williamsburg Township did all the pioneer work with their own hands. The first African slave in the Township was a negro "fellow" named Dick, imported by Roger Gordon in 1736. From that time the men of the Township began to buy a few slaves. During the Revolution, there were more negro slaves than whites in the Township. No herdsman or planter owned very many, yet every one owned a few. A great many of these slaves escaped or were taken away by the British during the War, yet a large majority remained loyal to their masters and refused to leave their plantations.

Many of the French Huguenots on the Santee and the English and Scotch on Black Mingo had a considerable number of negro slaves. These Africans, at this time, were useful only for the cultivation of the soil; and until the production of cotton and tobacco assumed considerable proportions, emancipation was seriously considered and contemplated. There was an unwritten as well as a written law in the State that slaves should not be taught mechanic trades. This was later annulled by common consent.

In 1790, Theodore Gourdin was the largest slave owner in Williamsburg. He had one hundred fifty slaves of his own, and thirteen belonging to the estate of John James. Stephen Ford owned ninety-eight; Moses Murphy, eighty-seven; John Baxter, eighty-three; Anthony White, seventy-three; William Goddard, seventy; Benjamin Porter, sixty-seven; Allen McKnight, fifty-eight; Susannah McCrea, fifty-two; Hugh Montgomery, fifty-two. None of these, except Mrs. McCrea and Mr. Montgomery, lived within the Township; and their plantations were in the extreme northeastern corner near the rice planting district in Williamsburg.

In 1790, there were eighty men in Williamsburg who owned more than twenty slaves. These men rapidly increased the number of their slaves; and most of them, within the next thirty years, became wealthy planters.

James Snow did not own any slaves, but he had seventy-seven free persons on his plantation. The term "free persons" then included those bound for a term of years to service. Mr. Snow was a man of considerable wealth. He sold his slaves and experimented with indentured labor. In so doing, he lost much of his property and was not regarded with favor by the community.

Theodore Gourdin was probably the wealthiest man in Williamsburg prior to 1830. It is said that at one time he could walk from Lower Saint Mark's Church on the Clarendon-Williamsburg line to the town clock in Georgetown, a distance of about seventy-five miles, without stepping off his own land. Mr. Gourdin was a useful, public spirited citizen. He served the district and the State in many capacities. He was a man of culture and owned a large library.

Colonel John Baxter was one of the heroes of the War of the Revolution. He was a man of liberal learning and a successful planter. He owned land all over Williamsburg and Georgetown Districts.

Colonel Anthony White lived in the Indiantown section. He was an enthusiastic churchman as well as a successful planter. He was Colonel of the Williamsburg-Georgetown regiment of militia and sheriff of the district in 1798.

William Goddard lived in the northeastern section of the County. His name died out in this County nearly a century ago, but he left a large number of descendants among the Britton, Nesmith, and other clans in the County.

Allen McKnight lived near Indiantown. His clan name still lives in Williamsburg and he has a number of descendants of other names who are now prominent.

Susannah McCrea was the widow of Alexander McCrea. Her husband's estate had been divided at this time and her several sons and daughters had already received their share of the slaves. Her son, Thomas McCrea, Jr., soldier in the Revolution under Marion, became one of the largest landowners and planters in the district. When one begins to abstract titles to land in Williamsburg County, he will probably think that Thomas McCrea, Jr., must have inherited an enormous quantity of land and purchased all that was offered for sale in his day.

Stephen Ford lived near the Georgetown line and finally moved to the town. A large number of his descendants live now in Georgetown.

Moses Murphy lived in the Indiantown section. He has hundreds of descendants now living in Williamsburg County.

Benjamin Porter lived on Black River, south of the Black Mingo. Hugh Montgomery's plantation was a part of that now owned by the heirs of W. J. B. Cooper.

In 1800, the Williamsburg District was almost entirely an agricultural and a cattle raising section. The people had just begun to cultivate cotton and tobacco in considerable quantities. But few slaves had been required for the production of indigo and for the herding of cattle. They were necessary to cultivate cotton and tobacco. From the beginning of the production of these two commodities on a large scale, the value of slaves in Williamsburg increased rapidly and the planters began to import as many as they could purchase.

There were several tobacco warehouses in the State where this product was inspected. Williamsburg sold most of its tobacco in Charleston and in Georgetown. The planter in Williamsburg packed about twelve hundred pounds in a strong hogshead, through which hogshead he ran an axle, placing two wheels and a pair of shafts. Between these shafts he hitched a mule, and this hogshead was rolled to Charleston over Murray's Ferry or to Georgetown over Brown's Ferry. This tobacco was a heavy variety, somewhat resembling burley, produced at the present time in Kentucky. It was cured in the sun. It averaged about seven cents per pound. Sometimes, however, the price was much greater. In 1823, it sold for forty cents per pound.

Nearly all of the planters in Williamsburg purchased their supplies from Georgetown during this period. Some of them, however, did their business in Charleston. It was their custom to send their cotton and tobacco to factors in these two cities and draw drafts on these factors for whatever money they needed, and to give orders to merchants for what they desired. Settlements were made with these factors and merchants once a year. If the planter did not feel disposed to make a settlement once a year, his factor and his merchants allowed him to carry over his account until the following year. At this time, nobody in Williamsburg even considered paying accounts oftener than annually, and this custom was almost binding for a century. It resulted in serious consequences to the commercial interest of Williamsburg and its hang-over influence, even unto this day, is a disturbing factor.

In Kingstree, there were few establishments called stores. Patrick Cormick, William Bracey, Samuel Fluitt, and Thomas Rodgers owned these places. These merchants carried lines of hunter's supplies, which consisted largely of rifles, powder, shot, and knives. All of them had large stocks of whiskey. In fact, this whiskey was their principal excuse for being. Kingstree was hardly a village at that time. Nearly every plantation in the district had about its mansion house more buildings than in 1810 could be found within the territory now making up the corporate limits of Kingstree. In 1810, Kingstree was made a postoffice. Very few pieces of mail came through the office for many years. One of the first of these was a letter from William Gordon Flagler, who was attending school in Concord, N. C., to his parents, Captain William and Mrs. Margaret Gregg Flagler. This letter is now in the possession of the grandson of this student, Alonzo W. Flagler, a venerable citizen of Williamsburg.

There are now three buildings standing in Kingstree that were erected prior to 1830, the Court House, the Nelson house, and a part of the Harper home. In 1820, Joseph Scott and William Reed established a sawmill on "The Branch" in the northeastern part of the present limits of the town of Kingstree. This was the first sawmill established in Williamsburg. Up to that time all lumber had been made by whip saw, worked by man power. This sawmill furnished most of the lumber from which the reunited Congregation of Williamsburg built its meeting house in 1828. Some, however, came from the Bethel Meeting House, which was torn down when the congregation "turned again home."

Later, Joseph Scott established a steam sawmill on his wife's plantation on Finley Bay, where was used the first steam engine brought into Williamsburg District. The whistle was a most important part on the steam engines of that day. It is said that for years when Joseph Scott's whistle blew on Finley Bay, all Williamsburg, man and beast, stood at attention. Planters for miles around abandoned their noon day horns and gongs, for when this steam whistle sounded, it was twelve o'clock in all the land.

Willtown, on Black Mingo, was the first village settlement in ancient Williamsburg. It had a beautiful location in a rich and prosperous section and an excellent water way to the sea. James Fowler, a rich merchant in Charleston and a rice planter on Black Mingo, established a trading post at Willtown in 1750. He exchanged tape and buttons and rum and molasses for the cow hides, deer skins, and tobacco the people of Williamsburg brought. About that same time, Dr. John Augustus Fincke settled at Willtown and began the practice of "physic." He established an inn and was as celebrated as "Mine Host" as a healer of diseases. He practised medicine for everybody within a radius of thirty miles of Willtown. Men came from a greater range than this to refresh themselves at his "Barr and Board." From Dr. Fincke's old account books and the inventory made of his estate after his death in 1766, one may know the names of nearly every man in that country,—when he elected to "celebrate" a week, and when his babies came.

Willtown reached its zenith about 1800, even though a commercial traveller from Europe then described it as "a miserable hamlet with about thirty houses and eight stores." Among the merchants at Willtown at that time were: James Zuill, Thomas McConnell, John Mason, Hugh Paisley, John King, and Captain John Brockinton. These merchants had large storehouses, and lines of sloops, flat boats, and pettiaguas running to Georgetown, from which place their own schooners carried the country produce they had collected at Willtown to Europe and brought back manufactured supplies. One might purchase from these merchants at Willtown almost any article he could find even in metropolitan markets.

The first postoffice established in Williamsburg District was at Willtown. Willtown lay on the post route which Benjamin Franklin established from Savannah, Ga., to Wicasset, Maine. Since Willtown was on this post route from North to South, was a stopping place for travellers in those days, and since there were many wealthy cultured people living in the community, it became one of the best known points in South Carolina. Patrick Dollard had an inn there. He was a witty Irishman and a genial host. Travellers anticipated their reception and treatment at his inn. He told them wonderful tales and fed them on well-prepared fish and game, for which this community is famous. In 1785, Bishop Asbury stopped at this old inn on his first visit to South Carolina, and he recorded in his diary that he was there "well used." Aaron Burr frequently halted there for refreshment and rest while he was visiting his daughter, Theodosia, who married Governor Alston of South Carolina and whose unknown fate is the subject of some of the most pathetic tales told.

In 1819, the rivalry existing between Thomas McConnell and John Dozier had reached such proportions that it was the subject of action on the part of the Legislature in that the public roads leading into Willtown were discontinued and the bridge over Black Mingo was moved some miles below Willtown to Shepherd's Ferry. This action killed Willtown. From that time onward, these storehouses were one by one abandoned and were burned or fell into decay. Cleland Belin, however, began a mercantile business there about this time and was a great merchant for half a century.

A postoffice was established at Indiantown in 1818. It was kept by George McCutchen on the Kingstree road about three miles from the church. This mail route extended from Sumter to China Grove where it met the stage line from Cheraw to Georgetown. Indiantown at this time began to support a school. Levy Durant of Georgetown taught in the church for several years and until the Indiantown Academy was built. There were many men in Indiantown who owned a considerable amount of property. James McFaddin was banker for the section. He always kept money at hand and grew wealthy "shaving notes."

Puritanism was introduced into Williamsburg by Dr. James W. Stephenson, who was pastor of the Bethel Presbyterian Church at Kingstree and of the Indiantown Presbyterian Church from 1790 until 1808. He had been impressed somewhere before coming to Williamsburg with the principles of Arminianism. He, doubtless, believed that he preached Calvinism. His words may have been Calvinistic but his thoughts and his personality emphasized the responsibility of the individual. He began Christianizing negroes. Calvinism never thought of negroes as of the elect, but of them as "being left to act in their sin to their just condemnation, to the praise of His glorious justice." Calvinistic ministers had preached in Williamsburg for three score years before Dr. Stephenson came, and not one of them had said a word about the saving of the souls of slaves.

These Scotch-Irish Presbyterians of 1730 were about as far removed from Puritanism as were the Roman Catholics. The fact is, the average Scotch-Irish Presbyterian who came to Williamsburg, while he talked a great deal about his religion and had absolute faith in his church, yet he was restrained in his daily conduct by his religion and by his church about as little as any man who ever lived in the world. He said and did very nearly what he wished. It is true that the Session of Elders of his church would sometimes call him before it, making him confess his sins and fall down on his knees before the congregation and receive reproof for his irreligious conduct before receiving communion, but this was so common that offenders did not consider it too seriously. One usually offended again whenever it suited his will.

When Dr. Stephenson came to Kingstree in 1790, he found people here and at Indiantown much given to wordly amusements, frivolity and unpuritanlike conduct in general. They loved horse racing and frequently held races. Probably the largest crowds of people Dr. Stephenson saw in Kingstree the first ten years he lived there were gathered about the old race course. Sometimes, men of Kingstree drank more whiskey than was good for them and every man kept a barrel of whiskey in his home. Nobody then thought of apologizing for offering a caller a drink of good whiskey, and most frequently the caller took two drinks. Dr. Stephenson found that dancing parties were frequent and sometimes grand balls were held in the community. The most saintly men and women out of his flock even attended these dancing frolics and sometimes he saw one of his elders, more than four score years of age, indulging in the pastime.

In short, Dr. Stephenson found a band of rollicking cavaliers in these parts and his greatest sorrow lay in the fact that Dr. James Malcolmson, minister of the faction of the congregation controlling the old Williamsburg Church, rather encouraged these wordly amusements. Furthermore, Dr. Malcolmson actually scorned the camp meeting Dr. Stephenson engineered at the Sandhills. Dr. Malcolmson even was chairman of a board that conducted a lottery for the building of the Williamsburg Academy. The slave owners in Dr. Malcolmson's congregation allowed their negro slaves to work on Sundays land which their masters had given them for producing crops. Dr. Stephenson's congregation had just seceded from Dr. Malcomson's congregation and had seen the new Light. Dr. Stephenson preached about all these things which Dr. Malcolmson's congregation did and when Dr. Stephenson left for Tennessee with his congregation in 1808, he took with him most of the people in Williamsburg whom he had succeeded in making Puritans. Dr. Stephenson, however, sowed the seeds of Puritanism and helped lay the foundation for Arminianism in this district.

By 1800, Williamsburg had recuperated from its losses in the Revolutionary War and began an era of prosperity which continued until the Confederate War. While some of the paragraphs in sermons preached by Dr. Stephenson indicated that the people of Williamsburg lived riotous lives, the fact is, they were conservative in all things. While they enjoyed horse racing, dancing, and some of them even an occasional drink of good whiskey, the vast majority of the people did only those things which were conducive to strength and to progression. There were many lovers of blooded horses in this district. Major John James had introduced some of the best strains of Arabian blood many years prior to the Revolution and there were some excellent horses on the plantations at this time. John Keels, on Mount Hope Swamp, had some very fine horses. He kept a race track on his own plantation. Samuel Tisdale in the Cedar Swamp section owned a race track. Captain John James had one. James Burgess, of the Pudding Swamp section, sometimes entertained his friends on his plantation race track.

At one of the dances held in Kingstree in 1805, John and Samuel McGill of Williamsburg, who had been working as apprentice carpenters under Colonel David Gordon in Sumter for about seven years, introduced short hair for men in Williamsburg. Up to this time, all men had worn queues. When these two young men entered the ball room, their short hair created a sensation. The wearing of queues by the men of Williamsburg up to this time indicates a distinct English influence in the district. Until this day, stories are told of the dances that were held at the homes of Samuel McGill and of Colonel William Cooper of Indiantown, of Joseph Scott and Samuel Fluitt at Kingstree, and of Major James Campbell and Francis Lesesne of Campbell Swamp.

State of South Carolina.

Pursuant to an order of the Hon. Thomas Broughton, Esq. Lieutenant Governor, and his Majesty's Surveyor Genl. bearing date 8th August 1735, I have admeasured and laid out a general plan of the town of Williamsburgh in Craven County, containing 350 acres of land, the river swamp fronting the town including. Butting and bounding North-degree Westerly on lands laid out to David Johnson and Jane Ervin — to the South 75 degrees westerly on Black River — to the North and East on land laid out unto Roger Gordon and John Henderson and to the South 15 degrees on Archibold Hamilton, and hath such shapes and marks, forms, and numbers of lots as are represented in the above described plan.

Given under my seal the 25th day of August, 1737.

'Anthony Williams.
Dep. Surveyor–

Town of Williamsburg.

Lands laid out to David Johnson					Lands laid out to Jane Ervin					
					346	347	348	349	350	351	352	353
					313	314	315	316	317	318	319	320
					280	281	282	283	284	285	286	287
					247	248	249	260	261	262	253	254
					214	215	216	217	218	219	220	221
181	182	183		184	185	186	187	188	189
153	154	155	JEFFERSON STREET	156	157	158	159	ADAMS STREET	160	161
125	126	127		128	129	130	131		132	133
59	60	61		62	63	64	65		66	67
92	93	94		95	96	97	98		99	100
26	27	28		29	30	31	32		33	34
16	15	14		13	12	11	10		9	8
387	388	389		390	391	392	393		394	395

SWAMP

MSBURG, 1801.

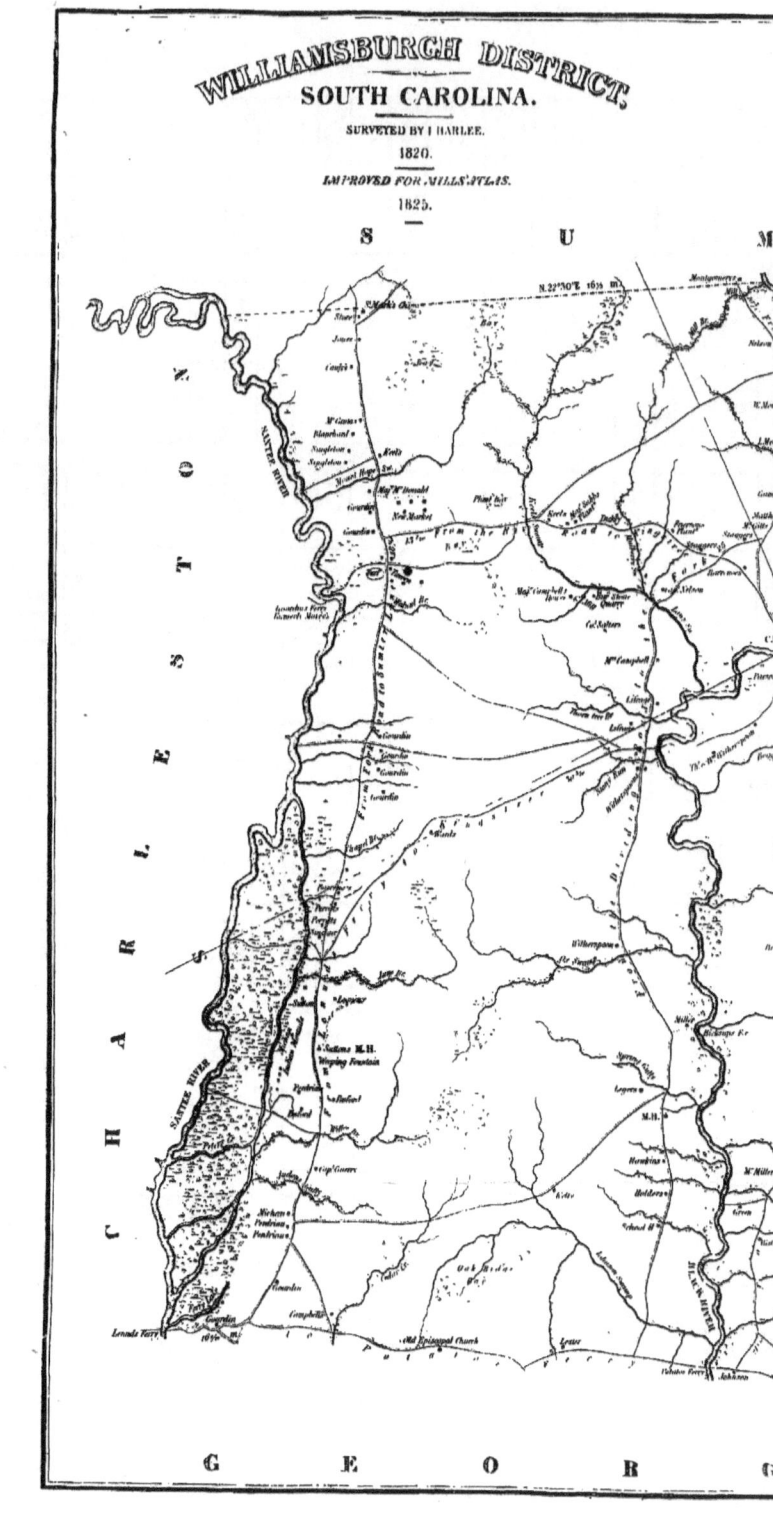

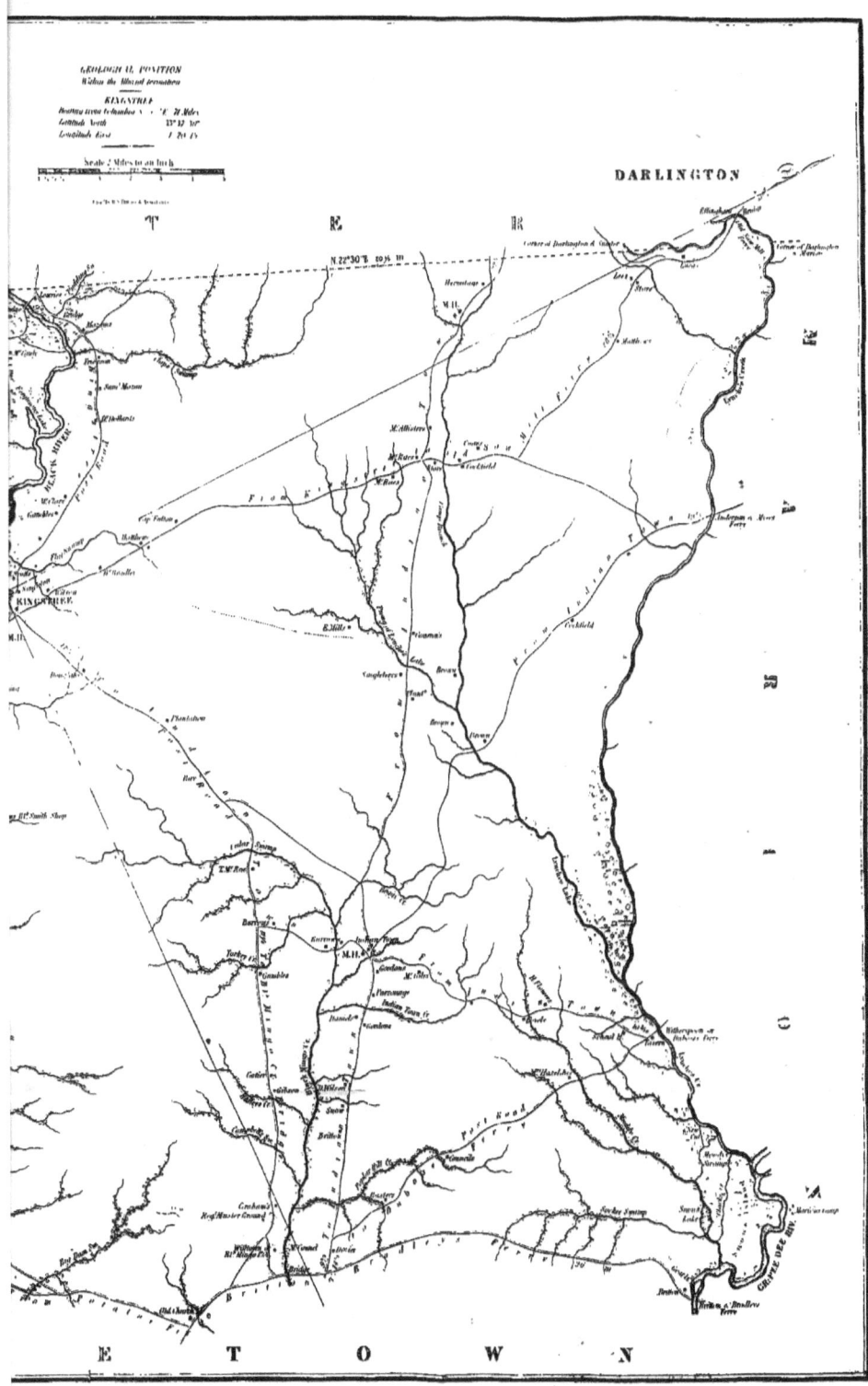

In 1830, property was probably more equally distributed in Williamsburg than in any other district in South Carolina. There were practically no poor whites here. Everyone, except overseers, owned a plantation, and these plantations were miniature empires. A sufficient number of the sons of overseers to supply the demand remained. The surplus went West. Some of this surplus became the bitterest element of the abolition party in Kansas and Nebraska of later years. "Free schools," designed for people too poor to have their children taught to read and write, were authorized in South Carolina in 1811. There were none of these schools in Williamsburg.

Lands were worth from $2.00 to $3.00 an acre; slaves from $500.00 for an ordinary farm hand to $3,000.00 for a skilled blacksmith, carpenter, or patroon. Black River was navigable for flatboats carrying a hundred bales of cotton for some miles above Kingstree. Black Mingo was navigable up to the site of the old Indian village on Indiantown Swamp. There were three times as many slaves as whites in the district.

Up to this time, when a man died he usually willed all of his land to his eldest son and provided for his other children out of his personal property. Many of the younger sons took their property and migrated into other states. A number of these younger sons founded families in Western South Carolina, and in Georgia, Florida, Alabama, Mississippi, Louisiana, Texas, and Tennessee.

CHAPTER XXI.

INDIANTOWN CHURCH, 1819-1830.

The Session of Elders of Indiantown Presbyterian Church was the supreme court of all that section. In civil as well as religious matters, the people required no other tribunal than this ecclesiastical court. No Sanhedrim at Jerusalem nor College of Cardinals at Rome, in its time and place, ever exercised more complete control than did the Session of Elders at Indiantown. A remarkably conservative citizenship has composed the Indiantown Congregation in all its history. It is very possible that no other community in this country has for so many years required so little interference by civil authority. The unwritten law is so high in conception and so strong in execution that hardly ever is it necessary for the State to use its authority in Indiantown.

The Session Records of Indiantown Church from 1819 are complete and existing. On February 12, 1819, the Reverend Robert Wilson James, a graduate of Princeton, and a licentiate of the Presbytery of Harmony, was ordained pastor of the Indiantown Church and of the Bethel Church at Kingstree. At this time, the old Williamsburg Presbyterian Church was maintaining a feeble organization and had not had a minister for a score of years. The other faction of this old Williamsburg Church, the Bethel Church, had lost most of its leading members by removal to Maury County, Tennessee, and to other states. Indiantown Church was the only strong militant congregation worshipping in Williamsburg District.

For eighteen years, from 1790 until 1808, Indiantown enjoyed the ministry of the Reverend James W. Stephenson. Dr. Stephenson had a remarkable influence upon Indiantown. He came very near Puritanizing it in a single score of years. The other ministers who had followed Mr. Stevenson up to the time of Mr. James' coming were all good men and the church was in excellent condition when he was ordained. Some of these old records in the Session Book here are copied:

"The following infants were received into the church by Baptism, February 22, 1819: Calvin, son of Hugh and Elizabeth Hanna; Alexander James, son of Alexander and Martha McCants; William Hitch, son of John and Jane Price; Mary Scott, daughter of George and Jannet Barr; Frances Jane, daughter of Alexander and Jane McCrea; Samuel Davis, son of Mary Ann and Samuel McGill; Alexander Washington Jackson, son of William and Susan Graham. In the summer and fall of 1819, the following infants were received into the Church by baptism: David Flavil, son of Samuel J. and Jane Wilson; David Edward, son of David D. and Mary Wilson; Sarah Margaret, daughter of William and Esther Daniel; Jane McGill and Elizabeth, daughters of Enos and Mary McDonald. This year Hugh Hanna, George Barr, George McCutchen, Jr., and Samuel J. Wilson were elected and ordained to the office of Ruling Elders. In November, applications for membership from two black men received attention. Upon recommendation of their masters and after satisfying the Session as to their knowledge and piety, Cupid was first admitted to the ordinance of baptism and then to the Lord's Supper; Hannibal, having been previously baptized in the Methodist Church, was admitted to the Supper."

"At this meeting of the Session of Elders, a young woman in the community who had, some years before that time, been charged with incest, applied for membership in the Church, making full confession before the Session. The Session was uncertain about receiving her into full membership and referred the case to the Presbytery, to which the Presbytery at its next meeting replied, 'The opinion of the Presbytery in the above case is, the person in question may be correctly admitted to the communion of the Church, upon giving satisfactory evidence of experimental piety; and that it be recommended to the Session to receive a public confession of penitence for the crime above alluded to. Signed: John Cousar, Moderator.' This recommendation was made known to the applicant, but she declined to make a confession of her crime before the congregation and she was not admitted to membership."

April 30, 1820, "At a meeting of the Session, the Eldership came to the determination to take into consideration and to state formally to this Church Judiciary the conduct of some members that were guilty of unchristian practices. At a meeting held in May, the following members were reported: Hugh Paisley, charged with intoxication; John J. McCullough, intoxication; Robert Brown, gambling and fighting; John S. Dick, intoxication; Samuel James, intoxication; Sam, a black man, theft.

"The Session adjudged it most proper that Hugh Paisley shall be conversed with by two of their members in a private manner referring to his crime. George McCutchen, Sr., and Samuel J. Wilson were appointed for this purpose. The Session adjudged that John J. McCullough should be warned of his crime, reminded of his relation to the Church and informed that the Church would proceed farther in the case without his reformation. George McCutchen and James Daniels were appointed to converse with him. The Session adjudged that Robert Brown should be warned of his conduct by a private letter. Hugh Hanna and George Barr were appointed to converse with James Barr and warn him that he had scandalized his Christian profession and that the Session would find it necessary to exclude him from the communion, unless he manifest the fruits of repentance and reformation. The Reverend Robert W. James was appointed to converse with John S. Dick and Samuel James and warn then against their alleged crimes. Captain John James was instructed to collect the evidence against Sam, the black man, and lay it before the Session.

"The committee appointed to wait on James Barr reported that he would not hear or attend to the warning of the Church. Samuel James acknowledged his offense and professed repentance for it. John J. McCullough acknowledged the crime made to his charge, admitted its being a crime, but excused himself as being under the decree of God. He made a promise that he would endeavor to amend. The Session did not accept Mr. McCullough's excuse and refused to admit him to partake of the Communion of the Lord's Supper until he had further acknowledged his crime and repented. Hugh Paisley came before the Session, acknowledged his crime, was permitted to make profession of his repentance agreeable to the form prescribed in the Book of Discipline. James Barr was suspended. The black man, Sam, was rebuked but permitted to retain his privileges in the Church."

This entry is found in the records of the next meeting of the Session, "The Session of this Church has to lament the apostacy of Hugh Paisley, who has again been guilty of intoxication and appeared in that condition in the presence of the whole church on the Sabbath Day." It was then resolved that Hugh Paisley be cited to appear before the Session on the 2nd day of February for trial for his crime.

"2nd of February, 1821. The Session at this time finds itself at a loss on the cases of two negro men who have been in communion with the Church and whose wives have been removed from them by their owners. These men have taken other wives. The Session is at a loss to determine on the propriety of their conduct. It refers their cases to the Presbytery and suspends them until its opinion is known.

February 4, 1821, James Daniel, a Ruling Elder in this Church came forward, confessed to the Session that he had been overtaken with the crime of intoxication and professed a sincere repentance. The Session deemed it advisable that James Daniel, in consequence of his standing as an officer of the Church, should make public confession of his crime and repentance.

"October 10, 1822, three black persons in connection with the Methodist Church made application for membership in this. It was the voice of this Session that if they fell under its jurisdiction, it should be satisfied with their piety and knowledge. They were accordingly examined, but being very deficient in knowledge so far as this Session could judge, they were for the present excluded.

"June 1, 1823, the Sacrament of the Lord's Supper was administered and the following black members received into full communion: Sena, Phœbe, Jannet, Cupid, and Jenny, of the Methodist Society.

"October 29, 1823, charges next were exhibited against Entrum, a black man on the plantation of Mr. Hugh McCutchen. Entrum was charged with adultery. Two witnesses supported this charge and his own statements amounted to a confession. The Session, after giving the parties a full hearing, decided that Entrum should be suspended from the Church.

"The Pastor of the Church now laid before the Session plans for carrying into operation a Bible class, a Sunday School, and a regular catechizing of the black people, which plans were concurred in and measures taken for their early commencements.

"January 22, 1825, David Wilson, a Ruling Elder of this Church, with Sarah Florilla Wilson, his wife, took their dismission from this Church to remove with their family, James Stephenson, Thomas Edwin, Robert Manton, Samuel Addison, and William McClary, to the State of Alabama.

"December 31, 1825, it has pleased Almighty God, the great head of the Church, to remove from us our venerable fathers, Captain John James, Mr. James Daniel, and Mr. George McCutchen, Sr. While the surviving members of the Session of Indiantown Church feel the heavy affliction and deeply deplore the loss of these very respectable, much esteemed, and good, useful Church officers, they must, at the same time, express their gratitude to a Good and Gracious God for their long spared lives, for the services they were enabled to render by their exemplary and pious conduct, but, above all, for preparing them, as we trust, for glory and honor with Himself.

"Captain John James, after filling useful stations in State, as well as Church, with honor to himself, and having through life manifested great liberality of mind and generosity of conduct, was removed by death on October 12, 1825, in the sixty-ninth year of his age.

"Mr. James Daniel was removed from life and from his services among us as a Ruling Elder, September 12, 1826, aged seventy-eight. His life was a retired one, but useful in his sphere. Sound principles appear to have possessed his mind and under the influences of these, the tenor of his life was uniform, unpretending, conscientious, and faithful in all his duties.

Mr. George McCutchen was called from this scene of earthly existence on the 26th day of November and in the seventy-third year of his age. Blessed by his God with a calm and discriminating mind, a paternal temper, and a satisfied and placid disposition, his life was to us, dignified, pious, and lovely.

"It having been made known to the Session and Church by the present Pastor that he intended to resign his pastoral charge in this congregation in the ensuing April, this having been signified almost twelve months ago, it was deemed expedient to take another Pastor. This business was referred to the Reverend R. W. James to correspond or communicate with certain gentlemen on this subject as preparatory to this business.

"It was determined in the Session that there should be a meeting of the Congregation, called for the purpose of electing five more Ruling Elders to our Session on January 29, 1827.

"February 10, 1827, the Congregation met according to appointment and elected Benjamin Britton, James McFaddin, Hugh McCutchen, William McFaddin, and David D. Wilson as Ruling Elders in the Church. David D. Wilson only accepted the appointment and was ordained the 13th of November, 1827.

"Our Pastor, Reverend Robert Wilson James, previous to this, made known to the Congregation his intention of giving up the charge of this Church in May, 1827.

"November, Sam, a black man, belonging to William E. James, was restored to the privileges of the Church by making public acknowledgement and confessing repentance for the crime of fishing on the Sabbath Day.

"October 25, at a meeting of the Session, the following members were admitted to the Ordinance of the Lord's Supper, namely: Alexander McCrea, Jane J. McKnight, Agnes K. Singletary, Sarah A. B. Singletary, Elizabeth Pressley, Sarah Gotea, Mary M. McGill, Sarah A. James, William Pressley, Elizabeth M. Pressley, John J. Clark, Jane P. Clark, Samuel E. Graham, Martha M. Graham, Margaret E. McCrea, Jane E. McFaddin, Elizabeth M. Wilson, Sarah R. J. Snowden, and Jane Barr.

"October 28, Adam Smith was suspended for intemperance on the 14th of March and for want of candour in not stating his reason for not communing on a former occasion when present.

"October 28, Samuel James was suspended for intemperance on the 14th of March. The suspension of Samuel James was continued and the next Session unanimously decided that on some day, just previous to the next Sacrament in April, the Session would receive the said Samuel James in full communion in case of his amendment; or if, at that time, there be not satisfactory evidence given of reformation, the Session will proceed to excommuniate the said Samuel James from the sealing ordinances of the church. And further resolved by the Session, that a copy of these minutes be handed to Samuel James within the space of a few days, signed by the Moderator, and all the Session."

CHAPTER XXII.

THE NULLIFICATION MOVEMENT, 1832.

When the Treaty of Peace between the United States and Great Britain was signed in 1783, the United States were thirteen independent republics bound together by a "rope of sand." These thirteen independent states covering a vast territory were settled by peoples of widely differing European nations, of many classes, religions, occupations, and characteristics. The means of communication among these thirteen states were practically impossible. A journey over land from Boston to Savannah by the most rapid means of travel required many weeks and could be made only by strong and daring men inured to hardships and unaccustomed to fear.

In 1789, these thirteen independent American states united into one state and adopted the Federal Constitution. This union was effected after many years of fasting and praying by the righteous, of scheming and dreaming by politicians, and laboring and compromising by statesmen. There were two well defined schools of political thought in almost every one of these thirteen states from the time of the actualization of their independence. One school believed that the success of this new thing in nations depended on a strong central government in which the thirteen states should play but minor parts. The other faction believed just as sincerely that the central government should be largely formal and possess but nominal authority and power. The economic interests of the northern section and the southern section of the territory of these United States were widely different. The North was better suited for manufacturing and commerce and the South for agriculture and stock raising.

This new government of the United States required money for supporting its many agencies or functions. A tax on imported goods was adopted in the beginning to raise the required revenue. This tax on imported goods actually subsidized manufacturing and commerce, but it placed a heavy burden on agriculture and stock raising. The tariff question was from the beginning, and has continued until this day, the direct or the indirect cause of nearly all the conflicts which have befallen the American people. The sections were first divided on this matter and still divide on it as interests conflict in the ever changing economic conditions in the various parts of the nation.

If some statesmen of 1789 could have written into the Constitution of the United States an article that would have, without favoring any section, produced revenue sufficient to maintain the Federal Government in all of its activities forever, in all probability the "States' Rights" question would have been the subject of nothing more than fanciful, theoretical, senatorial orations, and the slavery matter of little more than long winded sermons by sharp nosed Puritans, "full of sound and fury, signifying nothing."

South Carolina was the one state of all the thirteen most grievously burdened by the taxes, known as the tariff, levied and collected by the Federal Government. South Carolina was, is, and will be, a state dependent largely on agriculture and animal husbandry, and there is no portion of South Carolina more entirely devoted to agriculture and stock raising than is Williamsburg.

About 1830, the tariff then in force was especially burdensome to South Carolina; and in 1832 a State Convention was held in Columbia and declared the tariffs of 1828 and 1832 null and void, and that if the United States Government attempted to enforce them, South Carolina would set up a government of its own. The great leaders of the Nullification in South Carolina were Calhoun, Hayne, McDuffie, and Hamilton; the Unionist leaders were Legare, Grimke, Pettigru, and Elliott. Practically everybody in South Carolina opposed any tariff except for revenue. The division between the Nullifiers and the Unionists in South Carolina lay in the means to be used for opposing the ever increasing tariff. The Nullifiers claimed that the Constitution was a compact between the states as equals, that this Constitution had granted certain powers to the general government and reserved all others to the states; and that when the Federal Government should exceed its granted powers, any state had the right to veto such action. The Union party held that the Constitution was for the government of the American people as a whole, and that no state had the right to nullify any act of the National Government.

In Williamsburg District, the lines between the Nullifiers and the Unionists were clearly drawn. In Kingstree, Dr. James Bradley was Unionist leader; allied with him were the Scotts, Fultons, and Witherspoons. Dr. Thomas D. Singleton was the leading Nullifier and with him were the Gourdins, Nelsons, and Salters'. On the Santee, Dr. William Buford and Major Morgan Sabb were Unionists, while the Campbells, Gourdins, Keels, and McDonalds were Nullifiers. Anderson Township, under the leadership of Matthew L. Martin, was almost unanimously Union; on Black Mingo, the Doziers and Captain Jack Graham were Unionists, and the Nesmiths and Brockintons were Nullifiers; the Johnsonville section was composed largely of Unionists under the leadership of the Johnsons, Haseldens, and Coxs; the Lake section, in its northern and middle portions, under the leadership of A. F. Graham, Samuel E. Graham, the Cockfields, McCallisters, Matthews', and Rodgers, was largely for Nullification, while its lower and eastern portions, under the leadership of James Graham, the Singletarys, and

Browns, largely espoused the Union cause. Indiantown was almost as a unit favorable to the Union cause. Many of the old families of the district were seriously divided on this question, as were the Grahams, Mouzons, McClarys, and Hannas.

The feeling between these two factions in Williamsburg grew intense. The Nullifiers denounced the Unionists as submissionists or cowards, and the Unionists retorted that the Nullifiers were "all smoke and no fire." The Nullifiers adopted as a badge a cockade made of white and blue ribbons representing a palmetto tree and wore these badges on the side of their hats. Great public dinners were given by each party in the several sections of the district. Sometimes, both parties held their feasts on the same day and at the some place. At these dinners, fiery orators addressed the multitudes and frequently feeling ran so high that rioting was begun.

Many were the fisticuff fights occurring between partisans at this time. Tradition tells of some of these. Among them, that between W. G. Gamble, Nullifier, and Colonel William Cooper, Unionist, which occurred at Kingstree; one between Robert W. Fulton, of Kingstree, and John F. Graham, at the crossroads in the vicinity of Cades. Another between Sam Graham, Unionist, and C. W. Cades, Nullifier, at the same place. Among the orators who addressed the Union gatherings in Williamsburg, were Dr. James Bradley, Colonel David D. Wilson, and Honorable Thomas R. Mitchell, while the most important Nullifier speakers were Dr. Thomas D. Singleton and Peter Gourdin.

As evidence of how nearly these two factions in Williamsburg were equal, Dr. Thomas D. Singleton and Colonel David D. Wilson were candidates for the Senate from Williamsburg, and when the vote was tabulated it was found that each of them had received the same number. Members of the Legislature from Williamsburg elected that year were Dr. T. D. Singleton, William Cooper, and Joseph Bradley, two Unionists and one Nullifier. The Nullifiers elected all three of their delegates to the Nullification Convention which was held in November, 1832. The delegates from Williamsburg to this Convention were Peter Gourdin, Dr. T. D. Singleton, and William Waites.

CHAPTER XXIII.

PURITANISM, CALVINISM, AND ARMINIANISM.

Williamsburg was wealthy in 1830. This was the first time within two hundred years these Scotch-Irish had not been enthralled by a superior force, when they were free and able to act. Calvinism had been thrust upon them in the most strategic period in their history, when they were torn and bleeding and bereft of all worldly goods, and it must have seemed that God had forgotten them. John Knox then came and preached Calvinism to them, declaring unto them that they were God's own elect, "predestinated and foreordained" as His own elect. How easy was it then for the Church of Scotland to embrace Calvinism!

Economic independence is indispensable for religious progress. Circuit riders, following Bishop Asbury, had been preaching the doctrine according to St. James and the Dutch theologian, James Arminius, but until about this time few men had reached the financial condition where they felt able to fight for a faith. Besides, these Scotch-Irish had a most comforting religion in Calivnism. Did not the whole weight of responsibility for their salvation rest on God? Had not God "elected" them from the foundation of the world? Nobody but a fool would believe that a man had to work out his own salvation when it was so plain and simple that "This effectual call is of God's free and special grace alone, not from anything at all foreseen in man, nor from any power or agency in the creature, coworking with His special Grace, the Creature being wholly passive therein."

The Baptists, until about 1830, had been dominated by Calvinism. They had made no inroads on the Presbyterians in Williamsburg. The preaching of baptism by immersion only had not been sufficient to disturb these

Presbyterian Congregations. The Church of England in South Carolina had not been vitally interested in bringing these "poor Protestants" into communion with them in 1730, nor had its successor, the Protestant Episcopal Church, seemed to care much about these "back country" people in 1830.

In 1830, the Presbyterian Church in Williamburg believed this district its very own. Ever since the War of the Revolution, it had been rightly confident that the Protestant Episcopal Church would not disturb the realm. It knew that the Baptist Church would not seriously interfere with its undisputed sway so long as it offered only immersion as an inducement. But the continual coming of the Methodist circuit riders began to weary the Presbyterian leaders. Not that these circuit riders had made many converts to their faith, especially from among the "elect," but their continual coming and fervent preaching disturbed them. About this time, too, many Baptist preachers were losing faith in Calvinism and proclaiming "Whatsoever a man soweth that shall he also reap."

The old breach in the Presbyterian Congregation at Williamsburg had just been healed, a new church erected, and the Indiantown Church seemed approaching the full meridian of its glory and power. These two Presbyterian Churches were the only religious organizations in the district that were, to all appearances, worthy of more than a name. But the Presbyterians decided it would be wise to begin preaching Calvinism in all its intensity. Then at least ninety-five per centum of the church membership of the district was Presbyterian.

The Reverend John M. Ervin, who came from North Carolina as pastor of the Williamsburg and the Indiantown Churches in 1828, was the second Puritan Presbyterian preacher who came into Williamsburg, and who undertook to impress ideas of religion that had not grown out of the people of the community. Mr. Ervin, when he came, was in the prime vigor of manhood, tall and slender, and sharp faced, "with a long grey beard and a glittering eye." He found in the reunited church at Williamsburg that "conquered Greece had captured Rome," for that the seceders of the Bethel Congregation with their Puritan tendencies, somewhat influenced by Arminianism, had become the dominant element in the ancient Williamsburg Church. In his Indiantown Congregation, his board of elders were men of strongly pronounced Puritan tendencies. Nearly everybody in both of these congregations believed that the Presbyterian Church should completely dominate temporal as well as spiritual affairs.

Mr. Ervin found that there was in this section much not in consonance with his notions of religious conduct. Especially at Indiantown did he find many of his congregation given to enjoying such wordly amusements as dancing and horse racing. With the unreserved support of his Session of Elders in that Church, he preached powerful sermons against these practices. On the 8th of January, 1830, he and his Session of Elders published the following statement: "At a meeting of the Session of Indiantown Church, it was resolved to address the following to the communing members of this Society: Whereas, your Session has reason to believe that some of the members in full communion in this Church give encouragement to and take active part in balls or dancing frolics; and, Whereas the encouragement thus given to this amusement is a great grievance to some, perhaps to a majority of this Society, and if we mistake not, a stumbling block to others; and, Whereas, the General Assembly of our Church has expressly disapproved of this amusement as inexpedient among professors in our Church; the Session, after deliberately viewing these things in connection with its responsibilities as officers of this Church, does hereby declare to you its approval of the decision of this judicatory of the Church and that it will henceforth feel itself bound to view all professors of religion in this Church who encourage or take an active part in dancing as offenders against this Church and prosperity. Finally, brethren, we affectionately exhort you to abstain from all appearance of evil. Directed to be read by the Moderator next Sabbath." Signed, John M. Ervin, George Barr, George McCutchen, David D. Wilson, and Samuel J. Wilson.

At the next meeting of the Session, the Reverend Mr. Ervin was directed to admonish privately all those persons whose names may have come to his knowledge as having violated the resolution on the subject of dancing. At this meeting, no satisfactory evidence of the reformation of Samuel James having been produced, the Session excommunicated him, and the clerk was instructed to notify him of its action.

These actions on the part of this Session of Elders did not terrify some of the communing members of this Church and they continued enjoying themselves as if these edicts had not been promulgated. Finally, the Session of Elders appointed a committee of two, Reverend John M. Ervin and Elder D. D. Wilson, to "converse in a private manner" with Samuel McGill and to endeavor to bring him to repentance for his dancing and permitting dancing parties to be held in his home. This committee visited Mr. McGill, who "assumed principles and used expressions," a summary of which the committee made known to the Session previous to administration of the Lord's Supper on the next occasion. After hearing this committee report, he was warned by the Session not to come to the Lord's Table for communion.

After this, the Session cited Mr. McGill to appear before it to answer the following questions. "1. Do you acknowledge subjection to the government and discipline of the Presbyterian Church? 2. Do you acknowledge the permanent authority of the pastoral letters of the General Assembly of 1818 as far as it respects dancing? 3. Do you acknowledge that when an officer of the Church is properly authorized to converse with an offending member and the offense is confessed as a fact, that, in such a case, it is the immediate duty of the officers to endeavor to bring the offender to repentance and amendment by all proper means?"

May 30, 1830. "The Session at Indiantown met at twelve o'clock and continued in session until six o'clock in the afternoon, awaiting the result of Mr. Samuel McGill's deliberations on the admonitory letter addressed to him on the 16th instant, and also his decision on the propositions submitted to him on the 25th, and Mr. McGill did not appear nor was any communication received from him. After mature deliberation, the Session unanimously resolved to prefer the following charges against him:

"1. Samuel McGill is charged with obstinacy by avowing and adhering to the following as a principle in discipline, viz., 'that all we do is sin,' in direct opposition to the plain import of discipline read audibly in his presence. This obstinacy occurred on the 11th instant at his own house, and was persevered in during the stay of the committee, without any apparent charge of sentiment, in the presence of three members of his own family, the pastor of the Church, and D. D. Wilson, ruling elder, the two last being present on official duty with reference to a case of discipline with a member of his own family.

"2. Samuel McGill is charged with disrespect to the authorized expressions of the General Assembly of 1818, as contained in the pastoral letter on the subject of dancing. This disrespect was manifested in the day, at the place, and in the presence of all the persons above mentioned, and after it had been distinctly and audibly announced to him that these expressions were matters of permanent authority in the Presbyterian Church.

"3. Mr. Samuel McGill is charged with slandering an individual of this Session by plainly intimating that the Elder had used improper means to force an offending member of this Church to make promises of an amendment; and afterwards, as he asserted, the member did the same thing again, and then said Samuel McGill laid the criminality of the breach of promise on said member of Session. This slander was uttered on the day, at the place, and in the presence of all the persons mentioned in the first charge.

"The Reverened J. M. Ervin and D. D. Wilson are cited as witnesses to substantiate the above charges.

"Mr. Samuel McGill, you are hereby cited to appear before this Session on Thursday, the 9th day of June next, to answer the above charges."

Thus, the issue was clearly drawn. The moving spirit in the effort to eliminate dancing as an amusement and a recreation in Indiantown was the Reverend John M. Ervin, a minister who had lately come into the community and who had been trained under Puritanic conditions. He was a man of considerable force and ability and of a higher degree of learning than the average Presbyterian minister of his generation. He was supported and sustained by his Session of Elders, three out of four of whom were direct lineal descendants of the great John Knox, of whom it was said, "He never feared the face of any man." Colonel Wilson, of this board of elders, was one of the most uncompromising, influential, and vigorous men of his day in eastern South Carolina. He was colonel of the Pee Dee Regiment of militia and State Senator, and held other places of distinction and power. The other three members of this Session of Elders were wealthy, influential, educated, and uncompromising in their views. From the beginning, it was generally understood that this was a fight to the finish.

PURITANISM, CALVINISM, ARMINIANISM 277

The trial of Samuel McGill before this Session of Elders continued for nearly four years, during which time it was brought to the official notice of the Presbyterian organizations of highest rank in this country and attracted exceeding interest in the State of South Carolina.

This trial was conducted in strict compliance with canonical procedure, customs, and law, and the testimony recorded in full in the old Indiantown Sessional Record book. This trial and the records that were made of it indicate unmistakably the forensic abilities of the contending parties. Some of the questions asked Samuel McGill and his replies thereto show that it was a case of Greek meeting Greek, and some of them, when placed within their intensely serious and penetrating religious atmosphere, are now very amusing. For instance, question 9 in the direct examination of the prosecuting witness, the Reverend John M. Ervin, "Did you recommend any religious exercise in preference to dancing as an amusement?" Answer, "I did, I recommended the singing of hymns." Mrs. McGill was offered as a witness to the matters and things occurring at the time Mr. McGill was first rebuked at his home by this Session for dancing. Question 8 asked her was as follows: "Did this conversation exasperate Mr. McGill and determine him to take higher grounds in favor of the practice, or did it shake his confidence and cause him to yield the justification of the amusement?" Mrs. McGill's answer was "He remained much the same."

On the third charge against Mr. McGill, the following question was asked Mrs. McGill: "Who was the person that extorted the promise, and from whom was it extorted?" Answer, "George McCutchen was the person that extorted it and Leonora Montgomery was the person from whom it was extorted and violated it." The following is Miss Leonora Montgomery's evidence on third charge. "Did George McCutchen take you out at George

Cooper's and have a talk with you respecting dancing?" Answer, "Yes." "Were you not badly scared?" Answer, "Yes." "Did you not make a promise to him that you would not dance?" Answer, "Yes, I was so scared I hardly knew what I said." "Did you break that promise again?" Answer, "Yes." "Did you impute the blame to Mr. McCutchen?" Answer, "He did not attempt to frighten me into a promise." "Did he extort a promise?" Answer, "No."

Samuel McGill was found guilty of the crime of dancing and excommunicated. He appealed and his appeal has an interesting history. For all practical purposes, it was not sustained. "Whereupon, the Moderator read to him the decision of that judicatory and asked him if he were ready to receive the admonition and rebuke passed by this body on him. The censure itself he did not absolutely refuse, but gave the Session sufficient answer to believe that being interrogated as to his convictions of guilt or as to his penitence that he was still impenitent. The Moderator then proceeded to inflict censure so far as the Session judged expedient, but in so far as it could perceive, no satisfactory effect was produced on the offender."

The following letter shows some of the subsequent history in the case, "April 28th, We, the undersigned, Elders of the Indiantown Church, having for some years past been contending against a prevailing practice in the Church, which we deem unchristian, and when bringing discipline to bear upon offending members, we were plainly told by a member of full standing that he knew the mind of the congregation two times better than we did and that there were not three individuals in Indiantown Church that would sustain our proceedings, and, having received very little support or countenance from the congregation, we were induced to believe his statements measurably correct; and, moreover, at a house in

PURITANISM, CALVINISM, ARMINIANISM 279

the immediate vicinity of the Church (the heads of the family in full membership) at which a large number of the congregation attended a wedding, on the night previous to a three-days' meeting, at which the Sacrament of the Lord's Supper was administered, these practices were introduced and persevered in through the night, and to much excess that we believe it hopeless to proceed farther against such determined opposition, and as we cannot conscientionsly serve the Church as ruling elders, seeing the practices of dancing, excessive drinking, and their accompanying evils cannot be suppressed by us, and judging from the efforts already made that our influence is insufficient for this, or to promote the purity and edification of this Church; and, therefore, after mature reflection, we have unanimously resolved that we claim the constitutional privilege of ceasing to act as officers of this Congregation, (Confession of Faith, Book 1st, Chapter 13, Sec. 6 and 7), and now we earnestly pray the Great Head of the Church, the efforts of those who may be called to succeed us in His Providence, may be accompained with His Almighty power of blessing and make theirs more successful than ours have been." Signed, S. James Wilson, George Barr, George McCutchen, and David D. Wilson.

Early in the following year, 1835, the Indiantown Congregation met and elected William Daniel and Samuel Scott as Elders of the Church, the former board of elders having resigned. The Reverened Mr. Ervin also resigned as minister of the congregation. The new board of elders called the Reverened A. G. Peden to the charge. He accepted and was installed as its pastor. Samuel McGill was reinstated in the Indiantown Church and died in 1840 a communing member.

This trial of Samuel McGill for dancing was one of the most important and far-reaching events in the history of Williamsburg County. It shows the fundamental character of the people of Williamsburg, a character which has grown out of the same root for more than a thousand years. After this powerful session of elders with all the force that Puritanism could muster had spent all of its fury on Samuel McGill, his wife testified that "he remained much the same." Samuel McGill is Williamsburg.

It may have been expected that after this trial of Samuel McGill for dancing had resulted in a full and effective defeat for the forces of ultra-Puritanism in the dominant church congregation, Williamsburg District, that its people would have reacted into a season of riotous living such as occurred during the reign of the "Merrie Monarch" in England, but it was not so. Williamsburg remained "much the same." The records in old Indiantown Church continued to show births, baptisms, marriages, communion celebrations, and session meetings.

In 1836, the Williamsburg Church made application to the Indiantown Church for part of the services of the Reverened A. G. Peden. Mr. Peden was allowed for six months to preach twice each month in the Williamsburg Church.

On July 4, 1836, an education society was formed in Indiantown Church. The following officers were appointed: Reverend A. G. Peden, president; Colonel David D. Wilson, vice-president; Dr. Lee, recording secretary; and George Barr, treasurer. At this time, a collection was taken and from the proceeds, a substantial increase was made in the Church Library. At the end of this year, the Church increased its Session of Elders by electing the following: Colonel David D. Wilson, Captain Samuel J. Snowden, Alexander Knox, and John M. Fulton. It will be seen that the Church regarded the services of Colonel Wilson of great value and would not permit him to remain outside its official body.

About this time, the Indiantown Church began a progressive program. The congregation was wealthy and inclined to liberality. Collections were taken in the Church for various causes and much contributed to education and to foreign missions. On February 5, 1837, the ladies of this congregation gave $50.00 to constitute their pastor, the Reverend A. G. Peden, an honorary member of the Southern Board of Foreign Missions.

In 1840, the Reverend H. B. Cunningham was elected and ordained minister of the Church. During the pastorate of Mr. Cunningham, the Puritanic element in the Church began another campaign against dancing, as will be seen from the following entry of June 3, 1843: "In as much as some of the members of this Church are charged by common fame with dancing, the Session had conversed with them privately and some of them expressed a desire to make acknowledgment before the Session and it was agreed that they should have an opportunity of doing so. The following persons appeared, J. W. Scott, Miss Rebecca C. Scott, Miss Rebecca E. Gordon, and Miss Martha McCants, who acknowledged that they had danced, professed repentance, and promised to abstain from this practice in the future. Whereupon it was resolved that they be admonished by the moderator, and if they submit to this censure that their standing be declared regular. All of this was attended to immediately. Mr. John T. McCants also appeared and acknowledged that he had danced but said that he did not consider it a sin and therefore was not sorry. Whereupon it was unanimously resolved that he be suspended from the privileges of the church until he gives evidence of repentance."

Under date of February 18, 1844, the following entry is found, "Lisbon, belonging to Mr. A. J. McKnight, appeared before the Session on a charge of adultery, that is, keeping two wives, both of whom were present. Lisbon acknowledged that he was guilty and said he was sorry but did not seem to be really penitent, and, of course, he was suspended until he gives satisfactory evidence of repentance. Hagar, belonging to J. M. Fulton, one of the women implicated, said that whereas Lisbon came to see her, he told her he intended to make her his wife again, they having been separated several years, and believing him sincere in his professions, she had lived with him as his wife. In view of these statements, the Session did not think her case worthy of church censure. Candice, belonging to George Cooper, the other woman in the case, said that she lived with Lisbon as his wife because he solemnly declared to her that she was his wife and that he had no other.

"Believing these statements to be in the main correct, the Session did not feel that she should be debarred from church privileges; but, in as much as they had good reason to believe that she was visiting Lisbon at night, contrary to the wishes and orders of her master, she was required to promise faithfully that she would do so no more, with which requisition she complied. It was ordered that Lisbon's suspension should be published to the colored congregation this afternoon."

Another entry after the Reverend J. P. McPherson became pastor of the Church in 1844 follows: "Mr. McPherson stated to the Session that he had been requested to baptize the children of Mr. James and Mrs. Mary Ann Cooper, and that he had declined complying with that request because one of these children was seventeen years old and nearly, if not quite, grown, and therefore he deemed it proper that the Session should determine whether that member of the family was entitled to infant baptism according to our standards. Whereupon, after mature deliberation, it was resolved that in as much as the said child had arrived at that period of life when, according to our views of the Bible and of our Confession of Faith, an individual becomes a moral agent, it is in our judgment not proper that this member of the family should be entitled to infant baptism."

Here follows the entry of April 16, 1848. "A communication was received from Dr. H. L. Byrd, a member of our Church, dated Georgetown, S. C., March 30, 1848, giving a statement of a 'late unpleasant difficulty between Mr. Shakleford and himself' and referring to the correspondence which had been recently published in the Winyah Observer, and asking in the judgment, the honor of religion, and the interests of the Church might seem to require, and at the same time declaring his readiness to submit to any censure that we might think necessary to inflict and likewise most deeply deploring his connection with such an unfortunate affair and promising hereafter to 'keep all points guarded against difficulties of whatever characters.'

"After a careful reading of this communication in connection with the correspondence referred to by Dr. Byrd, and having heard statements from some members of the Session, who had learned all the facts in the case from persons residing in Georgetown, who may be considered as unprejudiced, the Session came deliberately to the following conclusion, viz.:

"That whilst Dr. Byrd's conduct is somewhat palliated by the peculiar circumstances of the case, yet we are constrained to feel, that he has acted very improperly and to an extent that cannot be justified by the laws of Christ's house; and while we fully believe that he has committed a great sin, for which he should humble himself in the dust before God; yet in as much as he voluntarily brought his case to the notice of this body and professes to be sincerely sorry for his conduct; and in as much as he has given us a promise to be more guarded in the future; whereupon, it was unanimously resolved that in as much as the ends of church discipline seem to have been accomplished, our pastor be directed to write to Dr. Byrd, setting forth our views on this whole subject and giving him such advice, counsel, and admonition as the case seems to require; and if he submit to this decision, his standing in the Church be declared regular. To this decision, Dr. Byrd cheerfully submitted."

The following entry was made for February 25, 1849. "In entire accordance with the views and wishes of Dr. S. D. McGill, the academy under his care was received under the supervision of the Session as a parochial school; and it was resolved that the pastor of the church visit said school frequently to catechize, talk to, and pray with the pupils and that he report its state and prospects to his body."

The following entry was made for July 22, 1849. "Session met and was constituted by prayer. Present, J. P. McPherson, Samuel Scott, D. D. Wilson, William Daniel, S. J. Snowden, and W. F. Blakely; and took into consideration the recommendation of the President of the United States that the first Friday in August next be kept as a day of fasting, humiliation, and prayer, calling upon all religious denominations to abstain as far as practicable from all regular occupations and to assemble in their respective places of worship, to acknowledge the infinite goodness of God which has watched over us as a nation and to implore His Almighty aid in His own good time to stay the destroying pestilence which is now wasting our land.

"The Session highly approving the said recommendation, resolved that the day be kept by the members of this congregation as a day of solemn fasting, humiliation, and prayer, that they abstain from their usual avocations, and that they urge it upon their servants to attend on that day the sanctuary of Almighty God. It was further resolved that the Sacrament of the Lord's

Supper be administered at this place on the Sabbath succeeding the first Friday in August, next."

This entry was made for April 5, 1851. "A communication was received from W. F. Blakely tendering his resignation of the office Clerk of Session and also resigning his office as an acting elder of this Church on the ground of his unacceptability to a portion of the church. Whereupon, it was resolved: 1st. that his resignation of the clerk's office be accepted and that the moderator be requested to act as temporary clerk. On motion of Colonel D. D. Wilson, it was resolved: 2nd. that his resignation of the office of ruling elder be accepted. On motion of Colonel Wilson, it was also resolved: 3rd. that his letter to the Session be inserted in our Session Book. Session adjourned, closed with prayer.

"April 6th. An extract of W. F. Blakely's letter to the Session of Indiantown Church. Gentlemen: From a sense of duty which I owe to myself and possibly the Church over which you so worthily preside. I am constrained to tender to you my resignation as Clerk of the Session. This step has not been taken hastily or unadvisedly; but after mature deliberation and much prayer for guidance on the issue. It is not that I have ever thought that the duties it devolves on the incumbent are onerous or burdesome; however responsible they may be, that has induced me to arrive at this conclusion. No, far from it. On the other hand, I have ever felt gratified when it has been in my power to contribute so far as in me lay to the general good of either Church or State.

"I hold the maxim, no man should live for himself alone, but causes of which none of you are ignorant and, of course, unnecessary for me here to enumerate or mention have influenced me in this matter. When an individual, however exalted he may be, or however humble be his condition, is called upon by others to perform services of any kind and fails to give the necessary satisfaction to those by whom he is employed or who may be disagreeable to all or any of those with whom he is associated, he should forthwith decline his position and give way to some more desirable than himself, is a duty so plain that it requires no sophistry to prove. Being convinced of the justness of my argument, I cannot in reason expect to exempt myself from doing that which I think to be the duty of another. I regret exceedingly that circumstances compel me to adopt the course I have; and that I no longer can consistently cooperate with you, nor share with you the responsibility. With my best wishes for you individually and for the Church over which you preside, I pray God to have you and it in His holy keeping and to build it up and strengthen it and deliver me from sowing the seeds of discord and confusion amongst His people. I now respectfully take my leave and again repeat that you have my best wishes and shall ever pray that the Almighty disposer of all events will ever bless you and graciously smile upon your labors. Hoping you may select from your respected body some one better qualified to discharge the duties of Clerk of the Session, I remain very respectfully, W. F. Blakely."

Mr. Blakely is still remembered as Squire Blakely of Indiantown Church. He was Clerk of the Indiantown Session of Elders for many years and his handwriting makes the pages, whereon he placed the records, strikingly beautiful.

Partly from the Session records and partly from abundant tradition, it seems that Nero, a slave, belonging to Captain S. J. Snowden, and a member of the Indiantown Church, gave the learned and austere Session food for thought. Nero was being tried for stealing two of his master's hogs, killing them, and concealing and eating the meat. Nero confessed his "crime" and thus sought to excuse himself. "It wuz dis way, Massuh

Colonel Wilson. Nero wen' to ole marster and axes ole marster for sum meat. Ole marster he say 'Nero, you go git sum meat from ole missus.' Nero he wen to ole missus and she say 'Nero, you have ter git dat meat from ole marster!' Den Nero wen to de Lord, case Nero wanted sum meat. De Lord say 'Nero, old marster got plenty ob hawgs down dar in de swamp. Ole Nero is marster's nigger and dem is marster's hawgs.' Nero wen down to de swamp dat nite and killed two ob marster's hawgs and et dem up." About that time, the Moderator of the Session looked into the eyes of its several members and, without waiting for a word from them, said, "Nero, you go home."

In 1852, the Reverend Daniel Baker, D. D., held a protracted meeting at Indiantown and one of the results was that the following persons were admitted to full communion: William J. Graham, Robert F. Blakely, J. M. Graham, Samuel J. Graham, E. P. Blakely, Elizabeth L. Blakely, Sarah J. Blakely, William S. McConnell, L. M. McConnell, Robert M. Cooper, Thomas Cooper, Samuel Cooper, James McCutchen, Thomas M. Britton, Janet Cooper, Amelia Burgess, Mary Nesmith, Joanna Nesmith, Sarah B. Hanna, and Joseph Fulmore.

On December 26, 1852, the following persons were granted certificates of dismission for the purpose of connecting themselves with the White Oak Church: Minto W. McGill, Sarah Elizabeth McGill, James Burgess, Janet D. Burgess, Amelia E. Burgess, Andrew J. Murphy, Mary Ann Murphy, Mary M. C. Burgess, Mr. and Mrs. J. B. Cooper, Mrs. Thermutas Cooper, and Mrs. E. W. Montgomery. At the same time, Messrs. George, John, Robert, and S. G. Cooper asked for certificates to unite with the White Oak Church, but these men were under the charge of "fighting" some time previous and their certificates were not granted at this time.

This fight was between the Messrs. Cooper and Messrs. S. J. Snowden, Jr., Italy Wilson, and others, opposing. It seems that both sides in the fight had acted strictly according to the Irish code and the whole of Williamsburg District became interested. The Indiantown Session of Elders investigated the matter for a long time and finally decided that it could not arrive at a just and righteous decision and dismissed the case against the Messrs. Cooper and they were given certificates for uniting with the White Oak Church.

On February 24, 1856, J. C. Dye, a member of the Indiantown Church, was charged before the Session as neglecting the ordinances of the Church; secondly, selling ardent spirits; third, permitting intemperance at his store, and cited to appear before the Session for trial. Mr. Dye appeared before the Session and confessed that he had sold ardent spirits and that he did not regard the selling of whiskey as wholly sinful in itself but led to sinful or bad consequences. Mr. Dye, having promised to abstain from selling ardent spirits in the future except for medicinal purposes and likewise having expressed his sorrow for the past error, was, after being admonished by the Moderator, restored to his former standing in the Church. This is the first recorded church opposition to the sale of whiskey in Williamsburg District. Until this time, whiskey had been sold by practically all merchants and without criticism by the religious bodies of the district. Some time prior to this, a chapter of the "Sons of Temperance" in the Indiantown community had been organized and this trial of Mr. Dye was one of its results.

During the late fifties, many of the men who had been leaders in the Indiantown Congregation for more than half a century, began resigning their offices in the Church and soon thereafter passing away. The first of these was Samuel Scott, who wrote, "My age and infirmity admonish me that I can be of little or no service to the Church by continuing to act any longer, now in my seventy-eighth year, and I therefore tender my resignation as an Elder and Clerk of the Session." Later, Captain S. J. Snowden was deprived of the power of speech by a stroke of paralysis and he resigned. Within a few years, William Daniel, James McCutchen, George Barr, and Captain R. H. Wilson, all men of long and valuable service in the Church, died.

Robert Strong united with the Williamsburg Presbyterian Church in 1799, and in 1830 was the oldest living communicant in point of church membership. There were then living the following members of the Church who had been enrolled prior to 1822: Daniel Frierson, Jane Frierson, Henry Frierson, Martha Mouzon, Nancy Mouzon, Elizabeth McGill, V. Tyson Fulton, James Bradley, Cecelia Bradley, Mary S. Wilson, Ezra Greene, Eliza Fulton, Joseph Scott, Sr., Mary Scott, Sarah Bradley, Martha Greene, Samuel Fluitt, Catherine McLean, Caroline Scott, Amelia Scott, D. R. McClary, Ann McClary, Charlotte Fleming, Elizabeth Knox, William Douglas, Mary H. Duke, E. M. Cantey, Mary McClary, Elizabeth Tisdale, William Lifrage, Nancy Lifrage, Mary Watson, Francis Gowdy, Martha Barrineau, Joseph Chandler, Susannah Chandler, Sarah Salters, R. G. Ferrell, Elvira Chandler, and Martha Graham.

The following joined the Church during the ministry of the Reverend John Covert in 1822: Eliza Brockinton, John Murphy, Margaret Strong, Margaret Scott, H. D. Shaw, Agnes Shaw, William Camlin, Elizabeth Camlin, Mrs. M. Davis, William G. Flagler, and Mary Flagler.

The following joined the Williamsburg Church after the union of the Williamsburg and Bethel Congregations had been effected in 1828, and during the ministry of the Reverend John M. Ervin; Samuel R. Mouzon, Sarah Devers, J. M. Fulton, James E. Fulton, T. D.

Singleton, Hester Singleton, M. M. Singleton, Susannah Staggers, Nancy Witherspoon, William R. Scott, J. T. Scott, Sarah Murphy, Emerline Burrows, Sarah E. McClary, D. S. McClary, M. M. McClary, J. H. Fleming, S. A. Knox, Joseph A. Scott, William D. Scott, Martha Troy, G. H. Chandler, John A. Gordon, Margaret Smith, Elizabeth Douglas, John Watson, Emma Watson, Isaac Nelson, Jr., Rebecca Scott, George Barrineau, Priscilla Barrineau, Caroline Troy, Albert Scott, A. F. Graham, J. C. Graham, Jane Miller, John Knox, and S. E. Graham.

Mr. Ervin gave most of his attention during his four years service in Williamsburg to the Indiantown Congregation. However, from the above, it will be seen that a large number of substantial members were added to the Williamsburg Church during his ministry.

The Reverend Alexander Mitchell, a native of Argyleshire, Scotland, succeeded Mr. Ervin in 1832. Mr. Mitchell contracted fever a few weeks after his arrival in Kingstree and died November 4, 1832. He was buried near Mr. Covert in the Williamsburg Cemetery.

The Reverend John McEwen succeeded Mr. Mitchell as minister of Williamsburg Church, but he served only a few months when he died on May 31, 1833.

In February, 1835, the Williamsburg Church secured the Reverend George H. W. Petrie, a native of Charleston and a graduate of the College of Charleston and of the Theological Seminary, as its minister. He served four years. The officers of the Church at that time were, Elders, Daniel Frierson, Isaac Nelson, Henry D. Shaw, David McClary, and James E. Fulton. Mr. Fulton was clerk of the Session and Mr. Nelson treasurer of the congregation. A great many persons united with the Church during his ministry.

The Session Records of the Williamsburg Church from the beginning of the minstry of the Reverend A. G. Peden in 1839, have been preserved. Mr. Peden's Session of Elders was composed of the following men: Isaac Nelson, Daniel Frierson, H. D. Shaw, James E. Fulton, E. W. Greene, W. Camlin, Joseph Chandler, and John A. Gordon.

During the ministry of Mr. Peden, the Session of Elders had one trial of considerable interest. On May 24, 1844, the Reverend Philip Pearson preferred charges of slander and defamation against Elder Daniel Frierson. The Moderator charged the members of the Session "regarding their characters as Judges of the Court of Jesus Christ and the solemn duty in which they were about to come."

The specifications were these: "Mr. Frierson had in a written communication to Reverend P. Pearson, accused said Pearson; first, with the crime of removing his neighbor's land mark; and, second, with having resisted the civil law." Elder Frierson plead not guilty. The witnesses were then called and sworn and the testimony heard on both sides. The parties discussed their cases. Elder Frierson was found guilty and excommunicated. Some time after this, Mr. Frierson wrote a remarkable letter to this Session applying for reinstatement in church membership. He confessed repentance and declared to the Session that he had from his youth up walked in the straight and narrow way, that he had diligently studied many of the prescribed theological works of that period, and that he had an earnest desire to enjoy communion with the Church. Mr. Frierson was again received into the Church.

The Reverend James A. Wallace became minister of the Williamsburg Church on May 20, 1848. Mr. Wallace came here from Cabarrus County, North Carolina, where he was born a son of the Reverend Jedekiah Wallace, himself a Presbyterian preacher. When Mr. Wallace took charge of the Williamsburg Church, it had renewed its youth and had become a leading factor in the social, political, and religious life of Williamsburg District. Soon after his arrival, he married Miss Mary Flagler, a daughter of one of the most prominent families in the district. When he began his ministry here, he firmly believed that Calvinism was the Key to the Kingdom of Heaven, and that the Presbyterian Church held this Key by the election of Almighty God.

Mr. Wallace knew that Cleland Belin had built the beautiful Black Mingo Baptist Church in 1843. This church, still standing near where Willtown once was, abandoned and open, is almost as beautiful and entire and clean as when Mr. Belin had it dedicated to God. It is a wonderful piece of workmanship, a fit place for God to dwell. But when one now looks above its sacred altar expecting to see the Burning Bush, his eye will fall on leather winged bats clinging to its frescoed walls. Mr. Wallace knew that Cleland Belin wore a black silk gown whenever he attended this church on official duty as its Senior Deacon; that he was "faultily faultless, icily regular, splendidly swell;" that his personality dominated the Church and the Black Mingo people regarded him with superstitious awe; and that the Presbyterians need not fear the "Belin Church." Mr. Wallace did not see that the same cancerous Calvinism with which he was about to revaccinate his Williamsburg Congregation was that very same virus out of which came the bats and owls to the Belin Black Mingo Baptist Church.

Mr. Wallace learned soon after he came to Williamsburg that Francis Asbury, Lemuel Andrews, John Bunch, William Capers, John Dix, Henry Hill Durant, John Gamewell, Hope Hull, George Huggins, William Kennedy, Cornelius McLeod, Hugh Ogburn, John R. Pickett, Frederick Rush, Isaac Smith, Alexander Walker, Henry Willis, and other Methodist circuit riders had been coming this way for more than half a century and had been preaching the Fatherhood of God and the Fellowship of

PURITANISM, CALVINISM, ARMINIANISM 293

Man; that Love fulfilled the Law; that Jesus Christ came to show Man his part in the Way to Life. The two little Methodist Churches, one at Ebenezer and the other at Suttons, did not disturb Mr. Wallace. It was the Arminian spirit that was touching the Rock of Calvinism in Williamsburg and making Healing Waters to flow.

Mr. Wallace was a rigorous Calvinist. He proclaimed with a Crusader's zeal the infallibility of the Philadelphia Confession of Faith and honestly believed it the most perfect theological statement in existence. Some quotations from this Confession of Faith show its nature: "God hath decreed in Himself from all Eternity, by the most wise and holy Councel of his own will, all things whatsoever comes to passe," Chapter III, Section 1; again in Section III: "By the decree of God, for the manifestation of His glory, some men and Angels are predestinated, or foreordained, to Eternal Life, through Jesus Christ, to the praise of His glorious grace; others being left to act in their sin to their just condemnation, to the praise of His glorious justice." Section IV: "These Angels and Men thus predestinated, and foreordained, are particularly, and unchangeably designed, and their number so certain, and definite, that it cannot be either increased, or diminished." Again in Chapter X, it said, "Those whom God has predestinated unto Life, He is pleased, in His appointed, and acceptable time, effectually to call by his word, and Spirit....This effectual call is of God's free and special grace alone, not from anything at all foreseen in man, nor from any power, or agency in the creature, co-working with his special grace, the creature being wholly passive therein, being dead in sins and trespasses....Elect infants dying in infancy, are regenerated and saved by Christ through the Spirit....So also are other elect persons, who are uncapable of being outwardly called by the Ministry of the Word." This was the doctrine on which nearly all of the people of

Williamsburg had been brought up and this was the foundation on which Mr. Wallace planned to circumscribe and include the District of Williamsburg.

No knight under the banner of the Cross ever charged the Moslem guarded walls about the Holy Sepulchre more valiantly than did Mr. Wallace that silent growing Arminianism in Williamsburg. He preached Calvinism more eloquently than Williamsburg had theretofore heard. He was a strong man. Somehow, Arminianism kept growing. The more furious the onslaughts of Mr. Wallace the stronger Arminianism grew. Mr. Wallace, one time, almost lost faith in himself. It seemed that the more fervently he preached and the more earnestly his congregation listened the larger Arminianism loomed. So, in 1852, after great effort, he secured the Reverend Daniel Baker, D. D., probably the most powerful Presbyterian evangelist of his age, to conduct a series of meetings at the Williamsburg Church.

"The meeting commenced on the 2nd Sabbath, the 8th of August, and continued nine days; the fruits of which were fifty-nine additions, and the conversion of some of the old members, one of whom is now a Ruling Elder. A few of these persons have apostatized; but in justice to the character of the work, not a greater proportion than of those who have been received from time to time. The character of our congregation is somewhat peculiar—partaking more than is usual of the feelings and habits of the old country. And those who have proved unworthy were mostly such as had been but little impressed, if at all, by Dr. Baker's preaching. They came to the meeting near the close, and united, I fear, only for the purpose of obtaining baptism for their children, and other church privileges. But not the least of the benefits arising from Dr. Baker's visit was the healing of the old schism in the Indiantown Church. Though a few families left, never to return, in consequence of Mr. McPherson's departure, those who had been worshipping with us returned, and the Church is now prospering. We have still received some valuable members from time to time." (Letter of Reverend James A. Wallace, of December 26, 1855.)

The members who united with the Church were as follows: John Armstrong, James Tisdale, N. G. Rich, D. M. Mason, S. C. Murphy, T. J. China, J. C. Matthews, John Murphy, Robert W. Fluitt, Sam Strong, William Kinder, Samuel M. Matthews, John P. Bradley, P. O. Fulton, T. J. Strong, Asa E. Brown, M. F. McCottry, S. E. Fulton, Thomas M. Fulton, J. N. Matthews, John Wheeler, S. J. Montgomery, D. Dukes, William McCullough, S. McBride Scott, Theodore M. Lifrage, Calvin McClary, James S. Brockinton, Mrs. E. S. Armstrong, Leonora McClary, Mary S. Fulton, Agnes Strong, Susan Strong, Rebecca Matthews, Eleanor Fluitt, Mary J. China, Mary McClary, Margaret Fluitt, Adelaide Dukes, Virginia Brockinton, Sarah S. Boyd, Mrs. Daniel Jones, Miss Margaret Tisdale, Miss Elizabeth Tisdale, Elizabeth Staggers, Isabella Dukes, Agnes Murphy, Mary Patterson, Jannet E. Murphy, Adeline S. E. Graham, Sarah C. McClary, Mary Lifrage, Jane McClary, Margaret Strong, Martha McCutchen, Franklin Boyd, Duncan M. Mouzon, and Robert McCants. Most of these members were heads of families and leading citizens in this community. After this meeting and the one at Indiantown held by Dr. Baker, which had similar results in that community, Mr. Wallace realized that the Presbyterian Church had as communing members nearly all of the influential people in the district. He looked on the field and called it fair.

That same year the Harmony Presbytery met in Sumter. Mr. Wallace attended. He was full of his conquest of Williamsburg. He told the other Presbyterian ministers how complete it was and they congratulated him. He was a shining light in that Presbytery. The Moderator called on him to lead in prayer. In this prayer, he thanked God that he had been instrumental in preventing the organization of a Methodist Church in the town of Kingstree. A. Isaac McKnight, one of the members of the Williamsburg Church, was present and heard that prayer.

Mr. McKnight was a lawyer and one of the leading citizens of Williamsburg District. Mr. Wallace's prayer set him to thinking. Mr. McKnight had heard the circuit riders preach and realized that they proclaimed a doctrine that worked in making good citizens in this world as well as sanctified saints for that which is to come. Some time thereafter, Mr. McKnight talked over this matter with some of the influential men of Kingstree and of the surrounding country and they agreed that a Methodist Church in Kingstree would prove a progressive factor in the community.

On January 31, 1853, the following deed was given and recorded at Book G, page 410, Williamsburg County Registry: Alexander Isaac McKnight "for and in consideration of the regard which I have and bear towards the Christian religion and also for and in consideration of the sum of $1.00 to me in hand paid by Thomas R. Mouzon, Samuel E. Graham, James H. Stone, William G. McCallister, and Thomas S. Lesesne, trustees of the Methodist Episcopal Church of the village of Kingstree, one town lot consisting of one-half acre of land bounded on the North by the lands of the said Alexander McKnight and running seventy yards or two hundred ten feet on said lands; on the East by the street leading to Broad Swamp bridges; on the South by the street which was parallel with the Main and Broad Street of the said Village of Kingstree; on the West by the lands of the said Alexander McKnight and running thirty-five yards or one hundred five feet on said land. Said land being in the shape of a parallelogram whose North and South lines are parallel and each one hundred five feet in

PURITANISM, CALVINISM, ARMINIANISM 297

length, all of whose angles are right angles; said half-acre of land or lot is known and designated in the town plat of the King's Tree by No. 159, according to the survey made of the said town of Williamsburg on the 25th day of August, A. D. 1737, by Anthony Williams, D. S., in obedience to an order of the Honorable Thomas Broughton, then Lieutenant Governor, bearing the date of the 8th day of August, 1735."

The Methodist Episcopal Church in Kingstree was built on the lot donated by Mr. McKnight that same year. B. P. Pendergrass had a sawmill near Kingstree and supplied the lumber; John Ervin Scott of Cedar Swamp had a force of carpenters on his plantation and they built the church. That same year, under the leadership of John Ervin Scott, Joseph B. Chandler, and Dr. John C. Williams, the Cedar Swamp Methodist Church was organized and built. Messrs. Newsom and Price erected at the same time the Methodist Church on the Green road about four miles west of the present town of Cades. The Rough Branch Methodist Church, several miles toward Indiantown from Cades, was built by John Frierson and others. A great many substantial men in Williamsburg, whose ancestors had been Presbyterians for generations, united with these churches and supported them.

Very soon after this time, William Staggers donated to John L. Rollins, James M. Staggers, John G. Pressley, and William Bradham, lot No. 401 in the Village of Kingstree, bounded "on the South by Main Street leading from the bridge across Black River; West by Black River; and on all other sides by lands owned by said William Staggers" and containing one-half acre of land "in trust to permit and allow the Baptist denomination to which the said John L. Rollins, James M. Staggers, John G. Pressley, and William Bradham now belong to enter upon and build a Church or meeting house for the use of the said denomination and to permit the members of the Baptist Church, which shall at the said meeting house regularly worship, and for the exclusive control of the said meeting house according to the usages and customs of the Baptist denomination." It is also provided in this deed that should the Kingstree Baptist Congregation desire at any time thereafter to change the location of its house of worship, that the congregation might sell this land donated by Mr. Staggers and use the proceeds in building another church. This deed was dated October 25, 1856.

The Baptists of Kingstree immediately erected a church on this lot and there worshipped until the church was moved to its present site on Academy Street. The lot on the river whereon the first Baptist Church was built was used as a burying ground for a great many years, and is now known as the old Baptist Cemetery. Twenty-one Confederate soldiers, who died here during the War between the Sections, are buried in one plot there and a modest monument stands to their memory.

Some other Baptist Churches were organized and built in the district about this time. Ebenezer Cockfield gave an acre of land on the west side of Lynch's Creek on the road to Indiantown in 1855 to the Baptist Church which was there erected. Aaron F. Graham conveyed on May 11, 1856, "one acre of ground lying on the public road leading to the Williamsburg Court House in the fork of two branches including the new Baptist Church or meeting house near the said Aaron Graham's present residence." Charles McCallister and S. C. McCutchen deeded to M. S. Feagin, Deacon, in behalf of the Midway Baptist Church "one piece of land containing one acre, a part of the Fullwood survey, lying in the Kingstree Swamp on the waters of Black River, one side being on the public road known as the Green road at or about Brown's Avenue." This was in October, 1860.

In 1857, the Reverend James A. Wallace preached a sermon in his church at Kingstree which in reality was a powerful oration seeking to convince his auditors that Williamsburg had been predestined for Presbyterians from the foundation of the world, and that no other religious denominations had any rights therein. In this sermon, he outlined the tradition of Williamsburg Township, and purported to give quotations from grants of King George to the Presbyterian Church, and asserted that grants were made herein only to people who worshipped according to the tenets of the Church of Scotland. No such grants were made by King George, for that the Church of England was the only Church recognized by law in South Carolina until the Declaration of Independence had been signed. The advocate in Mr. Wallace overcame the scholar in preaching this sermon.

This sermon was the supreme effort of Mr. Wallace to hold Williamsburg to Calvinism. It was published as Wallace's History of Williamsburg Church, and is a most treasured volume in many public and private libraries. It is intensely interesting to students of psychology and of history.

This sermon did not stay the hand of Arminianism in Williamsburg. It made hundreds of militant Baptist and Methodists. Mr. Wallace could not see that the hand of God Almighty had written Upharsin over the tabernacles of Calvinism. He lost faith in himself. His mercurial temperament overcame him. One day, while "cleanly weeding his corn" and a slave was ploughing a mule in an adjoining row, Mr. Wallace, without warning, brained the mule with a hoe, cutting that beast off in the blossoms of his sins, "unshriven, unhouseled, unaneled." His unconscious self saw Calvinism materialized in that hapless animal.

Mr. Wallace resigned as minister of the Williamsburg Church, a broken hearted man. One cannot help remembering Shakespeare's Cardinal Wolsey in connection with his resignation:

> "Had I but served my God with half the zeal
> I served my King, he, in mine age,
> Would not have left me naked to mine enemies."

And hear Mr. Wallace soliloquizing when departing for Arkansas:

> "Had I but served my God with half the zeal
> I served John Calvin's god, I should not now
> Be leaving for unknown lands."

Saul began a journey to Damacus. Paul arrived. Wallace the Calvinist began the journey to Arkansas. Wallace the Christian reached those fertile fields. It was a long way, that half thousand leagues in 1858. Thirty miles was a good day's journey, and frequently stormy seasons and swollen streams impeded onward movement. Somewhere along this way, the Reverend James A. Wallace saw a strange Light. It showed him that Calvinism was the theological monstrosity of the ages; that John Calvin created the only god unapproachable by man; that Hope hovers above a praying Igorrote, but Fear alone stalks and grins about a petitioning Calvinist. This Light showed Mr. Wallace that God is Love. He made a remarkable record in Arkansas preaching the Merciful Nazarene. It may be that Mr. Wallace never knew that he had been so wonderfully instrumental in saving a remnant of Williamsburg from Calvinism to the ancient Presbyterian faith, the same that grew out of the spirit of Abraham and Isaiah and Christ. It is possible that he always remembered he came to Williamsburg and found it ninety-five per centum Presbyterian, remained nine years and left his denomination in the minority. It is to be hoped that he realized that he had come for just such a time as this, and that his almost superhuman efforts had made Williamsburg know more certainly than any Arminianist how to give a cup of cold water in Jesus' name. No Presbyterian minister who ever came to Williamsburg drew more Light into this Land. God rest him!

Union Presbyterian Church was organized in 1857. That year William Lifrage granted to J. A. McCullough, W. J. J. Lifrage, and W. F. Rodgers, trustees of the Union Presbyterian Church, one acre of land on the Broom Straw road on which the church was built. Nearly all of the members of this Church had just withdrawn from the Williamsburg Church.

Elon Presbyterian Church was organized in 1856. Thomas China then granted to Henry Montgomery, S. J. Montgomery, and James Plowden, trustees, nine acres of land on the Coleman road on which the church was built. This congregation withdrew from the Brewington Congregation. The story is told that about this time a singing school master came into the Brewington community and everybody in the congregation enrolled in his singing school. Some proved apt pupils and learned new music and wanted to sing it in the Brewington Church. Part of the congregation failed to improve on account of the singing master's efforts, and finally refused even to attempt to sing the new songs, but clung to the old songs and the ancient tunes which had been used by their people since "the memory of man runneth not to the contrary." The faction that could sing the new songs and the faction that could not or would not became hostile to each other. The faction that clung to the old psalmody organized the Elon Church. The Elon Church prospered for about twenty years, when its organization was discontinued.

The Rehoboth Methodist Episcopal Church dates from 1857, when John W. Brogdon and wife, Mary B. Brogdon, conveyed to J. Warrington Oliver, W. J. R. Cantey, J. C. Strange, R. T. Lowder, T. J. M. Davis, R. J. Ragin, and M. M. Benbow, trustees, two acres of land whereupon this church was built.

The Bethel Presbyterian Church was built in 1858. Robert Epps gave the site and the building committee consisted of William H. McElveen, W. J. Burgess, and Daniel H. Smith. This Church was organized by the Burgess', McElveens, Smiths, Friersons, Fultons, Mouzons, and Kinders, who lived on the east side of Pudding Swamp and who heretofore had been members of the Midway Church Congregation. There were fifty-two members of this Church when organized. Samuel A. Burgess, William H. McElveen, W. S. Brand, were its first Session of Elders, and W. D. McFaddin and J. A. McElveen were its first deacons. The Reverend P. Pearson was its first minister. Samuel A. Burgess and William S. McElveen served the church as elders earnestly and faithfully for more than fifty years.

During this period between the War of the Revolution and the War between the Sections, Williamsburg District furnished many ministers of the Gospel. Among them may be mentioned, Robert W. James, William J. Wilson, E. O. Frierson, Elmo Kinder, Jeremiah Snow, R. G. McCutchen, and W. S. Hemingway. The three first named have been mentioned in this text. Mr. McCutchen migrated to the State of Indiana in 1856. Mr. Kinder was the son of Elder John M. Kinder, of Kingstree. The young man was graduated at the Columbia Presbyterian Theological Seminary in 1855, and died in the month following the completion of his education. Some of his old library books in Hebrew, Greek, and Latin may now be found in the Kingstree Carnegie Library. The Reverend W. S. Hemingway was graduated at Wofford College and was a Methodist minister of considerable influence and power. He preached the dedicatory sermon at Spring Street Church in the city of Charleston. He was a Chaplain in the Confederate Army.

In 1860, there were in Williamsburg, the following churches: Presbyterian: Williamsburg, Union, Elon, Bethel, and Indiantown; Methodist: Ebenezer, Union, Suttons, Kingstree, Rehoboth, Rough Branch, and Cades; Baptist: Black Mingo, Kingstree, Lynch's Creek, Black River, Midway, and the Free Will Baptist Church at Pine Grove. Midway and Brewington, Presbyterian, and Saint Mark's Methodist, were near the Clarendon-Williamsburg County line and served many of the people of the district.

From 1730 until 1860, probably no citizen of Williamsburg admitted being a member of the Roman Catholic Church. No person was permitted as an immigrant into the Williamsburg Colony until he had signed an oath that he was a Protestant. Even children from six years of age were required to subscribe to this solemn declaration regarding religious belief.

CHAPTER XXIV.

THINGS, POLITICAL AND SOCIAL, 1830-1860.

On the first day of December, 1922, there were a number of people living in Williamsburg who were born about 1830, and were, therefore, more than ninety years old. Several of these were of the highest types of citizenship, men and women whose minds were still keen and clear and strong and whose memories and judgments were remarkable. Among these were two physicians, Dr. James S. Cunningham and Dr. Isaac W. Graham. As an indication of the interest that these venerable men still held in things, each one read first in his family the newspaper as it came every morning.

These men and women who had lived in Williamsburg for more than ninety years seemed to regard the period between 1830 and 1860 as a wonderful epoch. While old men usually remember their youth as the greatest time in their lives, yet these old fellows had many reasons to give in arguing that from 1830 to 1860 was the halcyon period. There were no poor people in Williamsburg then except those willfully in want. Williamsburg's cupboards were full and its woodsheds overflowing. Kindly masters ruled from their mansion houses their large plantations, and in the evening negroes sang about the "great house" door. The only discord that marred this happy period grew out of arguments on religion and politics. Nobody then cared very much about the price of cotton or tobacco. If the world did not want to buy from Williamsburg, Williamsburg did not care. It had all it wanted. When a man owned more than one hundred slaves, he seemed to lose interest in acquiring temporal things and to devote his special attention to religion and to politics.

Public schools were authorized, but they were designed only for those people who were themselves unable to educate their children. Prior to 1860, all public schools in Willimsburg were more largely in name than in fact. Nearly every planter kept governesses and tutors in his home while his children needed them. There were some community, or parochial schools, like those conducted by Mr. North at Willtown, Mr. Durand at Indiantown, and Mr. Rowe at Kingstree. These schools were more in the nature of academies which the larger children in these communities sometimes attended. The young men were prepared for college at Reid's Academy in Concord, N. C. Bethany Academy in Iredell County, N. C. Yorkville Academy and at Waddell's Academy at Williston. The young men completed their education at the University of South Carolina, the University of North Carolina, the University of Virginia, Princeton, and at Davidson College, North Carolina, Wofford, and Furman Colleges. Medical students attended lectures at the South Carolina Medical College, Charleston. The young women were usually trained under governesses at home and some of them were sent to Salem Female Academy at Winston Salem, North Carolina, and others to Bradford Springs, Dr. Taylor's School at Darlington, and the Barhamville Female College near Columbia, South Carolina. A great many young men from this district received military and technical training at the Citadel, or South Carolina Military College, in Charleston.

Many are the interesting stories told of the College experiences at this time. Dr. Isaac W. Graham and the Reverend James E. Dunlap were students at the University of South Carolina in 1854. Dr. Graham says that a "bigger devil" than James E. Dunlap, in his younger days, never lived. One time, while they were there at the college, a number of students succeeded fairly well in making a night hideous. Among other things, they tore down and concealed within their rooms in the University tenements several sign boards that had rightfully reposed over the doorways of Columbia merchants. The next morning, the University marshal made a tour inspecting the rooms of the students, looking for these pieces of stolen property. Mr. Dunlap had some of them in his room and heard the marshal's footsteps approaching. Mr. Dunlap hurriedly threw the sign boards in the fire and began praying in the "holy tone" so often used in that period by pious preachers in their supreme flights of petitioning eloquence. The marshal heard Mr. Dunlap's marvelous praying and stood spellbound at the door until the sign boards had burned and Mr. Dunlap had ceased praying. Then the marshal entered and commended Mr. Dunlap for his exceeding religious fervor. He did not even look for any sign boards.

Some time during the presidency of Dr. Thornwell, the mess steward did not give the students so many biscuits as they wanted. The students claimed the right to take their meals outside of Steward's hall, but Dr. Thornwell refused and required them to fare where the authorities had provided. Practically all of the students of the University held a "Secession Convention" and unanimously resolved to withdraw from the University of South Carolina and enter the University of Virginia. Dr. Graham and Mr. Dunlap were two of these students engaged in this "Biscuit Rebellion," and so completed their college courses at the University of Virginia, graduating there in 1857.

Dancing, horse racing, and tournaments were the principal social recreations of antebellum Williamsburg. Nearly every planter in the district kept thoroughbred horses, and at least once every year each one thought he had developed a horse that could outrun any other horse in the world. These old men were firm in their convictions in this matter and usually staked a considerable amount of gold on their horses. Racing Days at Kingstree and Willtown and Murray's Ferry were time markers for the whole year. The whiskey distillers of western North Carolina knew these dates well and sent in covered wagons from Concord and Salisbury and Charlotte to Williamsburg sufficient supplies of "mountain dew" to accommodate the gentlemen in Williamsburg.

Tournaments were frequently held when the lords and ladies of Williamsburg appeared at their best. The young men who rode in the tournament impersonated in costume and conduct some favorite knight of ancient history. The herald called the turn in the list, "Earl of Sterling," "The Knight of Dalkeith," or the "Laird of Lochinvar." Out into the softened sunlight and on to the course the rider dashed on Selim of the proud Arabian line. The ladies witnessing held their breath and each one anticipated the winning of her knight and felt beforehand on her brow the crown as Queen of Love and Beauty. That night at the grand ball, the Queen was crowned and her descendants even now of the third and fourth generations know all about this wonderful occasion.

Some of these old Scotchmen had Irish blood in their veins and by virtue of it a sense of humor. Frequently, just after one of these tournaments, where so much pomp and ceremony and splendor had shone, they would stage a gander pulling on the field. Instead of rings, ancient, toughnecked, well greased ganders were suspended by the feet from the posts. The mock herald would call in stentorian tones the "Knight of Tater Hill" or the prince of "Punkin Centre," when out from the lists a clownish clad rider, his long eared steed essaying his utmost, would dash and try to gather gander necks along his way. The "Queen of Fun and Frolic" crowned by the winning gander puller was usually the fairest and fattest man available. It is said jolly John Brockinton, approaching four hundred weight in ordinary times, was prime favorite for this distinction.

Usually grand balls were closing events of Fourth of July celebrations at Kingstree, Willtown, and Lenud's, and sometimes the dances following wedding feasts were of considerable dignity and proportions; but the frequent plantation dances, where almost every one was a close cousin to every other, were the most pleasing and beautiful social affairs of this generation.

Many plantations had negro fiddlers who could make shouting Methodists as well as pious Presbyterians "chase the fox." Almost every young person in the district loved to dance, and perhaps the man who knows would say that nothing ever brought more light and love and joy to old Williamsburg than did these plantation dances of the long ago.

Tradition says Dick, the first African slave brought into Williamsburg, was a fiddler. Colonel Roger Gordon, his master, bequeathed him in his will to his daughter Sarah, who married Hugh McGill. Dick became fiddler facile princeps of all Williamsburg. Prior to Dick's coming into the McGill clan, it is not known just how strong the dance lure lived in them. It is certain, however, that since Dick began to fiddle for Hugh McGill, no McGill has ever been able to keep his feet from keeping time when a fiddle starts. Dick's spirit must even hover over the ground in which his body rests. He lived and died on what is now the Boyd plantation on Campbell Swamp.

Fundamentally religious in conception, but largely social in their working, were sacramental communion occasions and camp meetings. Bethel Congregation introduced camp meetings in Williamsburg amout 1800, but the Presbyterians soon abandoned them for biennial communion meetings. These communion occasions were held in the spring and in the fall of each year at all of the

Presbyterian Churches in the district. There were four days of religious services conducted, Thursday, Friday, Saturday, and Sunday. The congregations of Aimwell, Hopewell, Brewington, Midway, and Salem had been formed originally of people of the Williamsburg and Indiantown communities and were closely related by blood to these people. These communion meetings were announced many weeks before their occurrence, and large numbers from the surrounding Presbyterian Congregations embraced these opportunities of visiting their friends and relatives, as well as of participating in these great feasts of the Church. Frequently, visiting families would come in covered wagons and camp in the churchyard.

Ministers preached two long sermons every day and a most solemn religious atmosphere settled down about the churchyards. All the children of the community were baptized; all erring brethren humbled themselves in the dust before the congregation, received the forgiveness of the elders, and were restored to good standing in the Church. So called sinners were convinced that they were the peculiar elect and were then received into the rights and privileges of the Church. It was on these occasions that the Presbyterian Churches increased their membership.

Incident to these meetings was the deep social influence. About this time, men were exceedingly careful in guarding their daughters even from the appearance of evil. The young women were hardly ever permitted out of sight of duennas, and it was a rare occasion then when a young man could speak a word of love to a young maiden without its being heard by her protectors. Wooing in those days was exceedingly difficult and required practical diplomacy; but, on these communion occasions in this dim religious light, soft eyes could look love and the elders would not disapprove. The matches made were of great sociological value. The friendly relations continued through them, and the knowledge gained by this means of communication between the several communities in this section of South Carolina were of considerable import. Towards the end of this period, the Churches at Williamsburg and Indiantown held four of these communion occasions every year.

The Methodist denomination used camp meetings for evangelism from their introduction in 1800 until 1860. These camp meetings were held in Williamsburg at Popular Hill and at Suttons and sometimes in other sections of the district. The largest camp meetings held in South Carolina were those at Centenary Church in Marion District and at Remberts in the Sumter District. Hundreds of people from Williamsburg attended the meetings that were held at these two churches.

A well suited section of land was selected, usually a large live oak grove, and an immense bush arbor erected. The seats were simply strong pine boards placed on logs that had been lain at proper distances under the arbor. Frequently, more than a thousand people would listen, while seated under such conditions, to the burning eloquence of the evangelists.

During the latter part of this period, many of the wealthier Methodists maintained tents at these camp meetings. These tents were immense in size and partitioned into five sections. In one of these sections, the family lived and slept; in another, the cooking was done and the groceries stored; in the third was the dining room where all meals were served; sections four and five contained sleeping apartments for men and women, respectively. These two sections contained large numbers of mattresses and any one attending the services was gladly received for shelter during the night. All were invited to partake of any meal served. To these large tents every day came supplies in wagons from the owners' plantations and the best in the land was served. Every one who attended these camp meetings had a comfortable place to sleep and an abundance of food. Sometimes, thousands came to these camp meetings; and the social and political as well as the religious results were considerable.

Williamsburg between 1830 and 1860 was concerned deeply with certain fundamental political ideas. The States' Rights question was always before the people and everybody was deeply interested in national affairs in Washington. Local political matters received little attention. The men of Williamsburg voted only for members of the Legislature. The Legislature elected other office holders from governor to constable. The men of Williamsburg knew well how almost every one in the district would vote on stated occasions, when members of the Legislature were to be elected, and so it was difficult to induce many men of the district to take interest in elections and still more difficult to find men who were willing to leave their plantations for about two months every year to attend the session of the Legislature in Columbia.

In 1842, Williamsburg did not elect any representatives in the Legislature at all, nor did it elect any senator in 1846. During the period from 1830 to 1860, the members of the Senate and House of Representatives from Williamsburg were nearly all remarkable men. They were: Senators, D. D. Wilson, William Cooper, E. H. Miller, P. H. Moore, and S. J. Montgomery; House of Representatives, Joseph Bradley, T. D. Singleton, W. J. Buford, W. J. Campbell, Joseph Scott, Joseph R. Fulmore, Robert L. Mouzon, J. W. McCutchen, J. A. Salters, B. W. Bradley, S. J. Montgomery, H. M. McKnight, David Epps, J. C. Wilson, J. G. Pressley, W. M. Belser, and J. S. Brockinton. Among the county officers of this time were: Sheriffs, S. E. Graham, William R. Scott, D. B. Mouzon, William Carter, S. J. Bradley, W. R. Nelson, and W. N. Y. Rodgers; Clerks of the Court, R. G. Ferrell, William R. Scott, R. W. Rockingham, and W. R. Brockinton; Commissioners in Equity, T. D. Singleton, P. G. Gourdin, William R. Scott, William Flagler, Isaac Nelson, D. J. Porter, Dr. Henry Thorne, Reverend J. A. Wallace, Ikey Coleman, and R. C. Logan; Ordinaries, David McClary and N. M. Whitehead; Coroners, Samuel Fluitt, David McClary, Isaac Nelson, J. B. McElveen, and James McClary.

The American Grand Jury seems, of all good functioning governmental agencies in our Republic, that which most nearly approaches idealism in its working. When the average man takes his seat in a grand jury room, he seems then and there to be nearer both God and man than he can be elsewhere. Even the average American Grand Jury works nearly always as if it were conscious of both its human and its divine origin and responsibility. Nothing in American life is respected more than a Grand Jury.

There may have been in Williamsburg from 1830 to 1860 even more regard for its Grand Jury than other districts had. It is certain that this "grand inquest from the body" of Williamsburg was always heard when it spoke and that all good citizens asked for no higher authority for action than its suggestions.

At the fall term, 1833, of the Williamsburg District Court, the Grand Jury made the following presentment: "We, the Grand Jurors of the District of Williamsburg and State aforesaid, present as a grievous evil in our land the intemperate use of ardent spirits. Few causes, indeed, all other causes together, as the Grand Jury believes, have contributed as much as this to produce individual misfortune and distress and public crimes and misdemeanors. A candid exhibition of facts would doubtless lead to the lamentable conclusion that nine-tenths of the domestic evils which disturb the quiet of families and fully as great a proportion of the crimes and minor offences which fill up our Sessions dockets.

"Thus believing, without adding a word touching the great inroads on good morals and the permanence of our civil institutions, which this evil has made and is likely to make; this Grand Jury would earnestly, tho' with great deference, recommend to the Legislatures to grant all the aid and facilities which in their wisdom may be proper for them to grant in restraint of this great evil." Signed: Thomas Steele, Foreman, J. M. Pendergrass, William Brown, Jr., R. Morris, W. Parker, J. S. Dick, William Crapps, Samuel McKenzie, James Tedder, John M. Smith, John G. McKnight, Jesse Mild, George W. Cooper, Randall McDonald, B. R. Pendergrass, and H. D. Shaw.

It is very probable that this report of the Williamsburg Grand Jury, with its recommendation to the Legislature, was the highest recognition the cause of Prohibition had received in the State of South Carolina. It was time that something happened in Williamsburg. The Asbury kind of circuit riders had been preaching in these parts for nearly a half century that Man worked out his own Salvation.

"The Grand Jury for the District of Williamsburg for Fall Term, A. D. 1846, in the discharge of its duty would most respectfully make the following presentments:

"That in its examination of the Public Buildings of the District it finds nothing worthy of remarks, with the exceptions of the windows and doors of the Court House. It finds sundry panes of glass in the windows and lights of the circular room below the stairs broken and think they should be supplied. The cobwebs collected on the panes of the windows and other portions of the Court Room give it a dingy appearance and the Grand Jury think they should be kept away.

"The reports of the various boards of commissioners in the district, with the exception of the report of the Board of Commissioners of Public Buildings, have not been presented to the Grand Jury and of course it cannot express an opinion as to them.

"The Grand Jury presents the present system of Magistrates throughout the State as a great and growing evil. The Jury thinks that unless some change be made it would be better for the quiet and interest of the people that the whole system should be abolished. The change which this Grand Jury thinks advisable is in lieu of the present number, to have only one magistrate for each beat Company within the limits of the district and one extra magistrate for each Court House. The grievance complained is as to the number and as to the character of the magistrates appointed. This Jury thinks that by diminishing the number more competent persons than those who now fill the office may be obtained.

"The Grand Jury would advise an extension of the jurisdiction of the Ordinary in the matter of real estate. While the present law is continued, the rich may not complain, but the poor man has but slight consolation in the reflection that his hard earnings, instead of supplying the wants of them he leaves behind, find their way into the pockets of the officers of the Court of Equity. The forms of proceedings in that court are confessedly costly. The Jury is content that those who are able and willing should be permitted to pursue their rights before that Chancellor, but it deems it a grievance that the poor are not offered an option to adopt a cheaper course.

"The Grand Jury presents that Mr. Cleland Belin has obstructed the public road leading from the big Georgetown road to Black Mingo Creek by the erection of a house and the construction of a gate. The Grand Jury presents the obstruction as a nuisance and would suggest the names of Messrs. S. T. Cooper, J. B. Miller, W. F. Blakely, James Snow, as witnesses in relation to this nuisance. George Barr, Foreman."

"Judge John Belton O'Neal ordered the commissioners to repair the court house at once; that a copy of the report be served on the Senator and Representatives to be by them laid before Legislature and that a bench warrant issue for Cleland Belin."

"In 1848, the Grand Jury notes with pleasure the neat appearance of things about the court house and the general orderliness prevailing." Judge Wardlaw had been exacting in seeing the recommendations of former Grand Juries had been executed. It seems that at this time the county officers for the first time found it necessary to account for all fines and penalties collected. At a preceding term, every county officer was indicted for neglect of duty along this line. This Grand Jury of the Spring Term, 1848, suggested that "comfortable chairs replace the benches then in use for jurors and that the bar be made comfortable for lawyers and that this district might well model its court room and furnishings after the court room in Marion." A. W. Dozier was Foreman of this Jury.

From report of Grand Jury, Fall Term, 1854: "We present as our unanimous opinion that the Federal law abolishing the African slave trade is a public grievance. We hold it has been, and would be, if reestablished, a blessing to the American people and a benefit to the African himself. We hold further that this trade is consistent with the true policy of the South, and that slavery is authorized and sanctioned by Holy Writ, and experience has taught us that by introducing African slavery into these United States, the African has been elevated from a condition of absolute barbarism into one of comparative civilization; from a condition of heathen darkness into one of Christian light; from a condition of despotic and chaotic misrule into one of benign and regulated law. We hold that slavery is forbidden by no principle of policy or religion except that which springs from the frenzied imagination of fanatic philanthropy which arrogantly assumes to be purer and holier than what is written. We therefore recommend this subject to the consideration and action of the Legislature of the State, trusting that through its influence the evil complained of may be remedied." D. M. Mason, Foreman.

The Fall Term, Grand Jury, 1855, presented as a grievous nuisance the dragging of the mouth of Black River with seines by men from the North, so that Williamsburg was deprived of its normal and accustomed supply of fish in its waters. The Legislature is asked to remedy this evil condition.

Trading with slaves seems to have been the most common yet most serious offence general in Williamsburg in 1858. The Grand Jury that year asks the Legislature to pass an Act making trading with slaves punishable by whipping. Some of the richest merchants in the district at that time persisted in buying seed cotton at night from slaves. A pillory was erected on the Court House Square in Kingstree at this time for one of these offending merchants and he would have been placed in the stocks had not one man, his friend, suspected the purpose for which the structure was being erected and informed him in time for his escape.

The pillory had been used in the district at an earlier date than this, for a man convicted of "Assault with intent to murder" in 1815, was sentenced to one month in jail, fined fifty dollars, and to stand in the pillory fifteen minutes between twelve o'clock noon and two in the afternoon on the first Monday in April. In 1841, two white men, convicted of stealing three bushels of corn, were sentenced to receive on the first Monday in December, ten stripes; the first Monday in January, ten stripes; and the first Monday in February, ten stripes; and to be imprisoned for three months.

In 1859, the Grand Jury report contained the following: "We recommend that the Commissioners of Public Buildings apply to the Legislature for authority to sell a portion of the Eastern and the Western boundaries of the Public Square (Court House Square.) We find same unnecessarily large. We present the free negroes of the district as a nuisance and recommend that the Legislature pass some law that will have the effect of relieving the community of this troublesome element. We also present the present militia system as a nuisance and recommend that the same be abolished and another more efficient be substituted." Signed, D. D. Wilson, Foreman.

In the Williamsburg District in 1860, there were the following postoffices: Black Mingo, Camp Ridge, China Grove, Indiantown, Johnsonville, Kingstree, Lynch's Lake, Murray's Ferry, Santee, Natural Grove, and Parsonage.

Among the professional men of this period were: Lawyers, N. G. Rich, E. J. Porter, John G. Pressley, A. Isaac McKnight, and Samuel W. Maurice; Physicians, Dr. T. M. Mouzon, William Dollard, B. W. Bradley, S. D. M. Byrd, D. M. Mason, T. D. Singleton, Richard Jarrott, J. W. Staggers, S. J. Singletary, J. C. Williams, S. D. McGill, Isaac W. Graham, James S. Brockinton, John F. Brockinton, and Henry Thorne.

The Thirty-first Regiment of militia played a prominent part in the life of Williamsburg during this period. Once every month, the several companies met on their respective drill grounds in the many parts of the district and every Fourth of July all of the companies gathered on the Regimental Parade Ground at Black Mingo for regimental manoeuvres and a parade. These regimental meetings were occasions of great ceremony and were anticipated all during the year. Not only were then the several companies in the Regiment recruited up to legal strength and the Regiment drilled as a whole, but also on this day great barbecue feasts were enjoyed and usually the Governor of South Carolina delivered a patriotic address. On nearly every regimental muster day at Willtown the governor came, since it was a valuable opportunity for his own political future as well as the inculcation of patriotic principles. The Declaration of Independence was always read and patriotic songs were sung.

After the official and formal social events of the day had concluded, the "bullies" tried their strength and the district champion for the year was determined. Every section of the district had its "bully," the man who thought he could whip every other man in his community, at these regimental musters. The several communities brought out their respective champions and by a process of elimination in actual fist fights, the "bully" for the whole district was determined. These "bully" contests excited intense interest and formed the subject of conversation for the district for many moons. Sometimes, brigade reviews were held and the "bullies" from each regiment would meet in combat and the brigade "bully" would receive his laurel wreath.

On these regimental muster occasions at Willtown, the Governor of South Carolina was usually the guest of Cleland Belin. Mr. Belin was wealthy, had a beautiful home, and was one of the most unique characters that Williamsburg ever produced. His home was a splendid structure, finished and furnished in the similitude of a palace. He had considerable mechanical ability and supervised the erection of his residence. He required the builders to finish even its hidden corners with greatest care. Probably no other building erected in South Carolina up to that time was, from floor to roof, more nearly perfect. In his home, he gathered many objects of art and beautiful books and curiosities from the four corners of the globe. There were twelve bedrooms in his house.

In each one of these bedrooms, he had a grandfather's clock out of which fairies came at the end of each hour and danced and played on their little stages. These clocks in the several rooms were set successively five minutes ahead of each other so that every five minutes in the day in some room in the house fairies played. Mr. Belin's home excited great interest in this section of South Carolina. Thousands of people visited it every year and all of them, prince and peasant alike, received a cordial welcome.

Mr. Belin was a very successful business man and a man of considerable natural mental ability. His education was limited, yet some of his manuscripts and the inscriptions which he placed on monuments show a remarkable depth of thought and an excellent command of language. Governor Gist, after he had been entertained in Mr. Belin's home on one occasion, when returning to the Capitol, said in Kingstree, "If Cleland Belin had received a liberal education in his youth, he would have become the most powerful man in South Carolina."

Battalion musters were held in Kingstree and near Lenud's Ferry every year. On these battalion muster occasions, the Declaration of Independence was read and patriotic songs were sung. From the Revolution until the War between the Sections in 1861, it is probable that no part of the United States loved or regarded with greater veneration and respect than did Williamsburg what it regarded as the Constitution of the United States. That its interpretation was over-ruled by the supreme court of war detracts nothing from the splendor of its homage.

In 1837, when the Seminole Indian outbreak occurred, the Williamsburg Regiment of Militia furnished its quota of men. Among the volunteers at the first opportunity for service may be mentioned: John F. D. Britton,

Thomas R. Greer, J. L. Brown, W. G. Cantley, Samuel McGill, Winfield Scott, and E. P. Montgomery.

When war was declared with Mexico in 1844, a large number of the young men of Williamsburg volunteered and won everlasting fame as soldiers in the Palmetto Regiment. This Regiment was in the severest fighting at Buena Vista and Cherubusco, and sharpened its sabers on the walls of old Chapultepec.

Among the officers of the militia during this period, the following are outstanding: Colonels, D. D. Wilson, Washington Cockfield, William Cooper, and S. J. Montgomery; Captains, S. J. Snowden, John E. Scott, John G. Pressley, John Coachman, Leonard Dozier, John Green, and William G. Flagler. These men were very influential in civil as well as military affairs. Colonel Montgomery was commanding the Regiment at the beginning of the War between the Sections. He was also Senator from Williamsburg and died holding this high place. Colonel Washington Cockfield seems to have been one of the most spectacular officers of the day. The old men of present Williamsburg, who were then boys, remember him in full regimentals, his long waving plume and flashing sword, dashing about the Willtown muster ground on his coal black charger.

The one great curse of this halcyon period in Williamsburg was fever. Almost every year at least half of the people were incapacitated for business and for social activity on account of this malady. A few times typhus became epidemic and took a tremendous toll of human life. In 1815, the first epidemic occurred and hardly a home in the district was left untouched by the death angel. Again in 1854, it raged. At the spring term of the court in 1857, the district officers were ordered by the court to occupy their new quarters which had been recently added to the Court House. This order had not been obeyed when court convened in October. When the offending officers were served with the rule to show cause why they should not be punished for contempt, they showed to the satisfaction of the court that for three months prior to that time there had not been a sufficient number of people in the town of Kingstree unafflicted by fever to care for the actual needs of those who were stricken. But the great continuous curse of this period was malaria. Infected mosquitoes clouded the country. Dr. Isaac Graham says that when he was a small boy on Santee frequently he found difficutly in drawing a "bead" with his rifle on a squirrel up a tree on account of the mosquitoes swarming in the air.

Everybody in this country then had two residences. The house in which the family lived in winter was called its home. The place it lived in summer was either far removed from the swamps, or in the mountains of North Carolina. Women and children who lived near the swamps in summer were in great danger.

The old family graveyards filled during these periods tell fearful tales. Planters usually selected a square plot of about one-fourth an acre for their burying ground and there only the members of the family were interred. There are now hundreds of these old graveyards that show the father, mother, and five or more of their children of less than five years old buried by their sides. Diphtheria and malaria did their deadly work, so that in few families half of the children born reached maturity. The most pathetic tale told by these old tombstones is that of Cleland Belin and Sarah Margaret McFaddin. To them were born thirteen children before she died at forty years of age. Eleven of these thirteen are all buried in a row beside her, not one of the eleven having reached the age of five years. Mrs. Belin died before her husband and he placed a tombstone to her and one to each of their eleven dead children. He wrote the following inscription on the stone erected to her memory, "Sarah Margaret Belin, daughter of Mr.

William McFaddin, beloved wife of Cleland Belin, born 27 August, 1811, died 3 October, 1851. She was industrious, careful, and domestic in her habits, retiring in her manner, calm and tranquil in her demeanor, hospitable in her feelings, forgiving in her temper, and Christian in her principles."

It is said that when the French Huguenots first settled on the Santee River in Williamsburg, there were then quantities of mosquitoes infesting the section but that they were not infected with the germs that produced malaria. For many years these mosquitoes were not a serious menace to the community, but that some years after the introduction of African slaves, the malaria germ began to threaten the whole section, and, sooner or later, the pest made the section almost uninhabitable for Caucasians. It is believed that the malaria germ came into Williamsburg by way of the slaves imported from Africa.

Malarial fever, as it developed in the fifties, on the Santee, surpasses human capacity for description. When the germ once overpowered a human system, it was relentless. It took away life slowly and certainly. A man might be plowing in the fields when he first felt its force and from that moment he gradually failed. Some of the men and women of this period who overcame this malignant germ showed ever afterwards remarkable resistance to all the ills to which flesh is heir. One hears now the statement made, in opposition to the use of vaccines and mosquito exterminators, that a great many people who dwelt in the Santee swamps lived to be a hundred years old. These relators overlook the fact that nine average persons perished where one extraordinary physical specimen survived. Many years ago the mosquitoes were conquered, the fevers ceased to burn.

CHAPTER XXV.

TRANSPORTATION, 1830-1860.

Men called the ways over which they travelled in Williamsburg during this period roads. It is strange that men of their intelligence and their patriotic impulses and unlimited quantities of slave labor built no highways, but continued to worry along with ways over which they might go only at certain seasons of the year. The roads of this period wound in and out and around about the swamps. Much of the time they were half covered with water and boggy to an impassable degree. Perhaps these men of the prewar period had on their plantations about everything they wanted and did not see the necessity for roads.

With the slave labor at the command of Williamsburg during this period, and without effecting its production of cotton one bale, the district could have constructed roads that would have lasted like Indian mounds and have been for the good of a hundred generations. These planters usually had small boats that carried their cotton down the winding Wee Nee River to Georgetown. They seemed not to care that the courses these boats had to follow were a hundred miles. They could have, with a minimum amount of cost, straightened the river and made the distance less than half. Nor did they ever make any effective attempts to dredge the river. It is true that sometimes they would cut long pine trees that had fallen into the river and had become serious menaces to their sloops and flat boats, but this was about all that they did to improve the navigability of this natural highway. Black River has run by Kingstree for two hundred years without any businesslike effort undertaken to make its use valuable to the district.

The planters of Williamsburg marketed their cotton and tobacco at Georgetown since they could float these products down the river. Bringing back things up the river was a more difficult task and possibly this was a factor in the increasing wealth of the Williamsburg District during this period. It was much easier to carry things to market than to bring things from the market home. Always, except in emergencies, Williamsburg has chosen the easier way.

Some of the planters of Williamsburg lived at such a distance from the river that they transported their cotton and tobacco overland, crossing Black River at Brown's Ferry. A few marketed their products in Charleston, crossing the Santee at Murray's and Lenud's Ferries. All the district north of Williamsburg as far as North Carolina used the Murray's Ferry road through Kingstree and crossed the Santee there in going to Charleston and returning. Murray's Ferry was for a century one of the most important points in South Carolina. Usually in history rivers proved great blessings to the communities through which they flowed, but not so the Santee. It is a treacherous river, uncertain and dangerous. It was a barrier to eastern South Carolina for two centuries. Often passengers could not cross it at Murray's Ferry, and had to wait until its floods subsided. Sometimes when a crossing could not be effected at Murray's Ferry, it could be accomplished at Lenud's Ferry forty miles down the river. Lenud's Ferry was not used, however, from 1830 to 1860 so much as Murray's Ferry.

In 1856, the Northeastern Railway was built from Charleston northward through the Williamsburg District. The building of this railroad proved at once that it was an enormous factor in the life of Williamsburg District. On this railroad, planters could ship their produce and could go themselves in a few hours over the same distance that theretofore had required several laborious days. Very soon, the greater part of the business of Williamsburg was done in Charleston, and Georgetown ceased to be the trading seat of this district. Planters from Williamsburg shipped their cotton to factors in Charleston every fall. These factors sold their cotton and accepted their drafts from time to time. All of the cotton was thrown on the market about the same time and sold at such prices as the factors determined.

Planters of Williamsburg secured their supplies from merchants in Charleston almost entirely after the building of the Northeastern Railroad. These planters knew and were known to certain merchants in Charleston who filled the orders of the planters all during the year. If the cotton crop had been a good one, these merchants accepted their pay about November first. Nobody ever thought of paying bills oftener than once a year. If the Williamsburg planter had failed to make a good crop, the merchant permitted him to postpone payment until the following November. It was so easy to buy on order and pay days were so far away that just about the beginning of the War between the Sections, Williamsburg was enjoying a season of riotous living.

Bridging the Santee and completing the railroad through Williamsburg District was a tremendous task in those days when practically all labor was done by man power. Such engineering projects were also attended with great danger and several men lost their lives while this work was being done. Railroading was extremely hazardous in that experimental stage and often railroad men were killed in accidents. The supervising constructor of the Santee trestle, Mr. Littlefield, lost his life before completing his task. The first bridge built there in 1856 was a wooden structure and many miles of trestle work were required before the embankments were placed many years later. The first section boss was killed on this trestle within a year after trains began running. The first section boss in the Cades community was also killed in 1857.

The first train that ran through Williamsburg County is remembered distinctly by many persons now living. Celebrations were staged at its several stopping points in the district and multitudes of people, brass bands, and barbecue feasts greeted the day the locomotive whistle first startled the denizens of these swamps. Dr. D. C. Scott, then a six-year old boy living in the Cedar Swamp community, was brought by his father to see the first railroad train come into Kingstree. Dr. Scott's father had bought him a hobby horse in Kingstree that day and as the train was approaching, his father cautioned him to hold his horse or the train would frighten him. Every real horse in Kingstree that day was securely tied far away from the railroad.

At that time, people in Kingstree enjoyed seeing the trains pass. Some built their houses on Railroad Avenue for the purpose of witnessing railroad trains pass morning and evening. Seventy-five years later, when the great Atlantic Coast Line Railroad runs almost a continuous line of trains over its double tracks along Railroad Avenue in Kingstree, the descendants of these same people, who live in the houses which they built, are much disturbed by the passing of so many trains.

Up to this time, probably no other event in the history of Williamsburg, save the War of the Revolution, had such an immediate and far-reaching influence on the district as did the building of this Northeastern Railroad. The innkeepers in Kingstree and at Murray's Ferry and the ferrymen viewed the situation with alarm. All at once the line of travel from the North ceased coming through Kingstree and passing over Murray's Ferry, and it was not many years before the last ferry boat on the Santee had sunken and the ferryman's song forever hushed.

The building of the Northeastern Railway inflicted a serious blow on Georgetown. Up to that time, a considerable part of its trade had come from Williamsburg. This trade moved to Charleston almost at once after the railroad service began. Henceforth, Charleston and not Georgetown was the center of the commercial interest of Williamsburg.

Immediately after the Northeastern Railway was built through Williamsburg, there came "down here from North Carolina" a multitude of turpentine workers and distillers who began to develop the lumber and naval stores industries. These immigrants for the most part were a vigorous, hardy, and energetic people. They were about the first white people whom that generation in Williamsburg had ever seen who worked with their hands as well as their heads. This working of white people with their hands produced uncertain and conflicting opinions of them in Williamsburg. Some regarded these turpentine workers simply as "poor white trash" unworthy of notice. Others were not so sure. Williamsburg sold them turpentine rights at first for a song, but soon learned from the fortunes being made by these turpentine workers the value of a pine tree.

Richard H. Kellahan came into Kingstree without a dollar in the world. He was a likely looking youngster. M. J. Hirsch, Esq., a lawyer in Kingstree, took a fancy to him, bought him a pair of shoes and an axe and grubstaked him for three days. Mr. Kellahan went into the woods and chipped turpentine trees until he became a millionaire. Ferney Rhem "came down here from North Carolina" about 1847, settled on the Georgetown-Williamsburg County line and began to work turpentine. A few years later, he had a small empire in that section. When he died, he was one of the largest land owners in South Carolina and his descendants have been continuously adding to their estate. There were many others of these men who made fortunes and were influential factors in Williamsburg.

Among these "Tar Heels" who came to Williamsburg, Dr. McGill mentions J. F. Carraway, P. H. Bufkin, Isham Hinson, R. P. Hinnant, Augustus Haddock, John, James, and Edwin Harper, James, William, and Walter Bryan, James E. David, Thomas Edwards, Edward and Henry B. Johnson, S. B. Newsom, S. W. Mills, Hardy Hallimer, Samuel Moore, W. Lee, R. H. Kellahan, N. G. Pitman, Augustus Perkins, E. J. Parker, Jessie Turner, F. Rhem, W. T. Willoughby, Cicero and Hagard Whitfield, and W. K. Lane.

CHAPTER XXVI.

SLAVERY AND SECESSION.

There were two great ideas obtaining at the time of the creation of the American nation. For twelve years, there had been thirteen independent states along the Atlantic coast. It was realized that some form of union was necessary for the mutual protection of these states and for their highest opportunity for development. Until this time, a state had depended most largely on the personality of some individual leader, or king; and about him, the personalities of several lesser leaders, who dominated sections of the country, gathered. A strong king made a strong nation but the making of a strong nation usually worked unnecessary hardships upon the individuals composing this state.

The founders of the American Union were learned men. They knew the history of nations and had followed them as they rose and fell. One faction of the founders honestly believed that these thirteen states, along the Atlantic seaboard, should unite, surrendering to the Federal Union all of the powers inherent in a state and thus make the union one great state wherein all the powers of these thirteen smaller states should be amalgamated. This faction realized the practically unlimited possibilities of this great union existing in their minds. The individual leaders of this faction lived in the northern portion of these colonies where commerce and manufacturing predominated. They had much relationship with the other states of the world and saw very clearly how much better for them would be such a powerful state as the complete fusion of these thirteen states would make.

The other idea as to the formation of the American state obtained in the southern portion of the territory. The Southerners were planters and stock raisers. They lived largely on their plantations and had but little actual need for anything which they did not produce. The dominant element in this southern portion were extreme individualists by inheritance. They wanted to be let alone. They saw that economic conditions in so large a territory would result in inevitable clashes of interest and believed that the best thing for them would be to preserve, as far as possible, states' rights in their own section.

Sentiment, however, was by no means unanimous in either the northern or the southern sections of the American territory. The strong central government idea, however, predominated in the North, while the sectional rights idea maintained the ascendency in the South. Sentiment in the State of South Carolina was overwhelmingly in favor of the retaining all rights possible in the formation of the Federal Government.

Sentiment in Williamsburg District, however, was comparatively evenly divided. In the Constitutional Convention at Columbia, in 1788, when South Carolina joined the Union, Wiliam Wilson was one of the leaders in the promotion of the strong central government idea in the convention, while Patrick Dollard was equally enthusiastic and effective in his efforts for retaining everything which South Carolina could before adopting the Federal Constitution. Mr. Dollard eloquently opposed to the end the adoption of any Federal Constitution.

For several decades, Williamsburg had close relations with Charleston and Georgetown, where commerce and shipping interests predominated. In these two cities the strong federal union idea was in the ascendency in the beginning, and probably from them came the force that inclined Williamsburg until the tariff became unreasonable.

When the cost of maintaining the Federal Government became considerable and the levying of indirect taxes, popularly known as the tariff, became burdensome, sentiment in Williamsburg began to change; and later when the tariff in the beginning levied for the support of the Federal Union began practically to subsidize manufacturing and commercial interests and lay grievous burdens on stock raising and agriculture, the sentiment towards states' rights grew rapidly.

The first state action in South Carolina was the Nullification Convention in 1832. Sentiment about that time in Williamsburg was by no means unanimous. In fact, the more substantial element in the district did not favor the proceedings of the Nullification Convention.

When the manufacturing section of the United States secured control in the Congress and began to use a giant's strength like a giant, agriculture of South Carolina arose and asserted what it believed its rights under the American Constitution as adopted in 1789.

In the beginning and until the production of cotton in large quantities began about 1800, slave labor was not profitable in South Carolina, and up to this time the State had often considered the abolition of slavery. Gradually, from 1800, African slaves grew in value in South Carolina, since slaves had produced cotton and rice at a profit. African slaves were not profitable in the northern sections of the country. From about 1800 until 1860, the northern section of the country was just as eager to sell its slaves as the southern portion was anxious to buy, and it did not take many years of eager sellers and anxious purchasers to shift slavery to the South.

The conflict of these two ideas as to the American Union, the strong states' rights idea and the strong federal union notion, had inextricably mixed in it serious economic conditions due to differences of sectional interest. Each section soon began to consider only itself and gradually compromises of conflicting economic interests grew more and more difficult.

Slavery was the source of great power in the South. The North realized this. It is but a short way from the realization of an economic interest to the actualization of a strong religious sentiment to sustain and support it. It did not, therefore, take a long time for professional Puritan religious reformers to begin to preach and to pray about the evils of African slavery in the South. Some of them were sincere and honest, perhaps most of them, but like all reformers, they lost themselves in their own delusions. The power which slaves gave the South in Congress was the real reason for so many pathetic "Songs of Labor" which were written in the section where no darkies sang around the "Great House" door. The rabid Abolitionists at the North usually proclaimed only the inhumanity of African slavery in the South. The most charitable thing that may be said about them is that they did not know.

This is no defense of African slavery in the South. African slavery in the South did not grow out of missionary ideas for the promotion of the Christian spirit in the world, nor was it designed for the promotion of altruistic sentiment, but it did take a race of men that for thousands of years had roamed the pampas and plains and jungles of Africa like wild beasts, and, within a single century, bring forth multitudes of substantial Christian men and women.

In 1808, there was a shipload of Guinea negroes sold in Williamsburg, South Carolina. They spoke no language save that of grunts and nods. They knew not their right hand from their left. One hundred years later, in 1908, the descendants of these same Guinea negroes were prosperous citizens. Some of them owned considerable plantations and produced large crops of corn, cotton, and tobacco; some of them were members of the bar in New

York City; some were practising medicine; some were architects and builders. There is no other case of such remarkable development of a race recorded in history or told in tradition.

Slave owners in Williamsburg, South Carolina, were neither more nor less saintly, human nor inhuman, than other men of the world of their day and generation. When these savage Africans were brought to this district, they could not be disciplined or controlled and civilized and made serviceable only by the use of smooth tongues and gloved hands. It was necessary that the planter transform a wild man into a profitable workman within a short period of time that the slave might be profitable. This was a tremendous task and it was well done with as little physical force as was expedient. One now marvels that the transformation was often effected by these planters within such a short period of time. Slaves were required to render instant and unquestioning obedience and this proved their salvation. Out of this slave training, came some of the most noble characters, the most loyal subjects, and the most beautiful service ever seen in the world. One wonders now when he thinks that the son of a cannibal could become the "major domo" of a southern plantation. It required clear minds, strong arms, and endless patience to make Guinea negroes into serviceable citizens. South Carolina did it. It must not be thought for one moment that the transformation of these savages into good men and women was effected for other than utilitarian and economic motives, but the resulting love and loyalty fostered in this reformation often proved the most beautiful thing in the world.

Bill was the son of a negro captured in the jungles on the Congo, and sold as a slave on the block in Charleston. In the graveyard about the beautiful old Black Mingo Baptist Church, one now finds a marble slab on which is graven: "Sacred to the memory of Bill, a strictly honest and faithful servant of Cleland Belin. Bill was often intrusted with the care of Produce and Merchandize to the value of many thousand dollars, without loss or damage. He died 7th October, 1854, in the 35th year of his age, an approved member of the Black Mingo Baptist Church. Well done, thou good and faithful servant. Enter thou into Joy of thy Lord."

It must not be understood that slaves were always well and kindly treated. It must be realized that there were many thousand masters of so many thousand minds and hearts. It must be remembered, however, that nearly every one of these many thousand masters was essaying his utmost to make his slaves as valuable as possible and knew the value of good treatment and kindness in the development of the serviceability and dependability of his slave.

It is told of a large slave owner, one in Williamsburg District, that sometimes he moved up and down his line of slaves, while they were working in the fields, beating them promiscuously with his cane, and sometimes he knocked one senseless. It is told of another slave owner in the district that once he hanged a negro man up by the thumbs and used the claws of an enraged tom cat to lacerate the bare back of the suspended slave. These two stories are probably true. Each of these masters, however, would now be considered a paranoiac. At least half of the descendants of each one of them have spent a considerable part of their lives in sanitariums for the treatment of nervous diseases. That same master of whom the story is told of suspending the negro by the thumbs was seen one morning digging a ditch in a swamp while several of his slaves stood near on dry ground. A man passing asked the master why he did not make the negroes do the work. The master replied, "It might make the negroes sick."

SLAVERY AND SECESSION 335

In Williamsburg, slave owners fed and clothed their negroes the best they knew. The best physicians that could be secured were kept on the plantations and negroes were given every possible medical attention. They were too valuable to lose. Stories of cruelty and inhuman treatment of slaves in Williamsburg in individual cases may be true but the fact remains that the Williamsburg slave prepared his master's food, nursed his master's children, and closed his master's eyes in death. The master loved his negro and the negro loved his master, and out of their relations, grew much of the beauty of the world.

In 1835, petitions from the North began to flood Congress for the abolition of slavery in the District of Columbia and from this time until slavery was abolished in the United States, the activities of the abolitionists increased. Almost everything done by act of Congress in the city of Washington was tinctured with the slavery question and it was a continuous struggle between slavery and the anti-slavery forces to secure a majority in the Congress. The anti-slavery section was much larger in territory and in population than the slavery section. Every time, during this period, that new territory asked to be admitted into the Union, there was a fight as to whether it should be a free or a slave state; and for a long time states were admitted in pairs, one free and one slave. They could be admitted in no other way.

This continuous agitation on the subject of slavery, the means used for its abolition and the realization of the effect of its abolition on the South, made practically every southern planter a secessionist. Until about 1856, when the Dred Scott decision was delivered by Chief Justice Taney, there had been a great many union men in South Carolina, those who had steadfastly hoped and believed that the Union might continue and that the slavery question might be settled without secession. Some of the best men in Williamsburg District were among these union men. Love for the United States of America, until 1850, was nowhere greater than it was in Williamsburg. When the Unionists of Williamsburg realized that the Dred Scott decision would be nullified by some means, and when they fully understood the principles of the Constitution of the United States, supplemented by the decision of the Supreme Court, would be nullified in one way or another, then all Williamsburg saw that secession was the only way that states' rights, as had been and were being held in these parts, could be maintained.

In 1851, there was an election held in the State of South Carolina on the question of secession. The largest vote ever cast in the State was recorded at that time,— Secession 17,056; Cooperation, 24,914. The Secession party after its election renewed its efforts. A confidential letter distributed among the members of the Secession party, which letter was written by Maxcy Gregg, afterwards a distinguished general in the Confederate Army, contains the following paragraphs: "The defeat of the Secession Party has been effected by a coalition of Parties repugnant to each other in their principles, and by means most pernicious to the safety, as well as humiliating to the character, of the State of South Carolina.

"The Anti-Secession coalition is composed of two principal sections. The first, which is much the smallest (sic) in number and has heretofore been regarded as of inconsiderable power, is the Union Party. Adherence to the Union, at the expense of whatever submission and degradation may be required, is the object of this party. The success of the coalition thus far enures to the benefit of the Union Party.

"Another section of the coalition, and a much larger and more powerful one, consists of disunion men, who, sensible of the degradation and danger of our condition, desire to resist, and to form a Southern Confederacy, but regard

SLAVERY AND SECESSION 337

the cooperation of other States in the resistance either as indispensable or of such paramount importance as not to justify the separate action of South Carolina at the present time.

"Between these two sections is perhaps to be placed another class of men professing the resistance principles of the last as most popular, but really desirous of defeating all efforts for resistance and continuing in the Union. This class may at any moment, when their time serving propensities may prompt it, bring a great and sudden accession of power to the Union Party.

"Gloomy as is the prospect, it is not yet necessary to give up the cause of the State in utter despair. Submission is not yet to be contemplated as our inevitable destiny."

In 1852, a Secession Convention was held in the city of Columbia, at which the resolution as follows was adopted: "We, the People of the State of South Carolina, in Convention assembled, do declare and ordain, and it is hereby declared and ordained, That South Carolina, in the exercise of her sovereign will, is an independent State, acceded to the Federal Union, known as the United States of America, and that in the exercise of the same sovereign will, it is her right, without let, hindrance, or molestation from any power whatsoever, to secede from the said Federal Union; and for the sufficiency of the causes which may impel her to such separation, she is responsible alone, under God, to the tribunal of public opinion among the nations." The representatives from Williamsburg were S. E. Graham, A. W. Dozier, and D. M. Mason. Mr. Dozier did not attend this convention.

This convention shows the feeling in South Carolina at that time. It makes it very plain that all hope of remaining in the Union had not been lost, but just as clearly does it show the determined opposition to the encroachment on states' rights by the dominant element in the American Congress.

In 1854, Governor James H. Adams recommended that the African slave trade be opened. Committees were appointed by both branches of the Legislature to consider the matter and report at its next session. In this Legislature, a member of the committee appointed by the House of Representatives was J. Johnston Pettigrew, one of the most brilliant men that South Carolina ever produced. He read the minority report for this special committee of the House of Representatives. Trescot said that it was "a clear, complete, eloquent, and forceful exposition of the convictions of three-fourths of the slave holders of the South." Pettigrew's report is one of the greatest papers of the slavery regime. Many people in South Carolina hoped that such men as he would be able so to direct the opinions of the majority that secession and bloodshed would be avoided. The slave trade was not reopened.

There were at this time eighteen thousand slaves owned by negro masters in the United States and negro masters in the State of South Carolina more than that relatively proportionate number. There were some negro slave owners in Williamsburg. The descendants of Joshua Braveboy, a negro who had won his freedom on account of his services in the Revolutionary War, owned many negroes in this district.

The value of a good farm negro in Williamsburg in 1800 was $500.00; in 1820, $725.00; in 1840, $800.00; in 1850, $700.00; in 1860, $1200.00. Slaves who were well trained as house servants, horsemen, mechanics, carpenters, blacksmiths, and to other useful trades, frequently were sold for prices ranging from three to five thousand dollars in gold. In 1860, South Carolina stood third among the states in the Union in per capita wealth, $779.00 a head. The state taxation amounted to $1.85 per capita.

Slaves and general wealth were probably more evenly divided in Williamsburg County in 1850 than in any other district in the State of South Carolina. There were practically no poor people in the district and there were few who were very wealthy. There was no place in the district for a man who did not own slaves except as an overseer of slaves. Men who did not own slaves, except those who could find places as overseers on the plantations, did not remain long in Williamsburg. They migrated westward. Some of them went to Kansas and to California and usually became spitfire abolitionists. The doings of Kansas, Nebraska, and California had much more influence on the secession of the South and the abolition of slavery than did the preaching of ministers and the publishing of pamphleteers in Massachusetts and Ohio. Some of the very men who could find no place in Williamsburg were those most aggressive in the new states. There was, however, a class of white citizens in Williamsburg prior to 1860 who owned but a few slaves and who worked with their own hands. These were the turpentine men who began coming to this district in 1843.

From 1850 until 1860, however much the conservative element in South Carolina had labored to avert scession, it was known that such would finally result. The religious denominations in the country broke their bonds of union. There became a Presbyterian Church North and a Presbyterian Church South; a Methodist Church North and a Methodist Church South; and a Baptist Church North and a Baptist Church South. The Protestant Episcopal Church in the United States had no such bond of union as the Presbyterians, Baptists, and Methodists. Each diocese determined for its own territory its polity. It had, therefore, no reason for further disunion.

Theological diplomats of these several denominations declared one reason and another for these separations, but all their ex cathedra utterances were so thinly veiled by truth that the everlasting fact stood out unmistakable and clear. The ruling element in the membership of Methodist, Baptist, and Presbyterian Churches in the North held that slavery was wrong, and the dominant faction in those same churches in the South declared that slavery was right. These churches, and all other churches, by whatsoever name known, in every age and clime, follow the will of Man, their Creator, Preserver, and Promoter. Some of the most powerful sermons ever preached in Massachusetts were based on the doctrine that Slavery was the incestuous offspring of Sin and Death. Even more eloquent were some of the proclamations coming from South Carolina pulpits at the same time declaring that same slavery most pleasing to Almighty God. It is strange that so few men have ever realized that one must go straight to Almighty God to find the Truth.

Out of the ever increasing conflict and the more and more difficult compromising between the sectional ideas existing for three quarters of a century in the United States in the matter of relationship between the several states and the Federal Union, with the difficult economic condition and the resultant severity of feeling induced by African slavery, there came on November 6, 1860, the election of Abraham Lincoln as President of the United States. The southern section knew that it had lost on the forum and that it must resort to the field to realize its rights.

On November 7, 1860, the day after Lincoln was elected, the Grand Jury of the United States District Court in Charleston refused to function. When asked by the judge whether the jury had any presentments to make, Robert N. Gourdin, foreman, replied, in effect: "The verdict of the ballot-box on yesterday has swept away the last hope for the permanence of the Federal Government of these several States. In these extraordinary circumstances, the Grand Jury respectfully declines to proceed with its presentments." Whereupon, Judge A. G. McGrath arose, doffed his silken gown, and formally resigned his office, saying, in part: "So far as I am concerned, this Temple of Justice, raised under the Constitution of the United States, is now closed. If it shall never be again opened, I thank God that its doors have been closed before its altar has been desecrated with sacrifices to tyranny."

Governor Gist called the Legislature of the State in extraordinary session, recommended that the militia be reorganized, the whole military forces of the State placed in a position to be used at shortest notice, and every man between the ages of eighteen and forty-five be well armed, and that the services of ten thousand volunteers be immediately accepted. He designated November 21, as a day to be observed by all people of South Carolina in fasting and prayer, pleading for Divine guidance in the existing condition.

Secession clubs were immediately formed in every Militia beat in Williamsburg District. On December 16, 1860, the Secession flag was raised in Kingstree, and the three delegates which Williamsburg had chosen to represent it at the Secession Convention in Columbia on December 17, John G. Pressley, Anthony W. Dozier, and R. C. Logan, assembled to depart for the convention. About them, as they left the Court House for the train, there stood all Williamsburg. The district had gathered to express silently and unmistakably its verdict.

On December 20, every member of the Secession Convention from every district in South Carolina signed the Ordinance of Secession, dissolving the bonds between the State of South Carolina and the Federal Union. Shouts of deliverance coming from that Convention Hall in Charleston were sounded unbroken to the uttermost ends of the Commonwealth. That night bonfires burned and bugles blew in every city and hamlet in the land.

It was no simple matter that Williamsburg had consented and had aided in the dissolution of this Federal Union, which it had so valiantly served to create and which it had sustained with its best blood for three quarters of a century. It had not forgotten Marion and Mouzon and Macaulay and McCottry and James and Scott. Its children had played about patriots' graves in infancy and its old men had told tales of their heroism about every fireside in the land. The Declaration of Independence hung in every hall in the district and it had been read at public gatherings on every birthday of the nation. Secession came out of the depths of Williamsburg.

LIEUT. COL. JOHN G. PRESSLEY, C. S. A.

CHAPTER XXVII.

WILLIAMSBURG, C. S. A., 1861.

On January 1, 1861, at a gathering of the men and women of Williamsburg, the Wee Nee Volunteers were organized into a company for serving the State. It was some privilege to have the opportunity of placing one's name on the list of this company and of answering its first roll call. The men who were accepted were select men from every part of Williamsburg District. Communities contested for the number of representatives they should furnish and the list, which was finally made, contained names that were known at Tours, Hastings, Runnymede, Bannockburn, Black Mingo, Camden, Cowpens, and Yorktown.

Here is the first Muster Roll of the Wee Nee Volunteers that left Kingstree for Charleston, January 4, 1861: John G. Pressley, captain; Samuel W. Maurice, first lieutenant; R. C. Logan, second lieutenant; E. C. Keels, third lieutenant; D. B. McCreight, first sergeant; W. R. Brockinton, second sergeant; S. McBride Scott, third sergeant; G. F. McClary, fourth sergeant; W. A. China, fifth sergeant; John A. Keels, sixth sergeant; J. B. Montgomery, first corporal; S. I. Montgomery, second corporal; F. J. Lesesne, third corporal; T. S. Chandler, fourth corporal; H. Montgomery, Jr., fifth corporal; and S. F. Pendergrass, sixth corporal; privates: E. S. Armes, James Bradley, J. S. Brockinton, B. P. Brockinton, S. D. M. Byrd, R. J. Bradham, J. A. Bradham, R. H. Barrineau, F. W. Boyd, T. J. China, S. M. China, J. R. China, W. D. Cook, J .F. Cook, N. J. Conde, P. J. Creesey, S. W. Crapps, W. J. Cockfield, W. D. Duke, David Epps, A. W. Ezell, John Frierson, W. N. Fluitt, D. P. Fulton, J. M. Footman, W. J. Ferrell, J. A. Feagin, T. B. Fleming, J. W. Gamble, W. G. Gamble, William Guess, J. G. Green, R.

Henry, James Hopkins, Charles Jones, J. H. Keels, J. M. Kirton, S. W. Kirton, C. Lesesne, E. R. Lesesne, D. W. Logan, Calhoun Logan, H. J. Lynam, C. S. Land, D. C. McClary, S. B. McClary, S. A. McClary, J. L. McClary, William McCollough, J. S. McCollough, J. P. McElveen, Geo. G. McElveen, W. M. McCrea, T. A. McCrea, A. J. McCants, C. W. McClam, W. M. McKnight, E. R. Martin, J. J. Martin, I. J. Martin, J. T. Modlin, E. P. Montgomery, J. F. Montgomery, S. Montgomery, J. A. Montgomery, W. J. Montgomery, D. K. Mouzon, J. P. Mouzon, W. E. Mouzon, S. S. Mitchum, G. K. Mitchum, J. M. Morris, T. E. Ragin, Henry Ragin, J. A. Nexsen, E. B. Scott, W. P. Scott, W. N. Y. Rodgers, B. F. Scott, T. J. Strong, J. Y. Tisdale, J. S. Tisdale, S. Tisdale, George Wear, T. A. Wallace, A. Welch, L. E. Young.

The Wee Nee Volunteers entrained at Kingstree for Charleston on January 4, 1861. That very day the North, by proclamation of President Buchanan, was spending in fasting, humiliation, and prayer "to avert the alarming immediate political dangers and the fearful distress and panic in the land." For about two months, to President Buchanan and the North was Darkness visible. They remembered South Carolina and 1832, and hoped. But Andrew Jackson, a South Carolinian, was then President. Yet sixty more days and another South Carolinian, hardly knowing his own high birthright, came with the Day in the hollow of his hands.

During this sixty days, there was about as much uncertainty at the North as there was certainty at the South. The South said: "Cotton is King and the Nations of the Earth will fall down before him. Yankees will not fight. We can wipe up with one cotton handkerchief all the blood spilled; God is with us, for slavery is a divinely appointed institution."

South Carolina women wore bonnets of white and black cotton, long waving plumes fashioned out of fleecy staple, streamers ornamented with palmetto trees and stars embroidered in gold. Orators inspired the multitudes with tales of the heroism of the South Carolina forbears in the War of the Revolution. Ministers proved conclusively to them that African slavery was pleasing to Almighty God and that He would give victory to southern arms.

In the North, fanatical abolitionists who had crusaded for this condition for so many years, gloated over the blood stained fields they saw in the future. These frenzied abolitionists were about the only people, North or South, who were happy. They were frantic for the sight of blood. From afar they glutted their souls on it at Gettysburg.

There were many serious efforts made to avert the War. The North would not consent to the withdrawal of the Southern States. The South would not reunite with any territory opposing African slavery. Finally the North, with the New York Herald, realized, "The discussion of the right and the wrong in the matter, and the constitutionality of this thing, that thing, or the other, would now be a waste of time." This same paper, at the same time, said: "The longest purse and the largest population, when both races are equally brave, must tell in the end, and give the final victory to the North."

Finally, at four thirty o'clock on the morning of April 12, 1861, General Beauregard, commanding the Confederate troops at Charleston, fired on Fort Sumter, occupied by Union troops under Major Anderson. Major Anderson and his garrison of sixty-five men returned the fire. This was a beautiful battle. The bombardment lasted thirty-four hours. Once the Confederate flag was shot down from Fort Gregg. Samuel Montgomery and David Duke, of Williamsburg, volunteered and replaced it. The defenders of Fort Sumter saw this act of valor and ceased firing for a moment. When these two Williamsburg men realized their enemy recognized and respected their bravery, they both faced the foe, drew themselves rigidly to attention, and saluted him. Major Anderson capitulated on April 13, 1861, and on Sunday, April 14, 1861, marched his little force from the fort on to a waiting Union transport, his banners flying and his bands playing. As the transport made its way out of the harbor, the Confederate forces along the beaches uncovered, honoring a brave and chivalrous enemy. The War between the Sections had begun. Not a man on either side had been killed in the first battle.

The big guns fired during the Battle of Fort Sumter were distinctly heard in Williamsburg. At first these people along Black River thought the roar of the cannon was nothing more than a summer thunderstorm, but soon was realized the noise of battle. And Williamsburg was there!

When the six months time for which the Wee Nee Volunteers enlisted had expired, the company returned to Kingstree and was reorganized. On September 5, 1861, it joined the Twenty-Fifth South Carolina Regiment at Fort Johnson. The Muster Roll then showed; John G. Pressley, captain; Thomas J. China, first lieutenant, age 32; Calhoun Logan, second lieutenant, 25; Henry Montgomery, third lieutenant, 29; (Brevet second lieutenant); B. P. Brockinton, first sergeant, 36; J. M. Footman, second sergeant, 31; W. D. Duke, third sergeant; J. G. Tisdale, fourth sergeant; D. M. McClary, fifth sergeant; J. R. China, first corporal, 20; S. M. China, second corporal; J. L. McClary, third corporal; T. B. Fleming, fourth corporal; L. E. Young, fifth corporal; and J. C. Sanders, sixth corporal.

Privates: D. A. Allen, 37; E. G. Ard, 23; James Ard, Jr., 23; Joseph Ard, 25; S. Reuben Ard, 21; M. R. D. Baker; J. T. Barrineau, 25; Joseph Bradshaw; Jesse W. Braxton; S. W. Browder; H. J. Brown, 20; M. A. Brown;

J. M. Buckles; James M. Burgess; W. E. Graham, 16; J. F. Jones, 40; H. J. Cameron; J. W. Cameron; J. S. Coker; P. J. Coker; S. L. Coker; T. J. Cook, 24; W. D. Cook, 27; A. B. Cooper, 23; Jesse E. Christmas; E. G. Dennis, 32; S. R. Dennis, 22; B. F. Duke, 16; R. E. Duke, 20; E. S. Ellis, 30; J. H. Epps; J. J. Evans; R. E. Feagan; W. E. Fleming; G. S. Floyd; J. K. Gamble, 18; R. K. Gamble, 16; George Gist, 18; S. J. Graham; G. A. Guess, 30; S. S. James, 23; Joseph J. Jaudon, 22; John W. Jayroe, 18; Edward Johnson; Samuel M. June, 17; J. W. Kelly, 18; E. J. Kelly; W. J. Knox; James Land; Isaac E. Lee, 17; R. K. Liles; John Markey; J. M. Matthews, 20; S. A. McClary, 33; J. E. McCullough, 32; T. M. McConnell, 40; P. B. McCormick; Shadrack McKenzie; Charles Mitchum; G. K. Mitchum, 39; J. S. Mitchum, 38; S. E. Montgomery, 29; Samuel Montgomery; J. B. Parker; W. K. Parker; A. J. Parsons, 24; D. M. Smith, 29; E. W. Rush, 23; J. C. Sanders; W. J. C. Scurry; H. D. Shaw, Jr.; E. J. Singletary; J. E. Thigpen; W. H. Thigpen; W. W. Tisdale, 18; Hugh Tyler, 23; R. B. Walters, 23; G. H. Young, 18; L. E. Young; and W. H. Young, 23.

These enlisted in the company at Battery Island, February 26, 1862: D. E. Adams, 35; C. R. Barrineau; E. M. Barrineau, 16; G. W. Barrineau, 38; John Barrineau; R. H. Barrineau, 30; W. L. Barrineau, 22; J. A. Bradham, 21; I. M. Brown, 17; J. H. Burgess, 19; R. G. Burgess, 18; W. J. Burgess; E. R. Cook, 22; T. J. Dukes, 18; H. E. Footman, 17; H. S. Grayson, 18; W. E. James, 25; J. M. Grayson, 20; W. Guess, 32; J. B. Johnson, 17; W. M. Kinder; W. F. Lambert; E. R. Martin; I. J. Martin, 28; G. F. McClary; D. M. McClary, 30; E. R. Mouzon, 44; J. G. McCants, 17; Isaac Montgomery, 25; J. S. McCullough; W. M. McKnight, 28; J. B. Miller; J. T. Miller; E. P. Montgomery, 20; J. A. Montgomery, 22; J. B. Montgomery; J. F. Montgomery, 28; S. J.

Montgomery; S. R. Mouzon; F. R. Parsons, 30; W. H. Parsons, 32; J. M. Player, 30; E. M. Smith, 30; John Wilson, 23; and P. Wilson, 25.

These at Coles Island, December 30, 1861: J. A. Feagan, 22; H. S. Garner, 18; J. J. Johnston; W. D. Logan, 30; E. W. McClam; S. S. Mitchum.

At the same time, Captain Pressley reorganized the Wee Nee Volunteers in Kingstree in July, 1861, Lieutenant Samuel W. Maurice withdrew and became Captain of the Wee Nee Riflemen, which he organized. The Wee Nee Riflemen became a part of the Third Regiment, Pee Dee Legion, at Camp Harlee, near Georgetown. Follows a list of this company: Samuel W. Maurice, captain; R. C. Logan, first lieutenant; William McCullough, second lieutenant; S. Isaac Montgomery, third lieutenant; W. M. McCrea, first sergeant; D. M. Duke, second sergeant; S. B. McClary, third sergeant; S. S. Tisdale, fourth sergeant; E. P. Montgomery, fifth sergeant; R. A. Murphy, first corporal; T. F. Duke, second corporal; Alexander Montgomery, third corporal; S. W. Curtain, fourth corporal; N. G. Rich, fifth corporal.

Privates: W. J. Adams, J. E. Barrineau, J. A. Bradham, John Bradham, J. M. Brown, J. S. Brockinton, F. W. Boyd, Charles Boyd, R. W. Boyd, T. E. Barfield, A. E. Brown, F. G. Cantley, S. J. Carter, H. W. Carter, S. W. Crapps, William Cooper, Jr., J. J. Cooper, P. C. Creesy, J. S. Cunningham, T. J. Duke, S. Dreifus, L. Donath, J. L. Ferrell, H. E. Footman, Robert Gamble, A. F. Gardner, H. L. Grayson, William Guess, K. Guinna, L. Grendfield, R. Henry, R. H. Hudson, Edward Howard, Samuel Hanna, A. M. Jayroe, J. B. Johnston, J. M. Kirton, Joe Lewis, W. B. Lester, S. L. S. Lifrage, T. B. Logan, J. G. Martin, E. R. Martin, D .Z. Martin, W. J. Montgomery, J. B. Montgomery, J. F. Montgomery, John Morris, Augustus Morris, J. P. Mouzon, D. K. Mouzon, S. R. Mouzon, J. C. Murphy, S. D. McGill, R. B. McClary,

COL. JAMES F. PRESSLEY.

J. J. McCants, H. A. McCullough, John McCabe, T. A. McCrea, J. A. Nexsen, W. H. Pace, T. E. Ragin, R. F. Scott, J. F. Scott, J. E. Scott, J. M. Speights, Elias Speights, T. J. Strong, J. J. Steele, T. S. Steele, T. S. Stuart, M. Schwartz, W. J. Tisdale, J. H. Tisdale, J. T. Tisdale, R. S. Tisdale, and John Thompson.

The Tenth Regiment was mustered into service of the Confederate States, July 19, 1861, for a term of twelve months, at White's Bridge near Georgetown, South Carolina. The officers of the Regiment then were: A. M. Manigault, colonel, 36; James F. Pressley, lieutenant colonel, 26; A. J. Shaw, major, 32; C. I. Walker, adjutant captain, 19; B. H. Wilson, quarter master captain, 42; T. N. Britton, commissary and captain, 46; J. P. Cain, assistant surgeon and first lieutenant; W. T. Capers, chaplain and first lieutenant, 36; H. E. Huger, sergeant major, 17; J. F. B. Leighton, quarter master sergeant, 47.

Several companies were organized in Williamsburg in the early summer of 1861 and joined the Tenth South Carolina Regiment under Colonel Manigault.

Company E of the Tenth Regiment South Carolina mustered on July 19, 1861 at White's Bridge: James F. Carraway, captain, 34; F. M. Miller, first lieutenant, 22; F. M. Britton, second lieutenant, 23; J. F. D. Britton, third lieutenant, 45; J. P. Anderson, first sergeant, 23; D. D. Barr, second sergeant, 24; S. I. Wilson, third sergeant, 26; W. P. Nesmith, fourth sergeant, 27; J. T. McConnell, fifth sergeant, 26; Thomas M. Britton, first corporal, 29; I. W. Hughes, second corporal, 42; T. N. Martin, third corporal, 24; Thomas G. Altman, fourth corporal, 29.

Privates: R. H. Gibson, 24; C. W. Cockfield, 40; R. T. B. Abrams, 40; A. Akerman, 43; T. E. Altman, 24; E. G. Barrineau, 21; W. I. Britton, 18; T. J. Britton, 16; S. S. Britton, 19; J. W. Baxley, 38; W. I. Baxley, 33; J. F. Brockinton, Sr., 38; J. F. Brockinton, Jr., 17; J. S.

Brockinton, 17; Benjamin Beatty, 19; H. W. Blakely, 19; B. E. Britton, 23; J. H. Cockfield, 21; J. C. Conrad, 26; A. J. Council, 38; George Cumbee, 24; J. B. Freeman, 24; L. W. Fenters, 21; D. F. Fenters, 29; J. C. Fenters, 27; W. Daniel Fenters,. 18; J. J. Fenters, 20; Gilkee Fenters, 24; L. F. Fenters, 29; J. B. Godwin,. 17; N. H. Griggs, 35; David Greetless, 17; D. B. Hughes, 21; G. A. Howard, 21; J. W. Howard, 45; F. M. Howard, 17; W. B. Herdick, 19; W. J. Hewitt, 21; M. O. E. Hickson, 24; Daniel Johnson, 30; J. M. Johnson, 30; G. W. Johnson, 21; J. P. Johnson, 45; Gilbert Johnson, 18; R. H. Kimball, 45; Henry Young, 23; John Young, 21; J. C. P. Martin, 26; W. A. Marshall, 22; H. L. Marlow, 20; R. G. Martin, 30; J. F. Martin, 25; I. F. Martin, 36; E. Morris, 44; J. Z. McConnell, 26; H. T. McConnell, 17; John McNaemee, 26; E. I. Moyd, 26; J. G. Miller, 19; J. J. Miller, 18; W. H. Miller, 20; J. L. M. Smith, 21; B. S. M. Smith, 16; G. I. Nesmith, 16; Nathaniel Nesmith, 22; W. I. Pipkin, 27; Thomas Port, 35; E. T. Ray, 32; J. B. Russ, 39; W. C. Small, 40; J. H. Smith, 22; D. C. Tilton, 17; W. T. Wallace, 19; J. W. Sauls, 21; J. W. Cherry, 22; William W. Braswell, 22.

The Muster Roll of Captain J. R. Nettles' Company H, July 19, 1861, for a term of twelve months: J. R. Nettles, captain, 22; W. J. M. Lee, first lieutenant, 23; S. P. Burket, second lieutenant, 38; W. D. Fitch, third lieutenant, 20; J. C. Osborne, first sergeant, 43; E. M. Scurry, second sergeant, 36; J. M. Weaver, third sergeant, 29; E. S. Sauls, fourth sergeant, 27; J. T. Kirby, first corporal, 21; S. F. R. Godwin, second corporal, 19; J. J. McKnight, third corporal, 21; John McGee, fourth corporal, 26; Samuel Kirby, fifth corporal, 26; S. W. McClam, sixth corporal, 23; R. N. Brown, seventh corporal, 23.

Privates: G. W. Anderson, 41; S. W. Burrows, 22; W. P. Budden, 23; T. E. Burkett, 23; Moses Braveboy, 19; M. M. Braveboy, 23; J. W. Brown, 16; J. W. Carter, 22; J. M. T. Carter, 24; J. P. Cannady, 29; Allen Cook, 24; J. W. Cook, 34; E. W. Cook, 19; M. B. Coward, 18; D. C. Coward, 25; E. Cain, 26; W. Collins, 26; E. Carraway, 23; W. Carraway, 27; E. W. Daniels, 25; A. H. Evans, 35; J. E. Evans, 18; R. N. Flowers, 19; E. A. Flowers, 21; L. D. Floyd, 20; J. O. Filligan, 39; Alfred Gray, 21; N. Gray, 25; D. B. Godwin, 22; G. W. Graham, 25; G. D. Green, 25; W. M. Gause, 25; J. W. Huggins; J. I. Huggins, 20; A. J. Hatchell; T. H. Hatchell; J. N. Hatchell, 24; D. Hanford; M. Jones; G. W. James; L. Jones, 16; W. Jones, 18; T. Jordan, 15; D. P. Kirby, 27; R. W. Kirby, 25; J. M. Lacey, 18; M. C. Langston, 24; James L. Lee, 22; Hampton Lee, 20; John Laws, 19; C. W. Lee, 18; J. L. Lynch, 18; J. W. Lee, 19; W. C. Lee, 22; W. M. C. Lee, 19; N. D. Lee, 20; J. A. Lee, 22; B. Lee, 19; A. R. Lee, 20; Jason Lynch, 18; A. Lynch, 16; R. I. McKnight, 18; William Matthews, 60; A. M. Matthews, 20; H. Matthews, 19; P. McGee, 24; S. Miles, 38; M. Matthews, 21; G. W. Matthews, 21; F. Matthews, 25; John McKnight, 20; G. R. Matthews, 28; Elias Matthews, 18; R. M. Matthews, 19; S. I. Nettles, 17; Joseph Pate, 24; N. S. Parker, 30; Alex Parker, 28; G. W. Reed, 30; W. D. Smith, 39; S. D. Smith, 42; R. Spring, 26; J. J. Steele, 20; T. H. Wilkes, 23; S. A. Young, 20.

Company I, Tenth Regiment, enlisted on August 13, 1861, for a term of twelve months, at White's Bridge. There were about as many men in this company from Williamsburg as from Marion. H. M. Lofton, captain, 21; B. B. McKnight, first lieutenant, 21; S. S. Gasque, second lieutenant, 36; B. Poston, third lieutenant, 34; Jasper Bartell, first sergeant, 40; Andrew Poston, second sergeant, 32; T. J. Bostwick, third sergeant, 26; William

Bartell, fourth sergeant, 30; Ransom Turbeville, first corporal, 22; N. C. Hicks, second corporal, 16; G. C. Finklea, third corporal, 19; W. H. McWhite, fourth corporal, 17.

Privates: Jacob Atkinson, 34; C. T. Altman, 22; A. T. Altman, 42; D. J. Andrews, 39; B. Ard, 18; J. A. Askins, 18; B. J. Barnes, 37; J. H. Bostwick, 17; J. B. Brogdon, 18; E. E. Cain, 32; William Cain, 22; W. E. Carter, 27; James Calcobb; L. Cooper, 28; S. Cooper, 23; N. B. Cowls, 40; R. Finklea, 21; W. B. Finklea, 48; C. Flowers, 32; J. H. Flowers, 21; C. B. Foxworth, 32; D. W. Glassen, 32; J. J. Gordon, 45; A. B. Gordon, 40; J. B. Hanes, 19; D. P. Hanna, 24; J. R. Hanna, 28; E. Hanna, 18; J. H. Holland, 30; E. B. Hutchinson, 21; J. H. Hutchinson, 33; L. N. Hutchinson, 18; J. L. Hammond, 40; W. L. Hammond, 34; W. A. Lee, 16; W. E. McGee, 22; T. Mayville, 18; W. W. McKissick, 24; B. A. Poston, 18; W. Poston, 27; J. H. Poston, 30; J. L. Poston, 17; M. M. Poston, 25; T. W. Poston, 43; W. L. Poston; A. Poston; J. S. Powell, 42; S. C. Powell, 31; M. B. Prosser, 23; Nathan Prosser, 35; B. Shaw, 25; D. C. Smith, 24; S. B. Sturges, 25; John Tanner, 21; L. Tanner, 24; E. P. Wiggins, 16; S. Williams, 17; A. Willebard, 16; D. W. Woodson, 27.

Captain William B. Gordon's Company, for some time stationed as guard at the Northeastern Railway's Santee Bridge, afterwards became Company K, of the Twenty-Fifth Regiment. The Muster Roll of Captain Gordon's Company follows: William B. Gordon, captain; Francis J. Lesesne, first lieutenant; Samuel McDonald, second lieutenant; Charles Lesesne, first sergeant; Joseph W. Gamble, second sergeant; Edward R. Lesesne, third sergeant; Thomas H. Davis, fourth sergeant; William H. McConnell, first corporal; Jayhew P. Cooper, second corporal; James H. Brunson, third corporal.

Privates: Theo. M. Lifrage, Nicholas T. Altman, William J. Altman, Elihu Ard, John Ard, Benjamin Ard, Malachi Bradshaw, Thomas E. Blakely, Thomas W. Blakely, John J. Blakely, William J. Blakely, Isaac Browder, McKenzie Browder, Edwin Browder, Benjamin R. Browder, James W. Browder, Gadsden Browder, William T. Browder, Thomas E. Barfield, William R. Burdick, John Cubstead, John J. Cooper, John David, James E. Davis, Andrew J. Davis, John Davis, Jayhew P. Davis, Thomas B. Davis, Solomon Driefus, George Gamble, Louis Grendfeld, Benjamin Hix, John Hix, William Hodge, David Hodge, John H. Hodge, Thomas T. Keels, Jayhew H. Lamb, Samuel D. Lamb, Britton L. Land, Thomas S. Lesesne, George Martin, George K. McDonald, Major H. Mitchum, John B. Mitchum, John S. Mitchum, Charles M. Matthews, John N. Mims, John G. Player, Sylvester D. Player, Joel G. Rhodus, John A. Salters, William W. Smith, Francis N. Smith, William N. Stukes, James D. Thomas, George W. Ferry, Samuel Wilder, and John Wilder.

The Williamsburg Riflemen was organized September 16, 1861, by Captain J. B. Chandler, who resigned December 1, 1861, and Captain James McCutchen was promoted from First Lieutenant and commanded the Company during its battle service. It became Company G, Fifteenth Regiment, Colonel W. G. DeSaussure. Here follows the roll at its organization: J. B. Chandler, captain, 33; James McCutchen, first lieutenant, 31; William M. Haselden, second lieutenant, 21; Benjamin P. Barron, second lieutenant, 21; Thomas M. Fulton, first sergeant, 24; Martin V. Timmons, second sergeant, 24; William J. Wilson, third sergeant, 26; Hugh D. Gamble, fourth sergeant, 27; John J. Brown, first corporal, 20; William N. Johnson, second corporal, 20; Thomas J. Burrows, third sergeant, 18; Robert Nesmith, fourth sergeant, 19.

Privates: John B. Abrams, 31; Samuel R. Ard, 35;

Bartemus L. Barrineau, 47; John J. Barrineau, 16; Alexander Bradshaw, 24; John Brown, 30; Henry Browder, 21; Henry Buckels, 24; Lydford Buckels, 21; James H. Burns, 18; Asbury B. Carter, 22; John B. Carter, 21; George W. Carter, 42; James Collier, 30; William G. Cox, 23; John T. Cox, 22; David W. Cribb, 22; Flavius E. Cooper, 21; Tristam Eaddy, 28; John T. Eaddy, 21; William S. Eaddy, 21; Andrew J. Eaddy, 22; Benjamin F. Ferrell, 24; Andrew P. Flagler, 44; Josiah J. Gaskins, 24; Elias B. Gaskins, 30; Charles A. Gaskins, 22; Charlton H. Gordon, 22; William L. Graham, 23; Julius J. Hanna, 24; George W. Hanna, 21; Robert Hanna, 19; James F. Hanna, 23; John Haselden, 21; James Hudson, 19; Joseph A. James, 32; Edward H. Johnson, 22; Harvey H. Kinder, 20; Francis H. Lenerieux, 23; William W. Matthews, 20; Robert F. Maurice, 31; James McClary, 37; John J. Matthews, 18; Henry A. Poston, 25; A. Winfield Scott, 41; George C. Scott, 38; Palvey T. Stone, 24; James B. Stone, 17; Sidney B. Thompson, 24; John Thompson, 25; Nathaniel M. Whitehead, 38; Orlando R. Avant, 22; Abner H. Brown, 33; David L. Brown, 31; Jacob Whitehead, 17; William J. Christmas, 30; Gabriel G. Gist, 32; William J. Tilton, 18; James W. Scott, 44; George W. Carter, 47; Theodore G. June, 19; Adam H. June, 17; W. Augustus Perkins, 22.

The Williamsburg Light Dragoons was a militia organization commanded by Captain J. C. Wilson. When Governor Pickens called for volunteers to serve the State for twelve months, this troop of cavalry volunteered and was sent to Georgetown, where it became a part of the Harlee Legion. Four troops of cavalry were formed into a squadron, one of which was this Williamsburg troop and Captain J. C. Wilson was elected major. He was succeeded by Captain John Watson. At the expiration of the twelve months, Major Wilson was defeated for re-election as commanding officer of this squadron by

Major W. P. Emanuel. Whereupon, Major Wilson showed his manhood by enlisting in the Williamsburg troop as a private, and serving therein in such capacity until he was mortally wounded at Cold Harbor, and died in the Jackson hospital at Richmond several weeks later.

In this troop from Williamsburg were at least three men who had served as captains in the militia prior to the Confederate War. They were: Captain J. A. Salters, Captain J. C. Wilson, and Captain D. E. Gordon. This troop finally became a part of the Fourth Cavalry. This regiment was composed largely of the wealthier young men of the State. When they arrived in Richmond for participation along the battle line, nearly every individual soldier in the regiment had a negro servant attending him. The Confederate Government realized that it was sufficiently difficult to feed the soldiers without their negroes, so that these young men found it necessary to dispense with their servants and care for themselves. The regiment arrived in Virginia on Monday and on Friday it met the enemy at Haws Shop, where a number of men were killed, and on Monday, Tuesday, and Wednesday, it participated in the battle of Cold Harbor, one of the bloodiest battles of the War, and on Saturday, it met the enemy at Trevillian Station, where a number were killed, wounded, or captured. These were captured at Trevillian: Captain D. E. Gordon, S. R. Mouzon, James A. McCrea, B. P. Barron, John Coker, Robert Cade, and James Knox.

The story is told that Blackwell McClary, a private in this troop of cavalry, was very much afraid of "haunts," that his nervousness at night when in the vicinity of graveyards was a standing joke in the troop. The first time this regiment was shelled was at Cold Harbor, and this was as severe shelling as occurred during the war. This began unexpectedly and practically all of the men of Butler's Cavalry and their horses immediately undertook to move out of that shell fire, notwithstanding General Butler's orders, "Steady, men, steady." When the shelling had ceased and General Butler looked around him for his command, he saw about thirty troopers. All the others had departed. One of this thirty was Blackwell McClary. When the Williamsburg Light Dragoons reassembled, Blackwell McClary appeared before the men and told them in most emphatic language just what his opinion was of men who were afraid of exploding shells. Nobody ever attempted to taunt Mr. McClary about being afraid after this day.

In these three battles, occurring within ten days, Williamsburg Light Dragoons had a large number of men who were seriously wounded. They were all taken to the Jackson Hospital in Richmond, where many of them died. When their negro body servants had been left in Richmond, trooper Samuel R. Mouzon had succeeded in placing his negro, Peter, who was about sixty years old and one of the best servants in the country, in the Jackson Hospital in Richmond. When these wounded troopers from the Williamsburg organization found Peter there, they must have breathed a prayer of thanksgiving. Peter's master's brother, John P. Mouzon, lost a leg and was there. So was Major J. C. Wilson, who afterwards died, E. P. Montgomery, William Montgomery, E. R. Martin, and T. S. Nelson, and many others whom Peter had known and served in Williamsburg. Probably no other wounded men in the history of the world received more faithful service than did these men whom Peter knew and loved. God may have made men who served others more faithfully and beautifully than did these negro battle attendants their masters, but doubtless He never did. Ten of these old negro body servants of Williamsburg were living in 1923 and receiving pensions from the State of South Carolina: William Bragdon, Cæsar Chandler,

Richard Daggett, Charles Lee, Peter McCrea, George McCutchen, George Miller, Derry Montgomery, Joe Shaw, and Ned Washington.

The Williamsburg Light Dragoons, Captain John Watson, joined in July, 1861, the Pee Dee Legion, Colonel R. F. Graham. The Lieutenants were then G. P. Nelson, S. J. Snowden, and W. K. Lane. At the reorganization of the troop in October, G. P. Nelson was elected captain. He commanded the troop for nearly a year when he resigned and S. J. Snowden became the War Captain of this distinguished troop. It was officially known as Troop I, Fourth South Carolina Cavalry, Colonel B. H. Rutledge. Here is its muster roll: S. J. Snowden; W. W. Fluitt, first lieutenant; T. S. Nelson, second lieutenant; D. E. Gordon, third lieutenant; R. M. Wilson, first sergeant; J. H. Fluitt, R. S. Tisdale, S. L. Lifrage, J. H. McGavy, sergeants; J. D. Thomas, W. J. Hanna, S. W. Crapps, T. B. Fleming, corporals.

Privates: J. P. Adams, W. I. Adams, J. A. Arnett, B. L. Barrineau, J. E. Barrineau, W. J. Barrineau, John Bradham, J. R. Bryan, S. S. Blakely, E. P. Blakely, T. G. Britton, F. Brisket, R. A. Buckels, J. M. Bell, T. J. Coleman, P. Crapper, R. T. Cade, Samuel Cooper, J. M. Coker, J. S. Coker, James Colin, P. F. Duke, J. P. Davis, J. T. Davis, J. V. Epps, J. W. Edwards, W. E. Fleming, J. B. Fleming, J. M. Fulton, D. B. Fulton, J. W. Gordon, J. J. Flowers, R. K. Gamble, W. J. Gamble, W. S. Grayson, P. Holliday, T. J. Hughes, J. E. Hanna, J. Harper, E. C. Keels, W. J. Knox, J. S. Lifrage, Joe Lewis, J. E. McCullough, W. B. Lester, B. J. Lambert, R. B. McClary, J. J. Marshall, J. C. McClary, S. J. McClary, J. H. McClary, J. M. McClary, James McCrea, A. Mitchum, T. M. McCrea, R. A. Murphy, J. P. Mouzon, L. W. Mouzon, S. R. Mouzon, A. J. McCrea, T. M. McCutchen, W. R. Moyd, W. J. Morris, H. M. Morris, R. F. McCottry, J. H. Norton, S. M. Plowden, R. J. Patterson,

J. H. Parham, J. M. Porter, P. Reagin, T. E. Reagin, J. A. Salters, R. H. Shaw, W. F. Small, H. Singletary, W. D. Singletary, S. M. Singletary, T. J. Spooner, J. F. Spooner, S. J. Thorp, C. C. Thomas, J. B. Thompson, W. J. Thompson, J. G. Thomas, J. L. Turner, W. D. Perry, J. G. Tisdale, S. Thomas, W. J. Walters, O. H. Whitefield, F. W. Wilson, J. C. Wilson, C. C. Wilkes, J. Wilder.

Dr. S. D. M. Byrd organized a company during the summer of 1861, and soon thereafter became Major of Byrd's Battalion formed at McClellanville. When Major Byrd took command of the Battalion, Lieutenant C. S. Land was promoted captain of the company. Later this company became Company I, Twenty-Sixth South Carolina Infantry. Here is a roll of Captain Land's Company: C. S. Land, captain, 30; J. C. Graham, first lieutenant, 28; John A. Godwin, second lieutenant, 26; R. E. Cade, third lieutenant, 45.

Non-commissioned officers and privates: J. M. Thomas, 35; John L. Scott, 30; Thomas S. Stuart, 35; Thomas L. McClam, 18; Pleasant Matthews, 24; Robert F. Tilton, 18; W. L. Cameron, 38; John W. Cameron, 21; George V. Cameron, 18; Jacob D. Casselman, 39; Frank Collins, 25; Henry Collins, 17; John W. Collins, 19; Henry Carraway, 30; S. J. Coker, 28; J. J. Coker, 20; James W. Cockfield, 17; Josiah Cockfield, 37; William P. Cook, 20; Benjamin B. Dennis, 38; Benjamin R. Evans, 35; Joseph E. Evans, 18; S. W. Evans, 25; J. P. Floyd, 18; Joseph M. Godwin, 24; Henry E. Godwin, 18; John J. Godwin, 25; Samuel C. Godwin, 20; Thomas G. Gray, 23; Jefferson Gray, 17; Thomas Gray, 20; B. F. Gray, 16; John Graham, 17; Samuel J. Graham, 22; Hugh L. F. Graham, 25; Andrew J. Gaskin, 30; William G. Hicks, 50; George W. Hicks, 20; W. J. Hicks, 16; William J. Lee, 18; Isaac E. Lee, 20; Timothy Lee, 35; Ira Lee, 20; Simon Lee, 38; John E. Lynch, 18; George W. Lynch, 20; William E. Lynch, 21; J. Lazarus, 19; Benjamin Matthews, 25;

MAJ. C. S. LAND, C. S. A.

Madison Matthews, 25; James A. Matthews, 20; Dunnin Matthews, 17; Gordon Matthews, 36; Jefferson Matthews, 16; Ralston Matthews, 18; James S. Matthews, 17; D. K. Mouzon, 30; Jacob Miles, 30; Robert Miles, 17; Leonard Miles, 17; W. J. Miles, 40; J. W. Miles, 17; Joseph Miles, 16; Thomas Miles, 32; Benjamin Miles, 27; Wright Miles, 32; John J. McGee, 25; Gadsden G. McGee, 27; Daniel S. McKenzie, 16; William H. McKnight, 19; John H. McKnight, 17; Thomas M. McKnight, 22; James M. McCallister, 40; James E. McCallister; James C. Nettles, 22; William W. Odom 37; William H. Parker, 16; James R. Parker, 30; Jesse Parker, 18; Evander Pickett; John M. Powell; E. H. Sauls, 19; Evander G. Sauls, 15; John A. Smith, 25; Francis H. Smith, 28; Elias Speights, 25; Samuel A. Scott, 35; Henry B. Thomas, 34; William G. Williamson, 17; Henry J. Williamson, 17; John Yarborough, 36; William Young, 25.

Captain Land was promoted Major on December 9, 1864, by President Jefferson Davis "for distinguished valor and skill." Major Land commanded the picket line of Wallace's Brigade and on January 13, 1865, received high praise from the inspector general. In a letter to General Bushrod Johnson, referring to this report, General Robert E. Lee wrote on January 18, 1863: "I note with pleasure the commendation bestowed upon Major Land, 26th South Carolina Regiment, permanent commander of the picket line of the Brigade, who appears to be an efficient and capable officer."

There were a great many men from Williamsburg District who served in the Confederate Army in organizations recruited principally from other districts, and their names may not have appeared so far in the rolls of Williamsburg's Confederate Soldiers.

In 1861, Dr. Robert Gourdin organized a company from the Lenud's Ferry section. This company went to White's

Bridge in Georgetown and there volunteered for service in the Confederate Army. Dr. Gourdin was found physically unfit for military service—too old—and his company immediately broke up, the men uniting with other organizations. Many of those men joined Company A, of the Tenth Regiment, Captain Plowden C. J. Weston commanding. Among these were: N. B. Clarkson, James Sloan, E. Blakely, S. G. McClary, J. L. Blakely, W. J. Clarkson, Dr. I. W. Graham, W. G. Gamble, J. P. Gamble, J. E. Holmes, J. S. June, F. L. McCants, D. F. Michau, J. J. Morris, W. C. Ogburn, L. K. Pipkin, J. N. Row, J. C. Small, I. D. Singletary, W. H. West, John Wilson, and F. W. Wilson.

In the Fourth Cavalry: Ebenezer Row, John W. Marshall, 18; S. P. Morris, 36; James W. Rodgers, 49; David Harlee, 37; Riley Baxley, 48; William Baxley, 38; Jacob Benson, 30; James W. Newton, 40; James Epps, 18; L. D. Robinson, 42; N. P. Smith, 42; James Smith, 40; Ely Smith, 39; J. G. Smith, 37; R. Smith, 36; W. B. Smith, 45; Everett Smith, 50; Wesley Smith, 39; John Smith, 60; S. Smith, 37; A. E. Stephenson, 50; William Stone, 52; Evander Stocks, 48; John Lequeu, Robert Glass, Noah Michau, Fletcher Michau, V. E. Lifarge, William Henderson, and S. B. W. Courtney.

There were three cadets from Williamsburg at the Citadel in 1861. They volunteered as a part of Company F, Sixth Cavalry: Anthony W. Dozier, first lieutenant; Edward C. Dozier, corporal; and S. H. Owens, private. In the Seventh Cavalry from Williamsburg were: S. B. Green, D. Z. Martin, W. R. Godwin, John Ferdon, W. F. Thompson, J. W. Britton, W. H. Britton, W. T. Thompson, H. L. Crawford, Lieutenant W. D. Fitch, John Green, Richard Green, Thompson Green, J. D. Gordon, S. B. Gordon, Ely Rodgers, J. F. Rodgers, L. P. McCullough, J. F. Brockinton, James Hanna, and Sam Hanna.

These were in the Palmetto Battalion of Light Artillery: James A. Coward and Rix A. Coward; these in Gregg's Battery, Jacob Atkinson, and John J. Altman. These served in Inglis' Light Artillery: Lieutenant Texas B. Logan, James M. Nelson, E. S. Jones, G. Purvis Nelson, George O. Wheeler, John Shaw Tisdale, James J. Martin, Francis M. Britton, William B. Epps, James N. Fluitt, Richard M. Fulmore, Arthur Hammett, Frank M. Jones, James M. Kirton, S. W. Kirton, Samuel G. McClary, W. S. Camlin, T. J. Strong, William J. Thornhill, James E. Timmons, J. Y. Tisdale, Robert S. Tisdale, and Samuel Tisdale, and James Sloan; these in Gaillard's Light Artillery: Lieutenant W. R. Cooper, F. W. McCottry, J. H. Porter, J. H. Saunders, John W. Witherspoon, D. Barr, John Cooper, Robert Cooper, W. A. Cooper, William D. Fulton, and J. H. Kinder.

Captain Alexander Colclough's Company, D, of Colonel Blanding's Regiment, had a number of men of Williamsburg: Lieutenant W. Elliott Keels, R. J. Bradham, W. I. Connell, T. J. Etheridge, J. J. Ellis, J. J. Gamble, A. M. Gamble, W. J. Mouzon, J. S. Mitchum, T. G. Mitchum, H. J. Ragin, W. J. Ward, E. S. Arms, Robert Chandler, J. F. Chandler, A. W. Flagler, R. M. Footman, J. G. Green, T. M. Keels, G. T. Rollins, B. F. Scott, Lieutenant J. E. Scott, Lieutenant E. B. Scott, J. P. Thames, A. J. McCrea, D. M. Tisdale, J. M. McCullough, T. S. Chandler, W. S. Grayson, J. M. Grayson, Daniel Keels, N. McKenzie, W. M. McKnight, G. W. Morris, S. W. Mims.

Captain W. S. Brand was from Clarendon District, but about half of his Company, K, Sixth Regiment, were men of Williamsburg: Among these were: Lieutenant R. A. Flagler, Lieutenant E. B. Scott, Lieutenant Z. R. Fullmore, W. J. Ferrell, E. M. Graham, B. F. Scott, W. D. McFadden, J. P. Epps, W. W. Cunningham, J. H. Fullmore, S. W. Cockfield, T. S. Chandler, J. F. Chandler, B. S. Croft, A. W. Flagler, S. M. Flagler, R. M. Footman,

G. J. Graham, A. M. Gamble, G. S. B. Huggins, T. M. Keels, G. G. McElveen, J. A. McCrea, J. S. McCullough, W. McCullough, J. C. McCutchen, T. G. Mitchum, W. J. Matthews, J. Parker, S. J. Taylor, A. W. Williams.

In Captain D. W. Harrington's, these: William W. Cunningham, J. M. Gardner, John A. Graham, William W. Hair, M. E. Hodge, LeGrand N. Joy, Francis E. Joy, J. Harvey Wilson, L. P. McCullough, J. S. McCullough, J. A. McCrea, and N. W. Baggett.

These officers and men from Williamsburg: Captain William J. Taylor, Tenth Infantry; William J. Matthews, First Infantry; R. D. Rollins, Seventh Infantry; Frank Cox, Eight Infantry; Captain Peter C. Dozier, Chaplin J. E. Dunlap, of the Twenty-First Regimental Staff; Surgeon T. S. Hemingway, Staff, Seventh Cavalry; Thomas Burrows, Ben Ard, and E. H. Ard, Twenty-First Infantry; Jesse B. Ellis, Allen Miles, and John C. Scurry, Twenty-First Infantry; Nabor D. Lesesne, Charles Jones, George Weir, Samuel A. Jones, Robert A. Flagler, in Hampton's Legion; R. M. Footman, J. R. Hair, J. M. Gardner, J. G. Green, William Winkles, L. D. Winkles, in the Palmetto Sharpshooters.

These men of Williamsburg served in organizations as follows: R. E. Rodgers, Seventh Battalion; Lieutenant A. M. Snider, Hampton's Legion; Edwin Harper, Troop H, Seventh North Carolina Cavalry; John Todd, Company I, Fifty-First North Carolina Infantry; F. Thompson, Company F, Nineteenth Arkansas Infantry; R. W. Cow ard, Company E, Eighth Infantry; G. W. Ard and T. S. Ard, Company C, Second Arkansas Infantry; John A. Kelly, Company B, Second Infantry; Lieutenant Thomas M. Gilland, Third Infantry; Lieutenant William Epps, Fourth Cavalry; J. P. Shaw, Company B, Fourth Infantry; D. B. Young, Company E, Reserves; E. J. Player, Company K, Twenty-Third Infantry; E. J. Joye, Company K, Twenty-Third Infantry; P. W. Morris, Company

C. Ninth Infantry; J. E. Baker, Company A, First Artillery; G. W. Burgess, J. P. Burgess, R. W. Burgess, Company F, Twenty-Sixth Regiment; J. A. Burgess and J. C. Burgess, Company C, Ninth Regiment; S. H. Burgess and D. I. Burgess, Company C, Twenty-Fifth Infantry; J. W. Braxton, Company E, Seventh Infantry; G. T. Rollins, Company A, Ninth Regiment; F. M. Player, Company E, First Regiment; H. J. Lamb, Company E, Tenth Infantry; First Lieutenant J. G. K. Gourdin, Twenty-Second Carolina Infantry; Louis Jacobs, Hampton's Legion; M. J. Hirsch, Commissary Sergeant, Tenth Regiment, South Carolina Infantry; Daniel Conyers Nesmith, Fourth Georgia Infantry.

On December 31, 1861, there were more men from Williamsburg in the military service than there were voters in the district.

After the thrills that came with Secession on December 20, 1860, and the departure of the Wee Nee Volunteers under Captain John G. Pressley on January 4, 1861, there was comparative quiet in Williamsburg for about three months. The people seemed greatly relieved that South Carolina had withdrawn from the Union and believed that things would come out "all right." Williamsburg had "much goods" laid up for many years. It felt free. President Buchanan and the cabinet in Washington could worry, but Williamsburg would wait. Williamsburg listened to sermons preached in the old church at Kingstree by Reverend E. O. Frierson; at Indiantown by Reverend J. R. Gilland; in the Methodist Church at Kingstree by Reverend J. M. Little; and in the Black River Churches by the Reverend J. C. Stoll. These "fathers in Israel" told Williamsburg that the Lord was with the South and would see that right triumphed. Sometimes, Mr. Gilland played the fiddle for his younger congregation to dance.

The little "swamp rabbit" mail and passenger trains on the Northeastern Railway passed Kingstree morning and evening as theretofore. The coming of these trains were the events of the day. Everybody went to the station to meet them, hear local gossip, and get the "Mercury" or the "Courier." The Kingstree Star had suspended publication when the Wee Nee Volunteers left, for in that company was all its force, editor, printer, and devil. The Courier, January 8, 1861, said "Our esteemed contemporary, the Kingstree Star, is under temporary suspension—occultation by Mars—editor, foreman, and compositors are all in arms and are now near this City."

The booming of the big guns at Fort Sumter April 12, 1861, somewhat disturbed Williamsburg. But that was a bloodless battle, and its results were comforting. All the fighting might be just like that at Fort Sumter. And those days were just right for holding patriotic celebrations. Orators had eager auditors for the asking and abundant subjects for expression. Williamsburg dearly loved, and yet loves, fiery orations.

The Fourth of July celebrations that year exceeded in grandeur anything of the kind that had ever been held in Williamsburg. The pomp and circumstance and ceremony of war entered them. Stalwart men in uniform, mounted on spirited chargers, flashed shining sabers in the sunlight. Every woman had her hero. War looses so many feelings that one loves!

The celebration on the Santee on that Fourth of July was just like the others held at Kingstree and Black Mingo. There was a squadron of cavalry drilling and parading during the day, a dinner in the early evening, and a grand ball that night. Here were some of the toasts: 1. The Day Sacred to the Cause of Constitutional Liberty; 2. The Father of His Country; 3. The Confederate States of America, True to the Spirit of '76; 4. The President of the Confederate States of America,—a statesman and civilian wise in counsel and successful in arms; 5. The Army—free men who have gone to battle for their rights and the protection and sanctity of their homes; 6. The State of South Carolina, patriotic and brave, the first to throw off the yoke of a corrupt and fanatical government; 7. The Late United States—its government when administered in its integrity challenged our admiration and respect and had our most devoted loyalty and support: we mourn over its death by Northern fanaticism and misrule; 8. King Cotton—its Empire is the World; 9. The Institution of Slavery,—just, humane, wise, and Christian; one of Earth's greatest blessings to the benighted African and a cause of the prosperity and welfare of the South; 10. Woman—her sanctuary the home,—her mission, love, peace, and happiness. Many other toasts were given, all impressive of the fact that the people felt they were now really free and were celebrating the anniversary of the Fourth of July, 1776. At the grand ball that night, Williamsburg "had gathered there her beauty and her chivalry, and all went merry as a marriage bell."

The morning came and with it wild rumors of war. But these were nothing. Wild tongues had so often been loosed that no one seriously regarded them. Even the papers had begun to doubt their own startling stories printed day after day. The Richmond correspondent of the Courier, July 11, 1861, wrote: "There is an old Mokish law that when a man circulates a false report, his forehead shall be branded with a hot iron. With such retributive justice exercised just now, the countenance of every other individual in the community would be disfigured beyond redemption. Not that there is any intentional perversion of fact or a desire to mislead the public mind, but rather a diseased condition of the cerebellum which magnifies uncertainties a thousand times beyond their proper proportions. We have proofs of this daily. Let the mere skeleton of a rumor arrive in town, no matter from what source, and incidentally men, women, and children put on the seven-leagued boots of imagination and a historical monstrosity is created in half an hour worthy of an Arabian story teller. Before the day has expired, it will have become as contagious as the measles. By night, the telegraph wires will be flashing the epidemic to every hamlet in the South."

Out of all these wild rumors and incident doubting there came to Williamsburg on the afternoon of July 22, 1861, the Mercury and the Courier from Charleston, with headlines like this: "Terrible Battle. Southerners Victorious. Great Slaughter on Both Sides. Enemy in Full Flight and Closely Pursued. Battle Commenced four o'clock on the Morning of July 21, and lasted until seven o'clock in the evening."

A great shout went up at the Kingstree Northeastern Railway station that evening. In a moment, after the tumult of triumph ceased, some one saw following "Southerners Victorious" the words "Great Slaughter." And Williamsburg was there! Some one said, "Don't you know that Nabor Lesesne, and Charlie Jones, and George Weir, and Bob Flagler, and others from here were in Hampton's Legion, and Hampton's Legion was in the thickest of the fight?"

Nabor Lesesne had married Marian Ervin in 1860. Both of them were kin to half of the people of Williamsburg. They had Huguenot and Scotch-Irish blood in their veins, the best of Williamsburg. All Williamsburg knew and loved them both.

Later, a message came "Nabor Lesesne is wounded." Then a letter from him to his Marion, telling her he was comfortable in the hospital at Culpepper, and that she must conserve all her strength for the coming of a little life dearer to each of them than their very own. A few days later, a telegram read, "Nabor Lesesne is dead."

Wiliamsburg had made its first sacrifice on the altar of the Confederacy.

Heaven and Hell hovered about Nabor Lesesne as he died in that Culpepper hospital. He heard the shouts of victory that went up on the field at First Manassas and saw Marian singing saddened lullabies to their first born yet to be. The best and the worst of the world came to him in his dying moments. He passed unafraid.

All Williamsburg loved Marian Lesesne and the little Nabor Lesesne who came. Fifty years later this Nabor Lesesne was the most loved and respected man in Williamsburg County. He himself merited, as well as inherited, the veneration Williamsburg had for him.

After the battle of First Manassas, or Bull Run, Williamsburg realized that war had begun, and nearly every possible man in the district volunteered for military service. Many companies were immediately formed and were joined to South Carolina Vollunteer regiments.

Morale makes the soldier. There may be a hundred elements making morale, but certain fundamentals are essential. A soldier must be reasonably well fed, clothed, and equipped for fighting. He must be sustained by an unfaltering faith that his family at home has a fairly comfortable existence. When the "Conscript Fathers" of Williamsburg joined in decreeing the War between the Sections and called on the younger men of the district to offer themselves for service along the battle line, the young men volunteered. Many of these volunteers left wives and young children without capacity to support themselves. The old men of Williamsburg promised and fulfilled their sacred trust in supporting and sustaining these dependents of volunteer soldiers.

August 5, 1861, at the very beginning of the war, in accordance with previous notice, a convention of the citizens of Williamsburg was held in the Court House. Samuel E. Graham was called to the chair and Captain

J. C. Wilson was elected secretary. The chairman stated that the object of the meeting was for the discussion of ways and means and for the adoption of measures necessary for the proper support and maintenance of the families of such volunteers then in the service from this district as might need it.

Dr. James S. Brockinton offered the following preamble and resolution which was adopted by unanimous and heartfelt vote.

"Whereas: Many of our citizens have volunteered for service for the defense of our country, and, in a good many instances, have left families in indigent circumstances; and, whereas, the war now being waged against us has for its object the subversion of our institutions and the destruction of our liberties, it becomes the imperative duty of those of us who are not bearing the heat and burden of the day to sustain those that are; and that it is not a charity but a positive duty, which we owe to these brave men, to see that the families of those who need peculiar aid do not suffer.

"Therefore, resolved that an assessment upon the taxes of citizens, except the volunteers, is a just and equal way of raising sufficient funds."

On motion of John B. Pressley, Esq., Colonel David Wilson and Messrs. L. E. Graham and W. L. Lee were appointed a committee to investigate and to report the amount necessary for the immediate needs of the families of volunteers then in service. This committee reported that there were then two hundred and twenty persons needing help and suggested that $3,300.00 be made immediately available for distribution among them. The committee recommended that an assessment of 20 per centum on the taxes of citizens of Williamsburg be collected for the purpose of raising this amount.

The following persons were appointed for looking after the needy and for disbursing the funds raised for them:

for Black Mingo, J. A. Hemingway and John B. Pressley; for Andersons, S. E. Graham, John Lequex, Sr., and J. S. Singleton; for Kingstree, David Epps, W. R. Brockinton, S. J. Montgomery, and Thomas China; for Indiantown, Thomas M. McCutchen and W. C. Barr; for Lynch's Lake, N. M. Graham, W. J. Nettles, and J. L. Jones.

The following were appointed collectors of this voluntary tax of 20 per centum for their respective communities: Lynch's Lake, J. M. Coward, Benjamin Turner, and J. A. H. Cockfield; Black Mingo, John F. Nesmith, J. D. Daniel, and W. H. Johnson; Andersons, T. D. Muller, George McDonald, and John Watson; Kingstree, H. A. McCullough, W. H. McElveen, and H. Montgomery, Sr.; Indiantown, W. J. Brown, Thomas McCutchen, and Dr. J. A. James.

S. E. Graham was made permanent chairman of the association and Captain J. C. Wilson, secretary. Dr. John F. Brockinton was unanimously chosen as treasurer. This organization functioned all during the Confederate War. There is nothing more beautiful in all Confederate war history than the service which this association rendered.

It is possible that the idea in this association might have orginated elsewhere than in Williamsburg, but it is certain that nowhere else was it more splendidly materalized. This act of the citizenship of Williamsburg in voluntarily assessing, for the relief of the families of volunteer soldiers, the property of the District 20 per centum on its normal rate of taxation, seems a contribution to the progress of the world.

The women of Wiliamsburg were no less faithful in doing all they could for the families of volunteers about them than they were for sending relief to the soldiers in the field. There are no records of the thousands of things which those who were able contributed during this war for the sustenance of their less fortunate neighbors. There are some records, however, of the Soldiers' Aid Societies in the district.

On the 8th of August, 1861, the Cedar Swamp Soldiers' Aid Society was organized. The following is a list of the officers and members: President, Mrs A. M. Cunningham; vice-president, Mrs. M. G. McCrea; secretary, Miss Eugenia P. Scott; treasurer, Miss Mary J. Cunningham; members, Mrs. Mary Scott, Mrs Ellen McCottry, Mrs. Martha Chandler, Mrs. C. R. Flagler, Miss Rosa Flagler, Mrs Martha McCullough, Mrs. M. Gardner, Miss Sarah McCullough, Miss Addie Flagler, Miss Julia Scott, Mrs. Jane Sturgis, Mrs. Sarah A. McGill, Mrs. M. E. Chandler, Mrs. Sarah Brown, Miss Adeline Mitchum, Miss Elizabeth Mitchum, Mrs. Elizabeth Tisdale, Miss Mary Grayson, and Mrs. J. C. Williams. The committee to solicit aid was composed of the following: Mrs. Mary M. Scott, Mrs. Ellen McCottry, Mrs. Mary J. McCullough, Mrs. C. R. Flagler, and Miss Rosa Flagler. This committee reported at the meeting later in the same month $91.00 in cash and enough clothing to fill two large boxes.

At this meeting, the president of the society thanked the merchants of the district for liberal donations of cloth and other material for making supplies for the soldiers. She also urged the women of other districts to form other societies like this one at Cedar Swamp.

Immediately after the formation of the Cedar Swamp Society, the Lower Bridge Soldiers' Aid Society was organized. The following were officers: Mrs J. A. Salters, president; Mrs. H. D. Shaw, Mrs. John Watson, Mrs. J. A. Gordon, and Mrs. A. C. McKnight, vice-presidents; Mrs. J. B. McCollough, secretary; and Mrs. M. A. Bradford, treasurer.

These societies were then organized in all sections of Williamsburg. The boxes ladies societies from Williamsburg sent to these soldiers in the field contained almost every conceivable thing useful. Among these, may be mentioned: shirts, socks, mitts, scarfs, sheets, pillows, pillow cases, spreads, towels, blankets, wines, liquors, syrup, preserves, pickels, arrowroot, gelatin, tea, sugar, buttons, needles, tape, spool cotton, flax thread, hanks of yarn, Bibles, Prayer Books, pamphlets, Port wine, Madeira wine, blackberry wine, brandy, cordial, whiskey, honey, catsup, cocoa, chocolate, isinglass, nutmegs, cloves, allspice, pepper, sage, candles, soap, plates, tin pans, tin cups, spoons, knives, forks, tea pots, coffee pots, mugs, pitchers, and candle sticks.

In the old files of the Mercury and the Courier, published during the war in Charleston, may be found from time to time lists of contributions in money and in kind by individuals from Williamsburg. One of the items in these old lists runs as follows: "A coop of twenty-two chickens, eight from little Mary Brockinton and fourteen from the servants of Dr. John F. Brockinton."

Scotch loyalty to its very own came out in all its beauty when Williamsburg men went to war.

While Williamsburg had full storehouses on January 1, 1861, it was almost exclusively an agricultural and stock raising community, and some things that had been by custom imported soon became scarce. Salt, coffee, dyestuffs, and the clothing that the "elect" wore could not be purchased for many months after Union gunboats blockaded Southern ports. The following quotations are taken from The Macon Telegraph of September 25, 1861:

"The only trouble is salt, and to think that salt should be scarce with the Atlantic brine tub on our borders is a reflection on the intelligence and enterprise of the Confederate States. If a planter living beside a lake of cane juice should lament over the scarcity of sugar and syrup in his family, there would be but one response, 'you infernal fool, go get a kettle and boil down some of that cane juice.' Ditto, a people living beside a salt pond and too lazy to boil down or otherwise evaporate the water.

"To cheapen coffee, do not use the stuff. There is not one cook in five hundred who ever did anything else but abuse it. Some of the papers are recommending substitutes, parched beans, peas, rye, bread crusts, acorns, etc. Swamp mud with black water is just as effectual, but neither of them will make coffee any more than chalk will make cheese. If you must have a warm drink, take boiling water and put a little milk and sugar in it. Compared with what is called coffee, in nine cases out of ten, it is nectar of the gods to lager beer and does you no harm, while coffee fills your stomach with mud banks and shoals against which the bark of human life is often wrecked. The greatest humbug in the world as commonly understood and practiced is coffee. The practice should be suppressed by the Board of Health if there were no war to do it."

The scarcity of salt reached considerable proportions early in the summer of 1861. It was not very long before Williamsburg planters learned that they could evaporate the water of the Atlantic and secure the salt just as easily as they could boil out the cane juice into syrup and sugar. Soon the McClellanville coast was lined with squads of salt making slaves from the plantations of Williamsburg.

Williamsburg slaves wore, as a general rule, clothing made by themselves from the cotton and wool grown on their own plantations. These homespun goods had to be colored. Before the War, dyestuffs had been imported. When they could not be secured from the outside, the District had to filter from its own vegetation all the coloring matter used. About this time, the newspapers were full of recipes for making dyes. On July 23, 1861, the correspondent of the Courier from Graham's Turnout in Williamsburg submitted the following: "When a small boy, I recollect to have gathered bushels of the sumac berry on the mountains in this state for the purpose of having wool died black for the woof of our home made gears. There can be almost any quantity gathered in this section almost without any charge. Anyone wishing to try dyeing wool will find it one of the handsomest black dyes known to me."

The supply of imported fabrics that Southern gentlewomen wore began to fail after the blockade was made effective. All plantations kept making and were well supplied with homespun, a substantial clean looking serviceable kind of cloth. This had been the clothing of slaves. Early in 1861, two belles of Portsmouth, Virginia, appeared at a high social affair, clad in homespun dresses. Everybody said they were beautiful. Southern newspapers commented on their winsomeness in such simple raiment. Southern girls began to wear homespun dresses and glory in them. About that time, Miss Carrie Belle Sinclair, of Savannah, Georgia, composed a song which was sung all over the South. Soldiers went into battle with its words in their mouths and its spirit in their souls. Every young woman in Williamsburg knew it and hummed it as she stitched and knitted and prayed for her gray clad soldier in the field.

Somebody said "Give me to write the songs of a nation and I care not who makes its laws." But who writes the songs of a nation must be of that nation. It is interesting to note in connection with the authorship of this song that James Sinclair settled on the Santee in Williamsburg in 1725. It may be that something else shows more of the soul of the Southern girl of the sixties than "The Homespun Dress," but it is improbable. Here are the words to

THE HOMESPUN DRESS.

Oh, yes I am a Southern girl,
    And glory in the name;
I boast of it with greater pride
    Than glittering wealth or fame.
I envy not the Northern girl
    Her robes of beauty rare,
Though diamonds deck her snowy neck
    And pearls bestud her hair.

Hurrah, Hurrah!
For the sunny South, so dear!
Three cheers for the homespun dress
The Southern ladies wear.

Now Northern goods are out of date;
    And since Old Abe's blockade
We Southern girls can be content
    With goods that's Southern made.
We send our sweethearts to the war,
    But girls, ne'er you mind—
Your soldier love will not forget
    The girl he left behind.

The Southern land's a glorious land,
    And has a glorious cause;
Then cheer, three cheers for Southern rights,
    And for the Southern boys!
We scorn to wear a bit of silk,
    A bit of Northern lace,
But make our homespun dresses up
    And wear them with a grace.

And now, young man, a word to you,
    If you would win the fair,
Go to the field where honor calls,
    And win your lady there.
Remember that our brightest smiles
    Are for the true and brave,
And that our tears are all for those
    Who fill the soldier's grave.

About this time, the sale and exportation of cotton was one of the most important questions before the Confederacy. The newspapers were filled with arguments on both sides of the question. The factors of Charleston said to the planters of this and other states and printed it in capital letters that they should "send none of their cotton to America until the blockade is expressly removed from all the ports of the Southern States." According to information, one bank in Charleston had more than a million dollars balance in the Bank of England, and many other banks in Charleston and other cities in the South had large balances in banks in England and France. They said the South could finance the War without selling a bale of cotton. Cotton men believed they could compel the nations of the earth to recognize the Southern Confederacy and thus prove their statement that "Cotton is King." "When the hum of the spinning wheel mingles with the roar of the cannon, we will have two armies working out a complete and eternal independence of the South." "If cotton compels a recognition of the Southern Confederacy, cotton will indeed be king."

One of the saddest things of all this time was the fearful preaching of nearly all Southern ministers. They held up constantly and continuously before the soldiers and their mothers dreadful pictures of Death and Hell and pleaded with them to prepare to meet an awful God in a Day of Wrath. Not only did these probably well intentioned divines preach these orgiastic frenzies, but they also revelled in distributing among the young impressionable heroic men in the Southern Armies all manner of so called tracts wherein fanatical apostles of gloom had written their worst. The subjects of some of these tracts were: How Long Have You Been Sick; The Muffled Drum; The Crimean Hero; A Soldier's Legacy; The Soldier's Victory; How Do You Bear Your Troubles; Prepare to Meet Thy God.

These preachers evidently meant well. But the mental agony they induced on the field and about the firesides in the land no poet's pen can ever picture and no orator's tongue can ever tell. When one now reads in the soldiers' diaries and mothers' memoirs the fearful religious atmosphere pervading camp ground and castle in all this beautiful land, he wonders how Southern men ever mustered sufficient morale to move into battle. It is the most wonderful thing in all this war that valiant men came out of such impenetrable gloom. God may have forgiven these deadening "white vested Colonels of the Cross:" He may not.

The parents of many Williamsburg sons who went to war made the captains of the companies in which their sons enlisted promise that they would stay with these companies until the war ended. It was no little thing in a mother to turn over her favorite nor a father his first born to the god of war. These parents had confidence in these captains and these captains fulfilled their mission. So when the Tenth South Carolina Regiment in 1861 found it necessary to elect a major, all of the captains of the regiment declined the promotion, choosing to remain with their companies, and recommended that Lieutenant A. J. Shaw be made major, which was done.

There were more of Williamsburg's men in the Tenth Regiment of Infantry than in any other Confederate organization. There were three Williamsburg companies in it, and many Williamsburg men in other companies. Colonel A. M. Manigault, of Charleston, commanded the Regiment at the beginning, but these officers of the field and staff were from Wiliamsburg: Lieutenant Colonel James F. Pressley, Major A. J. Shaw, quartermaster, and Captain T. N. Britton, commissary.

The Tenth Infantry from July 23, 1861, to the end of the year, was stationed at Camp Marion, just below White's Bridge, two miles west of Georgetown. Here General

Marion had a camp during the War of the Revolution, and on this ground Colonel Horry whipped the Tories and the brave young Marion, the General's nephew, fell. While here, the Tenth was drilled and disciplined for war. Besides the officers, Lieutenants W. B. McKee, L. B. Stark, M. S. Elliott, J. L. Taylor, J. C. Neill, and A. Doty, of the Citadel, assisted as drill masters and helped instruct the men in the art of war. Surgeon T. S. Hemingway, of Wiliamsburg, a recent graduate of the Citadel, was instructor in the management of big guns and heavy field artillery.

A newspaper correspondent thus wrote from the camp: "The Tenth Regiment is fortunate in having Colonel Manigault to command it. Firm and resolute, he is at the same time kind and gentle. On the field his voice rings like a trumpet. He is a most courteous gentleman and genial companion. He bore himself with distinguished gallantry through the Mexican campaign and is the very man to lead the brave boys of the Tenth to victory.

"Lieutenant Colonel Pressley and Major Shaw are accomplished officers, Pressley a graduate of our Citadel and Shaw a soldier by constitutional inclination. Commissary, Captain Britton, has a difficult position which he fills most acceptably. The soldiers attend religious services, seeming to esteem it a pleasure and not a task to worship God. In the evenings, the encampment rings with sacred songs."

No military event occurred in Virginia in 1861 after the battle of Manassas in which South Carolina troops were engaged. About November 1, 1861, the Union forces took Port Royal from the Confederates. Williamsburg was there in Company G, Fifteenth Infantry, Captain J. B. Chandler. In the battle at Hilton Head, Andrew J. Eaddy, H. H. Kinder, and Henry Bowden, of Williamsburg, were seriously wounded and incapacitated for further military service.

From this time, the Union forces began closing in on the coast of South Carolina and keeping up continuous warfare. The defeat of the Confederate forces at Port Royal brought great grief to South Carolina and the blockade of the entire coast made war very real to all the people of the State. Williamsburg spent a serious Christmas 1861.

COL. JAMES McCUTCHEN, C. S. A.

CHAPTER XXVIII.

WILLIAMSBURG, C. S. A., 1862.

The first months of the year 1862 Williamsburg actually organized its military forces and disciplined its civilian population for the grim business of war. On February 1, 1862, the following companies from Williamsburg were in training camps: I. Company G, Fifteenth Infantry, Captain James McCutchen, enlisted for the period of the war; 2. Wee Nee Volunteers, Captain J. G. Pressley, in Colonel Hagood's First South Carolina Infantry, for one year from April 12, 1861; 3. Company E, Tenth Infantry, Captain J. F. Carraway, for twelve months from July 19, 1861; 4. Company H, Tenth Infantry, Captain J. R. Nettles, for twelve months from July 19, 1861; 5. Captain John Watson and his cavalry company in the Pee Dee Legion, for twelve months from January 1, 1862; 6. Captain S. D. M. Byrd and his company in Major Manigault's Battalion; 7. Captain William B. Gordon and his company known as the Ripley Guards stationed at the Santee Bridge doing local duty and enlisted for twelve months; 8. The Wee Nee Riflemen under Captain Samuel W. Maurice, Third Regiment, at Camp Harlee, Georgetown. There were in these companies about eight hundred men. There were then in companies formed in the surrounding districts more than three hundred men from Williamsburg. Of these eleven hundred men from Williamsburg then under arms, the one hundred men in Captain James McCutchen's company were the only ones from this district who had enlisted for the duration of the war.

The Wee Nee Volunteers commanded by Captain John G. Pressley became Company C of the Twenty-Fifth Regiment under Colonel Charles H. Simonton. Captain Pressley was then elected Lieutenant Colonel of this Regiment and commanded it in nearly all of its battle service. Colonel Simonton was commanding a brigade or on detached service in the Judge Advocate's Department for the greater part of the War. Captain Thomas J. China succeeded Captain Pressley in command of the Wee Nee Volunteers, and later, after Captain China had been killed, Captain Calhoun Logan commanded it.

James F. Pressley organized Company E, Tenth Infantry, but when the Tenth Infantry was formed, Captain Pressley was elected Lieutenant Colonel of this Regiment and Captain James F. Carraway succeeded him in command of the Company. When this Tenth Infantry commanded by Colonel A. M. Manigault was organized for the duration of the War, Captain Carraway of Company E resigned and Captain T. N. Miller succeeded him. Captain Miller died at Tupelo, Mississippi, in 1862, and Captain G. P. Anderson succeeded him. This Regiment in 1862 had in it for the duration of the War also from Williamsburg Captain J. R. Nettles' Company H. When Captain Watson's Company, Williamsburg Light Dragoons, became Company I, Fourth Cavalry, it was under the command of Captain S. J. Snowden. This year Captain Byrd was promoted, becoming Major of Byrd's Battalion in the Twenty-Sixth Regiment of Infantry. Captain C. S. Land succeeded him in command of the Company.

"In September of this year, there was a great demand for soldiers to defend our seacoast and companies composed of old men and broken down Confederate soldiers residing in our Congressional District were called into service. After two months at Fort Finger on the Pee Dee River, Colonel E. B. C. Cash's Regiment was ordered to report at Georgetown and thither we went. At an election for officers for the Williamsburg and Georgetown Company, the following men were chosen: S. D. McGill, captain; A. F. Gardner, first lieutenant; W. G.

Cantley, second lieutenant; W. J. Grayson, third lieutenant.

"Williamsburg was assigned as a guard around the colors of the regiment obtained by Major J. B. Chandler, a native of and interested in our County. At the organization of Company D, the following non-commissioned officers were appointed by its captain: W. D. Fulton, first sergeant; W. J. Lee, second sergeant; S. J. Strong, third sergeant; Jesse Carter, fourth sergeant; T. S. Stuart, fifth sergeant; J. M. Gordon, first corporal; R. F. Scott, second corporal; E. H. McConnell, third corporal; W. J. Stone, fourth corporal. The latter being quickly detailed in blacksmith shop, J. D. Harper was appointed in his place.

"At first, there were one hundred twenty-six men on roll, but a few were detailed from the company, as their services were required in other duties, occasioning a change among the non-commissioned officers. When the company was disbanded in February, 1863, at Kingstree, there were one hundred three men on duty and there they were paid off by the Captain for their services under him, including their commutation money, amounting to $6,935.41 in the aggregate.

"These have been preserved and below is the list of members of Company D, Second Regiment of Reserves: S. D. McGill, Jesse Carter, R. S. Tisdale, A. F. Gardner, T. S. Stuart, J. D. Harper, S. A. Scott, E. Baxley, D. Baker, W. Burrows, S. Cribb, L. Cribb, I. Coker, A. Carraway, L. J. Dennis, P. O. Eaddy, W. D. Fulton, J. Hathaway, J. G. Hanna, A. M. Jayroe, I. D. Byrd, W. H. Brown, I. R. Bradshaw, J. R. Crosby, I. Cribb, S. Cooper, W. J. Cameron, A. DuBose, R. I. Eaddy, R. W. Fulton, I. D. Ham, C. Hanna, J. H. Johnson, P. P. June, B. Lambert, S. R. Mitchum, W. G. Cantley, R. F. Scott, E. G. Cantley (Harper's substitute); W. J. Grayson, E. H. McConnell, J. Bradshaw, W. Altman, L. Brown,

I. M. Buckles, R. R. Blakely, C. Cribb, A. Cribb, W. M. Campbell, Z. T. Ham, W. Epps, G. Freeman, R. Gamble, J. E. Howard, J. F. Hanna, W. J. Baxley, I. K. Barfield, R. W. Burns, B. G. Blake, T. Cribb, John Cribb, S. Coltrain, W. B. Davis, D. Epps, I. W. Forbes, N. Graham, T. J. Hughes, S. D. Hanna, W. Jefferson, B. Kirby, J. C. Lesesne, E. J. C. Matthews, A. M. Matthews, W. A. Myers, Tim Prosser, J. E. Richburg, E. E. Stone, T. S. Thompson, R. Cribb, H. Lambert, W. J. J. Lifrage, John Matthews, D. McClam, L. E. Powell, R. Rodgers, Thomas Stone, R. G. Thompson, W. McClam, Isaac Poston, D. R. Russ, B. F. Singletary, W. G. Thompson, W. J. Wilder, W. P. Kennedy, A. J. Lambert, R. J. Morris, J. T. McCants, R. Pipkins, E. Pope, J. W. Scott, W. J. Stone, R. Williams, B. F. Westbury." (McGill's Reminiscences of Williamsburg.)

The second man from Williamsburg killed in the War was Benjamin Faneuil Scott, Sergeant of Company K, Sixth Infantry. He rushed on the field at Williamsburg, Virginia, on May 5, 1862, received from the first volley a wound in his thigh, was taken by the enemy sweeping the field and died in their hands. His cousin, Alonzo W. Flagler, saw him fall, but could give no further information of him. He was the eldest son of John Ervin and Mary Gordon Scott. His mother hoped as long as she lived that he might return.

On the Chickahominy River at Seven Pines, Fair Oaks, Gaines Mill, Savage Station, and at Malvern Hill, the following were killed: R. M. Footman, J. J. Gamble, A. M. Gamble, W. S. McFaddin, G. S. Croft, F. F. Parsons. These were wounded: J. S. McCullough, H. C. Floyd, J. H. Fulmore, W. S. Allen, R. M. Barron, D. Keels, J. A. McCrea, J. T. Elwell, A. F. Elwell, J. M. Gardner, John Green and S. B. Gordon.

At Second Manassas, these were killed: W. J. Matthews, R. Franklin Cox; wounded, W. J. Ferrell, G. S.

B. Huggins, and G. G. McElveen. Killed at Boonsboro, September 14, 1862: S. T. Chandler, John Hudson, William McCallister, J. McDonald, and George W. Spring. Killed at Maryland Heights, Lieutenant W. E. Keels. Wounded at Maryland Heights, Washington Venters. Wounded at Fort Sumter, November 2, 1862, E. Johnson. Wounded at Fredericksburg, December 13, 1862: G. S. Eaddy, H. D. Gamble, Lieutenant G. W. Barron, W. L. Graham, J. M. Graham, John Thompson, W. J. Wilson, Captain James McCutchen, and W. S. Eaddy. At Sharpsburg, September 17, 1862, were killed: W. W. Cunningham, Hugh Johnson, and Daniel Conyers Nesmith; wounded, Alonzo W. Flagler. Wounded at Corinth, May 26, 1862, William G. Gamble, W. J. Britton.

At Murfreesboro, December 31, 1862, killed: C. W. Cockfield, J. H. Cockfield, S. F. R. Godwin, T. J. Harrison, Reuben W. Kirby, Thomas Jordan, James M. Matthews, G. W. Matthews, James McMulken, W. J. Munn, Captain J. R. Nettles, Joseph B. Russ, R. Turbeville, and T. E. Williamson; wounded: W. J. Clarkson, John L. Nesmith, Francis L. McCants, C. B. Goude, Thomas Hathaway, W. J. Pipkin, Hampton Lee, John McKnight, Alexander Parker, G. W. Huggins, N. Gray, D. E. Coward, C. W. Daniels, G. R. Matthews, W. P. Scott, H. W. Blakely, and Benjamin Beatty.

Death may be a beautiful thing when a young man rejoicing in his strength rushes out to meet a valiant enemy and falls in the forefront of the battle line. There it is swift death or sweet victory, but where a young man wastes away with some loathsome disease in some pestilential hospital, when his strong comrades are outside responding to the clear call to fame, and the bugle notes with failing strength fall on his ears—this is death with all its sting.

From Williamsburg there had died of disease in 1861 the following: John B. Abrams, Washington Carraway,

J. W. Coker, B. F. Ferrell, L. W. Fenters, T. B. Fleming, E. A. Flowers, J. B. Flowers, Thomas M. Fulton, T. J. Gaskins, J. F. Gurgames, J. W. Hanna, John Haselden, George Jones, Henry Long, J. J. Matthews, R. W. J. McIntosh, Thomas Port, J. F. Welch, J. J. Whitehead.

The following died of disease from Williamsburg in 1862: D. W. Baxley, H. C. Baxley, J. W. Baxley, Thomas Boon, J. F. Bridgman, B. F. Britton, J. S. Brockinton, Lieutenant S. B. Brown, W. P. Budden, S. B. Burkett, E. E. Cain, S. T. Chandler, A. B. Carter, G. W. Carter, John H. Carter, J. W. Cook, S. Dye, J. C. Fenters, J. J. Fenters, D. F. Fenters, Andrew P. Flagler, L. B. Floyd, William B. Ferdon, J. B. Freeman, J. B. Godwin, L. Haines, W. B. Hardick, F. M. Howard, C. Houston, L. Jones, Amos Jones, Louis Jones, T. Jordan, C. W. Lee, W. C. Lee, P. D. Lee, John Marshall, J. C. P. Martin, W. S. McConnell, Robert McKnight, T. M. Miller, J. F. Moreton, T. N. Moreton, William B. Nesmith, W. J. Pipkin, Lieutenant E. B. Scott, E. M. Scurry, W. S. Wallace, Benjamin Ward, and William Wilson.

The Wee Nee Volunteers were stationed at Camp Glover on James Island and participated in the battle of Secessionville on June 16, 1862. This Company left James Island on December 14, 1862 and were transported by railroad to Wilmington, North Carolina. From Wilmington the Company was ordered to Kinston. On reaching Magnolia it was ordered to return to Wilmington, where it remained in barracks until December 31, on which day it left for Charleston, South Carolina, and was again stationed at Camp Glover. The officers of the Company at this time were Captain Thomas J. China, First Lieutenant Calhoun Logan, Second Lieutenant Henry Montgomery, Jr., Third Lieutenant B. P. Brockinton. Captain China was sick from July 13 until the end of the year, during which time the Company was commanded by Lieutenant Logan. The inspecting officer on James Island reported on the Company as follows: discipline, good; instruction, very good; military appearance, very fine; arms, good with exception of a few; accoutrements, good; clothing, very good.

The Tenth Infantry commanded by Colonel A. M. Manigault left South Island on March 31, 1862, for the West, where it was brigaded with three Alabama regiments and commanded by Brigadier General Trapier until December 1, 1862, when Colonel Manigault succeeded him. This Regiment had three Williamsburg companies in it and the other companies of the organization contained many Williamsburg men. On May 2 this Regiment formed the advance guard of Beauregard's army and checked the enemy at what was the first battle of Corinth. In August, General Beauregard was sent to Charleston and General Bragg commanded the Confederate forces in the vicinity of Chattanooga. The Tenth Regiment formed the advance guard of General Bragg's army at Munfordville and Perryville. After Perryville, Bragg returned to Knoxville to rest and recuperate his army. Then he recrossed the mountains and was attacked by General Rosecrans at Murfreesboro, or Stone's River, on December 31, 1862. In this battle the Tenth Regiment showed great valor and a large number of its men were killed or wounded. As a mark of especial distinction, this Regiment was allowed to retain the guns that it had captured and to have the names of the men of the Regiment who fell inscribed on them.

However much the Tenth Infantry suffered from battle during 1862, its losses from disease far exceeded its killed and wounded. It is difficult for one to understand the losses from disease that occurred during the summer and fall. Enterogastritis seems to have afflicted nearly all of the men and the physicians alternately prescribed blue mass and opium pills which had but little control of the condition. The men ate whatever they fancied and drank the first water they found. Thirty-five years later this country was considered as polluted with malignant disease germs when so many of the soldiers stationed at Chickamauga during the Spanish American War died of the same kind of diseases that had taken off so many of the Confederates.

William J. Clarkson, who was a merchant near Lenud's Ferry, enlisted in Captain Weston's Company of the Tenth Regiment when it was organized on July 19, 1861. Mr. Clarkson was the great grandson of Colonel William Floyd, one of the signers of the Declaration of Independence and a representative in the first Congress under the United States Constitution. Colonel William Floyd was the great grandson of Richard Floyd and his wife, Susannah, who in 1650 came from Brecknockshire in Wales to Massachusetts and afterwards settled on Long Island. Thus, it will be seen that William J. Clarkson, of the Tenth Regiment, had a long line of worthy American blood. He was educated and may be regarded as one of the highest type of private soldiers in the Confederate Army. Mr. Clarkson kept a diary from the time he left South Island with the Tenth Regiment on March 31, 1862 until he was severely wounded in the head and temporarily deprived of his sight at Murfreesboro on December 31, 1862. This diary is a remarkable piece of work. From it one may see something of the soul of the soldier of the Tenth Regiment during that period. These quotations are taken from this diary.

"March 31, 1862. Up very early—got breakfast—struck tents—then left for Mount Pleasant. Marched fifteen miles—this is a pretty place to camp—saw some pretty young ladies—two or three visited our camp that night.

"April 6, 1862. Went to Catholic Church this morning—the afternoon to the Methodist Episcopal Church—had inspection. The Colonel spoke to the Regiment in regard to some of its late conduct.

"April 9, 1862. Charleston is truly a mass of ruins. We have been reviewed by General Ripley. He appeared to like the looks of the Regiment very much.

"April 11, 1862. Left Charleston on steamboats—landed at a country wharf—marched through the city to the South Carolina Railroad—received many cheers on our way—tiresome trip to Augusta—some pretty places on the way.

"April 12, 1862. Left Augusta for Atlanta and arrived at daylight.

"April 14, 1862. Took breakfast at Dalton—liked the place very much—ordered to return in consequence of the enemy being in our way—take the back track for Atlanta. On our way to Atlanta—we again turn toward Chattanooga.

"April 15, 1862. Again we receive orders to return to Atlanta—shifted engines in Atlanta—many of us were left—Colonel Manigault appeared very much vexed. At Newman we were in a railroad smash—one was killed and twenty-eight wounded.

"April 17, 1862. Ladies request to have a dress parade, so the Regiment appeared on the grounds amidst a crowd. The people liked it very much.

"April 18, 1862. Arrived at Montgomery—it is a business looking place—eight hundred Yankee prisoners here. Two ladies sent me and some others a beautiful bouquet with their best wishes for our success and for safe return. Left Mobile on the steamer Saint Nicholas.

"April 19, 1862. We are now on the Alabama River—the scenery is quite picturesque—arrived at Mobile at one-thirty tonight.

"April 20, 1862. Billy Gamble and myself stole out of the boat and went up into the city. Like the looks of things very much—some very fine looking places and public houses, postoffice, custom house, and others. The

Bienville Park is very beautiful. The Battle House is the finest hotel in town.

"April 21, 1862. Ordered to leave for Corinth at four o'clock—expect soon to see the enemy. Our Regiment is truly in a state of confusion but I trust all things will work good for us and that our country will soon be at peace.

"April 22, 1862. Stopped at Whistler, a small manufacturing place. Ladies with bouquets appear.

"April 24, 1862. Arrived at Corinth at five-thirty—looks like there are many soldiers here. We are all worn out from the fatigue of travel, having been on the road for thirteen days. This is decidedly the filthiest place I ever saw. Nothing can be procured to eat for love nor money.

"April 26, 1862. I looked around at the breastworks that are around this place. It appears as if it would be impossible for the enemy to come in. This morning I ate one hard bread for dinner—this is what I call hard fare. After tattoo tonight the Regiment met at the Colonel's headquarters and Chaplain Capers had prayers. I truly hope God will hear, answer, and help us.

"April 27, 1862. Again partake of hard bread and bitter coffee for breakfast—had inspection this morning. I believe the Sabbath is truly a day of rest—may I do nothing today that I shall be sorry for hereafter. We received better rations today—molasses, flour, coffee, sugar, rice, and meat.

"April 28, 1862. I went down to the spring and for the first time tried to wash a few clothes—find it rather difficult. Various reports as to the fall of New Orleans are current.

"April 29, 1862. Various reports about the camp—hear that the enemy is quite near but I do not believe a word I hear.

"April 30, 1862. We expect an attack every day—I hope we shall be prepared to give the enemy a warm reception. Had a few instructions from our captain as to how we shall act and aim in battle—ordered to cook three days' rations. Noticed the Twenty-Eighth Alabama Regiment today. Its performance was very poor.

"May 31, 1862. Ordered to march at four o'clock tomorrow morning. We shall no doubt soon see the long looked for enemy and come together. If so, may God protect and shield us from danger.

"May 2, 1862. We are on the road for somewhere but I do not know where. Marched ten and one half miles over the worst road I ever saw—remained under arms all day—great excitement all the time. After dark I fell asleep, the ground for my bed and the starry heavens for my covering.

"May 5, 1862. No likelihood of anything to eat this morning—clothes still wet.

"May 6, 1862. Drank a cup of molasses and water—this kind of fare is not very pleasant—here all day and nothing to eat.

"May 7, 1862. Many reports about camp as to peace, fighting, armistice, and other things.

"May 8, 1862. Company being reorganized and the government is holding all those who have served twelve months—very unjust I think. Four o'clock we all marched out to face the Yankees on the road to Shiloh—some of our men fired on them—supposed to have killed a major—saw his horse and overcoat.

"May 9, 1862. After a few hours of sleep on the cold ground, we were called up at four-thirty—fell in but for no purpose—took another nap leaning against a tree—we are taken back to camp for rations and find we will be out of them for two days. Nine o'clock we are again on the road for Farmington—at twelve o'clock we opened a rapid fire on the enemy. We were in open field in full sight—feel calmer than I expected—three o'clock the firing ceases—we have driven the Yankees back through the field—saw four of the enemy that have been killed, awful sight—truly an awful sight to me to see the dead and wounded on the ground. This battle is considered to be a great victory. We have accomplished that for which we went—to burn and destroy the bridge at Farmington to cut off the communication of the enemy from the railroad.

"May 15, 1862. Over to the Fifth Georgia Regiment this evening—drank a quantity of beer—10¢ a cup. Various reports going the rounds—some say peace and some say war. My trust is in God.

"May 19, 1862. Our surgeon orders no one to come up on sick list who is suffering from colds or diarrhea. He is becoming quite harsh in his practice. Continual stir in camp.

"May 20, 1862. Very sick this morning—very much debilitated. The doctor comes to see me at ten o'clock and prescribes pills.

"May 21, 1862. Doctor prescribes pills again. Nothing else of interest.

"May 23, 1862. Expect to get furlough in order to recruit my health. Had a letter from home today—oh, that God may protect them and may we soon meet again, our country being at peace!

"May 27, 1862. The thoughts of staying at this hospital make me sick. Mr. Harmon, the Methodist preacher, carried me out to his home. The Harmons appear to be very fine but plain country people.

"June 5, 1862. News of victory in Virginia—likelihood of England and France interfering.

"June 12, 1862. Received haversack of eatables and bade the Harmons goodbye. I can never forget them for their kindness—I hope God will bless and reward them.

"June 13, 1862. Am at Jackson, the Capital of Mississippi—bought essence of ginger—looked at pistols being made—drank beer—lay about in the dirt all day—bought milk and ate snack—tried to get off on passenger train but being a poor soldier could not. Ate supper and at ten-thirty we were all crowded into box cars and left for Meridian.

"June 14, 1862. Arrived at Meridian at seven o'clock—looked about but find nothing but filth. It is truly tiresome staying about these one horse depots. At ten o'clock all aboard on filthy box cars again—travelled all night.

"June 15, 1862. Still on the road—detained in consequence of order given—had to run back for water—had a car smashed on our train and had to leave same—this way of treating a poor soldier is a shame—cars again tonight.

"June 17, 1862. Very little to eat—we have to cook it ourselves.

"June 20, 1862. Colonel is now very strict.

"June 22, 1862. On sick list—ate a piece of raw meat and raw liver for breakfast—this is indeed hard living. This holy Sabbath has been passed with little advantage to me—oh, that I may yet be allowed the privilege of enjoying this, the Lord's Day.

"June 26, 1862. Bade farewell to the sick list and to our quack doctors—was made to mark time for going to the creek for water—something new to me.

"June 27, 1862. Had a dress parade today—the regiment forming a square, which is something new.

"June 28, 1862. New clothes given out to all the company for common use, not dress parade. The Regiment looked well in round jackets and pants and grey caps.

"June 29, 1862. Washed and put on clean clothes—find lice on my undershirt. Oh, the filth!

"July 7, 1862. We are getting it rubbed in now.

"July 9, 1862. Reports that France and England have recognized our independence and that peace will soon be declared.

"July 14, 1862. Lequex and I took walk in the country —had a fine dinner, apple dumplings—bought a sheep for $12.00.

"July 15, 1862. Sheep meat for breakfast—helped on well.

"July 19, 1862. We were reviewed by Generals Bragg, Withers, Polk, and Hardee.

"July 28, 1862. Dreamed of peace and going home— hope it will all come to pass—bought some cider—lost $100.00 at a raffle.

"July 31, 1862. On the cars—tiresome travelling—no one is allowed to leave the cars even for water, but I violated orders and slept all night on the top of a car.

"August 5, 1862. Passed many ladies and received their good wishes for our success—many peaches and watermelons—stopped at Graniteville and got a fine supper at the hotel.

"August 6, 1862. On our way we stopped some time at Dalton and spent the night at Chickamauga, twelve miles below Chattanooga.

"August 7, 1862. Again see nothing but filth and soldiers—wrote to sister and gave her a slight description of this place.

"August 12, 1862. Ordered to wash clothes without soap. This is another unreasonable order which I do not obey. Dress parade and a perfect botch of the march off the field.

"August 13, 1862. Lequex, McCants, McNulty, and Alexander, and I walked out over the mountains to the country to various houses in search of eatables. At last we came up with a good dinner. We went to another house and picked some fine peaches.

"August 18, 1862. Rumor is very current that we return to South Carolina but of course it is false.

"August 24, 1862. Detailed to pull corn—hot work but had to do it—nothing to eat but two ears of corn. This is what I call hard times.

"September 14, 1862. It is truly no good and quite hard on me to be compelled to violate the holy Sabbath washing my clothes, but it is now three weeks since I put on any clean clothes, so I had to do this, it being my first opportunity.

"September 20, 1862. Amused at lice now.

"September 24, 1862. Bardstown, Kentucky, is a delightful place but the water is scarce. Our rations have been cut down again to one-half pound flour. Three of us went into the country and bought some peaches from a Lincolnite and ate fine dinner. I hear that Lincoln intends to free all the negroes on January first.

"October 3, 1862. Dr. Graham in guard house on account of some pumpkins. I cooked and ate the pumpkins.

"October 12, 1862. No enemy yet, thank God. God has been merciful to us all. Went up to the house and got rations of whiskey. The General and all hands 'full.'

"October 18, 1862. Marched eighteen miles—stopped at a creek—got rations of beef and half pound flour. Washed face and hands for the first time in over a week. Cooked my bread over top of an old lantern.

"October 21, 1862. Passed through the Cumberland Gap—saw the corner stone of Kentucky, Virginia, and Tennessee.

"October 22, 1862. Was amused at a soldier in a garden. The owner shot at him and the soldier ran out very rapidly. Rations of corn two ears to the man.

"November 5, 1862. Feel very sick, no money, no friends, in hospital all day. It is truly distressing to see the suffering at these hospitals.

"November 8, 1862. Sergeant Huckaby loaned me $2.00 —quite a friendly act.

"November 28, 1862. Sam Nesmith loaned me his shoes and socks.

"November 29, 1862. Dr. Isaac Graham went to Murfreesboro and was accepted by the board as surgeon of the Twenty-Sixth Alabama Regiment.

"November 30, 1862. Lieutenant White arrived and brought our boxes from home. Judge and I went to the creek, washed, put on clean clothes, and then we ate a hearty meal of butter, hominy, ham, cake, and other things.

"December 5, 1862. Colonel Pressley and staff now engaging in snow balling but it was too cold for me. I stay by the fire. I stayed up until after midnight to see the moon in total eclipse.

"December 13, 1862. Was reviewed on field about four miles beyond Murfreesboro by President Davis, General Bragg, and others. Our division alone was reviewed. This has truly been a day of interest, having seen the President of the Confederate States.

"December 19, 1862. Was compelled to see a poor man of the Twenty-Eighth Alabama Regiment shot for desertion—had twenty-eight guns fired at him—it was a cruel thing.

"December 20, 1862. Two years today since the secession of South Carolina—drew knapsack, and ate a hearty dinner. I hear that the enemy is evacuating Nashville, that Captain Weston has been elected Lieutenant Governor of South Carolina, and there is much talk of peace.

"December 25, 1862. Clear and pleasant—this is the first Christmas for me in the army—ate breakfast and reported at headquarters—wrote all day—very busy—wrote orders to have two men shot tomorrow. What a Christmas!

"December 28, 1862. Formed a line of battle waiting for the enemy.

"December 29, 1862. About ten o'clock the pickets begin to fight and then we engaged the enemy. Tim Harrison was killed.

"December 30, 1862. Almost continuous fighting for twenty-four hours.

"December 31, 1862. Battle still rages hot and heavy. The Tenth Regiment is ordered to advance and charge. We repulsed the enemy but they came back again. I was wounded—shot through the right eye and soon got off to the rear to the hospital. The wound is very painful."

The War in 1862 did not look to the folks at home like it did in 1861. In 1862, everybody realized that every energy must be utilized to win. Volunteering in the first part of 1861 was an easy matter. It was a serious step in 1862. A letter to the Courier of March 3, 1862, begins as follows: "As a daughter of Carolina and of the 'low country,' I write to beg that you will again appeal to our men. With dismay and grief, I learn that in Charleston it has been necessary to draft." The letter continues in the most appealing feminine manner. In Williamsburg, practically every man was a volunteer. There were, however, a few who attempted to remain at home. These were shown at once in no uncertain terms by the women that their place was on the field. If a man did not heed the warning of the women, the old men, using stern measures, soon made him look for the battle line.

In the spring of 1862, the people of Williamsburg planted all they could, and the slaves labored with increased zeal when they saw how "ole Massa" and "ole Missus" were working to send things to "young Massa" in "de wah." The slaves showed a loyalty to their masters all during the War that appeals most forcibly to a man. All war time there was an abundance of foodstuffs in Williamsburg.

The plantations were searched for everything that could be used by the Confederate Government. This letter was published by the Mercury: "Indiantown, S. C., March 29, 1862. Richard Yeadon, Esq. Dear Sir: I have this day sent to you by the Northeastern Railway about forty pounds of lead and brass of my own, and fourteen pounds for Mrs. Isabelle Garland, for the use of the government. Also, four patchwork quilts from four ladies of Williamsburgh, to be raffled or sold and the money applied to the ladies' gunboat, Palmetto State. Very respectfully, W. J. B. Cooper."

From the captain commanding came this letter to the Mercury: "I beg space to return thanks of the Wee Nee Volunteers to Mrs. J. F. Brockinton and to the ladies of the Elon Church Soldiers' Aid Association for valuable contributions of clothing and blankets. These substantial evidences of the regard and sympathy of the ladies of our native district have been gratefully received; and to be as brave in the defense of them and their homes as they are untiring in their efforts to serve us shall be our aim."

J. M. Thomas, of Myersville, was collector of Confederate War taxes in Williamsburg during 1862. The appointments to the Citadel that year were B. S. Nesmith and Thomas McCutchen. The Methodist circuit riders in the district were the Reverends John W. Murray and Henry J. Morgan. The Reverend W. A. Hemingway was chaplain of the Twenty-First Infantry in the field and the Reverend Jeremiah J. Snow, chaplain of the Sixth Infantry.

CHAPTER XXIX

WILLIAMSBURG, C. S. A., 1863.

District officers, as agreed to by the Legislature at its late session, for Williamsburg District in 1863, were: Magistrates, Samuel W. Maurice and R. G. Ferrell; Commissioners of Free Schools, W. G. Gamble, W. P. Nesmith, S. C. McCutchen, D. D. Wilson, and J. A. McCullough; Commissioners of Public Security, Dr. James S. Brockinton, John E. Scott, W. J. Goodwin, J. A. Salters, and J. A. McCullough; Commissioners of Roads, Andrew Jayroe, S. T. Cooper, J. A. Hemingway, W. G. McKnight, J. J. M. Graham, B. P. Brockinton, S. A. Douglas, W. C. Barr, J. D. Singletary, J. E. Fulton, R. J. Eaddy, E. H. Britton, J. E. Scott, D. Z. Martin, J. W. Keels, H. Sauls, John Lequex, Sr., S. McBride Scott, J. P. Mouzon, J. M. Speights, W. R. Rodgers, F. W. Boyd, Edmund Baxley, W. M. Campbell, W. H. Cockfield, H. G. Gaskins, Reuben Jordan, James Maxwell, J. A. Nixon, G. K. McDonald, and W. J. Haselden, Sr.; Dr. J. F. Brockinton was collector of Confederate War taxes and W. G. Gamble was assessor.

Mr. F. W. Mackusie ran a stage line between Georgetown and Kingstree. He carried the mails. It was said that the road from Kingstree to Georgetown was far better than the old stage road from Gourdins.

The Reverend W. A. Hemingway, post chaplain of the General Hospital of the Fourth Military District, located at Georgetown, asks through the Courier for donations of poultry, eggs, syrup, potatoes, hops, and other things for the hospital. He states the hospital would furnish transportation for anything left at Kingstree with John E. Scott or with J. A. Hemingway at Cooper's Store.

In 1863, Williamsburg soldiers participated in all of the great battles fought between the Confederate and Union armies, and its losses in killed and wounded were heavy. These fell at Chancellorsville, May 24: killed, Reuben Ard, Oliver Baxley, John J. Brown, Palvey T. Stone, and Wiliam J. Wilson; wounded, E. V. Gaskins, W. L. Graham, E. H. Johnson, William McCallister.

These were wounded at the Rappahannock, May 12: Lieutenant William Haselden, J. H. Barnes, O. W. Baxley, E. H. Johnson, A. B. Marsh, J. J. Brown, P. T. Stone, L. Buckles, A. M. Gaskins, S. W. Koon; and these killed, W. J. Wilson, William Brown, R. Ard, and William Duke.

At Gettysburg, July 1-3, the casualities were, killed: John Ard, John Floyd, J. Cleveland Cockfield, Frank Cox, John F. Eaddy, J. G. Gist, Francis Lenerieux; wounded, Lieutenant M. O. Timmons, F. N. Lenerieux, T. J. Burrows, W. D. L. Abrams, J. B. Carter, D. W. Cribb, J. F. Eaddy, H. A. Poston, J. L. Venters, Abram Willis, John B. Carter.

These killed and wounded at Battery Wagner, September 3-7: killed, Nelson Dennis, S. R. Dennis, J. F. Kirby, S. D. Lamb, E. Lynch, Lieutenant S. N. McDonald, Lieutenant H. J. Montgomery, Henry Ragin; wounded, G. F. McClary, J. J. Jaudon, W. H. McConnell, J. J. Baggett, S. R. Dennis, J. F. Montgomery, S. M. China, J. G. Player, E. Ard, B. Ard, J. F. McClary, W. H. Parsons, J. B. Miller, S. W. Browder, W. E. James, W. M. McKnight, J. F. Scott, B. M. Guess, E. G. Ard, H. M. Pressley, E. S. Ellis, Captain W. B. Gordon, E. R. Lesesne, J. H. Lamb, S. G. Cooper, S. T. Player, J. T. Player, George Martin, George Terrey, J. A. Bradham, A. B. Cooper, D. J. Jaudon, C. Lesesne, J. H. Lamb, P. N. Altman, L. Player, J. E. Scott, T. J. China.

At Chickamauga, September 20, 1863, Williamsburg's losses were, killed: C. T. Altman, Isaac B. Cook, Washington Collins, Daniel Fenters, Nathaniel Fenters, T. H. Gibbons, John A. Graham, M. C. Langston, J. R. Miles, Pleasant Matthews, Nathaniel Nesmith, Arthur B. Scipper; wounded: Thomas A. Matthews, D. M. Cook, G. L. Ellis, S. S. Guild, Solomon Hennesy, J. McLawhorn, William C. Ogburn, E. T. Porter, Thomas Altman, Paul W. Johnson, William Laney, John C. Laws, Lieutenant A. Poston, Lieutenant E. S. Sauls, S. Kirby, J. Brogdon, W. H. Poston, B. D. Poston, C. B. Foxsworth, S. D. Smith, H. Matthews, M. Jones, P. McGee, A. C. Osborn, J. W. Moore, C. T. Altman, W. D. Coleman, D. W. Johnson, William Lenerieux, James McCall, James Middleton, G. W. Scipper, John Rodgers, J. J. Huggins, R. B. Giles, J. F. Brockinton, J. Price, R. Collins, Rix A. Coward, James A. Coward.

At Chattanooga, November 23, were, killed: James M. Johnson, James H. Smith, Benjamin Ward.

At Missionary Ridge, November 25, were, killed: Harvey Barfield, Jesse Floyd, W. H. Poston; wounded: Louis H. Pipkin, Louis E. Burket; and a large number of men were here captured, some of whom were: M. M. Braveboy, John M. Brown, Eric Cain, John J. Huggins, John McKnight, Harvey Matthews. Pleasant McGhee, and E. C. Osborn.

It is most pathetic to remember that in all these terrible battles of Chickamauga, Chattanooga, Missionary Ridge, and the others that had preceded them, Williamsburg soldiers were equipped only with smooth bore rifles, while their enemies had an abundance of Enfields. How these men went into battle with such fearful odds against them reveals their heroic character. Until after the battle of Franklin, the Tenth Regiment, except Captain Weston's Company A, which he equipped with Enfields out of his own pocket, had only smooth bore rifles with which to fight men armed with the best weapons of the age.

These soldiers of Williamsburg died of disease in 1863: J. A. Arnett, J. E. Barrineau, W. J. Blakely, T. W Blakely, John W. Calder, A. J. Cook, E. W. Cook, J. T. Cox, J. J. Fillyaw, E. A. Flowers, J. B. Flowers, L. D. Floyd, W. J. Gamble, Andrew P. Flagler, G. W. Graham, A. Gray, J. P. Davis, W. S. Hardick, A. J. Hatchell, Jasper Hatchell, J. N. Hatchell, T. H. Hatchell, M. J. E. Hixon, W. Hodge, G. W. Johnson, A. Jones, M. Jones, J. M. Lacey, A. R. Lee, D. Lee, William C. Lee, J. A. Lee, W. C. Lee, J. W. Lee, J. H. Lee, A. Lynch, J. M. Lynch, Robert Matthews, H. H. Matthews, A. Matthews, M. Matthews, G. W. Matthews, F. Matthews, Pleasant Matthews, R. M. Matthews, J. C. McGee, S. Miles, C. H. Mitchum, S. J. Nettles, N. G. Parker, G. W. Reed, John L. Scott, E. M. Scurry, James Sauls, J. H. Smith, R. Spring, Benjamin Ward, George C. Wheeler, T. H. Wilkes.

It was during the three days fierce fighting at Battery Wagner that Junius E. Scott performed feats of valor for which he was given a commission as lieutenant and presented with a sword by General Hagood. Young Scott had volunteered at sixteen years of age in Captain Colclough's company, but was sent home after a few months on account of the enforcement of the law against receiving volunteers under eighteen. He then went to Wofford College until he could again re-enlist, when he joined Captain China's Wee Nee Volunteers. At Battery Wagner, young Scott carried messages from Fort Wagner to Fort Gregg during the long drawn out battling. It was for his heroism in these things that he was cited for valor and commissioned. He was again cited for valor in the Virginia campaign of the Twenty-Fifth South Carolina Regiment.

S. I. Montgomery was promoted from Sergeant to Lieutenant September 19, 1863. After Lieutenant McDonald had been killed, Lieutenant E. R. Lesesne was promoted and Charles Lesesne succeeded him as Lieutenant on Sep-

LIEUT. JUNIUS E. SCOTT, C. S. A.

tember 14, 1863. On this date the three lieutenants of Company K, Twenty-Fifth Infantry, were all Lesesnes.

On the Muster Roll of Company E, Tenth Infantry, of October 31, 1863, Captain Anderson made this simple endorsement: "On the afternoon of the seventeenth, we took up line of march for the field of Chickamauga, in the battle of which the company took part, as is shown from the list of killed and wounded." The Company was then at the foot of Missionary Ridge. After the battle of Chattanooga, this Company had only eleven men fit for duty.

E. S. Sauls was promoted to Second Lieutenant March 13, 1863. Lieutenant W. J. M. Lee succeeded Captain Nettles in command of Company H, Tenth Regiment.

Colonel A. M. Manigault, of the Tenth Infantry, was promoted to Brigadier General in July 1863, and Lieutenant Colonel James F. Pressley was promoted Colonel and succeeded him as commanding officer of the Tenth. Colonel Pressley commanded the Tenth and the Nineteenth Regiments of South Carolina Infantry at Chickamauga.

In the fall of 1863, all white males between the ages of eighteen and forty-five years of age "who have furnished substitutes in the Confederate States Army, resident aliens, and others who have avoided conscription by reason of civil employment, contract or engagement" were required to report to the military authorities for forming regiments for state service. All men between ages of sixteen and eighteen and forty-five and sixty were also required to enlist in these regiments to "repel threatened raids of the enemy within this State."

On December 5, 1863, the following members of the Williamsburg Presbyterian Church were dismissed by order of Harmony Presbytery for the purpose of organizing Union Presbyterian Church: Ann Lifrage, Mary A. Lifrage, W. J. J. Lifrage, C. R. Montgomery, J. S.

Lifrage, J. M. Shaw, Sarah A. Gordon, J. W. Gordon, Margaret P. Frierson, Sarah Frierson, Sarah M. Gordon, Jane M. Salters, Mary E. Salters, John Watson, M. E. Watson, J. A. Salters, M. I. Rodgers, D. E. Gordon, W. B. Gordon, W. F. Rodgers, W. J. Montgomery, Edward McDonald, Mary McClary, Hester McDonald, M. E. McClary, Daniel Barrineau, T. M. Lifrage, H. D. Shaw. The following colored persons were also dismissed to join Union Church: Pompey, belonging to W. F. Rodgers; and Peggy Ann, belonging to J. A. Salters.

After these members of the Williamsburg Presbyterian Church had withdrawn, and among them Elders H. D. Shaw and John A. Salters, S. J. Bradley was the only elder in the Williamsburg Church. About this time, the Reverend D. M. McClure became minister of the Williamsburg Church, which he served for two years.

CHAPTER XXX.

WILLIAMSBURG, C. S. A., 1864.

When one understands the almost superhuman veneration that has always "hedged about" ministers of the gospel in Williamsburg and this "low country," and reads the following extract from an editorial in the Charleston Courier of January 19, 1864, he will obtain some faint suggestion of the intensity of existing feeling that this country should do its utmost to win the war.

This editorial begins: "The propriety of conscripting the ministers has been discussed. We think it, first of all, very doubtful whether there is any need for the extension of the conscription as to ages or classes. We firmly believe that a faithful enforcement of the original conscription from eighteen to forty-five years, with the discontinuance of substitution, unless in special cases, to be decided not by the amount of money nor the position of influence of the conscript, but on just discrimination and sound discretion before a competent board, would give us an army sufficient and efficient, if properly organized, disciplined, and managed. We see all around us not occasions for new laws, but urgent occasions for the faithful execution of extant laws." The editorial continues, favoring ministers and all other able bodied men enlisting in combat units.

South Carolina sustained a great loss when Captain the Honorable Plowden C. J. Weston died of consumption on January 25, 1864. He was captain of Company A, Tenth Regiment, in which were many soldiers from along the Santee in Williamsburg. He equipped his company at his own expense according to the latest and most approved designs both in clothing and arms, and his company was the only unit in the regiment reasonably well armed until the time of his death. Captain Weston was born in

England while his parents, from the oldest families in Georgetown, were spending the summer in the old home of the family in the "Mother Country." Exposure incident to his military service in the Western campaign under General Bragg caused his death. He was Lieutenant Governor of South Carolina and had come home to preside over the Senate of 1863 when stricken.

The reaction from the Confederate losses in 1863 came early in 1864 on economic conditions. Confederate currency began to depreciate. The newspapers in Charleston said on May 28 that they could receive bills only at actual current valuation, one-third discount, stating they had deferred this action for some weeks after these bills had ceased to pass at par.

The prices of articles in Kingstree at that time may be realized from the following: Sugar, $5.00 per pound; flour, $1.00; cotton, $1.00; cotton cards, $75.00 per pair; tobacco, $6.00. On July 6, at Mrs. Belser's sale, a large iron pot brought $105.00; an oven, $95.00; and a match of horses, thirteen years old, $3,100.00. At the close of the year, Mrs. McGill purchased some articles and here is her bill: 4 yards homespun, $24.00; 1 spool cotton, $3.00; 1 skein black flax, $3.00; 1 lead pencil, $3.00; 2 slate pencils, $3.00; 1 cake soap, $3.00; 1 dozen horn buttons, $1.50; 2 bunches yarn, No. 8, $140.00; 3 bunches yarn, No. 9, $210.00. About the same time, Dr. McGill bought 4 drinks of whiskey, wine glass size, $20.00, and 2 bottles apple brandy, $140.00. (These price lists were taken from Dr. McGill's Reminiscences of Williamsburg.)

This year the fields of Williamsburg brought forth abundantly and at the harvest time all its barns were overflowing. Notwithstanding conditions incident to the deflation of currency, the defeats in Virginia and Tennessee and Georgia, and the sorrow coming from the death of so many valiant young men, Williamsburg's old men, its women, and its slaves labored with that Scotch-Irish intensity that always comes out of emergency.

An independent company, which was organized in Williamsburg and Georgetown Districts on November 5, 1862, for state service, and commanded by Captain W. N. Y. Rodgers, was on March 11, 1864 reorganized and mustered into the Confederate service. This company was known as Captain Steele's company and played a considerable part in the history of this low country from its organization until the end of the War. Here is its roll of March 11, 1864: J. J. Steele, captain; J. M. Kennedy, first lieutenant; N. H. Welch, second lieutenant; T. S. Steele, second lieutenant; J. H. Fulmore, first sergeant; E. Kirby, second sergeant; G. W. Mills, third sergeant; E. E. Matthews, fourth sergeant; James Floyd, fifth sergeant; J. M. Woods, first corporal; R. Epps, second corporal; C. W. McClam, third corporal.

Privates: E. Baxley, 42; J. M. Bass, 38; R. A. Buckels, 26; J. H. Byrd, 44; J. D. Byrd, 44; J. F. Butler, 33; H. O. Britton, 18; S. Cooper, 38; S. Caselman, 40; W. F. Cox, 20; M. M. Cook, 43; W. A. Deffee, 17; C. W. DuBose, 25; J. J. Floyd, 42; J. W. Grayson, 20; John S. Graham, 18; H. G. Gaskins, 38; J. Gore, 42; J. E. Howard, 19; A. W. Hardee, 28; W. Jefferson, 39; R. J. Jordan, 37; W. H. Kennedy, 38; W. T. Kennedy, 17; D. P. Kirby, 28; J. F. Kirby, 19; H. Lenud, 43; J. Lee, 19; W. J. Lay, 17; W. E. Jones, 23; S. A. Long, 27; J. Long, 26; W. Matthews, 37; J. R. Matthews, E. E. Moore, 38; B. C. Moore, 37; J. P. Moore, 30; J. B. Montgomery, 23; J. T. Morse, 19; S. M. McClam, 44; W. McClam, 18; G. D. McCutchen, 40; W. C. McCutchen, 20; William E. Nesmith, 23; J. Powell, 40; W. R. Powell, 42; W. K. Parker, 40; T. E. Patrick, 17; S. R. Rodgers, 43; B. F. Singletary, 42; E. J. Singletary, 39; M. M. Sellers, 22; K. Smith, 17; J. E. Thomas, 42; J. C. Thomas, 37; M. D. Turbeville, 42; J. T. Vareen, 24.

Williamsburg's battle losses in 1864 were fearful. Captain China, commanding Kingstree's Own, the Wee Nee Volunteers, was killed on May 16, at Drury's Bluff. Lieutenant F. J. Lesesne was killed at Swift Creek May 9th. Captain W. B. Gordon, commanding the Ripley Guards, the Pride of the Santee, was killed at the Weldon Railway. Lieutenant W. H. Munnerlin was killed at Atlanta on July 30th. Colonel James F. Pressley, who had been acting as Brigadier General for more than a year was severely wounded at Atlanta. His brother, Lieutenant Colonel John G. Pressley, easily favorite hero of all Williamsburg, was so severely wounded at Walthall Junction on May 5th that his right arm hung limp by his side the remainder of his life. Lieutenant Calhoun Logan and Ensign J. M. Pendergrass were wounded at Drury's Bluff; Lieutenant Charles Lesesne at Swift Creek; Lieutenants Thomas J. Kirby and E. S. Sauls at Atlanta; Lieutenant Junius E. Scott at Weldon Railway; Lieutenants R. A. Flagler and R. S. Smith at Fort Harrison; Lieutenant T. G. Britton at Haw's Shop; Lieutenant T. M. Britton at Franklin; Lieutenant T. M. McCutchen at Trevillian; Lieutenant T. S. Nelson at Haw's Shop.

Here is a list of Williamsburg's losses in 1864:

Wilderness, May 5: killed, William McCullough and A. M. Gaskins; wounded, D. L. Brown, J. M. Graham, W. L. Graham, John Matthews.

Walthall Junction, May 6: killed, John Ard, E. Browder, John Davis, W. D. Duke, T. M. Lifrage, J. G. Player; wounded, Lieutenant Colonel John G. Pressley, Captain T. J. China, H. G. Nelson, John Pelt, W. E. Mitchum, Sam Mitchum, C. W. Matthews, E. Ard, W. R. Burdick, W. Dennis, D. Manton McClary.

Swift Creek, May 9: killed, I. Ard, J. L. Barthley, E. B. Bentley, W. R. Burdick, E. Browder, J. E. Cubstead, J. Davis, D. I. Dennis, W. D. Duke, J. A. Fagin, J. W. Gordon, Robert Lamb, Lieutenant F. J. Lesesne,

P. H. Lesesne, J. G. Player, M. M. Scott, H. H. Stukes, John Wilder; wounded, Lieutenant C. Lesesne, S. Mitchum, W. E. Mitchum, Isaac K. Gamble, John M. Grayson, John Wilson.

Spottsylvania: killed, John A. Altman, Henry A. Poston, Nathaniel M. Johnson; wounded, J. G. Cox, Frank Cox.

Drury's Bluff, May 14-16: killed, J. T. Barrineau, M. A. Brown, Captain Thomas J. China, B. F. Duke, J. A. Fagin, B. M. Guess, H. W. Matthews, J. E. Kaler, T. A. McConnell, J. F. Montgomery, Samuel Montgomery, William Hallford, D. M. Smith; wounded, J. H. Bradham, B. R. Browder, H. J. Brown, Lieutenant C. Logan, B. F. Duke, R. E. Duke, E. S. Ellis, J. A. Fagin, A. M. Gamble, W. E. Graham, William Guess, H. L. Grayson, J. W. Jayroe, D. S. McClary, S. A. McClary, J. N. Miller, Isaac Montgomery, J. F. Montgomery, C. G. Parsons, J. C. Parsons, Ensign J. M. Pendergrass, H. M. Pressley, D. M. Smith, H. Tyler, H. G. Wilson, John Wilson, R. B. Walters, J. Wisson, J. H. Young.

Haw's Shop, May 28: killed, S. W. Crapps, William Henry Davis, J. J. Marshall, Lieutenant T. S. Nelson; wounded, Lieutenant T. G. Britton, J. E. McCullough, J. P. Mouzon, R. J. Patterson, T. E. Ragin.

Trevillian: killed, T. J. Spooner; wounded, Lieutenant T. M. McCutchen, J. Harper, R. B. McClary.

Cold Harbor, June 30: killed, S. I. Barrineau, Major J. C. Wilson, John T. Burrows, W. J. Cox; wounded, R. S. Smith and Thomas McConnell.

Clay's Farm: killed, Jacob D. Casselman, John W. Collins, Hugh Gunther, Benjamin Matthews, William G. Williamson; wounded, John J. Godwin and Samuel A. Scott.

Atlanta, July 22: killed, G. S. Cook, G. Cook, A. J. Council, Washington Emanuel, G. W. Huggins, James S. June, J. F. LaRebour, J. M. Matthews, T. A. Matthews,

S. W. McClam, S. W. McClary, Lieutenant W. H. Munnerlin; wounded, J. T. Kirby, John J. McCallister, Colonel James F. Pressley, Lieutenant Thomas J. Kirby, Lieutenant E. S. Sauls, John J. McKnight.

Bermuda Hundreds: killed, F. F. Parsons.

Weldon Railway, August 21: killed, J. M. Brown, Alexander Cook, Captain W. B. Gordon, J. W. Jayroe, E. J. Kelly, R. W. King, William Cantey Lesesne, J. E. McCants, F. McCallister, J. S. Mitchum, J. W. Montgomery, Thomas Warren Montgomery, J. A. Odom, Thomas Odom, C. Powell, E. Powell, Barney Wallace; wounded, J. H. Bradham, J. R. Cook, H. D. Shaw, J. D. Young, W. H. Young, H. L. Graham, Edward Johnson, R. K. Liles, James B. Montgomery, James M. Young, Joseph C. Duke, I. Player, G. W. Terry.

Fort Harrison, September 21: killed, Samuel Flagler; wounded, Lieutenant R. A. Flagler, Lieutenant R. S. Smith, and J. C. McCutchen.

Franklin, November 30: wounded, Lieutenant T. M. Britton, J. L. Nesmith, Thomas Altman.

Petersburg, 1864: killed, R. W. Chandler, B. M. Guess, George W. Hicks, Ira Lee, Timothy Lee, John J. McGee, James E. McCallister, J. R. McKenzie, William J. Mills, John Yarborough; wounded, Samuel Cooper, Robert Nesmith, W. H. Young, Robert F. Tilton, John W. Cameron, W. J. Hicks, Isaac E. Lee, Leonard Miles, R. W. Chandler, R. D. Rollins, Ira Coker.

Nashville, November 15: killed, J. W. Brown, G. W. Burrows, J. W. Carter, J. T. Carter, F. S. McCants; wounded, J. E. Holmes, G. L. Ellis, L. H. Pipkin, S. J. McCants, T. L. Altman, W. A. Marshall, G. W. Scipper, W. J. Vareen, D. E. Coward, A. M. B. Coward.

Somewhere these men were killed in action. Records and tradition say one place and another. Wherever they fell, Williamsburg dust is forever there. Robert Anderson, Frank McCants, John Rodgers, J. Cooper, William

Game, John Garner, W. H. Bunch, W. D. Burrows, John Missola, G. B. Townsend, H. J. Ervin, S. B. Harris, D. S. Owen, J. C. Singletary, James A. Owens, H. D. Cusack, T. J. Blackwell, T. S. Chandler, W. J. Matthews, S. C. DuBose, J. C. Hyman, T. Hyman, W. T. Rowell, L. V. Scott, John Wilder, Jesse B. Ellis, Stacey June, W. J. Wilson, R. Ard, Henry Buckels, Thomas J. Burrows, T. E. Ragin, T. J. Harrison, Thomas Williamson, James Mulken.

In hospitals, in camps, in kindly homes of Virginia, Tennessee, Mississippi, Georgia, and North Carolina, these soldiers of Williamsburg died of disease during 1864: B. J. Avant, J. A. Guess, C. R. Martin, Joseph Ard, W. N. Boatwright, James Martin, E. R. Martin, William Montgomery, T. J. Hughes, E. C. Keels, J. H. McClary, W. D. Singletary, J. McKenzie, S. E. McCants, W. J. B. Wall, L. W. Cockfield, W. S. Allen, S. M. Flagler, William G. Christmas, Henry Gordon, Lieutenant J. R. China, S. S. Mitchum, M. R. D. Baker, W. D. Cook, E. S. Ellis, S. Edgar Montgomery, John Salters, S. W. Cockfield.

Out of all this suffering and death grew hatred for Abraham Lincoln, President of the United States. From the beginning, the Southern people seemed to realize that this man stood between them and the destiny they desired. They called the North Lincolndom and its people Lincolnites. The Southern people were about correct in their estimate of Lincoln's powerful personality. He seems to have been the only man of the War who could have controlled.

Hatred for Abraham Lincoln was, and is, powerful in Williamsburg. No man can measure what this hatred has wrought in Williamsburg. It is interesting to know how the newspapers fed this flame of hatred. In the Courier of November 9, 1864, appears the following under the caption: "God Bless Our Noble President."

"A Republican paper in the North exclaims 'God Bless Our Noble President.' To this a Western paper says:

"God bless our noble President.

"And for what?

"Bless him for being the poorest apology for a Chief Magistrate the world ever saw.

"Bless our noble President for being the only clown, buffoon, and story teller ever elevated to a position of influence in this country.

"Bless him for filling the land with smutty jokes, with vile mouthed and obscene stories which even blackguards by profession are ashamed to repeat.

"Bless him for over-riding all law, both human and divine.

"Bless him for his imbecile incompetency and for his success in ruining a great nation.

"Bless him for turning a war for the preservation of the Union and for the suppression of the rebellion into a wicked, murderous, crusade for cotton, negroes, and power. Bless him for making a million of widows and five millions of orphans.

"Bless him for robbing the North of its bone and sinew, and for using the bodies of those who have served for enriching the soil of rebel territory.

"Bless him for piling mountains of taxes upon us—for the stamps we use—for the depreciation of our currency—for the the poverty, ruin, and suffering in the land—for the thousands of women who have been forced into houses of prostitution—for the thousands of broken hearts—for the thousands of orphan children who will curse him forever—for the army of cripples—for the corruption in high places—for the trampling upon the liberties of a free people—for the freeing of negroes by a stroke of his pen—for continuing this war until slaves are free, thus proving the foolishness of his proclamation—for the failure of our armies—for the deprivation of its rights which has made America the home of the oppressed.

"Yes, bless our noble President."

President Jefferson Davis, of the Confederate States of America, was first severely criticized in the South in November, 1864. His proposition for immediately emancipating forty thousand slaves and training them for service in the army, giving them fifty acres of land each, and to continue emancipating them for service in the army, created great resistance of sentiment in the South. The real basis of the secession of the Southern States was economic. This fact is nowhere more clearly revealed than in the scorn President Davis received when he made this recommendation to the Confederate Congress.

However much contempt was shown for President Davis' proposition, when it was realized that Sherman would probably march through South Carolina on his way North from the Sea, many of the best men in the State warmly advocated training slaves into soldiers to resist him. This was not done.

November 16, 1864, was set apart by executive authority as a day of prayer, confession, and thanksgiving. The Courier said, "Various and checkered has been the character of our fears for the past six months, which gives rise to feelings of a diverse nature. The reverses that our armies have sustained have been so grave as to admonish us that our sins have provoked the wrathful displeasure of Almighty God. God has greatly humiliated us at the hands of our adversaries. All our victories and successes have come from God, it is at once our duty and privilege to implore the continuance of His favor."

At the time of all these serious national matters, it seems that soap and vinegar were scarce and that whiskey and potatoes were plentiful in Williamsburg. One man in the district showed how good soap could be made from myrtle wax; and another asserted that good vinegar, very much like white wine vinegar, could be produced by mixing three bushels of ripe persimmons, three gallons of whiskey, and twenty-seven gallons of water. William Gilmore Simms, the historian, endorsed this vinegar recipe.

Editor Fulton, of the Wilmington Journal, came to Kingstree in November 1864, and P. B. Mouzon, agent of the Northwestern railway, gave him twenty sweet potatoes that could not all be contained in a bushel basket. Editor Fulton went back to Wilmington and wrote about Williamsburg's sweet potatoes. The editor of the Charleston Courier read Editor Fulton's article and came to Kingstree immediately. Mr. Mouzon gave him a bushel of "uncommonly fine" potatoes, one of which measured twenty-four inches in length, and of "other respectable dimensions." The editor of the Courier wrote: "It appears that large potatoes are quite common in old Williamsburg, as we saw a negro with six of unusual size, for which he was asking $1.00 each. When told that his price was above the market, he consoled himself by saying that he would take them home and keep them until spring, when potatoes would be scarce, and he could readily get his price. How much like 'ole Mossa.' "

Williamsburg elected in 1864 as its delegation in the Legislature: Senator, James McCutchen; representatives, James F. Pressley and W. A. Hemingway. Colonel McCutchen declined the honor, preferring to remain with his regiment. Colonel Pressley was at home recovering from the serious wound receievd at Atlanta.

The Methodist Episcopal Church, South, at its conference in December, 1864, appointed Reverend J. W. Murray for the Kingstree Circuit and the Reverend J. C. Stoll for the Black River Circuit for 1865.

CHAPTER XXXI.

WILLIAMSBURG, C. S. A. 1865.

The ragged remnant of the splendid Southern armies that had gone to War in 1861 refused to surrender during the autum of 1864, although all but the spirit of the men had been crushed. Southern regiments had been so decimated that not even a full company of effective fighting men could be had from many of them. All possible old men and boys and others who had been doing state service were sent to Virginia in the vain hope of strengthening the thin gray line of battle.

Captain John Tucker's Company, afterwards Captain John McDonald's, that had been guarding the coast from the Pee Dee to the Santee until late in 1864, was sent to Virginia to unite with Company A, Seventh Cavalry. Among the men of Williamsburg who then became soldiers in the Seventh Cavalry were W. H. Britton, J. W. Britton, D. Z. Martin, W. F. Thompson, W. T. Thompson, Robert Godwin, S. B. Green, John Green, Richard Green, Thompson Green, Eli Rodgers, Claron Rodgers, Furman Rodgers, Stephen Rodgers, John Ferdon, James Hanna, Robert Abrams, Duncan Fitch, John Hill, and others. J. W. Britton, and Robert Godwin were killed in the battle of Farmville on the retreat from Richmond to Appamattox.

At Fort Fisher, these died of wounds: J. B. Johnson and D. Powell; these at Fortress Monroe, R. M. Footman and Edgar Montgomery.

William G. Gamble and J. T. Moreton were killed at Bentonville, North Carolina, in almost the last efforts Johnson made to resist Sherman. G. P. Anderson was wounded at Kinston, J. J. Miller at Jonesboro, and D. B. Fulton at Raleigh.

Kingstree's Own, the Wee Nee Volunteers, then Company C, Twenty-Fifth Infantry, was sent from Virginia on December 22, 1864, to reinforce Fort Fisher. This Twenty-Fifth Regiment spent Christmas Day, December 25, 1864, in Greensboro, North Carolina, on the way. The citizens of this city feasted this Regiment on roast turkey, barbecued pig, apple dumplings, and gave them all the real coffee and ripe apple brandy its men could contain. These things were prepared and served as only the old Pennsylvania Dutch in that Greensboro country knew how, and these broken veterans of a hundred battles enjoyed them and found in them faith to sustain their feelings that all good in the South had not been lost. There were at least three of the Wee Nee Company who enjoyed that Greensboro Christmas dinner in 1864 living in Williamsburg in 1923. They were Captain Calhoun Logan, Harvey J. Brown, and William M. McKnight. These venerable and distinguished men recall this dinner as one of their most precious war memories.

The Twenty-Fifth Regiment proceeded on its way from Greensboro to Wilmington, where it was captured with the Fort Fisher garrison on January 15, 1865. The officers were separated from the enlisted men and all were sent on barges to Fortress Monroe, from which point they were sent to Elmira prison, where they remained until the end of the War.

In Elmira prison, Williamsburg's soldiers fared remarkably well. When the Wee Nee men arrived, they found there a large number of their comrades from the district who had been taken in battles before that time.

Among these was Lieutenant Junius E. Scott, who had been wounded and captured at the battle of the Weldon Railway.

Lieutenant Scott fell in this battle on the Weldon Railway and his comrades saw him lying unconscious on the field with a bullet hole in his clothing over his heart.

They abandoned him as dead. But he had a New Testament and a wallet in his breast pocket. The bullet went through the Testament, but stopped in the wallet. The traumatism was, however, sufficient to deaden him temporarily. Lieutenant Scott afterwards said that when he first revived a big Irish Yankee soldier had him by the collar and was saying kindly, "Come on, sonny." Lieutenant Scott was then but a boy in years.

These old Williamsburg soldiers say that they had one pound of good white bread, some beans or peas, and bacon or beef, issued to them every day they were at Elmira, and that all prisoners who were reasonably well behaved were allowed considerable liberty on the streets of Elmira. Veteran Harvey J. Brown says one night he and a number of others did not arrive at the stockade until much later than permitted out. When they returned it was dark and a Yankee sentinel simply would not let them pass until they used a few brickbats on him. These offenders were courtmartialled and could, under military law, have been shot. Some of the offenders were required to walk with their heads through one hundred pound barrels for a few hours. But when Mr. Brown came on for punishment, all the prepared barrels were in use. The provost marshall looked about him and finally saw a log weighing about one hundred pounds lying near. He ordered Mr. Brown to shoulder that log and march with it. Mr. Brown took up the log and placed it as ordered. He remembered, however, that he had been wounded in that shoulder at Chafin's Farm, so he showed the scar to the Yankee officer, who smiled and said, "Go on back to your stockade."

Lieutenant Junius Scott was an excellent accountant and agreeable in association, so the Elmira prison officials soon began to use him as a clerk and secretary. William M. McKnight says one time there a number of sick prisoners were ordered South, that he was sick and extremely anxious to leave that cold country, but that his name did not appear on the list to go. Lieutenant Scott took in the situation and the night before the departure of the prisoners, slipped him the proper papers, and advised him how to avoid the officer counting the departing prisoners.

J. E. Rowe, a wealthy resident of Elmira, was a personal friend of Lieutenant Scott's father. Mr. Rowe was exceedingly kind to Lieutenant Scott while in prison and to many of his friends. Frequently, he gave Lieutenant Scott many delicacies for his friends, thus relieving the monotony of prison fare.

Veteran Brown says when he was discharged from Elmira prison, he was furnished transportation to his home in Cades, coming by way of steamer from New York to Charleston, from which place he came by railway train to the Santee River, was there ferried across and boarded a train for his home. This was the first train from Charleston to Florence after the War, on July 27, 1865.

When the Twenty-Fifth South Carolina Infantry surrendered to General Sherman near Greensboro on April 26, 1865, Captain E. R. Lesesne was commanding. There were then, besides Captain Lesesne, these officers present: Lieutenant H. L. Greer and Surgeon M. L. Horlbeck; non-commissioned, Sergeant S. M. China, Hospital Steward J. E. Farris; Commissary Sergeant M. J. Hirsch, and thirty-six privates. These men from Company C, the Wee Nee Volunteers, signed the rolls: Sergeant S. M. China, privates D. E. Adams, E. M. Browder, A. Bradshaw, F. W. Boyd, and E. R. Cook.

The following were the terms of the Military Convention entered into between General Joseph E. Johnston, commanding Confederate Army, and Major General W. T. Sherman, commanding U. S. Army in North Carolina, and signed for the Twenty-Fifty South Carolina Infantry by Captain E. R. Lesesne: "Greensboro, North Carolina, May

1, 1865. The officers and men whose names are borne on this roll have given their solemn obligation not to take up arms against the government of the United States until properly released from this obligation. And they are permitted to return to their homes not to be disturbed by the United States authorities so long as they observe this obligation and obey the laws in force where they may reside."

The Tenth South Carolina Infantry, then commanded by Lieutenant Colonel C. Irvine Walker, in which were most of the Williamsburg men, surrendered with Johnston's army to General Sherman on April 26, 1865, and signed the parole on May 1, 1865. The Twenty-Sixth South Carolina Regiment surrendered with General Robert E. Lee at Appamattox.

After General Lee had surrendered, the Confederate cause was generally regarded as hopeless by the forces in Virginia and nearly all the men came home as quickly as possible, without regard to formality, parole, or anything else. Veteran James Epps was one of these men who shouldered his rifle immediately and who moved southward by the most effectual method available. Mr. Epps has that rifle until this day. He has been for nearly four score years one of the best men, from every point of view, who ever lived in Williamsburg. His old comrades, simply because he has lived so completely within the law, human and divine, have tried a thousand times to convince him that his "walking away" with his rifle, without having formally surrendered, was a grievous wrong, but he has never admitted "the crime."

Those men of Williamsburg who were being held as prisoners of war were not released until some time after all Confederate Armies had surrendered and all its forces had quitted the field. These prisoners were held at various points in the Northern States, and as released were furnished with transportation and rations to their respective homes.

On six hundred Confederate officers the United States Army visited the sins of the South. Two of this Immortal Six Hundred, Lieutenants William Epps and David Ervin Gordon, were men of Williamsburg. The sufferings of these Six Hundred officers must have been far beyond the imagination of lesser men. The severest retaliation known to modern warfare was inflicted upon them. They were placed under fire of guns from their own forces and kept there for months. This was because the Confederate authorities placed some United States officers in the residence portion of Charleston where they would be exposed to the fire of the Union forces besieging that city. These Six Hundred were given only corn meal and pickles to eat for a considerable period since some Union prisoners of war in the South were not furnished with a sufficient ration. This Six Hundred had dangling before their eyes all this time the Oath of Allegiance to the United States and freedom.

Does anyone but the keenest physiologist realize how intense partial starvation is? How fiercely the hunger fires burn when some elements of food are withheld until certain organs of the body cry continuously for sustenance? And does even the most understanding psychologist know half how much spirit is controlled by continuous half unconscious suffering and physical disintegration? In all this War Between the Sections, no other men had such opportunity as these Six Hundred Confederate Officers to show their divine manhood. These Six Hundred suffered most.

Lieutenant William Epps kept a diary while these "Immortal Six Hundred" were undergoing the furies of retaliation. Here follow some entries made therein:

LIEUT. WILLIAM EPPS, C. S. A.

LIEUT. DAVID ERVIN GORDON, C. S. A.

."Fort Delaware, August, 1864.

"1. Today has been very interestingly spent—prayer meeting and Christian Association in the morning and preaching in the evening.

"2. Nothing of interest passed today—attended meetings as usual.

"3. Excitement among the Yanks today—some of the Rebs tried to make their escape last night—one poor fellow was, they say, drowned in the attempt. I hope the others were more successful. Just read an interesting book, title, 'May I Believe?'

"4. Low in spirits today—thinking of Dixie far, far away.

"5. Attended divine services as usual—felt that I was living at too great distance from God.

"6. Just read an interesting little book, 'Mary Searching for Jesus.'

"7. and 8. Nothing of interest to the mind except pleasant hours spent in religious exercises. Just finished reading 'Poor Henry.'

"9. and 10. The weather is so warm it is very uncomfortable in prison. Yesterday I was astonished when I looked out of the window and saw fifteen privates (Rebel prisoners) drawing a heavy two-horse plough in rough land, driven by the Yanks. Read an interesting little book, 'Only Believe.'

"11. In high spirits about being exchanged soon—it is rumored that six hundred officers leave here in a few days for Charleston, South Carolina.

"20. Six hundred leave today for Hilton Head.

"24. This morning about three o'clock ran aground just off Cape Romain Light House—about six hours before we could move. During the delay, we planned to capture the vessel, but gunboat came up and our victory was crushed.

"September 7. Today we landed on Morris Island and are now situated in tents between Batteries Wagner and Gregg with negroes to guard us.

"9. The Yanks are firing furiously at our Batteries. Fort Moultrie replied, dropping shells in beautiful style in and around Wagner and Gregg, except two that exploded over our prison, three pieces of which fell among our tents and caused a very unpleasant feeling among the Rebs. Fortunately none of us were hurt.

"20. Since the 9th, nothing of very great importance has occurred except our rations have been very short and generally unfit for even a dog to live upon. They consist of, for breakfast, two hard crackers and about an ounce of salt pork; dinner, half pint bean soup, two crackers, and sometimes meat; supper, one cracker and about one ounce of meat. Upon an average I think we get about five crackers and two and one-half ounces of meat per day.

"28. A change in the rations—now it is four and one-half crackers, one-half pint of bean soup, and about two ounces of meat per day. Sometimes, a half pint rice. Received a letter from home today.

"October 5. I have not witnessed a more pleasant feeling among the men since I have been a prisoner. A large amount of nourishment from the citizens of Charleston has just arrived and never were provisions more joyfully received. Every man has a smile on his face.

"16. Sunday—batteries on Sullivan's Island apparently practicing at our pen or something nearby, for several fragments of shell have just fallen among the tents.

"30. Captain E. S. Hall and Captain H. S. Lewis have been taken out of prison for a special exchange. A change in our rations since we left Morris Island—we get per day about nine crackers, a pint of rice or bean soup, and about two ounces of meat.

"November 1. Another change in rations—nearly a pound of rice, loaf bread, about four ounces of meat, a pint of good vegetable soup, and as much salt and sugar as we need.

"4. and 5. A large supply of tobacco and ten gallons of syrup received for general distribution among us, besides a great many private boxes. Nothing seems to revive prisoners more than such acts of kindness by our friends at home.

"19. Moved from Fort Pulaski on board the steamer Canonicus and sailed northward. We anchored off Hilton Head about seven p. m.

"20. At four p. m., disembarked from the Canonicus and marched about one-half mile near Skull Creek, where we are now quartered. Our tents are in an open field—three men to each tent. We are limited to about an acre of land and guarded by the One Hundred Forty-Fourth New York Volunteer Infantry—so far a very clever set of men. They issued coffee, sugar, and bread for supper and breakfast.

"24. Since the 20th, our rations have been short and issued raw, viz.: crackers (cooked), beans, and salt pork, sometimes grist or rice. Very little wood is furnished and that green, such as maple, sweetgum, and short leaf pine —oak occasionally. The weather being cold and scarcely wood enough for cooking purposes, we have suffered very much from cold.

"December 1. Rations issued raw again and green pine wood to cook with. Unfortunately, the Yankees have succeeded in recapturing the other three officers who escaped the guard a few nights ago.

"6. Received a letter and box of provisions from home. Many wounded Yanks have arrived here from Foster's expeditions.

"16. Rations of meat stopped—nothing issued to us but bread and not enough of that for two meals each day. We are not allowed to buy anything whatever, neither are we allowed to receive money, clothing, provisions, or anything whatever, that would add to our comfort. My watch was returned a few days ago that was taken from me at Point Lookout, Maryland, but minus the key, guard, and twenty dollars that was taken at the same time.

"20. Corn meal and pickles instead of molasses—camp kettles to cook in. The Yanks say they are retaliating on us for some of their officers who were treated badly at Columbia, South Carolina. Some of them who made their escape from Columbia arrived here a few days ago. Some of them said they were very roughly treated while others of the same party said they were well treated.

"25. Christmas dinner composed of dry bread, but fortunately we got some molasses and gravy from our friends that made us a good meal. We get nothing but corn meal, pickles and once in four days, one pound wheat bread.

"31. Weather very rainy and cold—many of us are suffering wonderfully from cold and hunger. It is astonishing that any government will treat prisoners of war as we are treated.

"January 1. Unwell and suffering cold and hunger—ten days rations of corn meal and pickles issued. We have not had any meat since December 16. Dogs, rats, and cats dare not show themselves in our prison—several cats have been killed and eaten among us lately.

"10. Corn meal and pickles issued again.

"17. My birthday—twenty-two years of age. We are still suffering from cold and hunger. My feet have been frost bitten and pain me considerably. A great many others of my fellow prisoners are suffering in a worse condition. No fire is allowed us at night, and, during the day, only enough to cook our small rations.

"20. Meal and pickles issued and a little flour instead of bread.

"27. Our rations increased by four ounces of salt beef and four ounces of Irish potatoes per day, in addition to the meal and pickles, but still kept under retaliation.

"February 1. Rations of pickles stopped—the others continued, except beef—pork instead.

"15. All are in very high spirits. Official news arrived today that we are all to be exchanged as soon as practicable. Oh! what a happy thought it is to feel that we are soon to be released from this unhappy prison life.

"18. The Confederate money returned that was taken from us when we were first captured.

"19. A salute of one hundred guns fired by the fleet off this harbor and thirty-eight fired from a land battery over the fall of Charleston, South Carolina.

"20. Full rations issued—sixteen ounces of bread stuff, half flour and half corn meal, ten ounces of meat, pork, and bacon, per day, and also some beans and soup.

"28. Provost Marshall inquired of each prisoner whether or not he wants to be exchanged or take the oath of allegiance to the United States.

"March 1. Ten days' rations issued.

"3. Very busy preparing our rations for a voyage—the rumor is that we leave tomorrow for Fortress Monroe.

"8. A steamer said to be loaded with Confederate prisoners passed up the James River to be exchanged. Oh, that our turn would come!

"11. Sadly disappointed—instead of being exchanged, we sail north for Fort Delaware.

"19. Since our arrival here it is said eight of our party have died and many others are suffering with the same disease, scurvy. Small pox has also made its appearance.

"24. Taken sick with pneumonia.

"25. Went to the hospital and was kindly treated by the surgeon.

"April 2. Salute of one hundred guns fired over the fall of Richmond.

"10. Bad news—reported that General R. E. Lee has surrendered himself and army to General Grant. At twelve o'clock, a salute of two hundred guns fired over the news.

"11. Received a suit of clothing and a check for $10.00 from Miss S. E. Wells, 94 West Eleventh St., New York City, N. Y.

"15. News arrived that President Lincoln was shot last night and died this morning at seven o'clock; also that Secretary Seward was assasinated and, it is thought, mortally wounded.

"16. All flags flying at half mast and a cannon fired every half hour in honor of the deceased President. Twenty Confederate officers brought in (prisoners).

"26, 27, 28. Oath of Allegiance to the United States offered us on condition that all who take it are to be speedily released. Of two thousand, about half have consented to take it. Three Confederate officers brought in from Johnson Island. The prison is very much crowded and we are all in a demoralized state of mind caused by the sad news of our late misfortunes. It is rumored that General Joseph E. Johnston, Confederate States Army, has surrendered to General U. S. Grant, United States Army.

"30. The above rumor confirmed, a great many are making application to take the oath, feeling that our cause is entirely hopeless, that being the only chance of deliverance.

"May 2. Oath again presented to those who refused a few days ago. All consent to take it except one hundred ten who still feel it their duty to remain in prison for the sake of our beloved country, the Confederacy. After neglecting my dear mother and family four years and suffering the hardships of a soldier's life and twelve months and seven days of prison life for what I thought was a just cause, but thinking all hope of success is gone now, I consent to submit to the will of a victorious people, to return home with a sad heart and a conquered spirit, subject to the mercy of a powerful enemy.

"16. It has been rumored here that President Davis and his staff have been captured.

"22. For several days past we have been laboring under some excitement about our President. Though the papers have mentioned it each day for several days, saying that he was captured in women's clothing, not until this morning could we realize the fact that he had been captured. General Wheeler and staff, also Colonel Lubbock, of President Davis' staff, arrived here this morning, who gave us the particulars of his capture. Colonel Lubbock says he was captured with the President and that it is all false about them being captured in women's clothing. We are waiting in suspense for our release.

"26. Received $20.00 from Miss S. E. Wells through Lieutenant L. C. Nowell, to whom I feel under many obligations.

"June 11. This day twelve months ago I was made a prisoner of war. I am now waiting anxiously to be released from prison.

"19. At seven a. m., released from prison feeling once more at liberty. At seven-thirty, leave on a steamer for Philadelphia. At four-thirty p. m., leave Philadelphia by rail for New York, arriving there at eight-thirty.

"20. I am stopping at the Libby House, 54-56-58 Warren Street, New York, M. Martin, Proprietor.

"22. Miss Wells furnished me $10.00 through L. C. Nowell.

"23. Called on Miss Wells and found her a very kind lady. She again sends me $12.50,—truly she is a friend indeed.

"25. At eleven-thirty a. m., on board the steamship Arago, which sails at twelve o'clock for Hilton Head, S. C. I have spent a very pleasant week in New York.

"26. Beautiful weather and we are sailing quietly but slowly southward.

"27. Arrived at Hilton Head, S. C., after a pleasant voyage.

"July 1. At eleven o'clock a. m., on board the Kingfisher to sail to Charleston, S. C. Arrived at Charleston wharf at two o'clock, p. m.

"2. Take the cars for Kingstree at five o'clock a. m. Arrived at Kingstree at three-thirty p. m. At four-thirty, arrived at home, found mother and family all well, once more a happy man."

General Hardee in command of about fifteen thousand Confederate troops had his headquarters in the present Harper home on East Main Street, Kingstree, during February, 1865. He was recuperating his army and refurnishing it with supplies for the purpose of opposing Sherman's Army in its effort to flank Lee's Army in Virginia. General Hardee impressed nearly all horses, mules, corn, flour, and bacon in Williamsburg for his army and caused much distress in the district. Some men said that even Sherman's Army afflicted a community less than Hardee's.

But General Hardee did not impress Mrs. Elizabeth Brockinton's carriage horses. Some one who preceded Hardee to Kingstree told her that General Hardee impressed all draught animals except blind mules with ingrowing hoofs. Mrs. Brockinton was one of the best housekeepers in this district and her cook could "boil 'em tender and bake 'em brown." When Mrs. Brockinton knew that General Hardee was approaching Kingstree, she sent her favorite carriage horses in charge of Uncle Joe into the thicknesses of Impenetrable Swamp. She herself went into the kitchen and mixed and baked things that looked good, smelled good, and she knew would taste good. She filled a big basket with these things and rode in an oxcart to General Hardee's headquarters with them. She asked the sentinel to present her compliments to the General with her request for an interview. An orderly transmitted her message. Perhaps he most respectfully stated to the General that a fine lady outside desired to see him, and gave him at the same time the unmistakable "high sign of good eats" known and recognized by men of all ranks from prince to pauper. The General received the lady and she soon returned with an order that her carriage horses should not be molested. The General accepted the basket. Uncle Joe returned those horses to her plantation, and she another day appeared at Hardee's headquarters in state, invited the General and his personal staff to dine at her home. This invitation was accepted. Further, this chronicler knoweth not.

Sherman took Columbia February 17, 1865. On February 18, 1865, after five hundred sixty-seven days of siege and one of the most stubborn resistances in history, Charleston was evacuated by the Confederate forces and taken over by the Union troops. The only hope held out was the defeat of Sherman by Johnston's army.

Dr. Samuel McGill, one of the most intelligent men of this district, recorded the following in his diary, and later commented thereon as quoted from his Reminiscences of Williamsburg:

"February 28, 1865. All is gloom and uncertainty and preparations are being made for the worst. Furniture and provisions are hidden against pending raids expected through the district, which is now at the mercy of our enemy. Our currency is valueless and merchants refuse to take it for goods. It is feared famine will possess the land; our army is demoralized and the people panic-stricken. All is gloom, despondency, and inactivity. The power to do has left us. All our possessions will go to pay the Yankee debt. To fight longer seems to be madness; to submit tamely is dishonor.

"March 1, 1865. News continues to get worse. The enemy is reported to have crossed Santee and burned

Mr. Staggers' fine house at Murray's Ferry in this district. They are composed of artillery, cavalry, and infantry, most of which are negro troops. They were expected at Kingstree yesterday to burn and destroy and pillage. No force is there to oppose them. Another force of Yankees is reported coming from Georgetown by Rope Ferry who have already seized government stores at Pine Tree, which has been the point of transportation of rice from Georgetown. The whole country is in the wildest commotion and many are fleeing to the woods with their wives and daughters, while a few have gone to meet the advance and to give battle.

"All during this month of March, 1865, we were all under such excitement and distress that we gave credence to the most fabulous reports, as we seek information of news from our neighbors. All communication from the outside was cut off and all that we could hear from our army was through sick soldiers, who had made their way through the Yankee lines and who gave woeful accounts of our starving and disheartened soldiers. On the road could be seen deserters from our army, who, believing the war virtually ended, were trudging their way through the country, homeward bound in squads, with their guns, prepared to defend themselves if molested.

"Georgetown was now in possession of the Yankees, and thither thousands of our negro slaves, who had been kind, faithful, and true to us during the war, were stealing away in the night. Each morning we could hear of such a negro 'run away and gone to the Yankees,' and no efforts were made to intercept them, owing in part to our inability to do so and the expected successful operation of President Lincoln's Emancipation Proclamation."

About April 1, 1865, Governor Magrath determined to make a desperate effort to prevent raiders going from Georgetown into the surrounding country, so he ordered all available troops in this section to report to Colonel

WILLIAMSBURG, C. S. A., 1865

James F. Pressley, then at home recovering from his Atlanta wound, for such service. On April 4, when these home guard companies, old men and boys, of the district, began assembling at Potato Ferry for this duty, Potter's Raiders from Georgetown had already entered Williamsburg and were laying waste the country south of Black River.

Potter's Raiders were composed of some organized Union forces, many self attached robber bands, and hundreds of plantation deserting negro slaves. It must have been the purpose of Potter to show General Sherman that his march to the sea might have been more horrible. It is doubtful if ever a more comtemptible force of cutthroats assembled than Potter's Raiders. The plantation deserting negroes in this aggregation of fiends knew where everything of value in the district had been secreted and these Raiders gloated over wanton and malicious destruction. These Raiders butchered all the cattle and sheep south of Black River and left their carcasses to rot in the fields and swamps. They burned all the homes and destroyed all the plantation shade trees aged by the centuries. When this nefarious band had destroyed everything visible about the home of Hugh Boyd and was departing for the next home for annihilation, one of these fiends happened to notice the Boyd Family Bible hidden away in some weeds. This fiend dismounted, seized that sacred morocco bound book, and tore half of its cover away, hacking its pages with his sabre. The Lynch family had several linen table cloths and other pieces of priceless texture, within which were woven the coat of arms of the family, which beautiful things had been sacredly treasured for more than two centuries. Potter's Raiders destroyed everything else about the place, but used these beautiful things as saddlecloths to show their own souls along their way.

Potter's Raiders did not cross Black River from the south. Williamsburg arose *en masse* and resisted them. Fortunately, Black River at that time was very high, and it was practically impossible to cross it except at points where bridges were. With Captain J. J. Steele's company as a nucleus, about sixteen hundred men gathered together under the command of Colonel James F. Pressley at the Lower Bridge on April 6, 1865. Among these men were Captain T. W. Daggett, Captain S. J. Snowden, Captain W. L. Wallace, Captain W. N. Y. Rodgers, Captain John E. Scott, Captain Samuel McGill, Lieutenant Furman Rodgers, Lieutenant Thomas M. Gilland, Lieutenant J. M. Kennedy, Lieutenant N. H. Welch, and Lieutenant T. S. Steele, Jr., all of whom had served in the organized army, and all of whom commanded companies of men. This force under Colonel Pressley reached the Lower Bridge a few hours before Potter's Raiders and tore up and burned the bridge. Many volleys were exchanged, but the Raiders on the south side realized that it would be impossible to repair the burned bridge or to cross on pontoons under such a fire as would play upon them from Colonel Pressley's forces. The Raiders camped that night on the south side of the river. During the night, Captain John E. Scott swam the river and scuttled some boats that were anchored on the south side, Colonel Pressley fearing the Raiders might undertake to use them in attempting to cross during the darkness. It was this night that Dr. David C. Scott, then fifteen years old, spent armed with a Confederate rifle in the trenches at the Lower Bridge, which night he remembers, regretting all his life that he had not been born a few years earlier so that he could have gone into battle in Virginia in the Confederate Army.

When Potter's Raiders realized the hopelessness of crossing at the Lower Bridge, they moved westward on the south side of the river, while Colonel Pressley's forces pressed forward to prevent them from crossing. The bridge at Kingstree was burned by the Confederates to prevent these Raiders crossing, as were all other bridges in Williamsburg District.

"For the next few weeks," says Dr. McGill, "no mind can comprehend the gloom and fearful anticipations of the whole district. Every man, capable of bearing arms, was in our little army, now away in Sumter District, and our whole district was at the mercy of negro raids, led by Yankees from Georgetown. Nor were we in any way relieved from the horrors of our situation until General Potter, hearing of Lee's surrender in Virginia, was on his way to Georgetown by the Santee River road, and most of our men had returned to their homes, to gather around them and defend their families, who had sought safer places than their homes were considered to have been."

On the same day that the Wiliamsburg District between the Santee and Black River was being raided by indescribable ruffians, and that part north of Black River was defending its section against these nameless things, the Union Army, with President Lincoln at its head, was entering Richmond, the late capitol of the Confederacy. On April 9, 1865, General Robert E. Lee surrendered with his army to General U. S. Grant at Appamattox Court House. The Confederacy had been crushed.

From the beginning of the War Between the Sections, Abraham Lincoln was the only master of men and events. He was the Thing that shattered the Confederacy. He alone had been able to direct all conflicting forces towards the End. On April 15, 1865, when most needed, he was killed by an assassin's bullet. Hate snatched the ruins of government from his dying hands and for a decade drove North and South ruthlessly towards Death and Hell.

There were some abolitionists in New York and Boston who realized that they did not have the blood basis to equal in culture some of the slave owning aristocrats in the

South. There were other abolitionists in Kansas and Nebraska and California who had been driven out of the South by economic conditions, even from the valleys of the Pee Dee, the Wee Nee, and the Santee. These two classes of abolitionists had not been sated with sufferings and gore at the Bloody Lake of Chickamauga and on the murderous slopes of Gettysburg. The green eyed hate in them made them ghouls, to gather mangled and emaciated Union soldier forms from Southern battlefields and prisons, and exhibit them continuously to the already hate maddened hordes of the North.

And there was no Superman among the conquerors when Lincoln was dead.

CHAPTER XXXII.

WILLIAMSBURG, U. S. A., 1865.

Williamsburg District on May 1, 1860, was the most Southern of all the South. Every man was a cotton planter. Several were physicians, a half dozen were merchants, two or three were lawyers, but every one owned and operated a plantation by virtue of African slave labor. There were practically no "poor whites" in the district. All of this breed had gone away into the far West and become militant abolitionists. Williamsburg then placed its trust in cotton and believed that it was king of the earth. The district did not even produce a sufficiency of corn and pork to supply its needs, although corn would grow with little cultivation and hogs would increase and fatten in the swamps without any care from man. Williamsburg preferred to produce cotton and from the proceeds of its sale to purchase whatever else it needed or desired. Williamsburg then was drunk with material prosperity and did not consider the danger incident to the production of one article. Nor does it seem that Williamsburg remembered that less than three generations before that time the world had lived for countless generations without using cotton products.

The people of Williamsburg had passed through three generations without doing manual labor. Their hands were untutored and soft and their minds were overcome by the delusion that working with the hands was dishonorable and consistent only with the condition of slavery. While negro slavery had brought a kind of prosperity to the South, it had undermined the foundation of substantial life and the fall was inevitable.

It must have been that Williamsburg District on May 1, 1865, was one of the saddest spots in the world. Between May 1, 1861 and May 1, 1865, Williamsburg District furnished twelve hundred able bodied men to the Confederate Army. This was more in number than it had men between the ages of eighteen and forty-five. Of these twelve hundred, more than three hundred were killed in battle or died of disease and more than three hundred of the remainder had been severely wounded in action. A considerable number had been so seriously weakened by the hardships of the camp that they were semi-invalids for the rest of their days. Of those Confederate soldiers who returned strong and healthy from the War, few actually knew anything about agriculture and stock raising, nor had the old men and the women who remained on the plantations of Williamsburg learned very much about these things during the War. Overseers and slaves had been most largely responsible for the cotton raising in Williamsburg. Slaves had, as a general rule, remained loyal to their plantations during the War and the usual conditions had obtained. The hands of the white people of Williamsburg were still soft and their muscles untrained on May 1, 1865.

The Emancipation Proclamation, which had been promulgated as a war measure by President Lincoln on January 1, 1863, became effective in the Southern States as their territory came under the rule of martial law by the United States forces. Until May 1, 1865, Williamsburg's Confederate law did not succumb. A few days before that time some of the farsighted men of the district realized what fearful conditions might result from the complete collapse of the Confederate Government and requested the United States military commander at Georgetown to station some troops at Kingstree for the protection of the people of the County. This was done.

When Captain Blake and his company of regular troops of the United States Army arrived at Kingstree, these soldiers immediately satisfied the best element in the district that the community should be controlled according to the rule of reason and in harmony with the highest ideals of the section. These troops most agreeably surprised the substantial citizens of Williamsburg as well as certain recently freed slaves who had expected these Yankee soldiers to consort with them and to effect their nefarious designs. These soldiers advised and virtually required negro slaves in the district to remain on their respective plantations and complete the cultivation and harvesting of the crop that had already been planted. These troops maintained order and compelled the negroes to conform even to a severer code than their masters had required. An insolent or "uppish" negro found no comfort or consolation in this Yankee camp, and frequently a former master was seen pleading for mercy for an offender. The venerable Samuel Ruffin Mouzon, whose family history and natural ability assure sound judgement, said in 1922, "This military law just after the War gave South Carolina the best government it has ever had." This opinion seems to prevail so far as Williamsburg is concerned among the few remaining men who were mature in that far away period.

During the military occupation of Williamsburg, the same civil officials who had been chosen under the Confederate Government continued to exercise the functions of their several offices under the direction of and with but little interference from the Federal soldiers in the district.

Political, social, and economic conditions in Williamsburg at the close of 1865 were sufficiently severe to test to the uttermost any people who ever lived on these mundane plains. Half of its virile young manhood had been sacrificed to the god of war and every home in the land was a house of mourning. Its heroic dead were already dust in Virginia and Tennessee and Georgia, but its living sacrifices moved about with their empty sleeves falling limp by their sides and crying continuously out of their silence. The natural rulers of the district saw above them always a stronger force than they could control. However faithful and efficient this military government may have been and however closely its commanders may have followed the best light before them, those people, who had hewn out of primeval forests this pleasant land and who had paid for its political freedom and independence with their own blood, could not find peace and rest in other than their own law. Economic conditions were indescribable. For more than a year Williamsburg had no money as a medium of exchange and primitive barter obtained. The Federal troops stationed at Kingstree immediately after Appamattox brought the first money that would pass as currency in the district and through these Federal troops for about six months came nearly all of the money in circulation in this section.

The natives of Williamsburg had a sufficient amount to eat all during the year 1865, but there were many refugees who came here from the coast absolutely penniless. There was some suffering for food among these people while their condition was unknown to the normal residents.

Samuel Ruffin Mouzon, who then lived and now lives on the Mouzon plantation eight miles west of Kingstree, was passing along the streets of Kingstree soon after the coming of the Union soldiers when he was accosted by Major Atkinson, a refugee lawyer from Georgetown, who had brought his family here to escape Potter-made conditions in Georgetown. Says Mr. Mouzon, "Major Atkinson told me that his children were crying for bread and that he must have something for them to eat and that no money could be had and that he was helpless." Mr. Mouzon went home and immediately sent Major Atkinson a bushel of meal, two hams, and a fat beef steer, writing him that he might pay for these things whenever it was convenient. A few days later when Mr. Mouzon was in Kingstree, Major Atkinson gave him some money, which he placed in his pocket and did not count until reaching home. He then found that Major Atkinson had paid him $49.00. Mr. Mouzon took $9.00 back to Major Atkinson, since prior to that time they had agreed on $40.00 as a price for the steer. Major Atkinson declined to accept the $9.00 on the ground that old Simon had been given the head, liver, and lights of the beef for butchering, that he had kept one hind quarter for himself and sold the remainder of the beef for $53.00 to the Yankees. Mr. Mouzon says that he had more than one hundred head of cattle in Pudding Swamp at that time.

However distressing conditions were at this time, observant ones saw beneath the lowest depth already reached a lower depth yawning to receive them. Alien military rule seemed to tax these high spirited Anglo-Saxons to the absolute limit, yet hating, unrestrained abolitionists had not done their worst. President Andrew Johnson undertook to execute Lincoln's reconstruction policy in the South, but he was no stronger than a hundred other men about him who had hate in their hearts and vengeance in their hands.

The reconstruction policy advocated by such Republican leaders as Governor Andrew of Massachusetts was thus summarized by him on January 2, 1866: first, prosecute peace as vigorously as we have prosecuted war; second, inflict no humiliation, require no humiliation of the South; third, enlist the sympathy and service of the natural leaders of the South in the work of reconstruction. For advocating this policy towards the South, Governor Andrew's name was stricken from the list of the Republican party leaders and the reconstruction Republican Congress, ignoring and over ruling the Executive, proceeded without let or hindrance to wreak its policy of vengeance on the Southern States.

This Congress made a condition precedent to the readmission of the Southern States into the Union that they should adopt constitutions and organize and then submit to the Congress the condition that the Congress might determine whether or not the petitioning state had conformed and was worthy of readmission. This Republican Congress took the command of the army out of the hands of the President and decreed that Federal troops should remain in the subdued Southern States so long as it willed. This Congress passed laws granting suffrage to every male inhabitant in the South over twenty-one years of age and not attainted by felony, excepting certain classes of men who had participated in the War. This Congress directed that Federal troops should be stationed in the South to effect this suffrage policy. Under these laws, Williamsburg District had more than five recently emancipated negro slaves to every one white man who could vote. The State of South Carolina had more negroes than whites who could cast ballots and thus determine the constitution and the laws required for readmission into the Union.

"Democracy is for angels." Thousands of years of recorded history and further ages of reliable tradition show that unlimited democracy is impossible in any considerable state. The beautiful so called democracies which have flourished from time to time along the ages have all been so limited that in fact they were aristocracies. This act of the Republican Congress in attempting to create an unlimited democracy had no precedent in history and will probably never be used as authority for foisting such an impossible scheme on any other people until the end of the world. This Congress undertook to place within the hands of negroes, who could neither read nor write, and whose experiences had been limited to slaving services on plantations, and whose ancestors had four generations before them been cannibals on the Congo, the rule and domination of the fairest land on earth. White men owned this fair land by virtue of birth right from worthy establishing ancestry.

Under the terms dictated for suffrage by this Republican Congress, there gathered in Columbia a convention in 1868 which adopted a constitution for the control and the government of South Carolina. This Constitution came out of the brains of men who were aliens in the State and from those men who, though born and raised within its bounds, had been attainted by the State, and hated the land in which they first saw the light. This Constitution was a monstrosity in the eyes of the men who had made the State and who loved it. This Constitution was submitted to the Congress created voters of South Carolina for three days, April 14, 15, 16, 1868. Unspeakable Republican politicians herded ignorant and illiterate negroes to the polls and voted them for the adoption of this Constitution. And this was the first day in the history of the State that the Constitution had ever been submitted to the people for ratification. Elections were held under this Constitution and General Robert K. Scott, a carpet bagger from Ohio, was chosen Governor of the State and a "black and tan" Legislature selected.

On July 29, 1868, General R. S. Canby, Federal military commander in the State of South Carolina, issued General Order No. 145 in which he stated, that "all authority conferred upon and heretofore exercised by the commander of the second military district under the aforecited law of March 2, 1867 (the first of the Reconstruction acts) is hereby remitted to the civil authorities constituted and organized in the States of North Carolina and South Carolina, under the Constitution adopted by the people thereof, and approved by the Congress of the United States."

Night and Chaos reigned.

CHAPTER XXXIII.

RECONSTRUCTION.

The last County officials of Williamsburg before the reconstruction were as follows: James McCutchen, senator; James F. Pressley and John A. Keels, representatives; Samuel P. Mathews, sheriff; William R. Brockinton, clerk; David M. Duke, ordinary; Julius P. Gamble, coroner and tax collector; magistrates, S. W. Maurice, T. B. Logan, R. G. Ferrell, W. W. Carter, and T. R. Greer; notary publics, W. H. McElveen, S. T. Cooper, W. F. Ervin, Edward J. Porter, and John G. Pressley; John A. Salters was collector of internal revenue and T. B. Logan, District Judge. These men were all Democrats and were elected to their respective offices by the Legislature of the State of South Carolina.

In 1868, an election was held in which all males over twenty-one years old, not attainted of felony, and not prohibited on account of service under Confederate Government, were allowed to vote. This almost unlimited democracy, which was forced upon Williamsburg, chose the following Republican officials: S. A. Swails, negro, senator; F. H. Frost, J. Pendergrass, and Fortune Guilds, all negroes, representatives; W. W. Ward, sheriff; F. C. Cooper, clerk of the court; Louis Jacobs, probate judge; L. Douath, coroner; C. Gewinner, W. J. Lee, and R. A. McMillan, commissioners; F. H. Frost, negro, school commissioner; F. H. Swails, negro, auditor; Philip Heller, treasurer; C. H. Pettingil, State constable; C. Rasted and F. H. Frost, negroes, assessors. In all this list of County officials, there was not one white man who was a native of Williamsburg District, nor one belonging to what Governor Andrew of Massachusetts called the "natural ruling element."

One with imagination must have seen the morning after these Republican officials had been clothed with authority the shade of the scholarly Colonel N. G. Rich hovering over the Williamsburg Court House and heard it wondering, "Is this the region, this the soil, the clime?"

From the reports of the Grand Juries let the labors of these Republican rulers be told, remembering that this ancient and honorable Anglo-Saxon institution was then dominated by illiterate and ignorant negroes and "scallawag" whites who would have concealed every injurious fact possible.

The Grand Jury of May, 1871, reported: "The prisoners have not been confined as a general thing, but they have been allowed to walk about in the streets wheresoever and whensoever they pleased, and yet the County has been required to pay large sums of money for guard duty. Until the new county jail, now in process of erection, shall have been completed, this Jury recommends that the prisoners be confined in the jails of neighboring counties." This Jury reported that some of the county offices were badly kept and "the books and papers examined show a system of corruption and theft stupendous to behold." "The most glaring corruption and inefficiency we have discovered is in the office of the County Commissioners. The books and papers of the office up to the 15th of April, 1870, are totally unintelligible and furnish no information whatever of the money received in the office from licenses, or what has been done with the money that has been received. The books of the present Board show that $1466.00 have been received for licenses this year and the Board accounts for only $512.15."

The Jury had the clerk and the board summoned and examined but they could not and did not make any explanation of what had become of the balance. "The books show upon their very face that upon many occasions when money was received, it was forthwith divided out between the members of the board and the clerk. Many irregularities were discovered, only a few of which we deem it necessary to mention, owing to the want of time; and we believe those we do mention will show the general maladministration and malfeasance of the parties in office. We find that written application was made to the board by C. M. Matthews and E. P. Montgomery for licenses to sell liquors, but no evidence appears on the books of a license ever being granted, though it is a fact within our knowledge that both of these parties have been engaged in the sale of spiritous liquors during the past year. We find also by the books that the members of the board have charged for as many as twenty days for service of each member of the board in the same month while we are informed that the law allows only compensation to them for one hundred days in the whole year. We examined this point and report that from the 15th day of April, 1870, to April, 1871, that J. P. Barrineau charged for 182 days; that William Scott upon the same period charged for 170 days. Ambrose Tisdale went into office last fall. From the last of November, 1870, to April, 1871, he charged for 54 days. We have not been able to find any evidence that any account was ever made out by the members of the board and submitted to the County Treasurer to be audited and approved by him as required by acts of the General Assembly. In short, we find the whole office and the transactions of the board to have been conducted in such a manner as to exhibit a total disregard to law, honesty, and propriety and we recommend the members of the board and the clerk to be indicted for official misconduct and malfeasance in office for reasons heretofore stated.

"We find that the former incumbent in the School Commissioner's office has failed to account for funds received and we recommend that the said F. H. Frost be indicted.

"We find in the Treasurer's office that no regard has been paid either to justice or law where claims against the County have been paid or they have been paid in such a manner as shows favoriteness, or corruption, or both. We find that the County Treasurer speculates with county funds for his own benefit. The result of this kind of conduct is that jurymen and witnesses, who are compelled by law to attend court, cannot be paid for their tickets and forced in many cases to sell them for from 25 to 50 per centum discount to pay their necessary expenses in attending the court. This is a great evil and some remedy ought to be provided, for favorites ought not to get all of the county money and allow others who happen not to be so fortunate either to wait for years or submit to the outrage of discounting or trading out their claims.

"Another great injustice we have discovered is that in some cases the Treasurer will receive from one party a certain amount of his taxes in county orders and from others he will take none, and in some instances he will take all or nearly all of the taxes in orders, thus admitting the possession of funds for the County. We, therefore, recommend that the Treasurer, for the various reasons stated, be removed from office and that he be indicted for official misconduct. We are informed and believe that it is a habit of the Clerk of Court to absent himself from his office very frequently for weeks at the time. We suggest that he be required to amend his conduct or that he be indicted.

"We have examined the bonds of the various officers required by law to give bonds and we find them entirely insufficient. The roads and bridges in the County are in a bad condition and in some instances almost impassable. Some of them have not been worked in two years. The poor farm we have not been able to visit owing to a press of other engagements and to its distance from the village of Kingstree. As it is an institution of very recent origin, we have not been able to ascertain anything definite as to the number of inmates or the manner in which it is conducted, but we look upon it as an institution of very doubtful propriety, as we fear it is calculated to do more harm to the County than good.

"In conclusion, we regret that there are and have been for some time past evidences of lawlessness in the County in which persons unknown to the Grand Jury have taken the law into their own hands for the redress of their aggrievances, which has produced in the County a feeling of insecurity and unrest, which is calculated to prove injurious to society. To correct these demonstrations or to guard against them, we are informed that many persons do congregate on each night at various cross roads and bridges with arms in their hands. It is calculated on each side to make matters worse than they now are, instead of correcting any supposed grievances. We believe in a time of peace that all violations of law should be submitted to the proper tribunal for the redress which the offended law does provide, and we therefore condemn all such demonstrations as inexpedient and dangerous to the very existence of society and peace of the country, all of which is respectfully submitted."

"On motion of Solicitor S. T. Atkinson, it was ordered that copies be served on all concerned and that the solicitor take as early steps as possible to institute such proceedings as may be necessary to bring to trial and punishment the several county officers and all persons that may be implicated in the official misconduct and corruption reported by the Grand Jury. Finally, it was ordered that a certified copy of the presentments be made by the clerk and be sent to His Excellency, the Governor of the State."

In 1867, the Williamsburg County Jail was burned. Within it were twenty-seven negro prisoners who perished in the flames. Sometime during the night, the one white prisoner incarcerated at the time set fire to the floor of the building, burning a hole therein, through which he alone escaped. Before the cries of the negro prisoners were heard, it was too late to save them. Their destruction was the most pathetic circumstance in the history of the County.

For seven years, under this Republican rule, Williamsburg County had no jail. Its offenders against the law were sometimes crowded into one of the offices of the Court House and there locked up, allowed to roam the streets at will or in charge of highly paid negro guards, or imprisoned in neighboring county jails. The cost of transporting the average prisoner to and from a jail in Charleston or Georgetown during this period was sixty dollars.

After the county jail had finally been completed at the usual Republican cost, the Grand Jury of 1875 reported that "There has been a great negligence upon the part of those charged with the custody of criminals and offenders against public peace and welfare." It finds that "in other respects the officers of law charged with the safe custody of criminals have been guilty of negligence or malfeasance and especial references are made to the escape of one Bill Shaw, convicted of a grave offence and sentenced to the penitentiary; also to the escape of one Charles Cooper, charged with murder, who was taken from the jail by the jailer and other persons in charge of the jail, without sufficient authority or warrant of the law, and carried to the Salters Depot on the North Eastern Railroad and there allowed to escape. Another prisoner, Tom James, confined in the jail on a charge of larceny, was suffered to go outside of the prison walls without a guard and thus effected his escape. These various instances of escape mark a course on the part of the officers of the law that seems to the Grand Jury to be criminally negligent and the public welfare demands, and the good order of government requires, that a strong investigation into the conduct of these public servants be made."

Spring term, 1875, the Grand Jury reported that although the County Commissioners have power to grant license to retail spiritous liquors in not less quantities than one quart, it is generally the habit of the county merchants all over the County to sell liquor by the drink.

November term, 1875, it said: "Our people find it difficult with the exercise of the greatest economy to make by agricultural pursuits a subsistence, and they earnestly look to and reasonably expect those who have the power to make the laws to exercise their best efforts to secure a good and economical government." This came after the statement, "This large sum proved insufficient to meet the obligations of the County incurred during the past fiscal year."

Presentment of Grand Jury, November term, 1876: "Since the last session of this honorable court, a committee of the Grand Jury, assisted by three citizens, has given fourteen days to inquiry into the county offices. Our attention has been confined to the office of the County Commissioners, School Commissioner, and the Treasurer. Our investigation reaches back but three years and covers but in part the transactions of those years. In the County Commissioners' office, we found 'confusion worse confounded' so that to refer to everything to which exception might be taken would be an endless undertaking. We therefore cite a few cases from the many as examples for the consideration of the court."

This committee of three was composed of T. M. Gilland, G. S. Cooper, and John E. Scott. The labors of this Jury and this committee saved the County many thousands of dollars and brought punishment to several gross malefactors.

There came out of Potter's Raiders to Williamsburg a Pennsylvania negro named Stephen A. Swails. It was not then known that he had been one of this band, but often suspected. Had it been known, the first one of at least a hundred men in Williamsburg who saw him would have shot him like a snake. Swails was an educated negro and had much natural ability. Almost from the hour of his arrival in Williamsburg until he was driven away by the outraged whites of the County, he had an uncanny influence over the negroes. He was elected the first senator from Williamsburg after the War and held this high office until South Carolina was redeemed from Republican rule. In 1872, Swails was elected president pro tempore of the State Senate and for nearly two years would have succeeded to the governorship of the State had anything happened to disqualify the carpet bagger in that chair.

There were no white people in Williamsburg who had been born here who were Republicans in this reconstruction period. There were a few men who had served in the Confederate Army from other parts of South Carolina who settled here after the War and who became Republicans. These men filled the lucrative offices in the County during the reconstruction period. As a general rule, during this time, negroes were elected to the Legislature. A half decently honest man could not make any money out of the legislative offices.

As a general rule, Republican office holders gave respectful consideration to all of the natural ruling element in the County. They were, however, placed in office by the negro vote and were never forgiven by many men who lived during the reconstruction period. The county officers of Williamsburg during the Republican rule were generally tolerable except from a financial standpoint and some of them were honest men. All of them, however, accepted what the Legislature allowed. The legislators of South Carolina from 1870 until 1876 seem to have done their utmost to confiscate all the property of the State and to have placed all confiscated property within the reach of the politicians and office holders of their time.

The members of the Legislatures of South Carolina between 1870 and 1876 seem to have been able to buy anything which their fancies dictated and charge same to the account of the State. In 1871, the State of South Carolina paid for members of the Legislature under the item "sundries, wines, liquors, cigars, groceries, and dry goods, $281,514.50." These "black and tan" legislators bought, on credit of the State, Heidseck, Verzenay, Moet and Chandon champagne; Mozelle, Chateau la Rose, Chateau la Fitte, Madeira, and Malaga wines; Otard-du-Puy Brandy, French Cognac, Cabinet Rye, Best Kentucky Bourbon, and Holland Gin. They smoked Brevas, Portugas, and Conchas, the best imported cigars, at the expense of the State. They fed themselves on Westphalia hams, Edam, Switzer, and English cheese, fresh Norfolk oysters, French chocolate, imported mushrooms, preserved ginger, gauva jelly, and brandied peaches on the account of the State of South Carolina. They bought Gothic chairs, marble top bureaus, finest plush velvet tete a tetes, English tapestry, Brussels carpets, Irish linens, Marseilles quilts, imported extra long silk stockings, whalebone, gold and diamond rings, and paid for them out of taxes collected by levies on the land in the State of South Carolina.

Printing the State laws from 1871 to 1873 cost South Carolina $1,160,565.00; newspapers for members of the Legislature during this period cost the State $19,749.00; stationery for the Legislature during the two years from 1871 to 1873 cost $108,865.39.

These unrestrained Legislatures were creating an impossible condition in South Carolina when a tax payers' convention was called in Columbia on February 17, 1874. Delegates attended from every County in this State. This convention called attention to the existing conditions under Republican rule to all the world, and honest public opinion from outside the State gave much aid to the long suffering "natural ruling element" in South Carolina. The members of this taxpayers' convention from Williamsburg were James McCutchen, S. W. Maurice, N. M. Graham, W. D. Knox, and T. M. Gilland.

Not only was the "bottom rail on top" during this reconstruction period and everybody in the County angry nearly all the time on account of political conditions, but economic conditions were most serious. A majority of the large land owners in the County actually had difficulty in securing a sufficient amount of currency to pay their taxes. Taxes on land during this period were confiscatory. Samuel Ruffin Mouzon says that the taxes on a certain plantation which he owned were $14.00 under the military government after the War and on the same land were $400.00 a year during reconstruction under negro legislation.

About the only thing produced in Williamsburg for market was cotton. Little of this was grown during this period for the reason that the whites either did not know how to produce it or would not do manual labor, nor did the negroes sober up from their political debauch sufficiently to work. The negroes who cultivated cotton, as a general rule, rented land from their former masters and worked as little as they could, producing but nominal crops. The prices they obtained for cotton were considerable. Just after the War, it brought $1.00 per pound.

What cotton was produced in Williamsburg during this reconstruction period caused more trouble in the County than everything else combined, within which is included, of course, the political disturbances. These negroes rented land, promising to pay the landlords out of the cotton grown on the land. As a general rule, these negroes were so careless in their working that their cotton crops amounted to little more than they had agreed to pay as rent. Seed cotton then sold at high prices. The average negro then had a very uncertain conception of honesty. He had spent nearly all of his life as a slave and had been accustomed to regard himself as "Massa's negro" and whatever Massa had as belonging to him. Nero, of Indiantown, answered satisfactorily the austere Session of Elders when he was charged with theft by using this idea.

There were in the County a number of white merchants who could not resist the temptation presented when negroes offered to sell them seed cotton, even though they knew that these negroes had not paid their landlords. Nearly all merchants at this time sold whiskey, and it was a very easy matter to shoulder a small sack of seed cotton at night and barter it to one of these merchants for a quart of whiskey. Some of these unscrupulous merchants even sent wagons about the country at night for the purpose of buying this seed cotton from the negroes, knowing full well that the negroes had stolen it.

This illicit sale of seed cotton resulted in most serious consequences all over the County. The civil authorities had little or no control over the condition. Negro juries would seldom convict either the reprobate merchant who had bought or the less guilty negro who had sold. Frequently plantation cotton gins were burned. The landlords exhausted all their legal remedies in trying to cure this situation without any appreciable results, except the burning of their cotton gins. It was then that the landlords used some measures that were not sanctioned by law. Many of these thieving merchants were given severe beatings and were otherwise shown that they were undesirable citizens. The great amount of trouble which the illicit sale of seed cotton has given in South Carolina explains the number and severity of the laws prohibiting its sale.

During this reconstruction period in South Carolina, when the negroes and their white leaders controlled and dictated the policy of all the agencies and functions of government, the "natural ruling element" could not have endured conditions had no Ku Klux Klan existed. This Invisible Empire which existed in the "Black Border" during the reconstruction was the most daring and successfully consummated scheme ever actualized. Clans were organized all over this section. While sometimes physical force was utilized by them, their great weapons were superstition and secrecy. That man who first realized that a few good actors, hooded and gowned in the costume of "haunts," could control and absolutely and religiously determine the conduct of thousands of negroes deserves an imposing monument in Dixie. A few of these clansmen visiting negro congregations at night, and performing sleight of hand tricks and mystical rites, generally proved all that was necessary to make all the negroes of such communities conscientiously observe whatever law and procedure they understood these clansmen to require. While it may be true that this Ku Klux Klan used severe measures in some cases, it is highly probable that even more than ninety-nine per centum of its efficiency came out of the superstitious awe with which it was regarded by all of the negroes and a majority of the worthless, ignorant whites. There is nothing more beautiful in American history than the service the Ku Klux Klan rendered in the Black Border during the reconstruction period. This organization more than anything else made women safe.

When all things are considered, it will be realized that negroes behaved remarkably well during this reconstruction period. They had just been freed by executive power, knew nothing of the rights and responsibilities of American citizenship, nor had any of their ancestors reached the point they themselves held just before emancipation. There have been cases in history where men have been enslaved for a time and, when suddenly emancipated, became worthy citizens. In these cases the races had reached a high degree of civilization before enslavement. The African negro had reached his highest development on the day of emancipation. By law African slaves in the South had been prohibited from learning how to read and write. A system of patrols had kept them on their respective plantations, reducing assembling and communicating among them to an inconsiderable minimum. When emancipated, they did not understand, they were "blasted with excess of sight," "drunk with sight of power." They had a vague, indefinable idea that they had been liberated by the Yankees, and probably a majority of them believed that their emancipation was a consummation desirable.

Immediately after emancipation there came among them that contemptible element that follows in the wake of armies to gather what it can from the helpless, dying, and the dead. These pale faced ghouls came and affiliated with the negroes, ate at their tables, slept with them, thus appealing through that strongest desire of all inferior races for social equality with a higher race. These indescribable things called white men gained a certain degree of influence among them. Further, these contemptibles, or by whatsoever name known, promised these negroes that the United States government would support them and would finally give them the lands of their former masters. They assured the negroes that they had but to possess the land, and that the Republican party would assist them in possessing it. These scallawags knew that Lincoln was dead and that there was no strong arm in the land to stay the fury of fanatical abolitionists. Perhaps some of their promises to the negroes had an iota of sincerity. These carpet baggers realized that there were more negroes in the State of South Carolina than there were whites, and they were satisfied that the national Congress, so long as dominated by fanatics, would make South Carolina a happy hunting ground for ghouls.

Negroes labored during this reconstruction period as little as possible. They were taught to obtain from the whites everything they could. Their unmoral condition was largely responsible for their errors both of ommission and commission. This tendency on the part of the negroes as nearly as possible to take all and give none had a serious influence on the landlords of the County. Landlords realized that their negro tenants endeavored by every means known to escape their commercial obligations. This knowledge and this continued practice on the part of negroes made many theretofore honest landowners swerve from the paths of righteousness in that some of them took all within their power from their negro tenants. The negroes at this time had a saying, "Naught's a naught, and five's a figger, all for the white man and none for the nigger." In a vast majority of cases, after the white men had computed the cost of feeding the negro all the year and added his rent, the proceeds of the negro's crop would not pay this amount. Sometimes, however, there was surplus which the negro should have received but which he did not get. The feeling that some few white landlords have in this year 1923 that they may make an inventory of what their negro tenants produce and take practically all is one of the most contemptible things the reconstruction period left in Williamsburg. There exists but a trace of this feeling, but the trace remains.

In 1876, the white people of the State of South Carolina realized that negro Republican rule in the State could no longer be tolerated and Scotch-Irish emergency action began. Many fanatical abolitionists had gone into the unknown between 1866 and 1876, and there was in the governor's chair in Columbia a former citizen of the State of Massachusetts, one of a high degree of intelligence and with some idea of righteousness. There have been times when it is said that even the Holy One "winked at things," and one can scarcely doubt now that Governor D. H.

Chamberlain really rejoiced at what South Carolina brought forth in that second '76. It must not be understood that Governor Chamberlain assisted the Democrats in South Carolina in forever redeeming the State from the rule of his party. It is true, however, that he might have done many more things than he did to have hampered and hindered that second Revolution in the State. He evidently looked on the desperate leaders of the white people with great admiration.

On December 23, 1875, the white citizenship of South Carolina began to write the last chapter in the history of negro domination in the State. Colonel Thomas Y. Simons, of Charleston, a member of the National Democratic Executive Committee, summoned each member of the Democratic State Central Committee to a meeting in Columbia on January 6, 1876. This committee charged one man in every county in South Carolina with the organization of the party in every precint, ward, and township in his respective county. These county organizers were charged with conducting the Hampton Redemption campaign of 1876. Captain Samuel W. Maurice was this man in Williamsburg. It was at this time that the Democratic clubs were organized in every community in South Carolina, which Democratic clubs have dominated the political policy of the State until this time.

The Democratic State Convention met in Columbia on May 4, 1876, although the white people were in the minority, to nominate and elect a "straightout" Democratic ticket. Prior to this time, some of the best men in the State had believed it expedient to compromise with the Republicans and thus secure the election of the best man from that party for governor. From Williamsburg, the members of this May convention were T. M. Gilland, James McCutchen, W. H. Nettles, and Thomas R. Greer.

A second convention was called for August 15, 1876, for the purpose of announcing a platform of principles, nominating candidates for state offices for the Democratic party, and for considering such other business as might come before it. From Williamsburg in this convention were W. H. Kennedy, S. T. Cooper, and J. A. May. It was this convention that nominated General Wade Hampton for governor and adopted the Democratic platform on which the white people of South Carolina stood and regained control of the State.

Williamsburg County was one of the Black Border counties of the State, so called for the reason that the blacks far exceeded the whites in number. While nearly every white native in every county in South Carolina did his absolute utmost during the campaign and election in 1876, the white people in these Black Border counties, of which Williamsburg was one, must be regraded as "first among equals" in their heroic endeavor and abundant accomplishment.

There was in Williamsburg in 1876 only one white native born Republican, and he shall be nameless here forevermore. Usually when a long contemplated action is consummated on a broad field, some men on account of their peculiar fitness and valor are outstanding in their services. Every native white man in Williamsburg, save one, in 1876 gave himself absolutely to the redemption of the State from negro domination, and whatever inequalities there may have been in effectiveness were due to differences in the power of individuals. Red Shirt organizations were formed in every part of the County. Captains of these bodies of men are even now, forty-seven years thereafter, justly proud of their titles. John A. Kelly, Esq., Captain of the Kingstree Red Shirt Company, and General Hampton's special officer for combat in the County, reveres his Red Shirt title beyond all others that he merits. The ancient cannon now on the Court House square in Kingstree was sent here for his use on the election day in November, 1876. Captain G. P. Nelson loaded this cannon on that day with a keg of nails and kept it pointed down Main Street, where thousands of negroes were congregated. It is said that Captain Nelson held his hand on the fuse of that cannon all day long and prayed most fervently from sunrise until sunset that some negro would "start something" that would give him an opportunity to drive those nails home.

Late in the afternoon on that election day, Major S. D. M. Byrd, of Scranton, then commanding the Red Shirt Company in his section of the County, considered how very calmly and quietly the election had been conducted in his precinct and feared that something might be going wrong in Kingstree, so he and his hundred red-shirted men began a forced march to Kingstree, arriving at the Court House just about the time the polls closed. Major Byrd was then in the fullness and splendor of manhood, six feet six inches tall, straight as an Indian, and powerful as a Roman gladiator. When he arrived at Kingstree, everything was very quiet. He was charged for action, so he hurried to the polls on the second floor in the Court House and, gathering one of the negro judges of election by the collar, carried him suspended at arm's length to the door, and kicked him clear the steps to the ground. This incident created no diplomatic disturbances. It simply gave zest to the day.

Since Williamsburg had so many more negro voters than whites, the Republican county candidates were elected, but on that day General Wade Hampton and a white man's legislature were chosen and South Carolina sang its song of deliverance from negro domination. The decade between 1866 and 1876 made the Republican party synonymous with negro domination to South Carolinians.

There is much of the heroic in the history of South Carolina. When one considers the War of the Revolution in this State, he must believe that human nature there and then reached its apex. When he surveys the period from

1861 until 1865, he wonders if men and women may go farther toward that which is most beautiful in service. But no man who knows the history of South Carolina of 1876 hesitates in deciding that this was the time when conditions called for most from men in the State, and found it. Even the most idealistic philosophers sometimes feel that "the end justifies the means." This year of our Lord, 1876, in South Carolina took men far afield from dilettante ethical idealism. It is a long, long story, the half of which has never been told. Men seem to have feared, even when they knew, to tell the whole truth; but when the God of Things, sitting as a refiner and purifier of silver, looked through those fierce fires into His Vessel, He saw His own image reflected.

CHAPTER XXXIV.

ANOTHER WILLIAMSBURG.

Williamsburg groaned and travailed in pain from 1866 until 1876 when another Williamsburg, the child of rape, was born. But the mother blood was strong and virile.

Antebellum Williamsburg was an aristocracy. Every planter had an overseer for his negro slaves, so there were practically as many men of the overseer class as of the planters. Sometimes these overseers doubted that God Almighty wisely ruled the Universe, but they never questioned the omniscience of their employers. The planters were all natives to the soil. Their ancestors had been granted this land before the American commonwealth was organized, and these descendants owned it by every rightful title. These overseers were "birds of passage." They came, they saw, they could not evercome. The stronger ones departed into the West. One-tenth of the population of antebellum Williamsburg absolutely controlled. The nine-tenths knew little and cared less about matters of State.

Another force made supreme this nine-tenths in Williamsburg during the Reconstruction. There is a law of Life, not known but felt, which spirit and matter obey in moving towards that "one far off divine event." The working of things under this law made what is known as the Reconstruction in South Carolina. The unlimited democracy which the abolition hate dominating element in the North forced on the South could not withstand the strength fighting it. The old aristocracy could not overcome the powers against it—all at once. By compromise, the old aristocracy yielded to the newly arrived Caucasians the right to vote, thus bringing about the white aristocracy since dominating.

One fearful result of unlimited white suffrage in Williamsburg and in South Carolina has been the lowering of the standard for qualification for public service. So many times the "natural ruling element" among the whites has been defeated at the poles that the majority of this class has seemingly lost interest in determining South Carolina's temporal affairs. The conservative class, prepared by blood and education, does not usually offer candidates for office, nor show a virile interest in elections. The outcome of this has been that the "bottom rail" is nearly always "on top." Certainly, many of the conservative class have held places of power in the new State, but never since the War between the Sections has the "natural ruling element" held complete control of South Carolina.

A dual state government was functioning in Columbia for some time after the election in November, 1876. The Democrats claimed that General Wade Hampton had been elected Governor and the Republicans maintained that D. H. Chamberlain had been legally chosen. Maxmilian Jacobs was elected Clerk of the Court and Louis Jacobs Sheriff of Williamsburg in 1876. Maxmilian's commission as clerk was signed by Wade Hampton as Governor of South Carolina while Louis' commission as sheriff was signed about the same time by D. H. Chamberlain as Governor of South Carolina. These commissions of the Jacobs brothers, as Williamsburg County officials, were both accepted by the Courts and are recorded on the same page in the Journal of the Court of General Sessions of Williamsburg County. Finally, General Hampton was recognized as the legally elected and duly qualified Governor of the State and Chamberlain and his nefarious crew surrendered. Then ended negro domination in South Carolina.

Williamsburg elected the Republican candidates in November, 1876, since negroes then voted and the County had an overwhelming negro majority. S. A. Swails, senator, John Evans, James Peterson, and William Scott, members of the House of Representatives, were all negroes. It must be remembered that although the county delegation from Williamsburg was composed of negroes, there was a working majority of white Democrats in the State Legislature. M. J. Hirsch was at this time elected Solicitor of this judicial district. Although placed in office by negro votes, Mr. Hirsch used common sense and good judgment in his official conduct.

Of these Republicans who controlled the County during the Reconstruction, Louis Jacobs and M. J. Hirsch had been faithful Confederate soldiers and, during their office holding under Republican commissions, they always showed reasonable consideration to the natural ruling element. The venerable H. J. Brown says that when his father, Levi Brown, was killed by negroes during this period, he reported the matter to Sheriff Jacobs and he was commendably zealous in fulfilling the functions of his office. Once during this period Major S. D. M. Byrd came to Kingstree for the purpose of paying his taxes. He had managed to secure $30.00 in money and that was about all the currency he could command. His taxes were due and he had computed them at about this amount. Major Byrd went to the office of the Tax Collector to pay them. The Tax Collector informed him that they amounted to $100.00. Major Byrd realized that this was extortion and became excusably infuriated, yet was powerless. He went over to the office of M. J. Hirsh, Esq., and told him his story. Mr. Hirsch took Major Byrd's $30.00 and went to the office of the Tax Collector and returned with a receipt in full for Major Byrd's taxes for that year. Williamsburg remembers much to the credit and little to the condemnation of Louis Jacobs and M. J. Hirsch, except that they were Republicans.

The Democratic party has elected every candidate for office in Williamsburg County since 1876. A result of the State election in 1876 was the amendment to the Constitution restricting suffrage by requiring an educational qualification or property ownership essential. The practical working of this constitutional amendment was the almost entire elimination of the negro as a voter in the elections in this State. Some negroes have voted in Williamsburg since '76, but the spirit of South Carolina has been and is that only whites shall cast ballots.

The transformation wrought by white control of the County within a very short period is shown from the Grand Jury reports of 1876, and those of 1880. In 1876, this grand inquest from the body of the County declared "confusion worse confounded" everywhere; that the County was fearfully in debt from the fraud and negligence of its officials; that the Republican built jail was defective in construction and insecure and that prisoners escaped at will; that the roads were generally impassable and almost all bridges dangerous; that the books and papers of the County Commissioners were unintelligible and showed shameless criminal use of public funds; that the treasury was empty and jurors were vainly hawking County orders about the streets of Kingstree; that crime was prevalent and the punishment of criminals almost entirely neglected.

The Grand Jury, May term, 1880, said: "We congratulate the good people of the County on the reduction of crime and the establishment of law and order in our midst. At the present term, but one bill of indictment has been submitted to the Grand Jury, which is high evidence of the law abiding condition of the County. This is truly a matter for congratulation and we can but hope that under the just administration of the law this excellent condition of things will continue." The Grand Jury,

March 1883, reported that the County was out of debt for the first time since 1866.

In 1883, the second story of the County Court House was burned. When the fire was discovered, the county officials who had their records in their offices on the ground floor very quickly removed their books and papers from these offices. The second story was burning for three days, during which time the officials learned that their offices were fire proof and began using them before the embers above had ceased to burn. It was then remembered that Architect Robert Mills, the same out of whose mind had come plans for the Treasury Building and the Washington monument, in the District of Columbia, had erected this old Court House in his younger days and that he builded well. Repairs were soon made by a committee composed of G. P. Nelson, S. I. Montgomery, and J. W. Gamble.

In 1901, an addition was made to the south end of the Court House, so that the building became as now, a dignified, substantial structure about fifty by one hundred feet. The Grand Jury, December 1901, said: "We congratulate the County upon the great improvements made in repairs, additions, and alterations of the Court House and offices and trust the good work will keep apace with the present progress of the County. Contractor W. R. Funk deserves the commendation of the citizens of the County for the good architecture and excellent work he has done. We recommend as a further improvement that a neat and substantial fence be erected around the Court House 25 feet from the Court House on all sides thereof, giving a good park to the town and keeping out horses and cattle from the square. We also recommend that parties who are now using a part of the public square for their own private purposes be made to pay a mere nominal sum as rent so that no question can arise against the County's title."

ANOTHER WILLIAMSBURG

There has been a continuous growth towards civic righteousness in Williamsburg since the Redemption of the second '76. Unmistakable evidence of its law abiding citizenship of forty thousand souls is found in the fact that all civil and criminal courts for the first two terms of 1923 were annulled for the reason that pending business did not warrant the sessions. Faithful and efficient county officers for more than forty years have helped make such a condition. Here follow their names.

In 1878, Captain S. W. Maurice was elected senator but died before the convening of the Senate. Major S. D. M. Byrd was chosen to succeed him and served until 1888, when Dr. A. H. Williams was elected. Dr. Williams died in 1908 and was succeeded as senator by W. L. Bass, who held office for one term of four years. E. C. Epps became senator in 1912 and served eight years. He was succeeded by Hugh McCutchen who died in office. S. M. Beasley filled his unexpired term. In 1922, S. A. Graham was elected senator.

The members of the House of Representatives since 1876 have been: 1878, J. R. Lambson, Z. R. Fulmore, and S. J. Graham; 1880, J. B. Chandler, T. M. Gilland, and Dr. Robert Henry; 1882, R. H. Kimball, William Cooper, and W. S. Camlin; 1886, J. B. Chandler, John A. Kelley, and Edwin Harper; 1890, H. E. Eaddy, S. A. Graham, and D. L. Brown; 1892-1898, J. H. Blackwell, E. R. Lesesne, and W. J. Singletary; 1898, George W. Davis, John S. Graham, and W. H. Kennedy; 1900, John S. Graham, C. W. Wolfe, and S. W. Gamble; 1902, J. D. Carter, Theodore B. Gourdin, and W. M. Keels; 1904, Theodore B. Gourdin, W. L. Bass, and P. S. Wall; 1906, W. L. Bass, John S. Graham, and Philip H. Stoll; 1908, W. B. Bryan, John S. Graham, and R. H. Kellahan; 1910, W. B. Bryan, J. Davis Carter, and J. S. Graham; 1912, B. B. Chandler, J. C. Graham, and R. H. Kellahan; 1914, R. J. Kirk, W. J. Smiley, and R. H. Kellahan; 1916,

J. J. M. Graham, S. A. Graham, and R. K. Wallace; 1918, S. O. Eaddy, S. A. Graham, and W. H. Welch; 1920, W. O. Camlin, D. E. McCutchen, and W. O. Godwin; 1922, E. L. Ard, W. T. Rowell, and F. R. Hemingway.

Dr. John F. Brockinton was the first Democratic sheriff after the Reconstruction. He was elected in 1880 and served until he died May 15, 1881. He was succeeded by his son, Joseph E. Brockinton, who held the office until 1892. James Dodd Daniel was sheriff from 1892 until 1900. George J. Graham was elected in 1900 and remained in the office until he retired voluntarily, being eighty years old, in 1920. Henry S. Gamble, incumbent, succeeded him.

The Clerks of the Court since 1880 have been: J. H. Keels, Swingle Graham, W. W. Grayson, C. W. McClam, B. C. Whitehead, S. McBride Scott, H. O. Britton, and John D. Britton, incumbent; Auditors, Thomas McCutchen, J. W. Ferrell, H. Z. Hanna, J. D. Daniel, and J. J. B. Montgomery since 1902; Treasurers, W. R. Brockinton, J. M. Cooper, R. D. Rollins, W. W. Johnston, J. W. Cook, and R. B. Smith; Superintendents of Education: Dr. S. D. McGill, Captain S. J. Snowden, J. J. B. Montgomery, N. D. Lesesne, William Cooper, J. G. McCullough, Raymond Speigner, J. V. McElveen, and M. F. Montgomery; Judges of Probate: J. P. Mouzon, C. W. McClam, W. W. Grayson, J. Z. McConnell, E. M. Smith, W. E. Hanna, S. McBride Scott, P. M. Brockinton, and W. E. Snowden.

Immediately after the War between the Sections, the office of County Judge was created for Williamsburg, and Lieutenant Colonel John G. Pressley elected Judge. He resigned to migrate to California in 1869, and Lieutenant Texas B. Logan succeeded him. Judge Logan soon resigned and moved to Tennessee, where he became a distinguished Jurist. Charles W. Wolfe, Sr., succeeded Judge Logan, holding the office until it was abolished by the "black and tan" legislature.

In 1880, the following were elected County Commissioners: W. E. Nesmith, C. W. McClam, and J. M. Owens, Sr. A. P. McCormick was Clerk to this Board. Among the commissioners since that time have been: J. W. Gamble, G. P. Nelson, S. I. Montgomery, J. J. Morris, T. S. Stuart, W. R. Brown, Robert Epps, Charles R. Lesesne, W. B. McCollough, J. J. Graham, B. B. Chandler, W. H. Campbell, W. W. Kennedy, R. D. Blakeley, S. J. Singletary, O. R. Eaddy, J. C. -Everett, L. P. Kinder, D. E. McCutchen, J. M. Brown, R. B. Fitch, B. N. Stuckey, H. D. Ferrell, Bartow Smith, J. T. Eaddy, C. A. Heins, J. W. Chandler, J. M. Williamson, R. W. Smith, and J. R. Barrow. Those who were clerks to the Board prior to 1905, when the clerk became a district official with the title of Supervisor, were: W. L. Bass, E. G. Chandler, J. J. Steele, J. J. B. Montgomery, J. N. Hammett, B. M. Montgomery, J. G. McCutchen. Among the Supervisors have been B. B. Chandler, J. J. Graham, J. N. Hammett, and S. J. Singletary, incumbent.

Democratic party primaries held some time before the general election in November determine things in South Carolina. Practically all whites are enrolled on Democratic club lists and nearly every one votes in the primaries. So certain are the candidates chosen in these Democratic primaries for election, that very few vote on regular election days. Some negroes are registered voters, not a sufficient number to stimulate interest in general elections.

When the amendment to the Constitution of the United States forced women suffrage on South Carolina, there were probably less than a dozen men in Williamsburg who would admit favoring it. So strong was the sentiment opposing the voting of women that not a candidate in Williamsburg in the campaign of 1922 would openly advocate the registering of women on the club lists, lest such create hostility towards him among the men. There were, however, about three hundred white women in the County who registered on the Democratic Club Rolls and voted in the August primaries. The first woman in Williamsburg who registered for voting was Mrs. Helen Scott Boddie.

In 1922, there were twenty-seven Democratic clubs in Williamsburg, with a total enrollment of 2,879 voters qualified for the primaries. These were as follows: Bethel, 33; Black River, 40; Bloomingdale, 44; Cades, 245; Cedar Swamp, 75; Central, 63; Earles, 158; Gourdins, 29; Greelyville, 249; Hebron, 92; Hemingway, 229; Indiantown, 102; Kingstree, No. 1, 380; Kingstree, No. 2, 241; Lanes, 79; Lenuds, 55; Morrisville, 54; Muddy Creek, 80; Nesmith, 38; Oak Ridge, 33; Pergamos, 83; Poplar Hill, 60; Salters, 112; Sandy Bay, 67; Suttons, 42; Trio, 150; Workman, 47; A. C. Hinds was chairman of the County Democratic Executive Committee and Walter Wilson was county member of the State Democratic Executive Committee.

CHAPTER XXXV.

PUBLIC EDUCATION SINCE 1880.

Dr. Samuel D. McGill became County School Commissioner on January 1, 1881, and filled that office for ten years. The other members of this school commission were T. M. Gilland and M. J. Hirsch. It was during this decade that public schools became rooted in the soil of Williamsburg. Prior to this time it had been considered beneath the dignity of the "better element" to patronize "free schools," and universal education had not been regarded as practical, possible, or even a "consummation devoutly to be wished."

Williamsburg was especially fortunate in having these three men to determine its school affairs during those ten formative years. This decade may be called the silent epoch in the history of the County. It was probably the most directing period this section ever experienced. Dr. McGill had taught private schools in various parts of the district for many years, knew everybody intimately, and had the saving sense of humor. Mr. Gilland was a trained lawyer, knew how to find facts out of conflicting testimony, and was firm and resolute in his convictions. Mr. Hirsch had remarkable skill in pouring oil on troubled waters. Hardly any man who ever lived in this County ever settled more teapot tempests than he. It will be recalled that when the Democrats elected Mr. Hirsch to this commission he was serving under Republican election as Solicitor of the district. Fortune Barr, a Democratic negro and an interesting mimic, said one day while entertaining a street crowd, "Mr. Hirsch he see de Republican ship wuz sinkin', made one jump en lit on de deck uv de Democratic boat."

This commission divided the County into seventeen school districts and appointed the following trustees for the schools in the several districts: 1. E. R. Lesesne, E. P. Montgomery, S. J. Taylor; 2. T. E. Salters, J. M. Cook, J. A. Ferrel; 3. J. J. Graham, A. W. Chandler, W. B. McCollough; 4. E. J. Parker, A. J. Parsons, R. P. Hinnant; 5. D. Z. Martin, J. W. Marshall, W. S. Camlin; 6. W. H. McElveen, J. B. Price, J. M. McClam; 7. J. A. Nexsen, A. J. Smith, William Scott; 8. W. D. Snowden, J. S. McCullough, Dr. J. R. Brockinton; 9. S. T. Cooper, J. C. Josey, Rev. J. M. Kirton; 10. J. McB. Graham, J. P. Epps, Rev. Ben Brown; 11. G. S. Barr, William Cooper, Julian Wilson; 12. Captain J. F. Carraway, W. D. Owens, J. B. Davis; 13. W. R. Singletary, S. Kirby; 14. D. L. Brown, J. A. H. Cockfield, T. E. James; 15. H. H. Singletary, M. L. Jones, W. J. Hatfield; 16. W. J. Lee, L. Stackley, H. Z. Graham; 17. B. C. Whitehead, R. A. Rouse.

The entire amount of money spent for all public school purposes in the County from January 1, 1881, until January 1, 1891, including buildings and repairs, furniture and fixtures, teachers' salaries and current expenses was $52,393.18. Three times as much money was used for paying teachers' salaries and current expenses in the Kingstree school alone in 1922 as was spent for all school purposes in the whole County in 1882. It must be recalled that Williamsburg County has since that time lost a considerable part of its most populous territory to Florence County.

Among the white public school teachers of that period were: J. L. Barley, Mrs. S. L. Barrineau, Miss Sue T. Barr, Miss C. A. Blackwell, Miss M. A. Brockinton, Miss L. A. Brockinton, Miss F. W. Britton, W. R. Brown, J. J. Brown, Mrs. M. A. Carter, Miss Dora V. Chandler, Mrs. Ella Collette, Mrs. M. E. Cockfield, Miss Mutie Cooper, Miss Mollie Epps, Isaac Epps, Rev. Martin Eaddy, Miss L. N. Ervin, Miss S. M. Ervin, Miss L. A. Elliott, Miss M. V. Graham, Miss A. M. Henry, A. W. Jackson,

Miss Sue R. Keels, Miss M. F. Keels, Miss M. R. Lifrage, N. D. Lesesne, Miss Augusta McConnell, Mrs. M. B. McConnell, J. Z. McConnell, T. M. McCutchen, W. W. Matthews, Miss M. L. Montgomery, J. J. B. Montgomery, Mrs. S. A. Nelson, J. W. Nelson, W. E. Nesmith, W. P. Nesmith, Mrs. N. O. Poston, Mrs. S. M. Salters, S. R. Mouzon, Mrs. Carrie Mouzon, T. M. Scott, Rev. J. W. Shell, E. J. Smith, Albert Singleton, Miss H. S. Singletary, W. E. Snowden, J. P. Shaw, Mrs. A. L. Simmons, S. J. Snowden, T. B. Gourdin, J. F. Watson, J. T. Wilder, Miss Florence Workman, Mrs. E. P. Wolfe.

Some of the colored school teachers were: Augustus Brown, J. D. Barr, J. S. Cooper, Mrs. L. M. Cooper, B. L. Cooper, J. S. Fulmore, Jack Gordon, Mrs. H. Hanna, W. M. Hanna, S. S. Hanna, Miss N. A. Harper, Miss M. E. Mouzon, H. H. Mouzon, M. M. Mouzon, M. D. McBride, James M. Eaddy, Miss R. Z. Montgomery, J. C. Pendergrass, W. J. Parsons, Mrs. M. A. Ransom, Dick Salters, J. E. Singletary, W. D. Scott, G. K. Summersett, and W. G. Wilson.

Charles W. Wolfe wrote in the issue of The County Record of August 23, 1906: "Kingstree's excellent school system may be said to owe its origin to the establishment of the Kingstree Academy, the forerunner of the present handsome and splendidly equipped school building. Prior to that time the efforts to tend and till the pedagogical field in Kingstree were haphazard and without concert of action or organization. Finally certain public spirited citizens with an eye to the town's present and future needs resolved to bring about improvement in the then existing educational conditions and as the result of their efforts the Kingstree Academy was built. This was in 1886.

The first principal was Mr. S. W. Williams, and in the order named followed Messrs. M. M. Lander, N. D. Lesesne, W. B. Duncan, E. C. Dennis, C. W. Stoll, T. O.

Epps, W. W. Boddie, and Ernest Wiggins. With the election of Mr. Boddie came the adoption of the graded school system and the merging of the old Academy into Kingstree Graded School. Then came an awakening along educational lines and an agitation for a new building, the outcome of which is the present structure, which may well be termed 'the pride of the town.' To show the spirit that animated the people in this matter, only two negative votes were cast in the election to issue bonds for the school building which was erected in 1904."

The board of trustees of the first graded school in Kingstree were: Dr. D. C. Scott, Chairman, Louis Stackley, M. J. Hirsch, Edwin Harper, and Louis Jacobs. Assisting the principal as teachers at that time were Misses Amelia Kennedy and Nina Riser. The school building then stood at the corner of Hampton and Mill Streets, where was in 1923 the Carnegie Public Library. In June, 1902, the first certificates for the completion of the course of study in the Kingstree school were awarded to Misses Bessie Harper, Pearl Koger, Lorena Ross, and Helen Scott. The three first named entered Winthrop College and the last the College for Women, Columbia, the following September, all graduating with high class rank in due time.

Miss Koger died of pulmonary tuberculosis soon after her graduation from Winthrop College. She was the only child of her widowed mother, Mrs. Ellen Koger. This writer helped Miss Koger learn Arithmetic, Algebra, and Geometry, Caesar, Cicero, and Virgil, something of Literature and of History. She had one of the brightest minds and one of the most beautiful personalities that he ever knew.

William Cooper was superintendent of education in Williamsburg from 1900 to 1910, during which time the first graded school in the County was organized in Kingstree, and later others at Johnsonville and Union, and modern school buildings erected for all three; many special districts were established and communities began contributing towards the erection of school buildings and voting special tax levies for supplementary support to their own institutions. During this decade a majority of the white people in the County, for the first time, believed that schooling for their children was actually worth some time and money. Furthermore, that small minority who in all the history of the County has educated its children in college, began to hope that it could depend on the public schools for the high school grades.

The next decade from 1910 to 1920 almost everybody in the County, white and colored, began to believe that schooling for their children was actually worth time and money, and many felt that it was worth much time and money. Sometime during the last days of this decade one or two parents in Williamsburg actually heard Yahweh's unuttered reply to Cain's first question, and realized their duty to give their children a sound and various learning, for the purpose of serving their fellowmen as well as for private profit and power. These one or two parents stretched the ribbon streak of dawn for Williamsburg's Day.

Once five righteous men would have saved Sodom. There were in Williamsburg in 1923 more than five men and women who, understanding, were educating their children for the highest degree of citizenship. There were a hundred others who, seeing, like Browning's beggar, were preparing to plunge. Jocund day for Williamsburg was standing tiptoe on the misty mountain top.

Following will be found a list of the school officials of Williamsburg in 1923. Some of those named as teachers were worthy of the designation: others "kept" school hours for wages. One cannot know who teaches from one who does not, until the harvest time. A real teacher starts growing out of a mind something that environment cannot stop. Sometimes a mind shows few recognizable signs of growth for many years, and then seemingly all at once brings forth fruit an hundred fold.

The County Board of Education in 1923 was composed of M. A. Shuler, J. G. McCullough, and M. F. Montgomery. Mr. Montgomery was Superintendent of Education. Following are the names of the white schools, their trustees, and the teachers:

Heineman: Dr. I. N. Boyd, W. E. Blackwell, and Walter Scott; Martha Burgess.

Suttons: S. B. Gordon, D. W. Gordon, and W. W. Michau; Mrs. Ruth Chandler and Pauline Boyd.

Sumter: J. M. James, W. H. Dennis, and Shelton Wilson; Clara Steele.

Turkey: R. W. Smith and W. O. Camlin; Mamie Lou Sharp.

Hemingway: B. J. Chandler, L. G. Day, and D. G. Huggins; W. D. Halfacre, Superintendent, E. L. Rodgers, Ida Lee Parler, Virginia Galloway, Lyde Kennedy, Dess Gowdy, Effie Zimmerman, Lucia Winn, Iva Geddings, Emmie Snow, Alma Deloach, Virginia Warren, Muriel Williams, and Blondelle Cockfield.

Muddy Creek: R. K. Johnson, W. A. Larrimore, and E. C. Cribb; Janie Newell, Pauline Stone, and Mrs. Mattie Stone.

Kingstree: Dr. D. P. Frierson, L. W. Gilland, and A. C. Swails; J. W. Swittenberg, Superintendent, A. H. Baldwin, H. Bucck, Laura Lynch, Lilla Babb, Agnes Erckmann, Varina McDaniel, Elizabeth Speigner, Mrs. M. F. Montgomery, Lillie Pruitt, Carrie Lancaster, Mrs. Bettie Gwin, Mrs. G. A. McElveen, E. O. Baker, and Mrs. Ira Calhoun.

Hebron: Bartow Smith, J. W. DuBose, and B. C. Baker; J. H. Felder, Wista McElveen, Mattie Felder, and Annie M. Epps.

Taft: J. H. Burkett, S. B. Timmons, and D. E. Cooper; Thelma Lockliear.

Greelyville: T. W. Boyle, F. Mishoe, and J. F. Montgomery; S. P. Stackley, Superintendent, H. N. Parnell, Effie Chandler, Thelma Lunn, Cornelia Risher, Mary Ratchford, Estelle DeHay, and Bertha Blakely.

Cades: V. G. Arnette, and W. I. Hodges; C. B. Kirkley, Mrs. C. B. Kirkley, and Mina Gasque.

Cedar Creek: John West, John Lucas, and W. W. Wilson; E. Omitt Walters.

Cedar Swamp: W. T. Phillips, R. F. Ward, and D. C. Brown; Mary McColl, Murtiss Gantt, Agnes Riggs, and Etna Camlin.

Pergamos: W. A. Fitch and Dr. L. W. Moore; T. O. Sease, Lucile Allen, and Louise Heins.

Rough Branch: W. H. Foxworth, J. J. M. Graham, Jr., and J. S. Rodgers; Caroline Young.

Salters: T. E. Salters, C. W. Boswell, and Walter David; Lou A. Ferguson, Ellen T. Chandler, and M. D. Cooper.

Fowler: H. M. Burrows, W. E. Burrows, and W. C. Wilson; Mrs. W. D. Hanna.

Lane: J. E. Plowden, Frank Baggett, and P. C. Shirer; A. R. Register, Evelyn Williams, Dorothy Williams, and Ethel Buchanan.

Earle: G. W. Camlin, R. M. Haselden, and J. W. Parsons; L. E. Smith, Lorena Lawrence, and Bertha Kennedy.

Nesmith: G. B. Cooper, W. J. Cooper, and J. M. Rodgers; Claudelle Willis.

Cantley: W. G. Cantley, J. M. Tisdale, and F. P. Guerry; Annie Redman and Maude Allene Kinder.

Aimwell: R. C. Flowers, W. J. Flowers, and R. C. Mitchum; Mabel Jackson and Gladys Avant.

Wayside: D. C. Scott, Jr., M. L. McClary, and R. J. Parrott; Ella Ferguson and Sara Burch.

Trio: W. T. Rowell and J. H. Rowell; J. D. Mackintosh and Eleanor Owings.

Wee Nee: J. B. Player, T. D. Gamble, and Hamer Stuart; Lucile Darwin and Pearl Wallace.

Belser: J. E. Baker, Fred Hodge, and J. H. Covington; Ruby Wallace.

Carlisle: T. S. Kelley and P. M. Brockinton; Belle Harper and Mrs. Edward Vause.

Mulberry: J. L. Ferrell, A. B. Spivey, and J. J. Bradham; Emma Lifrage and Allie Montgomery.

Johnson Swamp: Alfred Moore, Lex Taylor, and E. M. Lambert; Connie Thompson and Elizabeth Lewis.

Bethel: C. L. Burgess, J. S. Epps, J. D. Burgess; Mrs. J. M. Duke.

Singletary: J. J. Epps, W. P. Jordon, and L. R. Dickerson; J. S. Johnson.

McClary: J. F. Rodgers, D. H. Hanna, and J. A. Hanna; P. B. Lockwood.

Mt. Vernon: W. R. McCants and J. S. Frierson; Mrs. Leamie Boyd.

Spring Gully: M. L. Boyd, W. T. Evans, and Capers Boyd; Mrs. E. E. Bradham.

Piney Forest: S. R. Long, G. W. Godwin, and Mack Benton; Frances Plexico and Evelyn McConnell.

Penn: W. R. Chandler, E. J. Donnely, and W. M. Roberts, trustees.

Anderson: J. T. McCants, R. W. Blakely, and Henry Eliott, trustees.

King: T. A. Johnson, W. J. Epps, and Willie McClary, trustees.

Mingo: B. W. McElveen, W. H. Altman, and J. J. Poston, trustees.

Ox Swamp: J. B. Morris, O. L Thomson, and J. L. Foxworth, trustees.

Indiantown: H. P. Snowden, J. T. Gaskins, and W. E. Tanner; Mrs. S. D. Cunningham, Mrs. Ozzie Lovett, and Virginia Wilson.

Clarendon: B. E. McKnight, W. H. Baker, and W. H. Kennedy, trustees.

St. John: R. E. Turbeville, trustee.

Wilson: B. B. Chandler and D. D. Rhem, trustees.

Heywood: W. R. Pritchett, C. C. Daniel, and G. H. Lovett, trustees.

Cooper: G. J. Graham, J. B. Lovett, and Willie Cooper, trustees.

Barrineau: J. B. Osborne, W. H. Thigpen, and J. D. Floyd, trustees.

Spring Bank: G. F. Williamson, R. C. McElveen, and J. W. Stewart, trustees.

Marion Branch: W. A. Marshall, Richard McConnell, and Hugh Pipkin, trustees.

Sandy Bay: J. N. Coker, A. B. McKenzie, and J. N. McKenzie, trustees.

Black River: J. Ted Frierson, J. E. Duke, and D. H. Smith, trustees.

Wee Tee: O. C. Hinnant and W. E. Altman, trustees.

Bloomingvale: Marian McFadden and Ila Cooper, teachers.

Midway: Ollie Wade, Bertha Williamson, and Roberta Evans, teachers.

Oak Ridge: Adria Lewis and Mrs. Ruth Hardee, teachers.

Rock Branch: Gladys Wham and Erline Harrington, teachers.

Bennett: Mrs. J. O. Amaker, teacher.

Beulah: Sadie Bates, teacher.

Birch Creek: Madge Blakely, teacher.

Boyd: May Cook, teacher.

Lenud: Della Harrelson, teacher.

Moss Grove: Mrs. W. D. Daniel, teacher.

Mouzon: Iva L. Moyd, teacher.

Mt. Vernon: Mrs. Leamie Boyd, teacher.

Neverfail: Katie Lou Smith, teacher.

Poston: Mayme McConnell, teacher.

Smith Swamp: Mrs. G. E. Grier, teacher.

Warsaw: Thelma Marshall, teacher.

Union: Ellen Williams, teacher.

Retreat: Charlie Heins, I. C. Player, and J. A. Bradham, trustees.

There were one hundred twenty-one white school teachers in the County in 1923 and one hundred fourteen negro teachers. Of these white teachers twenty-three were teaching by virtue of special permit, and forty-three negroes. The State school law requires that all teachers in the public schools shall hold certificates before being paid public money for services, except by special permits which may be granted for one year to teachers. This exception practically nullifies the effectiveness of the certificate requirement. It makes it possible for a board of school trustees that wishes to employ some favorite who cannot pass the examinations required for a certificate simply to request the County Superintendent to issue a special permit for such person.

An official opinion states that 44% of the white teachers in Williamsburg were not qualified to teach above the sixth grade and 14% not qualified to teach primary grades. From a standpoint of methods of teaching, it is said on authority that only 50% of the white teachers of the County are qualified and 30% of the negro teachers.

The progress made in public school service in Williamsburg for the past score of years certainly has not been exceeded by that in any other county in the United States. Notwithstanding this remarkable improvement, the public schools of Williamsburg in 1923 hardly gave 50% efficiency for the money expended. There may be a hundred reasons for this condition,—the principal one that the citizenship of the County, not trained itself, requires school officials and teachers, who should be leaders and directors in the educational work, to conform and to follow rather than to lead. In other words, the schools are dominated by politics and a school official or a teacher who attempts to lead beyond where the parents know is immediately eliminated from public service.

Another reason for the inefficiency of Williamsburg's public schools is that the average Williamsburg parent seems to desire appearance more than reality in the schooling of his children. A popular teacher must necessarily give high grades and promotion to the children of the leading citizens of the community. The average citizen seems to regard paper grades and paper promotion for his children more desirable than sound and various learning. The people of Williamsburg almost without exception now know that the schooling of their children is necessary, but few of them realize what education is and how it must be obtained. With the money available for public schools in Williamsburg a wise and generous school dictator, one who knows the way and has power to will it, could work out the public school salvation in this County in a single decade.

There are some parents in Williamsburg who are obtaining real service for their children from the public schools. Some of the children trained in Williamsburg's schools are well equipped when they go to college, but these well trained are exceptions. All of the high schools in South Carolina compete every year in a debating contest for the Manning silver loving cup. These high schools also hold a recitation contest. In 1923 Jane Smyth Gilland and James F. Cooper won the Manning cup for the Kingstree High School, Miss Gilland winning the medal for the first debater and Mr. Cooper that for second. Miss Mary Catherine Epps won the medal for the second best recitation. Thomas Merriman won third prize for recitation. The Kingstree High School baseball team at the same time gave an excellent account of itself in the athletic contests of the State. These high school pupils have received excellent public school training. Their parents belong to that class that require service from the schools and receive it. It is the function of the public school to give good training to pupils whether the parents of these pupils are of sufficient education and intelligence to require it or not.

There are some teachers in Williamsburg who regard their work seriously and who make it a profession and a business. J. W. Swittenberg, B. A., Newberry College, 1895, came to Kingstree as superintendent of its schools in 1910, which office he was holding in 1923. Mr. Swittenberg has taught school consecutively for twenty-eight years. Since 1910 and under his administration, the Kingstree High School has granted diplomas to thirty-eight boys and seventy-one girls. Miss Agnes Erckmann of Charleston came as teacher of the first grade in the Kingstree Graded Schools in September, 1902, which position she has held continuously since that time. Miss Erckmann is also in charge of the Carnegie Public Library in Kingstree. During her long service in the Kingstree schools, she has been an influential factor in community life.

While the white schools of Williamsburg have made remarkable progress when compared with those of other parts of the country, for the past few years the negro schools in Williamsburg have accomplished even greater things. From 1918 until the present, 1923, the negroes of Williamsburg had made such exceptional improvement in their educational conditions that it seems spectacular. In 1918, the negroes, as a general rule, had a surplus of money for the first time in their history. Be it recorded to their everlasting credit that they chose to use this money to a large degree for the education of their children. They went about this work seriously and with more intelligently directed energy than they had ever shown in anything else. There was in June, 1923, but little difference between the school obtained knowledge of the average twelve year old white child and the average twelve year old negro child in Kingstree. There were living in 1923 in Williamsburg a number of negro teachers who had given long and faithful service in their schools. Among these may be mentioned Mary Murray, thirty years; Boston Cooper, twenty-five years; Hattie Frierson, twenty-five years; Lillie Cooper, forty-four years; William Mouzon, thirty years; J. S. Fulmore, thirty years; David Fulton had been principal of the colored schools in Kingstree for fourteen years.

There were fifty-eight school districts averaging about sixteen square miles each in the County in 1923. There were fifty-one white and fifty-nine colored graded schools, in which were enrolled 10,931 pupils. High Schools for whites were functioning in Kingstree, Hemingway and Greelyville, with a total enrollment of 909. There was neither a private nor a parochial school in the County. The total expenditures for all school purposes in Williamsburg in 1922, amounted to $143,023.56; value of school property, $237,215.

Desire for a liberal education was quick in Williamsburg in 1923.

CHAPTER XXXVI.

RELIGIOUS DENOMINATIONS, 1865-1923.

The several churches in Williamsburg were usually supplied with ministers during the War between the Sections, but most of them were without regular pastors during the Reconstruction period and for many years thereafter. Few churches were able to support a minister during these trying times. Even as late as 1891, when the Reverend R. W. Spigner was first licensed as a local preacher and sent to the Salters Circuit, for two years he was the only white minister of any denomination residing within that more than three hundred square miles of territory between the Santee and Black Rivers in Williamsburg County. And then he was licensed only to preach the gospel—was not authorized to administer the sacraments or even to marry a couple.

Most of the heat and burden of religious labor for one or two score of years after the War was borne by saintly men and women and by local preachers and exhorters. The outstanding local preacher of Williamsburg, earnest, eloquent, effective, was Daniel Durant, who died in 1922, more than four score years of age. He preached the simple gospel all over this County and his preaching brought forth fruit an hundred fold. Some of the especially outstanding Christian men and women of this Santee section of this period may be mentioned, William J. Clarkson, Mrs. Elizabeth Lesesne, R. P. Hinnant, Jack Parsons, Bradford Keels, Dr. Robert Henry, and Dr. James M. Burgess. All other sections of Williamsburg had such beautiful characters as these named from the Santee.

The Williamsburg Presbyterian Church, the oldest denominational organization between the Santee and the Cape Fear Rivers maintaining continuous unbroken service, remained on its ancient and original churchyard on the eastern boundary of Kingstree until the new building was erected on Academy Street in the town in 1890. In 1885, Mrs. M. L. Singleton deeded to the Williamsburg Presbyterian Congregation the one-half acre lot on which this new church was built. There is a limitation in this deed to the effect that "the said lot herein granted is to be used for church purposes and for none other." In 1913, this congregation replaced this frame church by the excellent brick building now used as its place of worship. The building committee was composed of Louis W. Gilland, chairman, H. E. Montgomery, secretary and treasurer, W. R. Scott, E. C. Burgess, M. F. Heller, R. B. Smith, R. J. McCabe, P. G. Gourdin, and D. J. Epps.

Since 1866, the following ministers have served the Williamsburg Presbyterian Congregation: Robert Bradley, William Banks, James McDowell, W. C. Smith, H. G. Gilland, J. E. Dunlap, E. E. Ervin, P. S. McChesney, J. W. Herndon, and John W. Davis. Mr. Davis was installed minister in 1920. In 1923, the Reverend W. C. Smith was living on his own farm at Reidville, South Carolina, all his faculties undiminished, and with physical strength sufficient, as he wrote, "to plough and weed corn." The Reverend P. S. McChesney in 1923 was pastor of the First Presbyterian Church in Anderson, South Carolina, and the Reverend J. W. Herndon was serving the Church in a city of West Virginia. All the others here named except the Reverend Mr. Davis, in charge of the Williamsburg Church, had been gathered to their fathers.

The Indiantown Presbyterian Church had as its stated supply from March 7, 1858, until March 26, 1867, the Reverend James R. Gilland. He was succeeded at that time by the Reverend James McDowell. In 1868, Dr. J. S. Cunningham was elected and ordained as elder on the third Sabbath in June. Dr. Cunningham served as one of this session of elders for a great many years. He was living, hale and hearty, and a faithful attendant of Indiantown Church in 1923, when more than ninety-two years old. In 1873, the White Oak Church was disbanded and its property and membership became a part of the Indiantown Church. There were thirteen members who became thus a part of the Indiantown Congregation.

All through these dark days of the reconstruction period Indiantown Church continued its careful supervision over the individuals of the congregation. So often as a man strayed from the straight and narrow way he was summoned before the session of elders, where he either professed repentance and humbled himself in the dust before the congregation or was excommunicated. The sessional visitations were continued. The records show that on August 8, 1874, the congregation was divided into four classes for this sessional supervision. The first class was assigned to Elder Wilson, second to Elder James, the third to Elder Cunningham, and the fourth to Elder McCutchen. On May 31, 1878, the Reverend Henry G. Gilland became minister of this congregation.

On November 23, the following persons were dismissed from the Indiantown Congregation for the purpose of uniting with the Lake City Presbyterian Church: J. T. Gaskins, Mrs. S. L. McCutchen, Mrs. T. M. Perkins, William C. Brown, Mrs. H. H. Singletary, Mrs. S. G. Gaskins, and the following children of Mrs. Singletary, John Duncan, Barfield, Lamar, and Virginia Vernon. The elders of the Indiantown Church at this time were J. D. Daniel, Colonel James McCutchen, T. M. McCutchen, P. D. Snowden, and Dr. J. S. Cunningham.

On August 24, 1889, the Reverend J. E. Dunlap became pastor of the Indiantown fold. Colonel James McCutchen died on September 25, 1897. He was born March 8, 1830, and ordained as ruling elder on November 6, 1853. It will be seen that he served on the official board of his church forty-four years. His son, Hugh McCutchen, was elected elder "in his room." Since Mr. Dunlap the fol-

RELIGIUOS DENOMINATIONS, 1865-1923   483

lowing ministers in order have served the Indiantown Congregation: A. C. Bridgman, R. L. Darnall, F. H. Wardlaw, and W. R. Pritchett, who was in charge in 1923.

In 1917, the old Indiantown Church building, which had stood as a place of worship since 1835, was remodelled. It was raised about ten feet and below the main auditorium twelve Sunday School rooms constructed of solid concrete. A modern heating plant for the Sunday School rooms and the main auditorium of the church was then installed.

Among the Presbyterian ministers who served Elon, Union, Central, and Gourdins in the long ago, old men now living remember Dr. Hampton DuBose, Dr. J. W. Flinn, Chalmers Johnson, and Augustus Henderson, John LaFar. Dr. Flinn was a young man when he preached in this County. Later he developed into one of the leading ministers of his denomination. For many years he was a professor in the University of South Carolina. Reverend W. I. Sinnott, formerly of Alabama, in 1923, was minister in charge of the churches at Union and Central and Lake City. He had been serving these congregations many years. Reverend R. H. Ratchford was minister of the Greelyville Church in 1923. Reverend Philip Pierson served Bethel Church from its dedication in 1858, until he died, while preaching in its pulpit, November 9, 1873. He was succeeded by W. B. Crawford, Robert Adams, R. D. Perry, A. M. Hassell, S. E. Bishop, W. H. Workman, and James McDowell, D. M. Clarke, and Dr. F. M. Hawley, Elders of this church in 1923 were G. W. Burgess, E. F. Epps, T. E. Duke, and R. C. McElveen, clerk of the session, who succeeded his father in 1906.

In 1923 the following were active Presbyterian Churches in Williamsburg County with the number of communicants in each: Williamsburg, 285; Indiantown, 167; Union, 95; Central, 118; Lanes, 47; Greelyville (McDowell Memorial Church), 110; Bethel, 125; McGill

Memorial Chapel, 62. Total Presbyterian membership in Williamsburg County, 1009.

About 1880, Miss Caroline Simons, an enthusiastic member of the Protestant Episcopal Church, came to Kingstree as a school teacher. She was the only communicant of this church in the town of Kingstree until in 1882, through her influence, Bishop W. W. Howe conducted services in the county court house, and confirmed a class of four, composed of Mr. and Mrs. P. B. Thorne, Miss Minnie Porter, and Mr. Charles Porter. For several years these five communicants from time to time obtained the services of missionary ministers and "kept the faith."

On the 29th day of June, 1882, William J. Lee and Virginia E. Lee granted to the Protestant Episcopal Church in South Carolina "all that lot of land in Kingstree measuring and containing in width on the front and back lines one hundred and five feet and in depth on the said lines two hundred and ten feet, bounded on the north by a lot of John Dozier, south by Church Street, east by Hampton Street, and west by land of W. J. Lee." It was provided in this deed that no part of this lot should ever be used as a cemetery or place for the interment of the dead.

In 1890 St. Alban's Episcopal Chapel was erected on this lot and has since been used by the Episcopalians. In 1887, Miss Simons married M. F. Heller. Although a Presbyterian himself, Mr. Heller joined in with Mr. Thorne and they were largely responsible for the building of this place of worship. The same force of carpenters built St. Alban's Chapel immediately after completing the Williamsburg Presbyterian Church. This Presbyterian Church donated the use of the pews of its old church to St. Alban's until St. Alban's secured some of its own. The Reverend E. C. Steele, Protestant Episcopal missionary, was largely instrumental in the establishment of St. Alban's. The Reverends H. M. Jarvis, R. W. Barnwell, H. B. Bull, Dr. Robert Wilson, and Dr. Walter

Mitchell were ministers of St. Alban's prior to 1922 when the Reverend John Ridout became rector. Messrs. Jarvis and Bull were resident ministers; the others named visited the charge at stated intervals.

In 1922 the handsome rectory of St. Alban's Church was built and furnished. In 1923, the Protestant Episcopal had only one place of worship in Williamsburg County, St. Alban's Church on Hampton Street in Kingstree, and thirty-one communicants.

On February 16, 1875, R. C. Logan conveyed to J. W. Staggers, W. J. Lee, and J. Marion Staggers, trustees Kingstree Baptist Church, a lot of land in the town of Kingstree immediately across Academy Street from the Methodist Church Parsonage, said lot two hundred ten feet on Academy Street, and one hundred fifty-five feet on Brooks Street in the form of a rectangle. It was expressly provided in this deed that no part of the lot conveyed should ever be used as a cemetery or place for the interment of the dead. It was at this time that the Kingstree Baptist Church was moved from its old location on Main Street near Black River. This Church was used by the Baptists in Kingstree until 1913 when it was removed and replaced by the handsome brick structure, the home of the denomination in 1923. The Reverend W. E. Hurt was minister of the Church while this new church was being erected and the building committee was as follows: Dr. W. L. Wallace, M. A. Ross, W. R. Funk, C. M. Hinds, J. B. Gamble, G. F. Williamson, J. F. Rodgers, A. C. Swails, and S. C. Anderson.

In 1878, Dr. Robert Henry conveyed to J. M. Keels, E. R. Lesesne, N. T. Pitman, W. S. Varner, and J. W. Nettles, trustees of the Mount Hope Baptist Church, four acres of land whereon the church stood at that time. This church served the people of the Greelyville community for many years and until it was moved into the town. There is yet about this old church a well kept burying ground still used by the Baptists of that section.

In 1884, Mary Cade, Sarah E. Cade, and Charles W. Cade conveyed to H. J. Williamson, Jacob Rodgers, and C. W. McClam, trustees of the Midway Baptist Church, one-half acre of land in the present town of Cades, and the Midway Baptist Church was then moved to this new location.

During the past fifty years, the Baptist denomination has had a remarkable growth in Williamsburg. In 1923, there were fifteen hundred seventy-five members of the missionary Baptist Church in Williamsburg County and this denomination had the following active growing congregations: Antioch, Hemingway, Bloomingvale, Cades, Cedar Grove, Kingstree, Johnsonville, Lanes, Mount Tabor, Trio, Taft, Paron, Piney Forest, Piney Grove, Spring Gulley, Pleasant Hill, and Nesmith.

The following have served as ministers in the County during this period: J. B. Hicks, Elijah Hicks, J. D. Andrews, H. L. Oliver, T. P. Lide, L. T. Carroll, J. T. Burrows, William Moss, J. L. Rollins, S. M. Richardson, Simon T. Russell, J. M. Weaver, J. W. Kramer, J. T. Rollins, W. D. Moorer, A. M. Pitman, F. W. Eason, J. W. Bishop, G. T. Gresham, C. F. Ramsbottom, J. Henry Snyder, W. E. Hurt, and E. A. McDowell. The following were Baptist ministers resident in Williamsburg and serving churches in 1923: J. W. Morris, B. D. Thames, Hemingway; J. A. Turner, Cades; F. C. Hawkins, Kingstree; J. R. Funderburk, Greelyville.

The Methodist Episcopal Church in Kingstree used the building erected in 1853 as its house of worship until 1911, when it was removed and replaced by the handsome church now standing. At that time the Reverend W. A. Fairy was minister and the building committee was composed of F. W. Fairey, Chairman; A. C. Hinds, Secretary and

Treasurer; J. F. McFadden, E. C. Epps, L. J. Stackley, P. H. Stoll, A. M. Gordon, and H. D. Reddick.

Hebron Methodist Church was built in 1874. W. E. Smith "for and in consideration of the love I bear for the Cross of Christ and for an earnest desire to promote His heritage on earth, I do give, grant, and by these presents convey unto W. D. Coker, Jesse Christmas, J. M. Kennedy, A. DuBose, C. W. DuBose, one acre of land on the East side of Long Branch and on the South side of the road leading by J. M. Coker's to Cades Turnout."

The Salters Methodist Church was built in 1875 on land donated by T. Edward Salters to W. S. Camlin, S. S. Britton, E. J. Park, J. M. Owens, and S. B. Green, trustees.

New Market Methodist Church was built in 1876 on land donated by G. D. Rhodus to W. R. Coskney, Joseph S. Cantey, William M. Tobias, Dr. James M. Burgess, and Gabriel D. Rhodus, trustees.

Concord Methodist Church was built in 1882 on land granted by D. Z. Martin to J. M. McCants, R. J. Morris, Charles Boyd, J. E. Timmons, Hugh Boyd, W. J. Jefferson, and William W. Boyd, trustees.

Prospect Methodist Church was built on one acre of land granted by James and Elizabeth Eaddy to William Johnson, James Snow, Edward D. Eaddy, B. H. Stone, and James H. Stone, trustees, on the sixth day of June, 1891.

Dr. Cleland B. Graham in 1901 deeded two acres of land to Jackson Gordon, Hugh Cooper, Sr., Thomas Pressley, Samuel McCutchen, William Morris, Benjamin Cunningham, D. S. Cooper, R. H. Cooper, trustees of Bethesda Methodist Episcopal Church.

S. E. Cade in 1901 donated one-half acre of land in the town of Cades to the following board of trustees for the use of the Methodist Episcopal Church, South, S. B.

Newsom, W. D. Coker, J. McB. Graham, W. Lawrence Graham, and R. Erasmus Cade.

In 1907 Orange Brewington conveyed to B. S. Smith, R. B. Marshall, and Lemuel Smith, trustees, one acre of land on which the church then stood for the use of the Elim Methodist Episcopal Church, South.

Among the Methodist ministers who have served the church at Kingstree and other churches in the County since 1876 may be mentioned: John A. Rice, R. W. Spigner, W. S. Martin, N. A. Brunson, W. B. Duncan, J. C. Counts, W. H. Hodges, W. H. Elwell, R. M. DuBose, W. B. Baker, H. J. Cauthern, J. B. Wilson, A. W. Jackson, D. A. Phillips, W. B. Justice, T. J. Clyde, J. E. Mahaffy, W. A. Fairy, J. T. Fowler, G. T. Harmon, Charles B. Smith, J. W. Daniel, W. W. Daniel, J. K. Johnson, B. S. Hughes, W. S. Heath, J. E. Clark, G. T. Rhoad, B. G. Guess, T. E. Derrick, J. W. Jones, M. F. Dukes, W. A. Massibeau, C. C. Derrick, and J. P. Inabnit.

In 1923 there were the following Methodist Episcopal Churches, South, active in Williamsburg: Kingstree, Trio, Suttons, Concord, Harmony, Greelyville, Lanes, Cedar Swamp, Elim, Beulah, Cades, Bethesda, Hebron, Pergamos, Workman, Mount Vernon, Salters, Hemingway, and Ebenezer. There were twenty-six hundred and thirty-eight communicants of this Church in the County.

It has been practically impossible to secure accurate statistics as to the membership of the Free Will Baptist Churches of Williamsburg. There were probably more than twenty places of worship for this congregation in the County in 1923. They were all small buildings in rural districts and several of them had considerable congregations. A conservative estimate of the number of members of this denomination, growing out of careful study for the purpose of securing accurate statistics, indicates that there were considerably more than seven hundred and fifty Free Will Baptists in the County in 1923.

Until the Constitution of the United States had been adopted in 1789, every person, man, woman, and child, who settled on land in Williamsburg, had been required to swear to and subscribe an oath that they were Protestants. The inhabitants of Williamsburg unanimously approved of this non-admission of Roman Catholics into the district. While the Constitution of the United States required religious freedom, public sentiment in Williamsburg continued strongly hostile toward Roman Catholics and much of this averse sentiment was existent in the County in 1923. There were, however, in Williamsburg in 1923 fourteen adults who were communicants of Roman Catholic Churches and twenty children who had been taken into this Church by baptism. Of these fourteen adults who were Roman Catholics, not one of them was born in Williamsburg County and only five of them were native born Americans. There has never been a Roman Catholic Church erected in Williamsburg County.

In 1923, there were twenty Hebrews in Williamsburg, still faithful worshippers of Jehovah, the God of Abraham and of Isaac and of Jacob. No Jewish temple has ever been erected in this County, but the Law that Moses brought from the summit of Sanai has ruled this land since Roger Gordon settled at the King's Tree.

This County has furnished a number of ministers and missionaries during the past fifty years, among whom were: Samuel Fulton, Presbyterian missionary to Japan; Darby M. Fulton, the past thirty years pastor of the First Presbyterian Church in Darlington; J. Screven Brockinton, a Presbyterian minister in New York, who died about 1915; N. B. Clarkson and G. F. Clarkson, Methodists; F. A. Budden, now pastor Bethel Methodist Church in Charleston; Ernest Epps, Methodist, serving on special board duty of his denomination; Miss Leila Epps, daughter of Edwin Epps, Methodist missionary to Brazil; and Miss Hannah Plowden, daughter of M. H. Plowden, Baptist missionary to China.

In 1923 the number of white church members exceeded the adult white population in Williamsburg. In the town of Kingstree there were only six white adults who were not members of a church, and every one of this six was a new comer into the municipality. These facts are remarkable. It must not be understood from all this that Williamsburg has actualized the Kingdom of Heaven within its domain, even though it is a good place in which to live. It is very much like other American communities, notwithstanding its almost unanimous church membership.

Ministers of Protestant religious denominations have labored in Williamsburg continuously since 1736. With two or three notable exceptions, they have preached that the Bible is the sole source of revelation of God to man, and that its King James version, supplemented by Ussher's chronology, must be accepted verbatim et literatim et punctatim upon pain of eternal Death. They have proclaimed the Roman triune divinity, making God synonymous with Fear, substituting the pope and king created Christ for the merciful Nazarene, and declaring the Holy Ghost too much clothed in power for human contemplation. Their Trinity is an arbitrary Thing working its will on helpless man for its own glory; their Heaven is a jasper walled city where these three awful Gods receive after death certain immortal souls to praise them forever; their Hell a lake of solid and liquid fire, where the worm dieth not and the fire is not quenched, into which are hurled the souls of those human beings who while on earth failed to please this awful Three.

Williamsburg ministers, almost without exception, have preached that this world exists only for life beyond the grave. "Love not the world, neither the things that are in the world" has been the basis of nearly all of their sermons. From these selections from songs these ministers taught the people to sing may be gathered some idea of their theology: "This world's a wilderness of woe, this world is not my home." "What is life? 'Tis but a vapor. Soon it is vanished away. Life is like a dying taper. Oh! my soul! Why wish to stay?" "We should suspect some danger nigh when we possess delight." "Oh could we die with those that die, and place us in their stead; then would our spirits learn to fly, and converse with the dead. We should almost forsake our clay before the summons comes, and pray and wish our souls away to their eternal home." "I am but a stranger here, Heaven is my home. Earth is a desert drear, Heaven is my home."

The Reverend Mr. Ervin, in 1830, recommended to Samuel McGill the singing of hymns instead of dancing as an amusement. Practically every minister who has preached in Williamsburg for the past century would have done the same thing. Their theology has made them preach that all human desires are evil and that the nearer a man can overcome them the purer his heart will be. Since these ministers preach the Bible is the sole source of knowledge of the origin and development of things, they have resisted strenuously everything along this line that biology, geology, and allied sciences have revealed. Probably there is not in South Carolina in 1923 a denominational college president who would openly admit to a Williamsburg audience that the theory of Evolution is earnestly taught in his institution. Nor would any of them admit thus that India, China, Chaldea, Egypt, or even Greece taught the world anything about God.

These ministers of Williamsburg have talked a lot of Jesus Christ, but little have they known the Nazarene. In their pulpits, they have preached that monstrous god made by mediaeval papal and consistorial bulls. Jesus of Nazareth taught unmistakably of God in man, of Heaven here and now, and of worship as the love and service of humanity. These ministers have preached that the Devil is in man, that this world is a lesser Hell, and that true worship consists mainly in attending church, supporting its institutions, and paying tithes. From their pulpits they have never established the connection between Jesus of Nazareth and human life, although Jesus was the most intensely human personality of all the ages. The most passionate appeals revivalists have ever made were based on what is to happen to one after death.

A circuit rider in Williamsburg said the other day: "I was often unable to preach in three of my churches during last winter. It was so cold and these churches had no stoves for heating them." Not one of these churches has less than fifty members, and there is not less than three high powered automobiles owned by individual members in each of these three congregations. There are ten members in each one of these three congregations any one of whom could have placed a stove in his church without considering the cost. Either these church members do not know Jesus of Nazareth or they are little concerned in promoting His cause.

Within the last few years, many men in Williamsburg have learned in spite of ex cathedra utterances that Jesus Christ is the most lovable character of the world and that His spirit shows the way, the truth, and the life. One of the most successful business men in Kingstree, a man of highest intelligence and most approved church standing, said the other day: "If every theological seminary in the country were burned to the ground and every book of theological learning abolished from the face of the earth, it would be easier to bring the world to a knowledge of Jesus Christ." This man was thinking of the Christ that he himself knew and of the monstrous god usually preached in Williamsburg as the only begotten Son of God.

A man naturally follows the customs of his fathers. Normally he accepts the religion that he finds and tries to work out his relationship with his God along established lines. It has always taken an unusually strong man to contribute something to religious life. The priesthood in all ages has been powerful and has not hesitated to use any means within its control to suppress and to destroy any individual who even attempted to approach God otherwise than he had been taught. Jesus Christ was crucified on Calvary because he showed the Sanhedrin a higher God than it had theretofore known. Since Christ was crucified, priests and sanhedrins in every age have crucified as far as they were permitted by the laws of the land every man who has dared to evidence a closer walk with God. Even so has it been in Williamsburg.

Almost without exception the ministers who have served in Williamsburg have been good men—far more human and divine than the mediaeval Christ they have preached. God only knows how earnestly they have labored and how much they have suffered—how often they have preached to vacant pews and looked into empty larders. The Reverend James Wallace has not been the only one who has realized that the more fervently he has preached the more certainly his congregation has turned away from his god. Their yoke has not been easy nor their burden light. The general moral influence of their lives on Williamsburg has been good, for they have lived better lives than their doctrine could have made. They have practiced a reasonable religion, and men have learned the way, the truth, and the life from their conduct much more than from their conversation. Their theology has been bad; their religion, good. Few of them have ever realized that active and productive faith comes only by way of understanding, and that the true God is best known to the man of the highest general mental development. Not many of them have ever touched the average normal man, and, not understanding, they have declared human nature altogether evil.

Many complaints from pulpits have been heard in Williamsburg that so few of the "most promising young men" enter the ministry. The reason is perfectly clear to everybody but "orthodox" theologians. The very highest type of mind finds its supreme delight in the contemplation of God. The best young men of the age would enter the ministry if they did not know that ordination to the priesthood means perpetual incarceration in darker prisons than mamertine walls can make. There were some of the "most promising young men" of Williamsburg in 1923 who were praying fervently for being allowed the privilege of preaching the Gospel, but whose divinely given honesty and intelligence absolutely prevented them from taking the required vows for ordination.

One of the most distinct outward evidences of the inward spiritual growth of the church members of Kingstree was the formation in 1921 of a denominational federation in which the Protestant Episcopal, the Presbyterian, the Baptist, and the Methodist churches, all in town, united for the purpose of holding union services in one of the four churches on the first Sunday evening in each month. In turn, these four denominations worship together at the several churches and the four ministers preach in order to these massed denominational congregations.

In 1921, the Baptist Church in Kingstree secured the services of the Reverend Frank C. Hawkins as its minister. Mr. Hawkins had just completed his theological course at Harvard, having learned of some of the leading men of this age. Mr. Hawkins began his work in Kingstree quietly and earnestly. He felt that Jesus of Nazareth was first of all a teacher, and that teaching God is the primary function of a minister. Mr. Hawkins taught his congregation that God is Love and that Love Law rules the

Universe. He taught his congregation the Christ that Peter and James and John and the lepers and the lame and the halt and the blind knew about blue Galilee. After about two years some people in Kingstree realized that Mr. Hawkins was preaching a more human Christ than they had theretofore known. These people could not understand the divinity of the Christ Mr. Hawkins preached. Whereupon, some of them began to declare that he denied the divinity of Christ and all other things religious teachers usually are charged with denying. The Reverend John Davis, minister of the Presbyterian Church, one of the four churches in the Kingstree federation, asked his elders in official session, whether or not their church should withdraw from the Union on account of the "unorthodoxy" of this Baptist minister. When this was written, June 1, 1923, this Session of Elders had not withdrawn from the Union.

"The morning light is breaking;
The darkness disappears."

CHAPTER XXXVII.

BANKING IN WILLIAMSBURG.

The people of Williamsburg continued to do their banking business in the city of Charleston until the first year of this century. But little money had been required to satisfy their demands. Until 1900, planters shipped their cotton to Charleston and drew drafts on their factors for all the required money. There had been a small demand for money in the County all during the years and this demand was supplied by individuals. After the War between the Sections, for a long time L. W. Nesmith kept some currency on hand and supplied this need in the County. After him came R. H. Kellahan, who had grown wealthy in the turpentine business. In 1900, when the establishment of a bank at Kingstree was seriously agitated, Mr. Kellahan stated that not more than $30,000.00 would be necessary to supply the demand in the entire County and thought that a bank in Kingstree would be useless.

The Bank of Kingstree opened for business on September 11, 1901, with a paid up capital stock of $15,000.00. It was the first banking institution established in Williamsburg County. The original board of directors were R. D. Rollins, H. P. Williams, John A. Kelly, and Dr. D. C. Scott. The first officers: Dr. D. C. Scott, president; John A. Kelly, vice-president; and E. C. Epps, cashier. The first banking house of this institution was a little room in the rear of Dr. Scott's old Drug Store on Academy Street. The furniture and fixtures consisted of one home made pine table, one broken legged chair, and one shot bag for currency. When Cashier Epps had more currency on hand at the close of business on a day than he was willing to trust in one of the iron safes then in use by the merchants in town, he took this shot bag of currency with him to his room and placed it under his pillow during the night. At the close of business on January 1, 1902, the deposits in this, the only bank in the County, were $11,043.99; loans and discounts, $3,567.00; profits, $542.59. In 1904 Director Rollins died and R. H. Kellahan was elected a member of the board of directors to fill the vacancy. In September, 1904, Nabor D. Lesesne was elected assistant cashier. In 1905, the capital stock was increased from $15,000.00 to $30,000.00. At that same time, H. P. Williams resigned as director and J. F. Cooper succeeded him. E. C. Epps resigned as cashier and Fred Lesesne succeeded him. Mr. Lesesne soon resigned when L. H. Fairey filled the vacancy made.

On January 1, 1906, the deposits in this Bank were $246,728.26; loans and discounts, $121,731.53; profits, $12,370.15. As soon as possible after the beginning of business by this Bank, it erected a building on Main Street, wherein it installed modern furnishings and equipment. It occupied this building until 1921, when it leased the ground floor of the Nexsen building, corner of Main and Academy streets, and there equipped very handsome banking quarters. During this time, J. F. Cooper and R. H. Kellahan had died and the number of the board of directors had been increased from four to six. Hugh Cooper, A. C. Hinds, F. W. Fairey, and W. E. Nesmith filled these vacancies. In 1920, J. A. Kelly, Esq., resigned as vice-president and Hugh Cooper succeeded him.

At the close of business April 3, 1923, the Bank of Kingstree had assets to the value of $654,656.95. Its capital stock was then $60,000.00, with a surplus fund of $15,000.00. The officers and directors were Dr. D. C. Scott, president; Hugh Cooper, vice-president; F. W. Fairey, cashier; R. D. Mills and B. V. Singleton, assistant cashiers; and Mrs. Charlton Kelly, stenographer; directors: Dr. D. C. Scott, Hugh Cooper, John A. Kelly, W. E. Nesmith, A. C. Hinds, and F. W. Fairey. Dr. Scott has served as president of this institution continuously from the time of its organization until the day this was written.

The Bank of Greelyville was organized in 1904 with a capital stock of $10,000.00. Its first board of directors were: T. A. Blakely, J. P. Gamble, T. W. Boyle, W. M. O'Bryan, S. J. Taylor, E. D. Rhodus, and J. F. Register. Its first officers: T. W. Boyle, president; W. M. O'Bryan, vice-president; J. F. Register, cashier. In 1907 the capital stock was increased to $15,000.00. C. E. Register served as cashier from 1909 until 1920 and as active vice-president from 1920 to 1923, when forced to resign on account of his health. In 1920 the capital stock was increased to $50,000.00.

The board of directors in 1923 was as follows: T. W. Boyle, W. M. O'Bryan, P. G. Gourdin, J. R. Haynesworth, and H. D. Ferrell. Its officers were: T. W. Boyle, president; W. M. O'Bryan, vice-president; and G. W. Greene, cashier. Mr. Greene became cashier of this Bank in 1920. During the eighteen years in which this Bank has been doing business, the original stock holders have received a total of 112 per cent. in cash dividends and stock dividends of 100 per cent. At the close of business on April 3, 1923, this Bank showed resources to the amount of $147,843.72.

The Bank of Williamsburg began business on January 8, 1906, with a paid up capital stock of $40,000.00. The following were officers: C. W. Stoll, president; F. Rhem, vice-president; and E. C. Epps, cashier. Board of directors, Charles W. Stoll, W. T. Wilkins, P. G. Gourdin, W. I. Nexsen, J. F. McFadden, F. Rhem, T. A. Blakely, and J. C. Graham. In 1913, capital stock was raised to $100,000.00 and a stock dividend of 50% declared. At the close of business on April 3, 1923, the Bank of Williamsburg showed as resources $665,517.96. At this time the directors were: C. W. Stoll, W. I. Nexsen, J. F. McFadden, Dr. I. M. Boyd, W. V. Strong, J. D. O'Bryan, and E. C. Epps. Its officers: C. W. Stoll, president; W. I. Nexsen, vice-president; E. C. Epps, cashier; C. W. Boswell, assistant cashier; R. N. Speigner, teller; Miss Dulcie Lifrage, stenographer.

The Wee Nee Bank of Kingstree began business on July 1, 1910, with paid up capital of $13,800.00 and deposits of $1337.31. The following were first officers: Hugh McCutchen, president; W. V. Strong, vice-president, and E. L. Montgomery, cashier. Directors, H. McCutchen, W. V. Strong, H. E. Montgomery, W. B. Cooper, W. R. Scott, T. K. Smith, and J. K. Smith. E. L. Montgomery resigned as cashier on May 1, 1911, and was succeeded by L. C. Dove, who served in such capacity until January 1, 1919, when he resigned and was succeeded by W. W. Holliday. In 1920 President Hugh McCutchen died and W. V. Strong succeeded him. Mr. Strong began to exercise his office just about the time that "Deflation" set in and for three months he labored continuously for the Bank in that trying financial period. At the meeting of the board of directors at the end of that year, Mr. Strong resigned, telling the directors that he would not serve again as president of that or any other bank for any monetary consideration, that he had more respect for his body and his soul than to crucify them with the troubles of a bank president. Mr. Strong decided at that time that henceforth he would live a farmer's life in the country.

At that time, Thomas McCutchen was elected president and L. W. Gilland, vice-president. At the close of business on April 3, 1923, the Wee Nee Bank showed its resources as $318,644.97. Its officers then were Thomas McCutchen, president; L. W. Gilland, vice-president; W. W. Holliday, cashier; and H. L. Prosser, assistant cashier, Directors: H. E. Montgomery, W. V. Strong, T. K. Smith, J. K. Smith, Thomas McCutchen, L. C. Dove, and L. W. Gilland.

The stockholders of the Bank of Lane met in the office of J. A. McCullough at Lane June 3, 1919. It was announced that all of the $25,000 proposed capital stock had been taken, whereupon the stockholders present elected the following directors: S. W. McClary, J. A. McCullough, H. P. Brown, R. L. Pass, J. C. Graham, J. B. Clarkson, and A. C. Hinds. The following were chosen officers: J. C. Graham, president; J. A. McCullough, vice-president; E. D. McCullough, cashier.

The above named officers and directors of the Bank of Lane were in charge on April 3, 1923, when the statement of the condition of the bank showed its capital stock $25,000.00 and its resources $67,625.25.

The Bank of Cades was organized in 1912 with the following board of directors: W. B. Wilson, F. L. Willcox, L. G. Brock, J. L. McFadden, W. E. Nesmith, Thomas Wilson, W. W. Singletary, V. G. Arnette, and H. F. Fenegan. The following officers were elected on June 12, 1912: W. B. Wilson, president; V. G. Arnette, vice-president; H. J. Fenegan, cashier. The Bank opened for business October 21, 1912, with a capital stock of $10,000.00.

At the close of business on April 3, 1923, this Bank showed as resources $50,268.75. The officers were V. G. Arnette, president; T. J. Cottingham, vice-president; and R. L. Coleman, cashier. Directors: V. G. Arnette, W. I. Hodges, T. J. Cottingham, W. E. Nesmith, and J. B. Wallace.

The Bank of Hemingway was organized in 1912 by Dr. W. C. Hemingway, H. L. Baker, H. E. Eaddy, and N. M. Venters. It began business with a capital stock of $15,000.00 and with the following as officers, Dr. W. C. Hemingway, president; F. E. Huggins, vice-president; and J. A. Doyle, cashier. Directors: W. C. Hemingway, H. L. Baker, J. E. Hemingway, W. C. Rollins, F. E. Huggins, H. E. Eaddy, J. M. Eaddy, N. M. Venters, and John Richardson, Jr. This Bank paid regular 8% dividends

BANKING IN WILLIAMSBURG 501

annually to stockholders until 1920, when the capital stock was increased from $15,000.00 to $50,000.00 and the old stockholders received that year 50% stock dividend and a cash dividend of 26%. The present officers of the Bank are: F. E. Huggins, president; George S. Hemingway, vice-president; and D. G. Huggins, cashier. Directors: F. E. Huggins, George S. Hemingway, W. D. Harmon, E. T. Gaskins, W. A. Lawrimore, A. E. Flowers, H. L. Baker, J. R. Newman, and D. G. Huggins.

The Bank of Trio began business with a capital stock of $30,000.00 on November 26, 1918, with the following officers and directors: Officers, W. T. Rowell, president; J. W. Moore, vice-president; and E. M. Pate, cashier; directors, A. C. Boyd, J. W. Register, J. H. Rowell, J. W. Moore, W. T. Rowell, H. N. Shepard, and E. C. Epps.

The statement of this Bank at the close of business on April 3, 1923, showed as resources $66,182.88. The following were then officers and directors: W. T. Rowell, president; J. W. Register, vice-president; E. M. Pate, cashier; J. H. Rowell, secretary; Miss Helen Hinnant, bookkeeper; directors: W. T. Rowell, J. W. Register, J. H. Rowell, A. B. Cooper, H. N. Shepard, J. W. Moore, and E. C. Epps.

The Farmers Bank of Greelyville was organized in 1919 with the following as officers and directors: Dr. J. F. Haselden, president; H. P. Brown, vice-president; and C. H. Rehberg, cashier; directors: H. D. Ferrell, I. C. Player, G. M. Beasley, W. N. Clarkson, J. R. Haynesworth, A. B. Spivey, C. A. Heins, J. W. Harrington, and H. P. Brown.

The resources of this Bank at the close of business on April 3, 1923, were $64,739.50. Its capital stock was then $21,450.00. The following were officers and directors: J. P. Gamble, president; H. P. Brown, vice-president; C. H. Rehberg, cashier; directors: E. B. Rhodus,

J. P. Gamble, W. N. Clarkson, J. W. Harrington, P. R. Keels, H. P. Brown, and I. C. Player.

The Peoples Bank of Hemingway began business on July 19, 1920, with a capital stock of $29,210.00 and with the following officers and directors: Officers, D. H. Oliver, president; J. M. G. Eaddy, vice-president; J. B. Bushart, cashier; directors: D. H. Oliver, J. M. G. Eaddy, S. J. Haselden, N. M. Venters, P. S. Thomas, G. F. Chandler, L. G. Day, R. W. Stuckey, and L. B. Johnson. On April 3, 1923, the resources of this Bank were $79,231.92 and the following were officers and directors: L. G. Day, president; G. F. Chandler, vice-president; J. B. Bushart, cashier; B. J. Chandler, G. F. Chandler, W. H. Harmon, S. J. Haselden, T. D. Powers, D. H. Oliver, J. M. G. Eaddy, and N. M. Venters.

There were ten banks doing business in Williamsburg County on April 3, 1923. Their combined capital was $465,660.00 and their total resources $2,264,711.89. At this time there were still a large number of substantial men in the County who continued to do a considerable part of their banking business in the city of Charleston and also a large number in the northern part of the County who were interested in the Lake City and Florence banks. When it is remembered that in 1900 there was not a banking institution in the County, the foregoing statements show a remarkable financial growth within a score of years. There was a fearful financial period that followed in the wake of the World War, called Deflation, and the banks in Williamsburg in common with all of the banks in rural sections suffered severely, but the innate honesty and the emergency energy of these "indwellers in Williamsburg" slowly but certainly worked out the salvation of all their banks and all of them now are going strong for a friendly future.

CHAPTER XXXVIII.

THROBBING WAR DRUMS CALL.

The Spanish-American War in 1898 did not arouse so much enthusiasm in Williamsburg as in some parts of the United States. This County, however, furnished a number of volunteers for this short, decisive conflict. Among those who served may be mentioned Surgeon John Boyd, Navy; Artificer J. C. Kinder, Fifteenth United States Infantry; Leroy Lee, Cosmo E. Brockinton, and Franklin L. McCullough, Heavy Artillery, South Carolina Volunteers; R. H. Tisdale, B. M. Mitchum, A. L. Epps, H. A. Strong, John West, Walter McElveen, Arthur Graham, Edward Shirer, Richard J. Ferdon, Charles E. Epps, W. O. Thomas, Robert Cox, R. L. Wise, John McCullough, and Willie Holleman, Second South Carolina Volunteer Infantry.

When the United States entered the World War on April 6, 1917, several men immediately volunteered their services, among whom were: Constant Miller, Eugene King, G. H. Wilkins, Clarence Allsbrook, Sam Caldwell, A. W. McIntosh, J. H. Oliver, W. J. Britton, J. D. Britton, J. H. Scott, S. D. McGill, Will McCullough, Tom Phillips, T. M. Chandler, W. G. Gamble, Deems Baylor, Motte Hanna, Desmore Tisdale, William Crawford, Jack McCullough, Charlie Blakeley, Earl Cook, Ed Vause, Neal Dufford, Carlyle Myrick, Isham Boykin, Joseph H. Ferdon, Laurie Lewis, Ozzie Lovett, Julius P. Gamble, Thad McCullough, Herbert Haselden, Bartow Burgess, Bennie Frierson, J. M. McDaniel, Navy; David Wilmotte Hanna; Walter Battiste, Navy; Edward C. Thompson, Navy; Hazel Strong; Clarence Brunson, Navy; B. H. Lesesne, Marines; A. D. Brown, Navy, on the Florida as sailmaker; John B. Ferdon, C. B. Ferdon, Jr. Nearly all of these men were veterans of the Mexican Border campaign of 1916.

Almost as soon as the United States entered the World War, Congress enacted legislation calling into the military service of the nation all men between the ages of twenty-one and thirty-one years of age and providing ways and means of recruiting these men. In every county in every state in the Union there was created a commission, known as the Local Board, and composed of three men, one of them an active, influential physician and the other two vigorous, substantial citizens. These local boards were charged with the registration, examination, and induction of every man into the military service. Under the law, certain classes of men, married men with dependent families, others regarded as more valuable in the industrial and commercial life of the nation than they could have been in military service, and yet other classes, were exempt from the military service. These local boards were charged with the duty of determining individuals for military service and those exempt under the law. These boards were popularly known as "Exemption boards." It has been often said that no man serving the country during the World War had more difficult duty to perform than the members of these local boards, nor did any governmental agency function more wisely and well than they. All the world wonders at the work they performed.

The Local Board for the County of Williamsburg was originally composed of J. D. O'Bryan, chairman, H. O. Britton, and Dr. T. S. Hemingway. Mr. O'Bryan resigned when he learned that he was within the "draft age" and volunteered. L. W. Gilland succeeded him. During the summer of 1917, Mr. Gilland was stricken with a serious illness which required his resignation. Leroy Lee was appointed as his successor and served until the end of the War. It is hardly possible for anyone who did not serve as a member of one of these County Local

LIEUT. COL. EDWARD C. REGISTER, U. S. A.

Boards to realize the task thrust upon them nor how trying were their labors.

There were many officers from Williamsburg in the World War. Following will be found something about them and their records in the military service.

John H. Woodberry was born near Hemingway February 22, 1890, was appointed cadet, United States Military Academy, West Point, March 1, 1910, graduated June 12, 1914, and was appointed Second Lieutenant, Eighth Cavalry. He was promoted Captain May 15, 1917; Major, Ordnance Department, January 12, 1918; and Lieutenant Colonel, Ordnance Department, August 2, 1919. After the War, he resumed his rank as Major of Ordnance, United States Army, where he now serves.

Philip H. Stoll resigned as Solicitor of this Judicial District, volunteered for military service and was commissioned Major in the Judge Advocate General's Department September 4, 1917. He was assigned to duty as Judge Advocate of the Twelfth Division, Camp Devens, Massachusetts. He was promoted Lieutenant Colonel and Judge Advocate October 10, 1918, serving until honorably discharged from the military service, February 6, 1919. Colonel Stoll was chosen, at a special election in 1919, member of the United States House of Representatives, and reelected in 1920, serving until March 4, 1923. He was a member of the Military Committee and favored Ford's Muscle Shoals project. Colonel Stoll was chairman of the Williamsburg Democratic Executive Committee from 1908 until 1918, was one of the organizers of the Bank of Williamsburg. He is a trustee and steward of the Methodist Episcopal Church in Kingstree. He married Miss Evelyn Cunningham and they have four children.

Edward Chauncey Register was graduated from the Citadel in 1905, attended the Medical College of Virginia in Richmond, Va., from which he was graduated in 1908. He was an interne at Roper Hospital, Charleston, S. C., until June 1909. He practiced medicine in North Carolina until March 19, 1910, when he entered the Medical Corps, United States Army. He was graduated from the Army Medical School in March 1911 and was sent to the Texas border. He married Miss Jeannie DuBose Heyward of Charleston, S. C., on June 1, 1911. From July 16, 1911 to April 26, 1913, he was stationed at Fort McPherson, Ga.; from June 3, 1913 until October 15, 1915, on foreign service in the Philippine Islands and China. On his return to the United States in November 1915, he was stationed at Fortress Monroe and Fort Screven, Ga., until March 11, 1916, when he was ordered into Mexico with Pershing's Expedition. He remained in Mexico until February 1917, was taken ill in March 1917, and was on sick report until February 1918, when he was ordered to Camp Lee, Petersburg, Va., Camp McArthur, Waco, Texas, and Camp Greene, Charlotte, N. C., with the medical department of the Air Service for a few months at each place. In August 1918, he was ordered to Washington for duty in the Surgeon General's office and had charge of the Medical Department of the Student Army Training Corps. In December 1918, he was ordered to Charleston, S. C., where he was in charge of the Medical Department of the debarkation of troops from Europe. In July 1919, he was ordered to France and assisted with the rehabilitation of the German prisoners. He assisted with the closing of the American hospitals in France and the disposing of the property to the French Government. In September 1919, he volunteered to join the American Polish Relief Expedition, organized for the purpose of fighting typhus fever, which was threatening to wipe out the entire population. He reported to Warsaw to Colonel Gilchrist and volunteered to go to Tarnopol, the very worst place in the whole country, to establish hospitals and disinfecting stations. With only an interpreter, he set out for Tarnopol. He found there a frightful condition but, in spite of almost overpowering obstacles, he established three hospitals and many disinfecting stations. Refugees poured through Tarnopol by the thousands and each one had to be examined. When he volunteered for the duty, he knew that forty-five doctors had already sacrificed their lives there. He was the only American there. He was taken ill with typhus fever on December 18, 1919, and died on January 3, 1920. He was given the Distinguished Service Medal by the United States. The Polish Government awarded him two decorations, one "The Polish Cross," the other "The Cross of the Valiant." He is buried in the Churchyard of St. Philip's Episcopal Church, Charleston, S. C. He is survived by his widow and one daughter, Jane DuBose Register, born April 29, 1912. He was First Lieutenant from 1910 to 1914; Captain from 1914 to 1918; Major from February 1918 to July 1918, when he was made Lieutenant Colonel, which rank he held at the time of his death.

Clarence D. Jacobs, M. D., was commissioned First Lieutenant of the Medical Reserve Corps June 5, 1917, and ordered into active service at Fort Oglethorpe, Georgia, August 4, 1917. He was transferred to Camp Lee, Virginia, October 1917. He was assigned to the Medical Detachment of the Five Hundred Eleventh Engineer Battalion in January 1918, when this organization was formed, and went to France with this battalion. He was commissioned Captain Medical Corps, United States Army, August 20, 1918, and promoted Major, May 2, 1919. He returned to the United States with the Five Hundred Eleventh Engineer Battalion in June 1919, and was then honorably discharged from the military service. Major Jacobs married Miss Banna L. Wilkins. They have three sons.

Benton McQueen Montgomery, M. D., volunteered and was commissioned First Lieutenant, Medical Reserve Corps, August 18, 1917, and assigned to duty with the One

Hundred Seventh Ambulance Company and later with the One Hundred Fifth Infantry. He served in the Dichebusch sector, Belgium, during summer of 1918, and in the battles breaking the Hindenberg line along the La Salle River, Jonc de Mer Ridge, and St. Maurice River September and October 1918. His duties required that he work "farthest to the front" in first line dressing stations and often he was attending wounded under shell fire. He was honorably discharged April 2, 1919. Dr. Montgomery married Miss Mayna Claffy of Orangeburg, S. C., and they have two children.

Delos D. McKenzie was discharged as a sergeant in the Marine Corps in July 13, 1917, to receive commission as First Lieutenant of Marines. His discharge as an enlisted man in the Marines shows that his service therein was of the highest degree. It shows him: "An expert rifleman; gun pointer of the first class; military efficiency, excellent; obedience, excellent; sobriety, excellent; service, honest and faithful; battles, Chateau-Thierry front, June 1 to July 6, 1918." After being commissioned, Lieutenant McKenzie was assigned to the Sixth Regiment of Marines and participated in battles of Marne counter offensive, Soissons front, July 18-19; was wounded July 19, by machine gun bullets and high explosive shell, and sent to hospital for ten weeks. He rejoined his organization September 20, and fought about Blanc Mont; Meuse Argonne offensive October 30 to November 11, 1918. From November 17 to December 13, he marched three hundred forty-two kilometres into Germany, occupying area of Coblenz Bridgehead.

Walter H. Harper, M. D., was commissioned first Lieutenant in the Medical Corps of the Naval Reserve Force in New York City August 12, 1918, and sent to duty at the Naval Proving Grounds, Indian Head, Maryland, where he started the Medical Hospital and remained in charge until he was honorably discharged from service in the Navy on March 26, 1919.

Junius M. McIntosh entered service as a civilian in the First Officers Training Camp, Fort Oglethorpe, May 15, 1917, and was commissioned Second Lieutenant in the Quartermasters Corps, August 15, 1917. He served at Camp Jackson and Camp Joseph E. Johnson until June 28, 1918. He sailed for France with the American Expeditionary Forces, July 6, 1918; on duty with them until July 9, 1919. On duty with Motor Truck Company 438, Motor Supply Train 414, Headquarters First Army Corps and Headquarters First Army. On duty in the following sectors and engagements: 1 Vesle Sector, Chateau Thierry Salient, August 11-13; 2 Toul Sector, August 20 to September 12; 3 St. Miheil offensive, September 12-16; 4 Verdun Sector, September 26; 5 Meuse Argonne Offensive, September 26 to November 11, 1918. He was promoted to First Lieutenant, May 3, 1919, and Captain on May 6, 1919. He was commanding officer of Motor Truck Company 441, when this organization returned to the United States on July 5, 1919. He was honorably discharged July 9, 1919, at Camp Upton, New York.

William Gadsden Gamble, Jr., was the first volunteer from Williamsburg when the call to the Colors was made in 1916 for service on the Mexican Border. He was then eighteen. He served as musician in the Second South Carolina Infantry, doing outpost duty on the Rio Grande River during the fall and winter of 1916. Honorably discharged as Sergeant Company D, Second South Carolina Infantry, July 16, 1917, and recalled July 25, 1917, being sent to Camp Jackson. From Camp Jackson he was transferred to the One Hundred Fifth Ammunition Train at Camp Sevier and later to the Ordnance Corps and made Ordnance Sergeant October 4, 1917. Later he was promoted to Chief Ordnance Sergeant. He sailed from the United States to France May 26, 1918, and served at the front from August 15 to November 11, 1918, participating in St. Mihiel offensive, Meuse Argonne offensive, Woevere offensive, Defense of Toul Sector and of the Woevere. He served in the Army of Occupation from November 11, 1918, until his return to the United States, March 26, 1919. He was honorably discharged at Camp Jackson, April 3, 1918. He married Miss Lucy Hammond in 1917, and they have three children.

J. D. O'Bryan entered second Training School, Fort Oglethorpe, Ga., August 1917, and after having served one month was discharged on account of underweight. He was inducted into service April 1918 and sent to Camp Jackson. In May 1918 he entered the Fourth Officers Training School at Camp Sevier when in July 1918 he was transferred to Machine Gun Training School, Camp Hancock, Ga. He was commissioned Second Lieutenant of Infantry in October 1918 and assigned to Company Twenty-Eight, Fourth Group, Motor Train Detachment, Camp Hancock, Ga. In November of 1918 he was transferred to Company Twenty-Seven, Fourth Group, Motor Train Detachment, and placed in command of Company, remaining there until discharged January 9, 1919. He married Mrs. Marian McCabe and they have two children.

D. W. Register was commissioned a First Lieutenant in the Medical Corps of the Navy in May 1917, served during the World War, and resigned in 1922. He was graduated in 1914 from College of Physicians and Surgeons, Atlanta, in 1914, and settled in Atlanta to practice his profession after his service in the Navy.

McBride McFadden enlisted at Fort Screven, Ga., on April 23, 1918. On May 1, 1918 he was sent to Camp Oglethorpe with the Seventeenth Infantry. He was transferred on May 15 to Fort McPherson, Ga. On July 15 of the same year he went to Camp Meade, Maryland, where he was appointed First Sergeant of Company C, Seventy-Second Infantry, about the eighteenth day of July. Soon

SERGEANT LEROY W. SMITH, U. S. A.

afterward, he was transferred to Field Artillery Central Officers Training School, Camp Taylor, Kentucky, and commissioned Second Lieutenant of Artillery on October 9; was instructor in the Fifty-Fifth Training Battery until November twenty-third, when he went to School of Fire, Fort Sill, Oklahoma, where he was graduated February 1, 1919. He joined the Second Field Artillery at Camp Taylor and remained there until discharged in August 1919, Second Lieutenant of Battery D.

Clinton A. Clarkson and Julius P. Gamble attended officers training camps and were commissioned as Second Lieutenants of Infantry. They served until the end of the War, when Lieutenant Gamble was honorably discharged from the military service, but Lieutenant Clarkson accepted a transfer to the Officers Reserve Corps, United States Army, electing to remain ready on call. Loraine Funk was commissioned a second lieutenant of Infantry and served during the war.

Leroy Watson Smith was born near Cades April 21, 1895. He entered the military service September 21, 1917, and became a Sergeant of Company F, 118th Infantry, Thirtieth Division. Shortly after his arrival in France, he was placed in charge of Battalion Scouts and was held responsible for their instruction. He developed this group of men into an effective force. He participated in the Ypres-Lys offensive and the Somme offensive, Ypres trench sector, Bellicourt, Montbrehain, Bohain, Branscourt, and St. Martins. Sergeant Smith was awarded by the United States government the Distinguished Service Cross for Valor under Fire, and the British Empire its medal "For Bravery in the Field." General Orders No. 6, paragraph 23, February 8, 1918, American Army in France, thus cites Sergeant Smith: "During the attack at St. Martin's Reviere, 17th October, 1918, this non-commissioned officer, soon after the jump off, collapsed from gas, but realizing that he possessed the only compass and that it would be impossible for his company to advance properly through the smoke and fog without its assistance, struggled along by his company commander, indicating the proper direction with his hands, being unable to speak. He declined to go to the rear, though violently ill at the time, and assisted in organizing those lost in the fog, and later led a patrol to establish liaison with the right flank under heavy machine gun fire. His bravery and devotion to duty was an inspiration to all of his comrades."

There were five men of Williamsburg killed in battle during the World War: Four white—Deems Baylor, October 14, 1918; William P. Camlin, October 17, 1918; David Wilmot Hanna, October 1, 1918; Thomas G. Norton, October 8, 1918; and one colored—Walter Paul, September 29, 1918.

The following white soldiers died of disease during the War: Edwin A. Cribb, July 11, 1918; Isaac E. Davis, November 9, 1918; Dewey H. Douglass, March 29, 1918; Henry Gilliard, October 5, 1918; Joe E. Jordan, September 22, 1918; Henry L. McCants, October 11, 1918; Herbert J. McCutchen, November 16, 1918; Henry C. Myrick, January 7, 1918; Ashton T. Nelson, October 2, 1918; Thomas T. Pope, October 12, 1918; John H. Scott, November 16, 1918; Daniel E. St. Louis, March 14, 1918; and James A. Thompson, October 6, 1918; Henry C. Williamson, February 10, 1918; John A. Ross, who died of pneumonia two days after being discharged from the service in 1919.

These colored soldiers died in the service: Israel Burgess, May 14, 1918; Nathan Burrows, October 1, 1918; Ben Cooper, October 3, 1918; Mose Cunningham, September 29, 1918; Walter Fulton, November 16, 1918; Ivory Gamble, October 25, 1918; Carter Johnson, October 8, 1918; Reddick McClam, September 23, 1918; William McClary, September 30, 1918; Henry G. McClary, January 27, 1918; John Montgomery, September 30, 1918; Felix

Moore, October 2, 1918; Richard Moultrie, October 10, 1918; Harpy Mouzon, January 27, 1918; Allen Ravebell, November 28, 1918; John Robinson, October 15, 1918; Alec Scott, June 14, 1918; Sam Tisdale, October 3, 1918; Philip Whitfield, June 28, 1918; and Richard Wilson, January 6, 1918.

Nearly all of the unmarried men, white and colored, between the ages of twenty-one and thirty-one years, in Williamsburg went into the military service during the summer and fall of 1917. The Local Board sent all doubtful cases to higher authority and there were practically none excused for industrial reasons. There were some representatives from almost every family in the military service on January 1, 1918. While in the beginning there was no special interest manifest in this County in the World War, there very soon grew that intense patriotic feeling always characteristic of Williamsburg.

E. C. Epps was chairman of the War Loan organizations in the County and had as his central advisory committee L. W. Gilland, A. C. Hinds, S. J. Deery, M. A. Shuler, N. D. Lesesne, I. A. Calhoun, G. A. McElveen, J. V. McElveen, L. C. Dove, J. D. O'Bryan, P. G. Gourdin, and G. T. Harmon. These men apportioned the Liberty Bonds to the several banks in the County and these banks sold them. P. G. Gourdin was chairman of The Committee for the Sale of War Savings Stamps.

The County was organized for the American Red Cross at the very beginning of the War with Dr. D. P. Frierson as County Chairman. Dr. Frierson had the misfortune to lose his dwelling house and all its contents by fire just about this time and the good people of the County decided that he was entirely justified in resigning. The Reverend G. T. Harmon was elected to succeed him. Mr. Harmon was peculiarly fitted by personality and interest for this work. He served during the War. Mrs. D. C. Scott was vice-chairman; C. W. Boswell, treasurer; Mrs.

P. O. Arrowsmith, secretary. The executive committee was composed of the officers and the following committee chairmen: Mrs. W. G. Gamble, extension; Mrs. W. W. Holliday, membership; Mrs. L. W. Gilland, publicity; Mrs. W. L. Taylor, junior membership; M. A. Shuler, finance; Mrs. D. C. Scott, woman's work; Mrs. W. E. Brockinton, civilian relief; Mrs. R. L. Bass, military relief. The standing committees were composed of the respective chairmen above named and the following: Finance, C. C. Burgess, current expenses, and G. A. McElveen, war fund; extension, W. E. Nesmith, Mrs. G. T. Harmon, Mrs. A. C. Hinds, and Miss Florence Jacobs; publicity, W. F. Tolley, F. E. Bradham, Mrs. J. W. Swittenberg; civilian relief, J. F. McFadden, Miss Selma Thorne, Thomas McCutchen, W. H. Welch; membership, Miss Mamie Jacobs, chairman, Miss Amanda Edwards, Miss Ossie Epps, Mrs. LeRoy Lee; junior membership, Miss Belle Harper, Miss Martha Jenkinson; woman's work, Mrs. W. T. Wilkins, purchasing and shipping, Mrs. T. E. Arrowsmith, hospital garments, Mrs. M. F. Heller, knitting, Mrs. W. E. Nesmith, surgical dressings, Mrs. J. B. Steele work room.

The Williamsburg Herald said: "The extension committee, working constantly, has organized twelve auxiliaries. Much praise is due to the chairman, Mrs. W. G. Gamble, and to W. E. Nesmith, first lieutenant." Auxiliaries to the Kingstree chapter were organized all over the County. At Lane, R. L. Bass was chairman; Cades, Dr. W. J. Haselden; Bethel, R. C. McElveen; Hebron, J. W. DuBose; Trio, W. T. Rowell; Salters, Reverend J. E. Clark; Mouzon, W. O. Fulton; Sandy Bay, J. N. McKenzie; Concord, Hugh Boyd; Cedar Swamp, J. G. McCullough; Greelyville, W. M. O'Bryan; Kingstree (colored), Reverend J. Holman; St. Mary's (colored), Sampson Reardon. Other auxiliaries were organized at Goodwill, St. Johns, Bethlehem, Oak Grove, Bethesda and Piney

Grove. All of the individuals on these committees gave loving and loyal service to their work. The chapter, however, passed special resolutions of appreciation for that done by Mesdames P. O. Arrowsmith, W. L. Taylor, and D. C. Scott.

The American Red Cross asked Williamsburg for $6000.00 in its second War Fund campaign. M. F. Heller was appointed chairman of the executive committee for securing this amount, and with him W. H. Carr and C. W. Stoll, and these special officers, Mrs. P. O. Arrowsmith, secretary, F. W. Fairey, cashier, Mrs. L. W. Gilland, publicity, S. J. Deery, speakers, Mrs. T. E. Arrowsmith, captain of women's team, W. R. Scott, captain of men's team, and the following auxiliary team captains; C. A. Heins, Miss Mellie Ferrell, J. N. McKenzie, Mrs. Garfield McKenzie, John Burgess, Mrs. Bishop Burgess, Mrs. V. G. Arnette, W. M. O'Bryan, Mrs. J. P. Gamble, Willie Cooper, Miss Pet Hanna, Alex Tisdale, Miss Beth McGill, W. D. Bryan, Mrs. B. A. Brown, W. T. Rowell, Miss Gertrude Anderson, W. O. Camlin, Miss Flossie Kellahan, Reverend J. C. Everett, Miss Emmie Ferrell, J. R. Barrow, Mrs. J. R. Barrow, W. M. Bradham, T. W. Boyle, Mrs. E. O. Taylor, W. D. Fulton, Mrs. T. Fulton, J. B. Wallace, Miss Olive Smith, S. L. Parsons, Miss Helen Hinnant, R. L. Bass, Mrs. W. McClary, G. W. Camlin, W. I. Hodges, H. P. Brown, Thomas McCutchen, S. A. Guerry, Mrs. T. M. Cooper, Elmer Rodgers, J. W. Register, and W. J. Smiley.

President Woodrow Wilson set apart by proclamation the week beginning May 20, 1918, as Red Cross week for all the United States. Since May tenth has always been since 1865 "big day" in Kingstree, special authority was obtained from the National Red Cross to begin here on that day. Chairman Heller and his associates prepared a programme for that day that brought a large number of people to Kingstree and $6400.00 was obtained, $400.00

more than had been asked. When the executive committee gathered together that evening, every one was pleased. C. W. Stoll arose immediately after the $6400.00 had been counted and said: "We have more money than the Red Cross asked us to give, but this campaign begins May 20. Let us work this whole county for funds for the Red Cross." And it was done. Mrs. L. W. Gilland, publicity chairman, kept writing articles for the county newspapers. S. J. Deery, speakers chairman, arranged for community meetings in every church and school house, white and colored, in the County and sent three good "four minute speakers" to each assembly. Among these speakers were M. A. Shuler, G. O. Epps, M. F. Montgomery, A. C. Hinds, J. Y. McGill, E. C. Epps, G. M. Beasley, L. W. Gilland, Hugh McCutchen, W. E. Nesmith, G. A. McElveen, W. E. Snowden, T. Olin Epps, Reverend G. T. Harmon, J. J. M. Graham, W. D. Bryan, F. E. Bradham, R. L. Bass, Reverend W. I. Sinnott, Thomas McCutchen, H. E. Montgomery, J. Monroe McKenzie, D. E. McCutchen, J. G. McCullough, R. C. McElveen, and Reverend E. A. McDowell. These speakers and the publicity newspaper work done by Mrs. Gilland aroused such beautiful sentiment that having been asigned a quota of six thousand dollars for the Red Cross the people of Williamsburg actually contributed more than thirty-six thousand dollars. Chairman Heller was given a vote of thanks for his effective work. Among the negroes who were especially active in Red Cross work in the County may be mentioned: Mrs. Flora Nesmith, Dr. W. L. Sellers, J. C. James, G. T. Martin, Samuel Fulton, H. P. Pressley, T. J. Pendergrass, Julius Holman, J. A. Salters, and David Frierson. The negroes contributed their full share of the amount donated to the Red Cross in this County and responded promptly whenever called upon for work.

During the War, financial conditions in Williamsburg were good and little aid beyond that furnished by the Government was required among the soldiers' families. The service which the Red Cross rendered in maintaining commucation between the soldiers in Europe and their families in this country was especially good. Thousands of comfortable things were made by the women of Williamsburg and sent through the Red Cross to the soldiers in the field. After the close of the War, Reverend E. A. McDowell became chairman of the Red Cross in the County. He was succeeded by S. J. Deery, who assumed charge about the time that the returned soldiers needed so much help in straightening out their accounts with the Government as well as securing certain benefits coming to them. A great many soldiers realized the results of being gassed and wounded more seriously after they had returned to their homes and begun their work than they had before they began to labor. It was during this time that the Red Cross employed Miss Daisy Varn, a trained Red Cross worker, as Home Secretary, and for two years the Red Cross rendered very effective service for returned soldiers. Mr. Deery declined re-election in November 1921 and Thomas McCutchen was chosen to succeed him.

CHAPTER XXXIX.

MANY THINGS.

> "The time has come," the walrus said,
> "To talk of many things;
>   Of shoes and ships and sealing wax,
>   Of cabbages and kings."

The "village of Kingstree," the county seat of Williamsburg, was not incorporated until 1866. The municipality then was made to include all that territory within one mile of the Court House, except that Black River should be its western boundary line. The corporate limits of the town have remained unchanged until this day, 1923. Until 1885, the "Branch" flowed almost at will over the eastern portion of the town and these low marshy grounds formed a most favorable breeding place for mosquitoes. In this year, when Captain G. P. Nelson was mayor, a canal was dug from the old Scott saw mill dam in the extreme northeastern corner of the town to Black River, in which channel all the waters in this section flowed rapidly into the river. Until this drainage work had been done nearly everybody who lived in Kingstree from May until November suffered from malaria and frequently typhus played havoc. Consequently, few people undertook residing in Kingstree at all; and those few nearly always migrated to the mountains of Western North Carolina for the mosquito season.

Until about 1900, one in Kingstree might have truly said with the Ancient Mariner, "water, water, everywhere, and not a drop to drink." It was then that artesian wells were bored all over the town, at street corners and at private residences, and these wells began and have continuously flowed the purest water obtainable. One may drink and enjoy enormous quantities of it without discomfort or damage.

In 1910, Kingstree installed a system of water works and sewerage and then completed the conquest of the mosquito, when it became one of the healthiest towns in the State. Malarial fever, typhoid and typhus are now practically unknown in Kingstree and health conditions are practically the same in summer as in winter. Nobody now goes from Kingstree to the mountains in order to escape malaria. Some families migrate every summer but they are impelled to do so by a long formed habit or for other considerations than health.

It was but a few years after Kingstree had been well drained and pure artesian water obtained that people commenced to regard the town seriously as a place for residence. The county, about this time, began to produce tobacco for market and increased the cotton crop. It was then that some enterprising citizens organized the Kingstree Real Estate Company and the Building and Loan Association, both of which entered largely into the growth of the town.

The Kingstree Real Estate Company was organized in 1905 with Dr. D. C. Scott, president; M. F. Heller, secretary and treasurer; J. F. Cooper, J. A. Kelly, M. F. Heller, and Dr. D. C. Scott, as directors. This company purchased sixty-five acres of land from the R. C. Logan estate, divided it into lots, and offered it for sale at reasonable prices. A number of the younger citizens of Kingstree immediately purchased lots and Newtown became within a short time a substantial addition to the old town of Kingstree. Among the first who erected residences in Newton were W. H. Carr, E. C. Burgess, Mrs. Lula Barr, W. M. Vause, and W. V. Strong. Some years later the Williamsburg County Fair Association purchased a part of this land and thereon erected the fair ground building and established the race track.

The Kingstree Building and Loan Association was organized January 10, 1905, with J. A. Kelley, president; C. W. Stoll, vice-president; W. H. Carr, secretary and treasurer, and the following board of directors: J. A. Kelley, LeRoy Lee, Louis Stackley, C. W. Stoll, W. I. Nexsen, W. H. Carr, and C. W. Wolfe. This Building and Loan Association proved a great factor in the upbuilding of the town of Kingstree. W. H. Carr, its secretary and treasurer, was tireless in his efforts and tactful and intelligent in managing its affairs. Probably three-fourths of the residences erected in Kingstree since its organization have been built in part through this company. Mr. Carr died in 1921 and Roland D. Mills succeeded as secretary and treasurer.

A few years after the establishment of a tobacco market in Kingstree, many serviceable brick stores were erected on Main and Academy streets; and again from 1918 to 1920, when the tobacco market became one of the largest in the State, many other brick mercantiles and four very large brick tobacco sales warehouses and several prizeries were erected.

In 1912 the Kingstree Electric Light and Ice Company was formed with P. G. Gourdin as president, E. C. Burgess, secretary and treasurer, D. C. Scott, Jr., as manager. Dr. D. C. Scott was the moving spirit of the organization. The service this company began very soon after incorporation made a distinct mark of progress on the town. In 1922, F. B. Adams purchased half of the stock in this Electric Light and Ice Company and began an aggressive campaign for distributing its products. M. A. Ross has been connected with this company as "general overseer" and "man of all work" ever since its organization.

Several miles of asphalt paving was done in the town of Kingstree in 1922. The only thing about this paving that caused regret to anyone was the removal of many of

HON. R. C. LOGAN

the beautiful old live oak trees planted in 1812 by Colonel Robert L. Witherspoon, who undertook, with much success, to "beautify certain streets in the town." Enough of these old oaks were left on Main and Academy and Church streets to keep them beautiful avenues for comfortable homes. The live oaks on Hampton Avenue were planted by Dr. D. C. Scott.

The County Record, the oldest newspaper in the County, was established by R. C. Logan in 1885. He was its editor for ten years when it was sold in succession to E. G. Chandler, W. E. Cooke, and Louis J. Bristow, each of whom was its editor for a short period of time. In 1898, the Record was purchased by Charles W. Wolfe, who owned and edited it until his death in 1915. The paper was then purchased by W. F. Tolley and R. K. Wallace. Mr. Wallace soon sold out his interest to E. C. Epps, who transferred his rights therein to L. F. Cromer. In 1923, the editor was W. F. Tolley; the owners, Tolley and Cromer.

R. C. Logan—always called "Colonel Logan"—and possibly if any Southern gentleman by virtue of worthiness as such and for community service ever deserved such high military title, this man was he,—aided in establishing in 1856 the first newspaper ever published in Williamsburg County. When he volunteered for service in the Confederate Army and went as Lieutenant of the Wee Nee Volunteers to Charleston in 1861, the Kingstree Star was suspended. After the War, he re-established it and ably edited it for a number of years during the dark days of reconstruction. Later The Star was edited by Herbert B. Cunningham. For many years, Mr. Logan was editor of the Greenville Mountaineer and for sometime connected with the Charleston News and Courier. He was the youngest signer of the memorable Ordinance of Secession of December 20, 1860, which severed the bond between the State of South Carolina and the Federal Union. He was commissioner in Equity from 1862 until the County administration fell into the hands of carpet baggers after the War. He was very active and powerful in fighting the carpet bagger administration in South Carolina, and was one in Williamsburg who never forgave the usurpers. He married Susannah Theresa, daughter of Joseph Scott, who, with four of their children, Mrs. P. B. Thorn, Walter B. Logan, George P. Logan, and Miss Maude Logan, survived him at his death on September 13, 1905. Mrs. Logan died in 1921 at more than eighty-three years of age. George P. Logan, a prominent attorney of Columbia, died in 1923.

Charles W. Wolfe was born near Benson April 14, 1870, and was educated at the Citadel and at Wofford College. He taught school in South Carolina for some years, his last labors along this line being as principal of the Bennettsville schools. After this time, he attended a business college in Atlanta. One day while a student there, the Governor of Alabama asked the superintendent of that business college if he had a student capable of becoming private secretary. The superintendent recommended Mr. Wolfe, who was appointed by His Excellency, the Governor of Alabama, as his private secretary, in which place Mr. Wolfe served with special distinction. In 1898, Mr. Wolfe was elected a member of the County delegation in the General Assembly and was Chairman of the Committee on Public Printing. He was editor of the County Record from 1898 until his death in 1915, during which time he made it outstanding as a weekly county paper. His editorials were read and approved by the leading men of the State. During the greater part of his maturer manhood, Mr. Wolfe was a continuous sufferer from physical maladies. This greatly handicapped his career. At the time of his death, he was easily one of the most popular men in the County and was generally regarded the most brilliant. He was descended from landgrave Thomas Smith, colonial governor of South Carolina, and from John Scott, of Williamsburg, 1732, the oldest English and Scotch-Irish blood lines in South Carolina.

About forty years after Appamattox, the surviving veterans of the War Between the Sections had grown old and one by one began silently "putting out to sea." The very term "Confederate Veteran" has ever been a synonym for veneration and respect, but the passing of these old heroes brought home to Williamsburg the duty of perpetuating the memory of its Dead and of honoring its Living Veterans of that War. Mrs. D. C. Scott (Martha Brockinton) and some other women organized in Kingstree a chapter of the Daughters of the Confederacy, with Mrs. Scott as its first President. These good women with organized effort at once began the beautiful labor. They gave new interest to the celebration of Confederate Memorial Day, May tenth, and made it forever a sacred day in Williamsburg. With Mrs. Scott as the moving spirit, the Daughters of the Confederacy and the citizens of the County erected in 1910 the handsome granite monument at the junction of Main and Academy streets in Kingstree to the memory of Williamsburg's Confederate Dead. The inscriptions on this monument were written by Charles W. Wolfe. In 1923, the Daughters of the Confederacy had a large, enthusiastic organization, with Mrs. T. S. Hemingway (Laura Cromer) as President. In this year, the John G. Pressley Camp of Confederate Veterans, Commander H. J. Brown presiding, at its meeting in Kingstree on May tenth, invited the sons and grandsons of Confederate Veterans to unite with the organization and make it perpetual. A large number of young men enrolled as members, each one pledging in his heart to keep alive the beautiful history and tradition of the Confederacy.

About 1910, Mrs. Scott joined in with the Pee Dee Historical Society as the executive from Williamsburg and assisted in publishing a revised and enlarged edition of Bishop Gregg's History of the Old Cheraws. She contributed the addenda from this county in that valuable work. She also organized in Kingstree the Margaret Gregg Gordon chapter of the Daughters of the American Revolution and was its first Regent. This organization revived much interest in the Revolutionary history of the County and has been instrumental in collecting and preserving data that would otherwise have been lost. Miss Marion McFadden was Regent of this chapter in 1923.

In 1917 the Williamsburg Presbyterian Congregation deeded to the Williamsburg Cemetary Association the lot of land, which it had secured from Roger Gordon in 1738 and which had been used as its churchyard, for a burying ground for the white people of Kingstree and the vicinity. This cemetery association was composed of four members from the Presbyterian Church: Mrs. D. C. Scott, Mrs. Christina J. Nelson, Miss Beulah Nelson, and Mrs. John S. Fulton; one member from the Baptist Church, Mrs. M. A. Shuler; one from the Episcopal Church, Mrs. W. G. Gamble; and one from the Methodist Episcopal Church, Mrs. Julia S. Kennedy. Mrs. Scott died October 8, 1922, and Mrs. Nelson became chairman of the Association. In 1916, R. H. Kellahan died and bequeathed this cemetery association $3000.00 for the use of this board of trustees in the upkeep of the graveyard.

The Kingstree Masonic Lodge, Number 46, was organized in 1859 with Samuel W. Maurice, Worshipful Master; Angus McKenzie, Senior Warden; William E. Smith, Junior Warden; and William C. Footman, Secretary. During Reconstruction days, Republican politicians succeeded in making some negro members of this lodge, whereupon all native white members withdrew. Later, the lodge roll was purged and the order once again became a force in Kingstree. In 1923, M. H. Jacobs was Worshipful Master, B. E. Clarkson, Senior Deacon, H. L. Prosser, Junior Deacon, and Donald Montgomery, secretary. In connection with this Lodge, should be named J. C. Lanham, a commercial salesman, who has been coming to Kingstree and Williamsburg for more than thirty years. Mr. Lanham is a highly intelligent member of a distinguished family. He has always been deeply interested in Masonry, and has done much towards helping the Kingstree lodge do its worthy work.

Cohen Whitehead, a negro, was the last of the Reconstruction postmasters in Kingstree. He was succeeded by Mrs. C. M. Chandler, who held office under Cleveland. She was succeeded by Louis Jacobs in 1898, who held the office until his death, October 13, 1913. He was succeeded by Louis Stackley, the incumbent. Assisting Mr. Stackley in 1923, under civil serice appointments, were Misses Annie Stackley and Agnes Fulton and Mrs. G. H. Wilkins. G. H. Wilkins was the Kingstree postman.

Since Reconstruction the mayors of Kingstree have been S. W. Maurice, Dr. J. F. Brockinton, W. H. Kennedy, M. J. Hirsch, R. H. Kellahan, Thomas M. Gilland, Louis Stackley, C. W. Stoll, J. A. Kelley, L. P. Kinder, Louis W. Gilland, M. A. Shuler, and W. R. Scott, incumbent. In 1923, the aldermen of Kingstree were: E. F. Martin, F. W. Fairey, L. D. Rodgers, H. A. Miller, T. E. Arrowsmith, and W. E. Jenkinson; J. F. Scott was town clerk; H. U. Kinder, chief of police, and T. E. Frierson, night policeman. L. R. McIntosh was chief of the Fire Department. The town had a simple brick building wherein iron cells were arranged for the safe keeping of violators of the law, but the doors of this jail were rarely ever shut except for the purpose of keeping dogs from sleeping on the cots therein.

There were three men about Kingstree within the past half century who were institutions in themselves—who knew Williamsburg past and present, and who contributed much in their day and generation to the amusement and entertainement of the people. Dr. Samuel McGill was the first of these. His "Reminiscences of Williamsburg" was published and will remain forever a moving picture of the County from 1820 to 1900. With glowing humor, Dr. McGill kept Williamsburg laughing for half a century, and his book preserves much of him and his pleasing personality. Probably, no man who ever lived in Williamsburg had a clearer view of the War between the Sections than he, nor did any one more than he help heal the wounds the War had made.

George S. Barr was a merchant and hotel keeper in Kingstree for many years. No man ever added more to the "gayety" of the town than he. As "mine host" his equal has never appeared in these parts. Every day for a score of years the people of Kingstree repeated what George Barr had said the previous night, and every night they gathered in his hotel lobby to hear him recount the things that had happened during that day. No lesser man than Charles Dickens is worthy to describe George Barr, and "here's hoping" that an understanding Dickens may give him to coming generations.

John James Brockinton Montgomery, alias "Daddy," has held continuous levees on the shady court house green for more than thirty years. Sheriff G. J. Graham listened to "Daddy's" tales every day for the twenty years he was sheriff, and now when this venerable citizen comes to Kingstree he has not spent a "perfect day" until "Daddy" has entertained him with a story. Mr. Montgomery has been auditor of Williamsburg since 1900, and few politicians even years ago had the hardihood to attempt to disturb his place. For many years, nobody has offered as a candidate against him. Mr. Montgomery knows taxation as applied to Wiliamsburg and his office has always been kept along model lines. He knows the "previous condition of servitude" of every white man in Wiliamsburg and every man likes to hear him tell stories about every other man. He is dean of the Court House contingent and no man questions his kindly rule.

Among the physicians who have lived in Williamsburg during the period from the War between the Sections until the present time may be mentioned: W. S. Boyd, Sr., T. S. Hemingway, John F. Brockinton, James S. Brockinton, W. L. Wallace, James Staggers, R. F. Maurice, Samuel McGill, Robert Henry, James Bradley, J. A. James, W. D. Rich, S. D. M. Byrd, J. W. Graham, Richard Fulmore, A. H. Williams, Henry DuBose, D. C. Scott, Robert Gourdin, J. F. Pressley, Van Epps, W. G. Gamble, J. M. Burgess, W. V. Brockinton, R. J. Fulton, C. D. Jacobs, T. M. Mouzon, T. S. Hemingway, J. M. Mason, W. S. Boyd, William S. Boyd, Isaac Boyd, W. L. Sellers, W. S. Lynch, J. F. Register, B. M. Montgomery, W. H. Woods, E. O. Taylor, E. T. Kelley, Maurice Scott, Walter H. Harper, O. F. Hagan, A. M. Willcox, T. Cuyler Harper, J. D. Eaddy, H. O. Byrd, R. W. Sease, W. L. Whitehead, W. C. Rogers, John Rhett Brockinton, R. L. Cockfield, T. B. Harper, W. M. O'Bryan, Charles H. Pate, W. J. Haselden, J. F. Haselden, J. C. Moore, W. C. Hemingway, P. S. Thomas, A. G. Eaddy, John W. Staggers, S. B. W. Courtney, J. H. Pratt, H. L. Baker, L. B. Johnson, C. D. Rollins, John Boyd, and Carl Epps.

Among the dentists may be mentioned M. D. Nesmith, C. D. Haddon, R. C. McCabe, R. J. McCabe, Jack McCullough, J. A. Cole, D. Z. Rowell, Frank O. Lentz, and A. M. Snider.

Among the lawyers natives of the County or who practiced here: S. W. Maurice, George P. Logan, E. J. Porter, Paul A. Cooper, E. H. Williams, E. G. Chandler, J. S. Wilson, John O. Willson, Texas Logan, John Hughes Cooper, Barron Greer, R. J. Kirk, H. J. Haynesworth, T. M. Gilland, John A. Kelley, LeRoy Lee, A. C. Hinds, J. Capers James, M. A. Shuler, L. W. Gilland, J. Z. McConnell, J. D. O'Bryan, Philip H. Stoll, M. J. Hirsch,

E. L. Hirsch, F. R. Hemingway, W. W. Boddie, John Barron, B. P. Barron, R. K. Wallace, F. W. Fairey, C. E. St. Amand, W. O. Godwin, P. N. Becton, Junius McIntosh, Robert Pierson, E. L. Ard, C. W. Stoll, Hoxie G. Askins, J. D. Gilland, W. Furman Dargan, R. D. Epps, Timothy Dargan, W. L. Bass, John G. Pressley, D. A. Brockinton, and Heyward Brockinton. Colonel John G. Pressley migrated to California in 1869 and there became a distinguished jurist. Judge John S. Wilson moved to Manning as a young man. For more than twenty years, he has been a distinguished circuit judge.

Dr. John O. Wilson became a powerful minister in the Methodist Episcopal Church, South, and was one of the three who determined the legal polity of the Methodist Church in the Southern States. He died in 1923 while President of Lander College.

During the late seventies, Major C. S. Land worked the Southern portion of the County for naval stores products. He built a tramway for transporting logs from Lane to the western boundary of the County. In 1880, he sold this right of way to the Atlantic Coast Line Railway and immediately a standard gauge railroad was built from Lane westward through the County on to Sumter. In 1881, the first trains were put in operation on this railway. This railroad played a considerable part in the development of this Santee section. Along this railway was a section of country known as "Clocktown" for many years. It was told that soon after the War some agents selling seven-day clocks of considerable proportions and telling everything from one's "fortune" to the second of time went through this country and sold these clocks to all the inhabitants thereof. Some of these inhabitants, the story goes, lived in dwellings that could not contain these clocks so that some of the clocks were fastened to large pine trees nearby these dwellings. Nobody ever lived in "Clocktown," but it was well known in the County.

About 1870, S. J. Taylor and S. J. Hutson had the town of Greelyille incorporated and S. J. Taylor was elected the first intendant. It was then depending largely on the turpentine industry. Later it developed into a flourishing town. The first postmaster of Greelyville was Wade S. Varner; second, W. H. Campbell; third, H. D. Oliver. In 1899 Fred Mishoe became postmaster and still holds the office. Among those who have served as station agents at Greelyville have been Wade S. Varner, W. H. Campbell, Frank Welch, and David Sasser, Fred Mishoe, W. H. Hodges, T. S. Brunson, and W. D. Matthews. The first Masonic Lodge at Greelyville had as its officers: B. E. Clarkson, Worshipful Master; C. E. Hilton, Senior Warden; and D. A. Johnson, Junior Warden. The first drainage district for the purpose of reclaiming swamp lands in Williamsburg County was established in the Greelyville section. Its principal promoters were T. W. Boyle and E. B. Rhodus. About twenty thousand acres of excellent farming lands have been added by the efforts of this project. The Mallard Lumber Company has been of much service in the development of this Greelyville District.

H. J. Brown, more than four score years old, Coroner of Williamsburg County, Commander of John G. Pressley Camp of Confederate veterans, Deacon in the Baptist Church, and for many years Superintendent of the Baptist Sunday School at Cades, has lived through more than the allotted time of man in the Cades section and knows its history. When asked about Cades, he replied, "I was ten years old when I came to Cades in 1852. It was then known as Camp Ridge and C. W. Cade was postmaster. He kept the office at his home where H. L. Poston now lives. He had three boys about grown and they carried the mail on horseback to Santee Postoffice and to Darlington once every week. General Marion had a recuperation camp during the Revolution in the field on the opposite side of the road from where Larry Poston has recently settled. This place was called Camp Ridge from this fact. About the time my father moved to Cades, several other families came and joined with the other residents and built a school house near where M. Clark now lives. The patrons of this school were: on the north, Littleton Dennis, R. B. Green, Levi Brown, and Patrick Parker; on the east, C. A. Cade, John F. Graham, and Brown Graham; on the south, John Frierson and James E. Fulton; on the west, Martin S. Feagan and Benjamin Baker. Some of these men lived four miles from the little log school. The first teacher was named Palmer and boarded at Mr. Cades. The next teacher was Mr. Andrew Cade, and then came J. A. Feagan. These men taught three months in the year. In 1856, the Northeastern railway came through Cades, but it did not establish a depot for many years. Several turpentine stills were in operation, however. The first section boss on this railroad was named Pettit. He was killed by a train before his year was up. Charles DuBose was the next postmaster. He was succeeded by J. N. Sauls in 1883. E. H. Sauls became postmaster in 1887 and it was at this time that the name of the postoffice was changed from Camp Ridge to Cades. The railway then built a station house at this point and several stores were in operation. T. P. Fulmore became postmaster in 1907. He was succeeded by V. G. Arnette in 1913. L. G. Brock succeeded him and then came R. E. Tart, who was succeeded by W. J. Smiley, incumbent. There is a handsome graded school building, two churches, five stores, two meat markets, and a bank at Cades, which is in the midst of a good farming community. Its citizens are law abiding and prosperous."

Captain John A. Salters owned the plantation on which Salters depot was established and for him the town of Salters was named. Prior to the Civil War, mail was brought on horseback from Kingstree to William Lifrage's place just south of Black River where S. P. Britton now lives and the postoffice was called Black River. Theodore M. Lifrage was postmaster. During the War, this postoffice was discontinued. About 1870, Maxmilian Jacobs had a postoffice established about two miles south of Salters depot. It was called Dixie. This postoffice was in existence about one year. In 1873 a postoffice was established at Salters depot. Mrs. M. J. Rawlinski was postmistress until 1877 when Dr. R. F. Maurice succeeded her. He was postmaster until February 5, 1879, when J. G. Lifrage, incumbent, took charge. He has held this office continuously for more than forty-four years.

In 1883 W. D. Bryan, W. R. Bryan, and James Bryan lived on the railway in the sutheastern part of the County. They established a postoffice with James Bryan as postmaster and called it Trio. Helen M. Hinnant was incumbent in 1923.

In 1881, James Fowler Cooper had Fowler postoffice created and was postmaster until his death in 1914, when his brother, Hugh M. Cooper, incumbent, succeeded him. Cooper Brothers, merchants and planters, have their headquarters at Fowler.

Nesmith postoffice was established October 1, 1907, with R. J. Nesmith as Postmaster. B. L. Nesmith succeeded him December 31, 1912. This place was given its name from the old family so numerous in that vicinity.

Henry postoffice was named by J. J. Snow, a prominent scion of distinguished family in those parts. W. T. Turbeville became postmaster when the office was created in 1913 and is the present holder.

C. J. Rollins was the first postmaster at Lamberts. This post office was established about 1900. In 1913, Lamberts was changed in name to Hemingway, in honor of W. C. Hemingway, father of Dr. W. C. Hemingway, who was accidently killed by an explosion in his laboratory in 1921. Hemingway has grown into a considerable town within the past decade. The Masonic Lodge at Hemingway was formed at Indiantown in 1872, with John Frierson, Worshipful Master, H. L. Hanna, Senior Warden, and D. L. Keith, Junior Warden. Its headquarters were changed to Hemingway about ten years ago, but it is still known as the Indiantown Lodge, No. 165. Its present officers are: Z. H. McDaniel, Worshipful Master, R. A. Hughes, Senior Warden, D. H. Oliver, Junior Warden, and W. F. Hanna, secretary.

For a long time, young women have been coming into Williamsburg as school teachers every year. Many of the best of them have married Williamsburg men, and almost without exception, they have proved valuable in home, church, and general community service. Possibly no one influence working in Williamsburg has been more wholesome and elevating than these educated women brought from other districts. Among them may be named Mesdames M. F. Heller, J. J. B. Montgomery, LeRoy Lee, W. V. Brockinton, P. O. Arrowsmith, R. K. Wallace, T. S. Hemingway, John S. Fulton, L. F. Rhem, J. Y. McGill, D. E. Evans, Hugh M. Cooper, Stuart Cunningham, John Cunningham, John Foxworth, J. B. Allsbrook, S. W. Mimms, Dodd Daniel, W. W. Holliday, J. H. Epps, Robert Montgomery, G. A. McElveen, D. M. Ervin, L. S. Dennis, W. S. Boyd, Wilbur Eaddy, and Lawrence Swails.

To all outward appearances, Williamsburg in 1923 was almost perfectly Puritan. More than ninety-nine per centum of all the social gatherings in the County were under the auspices of church or patriotic organizations. Churches had many societies and the frequent meetings of these absorbed most of the "herding" energies of the people. Christian Endeavors, Epworth Leagues, and Young Peoples Unions almost circumscribed the social activities of the younger element; while Missionary Societies, Ladies' Aid Societies, and the like, almost encompassed the field for the matrons. The men of the

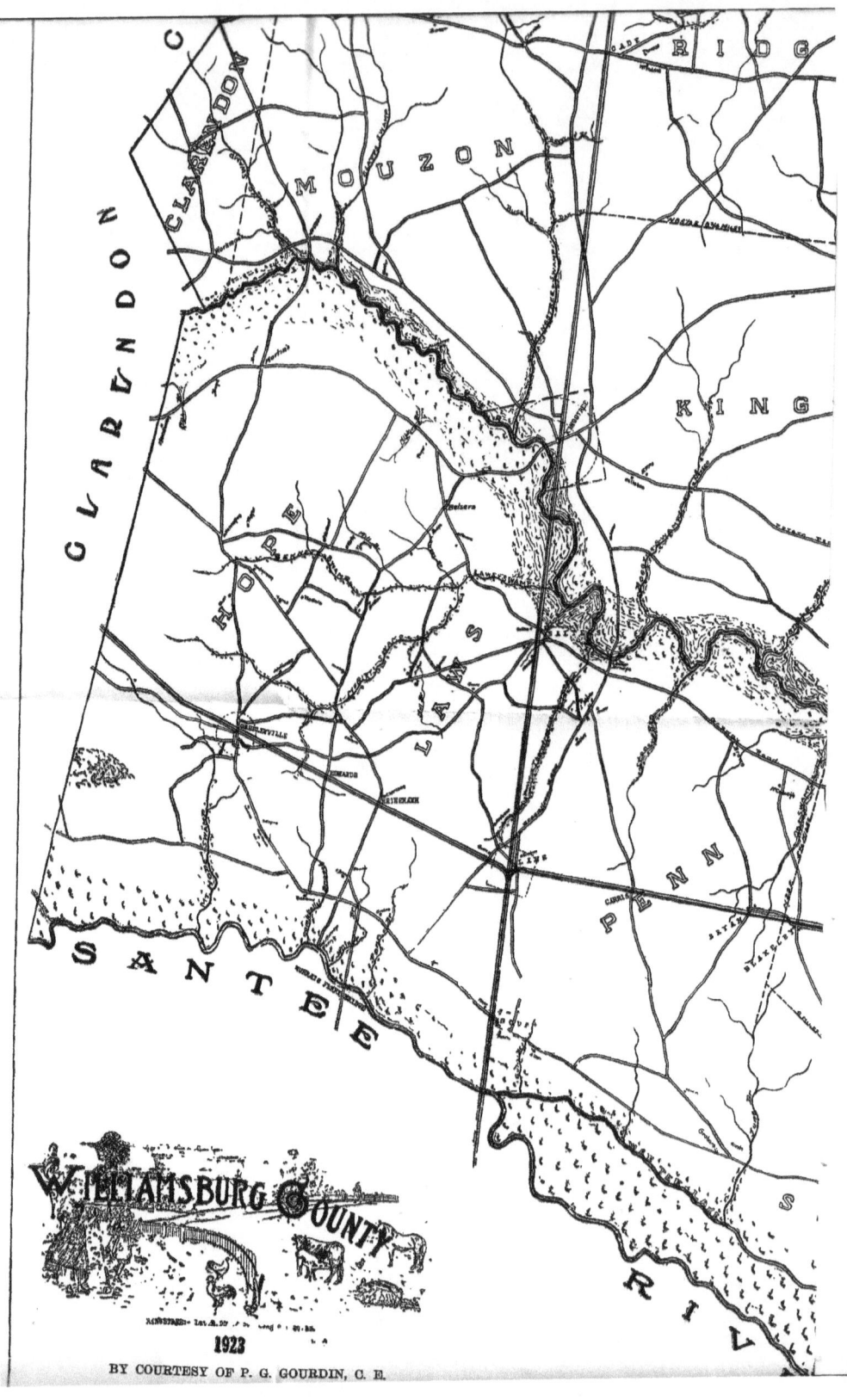

County had no social gatherings, except about once every year one of the very few fraternal lodges of the County usually gave a "Pine Bark Stew." A notable exception to the general social inactivity among the men was the "Pine Bark Stew" D. J. Epps usually gave about a hundred of his friends every May Day. Mr. Epps cooked and served Black River bream fit for a gathering of the gods. The taste of his stew always lingered in a man and lured him to return to the King's Tree on the Wee Nee. It has been customary in Wiliamsburg for more than a century for every minister to preach two or three sulphuric discourses every year on the subject of "worldly amusements," this term being applied to almost every social activity not under the patronage of denominational, patriotic, or fraternal organizations. It has not been possible for many years for the young people of the County to maintain a dancing club, or a card club; and almost any individual who encourages his children to participate in such entertainment as dancing or card playing is openly denounced as an advocate of the Devil. Participating in a game of golf or of tennis on Sunday would probably result in a social and commercial boycott in Williamsburg.

CHAPTER XL.

GENERAL PROGRESS.

There were very few men that, prior to the emancipation, had depended upon slave labor who emerged from the reconstruction period with any material thing of economic importance except land, and land then had but a nominal commercial value. W. B. McCollough says his father often told him that if a new comer desired very much to buy a tract of land, he might be induced to pay fifteen cents per acre; if the land owner were hard pressed for money, he would probably sell for ten cents per acre; but that where the land owner was neither practically forced to sell nor the purchaser over zealous to buy, the price was usually about twelve and one-half cents per acre.

A considerable portion of the present county of Williamsburg was swamp land until about 1900. When the pioneers settled here about 1730, it seems that nearly every one of them built his home within a stone's throw of a swamp and he buried his dead overlooking water. Hundreds of earth mounds showing the locations of the original adobe houses and the deeply ditched graveyards prove these statements. Neolithic peoples known as kitchen-middens of about ten thousand years before Christ lived on the lowlands of Scotland, from whence came these original settlers in Williamsburg. Was it a race instinct that placed these pioneer homes in Williamsburg overlooking swamps?

In the beginning, the mosquitoes that infested these sluggish waters seems to have been more annoying than harmful. Later, these little insects became infected by all kinds of fever producing germs and threatened the life of the swamp dwellers. It became necessary that every white family move out of the infested area during the mosquito months, and this proved a serious economic factor. Some of the wealthier men sent their families to the mountains every summer; others, unable to do this, built summer homes as far as possible away from the swamps. Later, everybody in Williamsburg began residing permanently, winter and summer, on the highlands rather than in the low lands. One hundred years ago, a man might have travelled across Williamsburg without having seen a residence from the public roads: now the homes are nearly all located on the highways.

Some planters before the War between the Sections undertook to drain their swamp lands, but these were very few in number. There was so much land available that nearly everybody elected to plant small patches here and there where water would not interfere.

These high lands planted produced but little per acre unless fertilized, and from the War until about 1900 not very many farmers in the County had been able to purchase the necessary commercial fertilizer. At first, Peruvian guano was used by planters. The cost of this was almost prohibitive; and besides, some wiseacres thought that this mixture actually destroyed the vitalizing elements in the soil. Later, commercial fertilizers gradually grew into use and the production of cotton increased. The soil of Williamsburg responds promptly and effectively to the intelligent use of chemical fertilizers.

Comparatively little land had been cleared for cultivation up to 1900. It was about that time that nearly everybody began to realize that the swamp lands were much more fertile than the sand hills, and the drainage of the lowlands became a serious undertaking. Draining the swamps helped in the conquest of the mosquito as well as added greatly to the productiveness of the section. It was about 1890 when the first artesian well in the present limits of Williamsburg was bored at Hebron Methodist Church. This well has been flowing continuously since that time. It was soon found that pure artesian water could be secured all over the County at depths from fifty to five hundred feet, and wells were located in all the towns, at most of the churches, and on many plantations within a decade. Theretofore surface drinking water had always been a menace to the health of the section.

With an abundance of pure and delightful artesian water all over the country, with the mosquito relegated to stagnant fens and moors far away from habitation, the health conditions rapidly improved and creative energy and productive ambition resulted in progression. Better lands planted produced more abundant harvests. About 1900, considerable visible material manifestation of economic development was evident.

About the only people in Williamsburg who accumulated any property between 1866 and 1876 were those who worked in the turpentine business. These men depended most largely on white labor. Nearly all of them had migrated into Williamsburg a few years before the beginning of the War between the States. Among these dealers in naval stores and pine products who made fortunes may be mentioned Captain J. F. Carraway, J. R. Lambson, R. H. Kimball, Edwin Harper, James Harper, R. H. Kellahan, Major C. S. Land, J. H. Pittman, and Dr. John F. Brockinton. Dr. Brockinton was the only man named in this list who was a native of Williamsburg.

As a rule during this time from 1876 to 1900, the masters of plantations were losing them little by little as necessity forced them from time to time to convey to others their inheritances. As late as 1905, Charles W. Wolfe said, "Negro labor is yet worse than nothing." It did not produce so much as it utilized. The whites began the period laboring under the delusion that manual labor degraded, and it was exceedingly difficult for them to realize that a gentleman might work with his hands. Many years passed before either the negro or the white man could reasonably adjust himself to the changed conditions. This was the most trying era in the history of Williamsburg.

Cotton was practically the only thing produced for market during this period. It was grown in ever increasing quantities, but the price received had gradually diminished from one dollar per pound just after the War to four cents per pound in 1897. All this time it must have seemed to the "indwellers in Williamsburg" that the gods had determined to enslave them forever. Planters had accounts with the merchants in Charleston and these accounts usually absorbed all the proceeds from the sale of their cotton every November. The planters of Williamsburg by this system of marketing almost surrendered their independence to cotton factors and merchants in the City of Charleston. These cotton factors and merchants determined the price they charged for supplies and also the price they paid the planters for their cotton. Actual results from the negro labor and this system of marketing show that the cotton planter in Williamsburg was between two mercilessly grinding millstones; that he, out of the substance which his ancestors had accumulated prior to the War and what his own energy could produce, fed and clothed freed negroes for a generation, as well as enriched cotton manipulators who kept him bound in economic chains.

Soon after the War between the Sections, the News and Courier, Charleston, undertook to promote the cultivation of tobacco in the State. Among other things, it offered a prize of considerable value for the best specimen of tobacco grown in South Carolina. A great many men in various parts undertook to win this prize. It was awarded to Dr. Robert F. Maurice for his exhibit produced on his plantation in what is now the McCollough community, south of Black River, in Williamsburg.

Although it was known that the soil and climate of Williamsburg were peculiarly adapted to the cultivation and production of tobacco, it was thirty years later before it was undertaken. Sheriff J. E. Brockinton was the first man in the County to grow the "golden weed" for market. This was about 1900. In many ways Sheriff Brockinton was a valuable man in Williamsburg. His experiments growing early vegetables for market brought much light along this line and were instrumental in promoting the valuable trucking industry in the County.

It was not long after Mr. Brockinton made some pleasing sales of tobacco before men in every section of the County began to grow it, and almost at once it became a considerable economic factor. Among the first tobacco planters of this time in Williamsburg, may be mentioned: J. E. Brown, J. Y. Mc Gill, Percy Snowden, B. N. Stuckey, J. B. Player, Solon Nesmith, J. B. Gamble, J. B. Tallevast, F. Rhem, and sons, J. C. Graham, R. D. Gamble, W. E. Lesesne, J. L. Lesesne, J. J. Bradham, W. O. Camlin, R. W. Smith, J. L. Thomas, W. J. Smiley, B. E. McKnight, William P. McKnight, J. S. Evans, and D. I. Burgess.

For the first few years Williamsburg tobacco planters marketed their crops in Florence and Lake City. In 1909, W. K. McIntosh and D. J. Epps each operated a tobacco sales warehouse on what is now, 1923, the Williamsburg County Fair Association grounds. In that season, one and three-fourths million pounds of tobacco were sold in these two warehouses. The building now used by the Fair Association for exhibits was one of these two sales warehouses. The other building was removed to the corner of Hampton and Mill Streets in Kingstree, where it was used as a sales warehouse until the brick Central Warehouse now standing replaced it.

In 1918, Williamsburg County produced eleven million pounds of tobacco and sold it for the average price of $33.20 per hundred. This crop of tobacco was all placed on the market during the month of August and the first week in September of that year and brought $3,652,000.00

into the County during that short time. There were four warehouses selling in Kingstree that year and several others in the smaller towns in the County. During that five weeks in 1918, Nelson's Warehouse in Kingstree paid out to farmers for their tobacco $989,752.52. This was, however, the largest sales warehouse in the County. It was owned and operated by W. K. McIntosh, E. J. Hester, E. C. Burgess, and L. F. Rhem. There were sold in 1918 in Kingstree during that memorable five weeks seven and one-half million pounds of tobacco.

Williamsburg produced that year an enormous cotton crop and it sold for about forty cents a pound. Those old men in Williamsburg who had been conscientious, consistent, continuous apostles of gloom for three or four score of years rubbed their eyes on Christmas morning and some of them actually admitted that Williamsburg was the promised land. That year and the next Williamsburg had an abundance of everything.

The census of Williamsburg County, 1920, shows its total population as 38,539, male 19,029, female, 19,510. There were only thirty-eight persons of foreign birth in the County, less than one-tenth of one per centum. There were 13,046 whites and 25,452 negroes, one Indian, and two Chinese. In 1920, the percentage of white population was 33.9; negroes 66; foreign born less than .1. In 1910, the percentage of white population was 38.2; the negro, 61.7. In 1920, there were 3006 white males and 4775 colored males over twenty-one years of age in the County. There were 7,232 dwelling houses in which there lived 7,318 families. The census valuation of all 1919 crops was $12,529,167.00; cereals, $2,035,529; seeds, $30,137; hay and forage, $288,410; vegetables, $283,030; fruits and nuts, $11,112; all other crops, $9,880,949. There were 992,260 bushels of corn, 37,102 bushels of oats, 2,159 bushels of wheat, 168 bushels of rice, 7,173 bushels of peas, 11,707,464 pounds of tobacco, 28,511 bales of cotton, 23,302 gallons of syrup, 38,137 pounds of grapes, 1,706 pounds of figs, 4,876 pounds of pecans produced and harvested.

For more than a century Williamsburg has lived and moved and had its being in cotton. The cotton crop has been for this period of time the barometer for Williamsburg. The tobacco money that flooded the County in 1918 was regarded as "pin money" and was used in riotous living. Men bought high powered automobiles and gold bound talking machines. Women spent their part for jewel studded slipper heels, parlez-vous petticoats, and Poiret gowns. There were, however, some few men in the County who took advantage of these money floods and saved. This County is fundamentally a mixture of Scotch-Irish and French Huguenots and both of these races have always realized that hard times will come.

Following closely on this period of unparalleled prosperity in material things, there came "Deflation," two long rainy seasons and the boll weevil. Any one of these three might have brought financial gloom to Williamsburg, but concurrent as they were and concomitant as they seemed, they produced a condition in Williamsburg about which the most presistent pessimist could not complain. The moneyed men of Williamsburg declared that they had passed through panics and however much they had suffered from them they would ever thereafter welcome a panic in preference to "Deflation." It rained almost every day during July and August 1920 and 1921 and these excessive rains gradually injured the tobacco crops and created just the climatic condition most favorable to the ravaging boll weevil. For many years cotton planters in Williamsburg had read accounts of the fearful destruction wrought by this little pest that had crossed the Rio Grande River from Mexico into Texas and had been making its way northward leaving cotton famine in its wake. One day early in July, 1921, the cotton planters realized that the boll weevil was here. There was dole in Astolat and well there may have been. In 1920, Williamsburg produced thirty-seven thousand bales of cotton. In 1921, it produced two thousand seven hundred. Besides all this, the tobacco produced was very light in weight and its price was less than eight cents per pound. Pessimistic preachers were fulsome on dry goods boxes in Williamsburg. "We are ruined" and "I told you so" could be heard from morn till noon, and from noon till dewy eve, and from dewy eve until far into the night.

"Blackberry time" had been for ages blissful negro days until the boll weevil came. Some joker started the story that somewhere once upon a time a mother boll weevil laid some eggs in some blackberries, which blackberries some negroes ate, and those negroes immediately died. This story was heard by every Williamsburg negro and thereafter the blackberry season became a period of mourning in all the land. Uncle Solomon Wilson said, "Boll weebil bite outen de cotton boll—hit die; boll weebil bite outen de nigger—he die. Nigger, let dem blackberries 'lone."

Negroes and superstitious whites believed the boll weevil a curse of God and were exceedingly doubtful about combating the pest. Some subtle negro, however, succeeded in satisfying these ignorant ones that placing poison for destroying the insect, under orders from employers, absolved them from the evil of "gwine 'ginst Gawd." It is remarkable how far the superstitious element was aroused by the boll weevil all over South Carolina. The Governor of the State, by proclamation, set apart Sunday, June 10, 1923, as a day of prayer and supplication to God to stay the destroying power of this little insect. This day was so observed by many congregations in Williamsburg.

It will be remembered that in the darkest days of the War of the Revolution in Williamsburg there came an hour when these Scotch-Irish gathered together in little groups, looked seriously into each others' faces, and some one said "something must be done." After the price of cotton had dropped from forty-two cents per pound in 1920 to nine cents in 1921 and its production in the County had fallen more than ninety per centum in a single twelve-month, and the tobacco crop, when planted they expected to produce eight hundred pounds an acre and receive thirty cents per pound, actually produced four hundred pounds per acre which they sold at about eight cents per pound; these same Scotch-Irish gathered together in small groups and some one said, "something must be done."

In the fall of 1921, the Williamsburg County Fair Association offered a prize for the best display of various articles produced on a farm in the County. Young Henry W. Haselden, of Hemingway, who cultivated the Lieutenant Haselden farm of eighty acres, won that prize. His exhibit showed the following articles produced on that eighty acres that year: four varieties of corn, long and short staple cotton, oats, rye, sorghum, peas, wheat, ribbon cane, rice, soy and velvet and soja beans, Irish and sweet potatoes, tobacco, watermelons, cantaloupes, squash, cucumbers, pumpkins, okra, gourds, hops, hay, fodder, pecans, acorns, hickory nuts, walnuts, rutabagas, peanuts, chufas, mulberries, egg plants, collards, mustard, hot and sweet peppers, carrots, radishes, beets, figs, onions, lettuce, tomatoes, lima beans, string beans, cabbage, artichokes, sugar corn, pie squash, grapes, grape preserves and jelly, grape acid, canned and preserved pears, canned and preserved apples, plum jelly, apple butter, peanut butter, blackberry and cherry and orange and lemon jelly, pepper hash, sweet pepper pickle, cucumber and pear and peach pickle, hams, butter, sausage, lard, eggs from hens, guineas, turkeys, and ducks, apples, peaches, pears, grapes, Japanese persimmons, strawberries, blackberries, raspberries, cured pork and dairy products of all kinds.

All of these things were well arranged and exhibited in a booth and naturally attracted much attention. Men looked over the things and remembered that they themselves had produced on their farms that very year some things that young Haselden had not. They talked about what Haselden's eighty acres had grown and knew that he had marketed $6,000.00 worth of produce from his farm that year. They realized that all of the things Haselden showed, and more, could be grown in marketable quantities at a profit on any small farm in Williamsburg County. And they found out that Haselden was born in 1897, the youngest of seven sons and one of twelve children of J. P. and Martha Donnahue Haselden; that he had received only the common school education afforded by the old Johnsonville school; that he had never been away from home in his life except to serve in the World War; that this youngster was of good old average Williamsburg blood and breeding. They thought about that $6,000.00 farm income, besides surplus products saved in sufficient quantities for the following year, and remembered the low prices of cotton and tobacco that year.

In Haselden's and competing exhibits in that 1921 County Fair were a hundred things declaring "something can be done." Williamsburg realized that it had depended on cotton for more than a hundred years and that the average negro and the thriftless white would find it difficult to place their faith in anything else. It was determined to fight the boll weevil in every way to conquer the insect, but anyway starvation was impossible in this favored land and prosperity was comparatively easy without cotton. Every conceivable means for fighting the boll weevil was utilized. Some of them were fanciful inventions—calcium arsenate dusted on the young cotton plant, or placed thereon in combination with molasses, was most frequently used. There was more than one man in the County who took Uncle Caesar's advice about raising cotton under boll weevil influence, which was, "Plant 'um early, work 'um fast." These men produced cotton successfully in 1922, without using poisons. The old story of the father who told his son he had hidden a great treasure in his vineyard, one could not help recalling, when he saw Williamsburg farmers during the fall and winter of 1922-23 clearing off the hedges and ditchbanks in order to destroy hibernating boll weevil. On these cleared hedges and ditchbanks rows of cotton were planted in 1923. Just how many bales of cotton these theretofore uncultivated places will produce cannot now be counted. The boll weevil invaded Coffee County, Georgia, several years ago and some of its citizens seemed to believe all was lost. A few years later a monument at the county seat was erected to the boll weevil for that the little pest had taught the county how many things it could produce at a profit and how vain a thing depending on cotton alone could prove. The coming of the boll weevil has already taught Williamsburg the same lesson—and more. Its people have been driven to diversification of farm products, something that the Clemson College Extension workers found possible to teach but few. One of the most beneficent results of the boll weevil plague has been the convincing of a majority of the farmers of the County that they do not know all things and that even they may learn something that their fathers did not tell them.

Road building began in Williamsburg in 1920 when the National Highway was projected through this County from North to South. Later, real highways from East to West were constructed, and then others. The United States Government furnished half the cost of building this road from Cades to Manning, the first undertaken. It was astonishing to see the number of landowners along this way who resisted the project with all their power. Three years later, all parts of the County were pleading for modern highways.

The building of Murray's Ferry bridge over the Santee, connecting Williamsburg with the South, in August 1923, was one of the most important acts in the history of the County. This bridge had been badly needed for a century, yet when the county delegations of Charleston, Berkeley, and Williamsburg had the bill passed making this project materialize, a large number of people in each of the three counties breathed vengeance against their delegations. These people, however, soon realized the wisdom of their legislators and everybody approved before the completion of the bridge. Hugh McCutchen was senator, and W. H. Welch, S. C. Eaddy, and S. A. Graham composed the Williamsburg County delegation in the legislature when the Santee River bridge bill was passed in 1920. On the Charleston delegation at that time as a member of the House of Representatives was D. Arthur Brockinton, a native of Williamsburg. Senator Arthur Young and Representative William Burguson, of Charleston, and Representative W. H. Welch, of Williamsburg, were the three active men of these delegations in securing the appropriations that made the Santee Bridge possible.

The Santee Bridge Commission was composed of three men from Charleston, two from Berkeley, and two from Williamsburg. This County's representatives on the commission were Peter G. Gourdin and Samuel A. Graham. Mr. Gourdin, a civil engineer of rank in his profession, with a first hand knowledge of Eastern South Carolina, physically and economically, proved a most valuable member of this commission. Mr. Graham had been interested in having a bridge built over the Santee at Murray's Ferry for many years; and during its construction in 1922 and 1923 gave it almost daily personal attention. His plantation is near the bridge and his home was always open to the commission.

The land owners of the Kingstree (or Broad) Swamp section of Williamsburg and Florence Counties had the territory incorporated in 1923 and voted about $200,000.00 in bonds for draining their lands according to the survey made by P. G. Gourdin, C. E. When completed, this will be one of the largest drainage systems in the state, with the main drain canal running from Kingstree to Olanta, a distance of 21 miles, and necessary laterals to drain smaller adjoining swamps. This project will give approximately 50,000 acres of fertile virgin land for agricultural purposes, and will doubtless result in stimulating the draining of a million other acres in Eastern South Carolina. Mr. Gourdin has been working quietly but effectively for many years for the consummation of drainage systems, and the indications are that his dreams will come "true." W. E. Nesmith and J. N. McKenzie, of Williamsburg, and J. C. Young, of Florence, are the Commissioners of the Kingstree Swamp Drainage District, and have had the work begun.

Out of the storm and stress of financial conditions of 1922 there came the Tobacco Growers Co-operative Association and the Cotton Growers Association, designed for the intelligent marketing of these two commodities. Ever since 1800, practically all of the cotton produced in Williamsburg had been placed in the market within sixty days, during the months of September and October, of each succeeding year. The Cotton Growers Association was designed to collect the cotton of individual planters and to distribute it into the markets of the world as needed.

All of the tobacco grown in Williamsburg until 1922 had been sold during the month of August and the first week in September. Buyers came to the markets every year from North Carolina and Virginia and forced the tobacco planters to cure and sell all of their crop within sixty days. Tobacco sales warehouses were then "hurrah grounds" where tobacco buying was more of a gambling game than anything else, with everything in favor of the buyer. Farmers rushed their products from their curing barns to the sales floors, knowing little of the grade or value of their offerings, and buyers always played "safe."

In 1922, a majority of the tobacco planters of Williamsburg joined the Co-operative Association and sold their tobacco through its agency. W. K. McIntosh was manager and W. T. Wilkins, assistant manager, for the local branch. There was no tobacco sold in Kingstree in 1922 except through the Association. Two independent sales warehouses were operated in Kingstree in 1923. Williamsburg tobacco farmers united with the Co-operative Association largely through the influence and labors of E. C. Epps, director in the Association under appointment by the Governor of South Carolina. Mr. Epps is a successful banker. He has seen for many years the fearful results coming from individual unorganized sales of farm products and believes the economic salvation of tobacco and cotton growers abides in co-operative marketing. Since he accepted appointment as director in the association, Mr. Epps has become a crusading co-operative association worker. He has made speeches all over the tobacco district in South Carolina and has proven his right to leadership in the association in the State.

In the beginning of the World War, wise men planted things on every available lot of land in the country. One saw tomatoes and beans growing close by governors' mansions in many of the capital cities of the country. In the beginning of 1923, Williamsburg planted everything everywhere—more things on more ground than theretofore in its history. Until the day this was written, June 20, 1923, it has seemed that especial natural favors have supplemented its labors.

In 1922, Williamsburg produced 10,320,000 pounds of leaf tobacco, ranking first among the counties of South Carolina. This date, 1923, there were more acres of better tobacco growing in Williamsburg than at the same time last year. There were, too, more acres of cotton, corn, sweet potatoes, peas, vegetables, fruits, and flowers, and all in better condition. There were more high grade cattle and hogs and chickens and other things than one year ago.

Men and women had been and were continuing learning rapidly the value of the things that they produce and how to secure better prices for them. Not only had the men actually realized that by co-operative marketing their cotton and tobacco commanded more money, but also they had learned that on their plantations they produced many things that were salable, and that butter and eggs and pork and poultry money is just as useful and valuable as that obtained in any other way.

In 1923, more young men and women from Williamsburg were graduated from the colleges of the country than in any two years of its prior history. More pupils were in the high and graded schools of the County, and far better work was done by them. An unusual number of these school boys and girls made remarkable progress and records during the year, and recent college honor rolls have been full of Williamsburg names. But, for the first time in its history, the parents of Williamsburg have been learning far more rapidly than their children. Preachers and prophets from Clemson College had been coming here for many years, but these old farmers would not hear them. "Deflation" and the "Boll Weevil" came two and one-half years ago. These old farmers sneered and cursed and complained under their schooling; but, about Christmas time 1922, they could read the handwriting on the wall. It declared, "Produce—in God's name, produce!"

Williamsburg has left its "outgrown shell by life's unresting sea."

INDEX

(In this index, no attempt has been made to show the different persons bearing the same name. For example, there are several men named William Cooper indexed under that name. I am grateful to Mrs. Lunette Burbage Cates, Mrs. Carrie Lancaster Swails, Miss Maude Allene Kinder, and Miss Adeline Shuler for very faithful work in making this index.—W. W. B.)

Abolitionists, 345.
Abolition Petitions, 335.
Abrams, Isabelle, 243, 246.
Abrams, John B., 353, 383.
Abrams, Robert, 413.
Abrams, R. T. B., 349.
Abrams, Thomas B., 243.
Abrams, W. L. D., 398.
Academy in Kingstree, 175.
Acadians, 56.
Acheson, Mary 76.
Act Resurveying Williamsburg, 139.
Adair, Alexander, 115.
Adair, Benjamin, 115.
Adair, James, 115.
Adair, John, 115, 118.
Adair, Samuel, 142, 153, 154.
Adams, D. E., 347, 416.
Adams, F. B., 520.
Adams, James, 21.
Adams, James H., 338.
Adams, J. P., 357.
Adams, John, 154.
Adams, Joseph, 199, 225.
Adams, Margaret, 154.
Adams, Robert, 79, 483.
Adams, Sarah, 79.
Adams, W. J., 357, 348.
Aimwell Church, 48, 119, 185, 210.
Aimwell School, 473.
"All for White Man," 453.
Allsbrook, Clarence, 503.
Allsbrook, Mrs. J. B., 532.
Altamaha, 3.
Alston, Governor, 253.
Akerman, A., 349.
Alexander, James, 145.
Alexander III, 29.
Allen, David, 19, 45, 46, 62.
Allen, D. A., 346.
Allen, Henry, 154.
Allen, John, 62, 154.
Allen, Lucile, 473.
Allen, Matthew, 211.
Allen, W. S., 382, 409.

Alling, Matthew, 230.
Allison, James, 115.
Allison, John, 208.
Allison, Robert, 21, 153.
Allison, Sarah, 154.
Allison's Ferry, 208.
Altman, A. T., 352.
Altman, C. T., 352, 398, 399.
Altman, Jane, 154.
Altman, John A., 407.
Altman, John J., 361.
Altman, Nicholas T., 353.
Altman, T. E., 349.
Altman, T. L., 408.
Altman, P. N., 398.
Altman, Thomas, 399, 408.
Altman, Thomas G., 349.
Altman W., 381.
Altman, W. E., 475.
Altman, W. H., 474.
Altman, William J., 353.
Amaker, Mrs. J. O., 475.
Anderson, Alexander, 74.
Anderson, Ann, 74.
Anderson, David, 70, 71.
Anderson, Gertrude, 515.
Anderson, G. W., 351.
Anderson, G. P., 380, 413.
Anderson, James, 154.
Anderson, John, 21, 66, 70, 142, 115.
Anderson, J. P., 349.
Anderson Joseph, 66.
Anderson, Major, 345.
Anderson, Robert, 408.
Anderson, S. C., 485.
Anderson, Williams, 74, 154.
Anderson School, 474.
Andrews, D. J., 352.
Andrews', Governor, Policy, 437.
Andrews, J. D., 486.
Andrews, Lemuel, 292.
Antipaedo Baptists, 24.
Antrim, 27.
"Ardent Spirits," 312.
Appamattox, 417.

INDEX

Ardesoif, 96, 124.
Aristocracy, 458.
Aristocracy Republic, 215.
Armagh, 27.
Arminianism, 254, 271.
Arminius, James, 271.
Armes, E. S., 343, 361.
Ard, Barbary, 154.
Ard, Benjamin, 199, 352, 353, 362, 398.
Ard, Barnabas, 199, 233.
Ard, E. G., 346., 398.
Ard, E., 398, 406, 353.
Ard, E. H., 362.
Ard, E. L., 464, 528.
Ard, G. W., 362.
Ard, James, 199, 346.
Ard, I., 406.
Ard, John, 353, 398, 406.
Ard, Joseph, 346, 409.
Ard, Reuben, 346, 353, 398.
Ard, T. S., 362.
Ard, William, 233.
Arely, Andrew, 154.
Armstrong, Mrs. E. S., 295.
Armstrong, James, 10, 13, 21, 25, 66, 70, 75, 115, 118, 127, 143, 154, 179, 180.
Armstrong, John, 114, 115, 118, 295.
Armstrong, Mary, 79, 84.
Armstrong, William, 115.
Arnett, David, 21, 151.
Arnett, Mrs. Jane, 118.
Arnett, J. A., 357, 400.
Arnett, John, 115, 118, 179, 199, 227.
Arnett, V. G., 473, 500, 530.
Arnett, Mrs. V. G., 515.
Arrowsmith, Mrs. T. E., 514, 515.
Arrowsmith, T. E., 525.
Arrowsmith, Mrs. P. O., 513, 515, 532.
Asbury, Francis, 187, 271, 292.
Asbury's First Journey, 187.
Asbury's Experiences, 189.
Askins, J. A., 352.
Askins, Hoxie G., 528.
Asurbanipal, 27.
Athol, John, 21, 153.
Atlanta—Battle, 407.
"Auld Lichts," 173.
Atkins, J., 69.
Atkinson, Anthony, 23, 53.
Atkinson, Eison, 224.
Atkinson, Jacob, 352, 361.
Atkinson, James, 199.
Atkinson, Major, 436.
Atkinson, Mary, 23.

Atkinson, Stephen, 199.
Atkinson, S. T., 444.
Austin, Francis, 115.
Austin, Jennett, 226.
Austin, John, 115.
Austin, Thomas, 115.
Avant, Caleb, 23.
Avant, B. J., 409.
Avant, Francis, 53, 74, 154.
Avant, Gladys, 473.
Avant, Hannah, 23, 74.
Avant, John, 23, 74, 211.
Avant, Lydia, 74.
Avant, Mary, 23.
Avant, Orlando, 354.
Avant, Rebecca, 74.
Avant's Ferry, 211.
Averton, Mary, 79.
Axson, Elijah, 154.
Ayers, Thomas, 199.

Babb, Lilla, 472.
"Back Country," 132.
Bagnall, Ebenezer, 25.
Bagnall, Isaac, 239.
Bagnall, John B., 239.
Baggett, J. J., 398.
Baggett, Frank, 473.
Baggell, N. W., 387.
Bailey, James, 200.
Bailey, William, 163.
Baker's Meeting, 294.
Baker, B. C., 472.
Baker, Benjamin, 530.
Baker, Daniel, 287, 294, 381.
Baker, E. O., 472.
Baker, H. L., 500, 501, 527.
Baker, James, 234.
Baker, J. E., 363, 474.
Baker, John, 234. 245.
Baker, M. R. D., 346, 409.
Baker, W. B., 488.
Baker, W. H., 475.
Baldwin, A. H., 472.
Ball, Elias, 104.
Ballentine, John, 21, 69, 152.
Ballentine, James, 200.
Banks, William, 481.
Banking Growth, 502.
Banking in Country, 496.
Bank of Cades, 500.
Bank of Greelyville, 498.
Bank of Hemingway, 500.
Bank of Kingstree, 496.
Bank of Trio, 501.
Bank of Williamsburg, 498.
Baptist Churches, 486.

INDEX

Baptist Ministers, 486.
Barber, John, 155.
Barfield, Charles, 154.
Barfield, Harvey, 399.
Barfield, J. K., 382.
Barfield, T. E., 348, 353.
Barefoot, John, 155.
Barhamville Female College, 305.
Barrineau School, 475.
Barrineau, Arthur, 155, 200, 221.
Barrineau, B. L., 354, 357.
Barrineau, Charles, 240.
Barrineau, C. R., 347.
Barrineau, Daniel, 402.
Barrineau, E. F., 244.
Barrineau, E. G., 349.
Barrineau, E. M., 347.
Barrineau, Fereby, 221.
Barrineau, George, 290.
Barrineau, G. W., 347.
Barrineau, Isaac, 142, 152, 155, 200, 221, 244.
Barrineau, Jesse, 221.
Barrineau, John, 347..
Barrineau, J. E., 348, 357, 400.
Barrineau, J. J., 354, 407.
Barrineau, J. P., 442.
Barrineau, J. T., 346, 407.
Barrineau, Levi, 200, 235.
Barrineau, Manuel, 200, 221.
Barrineau, Margaret, 200, 221.
Barrineau, Martha, 289.
Barrineau, Priscilla, 290.
Barrineau, Risdon, 200.
Barrineau, R. H., 343, 347.
Barrineau, Sarah, 221, 244.
Barrineau, Mrs. S. L., 468.
Barrineau, W. J., 357.
Barrineau, W. L., 347.
Barker, John, 155, 200.
Barker, Mrs. Thomas, 95.
Barley, J. L., 468.
Barnes, B. J., 352.
Barnes, John, 21, 153, 155.
Barnes, J. H., 398.
Barnwell, R. W., 384.
Barr, Caleb, 74.
Barr, Daniel, 229, 361.
Barr, D. D., 349.
Barr, Elizabeth, 229.
Barr, Esther, 74.
Barr, George, 21, 49, 198, 244, 245, 259, 274, 279, 280, 289, 468, 526.
Barr, Isaac, 74.
Barr, Jacob, 74.
Barr, John, 74, 76, 79, 199, 229, 244.
Barr, James, 70, 74, 155, 199, 229.

Barr, Jane, 229, 264.
Barr, Jannet, 245, 259.
Barr, J. D., 469.
Barr, Lula, 519.
Barr, Margaret, 74, 76, 79, 143.
Barr, Matthew, 153.
Barr, Mary, 259.
Barr, Nathaniel, 74.
Barr, Rachael, 74.
Barr, Silas, 74.
Barr, Sue T., 468.
Barr, W. C., 369, 397.
Barr, William, 74.
Barron, B. P., 353, 355, 528.
Barron, John, 528.
Barron, G. W., 383.
Barron, R. M., 382.
Barrow, J. R., 465, 515.
Barrow, Mrs. J. R., 515.
Barry, Joseph, 21.
Bartell, Jasper, 351.
Bartell, Jacob, 154.
Bartell, William, 352.
Bartley, E. B., 406.
Bartley, J. L., 406.
Barton, Mary, 23.
Barton, William, 23.
Barwell, Evans, 157.
Basnett, John, 21, 150.
Bass, J. M., 405.
Bass, Mrs. R. L., 514.
Bass, R. L., 515, 516, 574.
Bass, W. L., 463, 465, 528.
Bates, Benjamin, 21, 152.
Bates, Isaac, 154, 155.
Bates, Sadie, 475.
Bates, Sarah, 246.
Bates, Tobias, 246.
Battiste, Walter, 503.
Battle of Black Mingo, 104.
Battle of Cold Harbor, 355.
Battery Island, 347.
Battle Losses, 406.
Battle of Lower Bridge, 109.
Battle of Mount Hope, 109.
Battalion Musters, 319.
Battle of Tarcote, 107, 121.
Battle of Trevillian, 355.
Battle of Williamsburg, 382.
Baxley, D. W., 384.
Baxley, E., 381, 397, 405.
Baxley, H. C., 384.
Baxley, Joshua, 200.
Baxley, J. W., 349, 384.
Baxley, O. W., 398.
Baxley, Riley, 360.
Baxley, William, 360.

Baxley, W. J., 349, 382.
Baxter, Ann, 74.
Baxter, Charles, 25, 74.
Baxter, Israel, 115.
Baxter, James, 207.
Baxter, John, 49, 69, 76, 119, 131, 114, 143, 154, 247, 248.
Baxter, Robert, 122.
Baylor, Deems, 508, 512.
Beard, Thomas J., 149, 150.
Beard, Henry, 154.
Beasley, G. M., 501, 516.
Beasley, S. M., 463.
Beatty, Benjamin, 350, 383.
Beaufort, 2.
Beauregard, General, 345, 385.
Becky, D. N., 231.
Becton, P. N., 528.
Bedon, Henry, 25.
Bedgegood, Nicholas, 195.
Belin, Allard, 119, 127.
Belin, Cleland, 195, 196, 225, 242, 292, 318, 321.
Belin, Elam, 253.
Belin, James, 118, 119.
Belin, James F., 242.
Belin, John, 242.
Belin, William, 196.
Bellune, Francis, 158.
Bellune, Jane C., 224.
Bellune, Matthew, 196.
Bell, J. M., 357.
Bell, Raphael, 230.
Belser, W. M., 311.
Belser School, 474.
Benton, Ann, 231.
Benton, Cress, 155.
Benton, David, 225.
Benton, Elijah, 233.
Benton, Elizabeth, 233.
Benton, John, 199, 233.
Benton, Joseph, 199.
Benton, Mack, 474.
Benton, Mary, 231.
Benton, Martha, 233.
Benton, Moses, 199, 231, 233.
Benton, Rachael, 233.
Benton, Robert, 200, 233.
Benton, Sarah, 231, 233.
Benton, Simon, 231.
Benton, Susannah, 233.
Benton, Vila, 233.
Benton, William, 199.
Bennett, Henry, 23.
Bennett, Rebecca, 23.
Bennett, Samuel, 115, 118.
Benbow's Ferry, 208.

Benbow, M. M., 302.
Bennett's School, 75.
Benson, Jacob, 360.
Bentonville, 413.
Bethel, Bequest, 236.
Bernard, Matthew, 21.
Bernard, Paul, 155.
Berry, James, 155.
Berry, Lydford, 155.
Berry, Thomas, 155.
Berwick, James, 70.
Bethany Academy, 305.
Bethel Church, 176, 179, 302.
Bethel Congregation, 176, 179.
Bethel faction, 177.
Bethel School, 474.
Bethesda Church, 487.
Beulah School, 475.
Bible Class, 262.
Bible Desecrated, 429.
Bible Society Formed, 180.
"Big Four" Captains, 130.
Bigamy (?) among Slaves, 261.
Biggen, James, 154.
Bignion, Joseph, 21, 45, 152.
Bill, Son of a Cannibal, 333.
Bineau, Michael, 155.
Birds of Passage, 458.
Birch Creek School, 475.
Birch, Joseph, 155.
Biscuit Rebellion, 306.
Bishop, J. W., 486.
Bishop, S. E., 483.
Blackberry Time, 541.
Blackborn, Gabril, 155.
Blackmon, James, 208.
Blackwell, C. A., 468.
Blackwell, J. H., 463.
Blackwell, Mary A., 245.
Blackwell, Michael, 200, 205.
Blackwell, Thomas, 200.
Blackwell, T. J., 408.
Blackwell, W. E., 472.
"Black and Tan" Legislature, 439.
Black Border Counties, 455.
Black River, 3, 59.
Black River Church, 18.
Black River P. O., 531.
Black River School, 475.
Black Church members, 262.
Black Mingo, 24, 187.
Black Mingo Bridge, 210.
Black Mingo Church, 48, 52, 172, 176, 195, 292.
Black Mingo Congregation, 76.
Black Mingo Ferry, 207.

INDEX

Blake, B. G., 382.
Blake, Captain, 434.
Blake, James, 246.
Blake, Jane, 246.
Blake, John, 246.
Blake, Joseph, 75.
Blake, Mary, 246.
Blake, Sarah, 76.
Blakely resigns, 285.
Blakely's letter, 285.
Blakely, Bertha, 473.
Blakely, Catherine, 239.
Blakely, Charlie, 503.
Blakely, Dorothy, 233.
Blakely, Elizabeth, 75, 77, 84, 287, 360.
Blakely, E. T., 287.
Blakely, E. P., 357.
Blakely, H. W., 350, 383.
Blakely, James, 21, 47, 75, 142, 143, 179, 180.
Blakely, Jannet, 84, 179, 180.
Blakely, John, 21, 47, 66, 75, 115, 143, 179, 199, 200, 226.
Blakely, J. J., 353.
Blakely, J. L., 360.
Blakely, Madge, 475.
Blakely, R. D., 465.
Blakely, Robert F., 287.
Blakely, R. R., 381.
Blakely, R. W., 474.
Blakely, Sarah, 287.
Blakely, S. S., 357.
Blakely, T. A., 498.
Blakely, Thomas, 353.
Blakely, Thomas W., 353, 400.
Blakely, W. F., 284.
Blakely, William J., 353, 400.
Blakeway, Sarah, 69.
Blanding, Colonel, 361.
Blanchard, Benjamin, 200, 224, 228, 244.
Blanchard, Catherine, 233.
Blanchard, Henry, 242.
Blanchard, William F., 224.
Bland, Thomas, 155.
Bliss, John, 21, 151.
Bloomingvale School, 475.
Blunt, Jesse, 200.
Blunt, J. G., 155.
Bluset, Daniel, 25, 70.
Boatwright, W. N., 409.
Boddie, Helen Scott, 466.
Boddie, W. W., 470, 528.
Boggy Swamp, 13.
Boisseau, Marian, 84.
Boll Weevil, 544.

"Boll Weevil" Pest, 540.
Boll Weevil Superstition, 541.
Bolling, John, 142.
Bonneau, Anthony, 92.
Bonneau, Paul, 25, 71.
Bonnell, John, 53.
Bonnell, Mary, 56.
Boone, Capers, 155.
Boone, John, 25, 155.
Boone, Mary, 155.
Boone, Robert, 155.
Boone, Thomas, 25, 155, 188, 207, 384.
Boonesboro, 383.
Booth, Robert, 155.
Borland, Archibald, 75.
Borland, Elizabeth, 75.
Borland, Jean, 75.
Borland, John, 21, 115, 142.
Borland, Mary, 75.
Borland, William, 75.
Bossard, John, 210.
Bostwick, Ann, 229.
Bostwick, Elijah, 228.
Bostwick, Henry H., 199, 227.
Bostwick, J. H., 352.
Bostwick, Jonathan, 21, 155, 200, 222.
Bostwick, T. J., 351.
Bostwick, William H., 228.
Boston Tea Party, 95.
Boswell, C. W., 473, 499, 513.
Bottom Rail on Top, 449.
Botsford, John, 195.
Bouquets from Ladies, 387.
Boutwell, Joseph, 155.
Bowden, Henry, 378.
Bowen, Bishop, 186.
Bowen, Margaret, 161.
Bowlee, Margaret, 162.
Boyd, A. C., 501.
Boyd, Capers, 474.
Boyd, Charles, 348, 487.
Boyd, Eleanor, 236.
Boyd, Evans, 155.
Boyd, Franklin, 295.
Boyd, F. W., 343, 397, 416.
Boyd, Hugh, 200, 236, 429, 487, 514.
Boyd, I. N., 499, 527.
Boyd, James, 24.
Boyd, John, 115, 118, 143, 152, 155, 199, 503, 527.
Boyd, Mrs. Leamie, 475, 474.
Boyd, Mrs. Martha, 118.
Boyd, Mehitable, 24.
Boyd, M. L., 474.
Boyd, Pauline, 472.

Boyd, R. W., 348.
Boyd School, 475.
Boyd, W. S., 527.
Boyd, Mrs. W. S., 532.
Boyd, William W., 487.
Boykin, Isham, 503.
Boyle, T. W., 473, 498, 515, 529.
Bracey, William, 138, 143, 145, 146, 152, 155, 250.
Bradford, John, 115.
Bradford Springs School, 305.
Bradford, Mrs. M. A., 370.
Bradham, Benjamin, 200.
Bradham, F. E., 514, 516.
Bradham, J. A., 398, 343, 347, 348, 476.
Bradham, J. H., 407, 408.
Bradham, J. J., 474.
Bradham, John, 348.
Bradham, R. J., 343, 361.
Bradham, William, 297, 515.
Bradley, Aaron, 200.
Bradley, Cecelia, 289.
Bradley, Elizabeth, 118, 126, 235.
Bradley, Jane, 74.
Bradley, Jannet, 230, 235.
Bradley, James, 20, 21, 45, 46, 66, 74, 101, 115, 133, 142, 144, 146, 151, 155, 179, 183, 199, 225, 230, 232, 233, 235, 268, 269, 289, 343, 527.
Bradley, John, 66, 70.
Bradley, John P., 295.
Bradley, Joseph, 80, 270, 311.
Bradley, Mary, 74, 230, 235.
Bradley, Robert, 233, 235, 481.
Bradley, Robert W., 230, 311, 317.
Bradley, Samuel, 66, 74, 85, 230.
Bradley, Sarah, 230, 235, 289.
Bradley, S. J., 311, 402.
Bradley, Thomas, 66.
Bradley, William, 66.
Bradley, William W., 230.
Bradshaw, A., 354, 416.
Bradshaw, Amelia, 235.
Bradshaw, Asa, 200, 235.
Bradshaw, James, 221.
Bradshaw, John, 357, 381.
Bradshaw, Joseph, 346.
Bradshaw, J. R., 381.
Bradshaw, Levina, 221.
Bradshaw, Silas, 235.
Bradshaw, Malachi, 353.
Bradshaw, Moses, 235.
Bradshaw, Samuel, 200, 235.
Bradshaw, Mary, 200.
Brady, John, 138, 149.

Brady, William, 89, 216.
Bragg's Army, 385.
Brogdon, J., 399.
Brand, W. S., 302, 361.
Brass, 396.
Braswell, William W., 350.
Braveboy, Joshua, 115, 154, 338.
Braveboy, Morris, 199, 351.
Braveboy, M. M., 351, 399.
Braxton, J. W., 346, 363.
Brewington, 121, 185, 186.
Brewington Road, 208.
Brewington Singing School, 301.
Brewington, Orange, 488.
Brick Mercantiles, 520.
Bridge at King's Tree, 62.
Bridgman, A. C., 483.
Bridgman, J. F., 384.
Brisket, F., 357.
Bristow, Louis J., 521.
Britton's Ferry, 139.
Britton's Ferry Road, 208.
Britton, Ann, 74, 75.
Britton, Benjamin, 74, 196, 200, 210, 211, 222, 244, 264.
Britton, B. E., 350.
Britton, B. F., 384.
Britton, Daniel, 24. 75,
Britton, Daniel L., 74, 84.
Britton, Elizabeth H., 24.
Britton, E. H., 397.
Britton, Elizabeth, 74, 75.
Britton, Francis, 57, 74, 75, 84, 92, 200.
Britton, Francis M., 349, 261.
Britton, Miss F. W., 408.
Britton, Henry, 74, 84, 189.
Britton, Hester J., 24.
Britton, H. O., 405, 464, 504.
Britton, Jane, 75.
Britton, John, 74.
Britton, John F. D., 319, 349.
Britton, J. W., 43, 360.
Britton, John D., 464, 503.
Britton, Joseph, 74, 75, 84.
Britton, Martha, 74, 84.
Britton, Mary, 74, 75, 84.
Britton, Moses, 24, 57, 74, 75, 84.
Britton, Philip, 74, 75, 84.
Britton, Rachael, 75.
Britton, Rebecca, 74.
Britton, S. P., 531.
Britton, S. S., 349, 487.
Britton, Timothy, 75, 200.
Britton, T. G., 357, 406, 407.
Britton, T. J., 349.
Britton, Thomas M., 287, 349, 406,

INDEX

408.
Britton, Thomas, 74.
Britton, T. N., 349, 377.
Britton, W. H., 360, 413.
Britton, W. J., 349, 383, 503.
Brock, L. G., 500, 530.
Brockinton, Burrows P., 242, 343, 346, 384, 397.
Brockinton, Caroline M., 242.
Brockinton, Cosmo E., 503.
Brockinton, D. Arthur, 545.
Brockinton, Eliza, 289.
Brockinton, Elizabeth, 74, 426.
Brockinton, Hannah, 74.
Brockinton, James S., 241, 295, 311, 317, 343, 348, 350, 384, 397, 527.
Brockinton, J. Screven, 489.
Brockinton, John, 74, 77, 102, 115, 129, 132, 199, 242, 154, 155, 252.
Brockinton, John F., 241, 317, 349, 360, 369, 397, 399, 464, 525, 527, 536, 538.
Brockinton, Mrs. J. F., 396.
Brockinton, John R., 468, 527.
Brockinton, Joseph, 75.
Brockinton, Joseph E., 464.
Brockinton, Louise, 241.
Brockinton, Laura A., 468.
Brockinton, Martha, 200, 209, 242.
Brockinton, Martha A., 242.
Brockinton, Margaret, 468.
Brockinton, Mary, 74.
Brockinton, P. M., 464, 474.
Brockinton, Rachael, 75.
Brockinton, Richard, 74.
Brockinton, Sarah, 74, 75.
Brockinton, Virginia, 295.
Brockinton,, William, 25, 74, 75, 199, 234.
Brockinton, Mrs. W. E., 514.
Brockintodn, William R., 241, 312, 343, 369, 440, 464.
Brockinton, William S., 184, 237, 240, 241, 242.
Brockinton, W. V., 527.
Brockinton, Mrs. W. V., 532.
Brogdon, J. B., 352.
Brogdon, John W., 301.
Brogdon, Mary B., 301.
Brogdon, William, 356.
Broomstraw Road, 301.
Broome, John, 200.
Broughton, Thomas, 297.
Browder, B. R., 353, 470.
Browder, E., 353, 406.
Browder, Henry, 354.
Browder, Isaac, 353.
Browder, McKenzie, 353.
Browder, S. W., 346, 398.
Browder, Thomas, 200.
Browder, William T., 353.
Brown, Abner, 200, 230.
Brown, Abner H., 354.
Brown, Agnes, 232, 245.
Brown, Ann, 155, 224.
Brown, Asa, 237, 295, 348.
Brown, Augustus, 469.
Brown, A. D., 503.
Brown, B. A., 468.
Brown, Mrs. B. A., 513.
Brown, Daniel, 181, 199.
Brown, D. L., 354, 406, 463, 468.
Brown, Duncan, 191.
Brown, D. C., 473.
Brown's Ferry, 10.
Brown, Hesther, 23.
Brown, H. J., 346, 407, 414, 415, 460, 523, 529.
Brown, H. P., 500, 501, 502, 515.
Brown, I. M., 347.
Brown, James, 115, 155, 199.
Brown, Jeremiah, 154.
Brown, J. E., 538.
Brown, J. J., 353, 398, 468.
Brown, J. L., 320.
Brown, J. M., 348, 399, 408, 465.
Brown, J. W., 351, 408.
Brown, John, 53, 115, 150, 154, 155, 191, 195, 354.
Brown, Levi, 381, 400, 530.
Brown, M. A., 346, 407.
Brown, Moses, 57, 217.
Brown, Robert, 199, 260.
Brown, R. N., 350.
Brown, Sarah, 37, 199.
Brown, S. B., 384.
Brown, Thomas, 21, 218.
Brown, Thomas M., 150, 200, 222, 228.
Brown, William, 23, 84, 194, 199, 343, 398.
Brown, William C., 482.
Brown, W. H., 381.
Brown, W. J., 369.
Brown, W. R., 465, 468.
Brunson, Ann, 23.
Brunson, Clarence, 503.
Brunson, Daniel, 84.
Brunson, David, 84, 228.
Brunson, Isaac, 25, 62, 71, 84.
Brunson, James, 115, 118.
Brunson, James H., 352.
Brunson, John, 23.
Brunson, Joshua, 84.

Brunson, Josiah, 84.
Brunson, Mary, 84.
Brunson, Matthew, 84.
Brunson, Moses, 84.
Brunson, M. A., 488.
Brunson, Susannah, 84.
Brunson, T. S., 529.
Brunson, William, 115.
Bryan, James, 328.
Bryan, J. R., 357.
Bryan, Walter, 328.
Bryan, William, 328.
Bryan, W. B., 463.
Bryan, W. D., 515, 516, 531.
Bryan, W. R., 531.
Buchanan, President, 344.
Buchanan, Ethel, 473.
Buckles, Henry, 354, 409.
Buckles, J. M., 347, 381.
Buckles, Lydford, 354, 398.
Buckles, R. A., 357, 405.
Budden, Ann, 244.
Budden, F. A., 489.
Budden, James, 244.
Budden, John, 84.
Budden, Moses, 236.
Budden, Solomon, 199, 227, 244.
Budden, W. P., 351, 384.
Bueck, H., 472.
Buffkin, P. H., 328.
Buford, William, 84, 114, 120, 156, 191, 208, 226, 268.
Buford, William J., 244, 311.
Bull Run, 366.
Bull, H. B., 484.
Bull, William, 67.
Bullock, E. J., 155.
Bully Contest, 318.
Bunch, John, 292.
Bunch, W. H., 401.
Burbage, Jonathan, 154.
Burdick, Elam C., 224, 232.
Burdick, E. H., 224, 232.
Burdick, Fred A., 232.
Burdick, Sarah, 229.
Burdick, William R., 353, 406.
Burch, Sarah, 473.
Burgess, Amelia, 287.
Burgess, Bartow, 503.
Burgess, Mrs. Bishop, 515.
Burgess, Caroline, 221.
Burgess, C. C., 514.
Burgess, C. L., 474.
Burgess, D. I., 363, 538.
Burgess, E. C., 481, 519, 520, 539.
Burgess, G. W., 363, 483.
Burgess, Israel, 512.

Burgess, James, 145, 146, 147, 151, 187, 199, 200, 205, 208, 224, 230, 256, 287.
Burgess, James M., 347, 480, 487, 527.
Burgess, Jane, 221.
Burgess, Jannet, 229.
Burgess, Jannet D., 287.
Burgess, Jannet M., 229.
Burgess, J. A., 363.
Burgess, J. C., 363.
Burgess, J. D., 474.
Burgess, J. H., 347.
Burgess, J. P., 363.
Burgess, John, 25, 135, 136, 139, 141, 142, 145, 146, 147, 151, 152, 220, 230, 515.
Burgess, John D., 221, 233.
Burgess, Joseph, 115, 87.
Burgess, Louisa, 221.
Burgess, Margaret, 221.
Burgess, Martha, 472.
Burgess, Mary, 221.
Burgess, Mary M., 287.
Burgess, Pomelia, 221.
Burgess, R. G., 347.
Burgess, R. W., 363.
Burgess, S. A., 302.
Burgess, S. H., 363.
Burgess, Thomas, 229.
Burgess, W. J., 302, 347.
Burgess, William, 25, 115, 118.
Burguson, William, 545.
Burkett, J. H., 472.
Burkett, Louis E., 309.
Burket, F. B., 380, 384.
Burket, T. E., 351.
Burnett, Sabrine, 25.
Burns, James H., 354.
Burns, John, 118.
Burns, R. W., 382.
Burr, Aaron, 253.
Burr, Theodosia, 253.
Burrows, Emeline, 290.
Burrows, George, 21, 57, 66, 74, 153, 155, 200, 221.
Burrows, George W., 221, 408.
Burrows, H. M., 473.
Burrows, Jane, 74, 236.
Burrows, John, 83, 115, 155, 200, 229.
Burrows, John T., 407, 486.
Burrows, Joseph, 74, 155.
Burrows, Nathan, 512.
Burrows, Samuel, 74, 155.
Burrows, S. W., 351.

INDEX 557

Burrows, Thomas, 200, 229, 232, 362.
Burrows, Thomas J., 353, 398, 409.
Burrows, William, 74, 200, 115, 118, 218, 221, 223, 224, 240, 242, 381.
Burrows, W. D., 409.
Burrows, W. E., 473.
Burrows, William J., 224, 229.
Burton, Nancy, 155.
Bushart, J. B., 502.
Butler, Daniel, 70.
Butler, J. F., 405.
Butler, General M. C., 356.
Butler, Sarah, 154, 155.
Byrd, Ann, 222.
Byrd, Amea, 242.
Byrd's Battalion, 358.
Byrd, H. L., 283.
Byrd, H. O., 527.
Byrd, J. D., 381, 405.
Byrd, J. H., 405.
Byrd, Orpha, 222.
Byrd, S. D. M., 317, 343, 358, 379, 456, 460, 463, 527.

Cade, Adeline, 239.
Cade, Agnes, 239.
Cade, Andrew, 239, 530.
Cade, Charles, 239.
Cade, C. A., 530.
Cade, C. W., 269, 486, 529.
Cade, Elizabeth, 239.
Cade, Erasmus, 239.
Cade, Felix, 239.
Cade, Jane, 239.
Cade, Jannet, 239.
Cade, John, 239.
Cade, Mary, 486.
Cade, Robert, 200, 209, 222, 224, 235, 239, 355.
Cade, R. E., 358, 488.
Cade, R. T., 357.
Cade, S. E., 486, 487.
Cade, Violet, 239.
Cades Church, 487.
Cades Post Office, 529.
Cades School, 473.
Cain, Eric, 351, 352, 384, 399.
Cain, J. P., 349.
Cain, William, 352.
Calcobb, James, 352.
Calder, John W., 400.
Caldwell, Samuel, 503.
Calcot, James, 156.
Calcot, Henry, 156.
Caledonians, 171.

Calhoun, I. A., 513.
Calhoun, Mrs. Ira, 473.
Calhoun, James G., 224.
Calhoun, William A., 224.
Callebuff, Elizabeth, 156.
Callum, John, 156.
Calvin, John, 171.
Calvinism, 254, 271.
Calvin Knox faction, 172.
Cambrahan, Bryan, 231.
Cameron, Bryant, 200.
Cameron, George B., 358.
Cameron, Henry, 244.
Cameron, H. J., 347.
Cameron, John, 25.
Cameron, J. W,. 347, 358, 408.
Cameron, Margaret, 244.
Cameron, W. J., 381.
Cameron, W. L., 358.
Camp Glover, 384.
Camp Branch, 107.
Camp Meetings, 310.
Camp Ridge settlement, 529.
Camlin, Camlin, 156.
Camlin, Etna, 473.
Camlin, Elizabeth, 289.
Camlin, G. W., 473, 515.
Camlin, Matthew, 142, 151, 156.
Camlin, William, 200, 212, 289, 512.
Camlin, W. O., 464, 472, 515, 538.
Camlin, W. S., 361, 463, 468, 487.
Camp, William, 21.
Campbell, Alexander, 23.
Campbell, Archibald, 156, 233.
Campbell, Avagbel, 66.
Campbell, David, 115, 118.
Campbell, Duncan, 115.
Campbell, George, 115.
Campbell, James, 115, 147, 153, 156, 200, 208, 216, 221, 218, 219, 231, 244, 256.
Campbell, Mary, 156, 232, 245.
Campbell, Priscilla, 24.
Campbell, Rebecca, 200.
Campbell, Sarah, 17.
Campbell, Thomas, 115.
Campbell, William, 21, 84, 115, 153, 231, 232, 244, 382, 397.
Campbell, W. H., 465, 529.
Campbell, W. J., 311.
Campbell, W. M., 231.
Canby, R. S., 439.
Cannady, J. P., 351.
Cannon, 455.
Cantey, Ann, 23.
Cantey, Charles, 118.
Cantey, E. M., 289.

558   INDEX

Cantey, Jane, 235.
Cantey, John, 115, 118.
Cantey, Joseph, 23.
Cantey, Joseph F., 186.
Cantey, Joseph S., 487.
Cantey, Mary, 23.
Cantey, Samuel, 23, 71.
Cantey, Thomas S., 235.
Cantey, William, 81.
Cantey, W. J. R., 186, 301.
Cantley, Charles, 25, 115.
Cantley, E. G., 381.
Cantley, F. G., 348.
Cantley, John, 156.
Cantley, Mary, 222.
Cantley, Robert, 222.
Cantley, Roger G., 226.
Cantley School, 473.
Cantley, W. G., 320, 381, 473.
Cantzor, John, 25.
Capell, Benjamin, 25.
Captains Decline Promotion, 376.
Captured at Trevillian, 355.
Capers, William, 192, 292.
Capers, W. T., 349.
Capers Describes Camp Meeting, 192.
Carge, James, 151.
Carlisle School, 474.
Carlisle, Alexander, 156.
Carne, 76.
Carolina, 1.
Carolina Divided, 2.
Carpet Baggers, 452.
Carroll, L. F., 486.
Carraway, A., 381.
Carraway, E. 351.
Carraway, Henry, 358.
Carraway, Isaac, 194.
Carraway, James, 38, 240.
Carraway, J. F., 328, 349, 351, 379, 468, 536.
Carraway, Washington, 383.
Carr, W. H., 515, 519, 520.
Carson, Agnes, 79.
Carter, Asbury D., 354, 384.
Carter, George, 235.
Carter, George W., 354, 384, 554.
Carter, H. W., 348.
Carter, Isaac, 235.
Carter, Jesse, 381.
Carter, Josiah, 156.
Carter, J. B., 398, 351.
Carter, J. H., 384.
Carter, J. M. T., 351.
Carter, J. T., 468.
Carter, J. D., 463.

Carter, J. W., 408.
Carter, Mrs. M. A., 468.
Carter, S. J., 348.
Carter, William, 156, 200, 311.
Carter, W. E., 352.
Carter, W. W., 440.
Carter, Zachary, 156.
Cash, E. D. C., 380.
Casselman, J. D., 358, 407.
Casselman, S., 465.
Cattle, 134.
Caswell, Elizabeth, 239.
Caswell, Joseph, 239.
Caswell, John, 239.
Caswell, Samuel, 239.
Cedar Swamp Aid Society, 370.
Cedar Swamp M. Church, 297.
Cedar Creek School, 473.
Censure-proof, 298.
Census, 1790, 154.
Census, 1920, 539.
Cetty, John, 200.
Chancellorsville, 398.
Chandler, Ann, 76.
Chandler, A. W., 468.
Chandler, B. B., 463, 465, 475.
Chandler, B. J., 472, 502.
Chandler, Caesar, 356.
Chandler, Mrs. C. M., 525.
Chandler, Dora V., 468.
Chandler, Effie, 473.
Chandler, Ellen T., 473.
Chandler, Elizabeth, 76.
Chandler, Elvira, 289.
Chandler, E. G., 465, 521, 527.
Chandler, George, 25, 115, 118, 200, 225.
Chandler, G. H., 290.
Chandler, Isaac, 52, 76, 115.
Chandler, Jesse, 115.
Chandler, Joseph, 25, 70, 241, 289.
Chandler, Joseph B., 297, 353, 378, 381, 463.
Chandler, J. F., 361.
Chandler, J. W., 465.
Chandler, G. F., 502.
Chandler, Martha, 370.
Chandler, Ruth, 472.
Chandler, Robert, 361.
Chandler, R. W., 408.
Chandler, Samuel, 76.
Chandler, Susannah, 241, 289.
Chandler, S. T., 383, 384.
Chandler, T. M., 503.
Chandler, T. S., 343, 361, 408.
Chandler, W. R., 474.
Chamberlain, R. H., 454, 459.

INDEX 559

Chaos, 439.
Chambey, William, 142.
Chapels of Ease, 57.
Charles II, 1.
Charleston, 2.
Chattanooga, 399, 401.
Cherry, J. W., 350.
Cheeseborough, John, 156.
Cherokees, 6.
Cherokee War, 70.
Chickahominy River, 382.
Chickamauga, 398, 401.
Chicken, Elizabeth, 93.
Chicken, William, 23.
China, John, 115.
China, J. R., 343, 346, 409.
China, Mary J., 295.
China, S. M., 343, 346, 398, 416.
China, T. J., 295, 301, 343, 346, 369, 380, 384, 406, 407.
China, W. A., 343.
Christian Education, 79.
Christmas, Jesse, 347, 487.
Christening Basin, 187.
Christianizing Slaves, 181.
Christmas, Jonathan, 23.
Christmas, Hesther, 23.
Christmas, W. G., 409.
Christmas, W. J., 354.
Chosewood, Alexander, 70.
Chovin, Alexander, 156.
Church Charges, 275.
Churches Divide, 339.
Church of England, 5, 44, 272.
Church of Scotland, 17, 45.
Churches and Churchmen, 44.
Church Act, 1706, 53.
Churches in 1830, 197.
Church Members, 490.
Church Societies, 532.
Church Torn Down, 174.
Churches in 1776, 58.
Church sues Church, 175.
Citation from Church, 274.
Citadel, 305.
Cited for Valor, 400, 505, 511.
Circuit Riders, 190, 292.
Circuit Rider's Story, 492.
Civil Officials, 1863, 397.
Claffy, Mayna, 508.
Clapp, Elizabeth, 75.
Clapp, Mary, 76.
Clapp, Sarah, 76.
Claims Presented, 142.
Clarendon School, 475.
Clark, Bartley, 56.
Clark, D. M., 483.

Clark, Henry, 156.
Clark, Joseph, 200.
Clark, James, 156, 264.
Clark, J. E., 488, 514.
Clark, John J., 264.
Clark, M., 530.
Clark, Sarah, 200.
Clark, Thomas, 115.
Clarkson's Diary, 286.
Clarkson, B. E., 72, 529.
Clarkson, C. A., 571.
Clarkson, G. F., 489.
Clarkson, J. B., 500.
Clarkson, N. B., 489, 360.
Clarkson, W. J., 383, 386, 360, 480.
Clarkson, W. N., 501, 502.
Clay's Farm, 407.
Clearing Black Mingo, 62.
Clegg, Lydia, 80.
Cleland, John, 69, 151, 153.
Clock Town, 528.
Clubs, Democratic, 465.
Clyde, T. J., 488.
Coachman, Benjamin, 228.
Coachman, Isaac, 228.
Coachman, John, 219, 228, 320.
Coachman, Joseph, 228.
Coachman, Margaret, 228.
Cobert, John, 176.
Cochran, William, 21, 143.
Cockfield, Ann, 200.
Cockfield, Blondelle, 472.
Cockfield, C. W., 349, 383.
Cockfield, Ebenezer, 298.
Cockfield, James W., 358.
Cockfield, Josiah, 156, 358.
Cockfield, Joseph, 200.
Cockfield, J. C., 398.
Cockfield, J. H., 350.
Cockfield, J. A. H., 369, 468.
Cockfield, Mrs. M. E., 468.
Cockfield, R. L., 527.
Cockfield, S. W., 369, 409.
Cockfield, Washington, 200, 320.
Cockfield, William, 25, 200, 237.
Cockfield, W. H., 397.
Cockfield, W. J., 343.
Coffee Scarce, 371.
Coker, Benjamin, 115.
Coker, I., 381, 408.
Coker, John, 355.
Coker, J. J., 358.
Coker, J. M., 357, 487.
Coker, J. N., 475.
Coker, J. S., 347, 357.
Coker, J. W., 384.
Coker, Nathan, 115.

INDEX

Coker, P. J., 347.
Coker, S. J., 358.
Coker, S. L., 347.
Coker, Thomas, 115.
Coker, W. G., 487, 488.
Cold Harbor, 407.
Coleman, George, 228.
Coleman, Ikey, 312.
Coleman, Jacob, 115, 200, 228.
Coleman, Robert, 156.
Colclough, Alexander, 361.
Cole, J. A., 527.
Coleman, R. L., 500.
Coleman, Samuel, 200, 228.
Coleman, Savannah, 228.
Coleman, T. J., 357.
Coleman, W. D., 399.
Colin, James, 357.
Collette, Ella, 468.
Collier, James, 354.
Collins, Alexander, 156.
Collins, Frank, 358.
Collins, Henry, 358.
Collins, John W., 358, 407.
Collins, Jonah, 25.
Collins, R., 399.
Collins, W., 351, 398.
Collum, John, 200.
"Colonels of the Cross," 376.
Colonial Elections, 213.
Coltrain, S., 382.
Columbia Made Capital, 215.
Comb, Annie, 156.
Commander, Hannah, 81.
Commander, James, 156.
Commander, John, 25.
Commander, Joseph, 25.
Commander, Rachael, 75.
Commander, Samuel, 12, 25, 209.
Commander, Thomas, 70.
Commons, 3.
Committee on Court House, 149.
Commissioners, Town, 139.
Co-operative Crusader, 547.
Cooper School, 475.
Cooper Store, 397.
Cooper-Snowden Fight, 288.
Copeland, Hugh, 151.
Copeland, John, 156.
Copeland, William, 21.
Conde, N. J., 343.
Confederate War Results, 434.
Confession of Faith, 293.
Confessions of Sins, 254.
Confiscation, 447.
Conflicting Ideas, 332.

"Confusion Worse Confounded," 446.
Concord M. Church, 487.
Conn, Mary, 125.
Connel, Thomas, 200.
Connell, W. I., 361.
Connell, Abram, 200.
Connor, Abraham, 235.
Connor, Adam, 144, 151, 156.
Connor, Archibald, 143, 144, 150, 151, 156.
Connor, Ann, 228.
Connor, John, 200, 21, 228.
Connor, Rachael, 243.
Connor, Sarah, 228.
Conrad, J. C., 350.
Conscription, 395.
Constitution of 1790, 213.
Constitution to Voters, 439.
Conyers, 109.
Conyers, Ann, 23.
Conyers, Daniel, 114, 120, 126.
Conyers, James, 25, 103, 114, 120.
Conyers, John, 23, 208.
Conyers' Lake, 120.
Conyers, Mary, 185.
Cooper, A. B., 347, 398, 501.
Cooper, Agnes, 84.
Cooper, Ben, 512.
Cooper, B. L., 469.
Cooper, Boston, 479.
Cooper, D. E., 472.
Cooper, D. S., 487.
Cooper Elizabeth, 84.
Cooper, F. C., 440.
Cooper, F. E., 354.
Cooper, George, 84, 156, 200, 223, 224, 221.
Cooper, G. B., 473.
Cooper, G. S., 446.
Cooper, G. W., 238, 343.
Cooper, Hugh, 487, 497.
Cooper, Hugh M., 531.
Cooper, Mrs. Hugh M., 532.
Cooper, Ila, 475.
Cooper, James, 84, 156, 200, 209, 282.
Cooper, J. F., 477, 497, 519, 531.
Cooper, J. J., 348, 353.
Cooper, John, 156, 200, 361, 408.
Cooper, Jane, 223.
Cooper, J. B., 287.
Cooper, Jannet, 287.
Cooper, J. P., 352.
Cooper, J. H., 527.
Cooper, J. M., 464.
Cooper, Lillie, 179.

INDEX 561

Cooper, Mrs. L. M., 469.
Cooper, Miss Mutie, 468.
Cooper, Mary, 223, 246.
Cooper, Martha, 86.
Cooper, M. D., 473.
Cooper, Nancy, 223.
Cooper, Paul A., 527.
Cooper, Robert, 361.
Cooper, Robert M., 287.
Cooper, R. H., 487.
Cooper, Samuel, 287, 352, 357, 381, 405, 408.
Cooper, S. G., 398.
Cooper, S. T., 397, 440, 455, 468.
Cooper, Thomas, 84, 287.
Cooper, Mrs. T. M., 515.
Cooper, Thermutas, 287.
Cooper, William, 21, 23, 49, 57, 200, 205, 218, 219, 221, 238, 244, 246, 256, 269, 270, 311, 320, 348, 463, 464, 468, 470.
Cooper, Willie, 475, 515.
Cooper, W. B., 499.
Cooper, W. A., 361.
Cooper, William J., 156, 222, 223, 243, 473.
Cooper, W. J. B., 249, 396.
Cooper, W. R., 361.
Cooper's Ferry Road, 208.
Cook, Alexander, 408.
Cook, Allen, 351.
Cook, A. J., 400.
Cook, Benjamin, 156.
Cook, B. M., 398.
Cook, E. R., 347, 416.
Cook, E. W., 357, 400.
Cook, Earle, 503.
Cook, G., 407.
Cook, Isaac B., 398.
Cook, Joseph, 156.
Cook, J. F., 343.
Cook, J. M., 468.
Cook, J. R., 408.
Cook, J. W., 351, 384, 464.
Cook, M. M., 405.
Cook, May, 475.
Cook, T. J., 347.
Cook, W. D., 343, 347, 409.
Cook, W. E., 521.
Cook, William, 153.
Cook, West, 115.
Cook, William P., 358.
Corbett, Emma, 226.
Cordes, Francis, 23, 199, 200, 228.
Cordes, Samuel, 115, 118.
Cormick, Ann, 225.
Cormick, Elizabeth, 225.

Cormick, Jane, 225.
Cormick, Patrick, 138, 149, 200, 225, 250.
Cornwallis, 100, 112.
Cornwallis' March, 100.
Corinth, 383.
Corn meal and pickles, 422.
Cornell, John, 153.
Corruption, Official, 441.
Coskney, W. R., 487.
Conscripting Ministers, 403.
Cottingham, Daniel, 115.
Cottingham, Dill, 115.
Cottingham, T. J., 500.
Cotton, 41, 375, 449.
Cotton Cultivation, 249.
Cotton Market, 537.
Cotton Growers Ass'n., 546.
Cotton is King, 344.
Cotton Planters, 433.
Council, A. J., 350, 407.
Cousar, John, 115.
Counts, J. C., 488.
Court House Built, 217.
Court House Burned, 462.
Court House Remodelled, 162.
Court Sermons, 217.
County Antrim, 27.
County Board of Education, 472.
County Down, 27.
County Fair Ass'n., 519.
County Judge, 464.
County Officers, 218.
County Orders, 443.
County Records, 469, 521.
Covert, John, 289.
Covert, Laura, 244.
Covert, Susannah, 244, 245.
Covington, J. H., 474.
Courtney, S. B. W., 360, 527.
Coward, A. M., 408.
Coward, D. C., 351.
Coward, D. E., 383, 408.
Coward, James A., 361, 399.
Coward, John, 200, 231.
Coward, J. M., 369.
Coward, M. D., 351.
Coward, Rix A., 361, 399.
Coward, R. W., 362.
Coward, Solomon, 236.
Cowls, N. B., 352.
Cox, Frank, 362, 398, 407.
Cox, J. G., 407.
Cox, John T., 353, 400.
Cox, Robert, 503.
Cox, R. F., 382.
Cox, William, 156.

Cox, W. F., 405.
Cox, William G., 354.
Cox, W. J., 407.
Craven County, 9.
Craven Regiment, 93.
Crapper, P., 357.
Crapps, S. W., 343, 348, 357.
Crapps, William, 156, 246, 343, 407.
Crawford, Casiah, 227.
Crawford, Colwell, 227.
Crawford, George, 70.
Crawford, H. L., 360.
Crawford, James, 21, 23.
Crawford, William, 503.
Crawford, W. B., 483.
Creesy, B. J., 343.
Creesy, P. C., 348.
Cribb, A., 382.
Cribb, C., 382.
Cribb, D. W., 308, 353.
Cribb, E. A., 512.
Cribb, Elizabeth, 23.
Cribb, E. C., 472.
Cribb, John, 23, 156, 382.
Cribb, L., 381.
Cribb, R., 106, 382.
Cribb, S., 381.
Cribb, T., 382.
Crockett, James, 54, 71.
Croft, B. S., 361.
Croft, G. S., 382.
Crop Failure, 1749, 41.
Cromer, L. F., 52.
Cromwell, Oliver, 32, 36.
Cromwell, Hester, 80.
Crosby, J. R., 381.
Crosby, Sarah, 156.
Crosby, Elizabeth, 81.
Crosby, Martha, 81.
Crosener, Alex H., 57.
Cruelty to Slaves, 334.
Cubstead, John, 353.
Cubstead, J. E., 406.
Cupid, a Slave, 259.
Cumbee, George, 350.
Cummings, David, 156.
Cummings, J. B., 230, 231.
Cunningham, Alexander, 156, 219, 240.
Cunningham, Arthur, 25, 148, 149, 152, 200.
Cunningham, Mrs. A. M., 370.
Cunningham, Benjamin, 487.
Cunningham, Evelyn, 505.
Cunningham, H. B., 281, 521.
Cunningham, James, 25, 156, 200.
Cunningham, J. S., 304, 348, 481.

Cunningham, John, 115.
Cunningham, Mrs. John, 532.
Cunningham, Mary, 156, 200, 370.
Cunningham, Mose, 512.
Cunningham, Mrs. S. D., 474.
Cunningham, Mrs. Stuart, 532.
Cunningham, W. W., 361, 362.
Currency Depreciates, 404.
Currency Scarcity, 436.
Curtain, S. W., 348.
Cusack, H. D., 409.
Cutt, Bridgett, 34.

Daggett, Richard, 357.
Daggett, T. W., 430.
Dale, Thomas, 21.
Dancing, 178.
Dancing Frolics, 274.
Daniel, C. C., 475.
Daniel, C. W., 383.
Daniel, Mrs. W. D., 475.
Daniel, Mrs. Dodd, 532.
Daniel, Esther, 259.
Daniel, E. W., 351.
Daniel, James, 57, 157, 201, 230, 260, 262, 263.
Daniel, James D., 369, 464, 482.
Daniel, John, 115.
Daniel, J. W., 488.
Daniel, Martha, 201.
Daniel, Sarah M., 259.
Daniel, William, 25, 200, 259, 279, 284, 289.
Daniel, W. W., 488.
Danner, John, 153.
D. A. R. Chapter, 524.
Dargan, Jeremiah, 195.
Dargan, Timothy, 528.
Dargan, W. F., 528.
Darnall, R. L., 483.
Darwin, Lucile, 474.
David, James E., 328.
David, Jannet, 233.
David, John, 233, 353.
David, Walter, 473.
Davidson, Agnes, 79.
Davidson, Alexander, 24.
Davidson, Elizabeth, 24.
Davidson College, 305.
Davidson, William, 157.
Davis, Abraham, 235.
Davis, A. J., 353.
Davis, George, 70.
Davis, George W., 463.
Davis, Anna, 24.
Davis, Isaac E., 512.
Davis, James, 103, 114, 115, 175,

INDEX 563

Davis, 406.
Davis, James E., 353.
Davis, J. P., 353, 357, 400.
Davis, J. B., 468.
Davis, Jefferson, 359, 411.
Davis, John, 24, 115, 353, 406.
Davis, John, W., 481, 495.
Davis, John G., 235.
Davis, Mary, 157.
Davis, J. T., 357.
Davis, Martha, 234.
Davis, Mrs. M., 289.
Davis, Robert, 115, 157.
Davis, Thomas, 70.
Davis, Thomas B., 353.
Davis, Thomas H., 352.
Davis, T. P., 218, 221, 225.
Davis, T. J. N., 301.
Davis, William, 25.
Davis, W. B., 382.
Davis, William Henry, 407.
Davison, Mary, 157.
Dawsey, D. D., 244.
Dawson, Ervin, 144.
Dawson, John, 150, 157.
Day, L. G., 472, 502.
Day of Fasting, 284.
Day, John, 157.
Day of Prayer, 411.
Deery, S. J., 513, 515, 516, 517.
Deffee, W. A., 405.
DeHay, Estelle, 473.
Deflation, 540, 548.
Democracy, 438.
Delegation, 1782, 131.
Delegation Provincial Congress, 92.
Democratic Clubs, 454.
Democracy Unlimited, 458.
Democratic Party, 461.
DeLoache, Alma, 472.
Dennis, B. B., 358.
Dennis, D. I., 456.
Dennis, E. C., 460.
Dennis, E. G., 347.
Dennis, Isaiah, 115.
Dennis, Littleton, 530.
Dennis, L. J., 381.
Dennis, Mrs. L. S., 532.
Dennis, Nelson, 398.
Dennis, S. R., 347, 398.
Dennis, W., 406.
Dennis, W. H., 472.
Denominational Outlook, 183, 197.
Dentists, 527.
Derrick, C. C., 488.
Derrick, T. E., 488.
DeSaussure, W. G., 353.

Deserter Shot, 394.
Devers, Sarah, 289.
Development, Township, 137.
Dial, John, 115.
Dial, Thomas, 21, 70.
Diary, Epps', 418.
Dick, a Slave, 247, 308.
Dick, Elizabeth, 76.
Dick, Jane, 76.
Dick, James, 66.
Dick, James M., 230.
Dick, Jannet, 76, 242.
Dick, Jean, 79.
Dick, John, 21, 66, 76, 79, 151, 153, 200.
Dick, J. S., 260, 343.
Dick, Mary, 76.
Dick, Margaret, 76.
Dick, Samuel E., 233.
Dick, Susannah, 76.
Dick, Robert, 76, 157.
Dick, William, 56, 76, 200, 225.
Dickerson, Joseph, 246.
Dickerson, L. R., 474.
Dickson, James, 153.
Dickson, John, 157, 200.
Dickey, Catherine, 233.
Dickey, George, 85, 157, 221.
Dickey, James, 26, 85, 201, 238.
Dickey, John, 26, 115, 118, 127, 133, 141, 143, 145, 157, 179, 180, 201.
Dickey, Mary, 26.
Dickey, Martha, 238.
Dickey, Martha E., 233.
Dickey, Samuel E., 201, 233.
Dickey, Sarah, 221.
Dickey, Sarah M., 233.
Dickey, Stuart, 157.
Dickey, William, 224, 235.
Died, World War, 512.
Digman, Robert, 157.
Dinkins, Sarah T., 24.
Dinkins, William, 24.
Discussion with Sticks, 217.
Dissenters, 24, 33.
Division on Tariff, 267.
Dix, John, 202.
Dixie Post Office, 531.
Dixon, Robert, 152.
Dobbin, Elizabeth, 118.
Dobbin, James, 224.
Dobbin, Jean, 124.
Dobbin, Sarah, 223.
Dobbin, William, 48, 57, 124, 157, 179, 201, 228, 231, 232, 235.
Dollard, Caroline M., 233.
Dollard, Louisa J., 237.

564 INDEX

Dollard, Patrick, 104, 135, 136, 157, 253.
Dollard, William, 201, 221, 230, 242, 317.
Donath, L., 348, 440.
Donegal, 27.
Donnelly, E. J., 474.
Donnelly, James S., 238.
Doty, A., 377.
Doughty, William, 186.
Douglass, A., 236.
Douglass, D. H., 512.
Douglass, Elizabeth, 238, 290.
Douglass, Eleanor, 222, 243.
Douglass, James J., 235.
Douglass, S. A., 397.
Douglass, Samuel, 201, 205, 157, 145, 146, 151.
Douglass, Sarah, 239, 157.
Douglass, Isaac M., 239.
Douglass, William, 201, 225, 289, 157, 145, 26.
Duel Government, 215, 459.
DuBose, A., 114., 381, 487.
DuBose, Charles, 530.
DuBose, C. W., 405, 487.
DuBose, Elizabeth, 24.
DuBose, Hampton, 483.
DuBose, Henry, 527.
DuBose, John, 70.
DuBose, J. W., 472, 514.
DuBose, Peter, 115.
DuBose, R. M., 488.
DuBose, Stephen, 24.
DuBose, S. C., 408.
Dowing, Ranatus, 157.
Dowen, James, 157.
Downing, Martha, 201.
Dove, L. C., 499, 513.
Doyle, J. A., 500.
Dozier, A. W., 315, 337, 360.
Dozier, Edward C., 360.
Dozier, Elizabeth, 20.
Dozier, John, 24, 196, 205, 210, 211, 218, 219, 226, 253, 484.
Dozier, Leonard, 205, 219, 245, 320.
Dozier, N. W., 341.
Dozier, Peter C., 362.
Drake, Thomas, 201.
Draughn, Hampton, 240.
Drew, Archibald, 79.
Drew, David, 76.
Drew, Margaret, 76, 77, 79.
Drew, Mary, 76.
Drew, Nathaniel, 21, 47, 62, 76, 77, 142.
Drew, Samuel, 76, 77.

Dreifus, S., 348, 353.
Driggers, Jobe, 246.
DuBush, John, 70.
Dufford, Neill, 503.
Duke, Adelaide, 295.
Duke, Benjamin, 57, 115, 118, 127, 201.
Duke, B. F., 347, 407.
Duke, David, 295, 345.
Duke, David M., 240, 248, 440.
Duke, F. E., 483.
Duke, Isabella, 295.
Duke, J. E., 475.
Duke, Jannet P., 241.
Duke, Joseph C., 408.
Duke, Mrs. J. M., 474.
Duke, Mary E., 240.
Duke, Mary F., 240.
Duke, M. F., 488.
Duke, Mary H., 289.
Duke, P. F., 357.
Duke, R. E., 347, 407.
Duke, Sarah, 240.
Duke, Thomas, 240.
Duke, T. F., 348.
Duke, T. J., 347. 348.
Duke, W. D., 343, 346, 406.
Duke, Thomas, 183.
Duke, William, 115, 225, 398, 406.
Duncan, W. B., 469.
Dunlap, James E., 306, 362, 481, 482,
Dunlap's Praying, 306.
Dunn, Jannet, 79.
Dunn, Sarah, 84.
Dunn, Sylvester, 84.
Durant, Benjamin, 147, 157, 201, 225.
Durant, Daniel, 480.
Durant, George, 152, 157.
Durant, H. H., 292.
Durant, John, 225.
Durant, John H., 233.
Durant, Letitia S., 233.
Durant, Levi, 253.
Durant, Martha M., 225.
Durant, Mary, 225.
Durant, Paul, 157.
Durant, Ruth, 224.
DuPre, James, 157.
DuPre, Josiah, 53, 208.
DuPre, Margaret, 200.
DuPre, Thomas, 200.
Durong, Joseph, 56.
Drainage, 529.
Drainage Needed, 535.
Draining Swamps, 545.

INDEX 565

Drainage Work, 518.
Dredging Black River, 212.
Dress Parade, 287.
Drunk with Power, 452.
Drury's Bluff, 406, 407.
Dwellings, Colonial, 90.
Dye, John, 115, 118.
Dye, J. C., 288.
Dye, S., 384.
Dyestuffs Scarce, 371.

Eaddy, A. G., 527.
Eaddy, A. J., 354.
Eaddy, Andrew D., 115., 118, 127.
Eaddy, Daniel S., 217.
Eaddy, Edward D., 235, 487.
Eaddy, Elizabeth, 246, 487.
Eaddy, Frances, 246.
Eaddy, G. S., 383.
Eaddy, Henry, 115, 235.
Eaddy, H. E., 463, 500.
Eaddy, James, 157, 201, 217, 235, 487.
Eaddy, James A., 246.
Eaddy, James D., 527.
Eaddy, J. M., 469, 500.
Eaddy, Jenny, 201, 246.
Eaddy, John F., 398.
Eaddy, John, 235.
Eaddy, John T., 354, 465.
Eaddy, J. M. G., 502.
Eaddy, Mary, 235.
Eaddy, Margaret D., 246.
Eaddy, Martin, 468.
Eaddy, O. R., 465.
Eaddy, P. O., 381.
Eaddy, R. J., 381, 397.
Eaddy, Samuel, 201, 217, 246.
Eaddy, S. C., 545.
Eaddy, S. J., 246.
Eaddy, S. O., 464.
Eaddy, Tristam, 354.
Eaddy, Mrs. Wilbur, 532.
Eaddy, W. S., 354, 383.
Earle's School, 473.
Early, Andrew, 144, 151, 157.
Early, Barbara, 201.
Eason, F. W., 486.
Easterling, John R., 196.
Ebenezer Church, 190, 197.
Economic Conditions, 38, 404.
Economic and Social Life, 247.
Edenton Tea Party, 95.
Edict of Nantes, 25.
Education, Colonial, 91.
Education, Desire, 479.
Education, Public, 467.

Education Society, 208.
Edwards, Amanda, 514.
Edwards, James, 177.
Edwards, Joshua, 195.
Edwards, J. W., 357.
Edwards, Thomas, 328.
Edwards, Simon, 157.
Effingham Mills Bridge, 209.
Effingham Road, 207.
Elders Resign, 278.
Eldridge, Jane, 69.
Elections, 465.
Elections after Revolution, 213.
Election, Negro, 440.
Election on Secession, 336.
Elim M. Church, 488.
Elliott, Miss L. A., 468.
Elliott, M. S., 377.
Ellis, E. S., 347, 398, 407, 409.
Ellis, G. L., 398, 408.
Ellis, Jesse D., 362, 409.
Ellis, J. J., 361.
Elmira Prison, 415.
Elon Aid Society, 396.
Elon Church, 301.
Elwell, A. F., 382.
Elwell, J. T., 382.
Elwell, W. H., 488.
Emancipation Proclamation, 434.
Emanuel, W. P., 355.
Empire, Invisible, 451.
Enfield Rifles, 399.
English at Black Mingo, 33.
Entram, a Slave, 262,
Episcopal Church, 272.
Epps, A. L., 503.
Epps, Annie M., 472.
Epps, Carl, 527.
Epps, Charles E., 503.
Epps, Daniel, 25, 185, 201, 230, 382, 238.
Epps, Daniel D., 233.
Epps, David, 238, 311, 343, 369.
Epps, D. J., 481, 533, 538.
Epps, E. C., 463, 487, 496, 497, 498, 499, 501, 513, 516, 521, 547.
Epps, Edward, 238.
Epps, Edwin, 490.
Epps, E. F., 483.
Epps, Ernest, 489.
Epps, G. O., 516.
Epps, Isaac, 468.
Epps, James, 238, 360, 417.
Epps, J. H., 347.
Epps, Mrs. J. H., 532.
Epps, J. J., 474.
Epps, John, 238.

566   INDEX

Epps, J. P., 361, 468.
Epps, J. S., 474.
Epps, J. B., 357.
Epps, Leila, 489.
Epps, Martha, 238.
Epps, Mary C., 477.
Epps, Miss Mollie, 468.
Epps, Ossie, 514.
Epps, Peter, 238.
Epps, Robert, 238, 302, 405, 465.
Epps, R. D., 527.
Epps, T. O., 470, 516.
Epps, Van., 527.
Epps, William, 362, 382, 418.
Epps, W. B., 361.
Epps, W. J., 474.
Erckmann, Agnes, 472.
Ervin, Mrs. D. M., 532.
Ervin, E. E., 481.
Ervin, Elizabeth, 119, 157.
Ervin, H. J., 407.
Ervin, Hugh, 57, 70, 110, 114, 119, 157.
Ervin, James, 115.
Ervin, James R., 119.
Ervin, Jane, 179.
Ervin, John, 57, 66, 114, 119, 157.
Ervin, John M., 183, 184, 197, 272, 274, 289.
Ervin, Miss L. N., 468.
Ervin, Margaret, 119.
Ervin, Marian, 366.
Ervin, Mary, 76.
Ervin, Rebecca, 126.
Ervin, Robert, 10, 21, 45, 142, 147, 157, 201.
Ervin, Samuel, 70, 119.
Ervin, Miss S. M., 468.
Ervin, W. F., 440.
Ervin, William, 227.
Etheridge, T. J., 361.
Evans, A. H., 351.
Evans, Benjamin R., 358.
Evans, Mrs. D. E., 532.
Evans, Frances, 157.
Evans, J. E., 351, 358.
Evans, John, 23, 460.
Evans, J. J., 347.
Evans, J. S., 538.
Evans, S. W., 358.
Evans, Rebecca, 23.
Evans, Roberta, 475.
Evans, W. F., 474.
Everett, J. C., 465, 515.
Eveleigh's Letter, 30.
Excommunication, 274.
Exemption Board, 504.

Exhorters, 480.
Extorting of Promise, 277.
Ezell, A. W., 343.
Fair Oaks, 382.
Fair Field, 172.
Families, Williamsburg, 21.
Fairey, F. W., 486, 497, 515, 525, 528.
Fairey, L. H., 497.
Fairy, W. A., 486, 488.
Faith in Cotton, 433.
Falcon, Peter, 157.
Farm Products, 542.
Farmers Bank, 501.
Farris, J. E., 416.
Farrington, Thomas, 69, 143.
Fathers in Israel, 363.
Fenegan, H. J., 500.
Fenters, Daniel, 399.
Fenters, D. F., 350, 384.
Fenters, Gilkee, 350.
Fenters, J. C., 350, 384.
Fenters, J. J., 350, 384.
Fenters, L. F., 350.
Fenters, L. W., 350.
Fenters, S. W., 384.
Fenters, W. D., 350.
Ferdon, C. B., 503.
Ferdon, James, 25, 70.
Ferdon, Joanna, 245.
Ferdon, John, 360, 413.
Ferdon, John B., 503.
Ferdon, John P., 245.
Ferdon, Joseph H., 503.
Ferdon, Richard J., 503.
Ferdon, William, 245.
Ferdon, William B., 384.
Feagan, J. A., 343, 348, 406, 407, 530.
Feagan, R. E., 347.
Federal Law, 315.
Felder, J. H., 472.
Felder, Mrs. John L., 186.
Felder Mattie, 472.
Felps, Samuel, 158.
Felps, William, 201.
Ferguson, Ella, 473.
Ferguson, Hugh, 115.
Ferguson, James, 25.
Ferguson, John, 115.
Ferguson, Lou A., 473.
Ferguson, Mary, 81.
Ferguson, Moses, 115.
Ferguson, Thomas, 115, 118, 127.
Ferrell, B. F., 354, 384.
Ferrell, Emmie, 515.
Ferrell, H. D., 465, 498, 501.

INDEX 567

Ferrell, J. A., 468.
Ferrell, J. L., 348, 474.
Ferrell, J. W., 464.
Ferrell, Mary, 201, 239.
Ferrell, Mellie, 515.
Ferrell, R. G., 183, 184, 196, 218, 238, 289, 311, 397, 440.
Ferrell, William, 239.
Ferrell, W. J., 343, 361, 382.
Ferry, George W., 353.
Fertilizer Introduced, 535.
Fever Epidemics, 320.
Fiddlers, 308.
Fillyaw, J. B., 351.
Fillyaw, J. J., 400.
Filth, 391.
"Filthiest Place," 388.
Fincke, J. A., 25, 252.
Finkley, Charles, 157.
Finkley, G. C., 352.
Finkley, John, 157.
Finkley, R., 352.
Finkley, Thomas, 157.
Finkley, W. B., 352.
Finley Bay, 89.
Finley, Mary Ann, 78.
Finley, Francis, 21, 153.
Finley, Robert, 21, 59, 150, 179.
"First among Equals," 455.
First Court House, 217.
First Court Trial, 217.
Fisher, Fort, 413.
Fisher, James, 21, 69, 143, 150.
Fishing on Sunday, 264.
Fist Cuff Fights, 269.
Fitch, Duncan, 413.
Fitch, R. B., 465.
Fitch, W. A., 473.
Fitch, W. D., 350, 360.
Flagler, Addie, 370.
Flagler, Andrew P., 354, 384, 400.
Flagler, A. W., 361, 382, 383.
Flagler, Mrs. C. R., 370.
Flagler, Margaret G., 81, 251.
Flagler, Mary, 289, 292.
Flagler, Mary M., 236, 237.
Flagler, R. A., 361, 362, 366, 406, 408.
Flagler, Rosa, 370.
Flagler, S. M., 361, 408, 409.
Flagler, William, 81, 147, 157, 201, 205, 219, 228, 251, 312.
Flagler, William G., 219, 251, 289, 320.
Flax Culture, 41.
Fleming, Agnes, 84.
Fleming, Ann, 158, 230.

Fleming, Charlotte, 289.
Fleming, Elizabeth, 11, 75, 77, 84, 226, 230, 237.
Fleming, Hannah, 225.
Fleming, Isabella, 11, 77.
Fleming, J. B., 357.
Fleming, Jannet, 11, 77.
Fleming, James, 11, 77, 84, 115, 140, 141, 143, 145, 147, 152, 153, 201, 226, 230.
Fleming, J. H., 290.
Fleming, John, 11, 21, 45, 46, 66, 77, 84, 115, 143, 145, 158, 201, 230.
Fleming, Mary, 179, 180.
Fleming, Penelope, 11.
Fleming, Pinckney, 230.
Fleming, P. B., 30.
Fleming, Samuel, 185.
Fleming, T. B., 343, 346, 357, 384.
Fleming, W. E., 347, 357.
Fleming, William, 11, 77, 115.
Flinn, J. W., 483.
Flowers, A. E., 501.
Flowers, Coker, 194, 352.
Flowers, E. A., 351, 384, 400.
Flowers, Harmon, 201.
Flowers, J. B., 384, 400.
Flowers, J. H., 352.
Flowers, J. J., 357.
Flowers, R. C., 473.
Flowers, R. N., 351.
Flowers, W. J., 473.
Floyd, F. W., 348.
Floyd, G. S., 347.
Floyd, H. C., 382.
Floyd, James, 405.
Floyd, J. D., 475.
Floyd, Jesse, 194, 399.
Floyd, J. J., 405.
Floyd, John, 398.
Floyd, J. P., 358.
Floyd, L. B., 384.
Floyd, L. D., 351, 400.
Floyd, Noah, 194.
Floyd, Richard, 386.
Floyd, Susannah, 386.
Floyd, William, 386.
Fluitt, Eleanor, 295.
Fluitt, I., 152.
Fluitt, J. H., 357.
Fluitt, J. N., 361.
Fluitt, Margaret, 295.
Fluitt, Mary, 244.
Fluitt, R. W., 295.
Fluitt, Samuel, 149, 150, 205, 228, 237, 244, 250, 256, 289, 312.

Fluitt, W. N., 344.
Fluitt, W. W., 357.
Flynn, Andrew, 181.
Folly, James, 201, 240.
Folly, Margaret, 240.
Folly, Mary, 201.
Footman, H. E., 347, 348.
Footman, J. M., 343, 346.
Footman, R. M., 361, 362, 382, 413.
Footman, W. C., 524.
Forbes, I. W., 382.
Ford, Elizabeth, 119.
Ford, John, 115.
Ford, Samuel, 70.
Ford, Stephen, 158, 247, 249.
Fordyce, John, 45, 54, 79.
Fordyce, Mary, 79.
Forrest, Thomas, 151.
Forrester, Anthony, 158.
Fort Finger, 380.
Fort Sumter, 383.
Fort Sumter, Falls, 345.
Fort Wagner, 400.
Fort, John, 232.
Founding of Indiantown, 50.
Fourth of July, 364.
Fowler, Elizabeth, 81, 83.
Fowler, Jane, 81, 83, 252.
Fowler, Joanna, 83.
Fowler, J. T., 488.
Fowler, Martha, 83.
Fowler Post Office, 531.
Fowler, Richard, 83.
Fowler, Sarah, 83.
Fowler School, 473.
Foxworth, C. D., 352, 399.
Foxworth, John, 532.
Foxworth, Thomas, 158.
Foxworth, W. H., 473.
Francis, Richard, 157.
Franklin, Battle, 408.
Franklin, Benjamin, 252.
Fraser, Frances, 226, 227.
Fraser, Hugh, 226, 227.
Fraser, Peter, 226.
Fraser, Robert, 115.
Fraser, William, 25, 115, 158.
Fredricksburg, 383.
Free Negroes, a Nuisance, 317.
Freeman, James, 157.
Freeman, J. B., 350, 384.
Freeman, G., 382.
Free Schools, 248, 257, 467.
Free Will Baptists, 194, 488.
Frost, F. H., 440, 442.
Frost, John, 244.
Fryer, Dure, 158.

Fryer, Joel, 157.
Frierson, Absolom, 115, 118.
Frierson, Aaron, 21, 70, 77.
Frierson, Ben, 503.
Frierson, Daniel, 184, 198, 233, 238, 241, 289, 290.
Frierson, David, 179, 516.
Frierson, D. P., 472, 513.
Frierson, Elias, 179.
Frierson, E. O., 302, 363.
Frierson, George, 115, 179, 241.
Frierson Graveyard, 130.
Frierson, Hattie, 479.
Frierson, Henry, 289.
Frierson, Hester, 238.
Frierson, James, 77, 115, 153, 241, 233.
Frierson, Jane, 289.
Frierson, John, 21, 23, 77, 103, 158, 179, 201, 343, 530, 532, 114.
Frierson, John J., 84.
Frierson, Joshua, 115, 179, 180, 241.
Frierson, J. S., 474.
Frierson, J. T., 475.
Frierson, Margaret, 179, 180, 402.
Frierson, Mary, 77, 84, 85, 88.
Frierson, Moses, 77, 179, 180.
Frierson, Philip, 114.
Frierson, Robert, 84, 103, 115, 140, 145, 146, 148, 158, 179, 180, 181, 201, 208, 212, 221, 225, 233, 234, 238, 245.
Frierson, Robert P., 236.
Frierson, Samuel, 158, 179, 180, 181, 238, 241.
Frierson, Sarah, 23, 85, 236, 402.
Frierson, Thomas, 45, 85, 88, 143, 152.
Frierson, T. E., 525.
Frierson Trial, 291.
Frierson, William, 20, 21, 45, 62, 71, 84, 85, 97, 114, 115, 135, 136, 139, 141, 143, 145, 146, 152, 158, 179, 180, 201, 207, 212, 219, 222, 238, 241, 242.
Frierson, William J., 480.
Fullwood's Company, 120.
Fullwood, John, 201.
Fullwood, Robert, 143, 144, 150, 151.
Fullwood, William, 115.
Fundamental Constitution, 1.
Funderburk, J. R., 486.
Funk, Loraine, 511.
Funk, W. R., 462, 485.
Furman College, 305.
Furman, Richard, 195.

INDEX

Futhy, Elizabeth, 25.
Futhy, Francis, 25, 56.
Futhy, Hardy, 23.
Futhy, Henry, 158.
Futhy, John, 57, 158.
Fulmore, James, 239.
Fulmore, J. H., 361, 382.
Fulmore, J. R., 311.
Fulmore, J. S., 469, 479.
Fulmore, Richard, 361, 527.
Fulmore, T. P., 530.
Fulton, Z. R., 361, 463.
Fulton, Agnes, 525.
Fulton, D. M., 489.
Fulton, David, 21, 77, 479.
Fulton, D. B., 357, 413.
Fulton, D. P., 343.
Fulton, Eliza, 289.
Fulton, George M., 226.
Fulton, James E., 198, 289, 397, 530.
Fulton, Jean, 77.
Fulton, John, 146, 147, 158, 180, 201, 207, 219, 230.
Fulton, J. M., 280, 282, 289, 357, 524, 532.
Fulton, Margaret, 235.
Fulton, Mary, 77, 295.
Fulton, Paul, 77, 118, 177, 180.
Fulton, Rebecca, 77.
Fulton, R. J., 527.
Fulton, Robert W., 269, 381.
Fulton, Samuel, 48, 77, 226, 489, 516.
Fulton, Samuel E., 181, 183, 201, 229, 234, 295.
Fulton, Mrs. T., 515.
Fulton, Thomas M., 295, 353, 384.
Fulton, V. T., 289.
Fulton, Walter, 512.
Fulton, W. D., 361, 381, 515.
Fulton, W. O., 514.

Gadsden, Christopher, 159.
Gaillard, Theodore, 62.
Gaillard, Thomas, 92.
Gaines Mill, 382.
Gallinippers, 189.
Galloway, Virginia, 472.
Gamble, A. M., 361, 362, 382, 407.
Gamble, Catherine, 239.
Gamble, George, 146, 153, 201, 353.
Gamble, Hugh, 115, 118.
Gamble, H. D., 353, 383.
Gamble, Henry S., 464.
Gamble, I. K., 407.
Gamble, Ivory, 512.

Gamble, James, 21, 33, 66, 115, 142, 201, 225, 240, 244.
Gamble, J. B., 485, 538.
Gamble, J. K., 347.
Gamble, J. J., 361, 382.
Gamble, Mrs. J. P., 515.
Gamble, John, 103, 115, 118, 159, 201, 230, 234, 245, 465.
Gamble, J. P., 360, 440, 498, 501, 502, 503, 511.
Gamble, J. W., 343, 352, 462.
Gamble, Mary, 242.
Gamble's Muster Feld, 208.
Gamble, R. D., 538.
Gamble, R. K., 347, 357.
Gamble, R. R., 245.
Gamble, Samuel, 229.
Gamble, Sarah, 229, 233.
Gamble, Stephen, 115.
Gamble, S. W., 463.
Gamble, T. D., 474.
Gamble, Robert, 103, 115, 145, 151, 158, 159, 225, 348, 382.
Gamble, William, 57, 114, 142, 151, 159, 201, 229.
Gamble, W. G., 269, 360, 383, 397, 413, 503, 343, 509, 527.
Gamble, Mrs. W. G., 514, 524.
Gamble, W. J., 238, 357, 400.
Game, William, 409.
Game Abundant, 40.
Gamewell, John, 292.
Gano, John, 195.
Gantt, Myrtis, 473.
Gapway Road, 209.
Gardner, A. F., 348, 380, 381.
Gardner, J. M., 362, 382.
Gardner, John, 158.
Gardner, Mrs. M., 370.
Garland, Mary A., 231.
Garner, H. S., 348.
Garner, John, 409.
Garner, Samuel, 115.
Garrison, John, 70.
Gaskin, A. J., 358.
Gaskin, Ezekial, 158.
Gaskin, James, 159.
Gaskin, Samuel, 237.
Gaskin, Sarah, 158.
Gaskin, Vincent, 159.
Gaskins, A. M., 398, 406.
Gaskins, Charles A., 354.
Gaskins, E. B., 354.
Gaskins, E. T., 501.
Gaskins, E. V., 398.
Gaskins, H. G., 397, 405.
Gaskins, J. J., 354.

Gaskins, J. T., 474, 482.
Gaskins, Mrs. S. G., 482.
Gaskins, T. J., 384.
Gasque, Aaron, 159, 210.
Gasque, Loveless, 210, 211.
Gasque, Minna, 473.
Gasque, Nathan, 210.
Gasque, S. S., 251.
Gause, Benjamin, 92.
Gause, W. M., 351.
Geddings, Iva., 472.
George II, 2.
George III, 123.
George's Feld, 89, 129.
George, Jesse, 115.
George, Richard, 115, 127.
George, Robert, 245.
George, William, 115.
German, Edward, 71.
Gettysburg, 398.
Gewinner, C., 440.
Ghouls, 432, 452.
Gibbons, Michael, 159.
Gibbons, T. H., 399.
Gibson, Alexander, 159.
Gibson, Daniel, 158.
Gibson, Ebenezer, 142, 144, 151, 159, 201, 205, 212, 221, 222, 223, 231.
Gibson, Elander, 223.
Gibson, Elisha, 151.
Gibson, Francis, 222, 231.
Gibson, George, 159, 223, 246.
Gibson, James, 115, 118, 159, 201, 223, 224, 229, 244.
Gibson, John, 158, 159, 201, 223.
Gibson, Martha, 244.
Gibson, R. H., 349.
Gibson, Robert, 62, 115, 118.
Gibson, Roger, 21, 143, 153.
Gibson, Sarah, 236.
Gibson, Susan, 230.
Gibson, Thomas, 159, 222, 223.
Gibson, William, 222, 223.
Gilbraith, James, 146, 152, 159.
Giles, Abraham, 25.
Giles, Hugh, 205.
Giles, R. B., 399.
Gilland, Henry, 512.
Gilland, H. G., 481, 482.
Gilland, Jane, 477.
Gilland, J. D., 528.
Gilland, J. R., 363, 481.
Gilland, L. W., 472, 481, 499, 504, 513, 516, 525, 527.
Gilland, Mrs. L. W., 514, 515, 516.
Gilland, T. M., 362, 430, 446, 449, 454, 463, 467, 525, 527.
Gillespie, Andrew, 115.
Gillespie, Daniel, 201, 229.
Gillespie, John, 159.
Gilley, John, 158.
Gilles, Major, 127.
Ginn, Shadrack, 158.
Girrard, Gabriel, 21.
Gist, George, 347.
Gist, G. G., 354.
Gist, J. G., 398.
Gladden, Mary, 153.
Glass, Alex, 227, 228, 232.
Glass, Elizabeth, 232.
Glass, J. A., 159.
Glass, Robert, 360.
Glassen, D. W., 350.
Glebe Lands, 44, 184.
Glenn, John, 201.
Glenn, Louis, 201.
Gloom, 427.
Glover, Moses, 201, 205.
Goddard, Francis, 21, 75, 142, 143, 150.
Goddard, Thomas, 57.
Goddard, William, 75, 158, 247, 248.
Godfrey, John, 25.
Godwin, D. B., 351.
Godwin, G. W., 474.
Godwin, H. E., 358.
Godwin, J. A., 358.
Godwin, J. B., 350, 384.
Godwin, J. J., 358, 407.
Godwin, J. M., 358.
Godwin, Robert, 413.
Godwin, S. C., 358.
Godwin, S. F. R., 358, 383.
Godwin, William, 115.
Godwin, W. J., 397.
Godwin, W. O., 464, 528.
Godwin, W. R., 360.
Going, Bathiah, 158.
Goode, C. B., 383.
Goode, John, 201.
Goodwin, Able, 158.
Gordon, Abraham, 153.
Gordon, A. B., 352.
Gordon, A. M., 487.
Gordon, B. E., 236.
Gordon, Catherine, 243.
Gordon, Charles F., 25.
Gordon, C. H., 354.
Gordon, David, 25, 223, 256.
Gordon, D. E., 355, 357, 402, 418.
Gordon, D. W., 472.
Gordon, Elizabeth, 77, 85, 201.
Gordon, Henry, 409.

INDEX 571

Gordon, J. A., 290.
Gordon, J. D., 360.
Gordon, John, 77, 85, 115, 118, 158, 159, 201, 211, 240.
Gordon, J. J., 352.
Gordon, Mrs. J. A., 370.
Gordon, J. M., 381.
Gordon, J. W., 357, 406.
Gordon, Jack, 469.
Gordon, Jean, 85.
Gordon, James, 70, 77, 114, 115.
Gordon, J. W., 402.
Gordon, Margaret, 77, 81, 85, 112.
Gordon, Moses, 77, 85, 115, 118, 140.
Gordon, Mary, 77, 85.
Gordon, Rodger, 10, 13, 21, 39, 45, 66, 70, 71, 77, 87, 114, 122, 143, 229, 247, 524.
Gordon, Sarah, 77, 85.
Gordon, Sarah A., 402.
Gordon, Sarah M., 402.
Gordon, Samuel, 201.
Gordon, S. B., 360, 382, 472.
Gordon, William, 25, 81, 112, 114, 122.
Gordon, W. B., 352, 379, 398, 402, 406, 408.
Gordon, Rebecca E., 281.
Gore, J., 405.
Gorman, Catherine, 158.
Gotea, Eleanor, 232.
Gotea, Elender, 230.
Gotea, Elizabeth, 222, 230, 241, 242.
Gotea, George C., 222.
Gotea, James, 159.
Gotea, Jane, 223.
Gotea, John, 21, 201, 211, 218, 222, 223, 230, 237, 246.
Gotea, Sarah, 264.
Gouge, John, 159.
Gourdin, Elisha, 78.
Gourdin, Esther, 78.
Gourdin, Isaac, 78, 84.
Gourdin, J. G. K., 363.
Gourdin, Peter, 25, 77, 84, 118, 269, 270.
Gourdin, P. G., 240, 242, 312, 481, 498, 513, 520, 545, 546.
Gourdin, R. L., 219.
Gourdin, Robert, 359, 527.
Gourdin, Robert M., 340.
Gourdin, Samuel, 78, 84.
Gourdin, Susan, 242.
Gourdin, Theodore, 25, 33, 78, 84, 118, 149, 150, 159, 175, 189, 199, 201, 207, 208, 209, 216, 247, 248.

Gourdin, T. B., 463, 469.
Gourley, Joseph, 158.
Government and Officials, 213.
Gowdy, Dess, 472.
Gowdy, Francis, 240, 249.
Gowdy, James, 144, 151, 201.
Gowdy, James M., 221, 222, 231, 234.
Gowdy, Mary, 221, 222.
Grady, Henry W., 90.
Graham, Aaron, 298.
Graham, A. F., 231, 243, 268, 290.
Graham, Adeline, 295.
Graham, A. J., 243.
Graham, Arthur, 503.
Graham, A. W. J., 259.
Graham, B. T., 239.
Graham, Brown, 530.
Graham, Charles N., 243.
Graham, C. B., 487.
Graham, D. B., 243.
Graham, E. M., 361.
Graham, Elizabeth 239.
Graham, G. J., 362, 464, 475, 526.
Graham, G. W., 351, 400.
Graham, H. L., 358, 408.
Graham, Hugh, 21, 142, 159, 225.
Graham, I. W., 304, 317, 360, 394.
Graham, Jannet, 242.
Graham, Jack, 268.
Graham, James, 115, 201, 223, 225, 231, 268.
Graham, John, 25, 114, 159, 179, 181, 189, 196, 201, 207, 218, 219, 224, 232, 225, 226, 227, 239, 241, 358, 406.
Graham, J. A., 362, 398.
Graham, J. C., 290, 463, 498, 500, 538.
Graham, J. F., 243, 269, 530.
Graham, J. M., 287, 383, 406, 468, 488, 516.
Graham, J. J. M., 397, 464, 465, 473.
Graham, J. J., 468.
Graham, J. S., 405, 463.
Graham, J. W., 527.
Graham, Miss M. V., 468.
Graham, Martha, 264, 289.
Graham, Nelson, 201, 382.
Graham, N. M., 369, 469.
Graham, Robert, 159.
Graham, R. G., 239.
Graham, R. F., 357.
Graham, Samuel, 269.
Graham, S. A., 364, 463, 464, 545.

INDEX

Graham, S. E., 218, 243, 268, 290, 296, 311, 337, 367, 368, 369.
Graham, S. J., 287, 347, 358, 463.
Graham, Sarah, 225, 241, 243.
Graham, Susan, 242, 259.
Graham, Sevil, 225.
Graham, Swingle, 464.
Graham, W. E., 347, 407.
Graham, William, 115, 118, 159, 201, 209, 219, 223, 225, 231, 242, 259.
Graham, W. J., 287.
Graham, W. L., 354, 383, 298, 406, 488.
Grand Jury Committee, 446.
Grand Jury, 312, 340, 441, 461.
Grant, Hugh, 159.
Grant, John, 25.
Grant, U. S., 431.
Graveyards, 321, 534.
Gray, Alfred, 351.
Gray, B. F., 358.
Gray, Jefferson, 358.
Gray, N., 351, 383.
Gray, Thomas, 358.
Grayson, L., 348, 407.
Grayson, H. S., 347.
Grayson, J. M., 347, 361, 407.
Grayson, J. W., 405.
Grayson, Mary, 370.
Grayson, W. J., 381.
Grayson, W. S., 357, 361.
Grayson, W. W., 464.
Great Mortality, 18.
Greelyville, 529.
Greelyville School, 473.
Gregg, Bishop, 75.
Gregg, Eleanor, 86.
Gregg, Fort, 345.
Gregg, Hugh, 159.
Gregg, James, 86, 158.
Gregg, Jannet, 86.
Gregg, John, 25, 31, 86, 122, 158.
Gregg, Joseph, 158.
Gregg, Margaret, 81, 86.
Gregg, Mary, 86.
Gregg, Robert, 86, 158, 222.
Gregg, William, 86.
Green, Benjamin, 115.
Green, Elizabeth, 23.
Green, Ezra, 289.
Green, Francis, 56, 74, 159, 210.
Green, G. D., 351.
Green, George, 21, 244.
Green, G. W., 408.
Green, Hannah, 228.
Green, James, 114, 115, 159.

Green, Jane, 24.
Green, Jannet, 244.
Green, John, 23, 159, 360, 382, 413.
Green, J. J,. 211.
Green, J. G., 243, 361, 362.
Green, John T., 133, 159.
Green, Joshua, 25.
Green, Lydia, 23.
Green, Mary, 240, 245.
Green, Martha, 289.
Green, R. B., 530.
Green, Richard, 56, 158, 360, 413.
Green, Church, 297.
Green, Robert, 201, 231, 237.
Green, Samuel, 158, 245.
Green, S. B., 360, 413, 487.
Green, Thompson, 360, 413.
Green, William, 23, 24, 54, 56, 74, 115, 159.
Greer, Barron, 527.
Greer, H. L., 416.
Greer, T. R., 440, 454.
Greetless, David, 350.
Gregg's Letter, 336.
Grendfield, L., 348, 353.
Grier, Mrs. G. E., 476.
Grier, James, 169, 210.
Grier, John, 159.
Griffis, David, 159.
Griggs, N. H., 350.
Grimes, William, 70.
"Ground for Bed," 389.
Guard House, 525.
Gresham, G. T., 486.
Guerry, Benjamin, 159, 228.
Guerry, F. P., 473.
Guerry, Lydia, 164.
Guerry, Peter, 23.
Guerry, S. A., 515.
Guess, B. G., 488.
Guess, B. M., 398, 407, 408.
Guess, G. A., 347.
Guess, J. A., 409.
Guess, William, 343, 347, 348, 407.
Guards, Ripley, 379.
Guild, Samuel, 244, 191.
Guild, S. S., 398.
Guilds, Fortune, 440.
Guinea Negroes, 432.
Guinna, K., 348.
Gunther, Hugh, 407.
Gurgamus, J. F., 384.
Gwin, Bettie, 472.

Haddock, Augustus, 328.
Haddock, C. D., 527.
Hagood, General, 400.

INDEX 573

Hagan, O. F., 527.
Hagan, O., 160.
Hagan, Z., 160.
Hair, J. R., 362.
Hair, W. W., 362.
Haines, L., 384.
Hanes, J. B., 352.
Hanes, Samuel, 160.
Hall, E. S., 420,
Hall, Thomas, 21, 150.
Hall, Richard, 21, 142, 150.
Hallford, William, 407.
Hallimer, Hardy, 328.
Halfacre, W. D., 472.
Ham, J. D., 381.
Ham, William, 160.
Ham, Z. T., 382.
Hamer, Stuart, 474.
Hamilton, Archibald, 10, 21, 143.
Hamilton, Christian, 28.
Hamilton, James, 114, 116, 127.
Hamilton, Major, 132.
Hamilton, John, 63, 66, 78, 102, 116, 127, 151, 202.
Hamilton, Margaret, 202, 225.
Hamilton, Robert, 147, 152.
Hamilton, William, 19, 57, 116, 142, 153.
Hambelton, Rebecca, 160.
Hamlin, Thomas B., 245.
Hammett, Arthur, 361.
Hammett, J. N., 465.
Hampton, Wade, 120, 459, 456.
Hampton Nominated, 455.
Hammond, J. L., 352.
Hammond, Lucy, 510.
"Handwriting on the Wall," 548.
Hanna, Elizabeth, 229, 259, 352.
Hanna, D. H., 474.
Hanna, D. P., 352.
Hanna, D. W., 503, 512.
Hanna, Calvin, 259, 381.
Hanna, G. W., 354.
Hanna, Mrs. H., 469.
Hanna, Hugh, 160, 201, 229, 259.
Hanna, H. Z., 464.
Hanna, James, 160, 201, 224, 360, 413.
Hanna, J. A., 474.
Hanna, J. E., 357.
Hanna, J. F., 354. 382.
Hanna, J. G., 381.
Hanna, J. J., 354.
Hanna, J. R., 352.
Hanna, J. W., 384.
Hanna, Motte, 503.
Hanna, Pet, 515.

Hanna, Richard, 116.
Hanna, Robert, 116, 146, 354.
Hanna, Samuel, 348, 360.
Hanna, Sarah, 287.
Hanna, S. D., 382.
Hanna, S. S., 469.
Hanna, William, 160, 201, 469.
Hanna, Mrs. W. D., 473.
Hanna, W. E., 464.
Hanna, W. F., 532.
Hanna, W. J., 357.
Hannibal, a Slave, 259.
Hanford, D. 351.
Harbin, Ann, 81.
Harbin, Francis, 81.
"Hard Living", 391.
"Hard Times", 393.
Hardec, A. W., 405.
Hardee, General, 426.
Hardee, Mrs. Ruth, 475.
Harlee, David, 360.
Hardick, W. B., 384.
Hardick, W. S., 400.
Hardger, Ann, 152.
Harden, Michael, 145, 146, 151, 161.
Harper, Belle, 474, 514.
Harper, Bessie, 470.
Harper, Edwin, 328, 362, 463, 470, 536.
Harper, James, 25, 328, 357, 407, 536.
Harper, John, 328.
Harper, J. D., 381.
Harper, Miss N. A., 469.
Harper, T. B., 527.
Harper, T. C., 527.
Harper, W. H., 508, 527.
Harmon, G. T., 488, 513, 516.
Harmon, Mrs. G. T., 514.
Harmon, Thomas, 160.
Harmon, W. D., 501.
Harmon, W. H., 502.
Harmon, William, 160.
Harmon, Shenneraft, 160.
Harrington, Drury, 25.
Harrington, D. W., 362.
Harrington, Erline, 475.
Harrington, J. W., 501, 502.
Harrington, Mary, 23.
Harrington, Thomas, 23, 161.
Harrison, 108.
Harrison, T. J., 383, 409.
Harrison, Tim, 395.
Harrison, Fort, 408.
Harrell, Louis, 160.
Harrelson, Della, 475.
Harrelson, William, 160.

Harris, S. B., 409.
Harshey, John, 151.
Hart, David, 160.
Hart, Oliver, 195.
Hart, Simon, 160.
Harvey, Judith, 161.
Harvey, Christopher, 21, 153.
Harvey, William, 21, 153.
Hartley, James, 160.
Haselden, Ann, 224, 237.
Haselden, Elizabeth, 224.
Haselden, Henry W., 542.
Haselden, Herbert, 503.
Haselden, J. F., 501, 527.
Haselden, John, 202, 224, 354, 384.
Haselden, J. P., 543.
Haselden, Martha, 543.
Haselden, Richard, 116.
Haselden, R. M., 473.
Haselden, Samuel, 26, 188, 190, 201, 224, 237, 244.
Haselden, S. J., 502.
Haselden, Thomas, 201, 237.
Haselden, William, 116, 398, 397, 514, 527.
Haselden, W. M., 353.
Haselden, Violetta, 237.
Hassell, W. M., 483.
Hatchell, A. J., 400, 351.
Hatchell, Joseph, 400.
Hatchell, J. N., 400, 351.
Hatchell, T. H., 400, 351.
Hatcher, Moses, 161.
Hathhorn, Ann, 225.
Hathhorn, Hesther, 225.
Hathhorn, Jean, 225.
Hathhorn, Mary, 225.
Hathhorn, Sevil, 225.
Hathaway, J., 381.
Hathaway, Thomas, 383.
Hatfield, W. J., 460.
Hatcher, Isham, 160.
Hate Rampant, 431.
"Haunts," 355.
Haw's Shop, 355, 407.
Hawley, F. M., 483.
Hawkins, Elizabeth, 229.
Hawkins, Frank C., 486, 494.
Hawkins, John, 202, 212.
Hawthorn, George, 202.
Hawthorn, Samuel, 202.
Haynesworth, H. J., 527.
Haynesworth, J. R., 498, 501.
Heath, W. S., 488.
Health Conditions, 536.
Heathley, Elizabeth, 19, 78, 125, 180.

Heathley, James, 144.
Heathley, Mary, 23, 78, 89.
Heathley, Robert, 116.
Heathley's Run, 62.
Heathley, William, 23, 78, 142, 152.
Herren, William, 160.
Hebrews, 489.
Hebron Church, 487.
Hebron School, 472.
Hedelston, John, 202.
Heineman, School, 472.
Heins, C. A., 465, 476, 501, 515.
Heins, Louise, 473.
Hell, 441.
Heller, M. F., 481, 484, 515, 519.
Heller, Mrs. M. F., 514, 532.
Heller, Philip, 440.
Hemmington, Jiles, 202.
Helms, Jonathan, 202.
Hemingway, Post Office, 531.
Hemingway School, 472.
Hemingway, F. R., 464, 528.
Hemingway, G. S., 501.
Hemingway, J. A., 369, 397.
Hemingway, J. E., 500.
Hemingway, T. S., 362, 377, 504, 527.
Hemingway, Mrs. T. S., 523, 532.
Hemingway, W. A., 396, 397, 412.
Hemingway, W. C., 500, 527, 531.
Hemingway, W. S., 302.
Henderson, Augustus, 483.
Henderson, John, 45.
Henderson, William, 360.
Henlin, Benjamin, 161.
Henlin, John, 23, 25, 161.
Henlin, Margaret, 23.
Henry, Miss A. M., 468.
Henry, Robert, 343, 348, 463, 480, 485, 527.
Henry Post Office, 531.
Hepburn, James, 74, 161, 202.
Hepburn, Elizabeth, 74.
Henson, Nancy, 221.
Herdick, W. B., 350.
Herdsmen, 249.
Herron, John, 21.
Herron, Robert, 47.
Herron, Eleanor, 160, 161.
Herndon, J. W., 481.
Hester, E. J., 530.
Hetchinhan, Eliza, 238.
Hetchinhan, Thomas, 238.
Hewitt, Anna, 224.
Hewitt, E. H., 147, 149, 202, 229.
Hewitt, Elizabeth, 224.
Hewitt, Francis M., 224.

INDEX

Hewitt, Jane M., 229, 232.
Hewitt, John, 151.
Hewitt, John G., 243.
Hewitt, John J., 224.
Hewitt, Mary, 224, 229.
Hewitt, Sarah, 224.
Hewitt, Thomas N., 224.
Heyward, Jean, 506.
Heyward School, 475.
Hicks, Elisha, 202.
Hicks, Elijah, 486.
Hicks, George W., 358, 408.
Hicks, Jesse, 202.
Hicks, J. B., 486.
Hicks, Micajah, 202.
Hicks, W. J., 358, 408.
Hicks, William G., 358.
Hickman, Joshua, 160.
Hickman, Isaac, 160.
Hickson, James, 229.
Hickson, John, 160, 161, 201, 229, 221.
Hickson, Moses, 229.
Hickson, M. O., 350.
Hickson, Peter, 160.
Hickson, R. S., 228.
Hickson, Solomon R., 229.
Hicks, N. C., 352.
Hiddleston, Mary E., 237.
Hiddleston, Thomas, 237.
Hiddleston, William, 152, 161, 202, 205, 218, 230, 240.
Highlanders, 39.
Highway Commissioners, 62.
Hill, Isaac, 160.
Hill, John 415.
Hill, Patience, 221.
Hill, Thomas, 179.
Hilton, C. E., 529.
Hinds, A. C., 466, 486, 497, 500, 513, 516, 527.
Hinds, Mrs. A. C., 514.
Hinds, C. M., 485.
Hinds, John, 114.
Hinnant, Helen, 501, 515, 531.
Hinnant, O. C., 475.
Hinnant, R. P., 328, 468, 480.
Hinson, Isham, 328.
Hirsch, M. J., 327, 363, 416, 460, 467, 470, 525, 527.
Hirsch, E. L., 528.
History, St. Mark's, 187.
Hitch, William, 223, 225.
Hix, Benjamin, 353.
Hix, John, 353.
Hix, William, 160.
Hixon, M. J. E., 400.

Hoddy, Elizabeth, 160.
Hodge, Benjamin, 116.
Hodge, David, 553.
Hodge, Fred, 474.
Hodge, James, 116.
Hodge, John H., 353.
Hodge, M. E., 362.
Hodge, William, 116, 353, 400.
Hodges, Elizabeth, 24.
Hodges, John, 24.
Hodges, W. I., 473, 500, 515.
Hodges, W. H., 488, 529.
Holliday, Joseph, 239.
Holliday, P., 357.
Holliday, W. W., 499.
Holliday, Mrs. W., 514, 532.
Holland, J. H., 352.
Hope, Ralph, 160.
Hopkins, James, 344.
Hopton, Sarah, 76.
Hopton, William, 76.
Hopewell Church, 125, 185.
Holliday, Daniel, 25.
Holliday, William, 25.
Holden, John, 151.
Holden, Shoemaker, 161.
Holden, Samuel, 161.
Holman, J., 514, 516.
Holland, James, 159.
Holleman, Willie, 503.
Holmes, J. E., 360, 408.
"Homespun Dress", 373.
Hoole, Hannah, 74.
Hoole, James, 25, 74.
Horn, Richard, 160.
Horry, Peter, 71, 108, 127.
Horton, Joseph, 228.
Horse Racing, 93, 178, 255.
Horlbeck, M. L., 416.
Housten, C., 384.
House of Mourning, 436.
Howard, Benjamin, 116.
Howard, Edward, 84, 116, 220, 348.
Howard, F. N., 350, 384.
Howard, George, 84, 350.
Howard, J. E., 382, 405.
Howard, John, 116, 160, 161, 202, 220.
Howard, J. W., 350.
Howard, Rachael, 161.
Howard, William, 220.
Howard, W. R., 202.
Howard, W. W., 484.
Howe's History, 178.
Hudson, Ann, 24.
Hudson, Benjamin, 160.
Hudson, Hannah, 160.

576   INDEX

Hudson, James, 354.
Hudson, John, 383.
Hudson, Joseph, 160.
Hudson, Ludowick, 24.
Hudson, R. H., 348.
Hull, Hope, 292.
Hull, Joseph, 161.
Humphries, John, 144, 146, 151, 153, 160.
Hume, Peter, 21.
Hume, Thomas, 70.
Huger, H. E., 349.
Hughes, Bridgett, 66.
Hughes, B. S., 358.
Hughes, D. B., 350.
Huggins, F. E., 500, 501.
Hughes, I. W., 349.
Hughes, Meredith, 33.
Hughes, Richard, 152.
Hughes, R. A., 532.
Hughes, Sarah, 160.
Hughes, T. J., 357, 382, 409.
Huggins, D. G., 472, 501.
Huggins, George, 292.
Huggins, G. W., 383, 407.
Huggins, G. S. B., 362, 383.
Huggins, John, 116.
Huggins, J. J., 351, 399.
Huggins, J. W., 351.
Huggins, Mark, 114.
Huggins, William, 114.
Huguenots, 25, 32.
Hundreds, Bermuda, 408.
Hunter, George, 21, 69.
"Hurrah Grounds", 546.
Hurt, W. E., 485, 486.
Hutchinson, Aaron, 160.
Hutchinson, Arthur, 160,
Hutchinson, E. B., 352.
Hutchinson, L. N., 352.
Hutson, John, 116, 194.
Hutson, Joe, 194.
Hutson, S. J., 529.
Hutson, William, 116.
Hydecker, J. A., 160.
Hyman, J. C., 409.
Hyman, T., 409.
Hymns Sung, 490.

Immortal Six Hundred, 418.
Inabnit, J. P., 488.
"Independent Order", 176.
Indians, 2, 6, 15, 71.
Indiantown, 33.
Indiantown Academy, 253.
Indiantown Church, 48, 52, 124, 174, 179, 197, 258, 481, 483.

Indiantown Church Destroyed, 178.
Indiantown Congregation, 49.
Indiantown Post Office, 253.
Indiantown School, 474.
Indiantown Session Records, 258.
Indigo, 41, 133.
Indigo Accident, 42.
Indigo Vats, 89.
Infants Baptized, 259.
Influenza, 41.
Irish Protestants, 39.
Ironmonger, Recten, 161.
Ivey, John, 161.

Jackson, Andrew, 177, 344.
Jackson, A. W., 468, 488.
Jackson, John, 161.
Jackson, Mabel, 473.
Jackson, William, 161.
Jacobs, C. D., 507, 527.
Jacobs, Florence, 514.
Jacobs, Louis, 363, 440, 459, 460, 470, 525.
Jacobs, Mamie, 514.
Jacobs, Maxmilian, 459, 531.
Jacobs, M. H., 524.
James I, 27.
James II, 123.
James' Battalion, 97.
James Island, 384.
James, Alexander, 114.
James, David, 116.
James, E. L., 243.
James, Elzabeth, 78, 124. 243, 245.
James, Elizabeth L., 245.
James, Esther, 78.
James, Gavin, 108, 116, 202, 246.
James, G. W., 351.
James, Henry, 239.
James, Ervin, 161.
James, James, 116.
James, J. C., 516, 527.
James, J. I., 239.
James, J. M., 472.
James, Jane, 125, 161, 202, 227.
James, Jannet, 11, 77, 78, 124.
James, John, 11, 12, 20, 21, 45, 46, 48, 50, 57, 66, 71, 78, 92, 93, 95, 96, 101, 104, 114, 123, 124. 128, 130, 131, 133, 159, 161. 181, 202, 210, 221, 227, 243, 256, 261, 263.
James, John T., 243, 245.
James, Johnson, 161.
James, Jones, 162.
James, Jean, 79, 124.
James, J. A., 354, 369, 527.

INDEX 577

James, Mary, 11, 12.
James, Mary E., 243.
James, Meek, 162.
James, Nathaniel, 116.
James, Perry, 160.
James, Philip, 195.
James, Robert, 78, 116, 161, 238, 258.
James, Robert W., 181, 243, 245, 264, 302.
James, Samuel, 78, 227, 202, 243, 244, 245, 265, 274.
James, Samuel W., 202.
James, S. S., 347.
James, Sarah, 78, 118.
James, Sarah A., 243, 245, 264.
James, Sarah J., 227.
James, T. E., 468.
James, William, 9, 10, 11, 12, 13, 20, 21, 35, 45, 46, 62, 66, 78, 87, 99, 118, 123, 142, 143, 161, 202, 246.
James, William D., 116, 120, 124.
James, William E., 238, 243, 245, 347, 398.
Jamison, Isabella, 23.
Jamison, John, 21, 23, 143.
Jamison, Robert, 116.
Jamison, William, 78.
Jarrot, Richard, 317.
Jarvis, H. M., 484.
Jaudon, David, 78.
Jaudon, D. J., 398.
Jaudon, Elizabeth, 78, 228.
Jaudon, Esther, 228.
Jaudon, James, 228.
Jaudon, Joanna, 201.
Jaudon, J. J., 347, 398.
Jaudon, Margaret, 23.
Jaudon, Paul, 23, 25, 78, 228.
Jaudon, Samuel, 228.
Jaudon, Sarah, 228.
Jayroe, A. M., 348, 381, 397.
Jayroe, John W., 347, 407, 408.
Jefferson, W., 382, 405, 487.
Jenkins, Ann, 85.
Jenkins, Dorothy, 24.
Jenkins, James, 161.
Jenkins, Margaret, 161.
Jenkins, Samuel, 25, 161, 202, 208.
Jenkins, Thomas, 24, 224.
Jenkinson, Martha, 514.
Jenkinson, W. E., 525.
Jerks, 103.
Jeuner, James, 23.
Johnson Swamp, 474.
Johnson, Fort, 346.

Johnson, Andrew, 437.
Johnson, Bushrod, 359.
Johnson, Carter, 512.
Johnson, Celia, 244.
Johnson, Cemmy, 224.
Johnson, Chalmers, 483.
Johnson, Daniel, 350.
Johnson, David, 10, 142.
Johnson, D. A., 529.
Johnson, D. W., 399.
Johnson, Edward, 222, 328, 347, 383, 408.
Johnson, E. B., 202, 229.
Johnson, E. H., 354, 398.
Johnson, Francis, 244.
Johnson, George, 161.
Johnson, G. W., 350, 400.
Johnson, Gilbert, 350.
Johnson, H. B., 328.
Johnson, Hugh, 383.
Johnson, Jacob, 161, 202.
Johnson, James, 202, 399.
Johnson, J. B., 347, 413.
Johnson, J. H., 381.
Johnson, J. M., 350.
Johnson, J. P., 350.
Johnson, J. S., 474.
Johnson, Joseph, 21.
Johnson, L. B., 502, 527.
Johnson, Mary, 202.
Johnson, M. M., 407.
Johnson, Paul W., 399.
Johnson, R. K., 472.
Johnson, Richard, 153.
Johnson, Robert, 3.
Johnson, T. A., 474.
Johnson, Thomas, 80.
Johnson, Thomson, 161.
Johnson, William, 21, 161, 202, 224, 227, 244, 487.
Johnson, W. H., 369.
Johnson, W. N., 353.
Johnson, W. W., 237.
Johnston, J. B., 348.
Johnston, J. J., 348.
Johnston, Joseph, 416, 424.
Johnston, W. W., 464.
Jolly, Archibald, 161, 202.
Jolly, Joseph, 161.
Jolly, Joshua, 25, 74.
Jolly, Mary, 74.
Jones, Amos, 384, 400.
Jones, Charles, 344, 363, 366.
Jones, Mrs. Daniel, 295.
Jones, E. S., 361.
Jones, Frank M., 361.

INDEX

Jones, George, 384.
Jones, J. F., 347.
Jones, J. L., 369.
Jones, J. W., 488.
Jones, Elizabeth, 24.
Jones, Richard, 24.
Jones, Ebenezer, 25.
Jones, John, 56, 62, 101.
Jones, L., 351, 384.
Jones, Mary, 161.
Jones, M., 351, 399, 400, 468.
Jones, Peter, 161.
Jones, Samuel, 161, 202, 362.
Jones, W. E., 405.
Jones, William, 161, 202, 224, 351.
Jordan, Abraham, 21.
Jordan, J. E., 512.
Jordan, R., 397, 405.
Jordan, Sarah, 202.
Jordan, Thomas, 251, 383, 384.
Jordan, W. P., 474.
Josey, J. C., 468.
Joy, E. J., 362.
Joy, F. E., 362.
Joy, L. M., 362.
"Jumping Exercise," 193.
June, A., 354.
June, J. S., 360, 407.
June, P. P., 381.
June, S. M., 347.
June, Stacey, 409.
June, Stephen, 161.
June, P. G., 354.
Justus, W. B., 488.

Kaler, J. E., 407.
Keels, Abraham, 116, 118.
Keels, Bradford, 480.
Keels, Daniel, 361, 382.
Keels, E. C., 343, 347, 409.
Keels, G. W., 239.
Keels, Isaac, 116, 162, 188, 202, 208, 239.
Keels, John, 116, 162, 202, 224, 228, 235, 256.
Keels, J. A., 343, 440.
Keels, J. H., 344, 464.
Keels, J. M., 485.
Keels, J. W., 187, 224, 397.
Keels, Mary, 186, 224.
Keels, Miss M. T., 469.
Keels, Peter R., 224, 239, 502.
Keels, Richard, 186, 224.
Keels, R. F., 224.
Keels, S. J., 239.
Keels, Sue R., 469.

Keels, Susannah, 228, 239.
Keels, T. M., 361, 362.
Keels, T. T., 353.
Keels, W. E., 361.
Keels, W. M., 463.
Keith, B. L., 532.
Keith, Harriet, 119.
Keith, Robert, 1.
Keith, Sarah, 162.
Keith, William, 162.
Kellahan, Flossie, 515.
Kellahan, R. H., 327, 328, 463, 496, 524, 525, 536.
Kelley, Mrs. Charlton, 497.
Kelly, Daniel, 118.
Kelly, Elizabeth, 224.
Kelley, E. T., 527.
Kelly, E. J., 347, 408.
Kelly, James, 116.
Kelly, John, 24, 116.
Kelly, John A., 362, 455, 463, 496, 497, 519, 520, 525, 527.
Kelly, J. W., 347.
Kelly, Samuel, 116.
Kelly, T. S., 474.
Kelty, James, 235.
Kelty, Jean, 235.
Kelty, John, 162, 202, 235.
Kennedy Faction, 175.
Kennedy, Alexander, 116, 118, 127.
Kennedy, Amelia, 470.
Kennedy, Ann, 241.
Kennedy, Archibald, 238.
Kennedy, Bertha, 473.
Kennedy, Bryan, 23.
Kennedy, James, 25, 116.
Kennedy, J. N., 405, 430, 487.
Kennedy, John, 70, 118, 202.
Kennedy, Joseph, 116.
Kennedy, Mrs. Julia S., 524.
Kennedy, Lyde, 472.
Kennedy, Martha, 241.
Kennedy, Mary, 23, 162.
Kennedy, Muldrow, 194.
Kennedy, Samuel, 21, 143, 144, 150, 151, 162, 172, 173, 175, 176.
Kennedy, Sarah, 238.
Kennedy, Stephen, 116.
Kennedy, Thomas, 116, 118, 241.
Kennedy, William, 241, 292.
Kennedy, W. H., 405, 455, 463, 475, 525.
Kennedy, W. P., 382.
Kennedy, W. T., 405.
Kennedy, W. W., 465.
Kerwin, Crafton, 21, 59, 63, 79, 142,

INDEX

143.
Kerwin, Mary, 79.
Kerwin, Thomas, 79, 114, 118.
Key to Heaven, 292.
Kimball, R. H., 350, 403, 536.
Kinder, Elmo, 302.
Kinder, H. H., 354, 378.
Kinder, H. U., 525.
Kinder, John M., 143, 152, 162, 202, 302.
Kinder, J. C., 503.
Kinder, J. H., 361.
Kinder, L. P., 465, 525.
Kinder, Maude Allene, 473.
Kinder, William, 295.
Kinder, W. M., 347.
King, Eugene, 503.
King, James, 25.
King, John, 252.
King, R. W., 408.
King's Tree, 8, 9, 13, 139.
Kingstree Academy, 469.
Kingstree B. Church, 397, 405.
Kingstree Battle, 104.
Kingstree B & L Ass'n., 520.
Kingstree Library, 478.
Kingstree Light Co., 520.
Kingstree Ferry, 211.
Kingstree School, 470.
Kingstree Incorporated, 518.
Kingstree Masons, 524.
Killed, C. S. A., 382.
Killed, World War, 512.
Kingstree Meeting House, 207.
Kingstree M. Church, 486.
Kingstree Militia, 70.
Kingstree's Own Company, 414.
"Kingstree Star", 364.
Kingstree Drainage District, 545.
King School, 474.
Kirby, B., 382.
Kirby, D. P., 351, 405.
Kirby, E., 405.
Kirby, J. F., 398, 405.
Kirby, J. T., 350, 408.
Kirby, R. W., 351, 383.
Kirby, Samuel, 350, 398, 468.
Kirby, T. J., 406, 408.
Kirk, R. J., 403, 527.
Kirkley, Mrs. C. B., 473.
Kirkley, C. B., 473.
Kirkpatrick, James, 162.
Kirton, James, 344, 348, 361, 468.
Kirton, S. W., 344, 361.
Knight, Catherine, 162.
Knox, Alexander, 280.

Knox, Archibald, 86, 116, 162, 185.
Knox, Elizabeth, 289.
Knox, Hugh, 114, 118.
Knox, John, 21, 36, 151, 162, 171, 174, 180, 271, 290.
Knox, Mary, 162.
Knox, Robert, 116.
Knox, Samuel, 86, 162, 202, 226, 290.
Knox, William, 162, 176, 217.
Knox, W. D., 449.
Knox, W. J., 347.
Koger, Pearl, 470.
Koon, S. W., 398.
Kramer, J. W., 486.
Ku Klux Klan, 451.

Labor, Negro, 536.
Labor, White, 536.
Lacey, Sarah, 162.
Lacey, James, 162, 235.
Lacey, J. M., 351, 400.
LaFar, John, 483.
Lake, Richard, 21.
Lake, Thomas, 150.
Lamb, Javin, 162.
Lamb, Joseph, 163.
Lamb, H. J., 353, 363, 398.
Lamb, Levi, 202.
Lamb, Robert, 406.
Lamb, S. D., 353, 398.
Lambert, A. J., 382.
Lambert, Ann, 56.
Lambert, B. J., 357.
Lambert, B., 381.
Lambert, E. M., 474.
Lambert, H., 382.
Lambert, W. F., 347.
Lambert's Post Office, 531.
Lambson, J. R., 463, 536.
Lancaster, Carrie, 472.
Land, B. L., 353.
Land, C. S., 344, 358, 359, 380, 528, 536.
Land, James, 347.
Lander, M. M., 469.
Land, Grants, 137.
Land Values, 257, 534.
Lansdale, Thomas, 143.
Lane, Elizabeth, 232.
Lane, Hannah, 162.
Lane, James, 56, 57, 232.
Lane, John, 21, 23, 53, 162, 202, 230, 232.
Lane, Rebecca, 162.
Lane, Sarah, 23, 232.

Lane School, 473.
Lane, Thomas, 205, 232.
Lane, W. K., 327, 357.
Lane, Bank of, 500.
Laney, William, 399.
Langston, M. C., 351, 398.
Lanham, J. C., 525.
LaRebour, J. F., 407.
Laroche, Paul, 53.
Larrimore, W. A., 432.
Latham, Amos, 162.
Law and Order, 461.
Law, Martial, 434.
Law, James, 21, 142.
Law, William, 85, 145, 151, 162.
Lawes, James, 66.
Lawlessness, 444.
Lawremore, William, 163.
Lawrence, Lorena, 473.
Lawrimore, W. A., 501.
Laws, John, 351.
Laws, John C., 398.
Lawyers in 1860, 317.
Lawyers, 527.
Lazarus, J., 358.
Layman, David, 162.
Learning, 548.
Legal Holidays, 92.
Legion, Pee Dee, 357.
Leighton, J. F., 349.
Leger, Francis, 233.
Lee, Andrew, 116.
Lee, A. R., 400, 351.
Lee, B., 351.
Lee, Charles, 357.
Lee, C. W., 351, 384.
Lee, D., 223, 400.
Lee, Elijah, 202.
Lee, Fernay, 163.
Lee, Hampton, 351, 383.
Lee, Ira, 358, 408.
Lee, Isaac, 347, 358, 408.
Lee, J., 162, 405.
Lee, J. A., 351.
Lee, J. L., 351.
Lee, J. W., 351.
Lee, Jesse, 187.
Lee, John, 24, 116, 118.
Lee, J. H., 400.
Lee, J. W., 400.
Lee, LeRoy, 503, 504, 520, 527.
Lee, Mrs. LeRoy, 514, 532.
Lee's Legion, 110.
Lee, Margaret, 24.
Lee, N. D., 351.
Lee, Needham, 162, 202, 207, 209.
Lee, P. D., 384.
Lee, Robert E., 359, 423, 431.
Lee, Sam, 162.
Lee, Simon, 358.
Lee, Sherrod, 202.
Lee, Timothy, 202, 258, 408.
Lee, Virginia, 484.
Lee, W. A., 328, 352.
Lee, W. C., 251, 384, 400.
Lee, W. J., 358, 484, 485, 381, 440.
Lee, W. L., 368.
Lee, W. J. M., 350, 401.
Lee, W. M. C., 351.
Leger, Ann, 23.
Leger, Daniel, 162.
Leger, James, 162.
Leger, John, 23, 25, 162, 232.
Leger, William, 162, 232.
Lemon, John, 66, 153.
Lenerieux, Francis H., 354, 398.
Lenerieux, William, 399.
Lentz, Frank O., 527.
Lenud, Abraham, 25, 71.
Lenud, C. C., 228.
Lenud, Henry, 116, 118, 405.
Lenud's Ferry, 25, 139, 187, 324.
Lenud's Ferry Battle, 100.
Lenud's Ferry Road, 207.
Lenud School, 475.
Lequex, John, 162, 244, 360, 369, 397.
Lequex, Peter, 25, 116, 118, 207.
Lequex, Samuel, 116, 162.
Lesesne, B. H., 503.
Lesesne, Charles F., 186, 220, 235.
Lesesne, Charles, 187, 244, 344, 352, 398, 407, 400, 406.
Lesesne, Charles R., 465.
Lesesne, Daniel, 116, 118.
Lesesne, Mrs. Elizabeth, 480.
Lesesne, E. R., 344, 352, 398, 463, 400, 416, 485, 468.
Lesesne, F. J., 343, 406.
Lesesne, Francis, 25, 33, 116, 256, 352.
Lesesne, Fred, 496.
Lesesne, J. C., 382.
Lesesne, J. L., 538.
Lesesne, John, 116.
Lesesne, Margaret, 235.
Lesesne, Mary, 118.
Lesesne, N. D., 362, 366, 367, 464, 469, 497, 513.
Lesesne, P. H., 407.
Lesesne, Thomas S., 296, 353.
Lesesne, W. E., 538.
Lesesne, William, 226, 228.
Lesesne, W. C., 408.

INDEX 581

Lester, Andrew, 114.
Lester, Ann, 78.
Lester, James, 116, 118.
Lester, John, 78.
Lester, Martha, 78.
Lester, Sarah, 227.
Lester, Robert, 212.
Lester, W. B., 340, 357.
Lester, William, 162, 202, 227.
Lever, James, 202.
Leviston, Elizabeth, 76.
Leviston, John, 48, 62, 63, 66, 71, 76.
Leviston, Samuel, 76.
Levy, Aaron, 154.
Levy, Lamb, 154.
Levy, William, 202.
Lewis, Adria, 475.
Lewis, Elizabeth, 474.
Lewis, Joe, 348, 357.
Lewis, Laurie, 503.
Lewis, Robert, 70, 71.
Lewis, Sarah, 85.
Lewis, H. S., 420.
"Liberty or Death," 96.
"Lice Amuse," 393.
Lide, T. P., 486.
Lifrage, Ann, 401.
Lifrage, Dulcie, 499.
Lifrage, Emma, 474.
Lifrage, J. G., 531.
Lifrage, J. S., 357, 402.
Lifrage, Margaret, 221.
Lifrage, Mary, 295, 401.
Lifrage, M. R., 469.
Lifrage, Nancy, 289.
Lifrage, S. L., 348, 357.
Lifrage, T. M., 295, 353, 402, 406, 531.
Lifrage, V., 360.
Lifrage, William, 221, 289, 301, 530, 202, 241, 244, 245.
Lifrage, W. J. J., 301, 382, 401.
Ligneager, Isaac, 162.
Liles, R. K., 347, 408.
Lincoln, Abraham, 340, 344, 431.
Lincolndom, 409.
Lincolnites, 409.
Lindsey, Patrick, 66, 21, 153.
Linson, Thomas, 162.
Liquor Selling, 446.
Liquor Selling Opposed, 288.
Little, J. M., 363.
Little, Robert, 153.
Lining, Doctor, 152.
Local Board, 504.
Local Preachers, 480.

Locke, John, 1.
Lockliear, Thelma, 472.
Lockwood, P. B., 474.
Lofton, H. M., 351.
Logan, Calhoun, 344, 346, 380, 384, 406, 407, 414.
Logan, George P., 522, 527.
Logan, Joseph, 228.
Logan, Maude, 522.
Logan, R. C., 312, 341, 343, 348, 485, 519, 521.
Logan, T. B., 348, 361, 440, 464, 527.
Logan, D. W., 344, 348.
Logan, W. B., 522.
Long, J., 405.
Long, Henry, 384.
Long, S. A., 405.
Long, S. R., 474.
Lord Bishop of London, 5.
Lord's Day, 6.
Lords Proprietors, 1.
Lottery in Kingstree, 175.
Lovett, G. H., 475.
Lovett, J. B., 475.
Lovett, Mrs. Ozzie, 474, 503.
Low Country, 214.
Lower Bridge, 18, 430.
Lower Bridge Aid Society, 370.
Lower Bridge Road, 61, 207.
Lowder, R. T., 301.
Lowry, David, 239.
Lowry, Elizabeth, 239.
Lowry, John, 162.
Lowry, Robert, 116, 118, 162, 202, 227, 239.
Lowry, Samuel, 239.
Lowry, William, 21, 41, 116, 239.
Lowry's Bridge, 211.
Loyd, John, 70, 141.
Lucas, John, 473.
Luiser, Thomas,
Lume, Charles, 221.
Lume, Thelma, 472.
Lynam, H. J., 344.
Lynch's Creek, 139, 187.
Lynch, A., 351, 400.
Lynch, E., 390.
Lynch, G. W., 358.
Lynch, James, 84.
Lynch, Jason, 351.
Lynch, J. L., 351.
Lynch, J. M., 400.
Lynch, John E., 358.
Lynch, Laura, 472.
Lynch, Thomas, 75, 76, 92, 95.

Lynch, William E., 358.
Lynch, W. S., 527.

McCauley, Amarynthia, 239.
McCauley, James, 22, 116, 118.
McCauley, John, 97, 114, 118, 128, 129, 131, 139, 141, 142, 144, 145, 152, 151, 219.
McCauley, Rachael, 239.
Macon Telegraph, 371.
Magistrate System, 314.
Mahaffy, J. E., 488.
Malcolmson, James, 148, 152, 175, 255.
Malcolmson, Samuel, 147, 149, 150, 151, 152, 203, 219.
Malfeasance, 445.
Mallard Lumber Company, 529.
Malone, Richard, 21, 152.
Malpess, Joel, 163.
Malvern Hill, 382.
Mammon, John, 165.
Manigault, A. M., 349, 377, 401.
Manning, James, 163.
Manning, William, 202.
Manual Labor, Delusion, 433.
Marion's Body Guard, 127.
Marion Branch School, 475.
Marion's Brigade, 98, 104, 111, 114.
Marion, Francis, 98, 104, 108, 121, 220, 529.
Marion's Headquarters, 105.
Marion Takes Command, 98.
Marion's Spy System, 100.
Marlowe, Charles, 164.
Marler, Joseph, 203.
Marlow, H. L., 350.
Marlow, James, 163.
Marlow, William, 164, 165.
Marlow, Richard, 163.
Market House, 140, 148.
Market, Tobacco, 520.
Markets of Williamsburg, 250.
Markey, John, 347.
Marriages, 5.
Marsden, Elizabeth, 164.
Marsh, Samuel, 237.
Marshall, James, 203.
Marshall, J. J., 357, 407.
Marshall, John, 116, 384.
Marshall, J. W., 360, 468.
Marshall, R. B., 488.
Marshall, Thelma, 476.
Marshall, W. A., 350, 408, 475.
March, John, 163, 165.
March, Tarena, 163.
Marler, Richard, 165.

Marner, Charles, 163.
Marsh, A. B., 398.
Martin, Abraham, 235.
Martin, C. R., 409.
Martin, David, 225.
Martin, D. Z., 348, 360, 397, 413, 468, 487.
Martin, Ebenezer, 235.
Martin, E. F., 525.
Martin, E. R., 344, 347, 348, 356, 409.
Martin, Francis Mann, 168.
Martin, George, 353, 398.
Martin, G. T., 516.
Martin, I. J., 344, 347.
Martin, James, 409.
Martin, J. C. P., 350, 384.
Martin, J. F., 350.
Martin, J. G., 348.
Martin, J. J., 344, 361.
Martin, Matthew L., 268.
Martin, R. G., 350.
Martin, T. N., 349.
Martin, W. S, 488.
Martin, Walter, 75.
Martin, Zachariah, 163.
Maryland Heights, 383.
Mason, B. M., 317.
Mason, D. M., 295, 316, 337.
Mason, J. M., 527.
Mason, John, 252.
Massachusetts Bay, 3.
Massibeau, W. A., 488.
Matthews, Abraham, 80, 203, 164, 400.
Matthews, Ann, 80.
Matthews, A. M., 351, 382.
Matthews, Benjamin, 358, 407.
Matthews, C. M., 353, 442.
Matthews, C. W., 406.
Matthews, David, 116, 203.
Matthews, Dunnin, 359.
Matthews, E. E., 405.
Matthews, Eleanor, 222.
Matthews, Charles, 351.
Matthews, Elizabeth, 80, 82, 203.
Matthews, E. J. C., 382.
Matthews, F., 351, 400.
Matthews, Gordon, 359.
Matthews, G. R., 351, 383.
Matthews, G. W., 351, 383, 400.
Matthews, H., 351, 399, 400.
Matthews, H. W., 407.
Matthews, Isaac, 80, 102, 116, 143, 150, 164, 199, 203, 227.
Matthews, James, A., 359.
Matthews, T. A., 407.

INDEX 583

Matthews, J. C., 295.
Matthews, J. M., 383.
Matthews, J. S., 359.
Matthews, Jane, 257.
Matthews, Jean, 80.
Matthews, Jefferson, 359.
Matthews, Jeremiah, 202.
Matthews, John, 21, 66, 80, 87, 150, 153, 163, 180, 203, 222, 226, 227, 229, 232, 382, 354.
Matthews, J. J., 194, 384.
Matthews, J. M., 202, 347, 407.
Matthews, J. N., 295.
Matthews, Jonah, 165, 203.
Matthews, J. L. R., 405.
Matthews, Joseph, 116.
Matthews, Moses M., 351, 359.
Matthews, Mary, 80, 227.
Matthews, Moses, 218, 227, 230, 400.
Matthews, Pleasant, 358, 398, 400.
Matthews, Ralston, 359.
Matthews, Rebecca, 295.
Matthews, Richard, 203.
Matthews, R. M., 351, 400.
Matthews, Robert, 400.
Matthews, Samuel, 116, 207, 440.
Matthews, Sarah, 80, 229.
Matthews, Susannah, 229.
Matthews, T. A., 398.
Matthews, W. D., 529.
Matthews, William, 80, 82, 116, 203, 351, 405.
Matthews, W. J., 362, 382, 408.
Matthews, W. W., 354, 469.
Maurice, R. F., 354, 527, 531, 537.
Maurice, S. W., 317, 343, 348, 379, 397, 440, 449, 459, 463, 524, 525, 527.
Maxwell, Dorothy, 79.
Maxwell, George, 79.
Maxwell, James, 397.
Maxwell, John, 203.
Maxwell, Samuel, 144, 145, 146, 151, 164.
May, Enoch, 165.
May, J. A., 455.
Mayes, Samuel, 116, 180.
Mayors of Kingstree, 525.
Mellett, Mary, 84.
Mellett, Peter, 70.
Merchants at Willtown, 252.
Merriman, Thomas, 477.
Messers, John, 164.
Methodist Churches, 296, 488.
Mexican War, 320.
Michau, Abraham, 23, 25, 80, 71, 219.
Michau, Alexander, 203, 227, 232, 235.
Michau, Ann, 227.
Michau, Charlotte, 227.
Michau, Daniel, 80.
Michau, D. F., 360.
Michau, Dorothy, 227.
Michau, Duplessus, 191, 203.
Michau, Fletcher, 360.
Michau, Hester, 80.
Michau, Julia, 80.
Michau, Lydia, 23, 80.
Michau, Manassel, 164.
Michau, Noah, 360.
Michau, Paul, 80, 164, 203, 227.
Michau, Peter, 165, 244.
Michau, Susannah, 235.
Michau, W., 80, 92, 116, 118.
Michau, W. W., 472.
Middleton, James, 399.
Middleton, Richard, 59, 87, 142.
Midway Church, 186, 298, 486.
Midway School, 475.
Migrations, 180, 257.
Mikell, Jane, 163.
Mild, Jesse, 343.
Miles, Allen, 362.
Miles, Benjamin, 359.
Miles, Joseph, 359.
Miles, J. R., 398.
Miles, J. W., 359.
Miles, Leonard, 359, 408.
Miles, Robert, 359.
Miles, S., 351, 400.
Miles, Thomas, 202, 359.
Miles, W. J., 359.
Miles, Wright, 359.
Militia, 218, 317, 320.
Miller, Alexander, 203.
Miller, Andrew, 117.
Miller, Constant, 503.
Miller, A. H., 311.
Miller, F. M., 349.
Miller, George, 357.
Miller, H. A., 525.
Miller, Henry, 212, 243.
Miller, Jane, 86, 243, 290.
Miller, J. B., 347, 398.
Miller, J. G., 350.
Miller, J. J., 350, 413.
Miller, John, 243.
Miller, J. N., 407.
Miller, J. T., 347.
Miller, Mary, 23.
Miller, Moses, 164, 202.
Miller, Samuel, 23, 202.

584 INDEX

Miller, Stephen, 165, 199, 202, 243.
Miller, Thomas, 203.
Miller, T. N., 380, 384.
Miller, William, 57, 86, 229.
Miller, W. H., 350.
Miller, Elam, 203, 223, 232, 238.
Mills, G. W., 405.
Mills, Jesse, 117.
Mills, John, 114, 117, 118, 122, 165.
Mills, R. D., 497, 520.
Mills, Robert, 217, 462.
Mills, S. W., 328.
Mills, Thomas, 117.
Mills, W. J., 408.
Milton, John, 37.
Mims, John, 246, 353.
Mims, S. W., 361.
Mims, Mrs. S. W., 532.
Mingo School, 475.
Mining Reservations, 9.
Ministers, 488, 489, 493.
Mingoes, 71.
Minutes of Church, 183.
Mishoe, F., 473, 529.
Missionary Ridge, 399, 401.
Mitchell, Alexander, 290.
Mitchell, Thomas R., 269.
Mitchell, Walter, 485.
Mitchum, A., 357, 370.
Mitchum, D. M., 503.
Mitchum, Charles, 347.
Mitchum, C. H., 400.
Mitchum, G. K., 344, 347.
Mitchum, H., 353.
Mitchum, J. B., 353.
Mitchum, J. S., 347, 353, 361, 408.
Mitchum, R. C., 473.
Mitchum, S., 406, 407.
Mitchum, S. S., 344, 348, 409.
Mitchum, S. R., 381.
Mitchum, T. G., 361, 362.
Mitchum, Thomas, 117.
Mitchum, W. E., 406, 407.
Missola, John, 409.
Modlin, J. T., 344.
Moffett, William, 117.
Mon, Jemima, 203.
Monk, T., 143.
Monk, Thomas, 69, 151.
Monroe, Fortress, 413.
Montgomery, Alexander, 348.
Montgomery, Allie, 474.
Montgomery, D. M., 465, 507, 527.
Montgomery, C. R., 401.
Montgomery, Derry, 357.
Montgomery, Donald, 525.
Montgomery, Edgar, 413.

Montgomery, E. L., 499.
Montgomery, E. T., 320, 344, 347, 348, 356, 442, 468.
Montgomery, Mrs. E. W., 287.
Montgomery, George, 66.
Montgomery, H. E., 481, 499, 516.
Montgomery, Henry, 79, 84, 66, 152, 239, 301, 343, 346, 384.
Montgomery, H. J., 398.
Montgomery, Hugh, 84, 117, 163, 247, 249, 369.
Montgomery, Isaac, 203, 228, 239, 347, 407.
Montgomery, J. A., 344, 347.
Montgomery, James, 117, 231, 239, 408.
Montgomery, Jane, 239.
Montgomery, Jannet, 79, 203.
Montgomery, J. B., 343, 347, 348, 405.
Montgomery, Jeleba, 80.
Montgomery, J. F., 344, 347, 348, 398, 407.
Montgomery, J. J. B., 464, 465, 469, 526.
Montgomery, Mrs. J. J. B., 532.
Montgomery, John, 202, 226, 229, 236, 239, 243, 512.
Montgomery, J. P., 221.
Montgomery, J. W., 408.
Montgomery, Leonora, 277.
Montgomery, Mary, 79, 84.
Montgomery, M. F., 464, 516.
Montgomery, Mrs. M. F., 472.
Montgomery, Miss M. L., 469.
Montgomery, Nathaniel, 80, 118, 163.
Montgomery, Norman, 116.
Montgomery, Robert, 63, 117.
Montgomery, Mrs. Robert, 532.
Montgomery, Miss R. Z., 469.
Montgomery, Samuel, 21, 33, 79,-80, 87, 118, 117, 127, 163, 344, 345, 347, 407.
Montgomery, Samuel S., 239.
Montgomery, Sarah, 79, 84.
Montgomery, S. E., 347, 409.
Montgomery, S. I., 343, 348.
Montgomery, S. J., 295, 301, 311, 320, 348, 369, 400, 462, 465.
Montgomery, S. F., 473.
Montgomery, T. W., 408.
Montgomery, W. J., 344, 348, 402.
Montgomery, William, 79, 80, 84, 153, 212, 239, 356, 409.
Montgomery, W. R., 243.
Monument Erected, 523.

INDEX

Moody, Joseph, 22.
Moody, James, 151.
Mooney, Daniel, 21, 142.
Mooney, John, 151.
Moore, Alfred, 474.
Moore, B. C., 405.
Moore, E. E., 405.
Moore, E. H., 311.
Moore, Felix, 512.
Moore, J. C., 527.
Moore, John, 21, 66, 142.
Moore, J. P., 405.
Moore, J. W., 399, 501.
Moore, L. W., 473.
Moore, Robert, 159.
Moore, Samuel, 328.
Moore, Sarah, 232.
Moore, William, 150, 164, 165, 203, 232.
Moorer, W. D., 486.
Moreton, J. F., 384, 413.
Moreton, T. N., 384.
Morgan, H. J., 396.
Morgan, Margaret, 151.
Morgan, William, 21, 150, 151.
Morland, Peter, 222.
Morley, George, 30.
Morris, Augustus, 348.
Morris, Benjamin, 117.
Morris, E., 203, 350.
Morris, George, 117.
Morris, G. W., 361.
Morris, H. M., 357.
Morris, J. B., 474.
Morris, J. J., 360, 464.
Morris, J. M., 344.
Morris, John, 117, 165, 203, 348.
Morris, J. W., 486.
Morris, P. W., 362.
Morris, R. J., 382, 487.
Morris, Robert, 202, 343.
Morris, S. P., 360.
Morris, Thomas, 117.
Morris, William, 117, 165, 243, 487.
Morris, W. J., 357.
Morritt, Thomas, 53.
Morse, J. T., 405.
Mosquitoes, 321, 534.
Moss, William, 486.
Moss Grove School, 475.
Motte, Stephen, 70.
Moultrie, Richard, 512.
Mouzon, Ann, 82, 220, 233.
Mouzon, B. B., 311.
Mouzon's Bridge, 208, 209.
Mouzon, Mrs. Carrie M., 469.

Mouzon, D. K., 344, 348, 359.
Mouzon, D. N., 295.
Mouzon's Dwelling Burned, 101.
Mouzon, Elizabeth, 82, 220.
Mouzon, E. R., 347.
Mouzon, Esther, 82.
Mouzon, Harpy, 512.
Mouzon, Henry, 25, 33, 82, 97, 102, 106, 114, 128, 149, 163, 203, 207, 208, 209, 233.
Mouzon, H. H., 469.
Mouzon, James, 82.
Mouzon, Jane, 82.
Mouzon, J. P., 344, 348, 356, 357, 397, 407, 464.
Mouzon, Louis, 82.
Mouzon, L. W., 357.
Mouzon, Martha, 289.
Mouzon, Mary, 224, 82, 220.
Mouzon, Miss M. E., 469.
Mouzon, M. M., 469.
Mouzon, Nancy, 289.
Mouzon, P. B., 412.
Mouzon, Peter, 82, 203, 208, 233.
Mouzon, R. L., 311.
Mouzon, Samuel, 82.
Mouzon, S. A., 230.
Mouzon, Samuel R., 203, 211, 218, 229, 233, 289, 348, 357, 436, 449, 469.
Mouzon, Sarah, 82.
Mouzon, Susannah, 82, 220, 233.
Mouzon, T. R., 296.
Mouzon, T. M., 317.
Mouzon, William, 233, 479.
Mouzon, W. E., 344.
Mouzon, W. H., 203, 225.
Mouzon, W. J., 361.
Mouzon, T. M., 527.
Mouzon's Toll Bridge, 211.
Mouzon School, 475.
Moyd, E. I., 350.
Moyd, I. L., 475.
Moyd, W. R., 357.
"Much the Same," 280.
Muddy Creek, 188.
Muddy Creek School, 472.
Mulberry School, 474.
Muldrow, David, 241.
Mulhollen, Jannet, 164.
Mulken, James, 409.
Muller, T. D., 369.
Munfordville, 385.
Munn, W. J., 383.
Munnerlin, W. H., 406, 408.
Munnerly, Jane, 202.

Murfee, Moses, 163, 164.
Murfreesboro, 383, 385.
Murphy, Agnes, 295.
Murphy, A. J., 241, 287.
Murphy, Archibald, 163, 203, 237.
Murphy, Catherine, 237.
Murphy, Edward, 117.
Murphy, Elizabeth, 228, 237, 241.
Murphy, James, 117, 241.
Murphy, J. C., 348.
Murphy, Jane, 237, 241.
Murphy, Jannet, 237, 241, 295.
Murphy, Jean, 237.
Murphy, John, 117, 237, 241, 289, 295.
Murphy, Mary, 23, 236, 237, 241.
Murphy, Mary A., 287.
Murphy, Mary C., 241.
Murphy, Michael, 23.
Murphy, Moses, 247, 249.
Murphy, Sarah, 241, 290.
Murphy, S. C., 295.
Murphy, R. A., 348, 357.
Murray, Daniel, 22.
Murray's Ferry, 18, 61, 207, 208, 324, 326, 544.
Murray's Ferry Road, 61, 207.
Murray, James, 207, 218.
Murray, John, 165, 396.
Murray, J. W., 412.
Murray, Joseph, 61, 207.
Murray, Mary, 479.
Murrell, Anthony, 80.
Murrell, Elizabeth, 80.
Murrell, Jonathan, 80.
Murrell, Martha, 80.
Murrell, Mary, 80.
Murrell, Sarah, 80.
Murrell, Susannah, 80.
Murrell, William, 80, 117, 127.
Murrell, W. M., 233.
Murrell, W. N., 232.
Muster Days, 92.
Myers, Daniel, 25.
Myers, James, 225, 231.
Myers, W. A., 382.
Myrick, Carlyle, 503.
Myrick, Henry C., 512.
Mt. Hope Church, 485.
Mt. Vernon School, 474, 475.
Mt. Zion College, 177.

McAlpin, Kenneth, 29.
McBride, Elizabeth, 82, 231.
McBride, Hugh, 116.
McBride, James, 83, 116, 144, 151, 163, 179, 203, 222, 231.
McBride, John, 82, 83, 125, 142, 143, 146, 152, 164, 223, 231.
McBride, M. D., 469.
McBride, Mary, 231.
McBride, Rebecca, 83, 126, 231.
McBride, Samuel, 83, 163, 231.
McBride, William, 83.
McCabe, John, 348.
McCabe, Mrs. Marian, 510.
McCabe, R. C., 527.
McCabe, R. J., 481, 527.
McCall, James, 399.
McCall, Martha, 244.
McCall, Mary, 473.
McCalla, Jannet, 79.
McCalla, Jean, 79.
McCalla, Margaret, 79.
McCalla, Sarah, 79.
McCalla, William, 79.
McCallister, Ann, 223.
McCallister, Catherine, 223.
McCallister, Charles, 26, 165, 203, 223, 298.
McCallister, Elizabeth, 225.
McCallister, Ezekial, 223.
MsCallister, F., 408.
McCallister, J. E., 359, 408.
McCallister, J. M., 359.
McCallister, John, 164, 202, 206, 222, 223.
McCallister, J. J., 408.
McCallister, Mary, 223.
McCallister, Robert, 222.
McCallister, Sampson, 223.
McCallister, Sarah, 223.
McCallister, William, 223, 237, 383, 398.
McCallister, W. G., 296.
McCants, A. J., 344, 259.
McCants, Alexander, 76, 164, 202.
McCants, David, 22, 116, 153.
McCants, F. L., 360, 383.
McCants, Frank, 408.
McCants, F. S., 408.
McCants, J. E., 408.
McCants, J. G., 347.
McCants, J. J., 349.
McCants, J. M., 487.
McCants, James, 84, 85.
McCants, H. L., 512.
McCants, John, 22, 62, 116.
McCants, J. T., 281, 382, 474.
McCants, Martha, 259, 281.
McCants, S. E., 409.
McCants, S. J., 408.

INDEX

McCants, Samuel, 203.
McCants, Thomas, 116, 118, 142, 151, 163, 203, 246.
McCants, William, 116.
McCants, W. R., 474.
McCarthy, Margaret, 164.
McCave, David, 203.
McChesney, P. S., 481.
McClam, Bryant, 203.
McClam, C. W., 344, 405, 464, 465, 486.
McClam, Daniel, 235.
McClam, E. W., 348.
McClam, J. W., 468.
McClam, Reddick, 512.
McClam, S. M., 405.
McClam, S. W., 350, 408.
McClam, Solomon, 203, 225, 235.
McClam, T. L., 358.
McClam, W., 382, 405.
McClary School, 474.
McClary, Alexander, 240.
McClary, Ann, 289.
McClary, Barkley, 116.
McClary, Blackwell, 355.
McClary, Calvin, 295.
McClary, D. C., 344.
McClary, David, 179, 181, 202, 218, 220, 237, 290, 312.
McClary, D. M., 240, 346, 347, 406.
McClary, D. R., 289.
McClary, D. S., 240, 290, 407.
McClary, Elizabeth, 226.
McClary, G. F., 240, 343, 347, 398.
McClary, Hannah R., 240.
McClary, H. G., 512.
McClary, J. C., 357.
McClary, J. F., 398.
McClary, J. H., 357, 409.
McClary, J. L., 344, 346.
McClary, J. M., 357, 240.
McClary, James, 240, 312, 354.
McClary, Jean, 295.
McClary, John, 116, 142, 144, 145, 146, 147, 151, 152, 164, 165, 182, 198, 203, 208, 240.
McClary, J. B., 212, 237.
McClary, J. J., 236.
McClary, J. R., 226.
McClary, Leonora, 295.
McClary, M. E., 402.
McClary, M. L., 473.
McClary, M. M., 290.
McClary, Margaret, 240.
McClary, Mary, 237, 240, 289, 295, 402.

McClary, Matthew, 116.
McClary, R. B., 348, 357, 407.
McClary, S. A., 344, 347, 407.
McClary, S. B., 240, 344, 348.
McClary, Samuel, 116, 202.
McClary, S. G., 237, 360, 361, 357.
McClary, S. W., 408, 500.
McClary, Sarah, 240, 290, 295.
McClary, Thomas, 116.
McClary, Willie, 474.
McClary, William, 512.
McClary, Mrs. William, 515.
McClary, W. D., 237.
McClelland, Andrew, 22.
McClelland, Bryce, 80.
McClelland, Christian, 78.
McClelland, Grizelle, 80.
McClelland, James, 20, 22, 45, 46, 47, 48, 66, 75, 76, 80, 143, 152.
McClelland, Jane, 142.
McClelland, John, 80.
McClelland, Leonard, 80.
McClelland, Mary, 80.
McClelland, Samuel, 80, 143, 152, 174.
McClinchy, Alexander, 22.
McClure, D. M., 402.
McConnell, Ann E., 240.
McConnell, Augusta, 469.
McConnell, Catherine A., 241.
McConnell, Dick, 230.
McConnell, E. H., 381.
McConnell, Ebenezer, 222.
McConnell, Evelyn, 474.
McConnell, Francis, 222.
McConnell, Francis, J., 240.
McConnell, George, 144, 147, 151, 202, 203, 229, 230, 232, 241, 242, 243.
McConnell, H. T., 350.
McConnell, Hugh, 116.
McConnell, J. T., 349.
McConnell, J. Z., 350, 464, 527.
McConnell, James, 116, 144, 203, 210, 223, 230, 232, 242, 243.
McConnell, James, D., 149, 150, 469.
McConnell, Jannet, 330.
McConnell, John, 116.
McConnell, John H., 150, 243.
McConnell, L. M., 287.
McConnell, Mamie, 476.
McConnell, Margaret, 223, 239, 48, 241.
McConnell, Mary, 74, 164, 202, 223, 230, 242.

McConnell, Mary B., 245.
McConnell, Mary R., 241.
McConnell, M. B., 469.
McConnell, Rachael, 232, 243.
McConnell, Richard, 475.
McConnell, Robert, 74, 140, 141, 142, 145, 146, 147, 151, 152. 164, 203, 232.
McConnell, Robert F., 240.
McConnell, Sarah, 230, 241, 242, 243.
McConnell, Sarah E., 241.
McConnell, T. A., 407.
McConnell, T. M., 347.
McConnell, Thomas, 23, 57, 116, 140, 141, 143, 144, 145, 151, 153, 163, 196, 203, 211, 225, 230, 232, 237, 242, 252, 253, 407.
McConnell, W. P., 232.
McConnell, William, 142, 152, 202, 222, 221, 239.
McConnell, William, G., 232, 239.
McConnell, William H., 352, 398.
McConnell, William S., 241, 287, 384.
McKenzie, J. M., 546.
McCormick, A. P., 465.
McCormick, Isabelle, 79.
McCormick, James, 79.
McCormick, John, 79.
McCormick, Mary, 23, 79.
McCormick, P. B., 347.
McCormick, Robert, 116.
McCormick, William, 22, 66, 79, 152.
McCottry, David, 203.
McCottry, Joseph, 223, 229.
McCottry, F. W., 361.
McCottry's Lake, 129.
McCottry, Mary, 203, 230, 242.
McCottry, M. F., 295.
McCottry, Nancy, 238.
McCottry's Riflemen, 101, 109, 129.
McCottry, Robert, 49, 66, 87, 97, 114, 128, 131, 165, 203, 223, 230.
McCottry, R. F., 357.
McCown, Alexander, 116.
McCown, David 79.
McCown, James, 51, 79.
McCown, John, 116.
McCown, Moses, 116.
McCown, Samuel, 116.
McCown, Thomas, 79.
McCoy, Charles, 70.
McCrady's History, 124.
McCracker, David, 163.
McCrea, A. J., 357, 361.

McCrea, Albert A., 236.
McCrea, Alexander, 22, 57, 63, 66, 79, 85, 123, 134, 203, 230, 231, 245, 246, 249, 259, 264.
McCrea, Ann, 80.
McCrea, Esther, 240.
McCrea, Farquher, 165.
McCrea, F. J., 259.
McCrea, James, 153, 164, 357.
McCrea, James A., 355, 362, 382.
McCrea, Jane, 259.
McCrea, Janet, 123.
McCrea, John, 56, 79, 116, 213, 219.
McCrea, Joseph, 79, 80, 160, 165.
McCrea, Mrs. M. G., 370.
McCrea, Margaret, 79, 264.
McCrea, Martha, 79.
McCrea, Mary, 80, 231.
McCrea, Peter, 357.
McCrea, Philip, 203, 235.
McCrea, Robert, 83.
McCrea, Sarah, 79, 240.
McCrea, Susannah, 164, 231, 247, 249.
McCrea, Thomas A., 231, 244, 249, 257.
McCrea, Thomas, 22, 33, 49, 57, 63, 66, 66, 83, 89, 116, 164, 202, 203, 220, 223, 231, 240, 249.
McCrea, William, 79, 83, 203.
McCrea, W. M., 348, 344.
McCreight, D. B., 343.
McCreight, James, 116.
McCreary, John, 116.
McCullough, Alexander, 203.
McCullough, E. D., 500.
McCullough, Elizabeth, 164.
McCullough, Elizabeth H., 230.
McCullough, F. L., 508.
McCullough, H. A., 349, 369.
McCullough, Henry, 64.
McCullough, Hugh, 116, 118, 142, 144, 151, 153, 165, 301.
McCullough, J. A., 397, 500.
McCullough, Mrs. J. B., 370.
McCullough, J. E., 347, 357, 407.
McCullough, J. G., 35, 464, 472, 514, 516.
McCullough, J. M., 361.
McCullough, J. S., 344, 347, 362, 382, 468.
McCullough, Jack, 503, 527.
McCullough, James, 56, 78, 116, 118, 144, 151, 163.
McCullough, James J., 203.
McCullough, Jane, 82.

INDEX

McCullough, John, 33, 22, 66, 116, 153, 164, 165, 202, 203, 220, 230, 503.
McCullough, J. J., 260.
McCullough, L. P., 360, 362.
McCullough, Martha, 370.
McCullough, Mary J., 370.
McCullough, Nathaniel, 22, 78, 116, 118, 153, 203, 229.
McCullough, Robert, 177, 179.
McCullough, Sarah, 370.
McCullough, Thad, 503.
McCullough, Thomas, 151, 230.
McCullough, T. J., 241.
McCullough, W. B., 465, 468, 534.
McCullough, William, 85, 116, 163, 179, 203, 220, 221, 222, 230, 295, 344, 348, 362, 406.
McCullough, Will, 503.
McCutchen, D. E., 464, 465, 516.
McCutchen, Elizabeth W., 238.
McCutchen, F. M., 482.
McCutchen, G. D., 405.
McCutchen, George, 26, 49, 57, 164, 198, 202, 221, 223, 231, 238, 240, 245, 253, 259, 260, 265, 274, 277, 279, 357.
McCutchen, Herbert J., 512.
McCutchen, Hugh, 203, 211, 218, 221, 223, 229, 238, 243, 245, 264, 463, 483, 499, 516, 545.
McCutchen, James, 22, 49, 116, 164, 203, 218, 287, 289, 353, 379, 383, 412, 440, 449, 454, 482.
McCutchen, J. C., 362, 408.
McCutchen, J. G., 465.
McCutchen, Joseph W., 238.
McCutchen, J. W., 311.
McCutchen, Martha, 295.
McCutchen, Mary, 241.
McCutchen, Mary J., 245.
McCutchen, Nancy, 238.
McCutchen, Robert G., 238, 302.
McCutchen, S. C., 298, 397.
McCutchen, Mrs. S. L., 482.
McCutchen, Samuel, 487.
McCutchen, T. M., 357, 406, 407, 460.
McCutchen, Thomas, 203, 238, 245, 369, 396, 464, 499, 514, 515, 516, 517.
McCutchen, W. C., 405.
McCutchen, William, 203, 223, 245.
McDaniel, Catherine, 243.
McDaniel, Daniel, 23, 71.
McDaniel, Elizabeth, 243.
McDaniel, Enos, 243.

McDaniel, Honour B., 243.
McDaniel, Isabella, 243.
McDaniel, J. M., 503.
McDaniel, James, 243.
McDaniel, John, 71.
McDaniel, Mary, 23, 243.
McDaniel, Randol, 243.
McDaniel, Thomas, 244.
McDaniel, Varina, 472.
McDaniel, Z. H., 532.
McDole, William, 22.
McDonald, Adam, 10, 13, 57, 163, 207.
McDonald, Archibald, 92, 114, 118, 120, 125, 163, 186.
McDonald, A. C., 234.
McDonald, Catherine L., 235.
McDonald, Daniel, 163, 226.
McDonald, Edward, 402.
McDonald, Eliza M., 235.
McDonald, Elizabeth, 24, 259.
McDonald, Enos, 246, 259.
McDonald, Esther, 84.
McDonald, E. J., 242.
McDonald, Francis, 116.
McDonald, George, 269.
McDonald, G. K., 353, 397.
McDonald, Hester, 402.
McDonald, Isabella, 245.
McDonald, James, 92, 116, 202, 246, 383.
McDonald, Jane, 165.
McDonald, Jane M., 259.
McDonald, John, 24, 71, 84, 116, 163.
McDonald, Laura, 186.
McDonald, Louisa A., 235.
McDonald, Mary, 245, 259.
McDonald, Mary E., 234.
McDonald, Mrs. Rachael, 118.
McDonald, Randol, 246, 343.
McDonald, S. M., 398.
McDonald, Sam, 163, 352.
McDonald, Sergeant, 110.
McDonald's Company, 413.
McDonald, Susan, 186.
McDonald, Susannah E., 235.
McDonald, T. E., 234.
McDonald, W. N., 224, 234, 235.
McDonald, William, 26, 153, 186, 199, 203, 234.
McDowell, Catherine D., 240.
McDowell, E. A., 486, 516, 517.
McDowell, Forgas, 165.
McDowell, James, 79, 114, 114, 116, 481, 483.
McDowell, John, 57, 23, 164.

INDEX

McDowell, Lucretia, 23.
McDowell, Samuel, 163.
McDowell, William, 116, 163, 164.
McElroy, Andrew, 203, 223.
McElroy, Elizabeth, 223.
McElroy, James, 223.
McElroy, John, 223.
McElroy, Mary, 142, 223.
McElroy, Samuel A., 223.
McElroy, William, 165, 179, 203, 223.
McElveen, B. W., 474.
McElveen, Mrs. G. A., 472, 532.
McElveen, G. A., 302, 513, 514, 516.
McElveen, G. G., 344, 362.
McElveen, Henry, 222.
McElveen, J. D., 312.
McElveen, J. P., 344.
McElveen, J. V., 464, 513.
McElveen, James, 204, 222, 229, 231.
McElveen, James H., 240.
McElveen, Jane, 222.
McElveen, John, 22, 85, 142, 290.
McElveen, Margaret, 222.
McElveen, Mary, 222.
McElveen, R. C., 375, 483, 514, 516.
McElveen, Rebecca, 241.
McElveen, Thomas, 222.
McElveen, Walter, 503.
McElveen, Wista, 472.
McElveen, William, 116, 164, 203, 222, 302.
McElveen, W. H., 302, 369, 440, 468.
McEwen, David, 22.
McEwen, James, 22.
McFadden, Edward, 116.
McFadden, James, 85, 203, 220, 226, 231, 236, 240, 245, 253, 264.
McFadden, Jane, E., 264.
McFadden, J. F., 487, 498, 514.
McFadden, J. L., 500.
McFadden, John, 66, 185, 85, 116.
McFadden, Marian, 475, 524.
McFadden, Mary, 85.
McFadden, McBride, 510.
McFadden, Robert, 85, 164.
McFadden, Sarah Margaret, 321.
McFadden, Thomas, 85, 116, 118, 185.
McFadden, W. D., 302, 361.
McFadden, W. S., 382.
McFadden, William, 116, 118, 202, 226, 264, 322.
McFadden, Hugh, 226.
McFarland, William, 25.

McGavy, J. H., 357.
McGee, Daniel, 202.
McGee, Elizabeth, 23.
McGee, Gadsden G., 359.
McGee, James, 22, 116.
McGee, J. C., 400.
McGee, John, 350.
McGee, John, J., 359, 408.
McGee, P., 351, 398.
McGee, Pleasant, 399.
McGee, Thomas, 115, 116.
McGee, W. E., 352.
McGee, William, 23, 57, 116, 164.
McGill, Beth, 515.
McGill, Elizabeth, 289, 203.
McGill, Elizabeth A., 244.
McGill, Hugh, 22, 77, 153.
McGill, J. W., 516.
McGill, Mrs. J. Y., 532.
McGill, J. Y., 538.
McGill, James, 203, 233.
McGill, J. G., 224, 149, 153, 220, 221, 228, 245.
McGill, J. B., 237.
McGill, John, 116, 118, 202, 246, 256.
McGill, Margaret S., 237.
McGill, Mary, 233.
McGill, Mary A., 246, 244.
McGill, Mary M., 264.
McGill, Mary N., 259.
McGill, Minto W., 287.
McGill's Reminiscences, 382, 526.
McGill, Roger, 70, 77, 164.
McGill, Samuel, 101, 102, 116, 164, 202, 229, 243, 244, 246, 256, 259, 274, 275, 276, 277, 278, 279, 320, 427, 430, 491, 526, 527.
McGill, S. D., 259, 317, 348, 380, 381, 284, 464, 467, 503.
McGill, Sarah, 77.
McGill, Sarah A., 370.
McGill, Sarah E., 287.
McGill, William, 202.
McGinnes, Alexander, 25.
McGinnes, A. J., 244.
McGinnes, Thomas, 116.
McGinney, Charles, 116, 118.
McGinney, Daniel, 24, 57.
McGinney, James, 163, 224.
McGinney, Samuel, 165.
McGinney, Susannah, 24.
McGrath, A. G., 341.
McGregor, A. L., 224.
McGregor, David, 31.
McGuirt's Branch, 192.

INDEX

McGirt, James, 23, 71.
McGirt, Priscilla, 23.
McGirt's Swamp, 18.
McGuirt's Swamp Road, 208.
McIntosh, A. W., 503.
McIntosh, J. D., 473.
McIntosh, John, 23, 70.
McIntosh, Junius M., 509, 528.
McIntosh, L. R., 525.
McIntosh, Lachlen, 166.
McIntosh, Mary, 23.
McIntosh, R. W., 384.
McIntosh, W. K., 538, 539, 547.
McIntosh, William, 185.
McIntree, Thomas, 163.
McIver, David, 25, 34.
McIver, John, 62.
McKable, Alexander, 165.
McKathan, Thomas, 62.
McKee, Adam, 86, 116.
McKee, Ann, 82.
McKee, Archibald, 82, 86, 143, 226.
McKee, Elizabeth, 82, 86, 226.
McKee, James, 164.
McKee, John, 163, 165.
McKee, Joseph, 85, 86, 118, 163, 179, 203, 226.
McKee, Martha, 86.
McKee, Philip, 225.
McKee, Robert, 116, 118.
McKee, Thomas, 116.
McKee, W. B., 377.
McKeithan, Donegal, 25.
McKinney, Thomas, 158.
McKenzie, A. B., 475.
McKenzie, Angus, 524.
McKenzie, Daniel, 241.
McKenzie, Daniel S., 359.
McKenzie, D. D., 508.
McKenzie, F. W., 397.
McKenzie, Mrs. Garfield, 515.
McKenzie, J. M., 409.
McKenzie, J. Monroe, 516.
McKenzie, J. N., 475, 514, 515.
McKenzie, J. R., 408.
McKenzie, John, 114, 122, 241.
McKenzie, Mary, 241.
McKenzie, Nancy, 241.
McKenzie, N., 361.
McKenzie, Peter, 241.
McKenzie, Sam, 194, 241, 343.
McKenzie, Shadrack, 347.
McKenzie, William, 122, 241.
McKindru, John, 163.
McKissick, Archie, 165.
McKissick, W. W., 352.

McKnelly, James, 164.
McKnight, Mrs. A. C., 186, 370.
McKnight, A. Isaac, 296, 317.
McKnight, Alexander, 34, 202, 222, 223, 224, 231, 238.
McKnight, Allan, 164, 247, 249.
McKnight, B. B., 351.
McKnight, B. E., 475, 538.
McKnight, H. M., 311.
McKnight, Isaac, 143.
McKnight, J. J., 350.
McKnight, John G., 343.
McKnight, James, 85, 163.
McKnight, Jane, 264.
McKnight, John, 66, 116, 164, 222, 351, 383, 399.
McKnight, John J., 408.
McKnight, J. H., 359.
McKnight, Mary, 85.
McKnight, Moses, 116.
McKnight, R. I., 351.
McKnight, Robert, 85, 116, 118, 165, 384.
McKnight, Thomas, 85, 163.
McKnight, T. M., 359.
McKnight, W. H., 359.
McKnight, W. M., 344, 347, 361, 398, 414, 415.
McKnight, W. G., 397.
McKnight, W. P., 538.
McKnight, William, 22, 66, 85, 153.
McLaughlin, John, 203.
McLaurin, John, 229.
McLeod, Catherine, 289.
McLeod, Cornelius, 292.
McMahan, Edward, 22.
McMelly, Mary, 165.
McBane, Daniel, 165.
McMillan, R. A., 440.
McMuldrow, Andrew, 117.
McMuldrow, David, 117.
McMuldrow, Hugh, 117.
McMuldrow, James, 117.
McMuldrow, John, 117.
McMuldrow, William, 117.
McMulkin, James, 383.
McMullen, Hugh, 163.
McMurray, Elizabeth, 228.
McMurray, James, 203, 228.
McMurray, Mary A., 228.
McNally, John, 25, 70.
McNaemee, John, 350.
McNealy, Henry, 203.
McNeedy, William, 63.
McPherson, Elias, 56.
McPherson, Elizabeth, 23.

McPherson, James, 23, 54, 56, 57.
McPherson, J. P., 282, 284.
McPherson, William, 116.
McQuoid, Elizabeth, 17, 81.
McQuoid, Robert, 17.
McWhite, W. H., 352.
McWhorter, C. G., 185, 191.

Nashville, Battle, 408.
Natural Ruling Element, 440.
Naval Stores Products, 528.
Negligence, Criminal, 445.
Negroes, 6.
Negro Body Servants Pensioned, 356.
Negro Labor, 453.
Negro Legislators, 447.
Negro Legislature, 448.
Negro Schools, 478.
Nero, a Slave, 450.
Negro Slave Owners, 338.
Nero Steals Hogs, 286.
Neill, J. C., 377.
Nelson, Ashton, T., 512.
Nelson, Beulah, 524.
Nelson, Mrs. Christina J., 524.
Nelson, Eleanor, 80.
Nelson, Elizabeth, 80.
Nelson, George, 49, 80.
Nelson, G. P., 357, 361, 455, 462, 465, 518.
Nelson, Helen, 49.
Nelson, H. G., 406.
Nelson, Isaac, 84, 117, 118, 144, 183, 184, 198, 204, 206, 212, 219, 232, 233, 244, 245, 290, 312.
Nelson, Isabelle, 80.
Nelson, James M., 361.
Nelson, Jane, 80.
Nelson, Jared, 80.
Nelson, John, 49, 80, 103, 114, 120, 121, 134.
Nelson, J. W., 469.
Nelson, Mary, 80.
Nelson, Matthews, 22, 80.
Nelson, Letitia, 165.
Nelson, Samuel, 80, 117.
Nelson, Mrs. S. A., 469.
Nelson, Thomas, 117.
Nelson, Warehouse Sales, 539.
Nelson, William, 62, 63, 71, 80, 115, 117, 118, 204, 206, 208, 233.
Nelson, W. R., 311.
Nelson, T. S., 356, 357, 406, 407.
Nesbit, James, 166.
Nesmith, B. L., 396, 531.

Nesmith, Daniel C., 363, 383.
Nesmith, Eliza, 204.
Nesmith, Elizabeth, 165.
Nesmith, Flora, 516.
Nesmith, G. T., 350.
Nesmith, Joannah, 287.
Nesmith, John, 25, 29, 76, 117, 127, 134, 149, 165, 175, 204, 216, 219, 222, 234, 369.
Nesmith, John F., 245.
Nesmith, John L., 383, 408.
Nesmith, Lemuel, 117, 127, 204, 234, 245.
Nesmith, L. W., 496.
Nesmith, Margaret, 240.
Nesmith, Martha, 234.
Nesmith, Mary, 234, 287.
Nesmith, Marie A., 245.
Nesmith, M. D., 527.
Nesmith, N. D., 165.
Nesmith, Nathaniel, 350, 398.
Nesmith, Post Office, 531.
Nesmith, Robert, 117, 127, 165, 204, 234, 245, 353, 408.
Nesmith, R. J., 531.
Nesmith, Samuel, 56, 76, 77, 84, 92, 117, 127, 165, 304, 224, 234, 245.
Nesmith, Sarah, 234.
Nesmith School, 473.
Nesmith, Solon, 538.
Nesmith, Thomas, 117.
Nesmith, W. B., 384.
Nesmith, W. E., 405, 464, 469, 497, 500, 514, 516, 546.
Nesmith, W. P., 469, 349, 397.
Nettles, Isham, 166.
Nettles, James C., 359.
Nettles, J. R., 350, 379, 380, 383.
Nettles, J. W., 485.
Nettles, Joseph, 117.
Nettles, Robert, 117.
Nettles, S. I., 351.
Nettles, S. J., 400.
Nettles, W. H., 454.
Nettles, W. J., 369.
Neverfail School, 475.
Newell, Janie, 472.
Newman, J. R., 501.
Newman, Thomas, 70.
Newsom, S. B., 328, 488.
Newton, James W., 360.
Nexsen, J. A., 344, 349, 397, 468.
Nexsen, W. I., 498, 499, 520.
New Town, 519.
The "New Built," 15.
New England Townships, **137**.

INDEX 593

New Enterprises, 519.
New Hampshire, 3.
"New Lichts," 173.
New York Herald, 345.
New Market Methodist Church, 487.
Nicholson, John, 22.
Nigger Fiddlers, 308.
Night, Thomas, 165.
Norton, Allen, 235.
Norton, Jacob, 204, 235.
Norton, J. H., 357.
Norton, Margaret A., 246.
Norton, Miles, 235, 246.
Norton, Thomas G., 512.
North Britain, 27.
North Carolina, 1.
North's Ferry, 208.
North, Thomas, 25.
North, Lord, 95.
North, William, 245.
Nowell, L. C., 425.
Nullifiers, 268.
Nullification Coventions, 267.
Nullification Movement, 266.

Oak Ridge School, 475.
O'Bryan, J. D., 499, 504, 510, 513, 527.
O'Bryan, John, 157, 166.
O'Bryan, W. M., 498, 514, 515, 527.
Odear, Samuel, 204.
Odom, Aaron, 204.
Odom, J. A., 408.
Odom, Thomas, 408.
Odom, William W., 359.
Officials, Colonial, 91.
Officers in World War, 505.
Ogburn, Hugh, 292.
Ogburn, W. C., 360, 399.
Ogelby, Daniel, 166.
Ogelby, Lewis, 166.
Oliver, D. H., 502, 532.
Oliver, H. D., 529.
Oliver, H. L., 486.
Oliver, H. J., 503.
Oliver, J. W., 301.
Oliver, Mary, 23.
Oliver, P. M., 239.
Oliver, Robert, 23.
Oliver, William, 117.
"On Credit of State," 448.
O'Neal, Henry, 25, 71.
O'Neill, John, 166.
O'Neill, John B., 315.
Original Settlers, 21.
Orr, John, 166.

Orr, Mary, 166.
Orr, William, 22, 85, 117, 153.
Osburn, A. C., 399.
Osborne, C. S., 232.
Osborn, E. C., 399.
Osborn, Jesse, 194.
Osborn, J. B., 475.
Osborn, J. C., 350.
Outgrown Shell, 548.
Oven, Dutch, 121.
Overseers, 257.
Owen, David M., 153.
Owen, D. S., 409.
Owens, James, 166.
Owens, James A., 409.
Owens, J. M., 465, 487.
Owens, Mary H., 224.
Owens, Peter, 166, 224.
Owens, S. H., 360.
Owens, Stephen, 224.
Owens, W. D., 468.
Owens, Zacine, 224.
Owens, Zachariah, 204, 208.
Owens, Jeremiah, 166.
Owings, Eleanor, 473.
Ox Swamp School, 474.

Pace, W. H., 349.
Paisley, Elizabeth, 238.
Paisley, Hannah, 204, 229.
Paisley, Hugh, 167, 204, 238, 252, 260.
Paisley, James, 81.
Paisley, Janet, 238.
Paisley, John, 81, 117, 165.
Paisley, Mary, 81.
Paisley, Peter, 167.
Paisley, Robert, 20, 48, 81, 85, 114, 133, 166.
Paisley, Sarah, 229.
Paisley, Sarah G., 238.
Paisley, Susannah, 229, 238.
Paisley, Thomas, 166.
Paisley, William, 81, 166, 167, 238.
Palatines, 39.
Palmetto Battalion, 361.
"Palmy Days," 304.
Parade Ground Divided, 146.
Parham, J. H., 358.
Park, E. J., 487.
Parker, Alexander, 351, 383.
Parker, E. J., 328, 468.
Parker, James R., 359.
Packer, Jannet, 76.
Parker, J. B., 347.
Parker, Jesse, 359.
Parker, John, 167.

Parker, J., 362.
Parker, N. S., 351.
Parker, Patrick, 530.
Parker, N. G., 400.
Parker, William, 204, 343.
Parker, W. H., 359.
Parker, W. K., 347, 405.
Parkison, John, 167.
Parler, Ida Lee, 472.
Parnell, H. N., 473.
Parnell, James, 117.
Parochial Schools, 305.
Parsons, Amos, 166, 204.
Parsons, A. J., 347, 468.
Parsons, Ann, 246.
Parsons, David, 245, 246.
Parsons, E. G., 407.
Parsons, Elizabeth, 204.
Parsons, Elizabeth P., 246.
Parsons, F. F., 382, 408.
Parsons, F. R., 348.
Parsons, Jack, 480.
Parsons, James, 117.
Parsons, J. C., 407.
Parsons, Joseph, 245, 246.
Parsons, J. W., 473.
Parsons, Mary, 204, 245.
Parsons, Sarah, 204.
Parsons, S. L., 515.
Parsons, Solomon, 204, 245.
Parsons, Mrs. Susannah, 118.
Parsons, W. H., 348, 398.
Parsons, W. J., 469.
Parsons, William, 167, 204, 246.
Parrott, R. J., 473.
Pass, R. L., 500.
Party Primaries, 465.
Pate, Charles H., 527.
Pate, E. M., 501.
Pate, Joseph, 351.
Patrick, James, 117.
Patrick, Joshua, 117.
Patrick, T. E., 405.
Patterson, Andrew, 26, 152, 166, 204, 231, 235, 237.
Patterson, A. L., 204.
Patterson, Jane H., 237.
Patterson, Jannet, 204, 237.
Patterson, John, 170.
Patterson, Margaret, 237.
Patterson, Mary, 295.
Patterson, Mary M., 229.
Patterson, Robert, 204.
Patterson, R. J., 237, 244, 357, 407.
Paul, Walter, 512.
Pawley, George, 70.
Payne, John, 166.

Pearson, Philip, 291, 302.
Peden, A. G., 279, 280, 281.
Pell, Gilbert, 166.
Pee Dee Regiment, 121.
Pee Dee River, 139.
Pelt, John, 406.
Pendergrass, Darby, 188.
Pendergrass, B. P., 297.
Pendergrass, B. R., 343.
Pendergrass, J., 440.
Pendergrass, J. C., 469.
Pendergrass, J. M., 343, 406, 407.
Pendergrass, Patrick, 117.
Pendergrass, S. F., 343.
Pendergrass, T. J., 516.
Penn School, 474.
Pennyfather, John, 151.
Peoples Bank, Hemingway, 502.
Perdreau, Abraham, 25.
Perdreau, Alexander, 227.
Perdreau, Elizabeth, 228.
Perdreau, John, 117, 118, 127, 164, 191, 204, 227, 232, 235, 244.
Perdreau, Samuel, 191, 204, 227, 228, 235.
Pergamos School, 473.
Perineau, Henry, 243.
Perkins, Augustus, 328, 354.
Perkins, Mrs. T. M., 482.
Perkins, David, 166.
Perkins, Lewis, 166.
Perkins, Mary, 166.
Permits, Teachers, 476.
Perrit, Abraham, 166, 207.
Perrit, Ann, 204, 221, 244.
Perritt, Edward T., 191.
Perritt, Francis, 166, 204.
Perritt, Francis W., 244.
Perritt, James, 166.
Perritt, Peter E., 204, 244.
Perry, John, 169.
Perry, Julia, 80.
Perry, R. D., 483.
Perry, W. D., 358.
Perryville, 385.
Peter, a Servant, 355.
Petersburg, Battle, 408.
Peterson, James, 460.
Petition, 67.
Petition, Black River, 59.
Petrie, George H. E., 290.
Pettiaguas, 252.
Pettingil, C. H., 440.
Pettigrew, James, 135, 136, 153, 166.
Pettigrew, J. J., 338.
Pettigrew's Report, 338.
Pewholders, Prince Frederick's, 53.

INDEX 595

Pewholder's voting, 173.
Philips, Anthony, 23.
Philips, D. A., 488.
Physicians, 527.
Physicians prior to 1860, 317.
Phillips, Tom, 503.
Phillips, W. T., 473.
Pick, 27.
Pickens, Ezekiel, 209.
Pickett, Evander, 359.
Pickett, John R., 292.
Pierson, Philip, 483.
Pierson, Robert, 528.
Pigott, Nathaniel, 166.
Pillory Erected, 316.
Pills, 390.
Pilkinton, DuRay, 166.
Pilkerton, John, 166.
"Pine Bark Stew", 533.
Pine Grove Church, 194, 197.
Pine Tree, 428.
Pine Forest School, 474.
Pipkin, Hugh, 475.
Pipkin, L. H., 399, 408.
Pipkin, L. K., 360.
Pipkin, R., 382.
Pipkin, W. I., 350.
Pipkin, W. J., 383, 384.
Pitman, A. M., 486.
Pitman, Isaac, 204.
Pitt, William, 95.
Pittman, J. H., 536.
Pittman, N. T., 485.
Pittman, N. G., 328.
"Plant 'um Early," 543.
Plat, Elizabeth, 167.
Player, E. J., 362.
Player, F. M., 363.
Player, I., 408.
Player, I. C., 502.
Player, J. B., 474, 538.
Player, J. C., 476, 501.
Player, J. G., 353, 398, 406, 407.
Player, J. M., 348.
Player, J. T., 398.
Player, L., 398.
Player, Sylvester D., 353.
Player, S. T., 395.
Player, Thomas, 70.
Plexico, Frances, 474.
Plowden, Edward, 10, 13, 22, 33, 57, 142.
Plowden, Hanna, 490.
Plowden, J. E., 473.
Plowden, John, 92.
Plowden, Mary J., 239.
Plowden, M. H., 490.

Plowden, S. M., 357.
Post Office in Williamsburg, 317.
Political & Social, 1745, 87.
Political Debauch, 449.
Political Thought, 266.
Pollard, James, 22.
Ponpon River, 3.
Pontovine, Samuel, 66.
"Poor Protestants," 35, 38.
"Poor Whites," 433.
Popery, 36.
Pope, E., 382.
Pope, Thomas T., 512.
Popular Hill Swamp, 196.
Population, 1920, 539.
Port, Benjamin, 166.
Port, Francis, 166.
Port Royal, 378.
Port, Thomas, 92, 250, 384.
Porter, Benjamin, 133, 167, 247, 249.
Porter, Charles, 484.
Porter, D. J., 312.
Porter, E. J., 317, 440, 527.
Porter, E. T., 399.
Porter, James, 80.
Porter, J. H., 361.
Porter, J. M., 358.
Porter, John, 22, 45, 46, 66, 80, 142, 166, 167.
Porter, Mary, 80.
Porter, Minnie, 484.
Porter, William, 166.
Postell, Henry, 153.
Postell, Hugh, 114.
Postell, James, 114, 131.
Postell, John, 117.
Poston, Andrew, 351, 352, 398.
Poston, B., 351.
Poston, B. A., 352.
Poston, B. D., 398.
Poston, H. A., 354, 398, 407.
Poston, H. L., 529.
Poston, Isaac, 382.
Poston, James, 166.
Poston, J. H., 352.
Poston, J. J., 474.
Poston, J. L., 352.
Boston, John, 166.
Poston, Joseph, 167.
Poston, Larry, 530.
Poston, M. M., 352.
Poston, Mrs. N. O., 469.
Poston School, 476.
Poston, T. W., 352.
Poston, W., 352.
Poston, W. H., 398, 399.

596 INDEX

Poston, W. L., 352.
Potatoes, 412.
Potato Ferry, 10, 189, 210.
Potato Ferry Road, 60, 207, 209.
Potter's Raiders, 429.
Potts, Ann, 80.
Potts, Elizabeth, 80.
Potts, Margaret, 80.
Potts, Mary, 80.
Potts, Rebecca, 204.
Potts, Sarah, 80.
Potts, Thomas, 25, 57, 80, 131, 166, 204.
Potts, William, 166.
Powe, Elizabeth, 119.
Powell, C., 408.
Powell, E., 408.
Powell, George, 25.
Powell, J., 405.
Powell, J. M., 359.
Powell, J. S., 352.
Powell, S. C., 352.
Powell, S. E., 382.
Powell, W. R., 405.
Powers, T. D., 502.
Pratt, J. H., 527.
Prelacy, 36.
Presbytery of S. C., 176.
Presbyterianism, 36.
Presbyterianism Regnant, 171.
Pres. Church of Williamsburg, 272.
Presbyterian Churches, 1923, 483.
Presbyterian factions, 172.
Presbyterian Ministers, 481, 483.
Presbyterian Missionaries, 55.
Presbyterians, 27.
Pressley, Ann, 11.
Pressley, David, 45.
Pressley, Eleanor, 82.
Pressley, Eliza, 237.
Pressley, Elizabeth, 241, 264.
Pressley, H. M., 398, 407.
Pressley, H. P., 516.
Pressley, Isabella, 77.
Pressley, James F., 237, 241, 349, 377, 406, 408, 412, 429, 430, 440, 527, 380.
Pressley, Jane, 82, 225.
Pressley, John, 22, 66, 77, 143, 151, 204, 225, 226, 230, 234, 237, 245.
Pressley, John B., 241, 368, 369.
Pressley, John G., 237, 297, 311, 317, 320, 341, 343, 346, 363, 379, 406, 440, 464, 528.
Pressley, Margaret, 82.
Pressley, Martha, 237.
Pressley, Mary B., 237, 242.

Pressley, Sarah, 82, 241.
Pressley, Susannah, 82.
Pressley, Thomas, 487.
Pressley, William, 22, 45, 66, 75, 82, 87, 153, 264.
Pressley, William J., 237, 241.
Price, Henry, 70, 166, 204, 226.
Price, J., 399.
Price, Jane, 224, 259.
Price, J. B., 468, 469.
Price, John, 204, 224, 259.
Price, Margaret, 226.
Price and Newsome, 297.
Price, William H., 259.
Prices of Articles, 404.
Prince Frederick's Church, 24, 53, 55.
Prince Frederick's Parish, 9, 53, 213.
Princeton, 305.
Princeton Seminary, 176.
Pringle, J. J., 141.
Pringle, Robert, 151.
Printing Cost, 1871, 448.
Prison, Elmira, 414.
Pritchard, Simon, 166.
Pritchard, Stephen, 166.
Pritchett, W. R., 475, 483.
"Produce," 548.
Products, 1920, 539.
Products, 1923, 547.
Prohibition Sentiment, 342.
Promising Young Men, 494.
Prospect M. Church, 487.
Prosperity, 539.
Prosser, H. L., 499, 524.
Prosser, Tim, 382.
Prosser, M. B., 352.
Prosser, Nathan, 352.
Prosser, Sarah, 235.
Protestants only Admitted, 303.
Provisions Furnished, 12.
Pruitt, Lillie, 472.
Public School Building, 149.
Puckett, J. R., 186.
Pudding Swamp Road, 61, 208.
Pulpit Hidden, 174.
Punch, Nicholas, 204.
Puncheons, 189.
Purtanism, 37, 180, 254, 271.
Puritanism Again, 281.
Puritanism Triumphant, 532.
Purse, William, 237, 238.
Purvis, Sarah, 24.
Purvis, William, 24.
Pygott, Nathaniel, 70.

INDEX 597

Qualifications for Voting, 213.
Queues Worn, 256.
Quorum, Justices, 92.

Race Courses, 256.
Race Track, 137.
Racing Days, 307.
Rae, Christian, 228.
Rae, John, 18, 78, 47, 48, 81, 75.
Rae, Rachael, 81.
Raffell, Margaret, 159.
"Ragged Remnant," 413.
Ragin, Henry, 344, 398.
Ragin, H. J., 361.
Ragin, T. E., 344, 349, 407, 409.
Railway, A. C. L., 528.
Railway, N. E., 324.
Railway, Weldon, 406, 408.
Rambert, Joachern, 167.
Ramsay's Revolution, 124.
Ramsbottom, C. F., 486.
Raney, Herbert, 167.
Ransom, Mrs. M. A., 469.
Raphield, James, 167.
Rappahannock, 398.
Rasberry, Nathaniel, 167.
Rasted, C., 440.
Ratchford, Mary, 473.
Ratchford, R. H., 483
Rawlinski, Mrs. M. J., 531.
Rawls, Elisha, 167.
Ravebelle, Allen, 512.
Rawdon, 108.
Ray, E. T., 350.
Reagin, P., 358.
Reagin, T. E., 358.
Reardon, Sampson, 514.
Reagin, William, 26.
Reardon, W. C., 241.
Reaves, Benjamin, 167.
Reaves, James, 167.
Reconstruction, 440.
Rectory, St. Alban's, 485.
Red Cross, 513.
Reddick, H. D., 487.
Redman, Annie, 473.
Redemption Campaign, 454.
Red House, 104.
Red Shirt Companies, 445.
Reed's Academy, 305.
Reed, G. W., 351, 400.
Reed, Hugh, 167, 207.
Reed, John, 114.
Reed, William, 135, 136, 167, 168, 206, 251.
Reese, Joseph, 195.

Reese, Thomas, 177, 179.
Reeves, Benjamin, 117.
Refugees, 436.
Regiment, Craven, 70.
Regimental Musters, 318.
Register, A. R., 473.
Register, C. E., 498.
Register, D. W., 510.
Register, E. C., 505.
Register, J. F., 498, 527.
Register, J. W., 501, 515.
Rehberg, C. H., 501.
Rehoboath M. Church, 301.
Reid, Mary, 204.
Reid, William, 204.
Religious Amusements, 277.
Religious Denominations, 480.
Rembert, Elijah, 189.
"Repel Raids," 401.
Repentance and non-repentance, 261.
Republican Congress, 438.
Republican Rule, 441,
Representatives in Legislature, 311.
Retaliation, 421.
Retreat School, 476.
Revolutionary Soldiers, 114.
Revolutionary War, 94.
Rhem, D. D., 475.
Rhem, Furney, 327, 328, 498, 538.
Rhem, L. F., 539.
Rhem, Mrs. L. F., 532.
Rhoad, G. T., 488.
Rhodes, John, 167.
Rhodus, Ann, 23.
Rhodus, Daniel, 84.
Rhodus, David, 221.
Rhodus, E. B., 501, 529.
Rhodus, E. D., 498.
Rhodus, G. D., 487.
Rhodus, Joel D., 353.
Rhodus, John, 221.
Rhodus, Joseph, 22, 23, 152.
Rhodus, Mary, 221.
Rhodus, Nathaniel, 221.
Rhodus, Solomon, 167, 221.
Rhodus, Thomas, 185.
Rhodus, William, 221.
Rich, N. G., 295, 317, 348, 441.
Rich, W. D., 527.
Riche, Anthony, 167.
Riche, James, 167, 204.
Richardson, David, 167.
Richardson, Elizabeth, 226.
Richardson, John, 500.
Richardson, J. B., 209.
Richardson, J. S., 226.

INDEX

Richardson, Richard, 71.
Richardson, S. M., 486.
Richardson, William, 226.
Richburg, James, 117, 118.
Richburg, J. E., 482.
Richburg, Margaret, 78.
Richburg, Rene, 25.
Rice Planting District, 248.
Rice, John A., 487.
Ridout, John, 485.
Rigden, Ephraim, 167.
Riggs, Agnes, 473.
Righteousness, Civic, 463.
Riser, Nina, 470.
Risher, Codnelia, 473.
Roads and Bridges, 443.
Road Building, 544.
Roads and Ferries, 207.
Roads in 1860, 323.
Roberts, Peter, 167.
Roberts, W. M., 474.
Rock Branch School, 475.
Rochingham, R. W., 312.
Robertson, Peter, 71.
Robinson, Ann, 204.
Robinson, John, 22, 117, 167, 207, 513.
Robinson, L. D., 360.
Robinson, William, 117.
Rodgers, Andrew, 117.
Rodgers, Claron, 413.
Rodgers, David, 226.
Rodgers, David P., 234.
Rodgers, Elizabeth, 360.
Rodgers, Eli, 413.
Rodgers, Elmer, 515.
Rodgers, E. L., 472.
Rodgers, Furman, 413, 430.
Rodgers, Isaac, 167, 204.
Rodgers, Jacob, 486.
Rogers, John, 117, 399, 204, 222.
Rodgers, James W., 360.
Rodgers, J. F., 360, 474, 485.
Rodgers, J. M., 473.
Rodgers, J. S., 473.
Rodgers, L. D., 525.
Rodgers, Mary, 224.
Rodgers, Mary A., 226.
Rodgers, Margaret, 222, 226.
Rodgers, Micajah, 167, 204.
Rodgers, M. I., 402.
Rodgers, Nathaniel, 117.
Rodgers, R., 382.
Rodgers, R. E., 362.
Rodgers, Shadrack, 167.
Rodgers, Stephen, 413.
Rodgers, S. R., 405.
Rodgers, Thomas, 149, 150, 204, 226, 250.
Rogers, William, 204, 226.
Rodgers, W. C., 527.
Rodgers, William F., 241, 301, 402.
Rogers, W. N. Y., 311, 344, 405, 430.
Rodgers, W. R., 397.
Rodgers, William T., 117.
Rollins, C. D., 527.
Rollins, C. J., 531.
Rollins, G. T., 361, 363.
Rollins, J. L., 297, 486.
Rollins, J. T., 486.
Rollins, R. D., 362, 408, 464, **496**.
Rollins, W. C., 500.
Rolls, Club, 466.
Roman Catholics, 27, 489.
Romish Wolves, 171.
Rose, Thomse, 241.
Rosecran's 385.
Ross, Jane, 143.
Ross, J. A., 512.
Ross, Lorena, 470.
Ross, M. A., 485, 520.
Rough Branch M. Church, **297**.
Rough Branch School, 473.
Roulet, John, 159.
Round O., 120.
Rouse, R. A., 468.
Row, Ebenezer, 360.
Row, J. N., 360.
Rowe, J. E., 416.
Rowell, D. Z., 527.
Rowell, Jeremiah, 26.
Rowell, John, 70.
Rowell, J. H., 473, 501.
Rowell, Rebecca, 204.
Rowell, William, 209.
Rowell, W. T., 409, 464, **473**, 501, 514, 515.
Roland, Abraham, 167.
Roland, Benjamin, 167.
Roland, Elizabeth, 167.
Rowlin, Margaret, 167.
Royal African Co., 6.
Royal, James, 167.
Rumors, 365.
Runnels, Mary, 76.
Ruel, Benjamin, 170.
Rush, E. W., 347.
Rush, Frederick, 292.
Russ, D. R., 382.
Russ, J. R., 350, 383.
Russell, Andrew, 167.
Russell, Jeremiah, 196.
Russell, Simon T., 486.

INDEX 599

Russell, Thomas, 167.
Rutledge, Andrew, 22, 69, 143.
Rutledge, B. H., 357.

Sabb, Anna, 82.
Sabb, Deborah, 82.
Sabb, Elizabeth, 82.
Sabb, Mary, 82.
Sabb, Morgan, 114, 117, 118, 132, 245, 268.
Sabb, Thomas, 82.
Sabb, William, 82, 102.
Sacramental Communion Meetings, 309.
Saddlecloths of Fine Linen, 429.
Salem Church, 48.
Salem Female Academy, 305.
Salem Black River, 181, 185.
Salt Scarce, 31.
Salters, J. A., 311, 353, 355, 358, 370, 397, 402, 440, 516, 530.
Salters, Jane M., 402.
Salters, John, 409.
Salters, Mrs. Mary, 118.
Salters, Mary E., 402.
Salters M. Church, 487.
Salters, Peter, 26, 117.
Salters Post Office, 531.
Salters, Sarah, 289.
Salters School, 473.
Salters, Mrs. S. M., 469.
Salters, T. E., 468, 473, 487.
Salters, William, 183, 184, 204, 218, 231, 232, 234, 239, 242, 245.
Sam, a Black Man, 260.
Saunders, George, 24.
Saunders, Hannah, 24.
Saunders, J. C., 346, 347.
Saunders, J. H., 361.
Saunders, William, 23.
Sand-Hills Camp Meeting, 182, 191.
Sandy Bay School, 475.
Santee Canal, 128.
Santee Circuit, 186.
Santee River, 3.
Santee River Road, 60.
Sasser, David, 529.
Sauls, E. H., 359, 530.
Sauls, E. S., 350, 398, 400, 406, 408.
Sauls, Evander G., 359.
Sauls, H., 397.
Sauls, James, 400.
Sauls, J. N., 530.
Sauls, J. W., 350.
Savage, Nathan, 168.
Savage Station, 382.
Savannah River, 3.

Sawmill, first, 251.
Seabrook, Thomas, 163.
"Searching eats," 392.
Sease, R. W., 527.
Sease, T. O., 473.
Seawright, James, 152.
Secession, 341.
Secession Clubs, 341.
Secession Convention, 1852, 337.
Secession Convention, 341.
Secession Flags, 341.
Second Bull Run, 382.
Second '76, 454.
Sectionalism, 214.
Seed Cotton Troubles, 450.
Sellers, M. M., 405.
Sellers, William, 117.
Sellers, W. L., 516, 527.
Seining in Black River, 316.
Seminole Indian War, 319.
Sere, Noah, 25.
Sessions of Court, 217.
Sessions, Edward, 205.
Sessions, John, 168, 204, 229.
Sessions, Richard, 205.
Sessions, William, 168.
Seven Pines, 382.
Sexton, Edward, 117.
Scallawags, 452.
Scarcity of Ministers, 480.
Scarf, Edward, 167.
Scarf, William, 168.
School Districts, 467.
School Funds, 1801, 468.
School Funds, 1922, 479.
Schools in County, 476.
School Officials, 1923, 471.
School Progress, 471.
Schwartz, M., 349.
Scipper, A. B., 398.
Scipper, G. W., 398, 400.
Scison, Ebenezer, 168.
Schoolmasters, 5.
Scotch-Irish, 27.
Scotch-Irish Colony, 10.
Scotch-Irish Migrate, 28.
Scott, Albert, 290.
Scott, Amelia, 289.
Scott, Arabella, 24.
Scott, Alexander, 66, 70, 81, 117, 168, 204, 205, 223, 513.
Scott, A. Winfield, 354.
Scott, B. F., 344, 361, 382.
Scott, Caroline, 289.
Scott, Katherine, 83.

INDEX

Scott, David C., 430, 470, 473, 496, 497, 519, 520, 521, 527.
Scott, Mrs. D. C., 513, 514, 515, 523, 524.
Scott, E. B., 344, 361, 384.
Scott, Elizabeth, 81, 83, 123, 229.
Scott, Eugenia P., 370.
Scott, George C., 354.
Scott, Gillespie, 201.
Scott, Helen, 470.
Scott, Hester Jane, 12.
Scott, Isabelle, 83.
Scott, James, 22, 66, 81, 117, 143, 152, 168.
Scott, Janet, 81.
Scott, Jannet, 83, 123, 204, 229, 246.
Scott, Jean, 83.
Scott, J. F., 290, 349, 398, 525.
Scott, John, 10, 22, 24, 29, 47, 66, 69, 76, 81, 83, 85, 87, 88, 97, 118, 123, 140, 141, 142, 149, 151, 152, 168, 179, 204, 205, 219, 220, 226, 229, 230, 231, 236, 523.
Scott, John Ervin, 40, 236, 297, 320, 349, 361, 382, 397, 430, 446.
Scott, J. H., 503, 512.
Scott, John L., 358, 400.
Scott, Joseph, 83, 97, 106, 114, 123, 143, 145, 147, 149, 152, 168, 205, 236, 251, 256, 289, 311, 522.
Scott, Joseph A., 290.
Scott, Julia E., 370.
Scott, Junius E., 398, 400, 406, 414.
Scott, J. W., 281.
Scott, James W., 354, 382.
Scott, Louisa, 233.
Scott, Margaret, 76, 83, 122, 123, 289.
Scott, Margaret G., 81.
Scott, Mary, 83, 123, 289.
Scott, Mrs. Mary, 370.
Scott, Mary G., 382.
Scott, Maurice, 527.
Scott, M. M., 407.
Scott, Moses, 83.
Scott, Rebecca, 290.
Scott, Rebecca C., 281.
Scott, R. F., 349, 381.
Scott, Rebecca Gordon, 236.
Scott, Robert K., 439.
Scott, S. A., 381.
Scott, Samuel, 81, 83, 117, 122, 204, 222, 231, 236, 245, 246, 279, 284, 288.
Scott, Samuel A., 359, 407.
Scott, Sarah, 83, 85.

Scott, S. McBride, 295, 343, 397, 464.
Scott, Susannah Theresa, 522.
Scott, Lieutenant, 409.
Scott, Thomas, 66, 81, 83, 117, 227.
Scott, Thomas G., 57.
Scott, T. M., 469.
Scott, Walter, 472.
Scott, W. D., 469.
Scott, Winfield, 320.
Scott, William, 22, 57, 70, 71, 81, 83, 117, 118, 153, 442, 460, 468.
Scott, W. D., 226, 290.
Scott, W. R., 236, 290, 311, 312, 481, 499, 515, 525.
Scott, W. P., 344, 383.
Scranton Red Shirt Co., 456.
Screven, Ann, 227.
Screven, Benjamin, 81, 82, 92, 118, 134.
Screven, Elisha, 24, 34, 35, 48, 69, 81, 195.
Screven, Elizabeth, 81, 83.
Screven, Hannah, 81, 82.
Screven, John, 195, 227.
Screven, Joseph, 81.
Screven, Joshua, 81, 82.
Screven, Rebecca, 83.
Screven, Robert, 24.
Screven, Samuel, 81.
Screven, William, 24, 34, 76, 81, 82, 195.
Scrime, Thomas, 210.
Scurry, E. M., 350, 384, 400.
Scurry, John C., 362.
Scurry, W. J. C., 347.
Scythians, 27.
Shackelford, Jean, 167.
Shade Trees Planted, 150.
Shannon, Samuel, 84.
Shaper, W. A., 214.
Sharp, Mamie Lou, 472.
Sharpsburg, 383.
Shaving Notes, 254.
Shaw, Agnes, 289.
Shaw, A. J., 349, 376.
Shaw, B., 352.
Shaw, Daniel, 23, 53, 117.
Shaw, David, 226.
Shaw, Elizabeth, 226.
Shaw, H. D., 183, 198, 240, 241, 289, 290, 293, 347, 402, 408.
Shaw, Mrs. H. D., 370.
Shaw, J. M., 402.
Shaw, Joe, 357.
Shaw, John, 226.
Shaw, J. P., 362.

Shaw, Lillie, 226.
Shaw, Peter, 226.
Shaw, R. H., 358.
Shaw, Sarah, 23, 226.
Shaw, William, 117, 226.
Shealds, John, 168.
Sheed, John, 168.
Shell, J. W., 409.
Shepard, H. N., 501.
Shepard, William, 25.
Shepard's Ferry, 104.
Sheriff, Henry, 47.
Sherman Takes Columbia, 427.
Sherman, W. T., 416.
Shirer, Edward, 503.
Shirer, P. C., 473.
Short Rations, 421.
Skrine, Thomas, 168.
Shuler, M. A., 472, 513, 514, 516, 525, 527.
Shuler, Mrs. M. A., 524.
Simon, Joseph, 161.
Sinclair, Carrie Belle, 373.
Sinclair, James, 25, 373.
Sims, David, 115.
Simms' Life of Marion, 124.
Simms, Thomas, 117, 118.
Simmons, Mrs. A. L., 469.
Simons, Caroline, 484.
Simons, Due, 168.
Simons, Mary L., 228.
Simons, Peter, 92.
Simons, Shadrack, 117, 208.
Simons, Thomas Y., 454.
Simonton, Charles H., 379.
Singletary, Agnes, 204.
Singletary, Agnes R., 264.
Singletary, Barfield, 482.
Singletary, B. F., 382, 405.
Singletary, Duncan, 482.
Singletary, Ebenezer, 168, 204, 205, 235.
Singletary, E. J., 347, 405.
Singletary, Elizabeth, 233.
Singletary, Eliza, 235.
Singletary, H., 358.
Singletary, Henry, 241.
Singletary, Hesther J., 241.
Singletary, H. H., 468.
Singletary, Mrs. H. H., 482.
Singletary, Miss H. S., 469.
Singletary, I. D., 360.
Singletary, Isaac, 149.
Singletary, Isaac F., 227.
Singletary, Jacob, 233, 246.
Singletary, J. C., 408.
Singletary, J. D., 497.

Singletary, J. E., 469.
Singletary, John, 238.
Singletary, John D., 205.
Singletary, Joseph S., 233.
Singletary, Lamar, 482.
Singletary, Lyda, 227.
Singletary, Richard, 26.
Singletary, Samuel, 204.
Singletary, Sarah, 238.
Singletary School, 474.
Singletary, S. J., 317, 465.
Singletary, S. M., 358.
Singletary, Sophronia P., 238.
Singletary, Virginia V., 482.
Singletary, W. D., 358, 459.
Singletary, W. J., 463.
Singletary, W. R., 468.
Singletary, W. W., 509.
Singleton, Albert, 469.
Singleton, Benjamin, 118.
Singleton, B. V., 497.
Singleton, Esther, 242.
Singleton, Esther G., 238.
Singleton, Mrs. Henry B., 186.
Singleton, Henry B., 242.
Singleton, Hester, 290.
Singleton, James D., 218.
Singleton, John, 24.
Singleton, John D., 235.
Singleton, J. S., 369.
Singleton, Mary, 24, 242.
Singleton, Mary B., 237.
Singleton, Mary M., 242.
Singleton, Matthew, 26.
Singleton, Mrs. M. L., 481.
Singleton, M. M., 232, 290.
Singleton, Richard, 117.
Singleton, Sarah, 237, 264.
Singleton, T. D., 218, 204, 225, 226, 228, 232, 237, 242, 245, 268, 269, 270, 289, 311, 312, 317.
Sinkler, John, 24.
Sinkler, Mary B., 24.
Sinkler, Peter, 117, 118.
Sinnott, W. I., 483, 516.
Skrines Ferry, 208.
Slaves, 41, 247.
Slaves, 1745, 87.
Slaves Deserting, 428.
Slave Labor Profitable, 331.
Slave Owners in Williamsburg, 332.
Slave Values, 257.
Slavery and Secession, 329.
Slaves value in 1860, 338.
Sloan, James, 360, 361.
Small, Christopher, 168.
Small, J. C., 360.

Small, W. C., 350.
Small, W. F., 358.
Small, William, 211.
Smiley, Samuel, 116.
Smiley, William, 117.
Smiley, W. J., 463, 515, 530, 538.
Smith, Abner, 168, 204, 231.
Smith, Adam, 168, 264.
Smith, A. J., 468.
Smith, Bartow, 465, 472.
Smith, Benjamin, 168.
Smith, B. S., 488.
Smith, B. S. M., 350.
Smith, Charles B., 488.
Smith, D. C., 352.
Smith, Daniel H., 302, 475.
Smith, D. M., 347, 407.
Smith, Elizabeth, 360.
Smith, E. J., 469.
Smith, Everett, 360.
Smith, E. M., 348, 464.
Smith, Francis H., 359.
Smith, Francis N., 353.
Smith, Henry, 168, 196, 205.
Smith, Henry J., 241.
Smith, Hugh, 168.
Smith, Isaac, 292.
Smith, James, 22, 117, 151, 168, 231, 360.
Smith, Jane, 238.
Smith, J. L. M., 350.
Smith, John, 117, 167, 168, 360.
Smith, John A., 359.
Smith, John H., 241, 350.
Smith, James H., 399, 400.
Smith, J. G., 360.
Smith, J. K., 499.
Smith, John M., 343.
Smith, K., 405.
Smith, Katie Lou, 475.
Smith, Lemuel, 488.
Smith, L. E., 473.
Smith, Leroy Watson, 511.
Smith, Margaret, 290.
Smith, Michael, 54.
Smith, Mollie, 231.
Smith, N. P., 360.
Smith, Noah, 204, 235.
Smith, Olive, 515.
Smith, Pat, 231.
Smith, R. B., 464, 481.
Smith, R., 360.
Smith, R. S., 406, 407, 408.
Smith, R. W., 465, 472, 538.
Smith, S., 360.
Smith, S. D., 351, 399.
Smith, Simon, 231.

Smith, T. K., 499.
Smith, Thomas, 168, 522.
Smith, Wesley, 360.
Smith, William, 117, 168.
Smith, W. B., 360.
Smith, W. C., 481.
Smith, W. D., 351.
Smith, W. E., 487, 524.
Smith, William W., 353.
Smith Swamp School, 476.
Smooth Bore Rifles, 399.
Smyth, Thomas, 168.
Snyder, A. M., 362, 527.
Snyder, J. Henry, 486.
Snow, Ann, 81.
Snow, Emmie, 472.
Snow Balling, 394.
Snow, George, 81.
Snow, Henry, 224.
Snow, James, 81, 117, 168, 248, 487.
Snow, Jeremiah, 302, 396.
Snow, John, 81, 134.
Snow, J. J., 531.
Snow, J. P., 469.
Snow, Mary, 23, 81.
Snow, Nathaniel, 52, 81, 224.
Snow, Philip, 233.
Snow, William, 23, 92, 117, 119, 168.
Snow's Island, 105, 110.
Snowden, Elizabeth M., 236.
Snowden, H. P., 474.
Snowden, James, 230.
Snowden, L., 152.
Snowden, Mary, 236.
Snowden, P. D., 482.
Snowden, Percy, 538.
Snowden, Samuel, 146, 152, 153, 204, 208, 236.
Snowden, Samuel J., 280, 286, 284, 289, 320, 357, 380, 430, 464, 469.
Snowden, Samuel M., 236.
Snowden, Sarah, 264.
Snowden, Thomas J., 236.
Snowden, W. D., 468.
Snowden, W. E., 464, 469, 516.
Snowden, William, 236.
Soap Scarce, 411.
Social Recreation, 306.
Society, Propagation of Gospel, 45.
Socinianism, 172.
Soft hands, 433.
Soldiers' boxes, 371.
Soldiers Families Aided, 368.
Soldiers in Field, 379.
Somerhoeff, John Peter, 24.
"Somerton", 35.
"Something must be done," 542.

INDEX

"Songs of Labor," 332.
Sons of Temperance, 288.
South Carolina Ind. Republic, 136.
S. C. Medical College, 305.
South Island, 385.
Spaniards, 2.
Spanish American War, 503.
Sparkman, Richard, 168.
Spears, William, 168.
Speights, Elias, 349, 359.
Speights, J. M., 349, 397.
Speigner, Elizabeth, 472.
Speigner, Raymond, 464.
Speigner, R. N., 499.
Speigner, R. W., 480, 488.
Spinning Wheel, 375.
Spit Fire Abolitionists, 339.
Spivey, A. B., 474, 501.
Spivey, William, 114.
Spooner, J. F., 358.
Spooner, T. J., 358, 407.
Spottsylvania, 407.
Spring, Ann, 167, 204, 222, 223.
Spring Bank School, 475.
Spring, Cornelius, 222.
Spring, George W., 383.
Spring Gulley School, 474.
Spring, R., 351.
Spring, Richard, 204.
Spring, Robert, 168, 204, 240, 400.
Spry, Elizabeth, 85.
Spry, Jean, 85.
Spry, John, 85.
Spry, Phineas, 60.
Spry, Rebecca, 85.
Spry, Royal, 85.
Stackley, Annie, 525.
Stackley, L., 468, 470, 520, 525.
Stackley, L. J., 487.
Stackley, S. P., 473.
Stage Line, 397.
Staggers, Barbary, 168.
Staggers, Elizabeth, 295.
Staggers, George, 242.
Staggers, James, 527.
Staggers, James M., 297, 485.
Staggers, John, 117, 118, 168, 205, 228, 233, 242.
Staggers, J. W., 317, 485, 527.
Staggers, Martin, 150, 153, 204, 225, 228, 242.
Staggers, Susannah, 290.
Staggers, William, 204, 242, 150, 297.
St. Alban's E. Chapel, 484.
St. Amand, C. E., 528.
Stamp Act, 94.

Standard Lowered, 459.
Stapleton, Levi, 167.
Stapleton, Sarah, 167.
Starnes, Charles, 168.
Stark, L. B., 377.
Starne, Charles, 22, 69, 151.
"Start Something," 456.
State Convention, 1787, 135.
Statement of Indiantown Session, 273.
States Rights Question, 311.
St. David's Church, 187.
Steam Engine, first, 251.
Steele, Clara, 472.
Steele, E. C., 484.
Steele, Mrs. J. B., 514.
Steele, James, 117.
Steele, John, 206, 231.
Steele, J. J., 349, 351, 405, 465.
Steele, Thomas, 204, 243, 343.
Steele, T. S., 349, 405, 430.
Steele's Company, 405, 430.
Steele, William, 117.
Stephens, Caleb, 205, 235.
Stephenson, A. E., 360.
Stephenson, James, 164.
Stephenson, J. W., 258.
Stephenson, John, 204.
Stephenson, Thomas, 180.
Stephenson's Labor, 178.
Stevenson, James W., 177, 181, 182, 254.
Stevens, Ruben, 167.
Stewart, Alexander, 117.
Stewart, Hugh, 117.
Stewart, J. W., 475.
Stewart, Mary, 230.
Still, Agnes, 78.
St. John's School, 475.
St. Louis, Daniel E., 512.
St. Mark's Church, 186.
St. Mark's Parish, 55.
Stocks, Evander, 360.
Stoll, C. W., 469, 498, 499, 516, 515, 520, 525, 528.
Stoll, J. C., 363, 412.
Stoll, Philip H., 463, 487, 505, 527.
Stone, Austin, 168, 204, 244.
Stone, B. H., 487.
Stone, Dottson, 205, 244.
Stone, E. E., 382.
Stone, James B., 354.
Stone, James H., 246, 296, 487.
Stone, Mrs. Mattie, 472.
Stone, Philip, 204, 235, 246.
Stone, Palvey T., 354.
Stone, Pauline, 472.

INDEX

Stone, P. T., 398.
Stone, Mary, 235.
Stone, Thomas, 382.
Stuart, Thomas S., 358.
Stone, William, 167, 360.
Stone, W. J., 381, 382.
Stone's River, 385.
Story, Mary, 126.
St. Patrick, 27.
Straight Out Ticket, 454.
Strain, Adam, 66.
Strange, J. C., 301.
Streets Paved, 520.
Streets in 1801, 148.
Stretch, Mary, 204, 232.
Strong, Agnes, 295.
Strong, Hazel, 503.
Strong, H. A., 503.
Strong, James, 242.
Strong, Margaret, 289, 295.
Strong, Robert, 117, 184, 204, 236, 240, 242, 289.
Strong, S. J., 381.
Strong, Samuel, 204, 236, 295.
Strong, Sarah, 228, 242.
Strong, Susan, 295.
Strong, T. J., 295, 344, 349, 361.
Strong, William, 242.
Strong, W. V., 499, 519.
Stuart, James, 22, 153.
Stuart, Lady Margaret, 171.
Stuart, Margaret, 30.
Stuart, Mary, 12.
Stuart, T. S., 349, 381, 465.
Stubbs, John, 22.
Stuckey, B. N., 465, 538.
Stuckey, R. W., 502.
Stukes, H. H., 407.
Stukes, William N., 353.
Sturgis, Jane, 370.
Sturges, S. D., 342.
Suffrage, Male, 438.
Sullivan, Esther, 78.
Sullivan, James, 85.
Sullivan, John, 78.
Sullivan, Joseph, 168.
Sumac Berry, 372.
Summersett, G. K., 469.
Sumter School, 472.
Sumter, Thomas, 135, 177.
Sunday School, 262.
Sunday School formed, 180.
Supervision by Elders, 482.
Surrender, Twenty-Fifth Regiment, 416.
Sutton, Ann, 244.
Sutton, Dorothy, 244.
Sutton, Elizabeth, 244.
Sutton, Hugh, 117.
Sutton, Jacob, 117.
Sutton, Magdalene, 244.
Sutton, Margaret, 244.
Sutton, Mary, 244.
Sutton, Robert, 188, 190, 191, 204, 232, 244.
Suttons Church, 190, 197.
Sutton School, 472.
Swab, J. G., 168.
Swails, A. C., 472, 485.
Swails, S. A., 440, 446, 460.
Swails, Mrs. Lawrence, 532.
Swails, F. H., 440.
"Swamp Fox," 108.
"Swamp Rabbit," 364.
Swan, Robert, 117.
Swift Creek, 406.
Swinton, Elizabeth, 80, 204.
Swinton, Hugh, 168.
Swinton, William, 4, 47, 53, 117.
Swittenberg, J. W., 472, 478.
Swittenberg, Mrs. J. W., 514.
Sykes, John, 22, 151.
Syms, William, 22, 45, 46.

Taft School, 472.
Tallevast, J. B., 538.
Talliessin, 171.
Tamplet, Isabel, 24.
Tamplet, Peter, 24.
Tamplet, Sarah, 191, 244.
Taney, Chief Justice, 335.
Tanner, John, 352.
Tanner, L., 352.
Tanner, W. E., 474.
Tar Heel, 328.
Tariff Question, 267.
Tarleton, 100.
Tarleton at King's Tree, 101.
Tart, R. E., 530.
Taxes Confiscatory, 449.
Taxpayers Convention, 448.
Taylor, O. E., 527.
Taylor, Mrs. O. E., 515.
Taylor, James, 22.
Taylor, J. L., 377.
Taylor, Lex, 474.
Taylor, Mary T., 231.
Taylor, Richard, 159.
Taylor, Ruffin, 143, 152, 169.
Taylor, S. J., 362, 468, 498, 529.
Taylor, Samuel, 114, 122.
Taylor, S. P., 233.
Taylor's School, 305.
Taylor, Mrs. W. L., 514, 515.

INDEX

Taylor, William, 208, 229.
Taylor, W. J., 362.
Tea, 94.
Teachers Marry, 532.
Teachers' Qualifications, 476.
Teachers, White Schools, 472.
Teaching of the Christ, 491.
Teapot Tempests, 467.
Tedder, James, 343.
Tenth Infantry, 376.
Tenth Regiment Mustered, 349.
Terrey, George, 398.
Terry, G. W., 408.
Thames, B. D., 486.
Thames, J. P., 361.
Thigpen, J. E., 347.
Thigpen, W. H., 347, 475.
Thomas, Alexander, 169.
Thomas, C. C., 358.
Thomas, David, 169.
Thomas, Edward, 117, 118, 207.
Thomas, Elizabeth, 205.
Thomas, Henry B., 359.
Thomas, James, 117.
Thomas, J. C., 405.
Thomas, J. E., 405.
Thomas, J. G., 358.
Thomas, J. M., 358, 396.
Thomas, J. D., 353, 357.
Thomas, Jesse, 169.
Thomas, P. S., 502, 527.
Thomas, S., 358.
Thomas, William, 117.
Thomas, W. O., 503.
Thompson, Alexander, 205.
Thomson, Archibald, 117.
Thompson, Connie, 474.
Thompson, Edward C., 503.
Thompson, Eleanor, 82.
Thompson, F., 362.
Thompson, Hannah, 205.
Thomson, James, 117, 169.
Thompson, James A., 512.
Thompson, J. B., 358.
Thompson, John, 23, 53, 169, 349, 354, 383.
Thompson, Martha, 23.
Thompson, O. L., 474.
Thompson, R. G., 382.
Thomson, Ruben, 169.
Thomson, Samuel, 159.
Thompson, Sidney B., 354.
Thompson, T. S., 382.
Thompson, W. E., 360.
Thompson, W. F., 413.
Thompson, W. G., 382.
Thompson, W. J., 358.
Thompson, William, 50, 117, 118, 205.
Thompson, W. and W. A., 205.
Thompson, W. T., 360, 413.
Thorne, Henry, 312.
Thorne, P. B., 484.
Thorne, Mrs. P. B., 484, 522.
Thorne, Selma, 514.
Thornhill, William J., 361.
Thorntree, 18.
Thorp, Janet, 237.
Thorp, John, 205, 224, 237.
Thorp, Samuel, 169.
Thorp, S. J., 358.
Tilton, D. C., 350.
Tilton, Robert F., 358, 408.
Tilton, William, 235.
Tilton, William J., 354.
Timmons, Isaac, 231.
Timmons, James, 169.
Timmons, James E., 361.
Timmons, John, 169.
Timmons, Levi, 169, 205.
Timmons, Martin V., 353.
Timmons, M. O., 398.
Timmons, Samuel, 233.
Timmons, S. B., 472.
Timmons, Simon, 231.
Timmons, T. E., 487.
Timmons, William, 231.
Tisdale, Alex, 515.
Tisdale, Ambrose, 442.
Tisdale, Desmore, 503.
Tisdale, D. M., 361.
Tisdale, Elizabeth, 289, 295, 370.
Tisdale, George, 344.
Tisdale, James, 146, 153, 169, 205, 222, 295.
Tisdale, Jane, 223.
Tisdale, J. G., 346, 358.
Tisdale, J. H., 349.
Tisdale, J. M., 473.
Tisdale, John J., 240.
Tisdale, J. S., 344, 361.
Tisdale, J. T., 349.
Tisdale, J. Y., 344, 361.
Tisdale, Margaret, 295.
Tisdale, R. H., 503.
Tisdale, R. S., 81, 349, 357, 361.
Tisdale, Samuel, 240, 256, 361, 513.
Tisdale, S. S., 348.
Tisdale, W. J., 349.
Tisdale, William, 240.
Tisdale, W. W., 347.
Tobacco, 34.
Tobacco Growers Ass'n., 546.
Tobacco Hogsheads, 250.

606 INDEX

Tobacco Industry, 538.
Tobacco in Williamsburg, 547.
Tobacco Planters, 538.
Tobacco Prizeries, 520.
Tobacco Produced, 249.
Tobacco Warehouses, 520, 538.
Tobias, William M., 487.
Todd, Elizabeth, 232, 245.
Todd, John, 362.
Tolley, W. F., 514, 521.
Tolls on Ferries, 209, 211.
Tomlinson, Nathaniel, 117.
Tomlinson, John, 117.
Tomson, Alexander, 169.
Tomson, George, 168.
Tomson, James, 168.
Tories, 131, 133.
Tories in Williamsbrug, 102.
Tournaments, 307.
Town Lots Advertised, 147.
Town Lot Owners, 150.
Town of Williamsburg, 9, 138.
Town of Williamsburg, 1788, 137.
Townsend, G. B., 408.
Townships, 3.
Tracts Distributed, 376.
Trading with Slaves, 316.
Trapier, General, 385.
Treating at Funerals, 178.
Treatment of Slaves, 335.
Travillian, 407.
Trial of Samuel McGill, 276.
Trio Post Office, 531.
Trio School, 473.
Troublefield, William, 22, 142.
Troy, Martha, 290.
Trucking Industry, 538.
Trustees, of White Schols, 472.
Truckers Company, 413.
Tucker, John, 169.
Turbeville, Charles, 24.
Turbeville, John, 24.
Turbeville, Margaret, 23.
Turbeville, M. D., 405.
Turbeville, Philadelphia, 24.
Turbeville, R., 383.
Turbeville, Ransom, 352.
Turbeville, R. E., 475.
Turbeville, Susannah S., 24.
Turbeville, William, 22, 23.
Turbeville, W. T., 531.
Turkey School, 475.
Turner, Amos, 169.
Turner, Benjamin, 169, 205, 231, 233, 236, 369.
Turner, Hugh, 233, 236.
Turner, J. A., 486.

Turner, J. L., 358.
Turner, John, 20, 168.
Turner, Mary, 242.
Turner, Phoebe, 236.
Turner, Ruben, 169, 236.
Turner, William, 205, 231, 236, 237, 240.
Turpentine Industry, 536.
Turnout, Graham, 372.
Tweed, Alexander, 135, 136.
Two Ears of Corn, 393.
Two Williamsburg Congregations, 174.
Tyler, Benjamin, 169.
Tyler, Hugh, 347, 407.
Tyler, Samuel, 168.
Tyrnes, 107.
Tyrone, 27.
Tyser, Richard, 85.

U. D. C. Organized, 523.
Unchristian Practices, 260.
Union Church, 196, 301, 401.
Unionists, 268.
Union School, 476.
Union Services, 494.
Unlawful Grants, 64.
University of N. C., 305.
University of S. C., 305.
University of Virginia, 305.
"Unorthodoxy," 495.
"Up Country," 214.
"Uppish" negroes, 435.

Vannalle, Esther, 83.
Vannalle, Matthew, 22, 83, 151.
Vareen, Ann, 81.
Vareen, Ebenezer, 85.
Vareen, Hannah, 85.
Varneen, Jane, 85.
Vareen, Jeremiah, 25, 85.
Vareen, J. T., 405.
Vareen, Martha, 81, 85.
Vareen, Mary, 85.
Vareen, Rachel, 85.
Vareen, Rebecca, 85.
Vareen, Samuel, 25, 81.
Vareen, William, 85.
Vareen, W. J., 408.
Varn, Daisy, 517.
Varner, W. S., 485, 529.
Vause, Ed, 503.
Vause, Mrs. Edward, 474.
Vause, W. M., 519.
Venters, J. L., 398.
Venters, N. M., 500, 502.
Venters, Washington, 383.

INDEX 607

Vinegar Scarce, 411.
Virginia, 1.
Volunteers, Citadel, 360.
Vote on Constitution, 135.
Vote on Ratification, 136.

Waccamaw River, 3.
Wade, Ollie, 475.
Waddell's Academy, 305.
Wagner Battery, 398.
Walker, C. I., 349, 417.
Walker, James, 170.
Walker, William, 54.
Wall, P. S., 463.
Wall, W. J. B., 409.
Wallace, Barney, 408.
Wallace, David D., 215.
Wallace, James, 117, 493.
Wallace, James A., 103, 291, 295, 312.
Wallace, J. B., 500, 515.
Wallace, Jedekiah, 291.
Wallace, John, 25, 53, 117.
Wallace, Michael, 117, 118.
Wallace, Pearl, 474.
Wallace Preaches Calvinism, 294.
Wallace Resigns, 299.
Wallace, R. K., 464, 521, 528.
Wallace, Mrs. R. K., 532.
Wallace, Ruby, 474.
Wallace, T. A., 344.
Wallace, W. L., 430, 485, 527.
Wallace, William, 117.
Wallace, W. S., 384.
Wallace, W. T., 352.
Wallace's History of Williamsburg, 299.
Wallace's Prayer, 295.
Wallace's Sermon, 299.
Wallace's Soliloquy, 300.
Walsh, Frank, 221.
Walters, E. Omitt, 473.
Walters, Jacob, 169, 205.
Walters, Patrick, 170.
Walters, Priscilla, 170.
Walters, R. B., 347, 407.
Walters, W. J., 358.
Walthall Junction, 406.
Walton, Caleb, 165.
War Loan Committee, 513.
Ward, Benjamin, 384, 399, 400.
Wardlaw, F. H., 483.
Ward, James, 169, 205, 238, 244.
Ward, Mary Grimke, 187.
Ward, R. F., 473.
Ward, W. J., 361.
Ward, W. W., 440.

Warehouse, Central, 538.
Warned from Communion Table, 274.
War Path through Williamsburg, 103.
Warren, Virginia, 472.
Warsaw School, 476.
Washington, Samuel J., 236.
Wateree River, 3.
Water Works and Sewerage, 519.
Watrons, Abner, 169.
Watson, 109.
Watson, Andrew, 205, 206.
Watson, Mrs. Catherine, 118.
Watson, David, 118.
Watson, Emma, 290.
Watson, George, 169.
Watson, Hugh, 169.
Watson, James, 117.
Watson, J. F., 469.
Watson, John, 47, 66, 81, 83, 101, 117, 118, 153, 222, 223, 226, 234, 242, 290, 354, 357, 369, 379, 402.
Watson, Mrs. John, 370.
Watson, Mary, 289.
Watson, Mary F., 242.
Watson, M. E., 402.
Washington, Ned, 357.
Watson, Robert, 117.
Watson, Sarah, 205, 234.
Watson, Sarah Ann, 234, 242.
Waxhaw Church, 177.
Wayside School, 473.
Weatherly, Isaac, 170.
Weaver, J. M., 350, 486.
Weaver, William, 170.
Wee Nee Bank, 499.
Wee Nee River, 8.
Wee Nees, 72.
Wee Nee School, 474.
Wee Nee Volunteers, 343, 414, 348.
Wee Tees, 72.
Wee Tee School, 475.
Weevil, Boll, 548.
Weir, George, 362, 344, 366.
Waites, William, 270.
Welch, A., 344.
Welch, Frank, 529.
Welch, J. F., 384.
Welch, W. H., 405, 464, 514, 545.
Wells, Artesian, 518.
Wells bored, 536.
Wells, Miss S. E., 424, 425.
West, John, 473, 503.
West, W. H., 360.
Westberry, B. F., 382.

Westberry, Jonathan, 25.
Westberry, William, 70, 170.
Weston, P. C. J., 360, 403.
Wemyss, 179.
Wemyss' Invasion, 103.
Weems' Life of Marion.
Wham, Gladys, 475.
Wheeler, George C., 400.
Wheeler, George D., 361.
Wheeler, John, 117, 295.
Whigs, 131.
Whipping Posts, 316.
Whitacre, Isaac, 170.
Whitby, George, 70.
White, Anthony, 23, 33, 53, 62, 71, 92, 170, 247, 248.
White, Blakely, 81.
White's Bridge, 377.
White, Daniel, 169.
White, George, 170, 213.
White, John, 71, 81, 118, 226.
White, Joseph, 245.
White, Mary, 23, 81, 240.
White, Nancy, 125.
White Oak Church, 287.
Whites only Vote, 461.
White School Teachers, 1887, 468.
White Schools, 472.
Whitehead, B. C., 464, 468.
Whitehead, Cohen, 525.
Whitehead, Jacob, 354.
Whitehead, J. J., 384.
Whitehead, N. M., 312, 354.
Whitehead, W. L., 527.
Whitfield, Benjamin, 244.
Whitfield, Cicero, 328.
Whitfield, Hagard, 328.
Whitfield, John, 22, 69, 142.
Whitfield, O. H., 358.
Whitfield, Philip, 513.
Whitfield, Thomas, 170.
Whitfield, William, 169.
Wiboo Swamp, 108.
Wickham, T. J., 169.
Wiggins, Ernest, 470.
Wiggins, E. P., 352.
Wiggins, Thomas, 146.
Wilder, John, 353, 358, 407, 409.
Wilder, J. T., 469.
Wilder, Samuel, 353.
Wilder, W. J., 382.
Wilderness, 406.
Wilkes, C. C., 358.
Wilkes, Ester, 170.
Wilkes, Lemuel, 170.
Wilkes, T. H., 351, 400.
Wilkins, Banna L., 507.
Wilkins, G. H., 503, 525.
Wilkins, Mrs. G. H., 525.
Wilkins, W. T., 498, 547.
Wilkins, Mrs. W. T., 514.
Will, Holograph, 220.
Willcox, A. M., 527.
Willcox. F. L., 500.
Willebard, A., 352.
William of Orange, 9, 28, 123.
Williams, A. H., 463, 527.
Williams, Anthony, 9, 22, 141, 297.
Williams, A. W., 362.
Williams, Daniel, 56.
Williams, Daniel J., 229.
Williams, E. H., 527.
Williams, Elizabeth, 83.
Williams, Ellen, 476.
Williams, Evelyn, 473.
Williams, Dorothy, 473.
Williams, Hannah, 169.
Williams, Henry, 22, 151.
Williams, Henry C., 512.
Williams, Hetty, 228.
Williams, H. P., 496, 497.
Williams, Jacob W., 228.
Williams, J. C., 317.
Williams, Mrs. J. C., 370.
Williams, John, 205.
Williams, J. G., 170.
Williams, Muriel, 472.
Williams, R., 382, 195.
Williams, Roger, 34.
Williams, S., 352.
Williams, S. W., 469.
Williams, Thomas, 145, 169, 205, 210, 238.
Williams, William, 170.
Williamsburg Academy, 175.
Williamsburg Battalion, 128.
Williamsburg Cemetery Ass'n., 524.
Williamsburg Church, 16, 46, 52, 78, 81, 172, 197, 401, 480.
Williamsburg Churches, 138.
Williamsburg Churches, 1860, 303.
Williamsburg P. Congregation, 45, 76, 143, 151, 152, 153.
Williamsburg Court, 216.
Williamsburg Congregations Reunite, 182.
Williamsburg County Created, 139.
Williamsburg District, 216.
Williamsburg Fair Ass'n., 542.
Williamsburg Light Dragoons, 354.
Williamsburg Preaching, 490.
Williamsburg Riflemen, 353.
Williamsburg Session Records, 290.
Williamsburg Tax Payers, 199.

INDEX 609

Williamsburg Township, 9, 39.
Williamsburg Was There, 346.
Williamson, Bertha, 475.
Williamson, G. F., 475.
Williamson, Henry G., 359.
Williamson, H. J., 486.
Williamson, J. M., 465.
Williamson, Sterling, 118.
Williamson, T. E., 383.
Williamson, Thomas, 409.
Williamson, William, 22, 118, 153.
Williamson, W. G., 359, 407.
Willis, Abram, 398.
Willis, Claudelle, 473.
Willis, Henry, 187, 292.
Willison, John, 16.
Willoughby, W. T., 320.
Wills, Colonial, 73.
Wills, Old, 220.
Willson, John O., 527.
Willtown, 71, 105, 195, 251.
Willtown Church, 197.
Willtown Post Office, 252.
Willtown road, 209, 211.
Wilson, Adam, 79.
Wilson, Avagale, 232.
Wilson, B. H., 349.
Wilson, Charles, 170.
Wilson, David, 10, 12, 20, 22, 45, 49, 66, 78, 142, 170, 205, 210, 236, 243, 244, 262.
Wilson, David D., 196, 198, 218, 238, 240, 246, 259, 269, 279, 264, 274, 275, 280, 311, 320, 368, 397.
Wilson, David E., 233, 259.
Wilson, David F., 259.
Wilson, E. D., 317.
Wilson, Eliza A., 236.
Wilson, Elizabeth, 243.
Wilson, Elizabeth M., 264.
Wilson, Elizabeth W., 233.
Wilson, F. W., 358, 360.
Wilson, Godfrey, 159.
Wilson, Grace, 169.
Wilson, Hugh, 118, 205, 226.
Wilson, H. G., 407.
Wilson, James, 114, 118.
Wilson, James E., 233, 236.
Wilson, James S., 262.
Wilson, Jane, 205, 227, 240, 243, 259.
Wilson, Jane I., 240.
Wilson, J. D., 488.
Wilson, J. Harvey, 362.
Wilson, John, 22, 69, 118, 142, 144, 145, 146, 151, 152, 169, 179, 181, 205, 243, 348, 360, 407.
Wilson, John C., 240, 311, 354, 355, 358, 368, 369, 407.
Wilson, John L., 243.
Wilson, John O., 528.
Wilson, J. S., 527, 528.
Wilson, John W., 233, 407.
Wilson, Julian, 468.
Wilson, Margaret, 77, 232.
Wilson, Mary, 85, 246, 259.
Wilson, Mrs. Mary, 118.
Wilson, Mary Grace, 233.
Wilson, Mary L., 240, 243.
Wilson, Mary S., 230, 233, 235, 289.
Wilson, P., 348.
Wilson, Richard, 513.
Wilson, Robert, 20, 49, 50, 48, 62, 66, 70, 85, 169, 170, 205, 228, 232, 243, 484.
Wilson, Robert D., 243.
Wilson, Robert H., 240, 289.
Wilson, Robert I., 181.
Wilson, Robert J., 229, 230, 234.
Wilson, Robert M., 262, 357.
Wilson, Roger, 77, 85, 226.
Wilson, Samuel, 142, 152, 169, 179, 181, 205, 206, 233.
Wilson, Samuel A., 263.
Wilson, Samuel F., 238.
Wilson, Samuel J., 198, 243, 244, 259, 260, 274, 279.
Wilson, Samuel M., 233.
Wilson, Sarah E., 240.
Wilson, Sarah F., 237, 262.
Wilson School, 475.
Wilson, Shelton, 472.
Wilson, S. I., 349.
Wilson, Thomas, 85, 232, 500.
Wilson, Thomas E., 236, 262.
Wilson, Virginia, 474.
Wilson, Walter, 466.
Wilson, W. B., 500.
Wilson, W. G., 469.
Wilson, William, 19, 22, 57, 92, 114, 134, 135, 136, 142, 152, 169, 170, 179, 181, 183, 205, 226, 227, 229, 231, 232, 234, 235, 383.
Wilson, William C., 233, 473.
Wilson, William J., 302, 353, 383, 398, 409.
Wilson, W. M., 263, 473.
Wilson, Woodrow, 515.
Wimper, John, 169.
Winchester, Elhannon, 195.
Windom, Jesse, 170.
Wingate, Edward, 118.
Winkles, L. D., 362.

Winkles, William, 362.
Winn, Jonas, 157.
Winn, Lucia, 472.
Winter, J. S., 161.
Winter, John, 221, 223.
Winter, Robert, 170.
Winyaw, 24.
Winyaw County, 139.
Werter, Susannah, 76.
Wise, R. L., 503.
Wisner, George, 205.
Wisner, Jannet, 237.
Wisner, Robert, 224.
Wisner, Robert P., 237.
Witherspoon, Ann, 19, 82.
Witherspoon Colony, 10.
Witherspoon, David, 11, 17, 18, 20, 22, 45, 46, 66, 97, 114, 126, 142, 152.
Witherspoon, Elizabeth, 10, 16, 19, 81, 123, 169, 180, 205, 234, 236.
Witherspoon, Esther D., 236.
Witherspoon, Esther L., 240.
Witherspoon's Ferry, 208, 210.
Witherspoon, Gavin, 11, 12, 20, 22, 48, 66, 78, 79, 81, 114, 118, 119, 125, 126, 142, 143, 152, 169, 170, 179, 205, 207, 222, 223, 226, 228, 234.
Witherspoon, George, 236.
Witherspoon, George W., 126.
Witherspoon, I. B., 181.
Witherspoon, James, 10, 19, 22, 48, 81, 89, 114, 125, 139, 140, 141, 142, 143, 144, 145, 146, 169, 179, 205, 222.
Witherspoon, James E., 227.
Witherspoon, James H., 126, 236.
Witherspoon, John M., 231, 234, 245.
Witherspoon, Jane, 18, 119.
Witherspoon, Jane James, 119.
Witherspoon, Janet, 10, 234.
Witherspoon, J. B., 210.
Witherspoon, John, 10, 16, 17, 19, 22, 30, 31, 45, 46, 82, 92, 114, 118, 125, 126, 143, 169, 185, 208, 211.
Witherspoon, John B., 227.
Witherspoon, J. R., 10, 236.
Witherspoon, J. R. D., 205.
Witherspoon, John W., 361.
Witherspoon, Joseph, 179, 205, 223.
Witherspoon, Langdon, 236.
Witherspoon, Mary, 11, 19, 26, 158, 234.
Witherspoon, Mary A., 236.

Witherspoon, Martha Ann, 126.
Witherspoon, Nancy, 290.
Witherspoon, Robert, 10, 11, 12, 15, 17, 19, 20, 22, 48, 49, 66, 81, 125, 141, 143, 145, 150, 151, 152, 153, 175, 180, 205, 226, 227, 236.
Witherspoon, Robert B., 205.
Witherspoon, Robert L., 126, 150, 180, 205, 218, 219, 521.
Witherspoon, Robert P., 179, 222, 234.
Witherspoon, Robert S., 181, 227.
Witherspoon, Samuel, 180, 234.
Witherspoon, Samuel M., 231.
Witherspoon, Sarah, 17, 142, 153, 169.
Witherspoon, Thomas, 19, 89, 180, 181, 205, 218, 226, 232, 234, 236.
Witherspoon, Thomas R., 234.
Witherspoon, William, 125, 152, 170.
Wofford College, 305.
Wolfe, C. W., 520, 521, 522, 523, 536, 463, 464, 469.
Wolfe, Mrs. E. P., 469.
Women, 1745, 87.
Women in Revolution, 112.
Woman Suffrage, 465.
Women's Work in War, 370.
Wood, William, 170.
Wood, Thomas, 25.
Woodberry, John, 118.
Woodberry, John H., 505.
Woodmason, Charles, 54, 71.
Woods, J. M., 405.
Woods, W. H., 527.
Woods, Willis, 205.
Woods, T. T., 149.
Woodson, D. W., 352.
Workers, Turpentine, 327.
Workman, Florence, 469.
Workman, John, 118.
Workman, Robert, 118.
Workman, W. H., 483.
Worldly Amusements, 255, 273, 533.
World War, 503.
Wounded, C. S. A., 382.
Wounded, Cold Harbor, 355.
Wyatt, James, 237.
Wyatt, Samuel, 237.

Yarborough, John, 359, 408.
Yeadon, Richard, 396.
York, William, 39.
Yorkville Academy, 305.
Young, Arthur, 545.
Young, Carolina, 473.

INDEX 611

Young, D. B., 362.
Young, Elizabeth, 170.
Young, G. H., 347.
Young, Henry, 350.
Young, James M., 408.
Young, John, 350.
Young, J. C., 546.
Young, J. D., 408.
Young, J. H., 407.
Young, L. E., 344, 346, 347.

Young, Matt, 70.
Young, Robert, 22, 142.
Young, S. A., 351.
Young, William, 62, 63, 79, 153, 359.
Young, W. H., 408.

Zimmerman, Effie, 472.
Zuill, James, 170, 205, 225, 252.
Zuill, John, 225.
Zuill, Margaret, 225.

www.ingramcontent.com/pod-product-compliance
Lightning Source LLC
Chambersburg PA
CBHW031357290426
44110CB00011B/195